The Study Book for the NEBOSH National Certificate in Construction Safety and Health

RMS Publishing
Victoria House
Lower High Street
Stourbridge
DY8 1TA

First Published January 2005

Cover design by Graham Scriven
Printed and bound in Great Britain by Raithby, Lawrence at the De Montfort Press, Leicester

ISBN 1 900420 58 9

Foreword

EDITOR: JOHN LACEY

With the continued poor record of the construction industry in regards to Health and Safety, it is of the utmost importance to make those within the industry aware of procedures to change both standards and culture.

This study book compliments training with a structured approach to give students the tools to allow positive safety management within the construction industry.

After many years within the industry, I have seen major improvements but there is always a need for step-change action. The NEBOSH Certificate in Construction will assist construction personnel in achieving such a step-change.

John Lacey, F.I.O.S.H., RSP, F.S.I.A., M.A.S.S.E.
Past President of IOSH and the Construction Specialist Group Past Chairman
Has been involved in and led by example construction health and safety,
in both the UK and other areas of the world for over 30 years.

Editor's Notes

Diagrams and photographs

A number of the diagrams included in the Study Book for the NEBOSH Certificate in Construction Safety and Health have been produced in hand-drawn format. In particular these are diagrams that students studying for NEBOSH examinations may be required, or find it helpful, to produce by hand at the time of examination. They are provided to help the student to get an impression of how to do similar drawings of their own. I hope that these diagrams show that such drawings are achievable by hand and also assist in illustrating a standard that might be expected in examination.

We have taken particular care to support the text with a significant number of photographs. They are illustrative of both good and bad working practices and should always be considered in context with supporting text. I am sure that students will find this a useful aid when trying to relate their background and experience to the broad based NEBOSH Certificate in Construction Safety and Health syllabus. They will give an insight into some of the technical areas of the syllabus that people have difficulty relating to when they do not have a strong technical background.

Where diagrams/text extracts are known to be drawn from other publications, a clear source reference is shown and ACT wish to emphasise that reproduction of such diagrams/text extracts within the Study Book is for educational purposes only and the original copyright has not been infringed.

Legal requirements

The Study Book has at its heart the fact that health and safety should be managed as a risk. However as one of the risks to a business is the risk of prosecution care has been taken to relate topics to current legislation. The level of treatment is targeted to cover the interests of the Certificate in Construction student. Legislation is referred to in context in the various units that comprise the Study Book and reflects the syllabus of the NEBOSH Certificate in Construction Safety and Health. In addition the book has a unit dedicated to legislation, Unit 20, and here the student will find a useful summary of the legislation required by the NEBOSH Certificate in Construction Safety and Health.

The NEBOSH Certificate in Construction Safety and Health does not examine the student's knowledge of Section numbers of the Health and Safety at Work Act or knowledge of Regulation numbers. These are referred to in the Study Book in order to differentiate different components of the law and to aid the student in referencing legislation in the workplace, if required by their work.

Syllabus

Each unit of the Study Book has a unit overview that sets out the aims of the units, the content, learning outcomes and any connected sources of reference. The Study Book reflects the order and content of the NEBOSH Certificate in Construction Safety and Health syllabus and in this way the student can be confident that the Study Book reflects the themes of the syllabus. In addition, the syllabus is structured in a very useful way, focusing on hazards, their control and core management of health and safety principles.

National Vocational Qualification

We are confident that those working towards national vocational qualifications will find this Study Book a useful companion for NVQ Level 3 in Occupational Health and Safety.

Acknowledgements

Managing Editor: Ian Coombes MIOSH – Managing Director, ACT; member of NEBOSH Advisory Committee; member IOSH professional Affairs Committee.

RMS Publishing and ACT Associates Ltd wish to acknowledge the following contributors and thank them for their assistance in the preparation of the Certificate in Construction Guide: Roger Chance, David Hitchen, Dean Johnson, Geoff Littley, John Lacey, Barrie Newell and Julie Skett.

NEBOSH Study Books also available from RMS:

NEBOSH General Certificate (2nd Edition)   ISBN 1 900420 38 4

NEBOSH Level 4 Diploma (1st Edition):
A. Managing Health and Safety   ISBN 1 900420 59 7
B. Hazardous Agents in the Workplace   ISBN 1 900420 60 0
C. Workplace and Work Equipment   ISBN 1 900420 61 9

NEBOSH Diploma Part 1 (6th Edition)
Risk Management   ISBN 1 900420 39 2
Legal and Organisational   ISBN 1 900420 40 6
Workplace   ISBN 1 900420 41 4
Work Equipment   ISBN 1 900420 42 2
Agents   ISBN 1 900420 43 0

NEBOSH Diploma Part 2 (3rd Edition)
Risk Management   ISBN 1 900420 44 9
Legal and Organisational   ISBN 1 900420 45 7
Workplace   ISBN 1 900420 46 5
Work Equipment   ISBN 1 900420 47 3
Agents   ISBN 1 900420 48 1

Contents

Figure List (including tables and quotes)

Unit 8

Unit 9

Unit 10

Unit 14

Unit 15

Unit 19

Unit 20

List of abbreviations

LEGISLATION

ASLIC	Asbestos (Licensing) Regulations 1983
CAWR	Control of Asbestos at Work Regulations 2002
CDM	Construction (Design and Management) Regulation 1994
CHIP	Chemicals (Hazard Information and Packaging for Supply) Regulations 2002
CHPR	Construction (Head Protection) Regulations 1989
CHSW	Construction (Health, Safety and Welfare) Regulations 1996
CLAW	Control of Lead at Work Regulations 2002
COER	Control of Explosives Regulations 1991
CoPA	Control of Pollution Act 1974
COSHH	Control of Substances Hazardous to Health Regulations 2002
CSR	Confined Spaces Regulations 1997
DSE	Health and Safety (Display Screen Equipment) Regulations 1992
DSEAR	Dangerous Substances and Explosive Atmospheres Regulations 2002
EPA	Environmental Protection Act 1990
EWR	Electricity at Work Regulations 1989
FAR	Health and Safety (First-Aid) Regulations 1981
FPA	Fire Precautions Act 1971
FPSPR	Fire Certificates (Special Premises) Regulations 1976
FPWR	Fire Precautions (Workplace) Regulations 1997
HASAWA	Health and Safety at Work etc Act 1974
HSCER	Health and Safety (Consultation with Employees) Regulations 1996
IER	Health and Safety Information for Employees Regulations 1989
IRR	Ionising Radiations Regulations 1999
LOLER	Lifting Operations and Lifting Equipment Regulations 1998
MHOR	Manual Handling Operations Regulations 1992
MHSWR	Management of Health and Safety at Work Regulations 1999
NRSWA	New Roads and Street Works Act 1991
NWR	Noise at Work Regulations 1989
PPER	Personal Protective Equipment at Work Regulations 1992
PUWER	Provision and Use of Work Equipment Regulations 1998
RIDDOR	Reporting of Injuries, Diseases and Dangerous Occurrences Regulations 1995
SMSR	Supply of Machinery (Safety) Regulations 1992
SRSC	Safety Representatives and Safety Committees Regulations 1977
SSSR	Health and Safety (Safety Signs and Signals) Regulations 1996
WHR	Working at Height Regulations 2004 (Draft)
WHSWR	Workplace (Health, Safety and Welfare) Regulations 1992

GENERAL

AC	Alternating Current
ACOP	Approved Code of Practice
AIDS	Acquired Immune Deficiency Syndrome
APF	Assigned Protection Factor
BATNEEC	Best Available Techniques Not Entailing Excessive Cost
BPEO	Best Practicable Environmental Option
BS	British Standards
BSC	British Safety Council
BSI	British Standards Institution
CAT	Cable Avoidance Tool
CCTV	Closed Circuit Television
CE	Conformité Européene
CITB	Construction Industry Training Board
dB	Decibel
DC	Direct Current
DIY	Do It Yourself
DSE	Display Screen Equipment
EA	Environmental Agency
EAT	Employment Appeal Tribunal
EC	European Community
EEF	Engineering Employers Federation
EH	Environmental Health
EHO	Environmental Health Office
EMAS	Employment Medical Advisory Service
ET	Employment Tribunal
ETA	Event Tree Analysis
EU	European Union
FMEA	Failure Mode and Effect Analysis
FRA	Fire Risk Assessment

FTA	Fault Tree Analysis
HAVS	Hand-arm Vibration Syndrome
HAZOP	Hazard and Operability Studies
HIV	Human Immunodeficiency Virus
HMIP	Her Majesty's Inspectorate of Pollution
HML	High, Medium and Low
HMSO	Her Majesty's Stationary Office
HSC	Health and Safety Commission
HSE	Health and Safety Executive
HSG	Health and Safety Guidance
IT	Information Technology
IEE	Institute of Electrical Engineers
ILO	International Labour Office
IOSH	Institute of Occupational Safety and Health
IPC	Integrated Pollution Act
ISO	International Organisation for Standardization
IT	Information Technology
KPI	Key Performance Indicator
LAAPC	Local Authority Air Pollution Control
LEV	Local Exhaust Ventilation
LTEL	Long Term Exposure Limit
MDI	Methylene Bisphenyl Di-isocyanate
MEL	Maximum Exposure Limit
MEWP	Mobile Elevated Work Platform
MSW	Municipal Solid Wastes
NEBOSH	National Examination Board in Occupational Safety and Health
NRA	National Rivers Authority
NVQ	National Vocational Qualification
OEL	Occupational Exposure Limit
OES	Occupational Exposure Standard
PAT	Portable Appliance Testing
PLC	Public Limited Company
PPE	Personal Protective Equipment
RCD	Residual Current Device
RES	Representatives of Employment Safety
ROSPA	Royal Society for Prevention of Accidents
RPA	Radiation Protected Advisors
RPE	Respiratory Protective Equipment
RRO	Regulatory Reform Fire Safety Order
RTFLT	Rough Terrain Fork Lift Truck
SEPA	Scottish Environmental Protection Agency
SNR	Single Number Rating
SR	Safety Representatives
SSW	Safe System of Work
STEL	Short Term Exposure Limit
SVQ	Scottish Vocational Qualification
TDI	Toluene Di-isocyanate
TUC	Trade Union Congress
UV	Ultra Violet
VCM	Vinyl Chloride Monomer
VWF	Vibration White Finger
WBV	Whole Body Vibration
WHO	World Health Organisation
WRULD	Work Related Upper Limb Disorder

This page is intentionally blank

Foundations in construction health and safety

Overall Aims

On completion of this Unit, candidates will understand:

■ the scope and nature of occupational health and safety in construction work.

■ the moral, legal and financial reasons for promoting good standards of health and safety within an organisation.

■ the legal framework for the regulation of health and safety in general, and in construction activities in particular.

■ the legal and financial consequences of failure to manage health and safety.

■ the basis of a system for managing health and safety in construction.

Content

Specific Intended Learning Outcomes

The intended learning outcomes of this Unit are that candidates will be able to:

1.1 demonstrate an awareness of the health and safety issues within construction work, and explain the significance of the nature of the work and its organisation on health and safety standards within the industry

1.2 explain briefly the moral, legal and economic bases for maintaining good standards of health and safety

1.3 outline the legal framework for the regulation of health and safety in general and in construction work in particular

1.4 describe the roles and powers of enforcement agencies and the judiciary

1.5 identify relevant sources of health and safety information, both within an organisation and from external agencies

1.6 outline the key elements of a health and safety management system

Sources of Reference

The Management of Health and Safety at Work (ACOP) (L21), HSE Books

Successful Health and Safety Management (HSG65), HSE Books

The Costs of Accidents at Work (HSG96), HSE Books

Managing Health and Safety in construction (ACOP) (HSG224), HSE Books

Relevant Statutory Provisions

The Health and Safety at Work etc Act (HASAWA) 1974 - sections 2 and 20-25, 33 and 39-40

The Construction (Design and Management) Regulations (CDM) 1994 - purpose and outline

The Construction (Health, Safety and Welfare) Regulations (CHSW) 1996 - purpose and outline

1.1 - The multi-disciplinary nature of health and safety

Health and safety is a fundamental aspect of running an organisation as it impacts on all the functions within the organisation, just as quality might. Health and safety embraces a number of disciplines reflecting the scope of its influence, including finance, insurance, health, personnel, production, design, purchase and information technology (IT).

The obstacles to success with health and safety are the same as with other business objectives, with an additional obstacle being that the main operational requirements of the organisation will tend (unless the organisation has the balance correct) to take priority, whether this is construction, manufacture or health care. Organisations tend to focus on the immediate costs of implementing health and safety rather than the benefits that can be gained from doing so. The constant struggle with protecting profits (or those wanting to budget) by not spending unnecessarily is something that those wishing to improve health and safety face daily. The competing and conflicting demands of organisations have an impact on their resources. Even something as important to the organisation as quality may divert resources from health and safety needs.

Successful organisations are realising the need to take an inclusive approach to heath and safety that balances effort between the three primary issues - technical, procedural and behavioural.

1.2 - Meanings of and distinctions between common terms

Health, safety, welfare and environmental protection

HEALTH

"a state of well being"

The term 'health' has been defined as a state of well being. It includes well being in a physiological and psychological sense. In occupational terms this would include not suffering from noise-induced deafness, mental fatigue or stress. There is an element of overlap with the terms 'safety" and 'health'; for example, it would be clear that someone who has experienced a fall could sustain a physical injury such as a broken bone (a safety issue). In addition, it would not be a surprise if someone observed that the injured party had a 'poor state of health' for the period that the injury affected them. Maintaining health includes attention to the various health hazards (agents) in the working environment that can affect the worker and others, for example, chemical and biological agents.

SAFETY

"absence of danger of physical harm"

The term 'safety' is considered to be the absence of danger of physical harm to people. The term would extend to other things that could be harmed in the workplace such as equipment, structures and materials. Attention to safety matters would typically deal with factors that can cause this type of harm, such as a fall from a height, fire, electricity, and moving plant & machinery.

WELFARE

"facilities for workplace comfort"

The term 'welfare' relates to the provision of workplace facilities that maintain the basic well being and comfort of the worker, such as eating, washing, toilet facilities and first aid.

ENVIRONMENTAL PROTECTION

"a measure used to prevent harm to the environment of the world"

The term 'environmental protection' relates to measures that are specifically focused on maintaining the general environment of the world. As such it focuses on such things as protection of plant life, animals, water, and land and air quality. Though the protection does not focus on the worker or other people directly by protecting the environment, people obtain a benefit.

Accidents, dangerous occurrences, near-misses and work-related ill-health

ACCIDENTS

"an unplanned, uncontrolled event which led to, or could have led to loss"

The term 'accident' relates to the variety of events that occur which have, or might have, a detrimental effect in the workplace. The detrimental effect could be a physical injury to a person, equipment damage or one in which no material loss had occurred (near miss).

DANGEROUS OCCURRENCES

"an accident not resulting in personal injury reportable to the enforcing authority"

The term is used in the Reporting of Injuries, Diseases and Dangerous Occurrences Regulations (RIDDOR) 1995. A dangerous occurrence is an event specified in the schedules to the regulations, that the regulations require to be notified and reported to the appropriate enforcing authority (e.g. collapse of a scaffold of five metres high or more).

NEAR-MISSES

"an accident that results in no apparent loss"

The term 'near-miss' refers to an event (accident) which did not result in personal injury, equipment damage or some other loss, but under slightly different circumstances could have done (e.g. building block falling off a scaffold and landing on the floor).

WORK RELATED ILL-HEALTH

"harm to a worker's health caused by their work"

The term refers to harm to a worker's health caused by their work and will include harm to health in a physiological or psychological way. This will include the types of harm listed in RIDDOR as notifiable diseases, e.g. dermatitis.

See also - Risk Assessment - Unit 5

Hazard and risk

HAZARD

"something that has the potential to cause harm (loss)"

"the potential to cause harm, including ill-health and injury, damage to property, plant, products or the environment, production losses or increased liabilities.

Figure 1-1: Definition of hazard. *Source: Successful Health and Safety Management, HSG65, HSE.*

An example would be that a substance would be a hazard in a particular way depending on the properties of the substance, e.g. a cement / concrete mix could present a chemical (alkaline) burn hazard.

RISK

"the likelihood of a given loss occurring in defined circumstances"

"the likelihood that a specified undesired event will occur due to the realisation of a hazard by, or during, work activities or by the products and services created by work activities"

Figure 1-2: Definition of risk. *Source: Successful Health and Safety Management, HSG65, HSE.*

a) The hazard presented by the substance.

b) How it is controlled.

c) Who is exposed, to how much and for how long, and what they are doing.

In the example of cement this may cause temporary injury, dermatitis or sensitise the skin resulting in a permanent effect where the skin is sensitized whenever the person comes into contact with cement in the future.

See also - Risk Assessment - Unit 5

Civil law and criminal law

TYPES OF LAW

English Law is divided into two types - criminal and civil law. In summary, criminal law deals with offences against the state and society whereas civil law settles disputes between individuals or organisations.

Criminal law

A number of sanctions may be imposed on a person or organisation found guilty of a criminal offence. These are prescribed by the relevant legislation. They may include restriction on activities or punishment. These sanctions are usually brought about by the State, though there is some scope to bring private prosecutions. In a case involving a contravention of health and safety legislation, such as the Health and Safety at Work Act (HASAWA) 1974, the prosecution is brought by the Health & Safety Executive (HSE) or Local Authority - Environmental Health Officer (EHO). In a criminal case the person charged is known as the accused. The outcome of a trial is a verdict of "guilty" or "not guilty" (or, in Scotland, "guilty" or "not guilty" or "not proven"). Penalties are intended as a punishment, although compensation may be ordered separately by the court.

Civil law

Civil law exists in order to regulate disputes between individuals over the rights and obligations people have when dealing with each other. There are many branches of civil law including contract law and the law of tort. Contract law deals with the legally binding relationships that individuals enter into whereas tort law is aimed at redressing the wrongs committed by one person against another. In essence, the word tort means 'a civil wrong'. Examples of torts include defamation and negligence. Comparisons of the two types of law are set out below.

	Civil Law	Criminal Law
Purpose	Resolve disputes of contract, tort (e.g. negligence)	Regulate crime
Remedy	Compensation	Punishment
Means used	Sue	Prosecute
Who hears case	Judge sits alone in most cases	Judge and jury (or magistrates)
Burden of proof	Balance of probability	Beyond reasonable doubt
Parties involved	Claimant/defendant	Prosecution/defendant
Status	Insurable	Not insurable

Common law and statute law

SOURCES OF LAW

English health and safety law has two primary sources, common law and statute law. Each has an influence on civil and criminal law.

Common law

Common law, rather than being laid down by Parliament, has traditionally grown up over the centuries. Principles derived from judgments made in earlier cases create binding precedents. Binding **precedents** are decisions made in a higher court that are binding on all lower courts. Thus, a decision made by the House of Lords is binding on all lower courts. Since 1966 the House of Lords is no longer bound to follow its own decisions but it would be rare for the House of Lords to overrule a previous precedent. The Court of Appeal binds all lower, criminal and civil courts (i.e. High Court, County Court, Employment Appeals Tribunals and Tribunals, Crown and Magistrates Courts). Decisions made by courts of equal status create persuasive precedent only. There is scope for the courts to interpret such precedents in the light of changing circumstances. This does allow some deviation from an established precedent, but the decision making has to be justified.

In civil cases a judge normally sits on his/her own and decides the case on the **balance of probabilities**, deciding whether the acts and omission involved foreseeable events or conditions and whether reasonable care was taken to avoid the loss.

Please note that in the workplace situation the term "foreseeable" usually refers to what should be foreseeable by a competent person.

Statute law

Statute law is a **source** of both criminal and civil law. Some statutes, such as the HASAWA are entirely criminal law. Similarly some statutes are actionable only under civil law (e.g. the Occupiers' Liability Act 1957). It must be understood, however, that many health and safety related statutes may be used both as a basis for prosecution and as a platform for civil actions relating to personal injury suffered in the workplace. *See breach of statutory duty in section - Employer's common law and statutory duties - later in this unit.*

Statute law consists of primary legislation (Acts of Parliament) and delegated legislation such as regulations (e.g. the Management of Health and Safety at Work Regulations (MHSWR) 1999 and Orders.

COMPARISON OF TWO SOURCES OF LAW

Common Law	Statute Law
Judge – made law through decisions of cases, builds up over time as cases heard set principles	Established by Parliament
Not written down	Written down and codified in Acts and Regulations.
Duty of reasonable care	A range of levels of care used e.g. reasonably practicable
In the area of health and safety, forms the basis of most civil cases	Failure to comply normally (but not always) constitutes a criminal offence, although it can also be used in civil actions unless specifically disallowed

1.3 - Scope and definition of construction

Types of work

"Construction site" - means any site where the principal work activity being carried out is construction work.

"Construction work" - means the carrying out of any building, civil engineering or any engineering construction and includes all of the activities identified in the Construction (Design and Management) Regulations (CDM) 1994 and the Construction (Health, Safety and Welfare) Regulations (CHSW) 1996. It does not include exploration for or the extraction of mineral resources.

"Excavation" - an uncovered cutting in the earth, as distinct from a covered cutting or tunnel. Defined in the CHSW Regulations as: any earthwork, trench, well, shaft, tunnel or underground working.

BUILDING WORKS

Building Works involve most trades within the construction industry such as ground workers, steel erectors, brick layers, carpenters, plasterers, etc all working closely together with the common goal of creating a new finished building or structure.

RENOVATION, REFURBISHMENT, ALTERATION AND MAINTENANCE OF EXISTING PREMISES

Renovation / refurbishment

Renovation / refurbishment works involves restoring an existing building or structure to a condition that is representative of its original condition or improved by repair and modernisation using more up-to-date materials and practices. As with new building works, this also involves most of the common trades normally used within the construction Industry.

Alteration

Alteration works are required when the layout of an existing building, structure or premises no longer suit the use for which it was originally intended. This can include elements of both new building works and renovation works. Alterations can comprise an extension to an existing structure or demolition and removal of sections of the internal structure to make premises more spacious.

Alternatively, an alteration may involve dividing the existing structure into smaller, separate sections by the introduction of partition walls of various materials (block-work, brick-work or studding and plasterboard).

Maintenance

Maintenance work is an essential element to ensure that the condition of an existing building, premises or structure does not deteriorate and that it remains in as good a condition as is possible. Works are normally carried out on a regular scheduled basis to deal with issues of wear and tear, but can also be required when and if a problem suddenly occurs that requires attention e.g. loss of roofing materials following a storm. Maintenance can be carried out on all components of premises to include the building, services, and any final building furnishing.

CIVIL ENGINEERING & WORKS OF ENGINEERING CONSTRUCTION

Civil engineering and engineering works normally relate to heavy construction activities requiring large items of plant and equipment such as cranes and excavators. This work will require specialist knowledge and experience in order to undertake activities such as highway construction, bridge construction, piling works, large foundations, large concrete structures, excavations and utility projects.

DEMOLITION / DECONSTRUCTION / DISMANTLING

The term demolition / deconstruction / dismantling refers to 'breaking down' or 'removing'. In construction this is applied to buildings and structures that are no longer required or are possibly derelict and unsafe. Demolition must be carried out in a well-planned and controlled manner in compliance with a safe system of work. Account needs to be taken of potential hazards that may arise from demolition (asbestos dust and falling debris). Any project that involves any element of demolition (full or part demolition) falls under the control of the CDM Regulations.

Range of activities

SITE CLEARANCE

Site clearance consists of preparing the site prior to the works being undertaken. This may involve removal of hazardous waste, obstructive trees, unwanted scrub and landscaping. Demolition activities may also be required as part of site clearance prior to construction works beginning.

Following completion of construction works site clearance will involve removal of all waste associated with the construction activities (e.g. brick & timber off-cuts, packaging, spoil) to a licensed waste disposal site. It will also include the removal of all plant and equipment used on the construction with the aim of leaving the site in a clean and tidy state ready for its intended use.

DEMOLITION AND DISMANTLING

Demolition / deconstruction / dismantling activities will generally also include a survey of the structure to be demolished in order to identify any potential contamination hazards that are concealed and are not obvious (asbestos dust, lead, chemicals, live utility services). Various techniques will be employed to carry out demolition, including 'piece meal' – large sections are demolished at a time by machines or demolition by hand - where items are broken into their individual parts to be reclaimed or reused. Where material recovery is not important long reach crane with demolition ball, long reach mechanical pincer jaw and explosive charges may be used in some cases. Protection should be ensured for all workers involved through controlled access to the area. The danger area should be defined and suitably fenced with controlled access only to authorised personnel. Demolition must be carried out in a structured sequence to prevent any premature collapse of the structure. Falling debris must not be allowed to fall onto any surrounding area or buildings.

EXCAVATION

Excavation consists of digging below ground level to various depths in order to create a cavity that can be used for exposure of buried utility services, trenching for installation of utility services, casting building foundations or ground investigations. Methods of digging used for excavation work include the use of hand tools (pick, fork, shovel), and also by using a mechanical excavator. Major excavations for basements, sub-structures etc, remain as a permanent part in the construction operation.

LOADING, UNLOADING AND STORAGE OF MATERIALS

Construction sites use a host of different materials in the construction process that will require loading or unloading by mechanical or manual means. These can be broken down into materials that are used or removed immediately at site (i.e. excavation spoil, concrete mix, mortar mix) and materials that are stored at site and used or removed at regular intervals as required (bricks, cement, sand, timber, sundries, waste disposal skips). Loading and unloading should be undertaken using the correct procedures that comply with site safe systems of work and wherever possible avoiding the need for manual handling. Storage requirements should be identified and planned for the whole project. This will need to consider security, safe position and suitable ground condition; protection from adverse weather and potential for falls from a height or into an excavation.

SITE MOVEMENTS

Construction sites contain various types of heavy mobile plant & equipment and large numbers of site workers. Construction sites projects should be well planned to take into account vehicles moving around the site. In particular consideration to safe access and egress would include issues of adequacy of space for manoeuvring and ensuring operator visibility. Routes for both vehicles and pedestrians should be provided and be suitably surfaced, clearly defined and separated.

FABRICATION

Fabrication at site can include steel erecting, welding and form-working. Quite often it can involve working at height (where specialist work platforms and fall arrest equipment should be used) and adequate control is essential to prevent the falling of materials and tools. A variety of specialist equipment may be required; e.g. welding machine, bolt gun, or nail gun, and such equipment should only be used by competent persons.

DECORATION

Decoration consists of applying various coatings, e.g. paints, wallpaper, and artex, necessary to create the final finished appearance to a building or structure. The tools involved with decoration are often handheld and not powered. Various access systems including mobile platforms are required for this type of work. .

CLEANING

Cleaning involves applying water, steam or various abrasive or chemical agents to the surfaces to be treated, e.g. walls, windows, floors, fabric. The method of application can require the use of various types of equipment ranging from vacuum cleaners, floor polisher through to high pressure jets. Consideration should be given to the correct disposal of waste materials.

INSTALLATION, REMOVAL AND MAINTENANCE OF SERVICES

Various utility services (e.g. electricity and water) are required on both existing and new construction sites, they are usually buried underground. In new installations this involves a gas great deal of liaison with the planner concerning the route the services will take and will involve excavation with heavy plant, loading and unloading of materials. New services are often connected to their source at a location that is situated outside the construction site boundary. Where this occurs, the additional hazard to the general public presents itself and suitable means of traffic control (e.g. signing, lighting), guarding and protection of the public (barriers, warning signs) will need to be employed.

LANDSCAPING

Landscaping usually takes place during the final stages of the construction phase, when there is little or no construction plant travelling around the site. Landscaping may include altering site levels and the introduction of trees, shrubs, grass turf / seed etc. The works generally consist of loading and unloading of materials, manual handling, and cleaning work (footways and roads). Note that care should be taken to avoid planting trees close to underground services or near to building footings.

The problems created by construction operations

Construction sites constantly change through the build phase, as the trades that are associated with the construction vary greatly at each stage. Consideration needs to be given to site induction for new workers as appropriate. The safe systems of work, risk assessments, site safety procedures and site inductions will need to be updated regularly to suit the most current situation. A construction site will always be an unfamiliar workplace with new hazards and dangers posed as each phase moves to the next.

1.4 - The moral, legal and financial arguments for maintaining good standards of health and safety

General argument

There are three good reasons for preventing accidents in the work place:

1)   Moral

Injury accidents result in a great deal of pain and suffering for those affected. Construction activities in the UK resulted in an average of two fatalities for each three week period during 2004. Clearly, we must all do what we can to avoid this.

2)   Legal

It is a legal requirement to safeguard the health and safety of employees and others that might be affected by the organisation's operations.

3)   Financial

Accidents at work cost a great deal of money, especially when we add in damage accidents (particularly when they interrupt production, downgrade the quality of our products or impair the environment). Costs can be enormous - and perhaps already are many times larger than we think.

The size of the problem

Every working day in Great Britain at least one person is killed and over 6000 are injured at work.

Health and Safety Executive (HSE) statistics reveal that 71 workers were killed in the construction industry during the year 2002/03. A breakdown of these 71 fatal injuries that occurred in 2002/03 indicates that falls from height remain the single biggest cause of death (47 per cent). This is followed by being struck by an object - other than a vehicle (15 per cent), electricity (10 per cent), transport (7 per cent), collapse (7 per cent) and other kinds (10 per cent). This breakdown of type of injury is consistent with previous years, although there has been a slight rise in the number of electrical accidents.

Every year three-quarters of a million people take time off work because of what they regard as work-related illness. About 30 million workdays are lost as a result.

Accidents and ill health are costly to workers and their families. They can also hurt organisations because, in addition to costs of personal injuries, they may incur far greater costs from damage to property or equipment, and lost production.

Employer's duty of care

The employer's duty of care in common law has been established for some time and obligates the employer to take *'reasonable care of those that might forseeably be affected by its acts or omissions'*. If the employer fails to meet this duty, they may be considered negligent. The duty extends to employees and to others (e.g. visitors) who might foreseeably be affected. This is sometimes referred to as the neighbour principle. It follows that employees have the right to work in a workplace and in a manner that provides reasonable protection from harm. This should not be interpreted to mean absolute safety.

The employer's duty in criminal law is established principally in the HASAWA and its associated regulations. These set out express duties to care for employees and others. The duties are qualified by terms such as 'so far as reasonably practicable'. *See also the section - Absolute and Qualified Duties - later in this unit.*

Employer's common law and statutory duties

In common law the employer must take reasonable care to protect employees. Wilsons and Clyde Coal Co. Ltd v. English (1938) *(The NEBOSH National Certificate in Construction Health and Safety does not require you to be able to quote case names)* is a notable precedent used to identify an employer's common law duties as the provision and maintenance of:

- A safe place of work.
- Safe appliances and equipment.
- A safe system of work.
- Competent and safety conscious personnel.

These duties are similarly reflected in criminal law in the statutory duties of HASAWA Section 2 of which emphasises the fact that plant (and equipment) must be provided and maintained such that it is safe and healthy. The duties under the HASAWA extend the need to provide a safe place of work to include means of access and egress to that place of work. The HASAWA requires systems of work, as well as plant, to be provided and maintained such that work is safe and healthy. The HASAWA does not specify that employees must be competent but expresses a requirement to provide information, instruction, and training. Though it is only implied, the purpose of this provision would be to ensure competence. These provisions are supported by a requirement for supervision, as necessary. If people were not competent a good deal of supervision would be required. The duties are qualified by terms such as 'so far as reasonably practicable'. *See also - Employers' Responsibilities - Unit 3 and Legislation - Unit 20.*

Criminal liabilities

In order to regulate work activities criminal law establishes criminal liabilities. These are the sanctions that can be taken against those found to be in breach of the law. Principally the legal options are split between the application (serving) of enforcement notices, which do not require the enforcing authority to go to court, and prosecution, which does.

ENFORCEMENT NOTICES

General points

The criteria for use are set out in sections 20-22 of the HASAWA. Enforcement notices are one of a number of options open to enforcing officers in order to regulate health and safety in the workplace. Before issuing a notice an officer will have considered the value of providing comment on compliance level and actions in oral and written form that is not a formal notice. There are two types of enforcement notice, an improvement notice and a prohibition notice. It should be remembered that both notices are a confirmation of non-compliance with legislation. When choosing to use a notice the enforcing officer has chosen not to prosecute for the offence at that point in time.

When an enforcing officer serves a notice he has a duty to inform a relevant employee representative of the circumstances, in addition to the person the notice is served on.

Improvement notices

An enforcing officer can serve an *improvement notice* if he/she is of the opinion that there:

- Is a contravention of one or more of the relevant statutory provisions.

OR

- Has been a contravention of one or more of those provisions in circumstances which make it likely that the contravention will continue to be repeated.

The effect of the notice is to require a specified improvement to take place in order to bring the situation back into compliance with the law.

In the improvement notice the enforcing officer must:
- State that he/she is of the opinion that there is or has been a contravention.
- Specify the provisions in his/her opinion which are contravened.
- Give particulars of the reasons for his/her opinion.
- Specify a period of time within which the person is required to remedy the contravention.

Examples of where an improvement notice may be used:
- Incomplete or no health and safety policy.
- Incomplete or no general risk assessment.
- Inadequate or no general training of managers.
- Restricted walkways or trailing cables in offices.
- Storage of oils causing risk of slipping.

The improvement specified must be complied with within the stated time. The responsibility to confirm compliance remains with the employer, the enforcing officer may or may not return to determine compliance with the notice. Notices are not 'lifted' by the enforcing officer but the act of being in compliance satisfies the notice. The notice must provide sufficient time for the employer to appeal therefore the time to improve must be in excess of the 21 days allowed to appeal. The time to make the improvement should reflect the scale and complexity of what is required. If the employer felt it did not this may be grounds for appeal.

Prohibition notices

If an enforcing officer is of the opinion that a workplace activity involves, or will involve, the ***risk of serious personal injury***, he/she can serve on the person responsible for the activity a ***prohibition notice***. The notice will usually take immediate effect and require the activity to cease. In circumstances where the enforcing officer considers the immediate stopping of the activity to be inappropriate (it may present its own risk) the notice can come into effect at a fixed date. A notice can relate to a system of work, equipment, workplace or a person.

A prohibition notice must:
- State that the Inspector is of the opinion that there is a risk of serious personal injury.
- Specify the matters which create the risks.
- Direct that the activities must not be carried out, unless the matters are remedied.

Examples of where a prohibition notice may be used:
- Unguarded machinery.
- Incomplete scaffold.
- Untrained personnel using high risk equipment e.g. rough terrain fork lift truck.
- Inadequate procedures for entry into a confined space e.g. sewers.

Appeals against notices

Right of appeal

A person on whom either type of notice is served can appeal to an Employment Tribunal (ET) within 21 days from the date of service of the notice.

The tribunal can extend this period on written application that it was not reasonably practicable for the appeal to be brought within 21 days.

Effect of appeal

a)   When an appeal is lodged against an improvement notice it ***is*** suspended.

b)   When an appeal is lodged against a prohibition notice it ***is not*** suspended until the tribunal hears the appeal and makes a decision.

When the appeal is heard the Employment Tribunal will consider the facts of the appeal and may make a number of responses in view of their findings. The options are to uphold the notice as originally defined, amend the notice (for example, the time to comply with an improvement notice) or quash it.

Employment Tribunals (ET)

An employment tribunal usually consists of a legally-qualified chairperson appointed by the Lord Chancellor and two lay members - one representing management interests and the other employees. These are selected from panels kept by the Department of Employment after nominations from employers' organisations and trades unions.

Employment tribunals deal with the following issues:
- Victimisation.
- Dismissal, actual or constructive, following a breach of health and safety law, regulation and/or term of an employment contract.
- Appeals against improvement and prohibition notices.
- Safety representatives and safety committees [time off, payment functions and training of representatives under the Safety Representatives and Safety Committees (SRSC) Regulations 1977].
- Representatives of employee safety [pay and time off under the Health and Safety (Consultation with Employees) Regulations (HSCER) 1996].
- Suspension from work for medical reasons [Employment Protection (Consolidation) Act 1978].
- Suspension from work on maternity grounds.

Appeals from employment tribunals lie to the Employment Appeal Tribunal (EAT), except in the case of health and safety notices, where appeal lies in the High Court. Appeal, in either case, is made on a point of law (not a point of fact).

Penalties for failure to comply

An advantage of formalising an enforcing officer's comment in the form of an enforcement notice is that failure to comply with the notice is an offence in itself, which carries a possible penalty of 2 years' prison sentence. In addition, the enforcement officer retains the right to prosecute for the original identified non-compliance with legislation.

PROSECUTION

Summary and indictable offences

Summary offences (minor)

Summary offences are those offences that the law recognises to arise from less serious breaches of law. It should be remembered that the HASAWA contains general duties that relate to all workplaces, all situations and all risks. It is logical that a prosecution may be deemed necessary in some situations that are straightforward and where relatively minor offences have occurred. The same point may be made with Regulations e.g. a straightforward failure to report an accident, required under RIDDOR might fit into this category. These offences are normally heard in the Magistrates Court.

Indictable (serious offences)

Indictable offences are more serious or repeated offences, and are tried in the Crown Court.

Criminal Courts

Magistrates Court

Magistrates' Courts are mostly staffed by lay magistrates who are not legally qualified and sit part-time. Stipendiary magistrates sit in large towns and are paid a stipend (a form of salary). Lay magistrates sit two or usually three to a court, a stipendiary magistrate sits alone. The Magistrates' Court deals with minor (summary) health and safety offences. Appeal from this court is usually to the Crown Court, but in some cases might be to the High Court (on a point of law). In addition, the Magistrates Court will consider indictable cases to determine whether there is sufficient evidence to support a charge.

The Crown Court

The Crown Court tries all serious (indictable) criminal health and safety offences, with a judge and a jury. It hears appeals and deals with committals for sentencing from magistrates' courts where they find they do not have sufficient power of punishment to match the crime.

From the Crown Court appeal on criminal matters is made to the Criminal Division of the Court of Appeal. As with the Magistrates Court, an appeal on a point of law may also be made to a Divisional Court of the Queen's Bench division (High Court).

The High Court

The High Court is staffed by judges (Justices of the High Court) who must be persons who have had right of audience in the High Court for at least ten years or a Circuit judge who has held office for at least two years. In hearing a case for the first time a High Court judge sits alone. A Divisional Court of two or more High Court judges sits to hear appeals from Magistrates and Crown Courts.

The Court of Appeal

The Court of Appeal is divided into Criminal and Civil Divisions. The Court consists of 35 Lords Justices of Appeal. Normally, three judges will sit together to hear appeals from the Crown Court. It does not conduct a complete rehearing of the case but reviews the record of the evidence in the lower court and the legal arguments put before it. It may uphold or reverse the earlier decision or order a new trial. A majority decision is given and dissenting judgements are stated.

The House of Lords

Apart from the limited jurisdiction of the European Court of Justice (of the EC), the House of Lords is the highest court of appeal in the United Kingdom. The court consists of between nine and twelve Law Lords who are life peers. A minimum of three (but normally five) Law Lords constitutes a court. A majority decision is given and dissenting judgments are stated. The Court hears appeals from both the civil and the criminal divisions of the Court of Appeal (and in certain circumstances directly from the High Court).

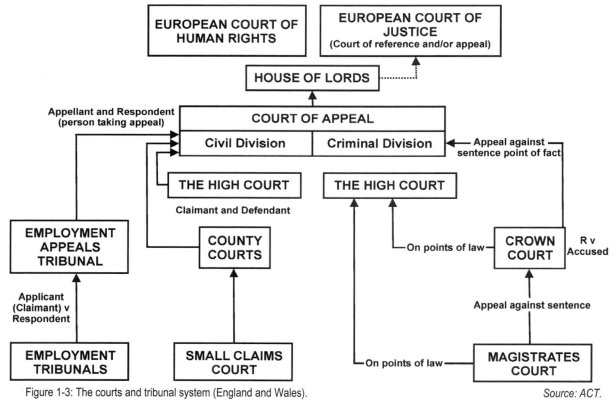

Figure 1-3: The courts and tribunal system (England and Wales).   Source: ACT.

Penalties

Health and safety penalties for the HASAWA and associated regulations are controlled by Section 33 of HASAWA. It sets out the following levels of penalty for different offences; essentially they are stated to be either summary offences or indictable offences. Some offences may be said to be triable either way; i.e. as summary or indictable depending on the seriousness of the circumstances of the breach.

Lower courts

In addition to this, magistrates may impose a prison sentence for an offence where a licence was required to be held, e.g. the removal of asbestos or for breach of an enforcement notice.

The maximum penalty on ***summary*** conviction for each offence is therefore:

For breaches of Sections 2-6 of HASAWA.	A fine of up to £20, 000.
For other breaches of HASAWA not specified above, or of other relevant statutory provisions under the HASAWA.	A fine of up to £5, 000.
For failure to comply with an improvement or prohibition notice, or court remedy order.	A fine of up to £20,000, and 6 months' imprisonment.

Higher courts

In the Crown Court, the maximum penalty for each ***indictable*** offence is an 'unlimited' fine (the court does not have a limit on what it can set).

For other breaches of HASAWA, or of other relevant statutory provisions under the Act.	Unlimited fines.
For failure to comply with an improvement or prohibition notice, or court remedy order.	2 years' imprisonment, or an unlimited fine, or both.
For contravening licence requirements or provisions relating to explosives.	2 years' imprisonment, or an unlimited fine, or both.

The maximum fine a magistrate can impose for health and safety offences is £20,000 per offence. This applies to breaches of Section 2-6 of the HASAWA and other sections relating to breaches of improvement/prohibition notices and court remedy orders. The maximum penalty for breaches of Section 7 of the HASAWA (relating to the employee), subordinate regulations and other sections of the HASAWA is £5000.

In addition to this, magistrates may impose a prison sentence for an offence where a licence was required to be held, e.g. the removal of asbestos or for breach of an enforcement notice.

The maximum penalty on ***summary*** conviction for each offence is therefore:

Employer /relevant duty holder	Sections 2 - 6	£20,000
Employees	Section 7	£5,000
Person in breach	Failure to comply with a notice	£20,000
		6 months in prison
	No licence	6 months in prison
	Other offences not listed	£5,000
	(e.g. breach of regulations)	

In the Crown Court the maximum penalty for each ***indictable*** offence is an 'unlimited' fine (the court does not have a limit on what it can set). In certain circumstances, e.g. contravening an enforcement notice the penalties are:

- A maximum of two years' imprisonment, or
- Two years' imprisonment and an indefinite fine.

Civil liabilities

NEGLIGENCE

General points

If an employee is injured at work then he may be able to sue the employer for the tort (civil wrong) of negligence. Negligence means failing to behave as a reasonable person would do in the same circumstances and can be an act or omission.

> You must take reasonable care to avoid acts or omissions when you can reasonably foresee would be likely to injure your neighbour.

Figure 1-4: Definition of negligence.   *Source: Donoghue v Stevenson (1932)*

Tests of proof

In order to prove the case and obtain damages (usually in the form of financial compensation) the injured party must show that:

- They were owed a duty of care.
- There was a failure to fulfil the duty to a reasonable standard (breach of duty).
- Damage, loss or injury directly resulted from the breach.

Duty owed

For example, a duty is owed by the employer to employees or someone that may foreseeably be affected by the employer's acts or omissions. This is part of what is sometimes called 'the neighbour principle'. Duties to other people depend on the circumstance. An example of where a duty might exist is where an employer occupies premises as an occupier then he would have a duty to lawful visitors.

Breach of duty

A breach of the duty of care is required when proving negligence. This depends on the standards of care that may be expected by the "reasonable man". In the case of an employer breaching a duty to employees this might include such things as failing to provide a safe place of work. ***See also - Employer's common law and statutory duties - earlier in this unit.***

Loss resulted

The injury (loss) was a result of the breach. Generally, the injury must be "reasonably foreseeable". There are exceptions to this rule; for example it is no defence to show that an injured person was unforeseeably weak ("the thin skull rule").

The loss must not be too remote from the breach and a direct causal link established by the facts of the case (on the balance of probability).

Contributory negligence

Where an injury is partly the fault of the injured person, their person may be said to have contributed to the injury and any damages he may recover will be reduced in proportion to his blameworthiness.

Vicarious liability

Vicarious liability (i.e. liability for the acts of a third party) is the principle that the employer is liable for the torts of their employees provided that they are committed during the course of the employees' employment. Thus if an employee causes damage or injury by not fulfilling a common law duty of care then the employer will be liable. This liability exists even if the employer has not been negligent.

This liability must be insured against under the Employer's Liability (Compulsory Insurance) Act 1969.

Civil courts

Small Claims Court

The small claims courts underpin the county court structure. A registrar typically hears cases. Personal injury claims of up to £5000 may be made to this court. Appeal is to the County Court.

County Court

County courts have civil jurisdiction only, but deal with almost every kind of civil case arising within the local area for which the court is established. County courts can hear cases in contract up to £25,000 and tort claims of up to £50,000 in the case of actions for damages relating to personal injury. They may exceed the limit with consent of both parties. In practice they deal with the majority of the country's civil litigation. The case is heard by a judge, on his/her own, and appeal is to the Court of Appeal.

High Court

The High Court deals with claims over £50,000 - it has no upper limit. The case is heard by a judge, on his/her own, and appeal is to the Court of Appeal.

Court of Appeal

The Court of Appeal hears cases referred from both the County Court and the High Court and the Employment Appeal Tribunal. Typically three judges will hear cases. It does not conduct a complete rehearing of the case but reviews the record of the evidence in the lower court and the legal arguments put before it. It may uphold or reverse the earlier decision or order a new trial. A majority decision is given and dissenting judgements are stated.

Appeal from this court is to the House of Lords.

House of Lords

The House of Lords, in the form of appointed Law Lords, sits to hear appeals from the Court of Appeal. Many important civil cases have been heard in the House of Lords. Cases relating to negligence heard in the House of Lords are very important because of the binding precedent they set to all courts below it. Precedent is particularly important to matters of negligence as it relies on the principles established by case law to guide acceptable behaviour.

Damages

The claimant, as part of the claim, will identify what loss they have sustained. In view of this they will seek damages from the other party. The damages may be seen as compensation, intended to put the claimant in the original position before the injury. This is a contentious area as the harm done to the claimant is often difficult to quantify in financial terms. Special damages include a figure for pain, suffering and loss of amenity. Special damages are awarded for the financial burden imposed on the claimant e.g. loss of earnings, medical costs and special care.

Defences against negligence

Primary defences

The main defences available are similar to the tests of proof.

No Duty Owed	It is difficult to show there is no duty for injuries an employer causes an employee. It is possible to show someone else had a duty, not you, e.g., contractor instead of employer, client instead of contractor.
No Negligence	Despite exercising reasonable care the accident still happened.
No Injury	The injury suffered by the plaintiff was not foreseeable.

Volenti non fit injuria

Volenti non fit injuria - translated from Latin this means 'to one who is willing no harm is done'.

Figure 1-5: Definition of volenti non fit injuria.   *Source: Murray v Harringay Arena (1951).*

(The NEBOSH National Certificate in Construction Health and Safety does not require you to be able to quote case names)

This is a complete defence to negligence by the defendant, and is used where the claimant agreed to run the risk of accidental harm. This true consent must be freely given and has been used in connection with spectators injured in the course of hazardous events, for example, motor racing. An employee, however, does not consent to any abnormal or unnecessary risks merely by accepting the job or continuing to do it. This defence is unlikely to succeed when defending claims made by rescuers who volunteered for the risk in order to safeguard others, whether or not the rescuers are members of the public or public service employees.

Statute of limitations

In general, legal proceedings in respect of personal injuries must be started within three years of the accident; after that time they are "statute barred". This time may be extended in special cases. For long-term health related cases the time is taken from the time the person had knowledge of the condition.

Direct and indirect costs of accidents and ill-health

There are many direct and indirect costs associated with accidents at work.

DIRECT COSTS

- Insurance.
- Court costs.
- Fines.
- Lost time of injured employee and continued payments to employee.
- Damage to the equipment, tools, property and plant or to materials.

INDIRECT COSTS

- Lost time by other employees who stop work or reduce performance.
  - Out of curiosity.
  - Out of sympathy.
  - Weakened morale.
- Lost time by supervisor or other managers.
  - Assisting injured employee.
  - Investigating the cause of the accident.
  - Arranging for the injured employee's production to be continued by some other employee
  - Selecting, training, or breaking in a new employee to replace injured employee.
  - Preparing accident reports, attending hearings, inquests courts.
- Interference with production leading to failure to fill orders on time, loss of bonuses, penalty schemes and similar causes.

In 1993 the HSE published a series of five case studies to illustrate just how much accidents at work could cost a company. The industries chosen were from a wide range of activities. The following table illustrates the losses identified.

		Total loss	**Annualised loss**	**Representing**
1	Construction site	£245,075	£700,000*	8.5% tender price
2	Creamery	£243,834	£975,336	1.4% operating costs
3	Transport company	£48,928	£195,712	1.8% of operating costs 37% of profits
4	Oil platform	£940,921	£3,763,684	14.2% of potential output

* represents length of contract.

Figure 1-6: Sample costs of accidents.   *Source: The costs of accidents at work, HSG96, HSE Books.*

The case studies also illustrated the difference between insured costs and uninsured costs. It was shown that uninsured costs were between 8 and 36 times greater than the costs of insurance premiums. The following 'Accident Costs Iceberg' represents the ratio of insured to uninsured costs incurred by the main contractor (1:11) during the building of a supermarket. HSE studies found that uninsured costs outweighed insured costs by up to 36 times.

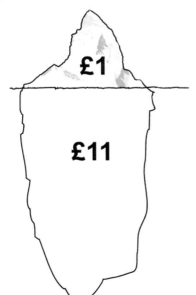

INSURED COSTS

- Employer's Liability
- Public / Third party liability
- Contractors all risks
- Plant and building damage
- Tool and equipment

UNINSURED COSTS

- Product and materials damage
- Emergency supplies
- Production delays
- Overtime and temporary labour
- Investigation time
- Supervisors' time diverted

Figure 1-7: Costs incurred by the main contractor (1:11) during the building of a supermarket. *Source: ACT / HSG96*

1.5 - The legal framework for regulating health and safety

The influence and role of the European Union as it affects UK health and safety legislation

The Council of the European Commission can, under the Treaty of Rome, issue Directives. These are to harmonise the laws of the member states, including those covering occupational health and safety.

Representatives of the member states meet to agree on the content of draft Directives. When they are agreed, they are presented to the European Parliament for ratification. The Directives impose a duty on each member state to make legislation to conform to the Directive and to enforce such legislation. The Directives are legally binding on the governments. Framework Directives set out the overall objectives and deal with individual objectives of Daughter Directives. In the UK the Directives are translated into Regulations. For example, we have the Working Time Directive translated into the Working Time Regulations.

The Single European Act identified the need to eliminate technical barriers to trade, such as the differing legal health and safety standards throughout the Community. The approach is to develop a philosophy of essential safety requirements and harmonisation Directives that establish those essential safety requirements. Further to this, there is recognition in the Act to encourage improvements in the working environment.

The structure of UK legislation

HEALTH AND SAFETY AT WORK ETC. ACT 1974 - (PRIMARY LEGISLATION)

The Health and Safety at Work etc. Act (HASAWA) sets out general responsibilities in a legal framework. It places responsibilities on people, covering all the main parties that contribute to health and safety in the workplace e.g. employers, employees, designers and suppliers. The duties are designed to be general rather than specific in order to make them widely applicable to all workplaces and all work activities. The HASAWA established means of regulation of behaviour in the form of enforcement notices and penalties, designed to match the circumstances that enforcing officers find. The general basis of the HASAWA is that measures taken should, as a minimum, reflect the level of risk for the issue being considered. Because the HASAWA sets out general duties its structure allowed for the creation of more specific legislation, in the form of regulations, to be made in order to set out specific requirements and to control specific risks. In turn the HASAWA made provision for the creation of approved codes of practice (ACOPs) to support its general provisions and the regulations made under the HASAWA.

HEALTH AND SAFETY REGULATIONS - (DELEGATED LEGISLATION)

These contain specific details. They give substance to the requirements of acts. The Secretary of State may make regulations, but is required to consult the Health and Safety Commission (HSC) and other interested parties. When the Regulations have been made, they are laid on the table of the Houses of Parliament to enable observation. It is usual for the Regulations to come into force after forty days, unless either House passes a negative resolution. Note: acts and regulations carry the full force of the law. Failure to comply with either can be both a criminal offence and a basis for civil action. ACOPs and/or guidance notes supplement acts and regulations.

APPROVED CODES OF PRACTICE

ACOPs are approved by the Health and Safety Commission with the consent of the Secretary of State and provide a recognised interpretation of how an employer may comply with the associated legislation. The code is not a piece of legislation and it does not have binding force. It is not a criminal offence to break it, nor will a breach of it automatically give rise to civil liability. However it can be cited in evidence and a person who breaks it is much more likely to be held negligent. Employers must either meet the standards contained in an ACOP or show that they have complied with an equal or better standard.

Examples of ACOPs are: "Managing Health and Safety in Construction – Construction (Design and Management) Regs", "Safe Use of Work Equipment" (which supplements the Provision and Use of Work Equipment Regulations 1998), "Workplace Health, Safety and Welfare" (supplementing the Workplace (Health, Safety and Welfare) Regulations) and "Rider Operated Lift Trucks – Operator Training".

GUIDANCE NOTES

The Health and Safety Executive sometimes issue guidance notes that are purely advisory and have no standing in law. The advice is generally more practical than that contained in an ACOP, and may be referred to in criminal and civil cases as persuasive argument of what may have been done to prevent a breach or injury.

Examples of Guidance Notes are those that accompany the Personal Protective Equipment Regulations (PPER) 1992 and the Manual Handling Operations Regulations (MHOR) 1992.

Absolute and qualified duties

GENERAL REQUIREMENTS

Statute law, because it is prescribed in a written form, provides an opportunity for the level of duty it expects to be specified. The level of duty specified will often relate to the level of risk of the issue being controlled and/or the knowledge we have that the specified action can be completed in the way that it would require. There are three distinct levels of statutory duty giving rise to criminal liability:

1. absolute   2. practicable and   3. reasonably practicable

ABSOLUTE STATUTORY REQUIREMENTS

Where the risk of injury is inevitable if safety precautions are not taken, a statutory duty may well be absolute. Absolute duties are worded as "shall" such as in the Provision and Use of Work Equipment Regulations (PUWER) 1998, Regulation 9, which requires that: "Every employer shall ensure that all persons who use work equipment have received adequate training for the purposes of health and safety…………"

PRACTICABLE REQUIREMENTS

This means they must be carried out if only limited by the current state of knowledge and invention, even though implementation may be difficult, inconvenient and/or costly. For example, the PUWER, Regulation 11, requires "The provision of fixed guards enclosing every dangerous part or rotating stock-bar where and to the extent that it is practicable to do so."

REASONABLY PRACTICABLE REQUIREMENTS

A statutory duty which has to be carried out as far as is reasonably practicable is one where there is a risk/benefit trade off. An employer is entitled to balance costs of remedy against benefits in reduction of risk and if the benefit is minimal compared to the cost, he/she need not carry out the duty. "Reasonably practicable" is a narrower term than "physically possible" and implies that a computation must be made, in which the quantum of risk is placed on one scale and the sacrifices involved in the measures necessary for averting the risk (whether in money, time or trouble) is placed on the other, and that if it be shown that there is a gross disproportion between them, the defendants discharge the onus on them to take that measure. It should be remembered that this would not mean no action at all is taken, just that a less costly and less effective measure would be used instead.

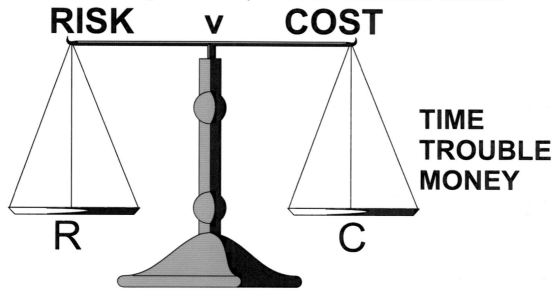

Figure 1-8: Reasonably practicable.   *Source: Corel Clipart.*

The roles and functions of external agencies

PARLIAMENT / HEALTH AND SAFETY COMMISSION

Parliament and the Health and Safety Commission (HSC) can only be an influence on organisations on a strategic basis. They rely on their operational arm, the enforcing authorities, to influence specifics. On behalf of the government the HSC identify the need for legal requirements, arrange drafts and consultation. They have an influence on law from the point of view that they decide what laws are appropriate and when they are to be introduced. As such they can control the quantity of law and the scope/extent of a given law. If organisations successfully lobby these bodies, they may be able to gain modification or delay.

HEALTH AND SAFETY EXECUTIVE

The Health and Safety Executive (HSE) is appointed as an enforcing authority. It's enforcing officers where possible take a monitoring role in the workplace but, where necessary, have a wide range of powers that enable them to enforce compliance. They will set out requirements orally or in writing as they see fit. If a more formal approach is required they will issue an enforcement notice or take steps to prosecute. In England and Wales they can take their own case in a Magistrates Court. Their field of responsibility is for the more technical workplaces such as construction, manufacturing, power generation, railways and farms. They also enforce the law in local authorities' workplaces. They are agents of the crown.

LOCAL AUTHORITIES

Local authorities have a similar remit to the HSE except that they enforce the law in simpler workplaces such as offices, shops and restaurants. Their enforcing officers (Environmental Health Officers – EHO) enforce health and safety law in HSE premises. The local authority appoints them.

FIRE AUTHORITIES

The fire authorities have a similar role to the HSE and Local Authorities, but for the narrow risk of fire. They are employees appointed by local authorities and enforce general fire legislation in all workplaces.

ENVIRONMENT AGENCY / SCOTTISH ENVIRONMENT PROTECTION AGENCY

The Environment Agency (EA) / Scottish Environment Protection Agency (SEPA) took over the responsibilities of HMIP, the NRA and the Waste Regulatory Authorities on April 1 1996. The EA is a Non-Departmental Public Body concerned with protecting and improving the land, air and water environment of England and Wales. It has a board and the board members are appointed by the Secretaries of State for the Environment and Wales and the Minister of Agriculture Fisheries and Food. The Scottish Environment Protection Agency has a similar role and function in Scotland.

The principal aim of the Agency is to protect and enhance the environment and to make a contribution towards "attaining the objective of achieving sustainable development". Objectives towards this aim include the adoption of an integrated approach to environmental protection and enhancement which considers impacts of substances on all environmental media and on natural resources.

INSURANCE COMPANIES

Insurance companies have become increasingly aware that they may have under valued the risks related to some companies they are insuring. This has caused them to look again at the risks and the factors that lead to claims. In conjunction with this they influence organisations to minimise the risks in order to control their level of premium. The new approach includes a focus on the status of management of health and safety in the organisation insured, which has been found to be a useful predictor of future loss.

The powers of inspectors under the HASWA

Enforcing authority inspectors (enforcing officers) are provided for in the HASAWA. Their role is to protect, enforce and advise on all matters related to health and safety management and standards. Here, the term inspector applies to either:

- Health and Safety Executive - e.g. Health and Safety Inspector, Agricultural Inspector or
- Local Authorities - Environmental Health Officer.

Although they are perhaps best known for their enforcement role, equal importance is placed on their role as advisors and for the dissemination of information on best practice.

POWERS UNDER THE HASAWA

- To enter any premises at any reasonable time.
- Take a constable or some other authorised person if there is an obstruction in the execution of his duty.
- To examine and investigate.
- Direct that a premises or part of premises remain undisturbed.
- Take photographs, measurements.
- Sample or retain unsafe articles and substances.
- To order the testing, dismantling and examination.
- Take possession of items.
- To require answers to questions with a signed statement, if necessary.
- To inspect and copy Statutory Books and documents or any other relevant documents.
- To provide assistance.
- Any other power.
- To serve
  - improvement notice, or
  - prohibition notice (may be suspended).
- Conduct own cases in England and Wales.

The scope and application of the Construction (Design and Management) Regulations

The scope of the CDM Regs extends to "construction work" on a "structure". These terms are defined in detail in the ACOP that accompanies the regs. The definitions are far too lengthy to repeat in full. However, the following is a brief extract from the ACOP.

"CONSTRUCTION"

The construction, alteration, conversion, fitting out, commissioning, renovation, repair, upkeep, redecoration or other maintenance, de-commissioning, demolition or dismantling of a structure.

The installation, commissioning, maintenance, repair or removal of mechanical, electrical, gas, compressed air, hydraulic, telecommunications, computer or similar services which are normally fixed to or within a structure.

"STRUCTURE"

Any building, steel or reinforced concrete structure, railway line or siding, tramway line, dock, harbour, inland navigation, tunnel, shaft, bridge, viaduct, waterworks, reservoir, pipe or pipe-line, cable, aqueduct, sewer, sewage works, gas holder, road, airfield, sea defence works, river works, drainage works, earthworks, lagoon, dam, wall, caisson, mast, tower, pylon, underground tank, earth retaining structure and any other structure similar to the foregoing.

The Regulations do not apply to projects where fewer than five people at any one time are expected to carry out construction work and where the local authority is the enforcing authority. Only the HSE enforce CDM, where the Local Authority is the enforcing authority, they hand over to the HSE as soon as CDM applies.

The Regulations apply to projects where five or more people at any one time are carrying out construction and where demolition or dismantling of a structure is taking place regardless of time or numbers.

Projects with a construction phase longer than 30 days or involving more than 500 person days of construction work are also notifiable to the Health and Safety Executive (HSE). Notification must be in writing and can be made using the form F10(rev).

Where there are fewer than five people CDM will still apply if the project is notifiable, e.g. a construction phase lasting 40 days with a workplace of 4.

The scope and application of the Construction (Health, Safety and Welfare) Regulations

These regulations came into force in September 1996. They replaced a lot of old legislation such as the Construction (General Provisions) Regulations 1961 and the Construction (Working Places) Regulations 1966 and introduce some new provisions. The Regulations cover a wide range of health and safety problems including:

- Provision of working platforms.
- Explosives.
- Prevention of falls.
- Support of excavations.
- Provision for high-risk activities such as roofwork and demolition.
- Emergency and fire procedures
- Good order.
- Welfare facilities.
- Transport routes.
- Inspections.
- "Construction site" - means any site where the principal work activity being carried out is construction work.
- "Construction work" - means the carrying out of any building, civil engineering or any engineering construction and includes all of the activities identified in paragraphs 1 and 2 above. It does not include the exploration for or the extraction of mineral resources.
- "Excavation" - means any earthwork, trench, well, shaft, tunnel or underground working.

1.6 - Sources of information on health and safety

Internal to the organisation

ACCIDENT/ILL-HEALTH DATA

Used properly, accident and ill-health data allow comparisons to be made both between organisations and by monitoring year on year performance. Analysis can be made to identify areas, situations of possible concern or the overall effectiveness of implementations of any control measures that may have been introduced. Data can be collected internally using accident books and report forms (e.g. RIDDOR) or from outside sources such as:

- The World Health Organisation (WHO).
- The International Labour Organisation (ILO).
- The Department of the Environment (Labour Force Survey).
- The HSE (including Statistical Services Unit and HSC Annual Report Statistical Supplement).

There are several methods of presenting data for analysis and some of the more common ones are given below. Methods should not be mixed and figures should only be used to compare like to like.

Accident/injury incidence rates

The HSE's formula for calculating an annual injury incidence rate is:

$$\frac{\text{No. of reportable injuries in financial year x 100 000}}{\text{Average no. employed during year}}$$

This is the rate per 100 000 employees. It does not allow for part-time workers or overtime and should only be used for a comparison of an annual calculation. There must be an adjustment made if shorter periods are to be considered.

Accident/injury frequency rates

Some parts of industry prefer to calculate injury frequency rates, usually per million hours worked. Using the hours worked rather than the number of employees avoids the problem of part-time workers and overtime causing a distortion as it does in the incidence rate calculation.

$$\frac{\text{No. of injuries in the period x 1 000 000}}{\text{Total hours working during the period}}$$

Accident/injury severity rates

$$\frac{\text{Total no. of days lost x 1 000}}{\text{Total hours worked}}$$

The injury severity rate does not necessarily correlate well with the seriousness of the injury. The data may be affected by the propensity of people in different parts of the country to take time off after a particular injury, e.g. food industry for poisoning.

Mean duration rate

$$\frac{\text{Total no. of days lost}}{\text{Total no. of accidents}}$$

Duration rate

$$\frac{\text{No. of hours worked}}{\text{Total no. of accidents}}$$

COST AND OTHER AND MANAGEMENT PERFORMANCE DATA

Cost and management performance data is generated by nearly all organisations. This internal information is often relevant to the health and safety management system and should not be overlooked.

COMPLIANCE DATA

The results of compliance visits by enforcing authorities can give a sometimes limited view of the organisation's compliance with health and safety legislation. Authorities such as the HSE, Employment Medical Advisory Service (EMAS), Environmental Health Officers and Fire Brigade are a good source of authoritative advice. This is usually of high quality but can be difficult to obtain. Some people are reluctant to seek advice from these sources as they do not wish to draw attention to themselves.

RESULTS OF AUDITS/INSPECTIONS

The aim of audits and inspections is to give management a detailed picture regarding the standards of health and safety management within the organisation. Thus audits and inspection are, essentially, confirmatory exercises which demonstrate that the health and safety management system is effective. The level and detail of audits/inspections carried out will depend on the type of organisation and its confidence in the existing management system.

Information from audits and inspections enables both symptoms as well as the cause to be identified and appropriate action taken. It is important to take this balanced approach where employees see that although they have a part to play in ensuring a safe and healthy workplace, it is also important that the things the organisation provides, including equipment and systems of work also be right and that action is taken to establish and maintain good standards. Auditors and inspectors can obtain information from three sources:

1. Interviewing individuals both about the operation of the health and safety management system and practices and their knowledge, understanding and perceptions of it.

2. Examining documentation for completeness, accuracy and reliability.

3. Visual observation of physical conditions and working practices to ensure conformity to legal and organisational standards.

External to the organisation

LEGISLATION (E.G. ACTS AND REGULATIONS)

These are available from the Her Majesty's Stationery Office (HMSO) and are prime sources which give the precise legal requirement. They can, however, be very dry and difficult to read without some legal understanding. It is also easy to miss changes and amendments unless an updating service is used.

New statutory instruments are published by the HMSO on the internet within 15 days of printed publication (http://www.hmso.gov.uk/stat.htm).

HSE AND HSC PUBLICATIONS

HSE Books publishes both approved codes of practice (ACOPs) and guidance notes. While failure to follow an ACOP is not in itself an offence, a defendant would have to show that the steps they took were equally effective thus transferring the burden of proof onto the defendant. Guidance notes, and other advisory literature, are persuasive in a law court; however they can set standards higher than the basic legal minimum. Lists of both priced and free publications are available from HSE Books.

The HSC/HSE also provides services such as a bi-monthly newsletter and an Autofax service. Autofax allows access to a number of free leaflets by dialling the appropriate number on a fax machine. These services are charged at premium telephone rates.

MAGAZINES

There are several occupational health and safety oriented magazines available from bodies such as ROSPA, IOSH and the British Safety Council. They are very useful for updating on new legislation and new publications as well as 'in depth' explanatory articles. The product and equipment advertising may also be useful.

INDUSTRY

Industrial bodies such as the Confederation of British Industry (CBI) and Engineering Employers Federation (EEF) often produce guidance and codes of practice for companies as do industrial training boards such as the Construction Industry Training Board (CITB) and the Paint Makers Association.

Manufacturers and suppliers of articles and substances have a legal duty to provide information under s.6 of the HASAWA and the Chemicals (Hazard Information and Packaging for Supply) Regulations (CHIP) 2002.

BRITISH STANDARDS INSTITUTE

The British Standards Institute (BSI) provides some high quality advice which is usually above the legal minimum standard. There is a distinct trend towards linking British Standards with legislation, for example, with the Safety Signs Regulations and BS 5378 as described in the communications module. There is also progressive harmonisation to European Standards (CEN) and the use of CE Marking.

TEXT BOOKS

These can be a useful reference but can quickly become out of date.

MICROFILM/COMPUTER DATABASES/SUBSCRIPTION SERVICES

These are a very comprehensive reference source which provides regular updates. Three well known services are:
- Microfiche – e.g. The Barbour Index.
- Computer compact disc read only memory – e.g. OSH-CD from the HSE; and
- Various reference books with a regular amendment service – e.g. Croner's Publications.

These types of service can, however, prove expensive for the casual user. When considering microfile computer and similar systems, the cost of the technology should be borne in mind as well as subscription charges.

ON-LINE COMPUTER SOURCES (THE INTERNET)

There is an increasing amount of information available on-line using a computer, modem and an Internet service provider. The World Wide Web provides a consistent interface with which to access information using software known as web browsers. These browsers allow the user to navigate through the Internet using hypertext links to jump from one page of information to another. Sites are found by the use of an 'address' known as an URL (unique resource locator). Many safety organisations are on the Web - including the HSE (http://.open.gov.uk/hse/hsehome.htm). There are also a number of relevant USENET newsgroups including sci.engr.safety (safety engineering), misc.health.injuries.rsi.misc (repetitive strain injuries) and sci.med.occupational (occupational medicine) which cater for people interested in these subjects. Newsgroups allow people to ask questions and post relevant information.

PROFESSIONAL BODIES

There are a number of safety related professional bodies such as the Institute of Occupational Safety and Health (IOSH). These provide local newsletters, regular meetings and a subscription to their magazine as part of the membership package. People who are interested in health and safety can join as affiliate members with no formal qualifications.

LAWYERS

Can provide expert legal advice but can be expensive and are rarely straightforward.

CONSULTANTS

These can be of variable quality and charge widely differing fees. As with selecting other types of contractor and service provider, safety consultants need to be chosen carefully. The HSE produces a free leaflet (INDG133(L)) giving further advice on selecting consultants.

TRAINING COURSES

In-house and external courses, seminars and exhibitions can prove a useful source of informations about developments and trends, as well as single topic issues.

1.7 - A framework for health and safety management

HSG65 - Successful Health and Safety Management

HSG65 - the HSE's Accident Prevention Unit first prepared Successful Health and Safety Management in 1991 and a second edition was published in 1997. The key elements of successful health and safety management are set out below and the relationship between them is outlined in the diagram.

POLICY

Organisations that are successful in achieving high standards of health and safety have health and safety policies which contribute to their business performance, while meeting their responsibilities to people and the environment in a way which fulfils both the spirit and the letter of the law. In this way they satisfy the expectations of shareholders, employees, customers and society at large. Their policies are cost effective and aimed at achieving the preservation and development of physical and human resources and reductions in financial losses and liabilities. Their health and safety policies influence all their activities and decisions, including those to do with the selection of resources and information, the design and operation of working systems, the design and delivery of products and services, and the control and disposal of waste.

ORGANISING

Organisations that achieve high health and safety standards are structured and operated so as to put their health and safety policies into effective practice. This is helped by the creation of a positive culture that secures involvement and participation at all levels. It is sustained by effective communications and the promotion of competence that enables all employees to make a responsible and informed contribution to the health and safety effort. The visible and active leadership of senior managers is necessary to develop and maintain a culture supportive of health and safety management. Their aim is not simply to avoid accidents, but to motivate and empower people to work safely. The vision, values and beliefs of leaders become the shared 'common knowledge' of all.

PLANNING

These successful organisations adopt a planned and systematic approach to policy implementation. Their aim is to minimise the risks created by work activities, products and services. They use risk assessment methods to decide priorities and set objectives for hazard elimination and risk reduction. Performance standards are established and performance is measured against them. Specific actions needed to promote a positive health and safety culture and to eliminate and control risks are identified. Wherever possible, risks are eliminated by the careful selection and design of facilities, equipment and processes or minimised by the use of physical control measures. Where this is not possible, provision of a safe system of work and personal protective equipment are used to control risks.

MEASURING PERFORMANCE

Health and safety performance in organisations that manage health and safety successfully is measured against pre-determined standards. This reveals when and where action is needed to improve performance. The success of action taken to control risks is assessed through active self-monitoring involving a range of techniques. This includes an examination of both hardware (premises, plant and substances) and software (people, procedures and systems), including individual behaviour. Failures of control are assessed through reactive monitoring which requires the thorough investigation of any accidents, ill health or incidents with the potential to cause harm or loss. In both active and reactive monitoring, the objectives are not only to determine the immediate causes of sub-standard performance but, more importantly, to identify the underlying causes and the implications for the design and operation of the health and safety management system.

AUDITING AND REVIEWING PERFORMANCE

Learning from all relevant experience and applying the lessons learned are important elements in effective health and safety management. This needs to be done systematically through regular reviews of performance based on data both from monitoring activities and from independent audits of the whole health and safety management system. These form the basis for self-regulation and for securing compliance with sections 2 to 6 of the HASAWA 1974. Commitment to continuous improvement involves the constant development of policies, approaches to implementation and techniques of risk control. Organisations which achieve high standards of health and safety assess their health and safety performance by internal reference to key performance indicators and by external comparison with the performance of business competitors. They often also record and account for their performance in their annual reports.

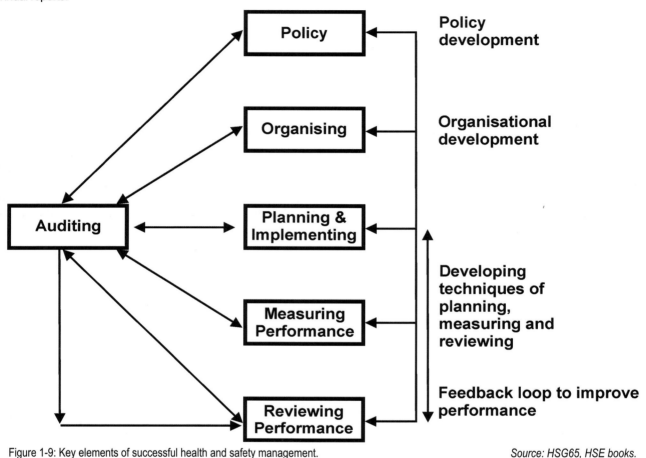

Figure 1-9: Key elements of successful health and safety management.   *Source: HSG65, HSE books.*

Policy

Overall Aims

On completion of this Unit, candidates will understand:

■ the importance of setting policy in health and safety.

■ the key features and appropriate content of an organisation's health and safety policy.

Content

Specific Intended Learning Outcomes

The intended learning outcomes of this Unit are that candidates will be able to:

2.1 explain the purpose of a health and safety policy

2.2 assess the appropriateness of an organisation's health and safety policy in terms of structure and general content

Sources of Reference

The Management of Health and Safety at Work (ACOP) (L21), HSE Books

Successful Health and Safety Management (HSG65), HSE Books

Starting Your Business (INDG324), HSE Books

A Guide to Managing Health and Safety in Construction, HSE Books

Relevant Statutory Provisions

The Health and Safety at Work etc Act (HASAWA) 1974 - section 2(3)

The Management of Health and Safety at Work Regulations (MHSWR) 1999 - regulation 5

The Workplace (Health, Safety and Welfare) Regulations (WHSWR) 1992

2.1 - The role of the health and safety policy

The Health and Safety at Work Act, etc (HASAWA) 1974 set out an obligation to manage the risks that organisations create, and a cornerstone of this was seen to be the establishment of an active health and safety policy. This has been consistently misunderstood and underestimated by many over the years since the HASAWA came into force. With the introduction of the Management of Health and Safety at Work Regulations (MHSWR) 1999 this has received a fresh focus. Without active management any attempt at organised accident prevention will be restricted and predominantly reactive. The overall intent of a policy will provide direction for an organisation, establishing a remit that will both guide the organisation to satisfy the goals set by it and to bind it so that it does not stray from the standards that it sets. This will influence the decisions made by an organisation, in that they will need to fall within the intent of the policy.

Organisations differ greatly in their goals, risks, structure and what they feel capable of committing themselves to. In the same way a policy is therefore a 'personal' thing setting out a particular organisation's position at that point in time.

2.2 - Aims, objectives and key elements of a H&S policy

AIMS

The aim of the policy of an organisation is to create a structure to its approach to health and safety.

OBJECTIVES

The objectives are to ensure clear definition of the organisation's goals, set out responsibilities for health and safety matters and describe the arrangements in place to ensure health and safety is achieved.

KEY ELEMENTS

A health and safety policy contains:

- A general statement of management commitment (What) - states the overall aims of the organisation in terms of health and safety performance.
- Details of the organisation (Who) - defining structure, role, relationships and responsibilities of individuals.
- Arrangements to control the risks (How) - expected to set the direction, scope and actions of an organisation to manage health and safety. Specifies the arrangements for achieving.

To be effective the policy should be:

- In a number of formats.
- Effectively communicated.
- Revised as appropriate.
- Monitored through audits.

The effective communication of the policy is important; all affected by it must understand it. In order to achieve this a good deal has to be done. Merely posting it or distributing a copy to employees is not enough. Training and briefings will be necessary, as a minimum, to ensure effective communication. For new employees this is often done as part of the induction process. The format, complexity and language used should be considered. Experience shows that no one form of document is adequate to meet everyone's needs; therefore the document is usually produced in at least a summary and a detailed format. If it is likely to be revised frequently, a loose-leaf scheme will be advisable for the detailed version. This is especially true when the names and contact telephone numbers of staff are included.

2.3 - Setting targets

A particularly effective way of demonstrating management commitment to health and safety is by communicating a policy statement of intent. It sets quantifiable organisational objectives for health and safety. In order to accentuate this commitment the statement should be signed and dated by the most senior member of the management team. Lack of firm management commitment of this kind leads to the perception that health and safety is not equal to other business objectives. The addition of a date to the statement will indicate the last time the statement was reviewed.

Organisations should translate their overall aims that are set out in the statement into objectives for the organisation, key parts of the organisation and key individuals. In line with other business objectives, health and safety objectives should be set out as quantifiable targets. An easily quantifiable item is the number of accidents occurring in an organisation. This is probably why people are attracted to targets for accident reduction; however it is important to look at the effect of such targets on accident reporting. Objectives should, ideally, be proactive; though it is not uncommon to have reactive objectives related to reduction in accidents as part of a group of objectives. Proactive objectives related to such things as manager training completed or risk assessments conducted are important to maintain progress on health and safety. Many organisations seek to compare their performance against other organisations, sometimes called 'benchmarking'. This is easiest done with performance indicators that are measurable, the most obvious of which are accident statistics. Though they are often unreliable for comparison in this way they are still used and limitations accepted. In more recent times organisations have compared other proactive factors such as the percentage of managers that hold a NEBOSH National Certificate in Construction Safety and Health.

2.4 - Organising for health and safety

It is usual to express the organisation by showing an organisational chart, allowing reporting/communication structures of line and function staff to be depicted. Clear identification of responsibilities for all levels of management, and duties of employees are necessary, as are the role and functions of health and safety professional staff. Part of organising for health and safety is to establish a clear perspective of the role and function of employee representatives and committees, including clarification of the communication lines and feedback loops.

The active involvement of managers in achieving health and safety is important for its success; this includes the role of the manager in ensuring compliance with the policy. It is necessary for managers to ensure resource is in place and work is being carried out in a safe and healthy way. It is essential therefore that they monitor the effectiveness of the policy and the practices used to achieve it.

2.5 - Health and safety arrangements

This section of the policy details the practical arrangements for planning, organising, and controlling hazards, as well as monitoring compliance with and assessing the effectiveness of the arrangements. The main headings of arrangements that could be detailed in the health and safety policy might include:

General arrangements:

- Allocation of finance for health and safety.
- Planning.
- Organising.
- Control of hazards - general e.g. risk assessments.
- Consultation.
- Communication.
- Competence.
- Accident and hazard reporting.
- Monitoring compliance.

Specific arrangements for hazards, such as those relating to:

- Fire.
- Electricity.
- Manual handling.
- Work at a height.

The specific style and scope of the policy needs to reflect that of the organisation. Though there will be some common elements, a policy from a construction company should be different to one for a charity that looks after dogs, as the risks they manage are different. Arrangements set out in a policy may not reflect well the circumstances of the workplace and as such may not be effective. It is essential that those affected by the arrangement be involved in its development. In addition, arrangements that are made can quickly become outdated by changes in the way that things are done in the organisation; this can undermine their effectiveness. It is essential that systems be in place to monitor and assess this.

Because it is useful to plan for arrangements to change it is worth producing documents in such a way that it is easy to identify changes. This can involve highlighting the different changes on the document, explaining the reasons for change, having a controlled number of copies of the document issued and recording that the changes have been issued to those that hold copies.

2.6 - Reviewing the policy

A number of circumstances may lead to a need to review the policy, for example, the passage of time, technological, organisational or legal changes and the results of monitoring.

As *time* passes the arrangements for control of health and safety are influenced by people finding different ways of doing the same thing. Arrangements as practised can therefore differ greatly from the original way it was set out in the policy.

Technological change is happening in the workplace all the time, and this can mean that arrangements may be set out against circumstances that do not exist anymore because equipment or substances have been altered. It might also be that the organisation has been able to take advantage of technological advantages in something, e.g. materials handling, yet the policy refers to the earlier way of working.

Changes in *organisation* have a specific bearing on the arrangements. For example, if reporting of accidents is set out in the policy and in relation to a certain post, this may be influenced by a reorganisation that removes the post. Similarly, changes in work patterns e.g. shift working could influence arrangements that have been made.

Legislation changes periodically and it is fair to say it usually reflects a strengthening of society's expectations. This may mean that specific arrangements set out in the policy may no longer conform with the law, in that it may be incomplete or not to a satisfactory standard. For example, the change to the Workplace (Health, Safety and Welfare) Regulations (WHSWR) 1992 that requires rest rooms to have "adequate number of tables and adequate seating with backs".

If *monitoring* methods are in place and are working they could identify a gap in a specific arrangement or that something is unclear or contradictory. This might be from enforcement action, professional advice such as an audit or following accident investigation.

2.7 - The legal requirements and guidance relating to health and safety policy and arrangements

Section 2 (3) of the Health and Safety at Work etc. Act 1974 requires all employers, except for the smaller organisations (currently those with fewer than five employees) to:

1. Create a written health and safety policy statement.
2. State the organisation and arrangement for bringing the statement into effect.
3. Bring the policy to the attention of employees.
4. Revise the policy as necessary.

The Management of Health and Safety at Work Regulations 1999 - Regulation 5 - Health and Safety Arrangements

Appropriate arrangements must be made for the effective planning, organisation, control, monitoring and review of preventative and protective measures (in other words, for the management of health and safety). Again, employers with five or more employees must have their arrangements in writing.

The Health and Safety Executive have set out guidance on managing health and safety in a document called "Successful Health and Safety Management" (HSG 65). It seeks to emphasise the importance of setting out policy on health and safety, supporting this with good organisation, establishing controls (arrangements), measurement of performance, review and audit.

Organising for Health and Safety in Construction

Overall Aims

On completion of this Unit, candidates will understand:

- the general health and safety roles and responsibilities of employers, managers, employees and other relevant parties.
- the particular duties and responsibilities of clients, designers, planning supervisors, principal contractors and contractors involved in construction projects.
- the need to consult with employees, and methods of consultation.

Content

Specific Intended Learning Outcomes

The intended learning outcomes of this Unit are that candidates will be able to:

3.1   outline the health and safety responsibilities of the various parties involved with work activities in general and construction work in particular.

3.2   explain the requirements placed on employers to consult with their employees.

Sources of Reference

A Guide to the Health and Safety at Work etc Act 1974 (L1), HSE Books

The Management of Health and Safety at Work (ACOP) (L21), HSE Books

Successful Health and Safety Management (HSG65), HSE Books

Managing Health and Safety in Construction (ACOP) (HSG224), HSE Books

A Guide to Managing Health and Safety in Construction, HSE Books

Safety Representatives and Safety Committees (ACOP) (L87), HSE Books

A Guide to the Health and Safety (Consultation with Employees) Regulations 1996 (L95), HSE Books

Relevant Statutory Provisions

The Health and Safety at Work etc Act (HASAWA) 1974 - sections 2-4, 6-9, 36 and 37

The Management of Health and Safety at Work Regulations (MHSWR) 1999 - regulations 7-9, 11, 12, 14, 15

The Construction (Design and Management) Regulations (CDM) 1994

The Safety Representatives and Safety Committees Regulations (SRSC) 1977

The Health and Safety (Consultation with Employees) Regulations (HSCER) 1996

The Reporting of Injuries, Diseases and Dangerous Occurrences Regulations (RIDDOR) 1995

3.1 - Legal & organisational roles & responsibilities

GENERAL POINTS

The Health and Safety at Work etc Act (HASAWA) 1974 covers all employment activities, apart from private domestic workers.

HASAWA applies to employers, self-employed persons, subcontractors, and visitors to places of employment, members of the public affected by the employer's activities, designers, suppliers, importers, employees, directors and managers. It also provides the Health & Safety Executive with various enforcement powers. Section 40 of the HASAWA requires that in any case relating to a failure to comply with a responsibility set out in the HASAWA to do something so far as is reasonably practicable, it is for the accused to prove that the steps they took satisfied the requirement.

More specific duties are expressed in the Management of Health and Safety at Work Regulations (MHSWR) 1999.

THE EMPLOYER'S RESPONSIBILITIES

All employers have a responsibility for those that might be affected by their undertaking, whether they are a small partnership of general practitioner doctors, a large charity that cares for animals, a medium sized limited liability construction company, a local authority, government department or a major multi-site public limited company (plc). In practice this is both a civil and criminal responsibility. The main responsibilities are set out below.

See also - Management of Health and Safety at Work Regulations (MHSWR) 1999 - Unit 20.

For the health, safety and welfare of employees

It should be noted that the employer's responsibility extends to situations where the employer's employees may be working in another person's premises, away from a main site or working from home.

Health and Safety at Work Act 1974

Section 2(1)

To ensure, so far as reasonably practicable, the health, safety and welfare at work of employees. This is a general duty which is expanded on by the following sections.

Section 2(2)

Ensuring, so far as **reasonably practicable**, the health, safety and welfare at work of employees through:

- Safe plant and systems of work e.g. provision of guards on machines and the safe use of the machine.
- Safe use, handling, storage and transport of goods and materials e.g. good manual handling of boxes, mechanical handling of trusses, storage of flammable gases or movement of goods by road.
- Provision of information, instruction, training and supervision e.g. provision of induction training, instruction on action in the case of fire and information on chemicals that are handled. Supervision is on an as necessary basis; inexperienced employees would require more supervision as would higher risk tasks.
- Safe place of work including means of access and egress e.g. aisles kept clear, safe ladders to a scaffold platform or emergency exit from a building. The requirements cover not only buildings but for example open air sites, boats, exhibition sites; the duty extends to the structure of any item.
- Safe and healthy working environment and welfare arrangements e.g. good lighting, appropriate temperature, washing facilities, seating and first aid.

Figure 3-1: Safe use, storage & transport.   *Source: ACT.*

Figure 3-2: Is this a safe place for this person?   *Source: ACT.*

MHSWR - Regulation 15 - Temporary workers

Fixed term contract

Consideration is given to the special needs of temporary workers. Employers are to provide those employed on fixed term contracts with particular health and safety information, such as on special qualifications required in order to perform the work safely, e.g. a fork lift truck driving qualification or any health surveillance required, e.g. for the effects of lead.

Temporary workers through employment businesses

Employers must provide information to temporary workers placed by employment businesses in the same way as with those on fixed term contracts. In addition, the employer must provide the employment business with information on special qualifications the worker will need and information on special features of the work that affect health and safety, e.g. work at a height or in a confined space. Further specific duties are placed on the employer by the HASAWA.

HASAWA 1974 - Section 2(3) - Health and Safety Policy

The employer has a duty to prepare and keep up to date a written **health and safety policy** supported by information on the organisation and arrangements for carrying out the policy. This policy should reflect how the employer is controlling risks. The health and safety policy has to be brought to the notice of employees. If there are fewer than five employees, the duty to have a written policy does not apply.

See also - Policy - Unit 2.

HASAWA 1974 - Section 2(4) - Appointment of safety representatives

Recognised Trade Unions have the right to **appoint safety representatives** to represent the employees in consultations with the employer about health and safety matters. See below for detail, in section on consultation.

HASAWA 1974 - Section 2(6) - Duty to consult

Employers must **consult with any safety representatives** appointed by recognised Trade Unions.

HASAWA 1974 - Section 2(7) - Safety committees

To **establish a safety committee** if requested by two or more safety representatives.

HASAWA 1974 - Section 9 - Not charge employees

The employer shall **not charge employees** for anything done or provided to comply with a specific legal obligation, e.g. provision of personal protective equipment, health surveillance, welfare facilities etc. This does not extend to anything that an employer may choose to do to provide health, safety and welfare standards beyond legal requirements. For example, a particular style of safety footwear that might be preferred by employees might cost more than a standard pair; In this case it would be usual to charge employees for the difference between the style they prefer and a standard pair. The same may be said for eye-sight correction glasses for display screen equipment.

MHSWR - Regulation 8 - Procedures for serious and imminent danger and for danger areas

Employers are required to set up emergency procedures and appoint competent persons to ensure compliance with identified arrangements, to devise control strategies as appropriate and to limit access to areas of risk to ensure that only those persons with adequate health and safety knowledge and instruction are admitted.

MHSWR - Regulation 9 - Contacts with external services

Employers must ensure that, where necessary, contacts are made with external services. This particularly applies with regard to first-aid, emergency medical care and rescue work.

For others affected by work activities

In addition to the employer's responsibility to its employees the employer has responsibilities to other people that are not employees. This covers a wide range of people including visitor, contractors, subcontractors and members of the public. The responsibility expects employers to have a mind to these people and how they might be affected by its activities. In so doing this will mean doing similar things to those that would keep employees healthy and safe. The responsibility extends to consideration of the fact that these people may not understand hazards they are exposed to or how they should be dealt with.

HASAWA 1974 - Section 3 - Employer's duties to persons not his employees

The employer shall so far as **reasonably practicable:**

a)   Not expose them to risk to their heath and safety e.g. an area used by a contractor on a busy site should be separated from hazards by barriers

b)   Give information about risks which may affect them e.g. providing an induction for contractors.

Visitors

Some of the practical steps that an organisation might take in order to satisfy its responsibility to ensure the health and safety of visitors to its premises are:

- Identify visitors by signing in and the provision of badges.
- Provide information regarding the risks present and the site rules and procedures to be followed, particularly in emergencies.
- Provide escorts to supervise visitors throughout the site and restrict access to areas where higher risk activities take place.

Many organisations issue badges to visitors. The main purpose of this is to ensure that visitors are clearly identified, but the issuing of badges may be combined with recording visitors and providing information on emergency procedures that can be included on the badge. In addition, badges may be used to identify regular contractors or people who may only have access to certain parts of the business, e.g. by differently coloured badges. It is important that badges are numbered and that at the end of the working day (or whenever) a note is made of outstanding badges to ensure that all are accounted for. Action should be taken to determine what has happened to the badge-holders. In organisations where it is common practice to issue badges to employees it is important that visitors' badges are noticeably different (e.g. in style or colour). Badges for employees and regular contractors should have a photograph of the holder in order to aid identification.

Contractors

Contractors are used to perform a wide variety of tasks on behalf of employers. Whilst the contractor may have duties of their own, the employer carries responsibility for the work done by contractors as part of the employer's undertaking. These responsibilities are both organisational and legal. In the organisational sense the employer commissions contractors to perform tasks on its behalf, and in doing this appropriately it is essential for good management that health and safety be included, along with provision of the service on time and with quality.

In addition, the employer will need to take reasonable care to control the work of contractors to discharge their duties at common law and reasonably practicable steps to discharge its duty under the HASAWA. These responsibilities work in harmony with the employer's responsibility to look after the contractor while the contractor is working in a workplace that the employer controls.

It is important to conduct risk assessments with contractors in mind and clearly define the task of the contractor in a way that includes health and safety issues. In this way the risks to a contractor can be identified and controlled. For example, if an employer needs a contractor to work at a height above the entrance to an office building using a scaffold, it is necessary for the employer to control this work such that it is conducted safely for the protection of contractors working on the scaffold and anyone passing near the scaffold. The provision of toe boards, guard rails, and lighting and the siting of the scaffold are factors that affect contractors and others.

The public

Employers need to be aware of the ways in which their work can affect the public and their responsibilities for control of these risks. The public may be visitors to the workplace by specific invitation or by straying into the workplace. The employer may invite and encourage the public into the workplace to enable them to purchase goods or services. It is important that the employer controls the exposure of the public to risks, such as slippery floors in shops, an unprotected excavation by the side of a pathway, operation of vehicle maintenance equipment in a garage, and a release of cement dust or dust from a demolition site to neighbouring houses.

DIRECTORS' AND SENIOR MANAGERS' RESPONSIBILITIES

Directors and senior managers implement the employer's responsibilities and are accountable for ensuring health and safety is established. In practice this will include ensuring that an appropriate health and safety policy is in place and that it is worked to; failure to do so may render the director or senior manager personally accountable.

HASAWA 1974 - Section 37 - Breaches by the body corporate

Where there has been a breach of legislation on the part of a body corporate (limited company or local authority) and the offence can be proved:

- To have been committed with the consent or connivance of, or
- To be attributable to any neglect on the part of any director, manager, secretary or similar officer of the body corporate, he, as well as the body corporate, can be found guilty and punished accordingly.

MIDDLE MANAGERS AND SUPERVISORS

In a similar way to senior managers, managers at all levels in an organisation are expected to ensure health and safety is effectively established in their area of control. If they fail to do this they could be held accountable for their failings. This may be seen as a separate accountability to that of senior managers or the employer. All could be prosecuted for the part they played in the situation. The HASAWA may be used to prosecute managers and supervisors. Section 36 of the HASAWA would be appropriate for the prosecution of middle managers, e.g. a store manager of a supermarket, and section 7 would be appropriate for prosecution of a supervisor. The supervisor plays a particularly important role on behalf of the employer in that they provide the supervisory control that ensures immediate causes of accidents (hazards) are identified and controlled. If they fail to take reasonable care in their provision of supervision they could be held accountable. *See also the section - employee's duties - later in this unit.*

HASAWA 1974 - Section 36 - Another person

Where the commission by any person of the breach of legislation is due to the act or default of some other person, that other person shall be guilty of the offence and may be charged with and convicted of the offence whether or not proceedings are taken against the first mentioned person. Case law indicates that 'other person' refers to persons lower down the corporate tree than mentioned in HSAWA section 37, e.g. middle managers, safety advisors, training officers, and may extend to people working on contract e.g. architects, consultants, planning supervisor.

Middle managers and supervisors carry a general duty to take reasonable care for those that might be affected by their acts or omissions. This would include responsibility for the health and safety of subordinates who might be affected by the way in which the manager or supervisor did their job. Failing to supervise effectively could be an omission, while directing someone to conduct a task without taking reasonable care to consider the risks could be seen as an act. *See also the section - Employees' Responsibilities - later in this unit.*

THE HEALTH AND SAFETY PRACTITIONER

The health and safety practitioner is appointed by the employer to provide advice and assistance to the employer in meeting the employer's responsibilities. The appointment of a practitioner does not remove line management responsibilities for health and safety but it provides support to line mangers in fulfilling these responsibilities. The health and safety practitioner is an employee and has responsibilities to take reasonable care for their acts and omissions when conducting their work, for example, failure to provide advice or agreed service such as an inspection or inadequate advice or service. This would apply equally to an occupational health nurse or fire specialist. The MHSWR place a legal duty on the employer to appoint competent persons to provide health and safety assistance.

MHSWR - Regulation 7 - Health and safety assistance

The regulation places an absolute duty on the employer to take the following actions:

- Appoint one or more competent persons to assist with compliance with health and safety legislation.
- Make arrangements for the persons to co-operate.
- Ensure the number of people appointed, time available and means at their disposal are adequate. Consider size of organisation, risks and distribution of the risks.
- Persons appointed that are not employees are provided with information.
- Persons appointed are informed of any person working under a fixed-term contract or employed in an employment business.

The regulations state that competence means having sufficient training and experience or knowledge and other qualities. The approved code of practice (ACOP) says employers should consider:

- Knowledge and understanding of work involved.
- Principles of risk assessment and prevention.
- Current health and safety applications.
- Capacity to apply to tasks required.
- Identifying problems.
- Promoting and communicating health, safety and welfare advances and practices.
- Understanding of relevant current best practice.
- Awareness of own limitations.
- Membership of a professional body or similar.

- Assessing the need for action.
- Designing and developing strategies and plans.
- Implementing these strategies and plans.
- Evaluating their effectiveness.
- Willingness and ability to supplement existing experience and knowledge.
- Holding competence based qualification (NVQ/SVQ).

The regulations do not require the self employed, who are themselves competent, to appoint anyone. The regulations do not require individuals in business partnership to appoint a person if one of them is competent.

EMPLOYEES' RESPONSIBILITIES

Effective health and safety requires the complete involvement of employees. Employees have responsibilities that reflect the part they play in ensuring health and safety. Their responsibility to take reasonable care is not as onerous as the employer's, reflecting the more limited role they play. In practice the requirement to take reasonable care is expressed in both criminal (HASAWA) and civil (common law) law. Day to day practical and useful things are expected of the employee, for example the wearing of any necessary personal protective equipment, washing hands after work, keeping their workplace tidy and free from hazards. Employees are expected to take an active part in preventing accidents; they must report hazards they identify and not interfere with provisions made for health and safety.

HASAWA 1974 - Section 7 - Employees' duties

These sections place general obligations upon all employees, whatever their position in the organisation.

Employees must:

- Take reasonable care of their own health and safety and that of others who may be affected by their acts or omissions, e.g. wear hard hat if necessary, not obstruct a fire exit, drive carefully or use guards on equipment.
- Co-operate with the employer (or any other person), so far as is necessary, so as to ensure that the employer can comply with his statutory obligations, e.g. report hazards or defects in control measures, attend training or provide medical samples for analysis.

HASAWA 1974 - Section 8 - No person

No person shall interfere with or misuse anything provided to secure health and safety - e.g. remove guard rail from scaffold, remove first aid equipment without authority or breach lock off systems.

MHSWR - Regulation 14 - Employees' duties

The regulations create additional specific duties:

- Every employee shall use any equipment, material or substance provided to him or her in accordance with any training and instruction.
- Within the limits of their training and instruction every employee shall inform their employer (e.g. via supervisory staff) of any (a) situation that represents a serious and immediate danger or (b) shortcoming in the employer's protection arrangements.

RESPONSIBILITIES OF PERSONS IN CONTROL OF PREMISES

HSAWA 1974 - Section 4 - Those in control of premises

Anyone in control of non-domestic premises or plant used by persons not in their employment shall, so far as is reasonably practicable:

- Ensure safe access and egress to premises and plant.
- Ensure that plant or substances in the premises, or provided for their use, are safe and without risk to health.

This is a wide-ranging responsibility and extends to some logical areas where the public or other workers need protection, for example, a self service launderette, a multi-story car park, an office block being built, or industrial units rented to employers. In addition it would extend to students studying in a college / university, or outside contractors who go onto premises under someone else's control to install / repair machinery. The duty is not imposed on employees who may have day to day 'control' on behalf of the person in control, for example, a caretaker, security staff or supervisor. However, such people must fulfil their general duties as an employee.

Civil law requires those in control of premises to take reasonable care of those that may be affected by hazards in the premises. This is further clarified by the Occupiers Liability Acts 1957 and 1984 that impose a general duty of care to employees, visitors and trespassers. An occupier may be someone that takes control of a premise or part of it on a temporary basis, such as a contractor or on a more permanent basis, such as a tenant of an office block. (The Occupiers Liability Acts are not examined as specific items in the NEBOSH National Certificate in Construction Safety and Health - only the concept of civil liability of the occupier is necessary.)

3.2 - The responsibilities of the self-employed

GENERAL POINTS

There are a great many self-employed people at work within construction today and they are frequently involved in work in other employers' (and the public's) premises. They carry a responsibility for the risks of their work that may affect those that work alongside them or the public. In addition, they are expected to take a responsibility for their own safety, for example, getting electrical equipment inspected and tested at intervals or making sure the ladder they use to access a scaffold platform is safe.

HASAWA 1974 - SECTION 3 - DUTIES OF THE SELF EMPLOYED

The self -employed shall so far as reasonably practicable:

- Not expose themselves to risks to their health and safety, e.g. wear personal protection.
- Not expose other persons to risks to their health and safety, e.g. keep shared work area tidy and not block fire exits.

3.3 - Responsibilities of "the supply chain"

GENERAL POINTS

It is essential that we recognise the importance of the influence of the supply chain on health and safety in the workplace. If a designer or manufacturer does not create articles that are safe by design or faults occur during manufacture they may easily pass down the supply chain and hazards will be introduced into the workplace. Small companies have to place a high degree of reliance on the supply chain to provide suitable articles and substances. The best way to deal with hazards is at source, e.g. at design and manufacture. In the same way, if an article or substance has residual hazards that the employer needs to take account of when using it, it is appropriate that the supply chain provide information on the hazards and controls to deal with them. This would include the provision of substance data sheets and instructions for the safe use of equipment.

HASAWA 1974 - SECTION 6 - GENERAL DUTIES OF SUPPLIERS, MANUFACTURERS AND DESIGNERS OF ARTICLES AND SUBSTANCES

This section places specific duties on those who can ensure that articles and substances for use at work are as safe and without risks as is reasonably practicable. The responsibility relates to both new and second hand articles as well as all substances (including micro-organisms) supplied to workplaces. The section covers:

■ Safe design, installation and testing of articles (including fairground equipment).
■ Substances are safe and without risks to health.
■ Carry out or arrange for tests or examinations to ensure safe design and construction of articles and to ensure substances will be safe and without risk to health.
■ Provision of information on use and conditions essential to health and safety, and information about new and serious risks which come to light is to be provided to those supplied.
■ Carry out research to minimise risks.
■ Erectors and installers of articles for use at work must ensure it does not make the article unsafe or a risk to health.

Importers and suppliers carry the same duties as designers and manufacturers. It would usually be enough for them to rely on the tests and examinations conducted by the manufacturer/designer. Importers would be expected to prove that the article had the same standard of health and safety as a United Kingdom (UK) supplier; conformity with European harmonised standards would usually be sufficient.

3.4 - The relationship between client and contractor

DUTIES TO EACH OTHER AND TO THE OTHER'S EMPLOYEES

General points

The principal duties are expressed in the above sections and show that a client has duties towards a contractor and their employees as visitors to their workplace. In addition, when a client commissions a contractor to conduct work relating to the client's undertaking the client retains responsibility to see that it is conducted in a safe and healthy manner. Clearly this may benefit the contractor's employees, other contractors' employees, the public and the client's employees. Sections 2 - 4 of HASAWA seek to control this. A contractor that agrees to a contract for service must provide appropriate health and safety standards when conducting the work - this will benefit all those that might be affected. It is the responsibility of both parties to build health and safety into the contract and work methods. To this end it is essential that they co-operate with each other, seeking to plan and co-ordinate activities.

MHSWR - Regulation 12 - Persons working in host employers' or self employed persons' undertakings

Host employers and self-employed people must ensure that people carrying out work on their premises receive relevant information. If reliance is placed on the employer of the visiting employees providing information a check should be made to ensure information has been passed on. The information should be enough to allow the employer of the visiting employee to comply with their responsibilities at law and would address the risks arising from the host employer's undertaking. In addition, information should identify people nominated by the host employer to help with emergency evacuation. Such employees would include those working under a contract of service and employees provided by temporary employment businesses under the control of a host employer.

Contractors

In the context of health and safety at work, the term contractor is commonly applied to those who visit the premises of others to conduct work. This is usually in connection with the repair, maintenance, refurbishment or installation of plant and equipment, or building alterations, and in this sense will be either an employer or self-employed person.

Contractors carrying out maintenance works are a significant cause of accidents in the workplace. In general, visiting contractors are less familiar with the workplace and associated risks than the indigenous workforce, yet often carry out more hazardous operations. In order to minimise the risk potential of such activities and to ensure that all concerned are made aware of their health and safety responsibilities, a detailed knowledge of relevant legislation / health and safety standards is essential, risks must be identified and effective control methods introduced.

Clients

Clients, as employers, are obliged both by criminal and civil law to protect their workforce and others from health risks and personal injury and to conduct all undertakings in such a way as to ensure that members of the public around or entering their premises are likewise protected. The main statutory provisions relating to health and safety with regard to managing contractors are embodied in the HASAWA, MHSWR, and the Construction (Design and Management) Regulations (CDM) 1994.

Clients contract operations for a wide range of situations, from activities such as window cleaning, catering or security to large-scale construction works, such as extensions to premises or the building of new premises on a "green field" site. Consultation with contractors prior to a contract being signed, commencement of work and during the course of the work is of the utmost significance if a safe and healthy site is to be maintained.

PLANNING AND CO-ORDINATION OF CONTRACTED WORK

It is essential that all contracted work be planned and co-ordinated. Contracted work carries particular risks in that workers may be unfamiliar with the workplace and work may be organised such that activities conflict with each other putting contractors or employees at risk. It is essential that a risk assessment of work activities be made foreseeing how they interact with each other. The MHSWR require that employers make arrangements to plan, organise, control, monitor and review activities that it controls. This would, naturally, extend to contract work commissioned by the employer.

PROCEDURES FOR THE SELECTION OF CONTRACTORS

There are six main elements to a management strategy for selection of contractors. The extent to which each element is relevant will depend upon the degree of risk and nature of work to be contracted. The elements are:

1. Identification of suitable bidders (preferred list).
2. Identification of hazards within the specification.
3. Checking of (health and safety aspects of) bids and selection of contractor.
4. Contractor agrees to be subject to client's rules.
5. Management of the contractor on site.
6. Checking after completion of contract.

3.5 - Joint occupation of premises

SHARED RESPONSIBILITIES IN THE CASE OF JOINT OCCUPATION

The occupier of premises has civil duties under the Occupiers' Liability Acts 1957 and 1984 regarding the state and condition of the premises. *(The Occupiers Liability Acts are not examined as specific items in the NEBOSH General Certificate in Construction Safety and Health - only the concept of civil liability of the occupier is necessary.)* When contractors are working on a premise it could be argued that they are joint occupiers with an employer under these Acts. Therefore both employer and the contractor have joint liabilities in 'common areas'. The occupier is not normally liable for dangers associated with the contractors' work activities, provided that in selecting the contractor he or she took care to ensure competency, and is satisfied that the works are being carried out properly.

In a similar way, considering criminal law, if more than one employer was in **control of premises** at the time that contracted work was being undertaken, these being the client and contractor, they may each be prosecuted for failing to meet responsibilities under section 4 of HASAWA.

Figure 3-3: Joint occupancy. *Source: ACT.*

Figure 3-4: Occupier's liability - to public.   *Source: ACT.*

CO-OPERATION AND CO-ORDINATION

MHSWR - Regulation 11 - Co-operation and co-ordination

Employers who work together in a common workplace have a duty to co-operate in order to discharge their duties under relevant statutory provisions. This will include consideration of each other when conducting risk assessments and provision of procedures for serious or imminent danger. For example, when establishing fire evacuation arrangements on a site with multiple occupancy the whole of the site should be considered. Each occupant should co-operate with a co-ordinated response. It is necessary for all employers and self employed involved in situations where they have a common workplace to satisfy themselves that the arrangements are adequate. Employers should ensure that all relevant employees and in particular, competent people appointed under the MHSWR are aware and fully take part. They must also take all reasonable steps to inform other employers concerned of risks to their employees' health or safety that may arise out of their work.

3.6 - Particular duties under the Construction (Design and Management) Regulations 1994

CLIENT DUTIES
- Satisfy themselves that the designer(s) are competent.
- Prompt (as soon as practicable) appointment of competent planning supervisor and principal contractor.
- Ensure adequate provision of resources and time to achieve a safe working environment.
- Provide information for inclusion in the pre-tender health and safety plan.
- Ensure the project health and safety file is available for any future construction work, and for handing on to a new owner.
- The client may appoint an agent to undertake his duties under CDM provided that:
  - He is reasonably satisfied that the agent is competent and,
  - That the Health and Safety Executive (HSE) are notified in writing of the appointment.

DESIGNER DUTIES
- Make clients aware of their duties.
- Ensure that structures are designed to avoid risks to health and safety while they are being built and maintained.
- Ensure where it is not possible to avoid risks that they are minimised.
- Provide adequate information about materials used in the design that could affect the health and safety of persons carrying out construction work.
- Co-operate with the planning supervisor and, where, appropriate, other designers involved in the project.

PLANNING SUPERVISOR DUTIES
- Ensure the HSE is notified if necessary.
- Ensure that a health and safety plan is prepared.
- Ensure that designers include among the design considerations, adequate regard to health and safety.
- Ensure co-operation between different designers.
- Be in a position to give advice to clients and contractors.
- Ensure that a health and safety file is prepared.
- Ensure that a health and safety file is delivered to the client.

PRINCIPAL CONTRACTOR DUTIES
- Take account of health and safety issues when preparing tenders.
- Develop the health and safety plan for the construction phase.
- Ensure co-operation between all contractors to ensure they comply with health and safety legislation.
- Take reasonable steps to prevent unauthorised access.
- Provide information to the planning supervisor for inclusion in the health and safety file.
- Enable employed persons to discuss health and safety issues.
- Arrange for co-ordinating the views of employed persons where this is important for health and safety.

CONTRACTOR DUTIES
- Must co-operate with the principal contractor.
- Provide relevant information to the principal contractor on the health and safety risks created by their works and how they will be controlled.
- Comply with directions given by the principal contractor and any rules in the Health and Safety Plan.
- Provide the principal contractor with any Reporting of Injuries Diseases and Dangerous Occurrences Regulations (RIDDOR) 1995 reports.

3.7 - Consultation with employees

DUTIES TO CONSULT

The primary responsibility to consult employees is set out in the HASAWA. This is further specified in regulations that express how this is done with regard to Trade Union Safety Representatives (Safety Representatives and Safety Committee Regulations (SRSC) 1977) and other, non-union employees (The Health and Safety [Consultation with Employees] Regulations (HSCER) 1996).

HASWA 1974 - Section 2(4)

Recognised Trade Unions have the right to appoint safety representatives to represent their member employees in consultations with the employer about health and safety matters.

HASWA 1974 - Section 2(6)

Employers must consult with any safety representatives appointed by recognised Trade Unions.

HASWA 1974 - Section 2(7)

Employers must establish a safety committee if requested to do so by two or more safety representatives.

FUNCTIONS, RIGHTS AND APPOINTMENT OF EMPLOYEE REPRESENTATIVES

Trade union appointed - Safety Representatives (SR)

Safety Representatives and Safety Committees Regulations (SRSC) 1977

The HASAWA made provision for the appointment of Safety Representatives by recognised trade unions and the formation of Safety Committees. The SRSC establish their functions, rights and appointment.

Functions

The SRSC Regulations grant safety representatives the opportunity to carry out certain functions as outlined below.

- To carry out investigations into potential hazards and dangerous occurrences.
- Examine the causes of accidents in the workplace.
- To carry out investigations into complaints by any employee they represent relating to health, safety or welfare.
- To represent the employees they were appointed to represent in consultations with the employer.
- To carry out inspections of the workplace
  - provided it has not been inspected in the last 3 months
  - when reasonable notice is provided in writing to the employer
  - at more frequent intervals if the employer agrees
  - or when a substantial change has occurred
  - or when new information is provided by Health and Safety Executive (HSE)/Health and Safety Commission (HSC)
  - or following an accident, occurrence or disease
  - inspect / copy documents relevant to those they represent
  - the employer is to provide facilities to assist.
- To bring to the employer's notice, any unsafe or unhealthy conditions, or unsafe working practices, which come to their attention whether during an inspection/investigation or day to day observation.
- To represent the employees they were appointed to represent in consultations with the Enforcing Authority inspectors.
- To receive information from an Enforcing Authority inspector on behalf of employees they represent.
- To attend meetings of safety committees related to matters affecting employees they represent.
- In order to fulfil the functions the safety representative should:
  - take all reasonably practical steps to keep themselves informed.
  - encourage co operation between their employer and his employees.
  - bring to the employer's notice, normally in writing, any conditions that come to their attention.

Rights

The SRSC set out duties on employers towards Safety Representatives - these in effect provide rights to the Safety Representative that make the provision of their function easier.

Information

The SRSC require employers to make any information within their knowledge available to safety representatives that are necessary to enable them to fulfil their functions. This should include:

- Information about the plans and performances and any changes that may affect the health and safety at work of their employees, e.g. the plan to re-organise the layout of a manufacturing site.
- Information of a technical nature about hazards to health and safety and precautions deemed necessary to eliminate or minimise them, e.g. about substances that workers are exposed to.
- Information which the employer keeps relating to the occurrence of any accidents, dangerous occurrences or notifiable industrial disease and any statistical records relating to such accidents, dangerous occurrences or cases of notifiable industrial disease, e.g. a copy of a report of an accident to an enforcing authority.
- Any other information relating to matters affecting the representative's employees, including any measurements to check the effectiveness of health and safety arrangements.
- Information on articles or substances which the employer issues to home workers.

Consultation

The SRSC were modified by MHSWR which place a duty on the employer to consult, provide facilities and assistance with regard to:

- Introduction of any measures which might substantially affect health and safety, e.g. the introduction of a new substance or a longer shift period.
- Arrangements for appointing persons to provide the employer with health and safety assistance e.g. a nominated person/organisation to provide health and safety advice.
- The appropriateness of information to be provided to employees as required to meet legislation requirements, e.g. related to substances workers are exposed to or the provision of an employee handbook/rule book on health and safety.
- The planning and organisation of any health and safety training required under particular health and safety laws; e.g. induction training or how to operate equipment safely.
- The health and safety consequences for employees of the introduction of new technologies into the workplace e.g. the computerisation of office processes or introduction of mechanical handling equipment to assist with manual handling.

Time off work to carry out functions and to attend training

The union appointing the safety representative may wish them to be trained on a Trades Union Congress (TUC) approved course. However, there is much to be gained by employers approaching the trades unions active in their workplace with the objective of holding joint courses. This has a particular advantage in that management may also be involved and the training could focus on the specific issues affecting the employer's organisation. In any event it is prudent for the employer to carry out company/industry orientated training to supplement the broad-based TUC course. The functions and training of the safety representatives may be carried out during normal working hours. The representative must receive normal earnings whilst carrying out their functions or training and this must take account of any bonuses that would have been earned if carrying out their normal work activities.

Appointment

A safety representative must be appointed by a recognised trade union in writing to the employer. This should set out the group of employees they represent. The safety representative should have experience in the workplace in question or a similar one for a period of 2 years and would cease to be a representative on leaving the union, the employer's workplace or on removal notified to the employer in writing by the trade union.

Appeals/complaint

A safety representative may make a complaint to an Employment Tribunal if:

- The employer has failed to permit the safety representative to take reasonable time off to perform their functions.
- The employer has failed to allow the safety representative to attend reasonable training.
- The employer has failed to pay him for the time taken to perform these functions or attend training.

The complaint to the Employment Tribunal must be presented within three months of the date when the failure occurred.

Elected - Representatives of Employee Safety (RES)

The Health and Safety (Consultation with Employees) Regulations (HSCER) 1996

The HSCER extend the rights of consultation on matters relating to health and safety to all workers regardless of trade union status. Employers can consult either directly with employees or, in respect of any group of employees, one or more elected representatives of that group. These are referred to as "representatives of employee safety" (RES). If the latter option is chosen, then employers must tell the employees the name of the representative and the group he/she represents. An employer that has been consulting a representative may choose to consult the whole workforce. However, the employer must inform the employees and the representatives of that fact.

Functions

Representatives of employee safety (RES) have the following functions:

- To make representations to the employer on potential hazards and dangerous occurrences at the workplace which affect, or could affect the represented employees.
- Make representations to the employer on general matters of health and safety.
- To represent the employees in workplace consultations with enforcing authority inspectors.

Rights

Information

If the employer consults employees directly then it must make available such information, within the employers' knowledge, as is necessary to enable them to participate fully and effectively in the consultation. If a representative is consulted, then the employer must make available all necessary information to enable them to carry out their functions. In addition, the employer must make available any record made under the RIDDOR which relates to the represented group of employees. This does not provide a right to inspect or copy any document which is not related to health and safety.

Consultation

Where there are employees not represented by the SRSC, the employer shall consult those employees in good time on matters relating to their health & safety at work. Essentially the matters on which the employees must be consulted are the same as those for safety representatives. In particular they must be consulted on:

- Introduction of any measures which might substantially affect health and safety, e.g. the introduction of a new substance or a longer shift period.
- Arrangements for appointing persons to provide the employer with health and safety assistance e.g. a nominated person/organisation to provide health and safety advice.
- The appropriateness of information to be provided to employees as required to meet legislation requirements, e.g. related to substances workers are exposed to or the provision of an employee handbook/rule book on health and safety.
- The planning and organisation of any health and safety training required under particular health and safety laws; e.g. induction training or how to operate equipment safely.
- The health and safety consequences for employees of the introduction of new technologies into the workplace e.g. the computerisation of office processes or introduction of mechanical handling equipment to assist with manual handling issues.

Time off work to carry out their function or for training

Representatives of employee safety must be given reasonable training in order to carry out their functions. Employers must meet the costs of the training and any travel and subsistence. They must also permit the representatives to take time off with pay during working hours in order for them to carry out their functions. Time off shall also be given, with pay, where this is required for any person standing as a candidate for election as a representative. Employers must also provide suitable facilities for the representatives to carry out their functions.

Appointment

It is the employer's decision as to the manner of consultation; if it is deemed that appointment of RES's is appropriate it is necessary to put this to employees to decide who they would like to appoint. This would be done by election, and it need not be a complicated or overly formal approach. Time off and suitable facilities are to be given where any person is standing as a candidate for election as a representative. It would be reasonable that RES's be appointed for local workplace issues and some of those be appointed for consultation on company wide issues.

See also - Legislation - Unit 20.

SAFETY COMMITTEES

Legal requirement

If two or more trade union appointed safety representatives request in writing the formation of a safety committee, the employer must implement this request within three months. Consultation must take place with the representatives making the request and recognised trade unions the members of which work in the workplace that the committee relates to.

Constitution

The employer must post a notice stating the composition of the committee and the workplace it covers where it may be easily read.

Objectives

- The promotion of co-operation on safety, health and welfare matters.
- Provision of a forum for discussion, ideas and recommendations to the employer.
- To promote and support normal employee/employer systems for the reporting and control of workplace problems.

Functions

- To review the measures taken to ensure health and safety.
- To review accident and occupational health trends.
- The examination of safety audit reports.
- To consider enforcing authority reports and information releases.
- To consider reports which safety representatives may wish to submit.
- To assist in the development of safety rules and systems of work and procedures.
- To consider the effectiveness of the safety content of employee training.
- To consider the adequacy of communication and publicity in the workplace.
- The provision of a link with enforcing authority.

Composition

The membership and structure of the safety committee should be settled in consultation between management and the trade union representatives concerned. This should be aimed at keeping the total size as compact as possible.

- Chairperson.
- Secretary.
- Management representatives.
- Employee representatives.
- Health & Safety practitioner.
- Other management e.g.: Project engineers, Planning engineers, Electrical engineers.
- Operational supervision.

Requirements for effectiveness

A basic requirement for a successful safety committee is the desire of both employee and management to show honest commitment and a positive approach to a programme of accident prevention and the establishment of a safe and healthy environment and systems of work. For any committee to operate effectively, it is necessary to determine clear objectives and functions. It is important to establish a committee that is balanced in representation of employees and management.

Frequency of meetings

This would depend on the nature of the organisation's business, the risks involved, how active the health and safety programme is, items on the agenda and other local considerations [such as a hierarchy of committees representing departments / locations / sites]. They tend to vary between once a month to every three months.

Minutes and agenda

The minutes must be circulated as soon as possible after the meeting. A suggested agenda is:

- Apologies for absence.
- Minutes of the previous meeting.
- Matters arising.
- Reports of health and safety practitioner
- Other reports e.g. fire officer, nurse, occupational hygienist.
- New items (and emergency items).
- Date of next meeting.

Reasons why safety committees are effective

- A clear management commitment.
- Clear objectives and functions.
- An even balance between management and employee representatives.
- Agenda agreed, distributed in advance and stuck to in meeting.
- Minutes or notes of the meetings being produced promptly and distributed in good time for actions to be taken before the next meeting.
- Personal copy of minutes provided to each member, each representative covered by the committee and the senior manager of the organisation.
- Effective publicity given to discussions and recommendations, including posting/displaying copies.
- Effective chairing of meeting enabling points to be raised but within the agenda; controlling points taken as any other business
- Full participation by members.
- Access to the organisation's decision-making processes through the chair and in that the committee's views are taken into account.
- Speedy decisions by management on recommendation promptly translated into action and effectively publicised.
- Regular meetings at a frequency that reflects the matters to be discussed.
- Meetings not cancelled or postponed except in very exceptional circumstances.
- Dates of meetings arranged well in advance and published to members, e.g. for a year period.
- Appropriate topics.
- Access to health and safety expertise.
- Sub-committees established where there is a need to focus in detail on specifics and report back.

Promoting a Positive Health and Safety Culture

Overall Aims

On completion of this Unit, candidates will understand:

■ the concept of health and safety culture and its various components.

■ how to assist in the development of a positive health and safety culture within a construction organisation.

Content

Specific Intended Learning Outcomes

The intended learning outcomes of this Unit are that candidates will be able to:

4.1   describe the concept of health and safety culture and its significance in the management of health and safety in an organisation

4.2   assess the effectiveness of an organisation's (and a site's) health and safety culture by use of relevant climate indicators

4.3   recognise the factors that could lead to a deterioration in health and safety culture

4.4   advise on methods for improving the health and safety culture of an organisation and of a site

4.5   outline the internal and external influences on a construction organisation's health and safety standards.

Sources of Reference

The Management of Health and Safety at Work (ACOP) (L21), HSE Books
Successful Health and Safety Management (HSG65), HSE Books
Reducing Error and Influencing Behaviour (HSG48), HSE Books
A Guide to Managing Health and Safety in Construction, HSE Books

Relevant Statutory Provisions

The Health and Safety at Work etc. Act (HASAWA) 1974
The Management of Health and Safety at Work Regulations (MHSWR) 1999
The Health and Safety Information for Employees Regulations (IER) 1989

4.1 - Definition of 'health and safety culture'

"The safety culture of an organisation is the product of individual and group values, attitudes, perceptions, competencies, and patterns of behaviour that determine the commitment to, and the style and proficiency of, an organisation's health and safety management."

Figure 4-1: Safety culture.

Source: NEBOSH Examiners Report.

4.2 - Correlation between health and safety culture and health and safety performance

The correlation between health and safety culture and health and safety performance can be illustrated by research that has been conducted.

For example, after the introduction of a safety programme in the range of forestry and logging organisations in Columbia, it was found by Painter and Smith (1986) that there were dramatic improvements in performance. The accident frequency rate was reduced by 75% and the workers' compensation costs were reduced by 62%. In further research, Lauriski and Guyman (1989) found that after a safety management programme had been introduced at the Utah Power & Light Company, lost time injury rates were reduced by 60% over a period of five years. From 1980 to 1988, the accident frequency rate was reduced from 40 to 8 per annum, while production more than doubled.

Research has shown that improvements in safety management are influential in achieving a positive safety culture. This leads to reduced accident rates, which is seen as a positive step forward, which is a further influence on the safety culture.

4.3 - Tangible outputs or indicators of an organisation's or site's health and safety culture

Developing and promoting a positive safety culture is an important aspect of health and safety management. A safety culture is an intangible thing, which has tangible manifestations. These manifestations can be measured.

Effective communication

Effective communication is a factor in achieving a positive safety culture; therefore effectiveness of communication can be used as a measurement. Considering a practical example: an organisation's safety policy must be communicated to the employees; therefore asking them about it will give an indication as to how well it has been communicated.

Leadership and commitment

Evidence of commitment by personnel at all levels of the organisation can be measured. The evidence can be shown by *the clear identification and acceptance of responsibility* for health and safety from the top. As Du Pont say: "The chairman takes the role of Chief Safety Officer." Areas that can be considered are: membership of safety committee and attendance; responsibilities accepted and taken seriously - whatever they should do they do; rules apply to everyone, for example the wearing of necessary PPE, etc. Measurement of what the organisation is achieving compared to the standards that have been set in the safety policy can be done by *safety audit.* Any shortfalls promptly dealt with are another indicator of a positive safety culture.

Equal priority

Evidence that health and safety is treated as an equal partner alongside other important business issues such as quality, finance, production, etc. The health and safety policy should be integrated with other corporate policies for, say, purchasing, training, etc.

Accident investigation

Findings of accident investigations can be used as a measurement of a safety culture. Root cause accident investigation can show where things are going wrong: have control measures considered the technical, procedural and behavioural aspects? Are they being implemented? Do the management controls need to be reviewed? Is everyone committed to working safely etc.?

The procedure for dealing with the findings of the accident investigation, that is, the recommendations for improvement and prevention is another way to measure the safety culture. For example

- Are people named for action?
- Are time limits set?

- Is there a system to check items have been actioned?
- Are the findings communicated to the employees?

Consultation

Proactive involvement of employees and/or their representatives in decision making e.g. when selecting access equipment for work at height. Discussion with employees about work methods and conditions of work will result in fewer or no complaints.

SPECIFIC TANGIBLE OUTPUTS INDICATORS

- Accidents.
- Absenteeism.
- Sickness rates.
- Staff turnover.
- Level of compliance with health and safety rules and procedures.
- Complaints about working conditions.

Measurement of these specific indicators may be easily done with direct labour employees, but this can present a greater challenge where workers are mainly contractors.

4.4 - Factors promoting a negative health and safety culture

Just as a positive safety culture starts with commitment from the top, a negative safety culture will develop from lack of it. There are, however, other factors involved which may lead to a negative health and safety culture.

When a company is *reorganising*, it is a time of upheaval, personal as well as corporate. Individuals and groups tend to be resistant to change, especially when they are unsure of the need for it. Lack of proper communication can lead to rumours of closure, redundancy or changes in the company's structure. The resulting fall in morale may lead to a lack of belief in the company's commitment. Reorganisation can also lead to people changing their position in the company structure with more, fewer or different responsibilities than previously. Without proper communication and necessary training this can lead to *uncertainty* and a mistrust of the company and its aims and objectives.

The company may state the aims and objectives, but the actions do not seem to be a clear way of achieving them. The aims and objectives may state a commitment to health and safety, yet the changes in work patterns do not allow for safe working. This could be from the point of view that production is seen as all-important and safety must be secondary or an 'add on' done only if time allows for it. A practical example would be if a company decided on a speed limit of five miles an hour for dumper trucks as a control to prevent accidents, but then increased the amount of material a driver had to move on a shift. This would be seen as mixed signals. On one hand, the company is showing commitment to safety by restricting the speed of the vehicles, but on the other, no one seems to care that the increased workload means that the drivers must break the speed limit to get their job done. The management and employees then have different aims and objectives and energy is exerted by each fighting the other. These *management decisions* prejudice mutual trust and lead to mixed signals regarding commitment to health and safety. This promotes a negative safety culture.

Organisations have a responsibility to set standards for health and safety performance when selecting potential contractors or suppliers. Any contracts entered into may represent or impose the equivalent requirements of a contract of service for employees. The system of awarding contracts, of itself, does not have a positive or negative influence on health and safety. Influence rather depends on the standards expected by the person that establishes the contract and those delivered by the contractor and finally by the level of monitoring / enforcement of the contract. In many organisations contractor approval has been used successfully to establish good health and safety standards in work activities that the client organisation has had trouble achieving with a history of resistant contractors. *Poor selection of contractors* who comply with health and safety will result in increased risks to others involved in the workplace and have detrimental effects on the safety of any operations or undertaking.

4.5 - Internal influences on health and safety

THE SIGNIFICANCE OF INTERNAL INFLUENCES

Internal influences on health and safety will depend on the maturity of the organisation concerning health and safety. This maturity and how it is displayed may be described as the culture of the organisation. The culture may be positive or negative, with many shades of grey in between.

MANAGEMENT COMMITMENT

Management commitment to safety should be clear, visible and cascade down from the most senior level in the organisation. The commitment should not just be a formal statement, but more importantly, be evident in the day-to-day activities of the company. This commitment must be known and understood by employees at all levels within the organisation. The correct attitude of a strong personality at a senior level within the organisation who leads by example, e.g. wearing a hard hat where required on site, will have a beneficial effect on a safety climate. Inevitably, junior employees will be influenced by that person's example.

CONTRACT COMPLETION DEMANDS

Contract completion targets are an integral part of running a construction business. The setting of targets (objectives) is a positive way of influencing an organisation, provided they are realistic and achievable. They are only considered realistic and achievable if they can be met in a safe and healthy manner. It is not uncommon for employees (including managers) to relegate health and safety by taking risks to achieve a completion target. Analysis of the situation often reveals such things as ill communicated health and safety objectives whereas completion targets are well defined. If senior management attention (monitoring) is singularly focused on completion targets, health and safety will inevitably suffer. Individuals may choose to take risks to meet their personal production targets, e.g. when involved in work such as 'job finish go home', where an employee might work faster than is reasonable in an effort to leave work earlier.

COMMUNICATION

The construction industry involves the services of a very wide range of specialist companies. Due to the range of trades required, this can result in a varying number of contractors being on site at any one time. It is of utmost importance that communication lines between all parties present on a construction site are known and open. Contractors carrying out different tasks have a duty to make their employees and others who may be affected by their activities, aware of any risks to health that may or may not be obvious, e.g. a contractor carrying out a heavy drilling operation wearing appropriate hearing protection next to an electrician running cable who is not wearing ear defenders. Workers on a construction site should make themselves aware of who are co-ordinating operations on site. Under the Construction (Design and Management) Regulations (CDM) 1994 this should include being informed of the identity of the planning supervisor and principal contractor in addition to any other important parties such as first aiders and health & safety representatives.

COMPETENCE

Every employer has a duty to ensure that employees at work are provided with competent and safe fellow workers and in order to achieve this, varying assessments and collation of evidence may be required to substantiate claims of competency. Competency can be defined as a balance of experience (not only of the type of work or job, but of the work area or location) and training. Information which may be held on file includes references, qualifications and records which chronologically demonstrate work experience. Competent workers improve health and safety working within the workplace and generate a culture of safety awareness.

EMPLOYEE REPRESENTATION

Internal influences of trade unions, where they exist in organisations, depend mainly on the views of the individuals that comprise the members, but in particular their representatives. In situations where appointed representatives deal with all union matters their efforts on health and safety may be diluted, particularly at times when pay is being reviewed and the representative is involved directly with collective bargaining. If the representative is appointed to deal with health and safety alone they will not be driven so much by payments as conditions of work e.g. negotiating more cash for 'dirty' jobs, rather than seeking better ways of working. Many union representatives have received significant training on health and safety matters and therefore have an opportunity to influence health and safety through knowledge. In some organisations, union representatives have received more training than managers. This can lead to misunderstanding and conflict with such managers who might feel at a disadvantage when carrying out their duties. In a similar way how an organisation communicates with non trade union employees either directly or through representatives of employee safety will have a bearing on employee perspective on commitment to health and safety promotion.

4.6 - External influences on health and safety

THE SIGNIFICANCE OF EXTERNAL INFLUENCES

There are many external influences on an organisation. They will have a varying influence depending on the status of the management of health and safety in the organisation. The status of health and safety management may be observed to be in one of three broad stages: 'young', 'immature' and 'mature'.

The young organisation will tend to be driven by events that are occurring and the pressures put on it by external organisations such as the enforcing authorities. The young organisation tends to see remedies as technical in nature and can be said to be operating at level one.

The immature organisation will tend to be driven by unplanned events, but is beginning to establish systems and practices in anticipation of events. The choice of preventive systems tends to be those required to comply with the law, e.g. conducting risk assessments and to be procedural in nature and is therefore seen to be operating at level two.

The mature organisation has spent considerable resource establishing active systems and practices. Unplanned events that result in actual loss are infrequent. Enhanced systems and practices are being established as the organisation observes opportunities for improvement. Attention is tending to be focused on preventive systems and practices that are behavioural in nature and is therefore seen to be operating at level three.

SOCIETAL EXPECTATIONS

Societal opinion tends to fall into two parts:

- Strategic influenced by the general mass of public concerning its tolerance of specific workplace hazards or situations (e.g. Display Screen Equipment or major disasters).
- Local influences tend to surround acceptability or unacceptability of the practices of a specific organisation. This is most acute following an accident and has had the effect of causing closure of some smaller organisations.

LEGISLATION

In the past, legislation has tended to be seen as a punitive influence. More recently, with the introduction of legislation that encourages preventive action and self-development, this perspective has softened. Balancing this is the move from specific prescriptive action for the organisation to comply with to management actions that must be carried out as duties by individuals (and the organisation). For legislation to influence organisations either they must want to comply or there has to be a real prospect of punishment for non-compliance.

ENFORCEMENT

Enforcement agencies have a significant role in influencing an organisation's level of performance concerning health and safety. If the focus of the enforcement agency is on technical specifics then organisations will tend to follow this lead and deal with these issues. It is therefore important that the enforcing agencies demonstrate the value of not only technical, but procedural and behavioural preventive measures. The relative influence of the enforcement agencies is highly dependent on them being sufficiently field active to contact a significant number of organisations. It would not be a balanced influence if the only time they were seen was following an accident. They should be seen by organisations before accidents occur to encourage planned preventive actions to be implemented.

INSURANCE COMPANIES

Insurance companies have become increasingly aware that they may have under valued the risks related to some companies they are insuring. This has caused them to look again at the risks and the factors that lead to claims. A focus on the status of the management of health and safety in the organisation insured has been found to be a useful predictor of future loss. This approach has been seen to influence many organisations and cause them to minimise the risks in order to control their level of premium increase.

TRADE UNIONS

Trade unions have had a significant influence on health and safety in previous years. In recent times their influence has subsided nationally as the number of members has reduced though they have remained influential in some industries/organisations. Union activities have, in recent times, tended to be distracted by other employment matters. There is now a renewed union interest in health and safety matters as it is beginning to be seen as a worthwhile way of servicing their members' needs. Unions have always maintained a profile of member support in making claims from employers concerning injury at work. As claims consciousness increases their role and influence will increase.

Trade Unions, through the Trade Union Congress (TUC), are represented on the Health and Safety Commission (HSC). Through this forum, they have an influence on strategic aspects of health and safety, contributing to the development of Regulations and Approved Codes of Practice (ACOPs).

STAKEHOLDERS

Stakeholders or shareholders of an organisation have a financial investment in that particular business and as a result wish to see their investment grow. Generally, stake / shareholders are not directly interested or involved in the day to day operations or undertakings of the business, but more likely to be concerned with the company's financial accounts and personal investment reward. Focus tends to be on increasing profits, which more often than not includes reducing overheads or making cutbacks. Additional pressures may be placed on the workforce following announcements of cutbacks or the need for profits to increase. Less resource may be available to undertake and fulfil a project safely or the workforce may feel under pressure to work faster, harder or longer in order to achieve profitability and gain job security. Some stakeholders / shareholders recognise that poor health and safety will result in lower profitability, such organisations generally invest considerably in risk management and are very successful in the marketplace.

ECONOMICS

The state of prosperity of an organisation or the country as a whole falls into the subject of economics. An economic 'climate' can be prosperous or in 'recession'. Although possible to vary greatly, in a prosperous, ascending or stable economy, industry generally is busy and productive, unemployment decreases and morale improves. However, a declining economy can plunge into recession, resulting in closure of business, higher unemployment and the morale of the population weakened by the thought of personal loss (i.e. job loss, repossession, loss of earnings, debt). The construction industry has historically suffered in this environment with, for example, a collapse of the housing market due to insufficient spending capability in previous years. The impact on struggling organisations may result in less time, effort and money spent on adequate resources and finance for health and safety measures, thus creating less safe working conditions. The additional 'knock-on' effect is that individuals in the workplace may subject themselves to hazards and risks that they would not normally subject themselves to in an attempt to try and remain in work, resulting in workers performing unsafe acts.

4.7 - Human behaviour

Individual, job and organisational factors

INDIVIDUAL FACTORS

Individual differences

All individuals are different. These differences will influence patterns of work behaviour and may limit the effectiveness with which an individual carries out a job. They will also influence how safely the work tasks are carried out. These individual differences arise from an interaction between the 'inherited characteristics' (passed on from the parents) and the various 'life experiences' through which the individual passes from the moment of conception.

- Experiences in the womb.
- Birth trauma.
- Family influences.
- Geographical location.
- Pre-school influences.

- Education - opportunities, quality, support.
- Occupational factors - training and retraining.
- Hobbies and interests.
- Own family influences - marriage, children.
- Ageing.

Any, many or all of the above will help to 'mould' the individual into a unique person different from all other individuals. The ways in which people differ are many and various and it is important to bear this in mind from the point of view of work effectiveness and safety. It is vital to know what a particular job entails (the job description) and to specify the characteristics required to enable a person to perform that job effectively (the personnel specification). Physical differences will need to be considered carefully when establishing controls for work activities, some differences may limit or prohibit individuals from certain tasks.

Summary of individual differences

Physical	Mental
Gender - e.g. females not exposed to lead.	Attitude - e.g. all PPE is uncomfortable.
Build - e.g. may restrict movement in a confined space.	Motivation - e.g. risks v reward.
Health - e.g. colour blindness.	Perception - e.g. do not respond to alarms.
Capability/strength - e.g. manual handling.	Capability - e.g. ability to follow safety instructions.

The significance of individual factors

Employees bring to their job personal habits, attitudes, skills, personality and so on, which in relation to task demands may be strengths or weaknesses. Individual characteristics influence behaviour in complex and significant ways. Some characteristics, such as personality, are fixed and largely incapable of modification. Others such as skills and attitudes are amenable to modification or enhancement. The person, therefore, needs to be matched to the job.

Important considerations within the personal factor category include the following.

a)   *Thorough task analysis* (especially for critical jobs) which should enable a detailed job description to be generated. From this, a specification can be drawn up to include such factors as age, physique, skill, qualifications and experience, aptitude, knowledge, intelligence and personality. Personnel selection policies and procedures should ensure the specifications are matched by the individuals.

b)   *Training* will produce an employee capable of working without close supervision with confidence to take on responsibility and perform effectively, providing that initial selection is done properly. Training should be carried out from induction and throughout the career of the individual to reflect not only changes in work, but to maintain, through refresher training, standards of performance. Self confidence and job satisfaction grow significantly when people are trained to work correctly under both routine and emergency conditions. This will not only benefit individuals themselves and their colleagues but greatly improve the achievement of organizational objectives. Training should aim to give all individuals the skills to allow them to understand the workings of plant and processes. It is not a once-and-for-all activity but in so far as procedures and processes change and complex skills (particularly when under used) deteriorate, is a regular contribution to individual performance.

c) *Monitoring of personal performance* in relation to health and safety. An old maxim states "That which gets measured, gets done". All work practices should be monitored through direct supervision. The degree of supervision or frequency will be risk based and will be influenced by many factors such as the experience or skill of the worker or the supervisor. Monitoring should not be at the task level only, but carried out by all of the management team, from the most senior down. This will ensure delegated tasks are performed correctly and ensure statutory requirements for health and safety are met.

d) *Fitness for work and health surveillance.* For certain jobs there may be specified medical standards for which pre-employment and/or periodic health surveillance is necessary. These may relate to the functional requirements of the job or the impact of specified conditions on the ability to perform it adequately and safely. An example is the medical examination of divers. There may also be a need for routine surveillance of the effects of exposure to workplace hazards, both physical, such as the effects of acute heat stress: or chemical, for example, absorption of organic phosphorous insecticides which may impair ability to control a tractor or aircraft. Medical surveillance is not a substitute for proper control of the hazardous agent.

e) *Review of health on return to work from sickness absence.* The recognition of the purpose of counselling and provision of advice during periods of individual need, such as dealing with anxiety or stress related to failure to achieve work objectives, in this context alcohol or drug abuse and the possible adverse side effects of prescribed drugs may be relevant stressors. Access to specialist assistance may be appropriate with the possible need for temporary or permanent re-deployment.

JOB / TASK FACTORS

Tasks should be designed in accordance with ergonomic principles to take into account limitations in human performance and physical ability. Matching the job to the person will ensure that they are not overloaded and that they will make the most effective contributions to the company. Physical match includes not only the design of the equipment associated with the task but the whole workplace and working environment. Mental match involves the individual's information and decision-making requirements, as well as their perception of the tasks. Mis-match between job requirements and workers' capabilities provide potential for human error.

The major considerations in the design of the job include the following.

a) Identification and comprehensive analysis of the critical (high risk) tasks expected of individuals and appraisal of likely errors;

b) Evaluation of required operator decision making and the optimum balance between the human and automatic contributions to safety actions.

c) Application of ergonomic principles to the design of man-machine interfaces, including displays of plant and process information, and suitable positioning, labelling of control devices and panel layouts.

d) Design and consistency of presentation of procedures and operating instructions.

e) Organisation and control of working environment, including the workspace, access for maintenance, lighting, noise and thermal conditions.

f) Provision of correct tools and equipment.

g) Scheduling of work patterns, including shift organisation, control of stressors such as noise or heat to reduce fatigue.

h) Arrangements to cover for absence and procedures for emergencies such as premature collapse of a structure or fire on a partial build project.

i) Efficient and suitable communications, both immediate and over periods of time.

ORGANISATIONAL FACTORS

As stated previously, organisations need to produce a climate that promotes staff commitment to health and safety and emphasises that deviation from corporate safety goals, at whatever level, is not acceptable.

Producing such a climate requires clear, visible, management commitment to safety from the most senior level in the organisation. The commitment should be not just a formal statement but be evident in the day-to-day activities of the company. This commitment must be known and understood by the employee. Individuals may be reluctant to err on the side of caution in matters that have safety implications if their decisions to do so are likely to be subject to unwarranted criticism from their superiors or their peers.

The attitude of a strong personality at a senior level within the organisation may have either a beneficial or an adverse effect on a safety climate. Inevitably, junior employees will be influenced by that person's example.

Health and safety procedures soon fall into disuse if there is no system of ensuring that they are followed. Too often procedures lapse because of management neglect, or operators are discouraged from working to them by peer groups or other pressures, such as production targets. Where managers become aware of deficiencies in safety procedures but do not act to remedy them, the workforce readily perceive that such actions are condoned.

Individuals may not understand the relevance of procedures or appreciate their significance in controlling risk. Sometimes procedures are faulty, irrelevant, or lacking in credibility. When accidents happen managers cannot blame individuals for taking short cuts which seemed safe and were allowed to become routine, if they have not explained the importance of, or monitored procedures they originally laid down.

To promote a proper working climate, it is essential to have an effective system for monitoring safety that identifies, investigates and corrects deviations. The introduction and operation of such systems requires considerable effort by managers and only by allocating adequate resources can they be confident that failures will be prevented or controlled.

In short, the organisation needs to provide:

■ Clear and evident commitment, from the most senior management downwards, which promotes a climate for safety in which management's objectives and the need for appropriate standards are communicated and in which constructive exchange of information at all levels is positively encouraged.

■ An analytical and imaginative approach identifying possible routes to human factor failure. This may well require access to specialist advice.

■ Procedures and standards for all aspects of critical work and mechanisms for reviewing them.

■ Effective monitoring systems to check the implementation of the procedures and standards.

■ Incident investigation and the effective use of information drawn from such investigations.

■ Adequate and effective supervision with the power to remedy deficiencies when found.

Attitude, aptitude and motivation

ATTITUDE

"the tendency to respond in a particular way to a certain situation"

Attitudes are another set of factors that constitute ways in which individuals differ one from another. Attitudes are not directly observable and can only be assessed by observing behavioural expression (physical or verbal behaviour).

Clearly, a person's attitudes will govern the way in which an object or situation is viewed and it will dictate the resultant response or pattern of behaviour. This is obviously very important when considering an individual's working patterns and any safety aspects associated with them. Attitudes, like other aspects of individual differences, are formed (not necessarily consciously) because of a lifetime of experiences and as such are not easily changed. A person's attitudes are not simply an aid to coping with their environment, but may determine how they wish to change what is there. Any attempts to change such a fundamental part of an individual's personality will be resisted. The individual will feel their very being is under threat. This is worth remembering in the context of safety propaganda campaigns.

"People's attitudes and opinions that have been formed over decades of life, cannot be changed by holding a few meetings or giving a few lectures".

Figure 4-2: Observation made by chairman Mao Tse Tung. *Source: "Little Red Book".*

Examples of attitudes affecting safe working:

1) It will never happen to me.

3) Its only the price of a plaster.

2) We have never had an accident.

4) I know my limits.

Everyone at work should attempt to change their own and their colleague's attitudes to health and safety from - Work safely because -

I have to. $\rightarrow$ I should. $\rightarrow$ I want to. $\rightarrow$ It is automatic.

Remedial action
- Train, and retrain when need for reinforcement is evident.
- Change by experience (involvement), e.g. selection of personal protective equipment (PPE).

APTITUDE

"a tendency to be good at certain things"

Aptitude is closely linked to personality. Some people are particularly good at certain things, for example, an individual may be good at working with his hands, while another may say they *"could not change a light bulb".*

Aptitude can be developed over time as a skill, but it is more likely to be part of that person's characteristics. This can be factor when placing people in particular jobs. A person with no aptitude for precision work, but superb at felling trees is 'an accident waiting to happen' if given the job of soldering electronic components.

MOTIVATION

"the driving force behind the way a person acts in order to achieve a goal"

In the context of the working situation there have been, over the years, many attempts to identify why people work. The earliest approach (by F. W. Taylor) was that people worked for money and fear of losing their livelihood. Financial reward was seen as the prime motivator. The more they were paid the harder they worked. This led to a new management philosophy:

■ Payment by results.

■ Piece work.

■ Incentive schemes.

■ Danger money.

From a health and safety management viewpoint, this theory is unsound since most bonus schemes encourage people to work **unsafely** by cutting corners, rushing to get the job done etc. with safe working practices the inevitable victim. Money **is** important but other factors are more important. e.g. social belonging, acceptance by one's peers. With this in mind, motivating people to adopt safe working practices should include:

■ Establishment of a positive health and safety culture where risk taking is frowned upon by all employees but especially supervisors and managers.

■ Setting realistic objectives with regard to accident rates.

■ Involvement in health and safety policy setting.

■ Clarification of responsibilities.

■ Developing a positive reward structure.

■ Monitoring health and safety performance.

■ Improving employees, knowledge of the consequences of not working safely (through information and training).

■ Showing the commitment of the organisation to safety (by providing resources and a safe working environment).
■ Involving employees in health and safety decisions (by consultation, team meetings etc.).
■ Recognising and rewarding achievement.

Positive motivation (i.e. employees working safely because that is how they want to work) tends to be more effective than negative motivation (i.e. employees working safely for fear of disciplinary action), although both have a place.

Remedial action
- Establish positive health and safety culture.
- Positive reward structure.
- Set clear objectives e.g. accident statistics.

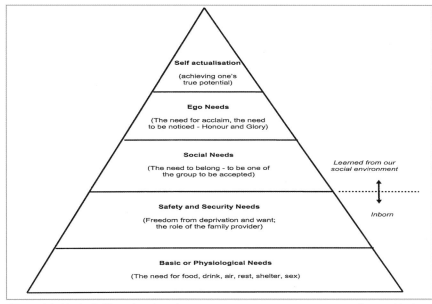

Figure 4-3: Maslow's hierarchy of needs   *Source: Maslow.*

(The NEBOSH National Certificate in Construction Safety and Health does not require detailed knowledge of Maslow's Hierarchy).

Perception of risk

PERCEPTION

"the way that a person views a situation"

Factors that influence the effectiveness are:

■ A boring, repetitive job may result in 'day dreaming' which may result in a lowering of the impact of a stimulus.
■ Warnings (or threats) may not be strong enough to get through the perceptual set.
■ Patterns of behaviour and habits can be carried from one situation to another where they are no longer appropriate or safe (e.g. we tend to drive too quickly after leaving a motorway).
■ Individuals can get 'used to' a stimulus and, if it is not reinforced, it ceases to command the attention and is ignored.
■ Intense concentration on one task may make paying attention to another stimulus difficult or impossible.

Remember: **We do not see what is there!**   **We do not see what we do not expect to be there!**

We see what we expect to be there!   **We do not see what we do not want to be there!**

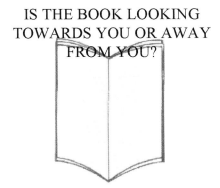

IS THE BOOK LOOKING TOWARDS YOU OR AWAY FROM YOU?

Figure 4-4: Examples of perception images.   *Source: Ambiguous.*

Remedial Action
- Information.
- Training.
- Instruction.
- Drills.

Process of perception

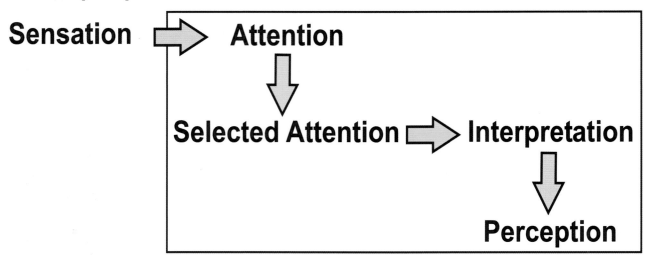

Figure 4-5: Model of perception.   Source: ACT.

Within each individual, these processes of attention and interpretation are closely interlinked. The factors that influence these processes and the way in which they operate are often referred to as the "perceptual set" of the individual.

Errors and violations

HUMAN ERROR AS A CAUSE OF ACCIDENTS

It is estimated that over 80% of accidents can be attributed, at least in part, to the actions or omissions of people. Many accidents are blamed on the actions or omissions of an individual who was directly involved in operational or maintenance work. This typical but short sighted response ignores the fundamental failures that led to the accident. These are usually rooted deeper in the organisation's management and decision-making functions. Our history teaches us much more about the origins of human failure. Attributing accidents to "human error" has often been seen as sufficient explanation in itself and something that is beyond the control of managers. Organisations must recognise that they need to consider human factors as a distinct element which needs to be assessed and managed effectively. The table that follows illustrates the influence of human factors in some recent major incidents:

Accident	Consequences	Human Contribution
Three Mile Island 1979	Serious damage to core of nuclear reactor.	Operators failed to recognise a valve that was stuck open due to poor design of the control panel. Maintenance failures had happened before but no steps had been taken to prevent a recurrence.
Space Shuttle 'Challenger' 1986	Explosion killed all 7 astronauts on board.	Inadequate response to internal warnings about the faulty design of a seal. Decision taken to go ahead with launch in very cold temperature despite faulty seal. Decision making result of conflicting scheduling/safety goals, mindset and effects of fatigue.
Herald of Free Enterprise 1987	Ferry sank killing 189 passengers and crew.	No system for checking that bow doors were shut. Inquiry reported that the company was "infected with the disease of sloppiness". Priority was to turn the ship around in record time.
Kings Cross fire 1987	Major fire killed 31 people.	Organisational changes had led to poor escalator cleaning. The fire took hold because of inadequate fire fighting equipment and poor staff training. There was a culture that viewed fires as inevitable.
Piper Alpha 1988	Major explosion on North Sea oil platform killed 167 workers.	Maintenance error that eventually led to the leak was the result of inexperience, poor procedures and poor learning. There was a breakdown in communications and the permit-to-work system at shift changeover and safety procedures were not properly practised.

Figure 4-6: Influence of human factors in recent major incidents.   Source: HSE.

CAUSES OF HUMAN FAILURE

There are two different types of human failure - errors and violations.

A **human error** is an action or decision that was not intended, which involved a deviation from an accepted standard, and which led to an undesirable outcome.

A **violation** is a deliberate deviation from a rule or procedure.

ERRORS

Errors fall into three categories: *1) Slips.*   *2) Lapses.*   *3) Mistakes.*

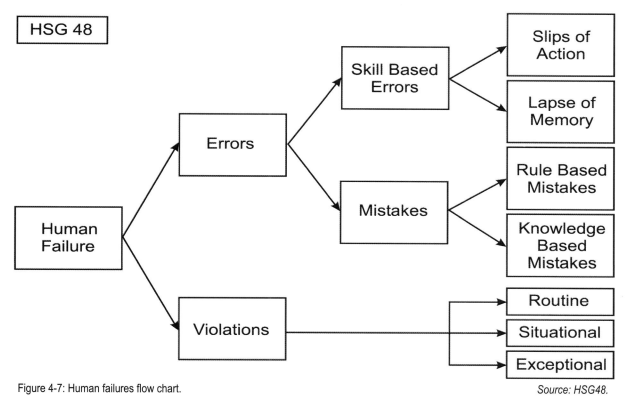

Figure 4-7: Human failures flow chart.

Source: HSG48.

Slips and lapses

Once we have learned a skill, there is little need for much conscious thought about what we are doing. We can carry out a task without having to think too much about the next step. We learn to ride a bike or drive a car in this way. We need to pay attention to the road and the traffic, but we manipulate the pedals and change gear without thinking about it. If our attention is diverted, we may fail to carry out the next action of the task, or we could forget the next action or lose our place resulting in an error.

Mistakes

Mistakes are a little more complex than slips and lapses. We may do the wrong thing believing it to be right. We have a tendency to use familiar rules or procedures, often when they don't apply. The wrong application of a rule to a situation can result in an error e.g. use of a water based extinguisher on electrical equipment on fire.

In unfamiliar situations, we may have to apply knowledge-based reasoning. If this is miscalculated or the situation is misdiagnosed, then a mistake may occur.

These errors typically occur with trained, experienced people, but also occur with untrained and inexperienced people. The untrained and inexperienced may base their decisions on misunderstandings and a lack of perception of risk.

VIOLATIONS

These violations are rarely acts of vandalism or sabotage, but are often carried out in order to get the job done e.g. using a convenient ladder of insufficient length. Many accidents, injuries and cases of ill health come about because of violations.

Routine violations

Routine violations are where breaking the rules or procedure has become the normal way of working. Not removing work cloth when taking refreshment breaks in a canteen facility. New workers come in and learn the incorrect ways, not realising they are wrong. The incorrect method may have come about because it is a quicker way to work or because the rules are seen as too restrictive. In one company, it was felt that the work could not be finished on time if all of the rules were followed.

Situational violations

Situational violations may occur with pressures from the job: time pressure, extreme weather conditions, wrong equipment, etc. Roof work may continue without edge protection, because the correct equipment has not been provided.

Exceptional violations

Exceptional violations occur when something has gone wrong. A decision has to be made to solve the problem and that might involve breaking a rule and taking a risk, e.g. temporary repair to equipment hydraulic lines that become permanent. It is erroneously believed that the benefits outweigh the risk.

Effects of age and experience

EFFECTS OF AGE ON BEHAVIOUR AT WORK

The design of the human body is uniform, allowing for differences of sex. The spine, joints, tendons and muscles work in the same way and will suffer after the same abuse, although to a varying extent. Individuals, therefore, have different physical capabilities due to height, weight, age and levels of fitness. They also have different mental capabilities, memory retention and personalities

The body will be affected, more or less, by tasks that involve bending, reaching, twisting, repetitive movements and poor posture. The aches, pains and fatigue suffered doing certain tasks will eventually impair the operator's ability and lead to degradation in performance. It is therefore essential to consider the task in order to match it to the individual so the level of general comfort is maximised. For example, when carrying out manual handling assessments it is important to look at the relationship between the individual, the task, the load and the environment.

EFFECTS OF EXPERIENCE ON BEHAVIOUR AT WORK

The experienced worker will know the hazards in the workplace and can make a decision on the risk he can take based on past experience. The problem with this is that his accident-free past may well be down to luck and that may change at any time. He may no longer see the hazards because of familiarity with them. More than half the fatalities from electrocution involve so-called competent people. The experienced worker will, however, be more aware of what can cause harm, unlike the inexperienced young person. It would be unethical to cause someone to have an accident in order to heighten their awareness of risk or so they could gain experience. Awareness must be heightened in other ways: training and education or simulation.

The influence of peers

Nearly all human beings need the company and social acceptance of their fellows. When we are in a group situation, it is very difficult to behave differently to others. The group will have established a norm for behaviour. The norm behaviour is what keeps the group together. There are two main groups, social and work. The social group is formed out of individuals with common beliefs, interests expectations etc. Individuals in the social group will be under its influence most of their time. Within the workplace we have groups of individuals working together often with common skills, but not always common beliefs. The work group is different to the social group; individual behaviour may be strongly influenced by their peers (others in the group) and personal choice may be changed by the peer pressure. This group behaviour is what sets the standard of performance and the method of achieving the particular work goal or situation. The observance of health and safety rules may strongly be influenced within a group. If the norm is to follow the rules, e.g. a pre flight equipment check on an aircraft before take off, then the rules will be obeyed. Conversely, if the norm is to flout the rules, e.g. failure to wear eye protection for a grinding operation, then the rules may well be disobeyed by an individual who may know the risks.

SUMMARY OF HUMAN BEHAVIOUR

Human failures:

Errors		Violations	
	■ Slips.		■ Routine.
	■ Lapses.		■ Situational.
	■ Mistakes.		■ Exceptional.

Control measures:

Individual factors:

- Increase skill and competence levels.
- Select staff according to their capabilities.
- Provide health surveillance wherever necessary.
- Job rotation to prevent boredom.

Job factors:

- Correct ergonomic design of tools and equipment.
- Prevent disturbances and interruptions.
- Provide clear instructions.
- Maintain equipment to a suitable standard.
- Minimise exposure to unpleasant working conditions such as noise, heat, adverse weather etc.

Organisational factors:

- Good work planning to avoid high work pressure.
- Adequate safety systems and barriers.
- Respond quickly to previous incidents.
- Consultation rather than information.
- Clear identification of responsibilities.
- Thorough management training.
- Create positive health and safety culture.

4.8 - Effecting cultural change

A general approach to effecting cultural change

THE "FOUR C'S"

The activities necessary to promote a positive health and safety culture are split into:

- Methods of *control*.
- Means of securing *co-operation*.
- Methods of *communication*.
- *Competence* of individuals.

Control

Control is achieved by:

- Getting the commitment of employees to clear health and safety objectives.
- Managers taking full responsibility for controlling the factors that could lead to loss.
- Nominating a senior figure to monitor the policy implementation.
- Allocating responsibilities to line managers and safety specialists.
- Encouraging safety representatives to make a contribution.
- Setting performance standards.

The emphasis is on a collective effort to develop and maintain systems of control before the event - not on blaming individuals for failures afterwards.

Co-operation

Pooling knowledge and experience through participation, commitment and involvement means that safety becomes everybody's business.

- Consult your employees and their representatives.
- Involve them in planning and reviewing performances, writing procedures and solving problems.
- Share information on loss and experience with contractors.

Competence

- Assess the skills needed to carry out tasks safely.
- Provide the means to ensure that all employees, including temporary employees, are adequately instructed and trained.
- Ensure that employees on especially dangerous work have the necessary training and experience to carry out the work safely.
- Arrange and encourage access to sound advice and help.

Communication

- Provide information about hazards, risks and any preventative measures.
- Discuss health & safety regularly.

Implementing the above "four c's" will greatly assist in ensuring a positive health and safety culture within an organisation.

SECURING COMMITMENT OF MANAGEMENT

Organisations should identify key performance indicator (KPI) standards for heath and safety. The standards should be achievable and designed not to compete with other organisational performance standards such as those set for production / service or quality. The standards must be agreed at the highest level within the organisation and standards for establishing management control must be established. The management controls must be designed to send a clear signal, that health and safety is an equal partner to the other organisational objectives. Management controls may take many forms, but should include system checks, such as random examination of completed permits to work, observations of high risk work activities or periodic tours. It should not be assumed that those that manage projects and quality issues are skilled in managing health and safety. Their competence should be confirmed through formal training in health and safety management.

PROMOTING HEALTH AND SAFETY STANDARDS BY LEADERSHIP AND EXAMPLE

Management actions at all levels should send clear signals to staff and others within the workplace of the importance of observing the health and safety standards which have been set. Leadership through example will include such issues as correct use of personal protective equipment, observance of rules, which might require special skills or training and commitment by seniors to attending health and safety training identified for development of subordinate managers.

USE OF COMPETENT PERSONNEL / CONTRACTORS

The organisation should identify the safety critical tasks and establish suitable controls. The task analysis should not only take account of engineering controls, such as guard design or fume extraction requirements, but the requirements of the personnel involved in the task. This will include ensuring that the relevant knowledge, skill and work experience is established, before an individual is put to work. Factors such as individual aptitude, dexterity and physical ability / endurance may also be important e.g. not everyone will be comfortable or able to work at height or in confined spaces. High-risk tasks may utilise simulation equipment to allow skill to be developed, at no risk to the individual or others, for example, the use of aircraft flight simulators. Similarly, it may be necessary for the trainee to be under close supervision (an instructor flies with a new pilot of an aircraft) until their skill can be demonstrated as appropriate through their displayed actions and ability.

Effective communication within the organisation

COMMUNICATION METHODS

It is the job of the middle manager/supervisor to translate decisions from superiors into concrete actions and, at the same time, be aware of the needs, desires, capabilities and expectations of subordinates in order to transmit them to superiors. Because of the higher levels of education amongst workers, the job of the middle manager has become harder. The days of imposing fines on and using discipline against workers are now seen as inapplicable to the modern organisation. The ideal is increasingly seen to be that of giving information and explanation. The emphasis must be on participation of all levels in all decisions.

One factor which prevents subordinates from communicating with their supervisors is a lack of trust. For some time it has been known that honest and open communication, the essentials of participation, correlate highly with workers' trust in management. A related issue, which grows out of trust, is the amount of influence workers feel they have in an organisation.

Bureaucratic organisations, by their nature, have error-amplifying characteristics. Democratic/participative organisations, on the other hand, contain error-reducing characteristics. This occurs because the perceived influence on what happens in the organisation increases for the workers. It is the ability to influence the decision-making process that is important for members of an organisation. Increasing worker participation increases the general level of job satisfaction.

Barriers to effective communication

It is imperative that verbal communication is clear, concise and easily understood. However this is not always the case and the reasons listed below are some of the barriers to effective verbal communication:

- Noise and distractions.
- Complexity of information.
- Language and/or dialect of the speaker.
- Sensory impairment (perhaps deafness).
- Ambiguity.
- Use of technical jargon.
- Mental difficulty.
- Inexperience on the part of the recipient.
- Lengthy communication chains.
- Inattention.

Some barriers to communication that may lead to employees failing to comply with safety instructions or procedures:

- Unrealistic or ill-considered procedures.
- Inadequate training.
- Lack of involvement in consultation.
- Peer group pressure.
- Risks not perceived.

- Mental and/or physical capabilities not taken into account.
- Poor safety culture in the organization.
- Complacency or lack of motivation.
- Other priorities and pressures.
- Fatigue and stress.

General principles of communication

Communication is a skill that we take for granted. Like any other skill, some people are better at it than others. The purpose of this document is to provide the reader with some of the basic principles. Communication is a two-way process where the needs of the receiver are equally as important as the needs of the speaker. Because it is a two-way process, both participants must be sure they are using the same language. The speaker should not assume that the receiver has understood what has been said. To ensure the success of the communication:

1) Direct yourself towards and reach the intended recipient.

2) Communicate in a form capable of being understood by the recipient.

3) Use open ended questions to investigate understanding.

4) Use closed questions, which yield yes/no answers, to confirm.

5) Use clear and unambiguous terms.

6) Be assertive but not aggressive.

7) Keep content concise.

8) Ensure the recipient understands.

9) Check to ensure understanding.

10) Budget time to encourage feedback.

All communication has two aspects:

Content   We can be influenced by the facts, opinions, suggestions put forward. We are influenced by the additional content.

Relationship   We are also influenced by the 'way' the content is presented and the relationship it suggests between the speaker and us.

Take, for example, the responses:

"We are unable to accept your findings as they do not take into account the rate of inflation," and,

"This is abysmal, we can't accept this!"

Both have approximately the same content but define very different relationships. This relationship aspect, which is part of all communication, establishes the way in which the content is to be received. When communication is assertive, the relationship is established as honest, direct and fair. Thus more detailed attention can be directed toward the content. Where it is aggressive, passive or devious, the relationship itself limits the content and the information that can be discussed.

Written communication

The primary purpose of written information is to communicate. The writer should, therefore, always have the reader in mind when producing the text. The use of plain English must be encouraged - this is particularly important for safety related material. One useful vehicle for conveying information is the *report.* A simple structure is as follows:

- Introduction and background.
- Main body of the report.
- Recommendations.
- Conclusions.

Introduction and Background This section includes the title page that should clearly identify the writer and the document. It should contain a brief explanation of the subject described in the document title and the reason for the document. Consider the aim of the report and inform the reader of the problems it intends to address.

Main Body of the Report This section deals with details, facts and findings. Keep the style simple and to the point. Avoid the use of jargon or embellishment. Inaccuracy, inadequate and sloppy presentation can distract the reader and lessen the impact.

Recommendations These should flow logically from the main body of the report. Recommendations should consist of a plain statement of action without repeating the arguments of the preceding section.

Conclusions This section should contain a summary of the main findings and inferences. The writer should end on a positive note.

USE AND EFFECTIVENESS OF VARIOUS COMMUNICATION MEASURES

Notice boards

A traditional communication technique is to post safety information on notice boards. The advantage of this method is that the communication is available to everyone in a particular work area. Notice boards should only be used to make general statements or to keep employees aware of current information or proposed developments. Notice boards should not be used where the currency or completeness of the information impacts on safety critical issues. The information must be kept up to date and maintained in a legible condition if it is to be effective. Notice board information relies on people's ability to read, understand and apply the information correctly. Care needs to be taken to ensure appropriate language(s) are used.

Safety propaganda

There are many forms of safety 'propaganda' which aim to sell the safety message. Their effectiveness in modifying human behaviour and attitudes has been the subject of much debate. Many professionals now view them to be of little value - however there is a marked reluctance to abandon them.

Films, videos

Films and videos are often used to renew attention during periods of training. The visual impact is a strong stimulus on the delegate, the video enables the training to expand experience outside the training room or the experience of the trainees. Shock videos are sometimes used to illustrate what might happen if procedures are not followed. It has been found that their effect does not change attitude in the longer term. A common use for videos is at site induction, for both new employees and contractor's access to high-risk locations.

Poster campaigns

Posters are sometimes seen as a cheap and visible way of showing commitment to safety. This attitude can be self-defeating if management place too much reliance on them. For example, the workforce can perceive this as an excuse for a proper safety policy.

To be effective messages must be:

Positive - posters exhorting people to 'be safe' or threatening dire consequences if a particular action is not taken are rarely effective. People are not necessarily rational or logical - particularly in giving priority to safety over even a small cut in take home pay or comfort. Messages should emphasise positive safety benefits by letting people know 'what's in it for them'.

Aimed at the correct audience - posters quickly blend into the background. This is compounded when messages are seen as irrelevant. Campaigns must be carefully targeted and posters positioned in order to have a captive audience. For example, a poster warning of the dangers of loose clothing being entangled in machinery should be sited close to the relevant machine.

Believable - messages should be relevant, credible and realistic. Peer pressure, which plays a large part in group behaviour, can be used to advantage if there is a general endorsement of the message.

Achievable - the aim here is to encourage simple steps towards a tangible and achievable end.

Care must be taken to avoid offending or distracting your audience away from the message. Sexual images can often offend both men and women. Similarly, pictures of horrific accidents can lead to a rejection of the message on the basis that it could not happen to them. Posters should be changed regularly to avoid them becoming wallpaper. An earlier study into how well a group of people remembered a poster campaign follows:

After one week:

- 90% of people remembered the general details.
- 45% remembered the specific message.

After two weeks:

- 20% of people remembered the poster.
- No one remembered the message.

Toolbox talks

Toolbox talks are often used in organisations which operate work on a continuous shift basis. Typical work sectors are major highway expansion such as the M25, chemical, food processing, police and continuous assembly, such as automotive manufacture. The technique is very good for fast communication on specifics. It relies on the cascade of information from supervisors or team leaders to their work group. Issues are normally kept to a minimum and two-way communication is very effective with individuals within the work group. Issues raised may be current, such as warning of some concerns over equipment reliability, or recent good or poor safety trends i.e. accidents. Other, future issues may be raised, such as proposed changes in personal protective equipment or work practice(s).

Memos e-mails

Memos are often used to communicate on short-term issues. The memo is an easier and faster vehicle to use than the more formal document change procedure. Safety related issues may be concerned with person, job or hours worked or work patterns. Written communication is effective in that it states what is to change and from when, but again relies on individual interpretation and understanding. It is often one way, as proof of issue is not always proof of receipt. As with memos, e-mails have similar limitations. Software is available to check whether the recipient has opened the correspondence, but not that it has been read, understood or actioned.

Employee handbooks

Employee handbooks are often issued to new employees at induction. They are useful in communicating site rules and information such as accident, injury-reporting mechanism. Similarly, they will often contain information on site emergency arrangements such as fire and first aid. To be effective a mechanism needs to be established to recall and reissue the handbooks when changes occur. Some organisations operate a loose leaf folder design. Consideration needs to be given to where each employee keeps the information provided.

Health and Safety Information for Employees Regulations 1989

The Regulations require that information relating to health and safety at work be furnished to all employees by means of posters and leaflets in a form approved by the Health and Safety Executive (HSE). Details of the enforcing authority and the medical advisory services should also be made available.

The approved poster *"Health and Safety Law - what you should know"* should be placed in a prominent position and should contain details of the names and addresses of the enforcing authority, medical advisory service, the name(s) of the competent person(s) appointed under Regulation 7 of the Management of Health and Safety at Work Regulations (MHSWR) 1999 and the name(s) of employee safety reps or Trade Union safety reps appointed under the relevant legislation. Any change of name or address should be shown within 6 months of the alteration.

The HSE may approve a particular form of poster or leaflet for use in relation to a particular employment and where any such form has been approved, the Executive shall publish it. If a poster is used, the information must be legible and up to date and the poster must be prominently located in an area to which all employees have access. If a leaflet is used, new leaflets must be issued to employees when any similar changes occur.

MHSWR Regulation 10 - INFORMATION FOR EMPLOYEES

Employees must be provided with relevant information about hazards to their health and safety arising from risks identified by the assessments. Clear instruction must be provided concerning any preventative or protective control measures including those relating to serious and imminent danger and fire assessments. Details of any competent persons nominated to discharge specific duties in accordance with the regulations must also be communicated as should risks arising from contact with other employer's activities. *See also – Regulation 11 of the Management of Health & Safety at Work Regulations – Unit 3.*

Before employing a child (a person who is not over compulsory school age) the employer must provide those with parental responsibility for the child with information on the risks that have been identified and preventative and protective measures to be taken.

Figure 4-8: On the 1st October 1999, the Health and Safety Executive introduced a new edition of their Health and Safety Law poster. All previous versions of this sign must have been replaced by the 30th June 2000. *Source: HSE Books.*

CO-OPERATION AND CONSULTATION WITH CONTRACTORS AND THE WORKFORCE

The employer has a duty to arrange to consult employees on matters of health and safety, in particular before any changes in arrangements are implemented. The employer does not have a duty to adopt any suggestions made by employees or their representatives. Both employees and employee representatives may take any grievance not settled to the local enforcer. An Employment Industrial Tribunal may settle certain disputes, in particular where the rights under specific regulations are in dispute i.e. those of Trade Union Safety Representatives, The Safety Representatives and Safety Committees (SRSC) Regulations 1977 or Representatives Employee Safety, The Health and Safety (Consultation with Employees) Regulations (HSCER) 1996.

Representatives of employee safety

The HSCER extend the rights of consultation on matters relating to health and safety to all workers regardless of trade union status. Employers have the option to consult employees directly or through elected representatives.

See also - The Health and Safety (Consultation with Employees) Regulations (HSCER) 1996 - Unit 3 and Unit 20.

Roles and benefits of worker participation, safety committees and employee feedback

Mayo identified that worker involvement had a significant, positive effect on individual performance.

Those organisations which recognise the importance of managing heath and safety have embraced the concept of good worker cooperation and participation at all stages of business development. This may be achieved through communication with employee representatives or on a one-to-one basis. One of the benefits of using employee representatives is the extra time, which can be made available to representatives over individual employees. This will enable the representatives to get to know the business and issues of health and safety better through structured training. Representatives will also be able to contribute to forums with management, such as safety committees. The roles and communication lines must be determined and monitored for effectiveness. Care needs to be taken that the right message is being communicated by representatives there may be a tendency to filter or dilute communication.

Figure 4-9: Site safety notice board.   *Source: ACT.*

Figure 4-10: Safety suggestion scheme.   *Source: ACT.*

Training

THE EFFECT OF TRAINING ON HUMAN RELIABILITY

General points

There is a legal requirement under section 2 of the HASAWA, namely, the employer must provide such information, instruction, training and supervision, so far as is reasonably practicable, to ensure the health and safety at work of all employees. This requirement, which is essential to underpin health and safety standards, is made more specific by Reg 13, Capabilities and Training, of the MHSWR. Employers need to take into account the capabilities of their employees before entrusting tasks. This is necessary to ensure that they have adequate health and safety training and are capable enough at their jobs to avoid risk. To this end consideration must be given to recruitment including job orientation when transferring between jobs and work departments. Training must also be provided when other factors such as the introduction of new technology and new systems of work or work equipment arise.

Training must be repeated periodically, where appropriate, be adapted to take account of any new or changed risks to the health and safety of the employees concerned, and take place during working hours. A safety-training programme should be instigated for all employees from director level down. This should include:

- Specialist training.
- Internal and external courses.

- Formal and informal training.

All the training should be recorded and the employer needs to recognise the importance of further training at each stage of a person's career. Training should take place at each stage of an individual's career.

Effects and benefits of training

Benefits to employee
- Better understanding and involvement raises staff morale / job satisfaction.
- Understanding of relevance of systems of work and controls reduces risk.
- Understanding of welfare arrangements aids health, safety and hygiene.
- Allows employee to reach experienced worker standard more quickly.
- Increases flexibility of staff.

Benefits to employer
- Reduces accident frequency and severity.
- Reduces injury related absenteeism.
- Reduces claims and insurance premiums.
- Reduces the chance of prosecution.
- Increases profits/benefit.

OPPORTUNITIES AND NEED FOR TRAINING PROVISION

Induction training for new employees

Induction training is generally defined as the information, instruction and training given when a person starts a new job, task or process. Its purpose is to orientate the individual to his or her environment in order to maximise both productivity and safety. Thus, a workforce that is aware of the risks is familiar with procedures and systems of work, knows how to recognise and report unsafe conditions. This ensures that the employee shares a common commitment to health and safety and it contributes strongly to a safer workforce. Induction Training for new employees should include:

- Review and discussion of the organisation's safety policy.
- Specific training requirements.
- Fire and emergency procedures
- Welfare facilities.

- First aid procedures and facilities.
- Personal protective equipment (PPE) provisions - limitations, use and maintenance etc.

Refresher training

As time passes a workers approach to health and safety can drift away from that intended by the employer. This may simply be because they have forgotten, sometimes because of infrequent use, or because they prefer to have a different understanding or way of working. It is important that regular refresher training be used to re-enforce the employer's desired approach. A common refresher period is three years, used for first aiders and lift truck operators. This may be an acceptable interval for some tasks but the period may need to be shorter for others. Refresher training needs to be provided to managers as well workers that use health and safety skills.

Job change / process change

Required at appropriate intervals to update techniques and ensure awareness of correct methods. Training will include information and skills relevant to:

- Introduction of new substances/processes.
- Changes in working procedure.
- Changes in work patterns.
- Review of risk assessments.

Required at appropriate intervals to update techniques, ensure awareness of correct methods and assess the behaviour of the workforce and their attitude. In addition, further safety training may be required following an increase in accidents/incidents.

Introduction of new legislation

Employers have a duty to bring to the attention of employees specific changes in legislation which may have an effect on their safety or the safety of others. Changes that may affect personal safety include revisions to HSE Guidance EH40, where a reduction in occupational exposure limits may cause employees to adopt more stringent exposure controls.

Introduction of new technology

The introduction of new technology will often require the adoption of new work practices. Such training will include developing skills to interpret equipment control layout and data display, e.g. the introduction of nets and airbag fall arresters, used in new builds.

Specific safety training

Specific training for certain employees will include:

- Safety systems of work e.g. permit to work procedure.
- First aid training.
- Equipment training e.g. dumper truck-driving skills.
- PPE training.
- Fire training.
- Safety inspections.

Supervisor and general management training

To ensure responsibilities are known and the organisation's policy is carried out. Key points that should be covered:

- The safety policy.
- Legal framework and the duties of the organisation.
- Safety inspection techniques.
- Cause and consequences of accidents.
- Accident prevention techniques.
- Disciplinary procedures.
- The use of reactive and active monitoring techniques.

Preparing for a training session

Training is a crucial area in health and safety and careful preparation prior to delivering a training session is vital to its success. One of the first considerations is to identify the particular aspect of health and safety that is to be addressed so that the objectives and the content (breadth and depth) of the training session can be established. Other factors to be considered are:

- The training style and methods to be used e.g. lecture, video, role play, group work, use of equipment, site visit etc.
- The target audience e.g. existing knowledge and skills, relevance, motivation, etc.
- The number of trainees.
- The time available.
- The skills required of the trainer.
- Audio-visual and other training aids required. (Make sure that they work and that you know how to use them!).
- The suitability of the training facilities e.g. location, room layout, size, lighting, etc.
- Provision of refreshments if necessary.
- How the effectiveness of the training is going to be evaluated, both at the time (e.g. course evaluation forms) and afterwards (e.g. greater compliance with procedures, reduction in accidents, etc.

Provision of short training sessions

Should include:

- Setting objectives.
- Preparation of the programme.
- Briefing of trainee(s).
- Presentation of the training session (using visual aids if possible).
- Review of the contents of the session.
- Follow up.

Preparing for training

When we train, it is important to prepare:

The trainer	Do we need lesson notes? Do we have enough time?	Equipment / materials	Is it all there and in good working order? Is there sufficient to demonstrate and for the trainee to practice?
Training area	Are we free from interruptions? Is it safe and healthy?	Trainees	Do they know their work is covered in their absence? Is this the right time for them? (not their lunch-break).

	Trainer	Group
Aids to learning	Visual aids Questions Praise Commitment Mnemonics	Physical comfort Interest Confidence
Barriers to learning	Lack of preparation Information overload Tutor disinterest Time of day	Lack of motivation Distractions Noise

The roles of penalties and disciplinary procedures

Penalties and disciplinary procedures are generally present as a visible deterrent to those who breach statutory regulations or company rules. Although they cannot physically safeguard against accidents in the workplace in themselves, they may provide harsh remedies for those who show ignorance towards them. These may be in the form of fines, loss of employment or custodial sentences. Disciplinary procedures should be clear and relate the punishment to the severity of the breach.

Risk Assessment

Overall Aims

On completion of this Unit, candidates will understand:

■ the process of risk assessment.

■ risk assessment recording and reviewing procedures.

Content

Specific Intended Learning Outcomes

The intended learning outcomes of this Unit are that candidates will be able to:

5.1   explain the aims and objectives of risk assessment

5.2   distinguish between high frequency/low severity events and low frequency/high severity events

5.3   identify hazards by means of site and workshop inspections and analysis of tasks

5.4   use accident and near-miss data in risk assessments

5.5   use a simple risk assessment technique to determine risk levels and to assess the adequacy of controls

Sources of Reference

The Management of Health and Safety at Work (ACOP) (L21), HSE Books

Five Steps to Risk Assessment - Case Studies (HSG183), HSE Books

Five Steps to Risk Assessment (INDG163), HSE Books

A Guide to Managing Health and Safety in Construction, HSE Books

Young People at Work (HSG165), HSE Books

Relevant Statutory Provisions

The Management of Health and Safety at Work Regulations (MHSWR) 1999

5.1 - Definitions of hazard and risk

HAZARD

"something that has the potential to cause harm (loss)"

For example, cement, site vehicles, etc. Following hazard identification, it is possible to establish that risks exist that are or are not acceptable. In order to establish the presence of a risk it is necessary to identify the existence of hazards that may give rise to unplanned risk.

RISK

"the likelihood of a given loss occurring in defined circumstances"

For example, cement in contact with the hands may result in dermatitis; a site vehicle being used by untrained personal might be overturned. The presence of hazards at a given level of risk may not be a cause for immediate concern. However, some situations may exist or arise where there is a significant danger of loss, which will require some prompt action to be taken to reduce the danger. The process of identification assessment is considered later.

5.2 - Objectives of risk assessment

GENERAL POINTS

Definition of term 'risk assessment'

"an identification of the hazards present in an undertaking and an estimate of the extent of the risks involved, taking into account whatever precautions are already being taken"

Objectives of risk assessment

A risk assessment has three objectives:

1) To identify all the factors which may cause harm to employees and others (the *hazards*).

2) To consider the chance of that harm actually befalling anyone in the circumstances of a particular case, and the possible consequences that could come from it (the *risks*).

3) To enable employers to plan, introduce and monitor preventive measures to ensure that the risks are adequately controlled at all times.

Risk assessment involves:
1. The identification of the hazards at work.
2. The evaluation of the risks from the hazards.
3. Deciding how to control the risks.
4. Implementing a control strategy.

Most people undertake risk assessment as a normal part of their everyday lives. Routine activities, such as crossing the road and driving to work, routinely call for a complex analysis of the hazards and risks involved in order to avoid damage and injury. Thus, most people are able to recognise hazards as they develop and take corrective action. People do, however, have widely different perceptions regarding risk and would find it difficult to apply their experience to the formal workplace risk assessments required by law.

The aim of this unit is to introduce the basic principles of risk assessment techniques in order to carry out the systematic, structured assessments needed to fulfil the requirements of modern health and safety legislation. The legal requirement to perform specific risk assessment is incorporated into many pieces of legislation such as the Noise at Work Regulations (NWR) 1989 and the Manual Handling Operations Regulations (MHOR) 1992. The MHSWR however set out broad general duties that apply to almost all kinds of work. Regulation 3 of The Management of Health and Safety at Work Regulations (MHSWR) 1999 requires employers to assess the risk to:

1. the health and safety of the employees.
2. to anyone else who may be affected by their work activity.

The assessment must be *suitable and sufficient* and should cover the whole undertaking; it should also be broad enough so that it remains valid for a reasonable period. Risks arising from the routine activities, associated with life in general, can usually be ignored *unless* the work activity compounds these risks. These general duties exist in conjunction with the more specific ones in other health and safety legislation. However, that will not mean that you have to do things twice. For example, if you have done a risk assessment to comply with the Control of Substances Hazardous to Health Regulations (COSHH) 2002 you will not have to do it again for the same hazardous substances to comply with the MHSWR. As a rule, a specific duty will take the place of a general one that duplicates it. *See also - Foundations in Construction Health and Safety - Unit 1.*

5.3 - Different types of incident

Distinction between different types of incident

ILL-HEALTH

The health and well-being of individuals may be affected by a number of work-related factors. Ill health may develop over a long period of time; these are commonly called chronic diseases. Typical examples of work-related ill health are asbestosis, pneumoconiosis and silicosis, where the ill heath effects may take several years to develop. More recently ill health effects have been related to work load and stress.

INJURY ACCIDENT

Some injury effects will be acute in nature and recognised immediately, such as strains or sprains of muscles or ligaments caused by inappropriate lifting of heavy items. Other common injuries include cuts, burns, and bruises.

DANGEROUS OCCURRENCE

The schedule to the Reporting of Injuries, Disease and Dangerous Occurrences (RIDDOR) 1995 lists incidents which must be formally reported to the relevant enforcement agency. They are significant events, such as the collapse of, the overturning of, or the failure of any load-bearing part of any lift or hoist; mobile powered access platform; access cradle or window-cleaning cradle; excavator; pile-driving frame or rig having an overall height, when operating, of more than 7 metres; or fork lift truck; the collapse of a scaffold of more than five metres high.

NEAR-MISS

A near-miss is an incident with the potential to cause harm, but where there is no measurable loss. A near-miss is classified under the term accident:

"an unplanned, uncontrolled event which led to, or could have led to loss"

It is important to analyse near miss to assess the potential of the event, had circumstances been different. This will enable corrective action to be put in place to prevent a reoccurrence of the incident.

DAMAGE-ONLY

Substantial damage occurs to property and materials at work annually. Often the most significant losses are associated with workplace fires, when the workplace may be destroyed, although fortunately only rarely are people injured. The study of the incidence of damage and potential losses may be a useful predictive tool to identify scenarios which might result in person damage. For example, a series of collisions into scaffold on a site with poor access and lighting may be predictive of a vehicle failure / scaffold collapse leading to personal injury. Such considerations enable the employer to take corrective action before any loss occurs.

THE DISTINCTION BETWEEN DIFFERENT INCIDENTS IN SUMMARY

An accident is an event which brings about a result. We must not think of injuries etc. as accidents, but rather as the results of accidents. In short, accidents result in losses of one kind or another: The following accident model is offered to illustrate the above statement. In a situation where a spanner falls from a height the following could result:

- Falls into a pile of sand and there is no damage or injury, *a near miss*.
- Hits an item of equipment, resulting in *damage*, but no injury.
- Hits a person causing cut and bruises to hand. *This is an injury accident.*
- If the person was working directly under the spanner when it fell there could have been a fatality*, or injury accident.*

This definition, therefore, includes "near-misses", i.e. where no injury or damage etc. occurs. The difference between a near-miss and a fatal accident in terms of time and distance can be very small indeed. It is therefore clear that the damage to persons or property is not the accident, but part of the effects of the accidents, the result or consequences of the accident.

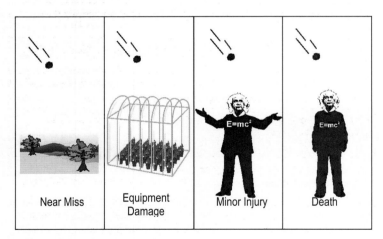

An old adage says: "Never waste an accident". Apart from being unpleasant and perhaps very costly, every accident constitutes an opportunity to correct some problem. For this purpose, a near miss is just as valuable as a serious injury/damage, in fact even more valuable and an excellent opportunity not to be missed.

Some years ago, a study of 1,750,000 accidents in 21 industries, led by Frank Bird, showed that there is a fixed ratio between losses of different severity and accidents where no loss occurred, i.e. near misses. This is illustrated in the pyramid model of incident outcomes - Frank Bird's accident ration study.

Figure 5-1: Results of an accident   Source: ACT.

Pyramid model of incident outcomes

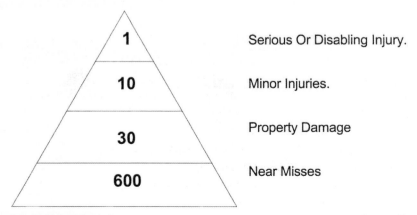

1	Serious Or Disabling Injury.
10	Minor Injuries.
30	Property Damage
600	Near Misses

Figure 5-2: Accident ratio study.   *Source: Frank Bird.*

The principle applies equally to other situations. The organisation, site or department that has most accidents is therefore, in the long run, likely to have the *most serious losses*. There is no escaping the ratio/pyramid.

The other lesson to be learned is that if you tackle the causes of minor loss accident, you will automatically reduce the serious loss accident causes as well.

Figures published by the Health and Safety Executive (HSE) show that annually in all work activities there are over 400,000 notified accidents of which approx. 500 are fatal. Reports published by the Chief Inspector of Factories showed that in manufacturing and service industries only, there are approximately 300 fatalities and over 9000 major injuries notified annually.

5.4 - Accident categories as causes of injury

The following are examples of hazards, together with some of the associated risks, which can occur in the workplace.

HAZARD	ASSOCIATED RISKS	SIGNIFICANCE
Slips/trips/falls	Fall of a person on the same level.	HSE statistics show that slips, trips and falls on the same level are the most common source of major injuries reported under RIDDOR.
Falls from height; falling objects	Fall of a person, object/material.	Falls from height (usually more than 2m) are by far the most common cause of fatal injuries.
Collision with objects	Bumps and bruises. Striking the head on low beams.	Although minor injuries they are very painful and can result in poor morale amongst the workforce if they happen frequently.
Trapping/crushing under or between objects	Serious injury caused by loss of load from crane, collision with site vehicles.	Due to the nature of the machinery involved, death or serious injury is often the result of incidents such as the loss of load from a crane.
Manual handling	Back strains, cuts, injury to joints.	Most of the "three day injuries" reported to the HSE are back strains that occur during manual handling operations.
Contact with machinery/hand tools	Parts being ejected from the machine. Trapping / crushing. Entanglement of clothing or hair.	All dangerous parts of machinery must be guarded so far as is practicable. Serious injury such as amputation can easily happen should contact with moving parts occur.
Electricity	Fire, shock, burns.	Static electricity or contact with live services can cause shock, burns and/or fire. Particular care should be taken during demolition activities to ensure that all services are disconnected.
Transport	Collision with people and/or property.	Only suitably trained and authorised people should be permitted to drive vehicles on site.
Contact with chemicals	Dermatitis, burns, poisoning.	It is very easy to underestimate the severity of diseases like dermatitis. Good personal hygiene is a must.
Asphyxiation/drowning	Drowning.	Strict precautions need to be taken to protect people who work above water or enter confined spaces (e.g. cellars).
Fire and explosion	Static electrical sparks causing explosions in say flammable or dusty atmospheres.	Permits to work must be used to control non routine work such as grinding and welding.
Animals	Anthrax, leptospirosis, psittacosis caused by coming into contact with animal hides, etc.	Many construction workers regularly come into contact with animal-borne micro-organisms during demolition work and when working in or near water.
Violence	Unhappy customers/clients, criminals, patients in hospitals.	A common problem, particularly for employees who come into contact with the public and those who are responsible for site security.

5.5 - Categorisation of health risks

CHEMICAL HAZARDS
Examples include:
- Acids and alkalis - dermatitis
- Metals - lead and mercury poisoning
- Non metals - arsenic and phosphorus poisoning
- Gases - carbon monoxide poisoning, arsine poisoning
- Organic compounds - occupational cancers e.g. bladder cancer

BIOLOGICAL HAZARDS
Examples include:
- Animal-borne - anthrax, brucellosis, leptospirosis
- Human-borne - viral hepatitis
- Vegetable-borne - aspergillosis (farmer's lung)
- Others (water/land) - legionella

PHYSICAL HAZARDS

Examples include:

Heat	-	heat cataract, heat stroke
Lighting	-	miner's nystagmus
Noise	-	noise induced hearing loss (occupational deafness)
Vibration	-	vibration induced white finger
Radiation	-	radiation sickness (at ionising wavelengths), burns, arc eye
Dust	-	silicosis, coal worker's pneumoconiosis
Pressure	-	decompression sickness

PSYCHOLOGICAL HAZARDS

Examples include: Work pressure, bullying,   - stress, alcohol / narcotic abuse

5.6 - The risk assessment process

A general approach to risk assessment

MANAGEMENT OF HEALTH AND SAFETY AT WORK REGULATIONS - REGULATIONS 3 AND 16 - CRITERIA FOR A 'SUITABLE AND SUFFICIENT' RISK ASSESSMENT

The Approved Code of Practice to the MHSWR states that in order to be suitable and sufficient a risk assessment must:

1)   Identify all the hazards and evaluate the risks from those hazards, taking into account current legal requirements.

2)   Record the significant findings.

3)   Identify any group of employees or single employees who are especially at risk.

4)   Identify others who may be specifically at risk e.g. members of the public, visitors.

5)   Evaluate existing controls, stating whether or not they are satisfactory, and if not, the action necessary.

6)   Evaluate the need for further controls including information, instruction and training.

IMPLEMENTING A RISK ASSESSMENT PROGRAMME

The key to carrying out an effective risk assessment programme is to have a systematic approach. Management must therefore:

1)   Commission, organise and co-ordinate the assessment in consultation with the workforce.

2)   Appoint competent persons (if not competent themselves) in consultation with the workforce to act as assessor(s).

3)   Provide all relevant information and resources to the assessor(s) to enable him/them to carry out his/their task efficiently.

4)   Provide full backing and support of all persons involved, e.g. local line management and the workforce.

5)   Inform the workforce of the results of the assessment, the measures recommended by the assessor(s), and the preventative and protective measures carried out or proposed.

6)   Check, in conjunction with the workforce, that the measures that have been carried out have been checked to ensure that they are sufficient and acceptable.

7)   Carry out improvement measures in order of cost benefits.

8)   Monitor the preventative and protective measures in order to ensure they are still sufficient and acceptable.

9)   Review and/or revise assessments whenever the equipment, material, procedure or workplace changes.

10)   Ensure that the workforce is informed of all reviews, revisions etc.

ASSESSORS

Assessments must be carried out by competent person(s). The number of competent persons required will depend on the size of the organisation and its geographical spread. The competent assessor must be able to demonstrate knowledge, training and suitable qualifications which are relevant to the organisation and have the ability to apply these qualities to practical situations.

HSE GUIDANCE ON RISK ASSESSMENT

The process of risk assessment typically involves the following 5 steps:

1)   Identify the hazard.

2)   Identify who and how harm might occur.

3)   Evaluate the risks.

4)   Record the significant findings.

5)   Review.

It is essential that there is a systematic examination of each activity, which could cause injury. It is important to ensure that all risks are considered. For ease of management, assessments could be categorised in:

- Groups e.g. machinery tasks, tasks involving substance, transport tasks.
- Geographical areas e.g. departments, sections, offices, or construction sites.

MODEL (GENERIC) RISK ASSESSMENTS

In cases where organisations have several locations or situations where the same activity is undertaken, then a model (generic) risk assessment could be carried out to consider the core hazards and associated risks of these. For generic assessments to be effective, they must:

1)   Be broadly appropriate to the type of work.

2)   Have the ability to adapt the model to the actual work situation.

3)   Have the ability to be extended to cover hazards and risks not referred to in the model.

Generic risk assessments are a useful aid. However, care has to be taken to ensure they are not accepted as being universally applicable without checking them against the actual circumstances being assessed by the assessor.

Identifying hazards

SOURCES AND FORM OF HARM

The first step is to identify the hazards. This can be done in many ways. The methods used will need to be assessed so all the hazards associated with a task can be identified and ranked in order of severity. For complex activities, it may be necessary to break the activity down into its component parts by, for example, job analysis. For a large machine, this could mean looking at:

- Installation.
- Normal operation.
- Breakdown.
- Cleaning.
- Adjustment.
- Dismantling.

The hazards associated with each part could then be identified more easily and thoroughly.

It is necessary to identify contingent hazard, which can arise from system, component, checking or maintenance failures, as well as continuing hazards, i.e. those present continuously, e.g.:

- Mechanical hazards.
- Electrical hazards.
- Thermal hazards.
- Noise and vibration.
- Radiation.
- Toxic materials.
- Ergonomic design.

Once the area/activity has been selected, the method(s) of hazard identification can be chosen. If a hazard is defined as being something with the potential to cause harm, then hazard identification can be carried out by observing the activity and noting the hazards as they occur in the actual work setting. This is seen to have advantages over carrying out a desktop exercise using the safety manual, for the use of a machine for example, as the operator may have developed his own method of working, contrary to instructions and training.

Another method of hazard identification may be a simple walk round an area, a tour, taking notes or using a checklist. Tours may be carried out daily, weekly or be ongoing. They may be formal or informal, but require a reporting and follow-up system in order to be effective. A further method is an inspection. This may be a specially set up or a routine scheduled inspection and involve someone familiar with the task/area and someone not familiar as a 'fresh pair of eyes'. It is more formal than a tour, takes place less often, and requires documenting. Hazards may also be identified during accident investigation, especially if the accident was not foreseen. An accident will not be wasted if it highlights previously unforeseen hazards. Accident statistics, from internal and external sources, can also be used for hazard information. There are other hazard identification techniques, which form part of the advanced risk assessment techniques:

- Hazard and operability studies (HAZOP), which are much used by the chemical industry at the design stage of processes and equipment.
- Reliability analysis and Failure mode and effect analysis (FMEA), which are inductive techniques.
- Fault tree analysis (FTA) and Event tree analysis (ETA), which are deductive techniques.

INSPECTIONS

The obvious purpose of safety is to identify areas where improvements are needed. Inspections may also affect the organisational safety culture, particularly where employee's views are sought as part of the inspection. In this way, employer's commitment to health and safety can be demonstrated, ownership of health and safety can be shared and employee morale can be increased by simple improvements being implemented at the time of the inspection.

Inspections involve examination of the workplace or items of equipment in order to identify hazards and determine if they are effectively controlled. Four different types of inspection are common:

- General workplace inspections - carried out by local first-line managers and employee representatives.
- Statutory inspections (thorough examination) of equipment, e.g. boilers, lifting equipment - by specialist Competent Persons.
- Preventive maintenance inspections of specific (critical) items - carried out by maintenance staff.
- Pre use 'checks' of equipment, e.g. vehicles, forklift trucks, access equipment - carried out by the user.

An important aid used by anyone carrying out an inspection is a checklist, i.e. a list of the "the way things ought to be". When a work area or item of equipment fails this test it is considered substandard and represents a hazard. Each substandard condition should be assessed and corrective action carried out and details recorded. Issues to be considered when creating a checklist should include: substances or materials being used, condition of traffic routes and means of access and egress, work equipment, work practices (manual handling, etc.), work environment, electricity, fire precautions, welfare provision including first aid arrangements and workstation ergonomics.

JOB / TASK SAFETY ANALYSIS

Job / task analysis is the identification of all the accident prevention measures appropriate to a particular job or area of work activity, and the behavioural factors which most significantly influence whether or not these measures are taken. The approach is diagnostic as well as descriptive.

Analysis can be:

1) Job based: operators of plant, fork lift truck drivers.

2) Task based: manual handling activities, housekeeping.

The results can be used to correct existing analyses and to improve such things as emergency procedures, reporting of information and the layout of work areas. The process of job analysis needs to be carried out methodically through a series of steps and the whole analysis should be documented.

LEGISLATION

Information about hazards can be obtained by considering a range of legislative documents including ACOPs and guidance notes. For example, the Fire precautions (Workplace) Regulations (FPWR) 1997, as amended, give information about fire hazards and escape routes. Likewise the Manual Handling Operations Regulations (MHOR) 1992 can be used to establish problems associated with lifting loads.

MANUFACTURERS' INFORMATION

Manufacturers are required to provide product equipment health and safety information. Information provided in relation to articles and substances must be relevant and kept up to date. Those that design, manufacture, supply or install have a duty to inform of any issues determined through research that may affect the users, including product liability aspects, safe operating and use of instructions. CHIP 3 requires suppliers to provide material safety data sheets that can then be considered when carrying out a risk assessment.

INCIDENT DATA

Statistics provide useful response information from past accident experience. Types include lost time, sickness absence, first aid records.

EXISTING WRITTEN INFORMATION

Policies, agreements, rules, regulations, procedures, methods, times, instructions and records.

JOB DESCRIPTIONS

The physical and mental requirements and limitations of certain jobs; past modifications to job descriptions; representations from operators on safety aspects of jobs directly affecting themselves.

PERSONAL EXPERIENCE

Experience of particular jobs, hazards, equipment, systems, or by specific trials and practice in problem areas.

INTERVIEWS AND DISCUSSION

To obtain subjective information, perceptions, ideas, feelings, informal roles and relationships, social norms, attitudes, levels of knowledge and skill the Safety Committee is a useful information source.

WORK STUDY TECHNIQUES

For example, activity sampling, surveys, method study, work measurement, process flows.

Identifying population at risk

A suitable and sufficient risk assessment will identify all those at risk. When judging numbers and types of people who might be affected it is important to remember certain groups of workers who may work unusual hours (e.g. security, cleaners, etc.). High risk groups include young people, pregnant women or nursing mothers.

GENERAL GROUPS AT RISK

This category includes vulnerable people that might be at risk from a particular hazard. For example, women of childbearing age (or more particularly any unborn foetus they may be carrying) may be deemed to be at risk from exposure to the hazards presented by lead. Other at risk groups could be the public (because of their lack of knowledge of the hazard/risk), young persons (16-18 years), workers that have come from other countries where language or work practices may be different to the UK or people with health conditions. The 'at risk group' depends on the hazard and the circumstances. The MHSWR require specific attention to women of childbearing age and the new or expectant mother.

The assessment must take into account the effect of any

- Process.
- Working condition.
- Physical, chemical and biological agents which may adversely affect the health and safety of the woman or baby.

Another specific group of people who must be considered are young people (under 18 years of age) and children (under compulsory school leaving age) - Regulation 19 of the MHSWR. These risk assessments must take into account their lack of experience, immaturity and consider any consequent necessary restrictions (e.g. exclusion from excessive noise). Where children are involved, the significance of assessments must be communicated to the people who have parental responsibility.

SPECIFIC GROUPS AT RISK

Site operatives

Typically these are individuals engaged in production type activities where they have little control over their environment or work routine. Issues include repetitive strain, slips, trips and falls, together with a variety of equipment hazards. Consideration of the task and issues of fatigue and loss of concentration are usually significant.

Surveyors

Site surveyors are engaged in a mixture of site and office based work. Activities at site are primarily for the collation of information to be used in construction drawings, and information used in construction specification documentation. They have little or no control over the day to day running of the operation.

Transport drivers

Transport drivers are responsible for the vehicle they are in control of, and are required to adhere to traffic routes, speed limits, and site rules. The vehicles used on construction sites can vary, but are usually heavy plant, with restricted vision. Dangers are pedestrian traffic, other site vehicles and unstable ground. All drivers must be adequately licensed and authorised for the vehicle they are operating on site.

Building inspectors

Similarly to site surveyors, building inspectors are engaged in a mixture of site and office based work. Activities at site are primarily for the inspection of works carried out with the aim of ensuring that all standards, specifications and quality are adhered to. They have little or no control over the day to day running of the operation.

Contractors

Arrangements for contractors need to be clearly established; the work to be done and limitations must be understood by all involved and only controlled deviation allowed. Typical issues may include consideration of location of equipment or materials, welfare or first aid arrangements.

Visitors / Public

Before visitors or members of the public are allowed into the work place issues of access, use of facilities, arrangements for escort or accompaniment must be established. Other issues include arrangements for safe evacuation. Certain workplaces such as places of sport have specific legal requirements such as the appointment of fire wardens.

Evaluating risk and adequacy of current controls

LIKELIHOOD OF HARM AND PROBABLE SEVERITY

After the hazards have been identified it is necessary to evaluate the risk. In order to do this, at least two areas must be considered - the consequence and the likelihood of harm. This requires a judgment for each hazard to decide, realistically, what is the most likely outcome and how likely is this to occur. It may be a matter of simple subjective judgement or it may require a more complex technique depending on the complexity of the situation.

1. **Consequence** - is there a risk of death, major injury, minor injury, damage to plant/equipment/product, or damage to the environment?
2. **Likelihood** - there is danger around us constantly, but we have in-built or applied safeguards. These may fail, be defeated or become inactive at various times. At these times, the hazard will be realised and the probability of this can be evaluated by such techniques as fault or probability tree analysis.

Factors affecting likelihood

In order to judge likelihood accurately, some or all of the following need to be considered:

- Competence of operators.
- Levels and quality of supervision.
- Attitudes of operators and supervisors.
- Environmental conditions e.g. adverse weather.
- Frequency and duration of exposure.

QUALITATIVE AND SEMI-QUANTITATIVE RISK RANKING

Qualitative

Qualitative risk assessment considers the probability or likelihood of failure. This analysis relies on failure rates and typically would consider such information as manufacturer reliability information for its components. It is useful at the micro and macro level.

Semi-quantitative

Semi-quantitative considers the relative effects of workplace risks for common task or operation. It uses the technique of risk ranking. It is useful at the macro level.

Risk ranking

Here associated risks are ranked in order. This normally consists of assigning a numerical value for consequence and likelihood typically in the range 1-5. The product of each risk is then listed and of those which are the most significant, the ones with the highest risk ranking number, are addressed first.

The purpose of ranking risks is to prioritise the need for action and to consider whether or not further action is required. Everyone has his own perception of risk because of his life experiences and background. A method is therefore required in order to have a common approach and attempt to overcome individual differences. We can rate and therefore rank a risk according to the consequence and likelihood of any loss resulting from a hazard. Thus:

Risk rating = consequence x likelihood

Where the:	Consequence	is the degree or amount of any resultant loss.
	Likelihood	is how likely this loss will occur.
	Risk rating	is the severity of the remaining risk after current controls have been taken into account.

Consequence categories

The consequence can be assessed on a scale of 1 to 5.

5.	Major	Causing death to one or more people. Loss or damage is such that it could cause serious business disruption (e.g. major fire, explosion or structural damage). Loss/damage in excess of (£_____).
4.	High	Causing permanent disability (e.g. loss of limb, sight or hearing). Loss/damage in excess of (£_____).
3.	Medium	Causing temporary disability (e.g. fractures). Loss/damage in excess of (£_____).
2.	Low	Causing significant injuries (e.g. sprains, bruises, and lacerations). Loss/damage in excess of (£_____) e.g. damage to fixtures and fittings.
1.	Minor	Causing minor injuries (e.g. cuts, scratches). No lost time likely other than for first aid treatment. Loss/damage in excess of (£_____) e.g. superficial damage to interior decorations.

The amounts in each of the above categories will depend on the size and type of organisation. Senior management in each case should decide these figures.

Likelihood categories

5.	Almost Certain	Absence of any management controls. If conditions remain unchanged there is almost a 100% certainty that an accident will happen (e.g. broken rung on a ladder, live exposed electrical conductor, and untrained personnel).
4.	High	Serious failures in management controls. The effects of human behaviour or other factors could cause an accident but is unlikely without this additional factor (e.g. ladder not secured properly, oil spilled on floor, poorly trained personnel).
3.	Medium	Insufficient or substandard controls in place. Loss is unlikely during normal operation, however it may occur in emergencies or non-routine conditions (e.g. keys left in forklift trucks; obstructed gangways; refresher training required).
2.	Low	The situation is generally well managed, however occasional lapses could occur. This also applies to situations where people are required to behave safely in order to protect themselves but are well trained.
1.	Improbable	Loss, accident or illness could only occur under freak conditions. The situation is well managed and all reasonable precautions have been taken. Ideally, this should be the normal state of the workplace.

Using the formula stated above (Risk Rating = Consequence x Likelihood) the risk rating can be calculated. It will fall into the range of 1 - 25. This risk rating is used to prioritise the observed risks.

The risk rating is then classified as follows:

Risk Rating   1 - 9   Low

Risk Rating   10 - 15   Medium

Risk Rating   16 - 25   High

Possible factors to consider in determining what further measures could be taken to reduce the risk include:

a)   Can the hazard be enclosed/guarded/segregated from people?

b)   Is there a safe system of work/written procedures/ adequate supervision?

c)   Is training required?

d)   Have people been informed/consulted/instructed?

e)   Is personal protective equipment required? Has it been provided?

RESIDUAL RISK

This is the risk which remains when controls have been decided; for example, whilst a fall from a height may be prevented by a guard rail, the potential to slip or trip may remain at a level.

ACCEPTABLE/TOLERABLE RISK LEVELS

Societal standards change and risk acceptability reduces each year within Europe. Legislation places a general duty to reduce the level of risk so far as is reasonably practicable. The standard "practicable" is looking to require employers to use any new improvements in technology.

GUIDANCE

When making a judgement as to whether controls are adequate care has to be taken to consider relevant guidance. This can be in the form of guidance to legislation, HSE guidance documents, industry standard guidance and relevant British Standards.

LEGISLATION APPLYING CONTROLS TO SPECIFIED HAZARDS

Duties to apply specific controls are found in the schedules to the Control of Substances Harmful to Health Regulations (COSHH) including exposure standards for substances in EH40. Similar requirements are provided in the Lead at Work (CLAW) and Asbestos at Work (AW) Regulations.

GENERAL CONTROL HIERARCHY

The principle is to address each risk in the following order of priority. Often a combination of measures will be used. The general control hierarchy is:

E liminate - the substance or work practice.

R educe - the use or frequency or substitute - for a lesser hazard or change the physical form.

C ontrol - at source, i.e. fume dust extraction, totally enclose.

P PE - a physical barrier between you and the risk.

D iscipline - follow the rules, obey signs and instructions.

PRIORITISATION BASED ON RISK

When risk potential has been identified prioritisation can be given to the order of work to mitigate the risk.

DISTINCTION BETWEEN PRIORITIES AND TIME SCALES

Often risks are of high priority, but the need to establish realistic time scales is also important. Often it is possible to carry out some aspects in the short and medium term to reduce the likelihood of a loss and remove the need to give everything considered a high priority for completion.

Recording

FORMAT

Employers with five or more employees are required to record the ***significant findings*** of their risk assessments in writing.

It should be noted that there are many forms and systems designed for recording assessments and while these may differ in design, the methodology broadly remains the same.

INFORMATION

The task/plant/process/activity together with the hazards involved, their associated risks and persons affected by them together with existing control measures, should be recorded. The necessary actions required to further reduce the risk are then dealt with and are usually recorded separately.

Some items, particularly those with a high-risk rating, may require a more detailed explanation or there may be a series of alternative actions. Information on risk assessments and any controls must be brought to the attention of those assigned the task of work. Risk assessment information should be included in lesson plans to ensure items are not missed when staff are trained or retrained.

No.	Hazard Identification	Associated Risks	No. At Risk	Existing Controls	Consequence	Likelihood	Current Risk Rating	Comments

Figure 5-3: Risk assessment form.

Source: ACT.

Reviewing

Any significant changes to a workplace, process or activity, or the introduction of any new process, activity or operation, should be subject to risk assessment.

The risk assessment should be periodically reviewed and updated.

Examples of circumstances that would require the re-evaluation of the validity of a risk assessment are:

- When the results of monitoring (accidents, ill-health effects, environmental) are not as expected.
- A change in process, work methods or materials.
- The introduction of new plant or technology.
- Changes in personnel.
- New information becoming available.
- As time passes - the risk assessment should be periodically reviewed and updated. A common approach would be no longer than 5 years.
- Changes in legislation.

MAINTAINING THE RISK ASSESSMENT

The risk assessment should be periodically reviewed and updated. This is best achieved through a combination of monitoring techniques such as:

- Preventive maintenance inspections.
- Safety representative/committee inspections.
- Statutory and maintenance scheme inspections, tests and examinations.
- Safety tours and inspections.
- Occupational health surveys.
- Air monitoring.
- Safety audits.

Routine analysis of accident and ill-health reports, damage accident reports, and 'near miss' reports can also provide a trigger to an earlier than planned review of risk assessments.

Principles of Control

Overall Aims

On completion of this Unit, candidates will understand:

- fundamental strategies for controlling site hazards and reducing risk.
- the various hazard control and risk reduction methods available.

Content

Specific Intended Learning Outcomes

The intended learning outcomes of this Unit are that candidates will be able to:

6.1   describe the general principles of control and a basic hierarchy of risk reduction measures that encompass technical, behavioural and procedural controls

6.2   develop and apply safe systems of work for general site activities

6.3   explain the role and function of a permit-to-work within a safe system of work

6.4   assess the adequacy of emergency procedures and provision.

Sources of Reference

Successful Health and Safety Management (HSG65), HSE Books

The Management of Health and Safety at Work Regulations (ACOP) (L21), HSE Books

A Guide to Managing Health and Safety in Construction, HSE Books

First-Aid at Work (ACOP) (L74), HSE Books

Safety Signs and Signals (Guidance) (L64), HSE Books

Personal Protective Equipment at Work (L25), HSE Books

Relevant Statutory Provisions

The Health and Safety at Work etc Act (HASAWA) 1974 - section 2

The Management of Health and Safety at Work Regulations (MHSWR) 1999

The Personal Protective Equipment at Work Regulations (PPER) 1992

The Health and Safety (Safety Signs and Signals) Regulations (SSSR) 1996

The Health and Safety (First-Aid) Regulations (FAR) 1981

6.1 - General principles of prevention

The general principles of prevention are contained in the Management of Health and Safety at Work Regulations (MHSWR) 1999.

In order to control the risks identified by the risk assessment, employers and the self-employed need to introduce preventive and protective measures. Regulation 4 of the MHSWR requires that "Where an employer implements any preventive and protective measures he shall do so on the basis of the principles specified in Schedule 1 to these Regulations". These are outlined below.

AVOIDING RISKS

If risks are avoided completely then they do not have to be either controlled or monitored. For example, not using pesticides or not working at height.

EVALUATING UNAVOIDABLE RISKS

Carry out a suitable and sufficient assessment of risks.

CONTROLLING HAZARDS AT SOURCE

Repairing a hole in the floor is much better than displaying a warning sign. Other examples are the use of local exhaust ventilation to remove a substance at source, the design of equipment so that movement is enclosed and does not create a hazard and the repair of a noisy bearing to control the hazard at source.

ADAPTING WORK TO THE INDIVIDUAL

This emphasises the importance of human factors in modern control methods. If the well-being of the person is dealt with, there is less chance of the job causing ill-health and less chance of the person making mistakes which lead to accidents. Consideration should be given to the design of any equipment used, frequently used controls should be close to the operator, start buttons should be positioned to avoid inadvertent use, stop buttons should be close to the operator and easy to operate in an emergency. All equipment should be clearly labelled. Consideration should be given to minimisation of fatigue. Alleviating monotonous work by breaks or task rotation can help the individual to remain alert and pay attention to the task.

ADAPTING TO TECHNICAL PROGRESS

This can lead to improved, safer and healthier working conditions, for example the provision of new non-slip floor surfaces or the bringing into use of less hazardous equipment such as new sound proofed equipment to replace old noisy equipment. In recent years this has included the use of waste chutes for removal of materials from scaffolds and the use of lower vibration equipment.

REPLACING THE DANGEROUS BY THE LESS/NON-DANGEROUS

For example, using a battery operated drill rather than a mains powered tool, providing compressed air at a lower pressure or providing water based chemicals instead of solvent based chemicals.

DEVELOPING A COHERENT PREVENTION POLICY

Taking a holistic stance to the control of risk, this involves consideration of the *organisation* through the establishing of risk / control identification systems, the *job* the use of task analysis and selection of the people, which includes consideration of human factors that affect an *individual* such as mental and physical requirements.

GIVING PRIORITY TO COLLECTIVE PROTECTIVE MEASURES OVER INDIVIDUAL PROTECTIVE MEASURES

Organisations with a less developed approach to health and safety may mistakenly see the solution to risks is to provide individual; protective measures such as warning people of hazards and provision of personal protective equipment - using the *'safe person'* (and healthy person) strategy. A more developed and effective approach is to give priority, where possible, to collective measures that provide protection to all workers such as provisions of barriers around street works or cleaning up a slippery substance spill rather than putting signs to warn workers - using the *'safe place'* (and healthy place) strategy. These two strategies are supported by a third strategy sometime called the *'safe system'* (and healthy system) strategy. This strategy establishes the correct way to do things in the form of rules and procedures, for example the rule that says 'clean up after you do work' in order that the place is left in a safe and healthy condition.

Reliance on only a safe/healthy person strategy is the weakest of controls. The preferred strategy is the safe/healthy place and priority must be given to using it where possible. By ensuring a safe/healthy place all people that find themselves in it will gain protection. This approach is reflected in the hierarchy used for safeguarding dangerous parts of equipment - our first priority is to provide guards around the dangerous parts (making it a safe place) and for the remainder that cannot be enclosed in this way we provide information, instruction and training to those that use the equipment (making the safe person). In practice, the most successful organisations use a combination of the three strategies, with the emphasis on making the place safe/healthy, supporting this with systems of work (procedures) and paying attention to the person element so that they support rather than undermine the other strategies. Many organisations that feel they have invested effort in getting the place and procedures right are taking a fresh look at the actions necessary to ensure the person is right also. Studies have shown that this too is a critical aspect of effective management of health and safety.

PROVIDING APPROPRIATE TRAINING, INFORMATION AND SUPERVISION

It is essential to distinguish between: information, instruction, training and supervision. This will ensure clarity of purpose for each and suggest the best way to communicate each effectively.

See also – Work equipment – hazards and control – Unit 12.

Information

Purpose   To improve awareness about health and safety generally and in relation to specific hazards, their controls and management performance to bring about these controls. In its self passive, it relies on the recipient to interpret.

Subjects

Legislation.	Accident statistics.	Names of appointed first aiders.
Company policy statements.	General hazards and controls.	

Means of communication

Bulletins and news sheets.	Team briefing.	Site signs and labels.
Notice boards, propaganda, films	Written material for visitors.	

Instruction

Purpose   To control employees, contractors and visitors behaviour with regard to general and specific health and safety arrangements. Typically one way, often no real check or understanding.

Subjects

Health and Safety rules.	Use of PPE.	Emergency procedures.
Policy, arrangements and plans.	Specific hazards e.g. smoking.	Reporting accidents.

Means of communicating   Formally using verbal, written and visual material, notice boards, induction and job training, direct issue of document, 'tool-box talks'.

Training

Purpose   To develop people, their attitudes, perception and motivation with regard to health and safety to ensure acceptable actions. Training should use two-way communication - information / instruction given and understanding checked. This may be by observation of a person's practical skill, for example by driving a fork lift truck or using a simulator, and / or by written or verbal assessment.

Subjects

Accident investigation.	How to set up your display screen workstation.	Use of personal protective equipment.
Conducting risk assessments.		
Conducting inspections/audits.	How to use work equipment e.g. rough terrain fork lift truck.	Manual handling techniques.
How to comply with instructions.		Emergency procedures.

Means of communicating

On/off the job.	Explanation, demonstration, discussion and practice.	One-to-one or group.
Internal/external trainers.		Written, oral and visual material.

Arrangements for induction

It is essential that systematic arrangements are in place to ensure a consistent standard of induction for health and safety on site. It is an important integral part of the prevention process, setting out standards of behaviour and workplace conditions for the site. It illustrates hazards that workers may create and helps to make them aware of what they may encounter on site. It must focus on the controls that should be used as well as the hazards that may be encountered. This creates an expectation of health and safety to be achieved and from each other. It provides confidence to the workforce that health and safety is an important part of doing work in the right way. It provides clarity of reporting chains for supervision and explains who workers can go to if they identify a conflict of interest with what is being expected and getting the work done. Some organisations use a health and safety passport system to confirm that people coming to site have received basic training in general health and safety, whilst this is an excellent approach it does not substitute for all of the site induction arrangements. It is still necessary for workers to know the relevant hazards and controls for each site that they are working on. For example this will mean knowing areas they can and cannot go to, the use of walkways, where rest facilities are, who the first aiders are and who they report hazards / accidents to.

Supervision

Supervision consists of the provision / re-enforcement of performance standards of employees to ensure health and safety. It includes monitoring that agreed work practices are followed and the use of motivation techniques such as involvement of the workforce in task design to help ensure compliance with the required actions.

The success of information instruction and training activities needs to be measured to enable updating to take place to cater for changes in the workplace. The supervisor has a crucial part to play in this monitoring process. It is important to balance the amount and timing of supervision against the work being done. It is generally appropriate that the level of supervision necessary increases with the level of risk related to the work. It can be said that when considering supervision of individuals it is important to take account of the competence of the person. In cases where a person has qualifications but has no experience and is therefore low in competence (e.g. a young person straight from college) then supervision must increase accordingly.

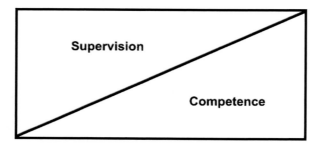

Figure 6-1: Competence v supervision.   *Source: ACT.*

SAFETY SIGNS

Role

The role is to ensure that employers provide and maintain standard signs and signals in the workplace where significant risks have not been avoided by other means to enable more consistent use, clearer communication and better understanding of information.

In order to avoid possible confusion due to language ability and reading skills, the shape, colour and symbols used on safety signs are governed by the Health and Safety (Safety Signs and Signals) Regulations.

Requirements of Health and Safety (Safety Signs and Signals) Regulations

The regulations require employers to provide specific safety signs whenever there is a significant risk which has not been avoided or controlled by other means, e.g. by engineering controls and safe systems of work. Where a safety sign would not help to reduce that risk there is no need to provide a sign.

They require employers to:

- Maintain the safety signs which are provided by them.
- Explain unfamiliar signs to their employees and tell them what they need to do when they see a safety sign.
- They require, where necessary, the use of road traffic signs within workplaces to regulate road traffic

The regulations do not apply in connection with transport or labelling of substances, other signs are to be used instead. They also do not cover the colour coding of pipe work containing hazardous substances, a system of marking is contained in BS 1710.

Categories and features

Signs are defined as those combining shape, colour and a pictorial symbol to provide specific health and safety information and instruction. The regulations require that safety signs comply with BS 5378 and fire safety signs comply with BS 5499.

The Regulations cover 4 main categories of signs:

1)	*PROHIBITION*	Circular signs. Red and white. e.g. - no smoking - no pedestrian access - no children - no unauthorised access.	 **Prohibition**
2)	*WARNING*	Triangular signs. Black on yellow. e.g. - toxic substance - site traffic - electrical hazard - deep excavation.	 **Warning**
3)	*MANDATORY*	Circular signs. Blue and white. e.g. - safety helmets must be worn - hearing protection must be worn - safety boots must be worn. - all visitors must report to site office	 **Mandatory**
4)	*SAFE CONDITION*	Oblong/square signs. Green and white. e.g. - fire exit - first aid - emergency assembly point - eye wash station.	 **Safe Condition**

Figure 6-2: Categories of safety signs.

Source: Safety Train.

Supplementary signs provide additional information. For example where a noise hazard is identified by a warning sign - 'hearing protection available on request' may be added as supplementary information.

Figure 6-3: Site signs. *Source: ACT.*

Figure 6-4: Warning sign. *Source: ACT.*

Figure 6-5: Mandatory PPE sign. *Source: ACT.*

Figure 6-6: Warning sign - site traffic. *Source: ACT.*

Supplementary safety signs can be used to mark obstacles e.g. the edge of a raised platform and dangerous locations e.g. an area where objects may fall or an area where work is going on that the public should not access. These may be yellow and black or red and white - in each case they consist of alternate colour stripes set at 45⁰. These supplementary sign must not be used as a substitute for other signs as defined above.

Figure 6-7: Hazard identification - obstruction. *Source: ACT.*

Figure 6-8: Hazard identification-restricted height. *Source: ACT.*

Signals

The regulations establish principles for acoustic, verbal and hand signals.

Acoustic signals have to be able to be heard and would usually be set at a level of 10dB above the level of ambient noise and at an appropriate frequency. Verbal signals can be used to direct hazardous operations and may be made by either human for example when directing lifting operations or artificial voices such as those used to indicate that a vehicle is reversing. Spoken messages must be clear, concise and understood by the listener. People involved need a good knowledge of the language used. Where English is not the first language of most staff the codes *(see next page)* used do not have to be in English.

Code word	Meaning
Start	Start an operation
Stop	Interrupt or end an operation
End	Stop an operation
Raise	Raise a load
Lower	Lower a load
Forwards	Move forward
Backwards	Move backwards
Right	Move to signaller's right
Left	Move to signaller's left
Danger	Emergency stop
Quickly	Speed up a movement

Figure 6-9: Codes for verbal signals.   *Source: Health and Safety (Safety Signs and Safety Signals) Regulations.*

Hand signals may be used to direct hazardous operations such as cranes or vehicle manoeuvres. It is essential that they be precise, simple, easy to make and to understand. A standard set of signalling codes as proposed by the Health and Safety (Safety Signs and Signals) Regulations (SSSR) 1996 are set out below.

Hand signals must be precise, simple, easy to make and to understand, and clearly distinct from other such signals.

Meaning	Description	Illustration

General signals:

START Attention Start of Command	both arms are extended horizontally with the palms facing forwards	
STOP Interruption End of movement	the right arm points upwards with the palm facing forwards	
END of the operation	both hands are clasped at chest height	

Vertical movements:

RAISE	the right arm points upwards with the palm facing forward and slowly makes a circle	
LOWER	the right arm points downwards with the palm facing inwards and slowly makes a circle	
VERTICAL DISTANCE	the hands indicate the relevant distance.	

Horizontal movements:

MOVE FORWARDS both arms are bent with the palms facing upwards, and the forearms make slow movements towards the body

MOVE BACKWARDS both arms are bent with the palms facing downwards, and the forearms make slow movements away from the body

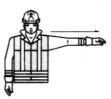

RIGHT
to the signalman's the right arm is extended more or less horizontally with the palm facing downwards and slowly makes small movements to the right

LEFT
to the signalman's the left arm is extended more or less horizontally with the palm facing downwards and slowly makes small movements to the left

HORIZONTAL
DISTANCE the hands indicate the relevant distance.

Danger:

DANGER
Emergency stop both arms points upwards with the palms facing forwards

QUICK all movements faster

SLOW all movements slower

Figure 6-10: Hand signals. *Source: Health and Safety (Safety Signs and Safety Signals) Regulations.*

POSTERS

There are many forms of information and health and safety propaganda which aim to sell the health and safety message. Their effectiveness in modifying human behaviour and attitudes has been the subject of much debate. Some professionals now view them to be of little value. However there is a marked reluctance to abandon them.

Poster campaigns are sometimes seen as a cheap and visible way of showing commitment to health and safety. This attitude can be self defeating if management place too much reliance on them. For example, the workforce can perceive this as an alternative to a proper health and safety policy.

To be effective messages must be:

■ Positive.
■ Aimed at the correct audience.
■ Believable.
■ Achievable.

6.2 - General hierarchy of control

ELIMINATION/SUBSTITUTION

Removal of the hazard in total from the working environment where possible, but this is not always practical. Reducing the hazard to an acceptable level by substituting something less hazardous/or reducing the strength of the hazardous material/or reducing the quantity in use/etc.

REDUCING EXPOSURE

Changing work methods

This may be achieved by utilising mechanical aids for repetitive and strenuous tasks, for example lifting equipment or rough terrain fork lift trucks to assist movement or carrying of loads. In some cases exposure to chemical used to coat surfaces may be reduced by arranging for the majority to be applied to materials before it gets to site, leaving only minor application where joints are made.

Changing work patterns

Reduction of exposure may be achieved by keeping the numbers at risk to a minimum by timing certain work so that other tasks are not taking place nearby or by rotating work to minimise the time of exposure for any one person, for example when reducing the exposure to radiation, noise or vibration.

ISOLATION/SEGREGATION

Enclose the hazard so there is a controlled interface between people and the hazard, for example fitting fixed guards around dangerous parts of a machine, provision of guard rails on scaffolds or barriers round streetworks.

ENGINEERING CONTROL

Control the numbers at risk by systems of working or by engineering methods, for example provision of an overload or over run device on a crane or hoist, control dust / fumes released into the atmosphere by local exhaust ventilation, or to limit the noise level emitted by use of sound insulation.

PERSONAL PROTECTIVE EQUIPMENT

Requirements

Personal protective equipment (PPE) is a low level control. It is often in the form of a simple barrier between the user and the risk, for example gloves and acid, and as such its effectiveness is subject to correct fit or adjustment. PPE is best used for low risk protection or as additional protection to safeguard against engineering control failure, for example breathing apparatus to protect against fume extraction failure when dealing with volatile toxic substances. It is important to determine the limitations of particular PPE before use. The main benefits include low cost and portability when considered against engineering strategies.

The Personal Protective Equipment at Work Regulations say:

■ Ensure PPE is suitable for hazard and person.
■ No PPE should be issued without adequate training/instruction.
■ Issue, obtain signature and record.
■ Set-up monitoring systems.
■ Organise routine exchange systems.
■ Implement cleaning/sterilisation.
■ Issue written/verbal instructions, define when and where to use.
■ Provide suitable storage.

Training and instruction will include both:

■ *Theoretical* - provision of a clear understanding of the reasons for wearing the PPE, factors which may affect the performance, the cleaning, maintenance and identification of defects.
■ *Practical* - practising the wearing, adjusting, removing, cleaning, maintenance and testing of PPE.

Benefits and limitations

"Whatever PPE is chosen, it should be remembered that, although some types of equipment do provide very high levels of protection, none provides 100%"

Figure 6-11: PPE quote.   *Source: Guidance on the Personal Protection Equipment Regulations 1992.*

PPE includes the following when worn for health and safety reasons at work:

■ Aprons.
■ Adverse weather gear.
■ High visibility clothing.
■ Gloves.
■ Safety footwear.
■ Safety helmets.

■ Eye protection.
■ Life-jackets.
■ Respirators.
■ Safety harness.
■ Underwater breathing gear.

There are some good reasons why PPE is used as a last resort:

■ PPE only protects the wearer and not others who may be in the area and also at risk.
■ The introduction of PPE may bring another hazard such as impaired vision, impaired movement or fatigue.
■ PPE may only be capable of minimising injury rather than preventing it.

Protection will depend upon fit in many cases, e.g. with respirators, breathing apparatus, noise protection devices. Factors that can influence fit are whether adequate training and instruction have been given and certain other individual conditions such as:

- Long hair.
- Wearing of spectacles.
- Stubble growing on men's faces which may have an adverse effect on protection.

PPE will not be suitable unless:

- It is appropriate to the risk involved and the prevailing conditions of the workplace.
- It is ergonomic (user-friendly) in design and takes account of the state of health of the user.
- It fits the wearer correctly, perhaps after adjustment.
- It is effective in preventing or controlling the risk(s) [without increasing the overall risk], so far as is practicable.
- It must comply with EU directives or other specific standards.
- It must be compatible with other equipment where there is more than one risk to guard against.

6.3 - Safe systems of work

EMPLOYER'S DUTY TO PROVIDE SAFE SYSTEM OF WORK

In criminal law the ***Health and Safety at Work etc. Act (HASAWA) 1974*** clearly requires the provision and maintenance of plant and systems of work that are, so far as is reasonably practicable, safe and without risks to health. The employer should also provide safe systems of work in order to fulfil his common law duty of care established in principles of negligence.

Definition of safe system of work (SSW):

"the integration of P eople, E quipment and M aterials in the correct E nvironment to produce the safest possible conditions in a specific work area"

This means that all work must be conducted in a safe way, but does not require that all work has to be prescribed in a written form. It is perfectly acceptable that a safe system of work be established and communicated orally at the time of the need to conduct the work e.g work for using a ladder to inspect a pipe joint. In contrast it does not mean that all systems of work can be specified orally. The higher the risks the more appropriate it is to specify safe systems of work in writing. This is reflected in the more formal approach to specifying a safe system of work for entry into a confined space, where the safe system of work is accompanied by a permit to work to provide higher assurance that it is followed correctly.

Components of the system (PEME)

People

Safe behaviour - sound knowledge, skills (both mental and physical), risk and control aware, willingness to conform with the system (motivation), resistance to pressures to behave unsafely, adequately trained, with job experience and supervised, working in harmony with each other.

Equipment

Good design and safety specification of plant, machinery and equipment - taking into account the work that it is to do, the environment and ergonomic factors, inspection and maintenance requirements.

Materials

Safe and healthy in both the raw state and as the finished product - appropriate purchasing and quality standards; consideration of use, handling, storage, transport and safe disposal of waste.

Environment

Establishing critical elements in the workplace that surround the people - effective control of heating, lighting and ventilation; safe levels of noise and vibration; effective control of dust, fumes, radiation, chemicals and biological hazards; effective means of access and egress and a good standards of welfare amenity provision (sanitation, hand washing, showers, clothing storage, catering, drinking water, and first aid).

THE ROLE OF COMPETENT PERSONS IN THE DEVELOPMENT OF SAFE SYSTEMS

It is important that those involved in the development process gain a perspective on the acceptability of the standards of proposed systems of work. This will mean consideration of the proposed safe system of work by people competent to provide a perspective. In a general sense this could be a health and safety practitioner who would be able to provide a general review of the proposed system of work against legal and practical requirements. In addition, depending on the technical complexity and the risks associated with the task, it may be necessary to get a perspective from someone that is competent in the technical health and safety issues involved for example an electrical specialist. Care should be taken not to presume the ***health and safety*** competence of specialist engineers or similar, this should be confirmed before involvement in the development process. The onus is on the employer to determine the competence of people who may be involved in for example development of safe systems of work, carrying out risk assessments, inspections, or issuing permits to work. Broadly, a competent person should have knowledge (practical and theoretical) and skill, as well as experience.

EMPLOYEE INVOLVEMENT IN THE DEVELOPMENT OF SAFE SYSTEMS

Employee involvement in the development of safe systems is essential to ensure their safe behaviour when working to the system. The employee knows all the practical difficulties in working to theoretical systems of work. Such as the absence of equipment specified or requirements that mean more people to do the task than are available. They have frequently encountered circumstances that make the work difficult and how they get round them, such as poor access/egress. By discussing proposed systems of work with employees it is possible to learn these practicalities and ensure the system of work takes account of them. Involvement in this way often ensures that the agreed system of work is followed.

IMPORTANCE AND RELEVANCE OF WRITTEN PROCEDURES

Where the safe system of work is complex or the risks of not working to it are high it is important to define what must be done in written procedures. This does not mean that written procedures have to be complicated or wordy some of the most effective are those that are clear, simple and easily understood.

The importance of creating written procedures is that they serve as a clear setting of standards of work, including how the risks of the work are to be combated. This is particularly relevant when communicating to a client how a contractor is going to conduct work safely. This will contribute to tender documents used to win work, to a construction stage plan to satisfy the Construction (Design and Management) Regulations (CDM) 1994. It will also enable supervisors and others that monitor health and safety to do so against clear standards of performance. Written procedures may relate to specific work to be done, such as carrying out a slitting operation or to general health and safety matters such as reporting accidents. The construction industry makes particular use of written procedures in the form of method statements. As the name suggests they are documents that express how work is to be conducted, the order of events, the health and safety considerations and the measures that will make it safe and healthy for those that might be affected.

It is important that procedures express how the work is done, not just how it should be done in theory. If there is a poor match between the procedure and what can be done in practice it will devalue that and other procedures and cause confusion. If a good match is achieved, in a manner that is clear to workers and supervisors, there is a higher chance that it will be complied with and the supervisor is more able to enforce it.

Job / task analysis is not only necessary to identify the hazards and controls, but is essential for preparing written procedures. These can then be translated into comprehensive training plans to ensure the correct skill and knowledge content for the work to be carried out safely.

THE DISTINCTION BETWEEN TECHNICAL, PROCEDURAL AND BEHAVIOURAL CONTROLS

In the workplace we use a variety of controls. In order to give emphasis to them and to help identify how complete our approach is to health and safety we group controls into a number of categories. The categories tend to reflect the main strategies used to improve health and safety. The categories reflect the strategies referred to in 6.1 above but use slightly different words. It is important to note that in order to deal effectively with a hazard we will need to use all three forms of control, to a greater or lesser degree, for example with the use of a hard hat for the control of a hazard of falling materials. It is important to see that the hard hat is a technical control that will afford a quantity of protection - the technical aspects of this come into play when we consider how long a hard hat lasts, what type is suitable for what work / person. Purchasing hard hats will not be effective if procedures are not in place to enable issue and replacement. These controls will be immediately undermined if we do not provide education and training to those that wear and enforce the wearing of hard hats in order to ensure the right behaviour of the wearer.

Risk control measures:

technical	(place)	(job)
procedural	(system)	(organisation)
behavioural	(person)	(person)

Technical controls include:

- Equipment - design (e.g. guarding) and maintenance.
- Access/egress - provision of wide aisles, access kept clear of storage items.
- Materials (substances and articles) - choice of packaging to make handling easier.
- Environment (temperature, light, dusts, noise) - local exhaust ventilation (LEV).

Procedural controls include:

- Policy and standards.
- Rules.
- Procedures.
- Permit to work.
- Authorisation and co-ordination of actions.
- Purchasing controls.
- Accident investigation and analysis.
- Emergency preparedness.

Behavioural controls include:

- Awareness, knowledge, skill, competence.
- Attitude, perception, motivation, communication.
- Supervision.
- Health surveillance.
- Personal protective equipment.

In practice, the most successful organisations use a combination of the three strategies, with the emphasis on making the place safe/healthy (providing technical controls) and supporting this with procedures and paying attention to the person. Many organisations that feel they have invested effort in getting the place and procedures right are taking a fresh look at the actions necessary to ensure the person's behaviour is right also. Studies have shown that this too is a critical aspect of effective management of health and safety.

DEVELOPMENT OF A SAFE SYSTEM OF WORK

Analysing the task

Assessment of the task must consider not only the job to be done, but the environment where it is to be done, to allow a full consideration of the hazards to be made. This may involve a detailed review known as *Job* or *Task Analysis.* Job/task safety analysis consists of a formal step by step review of the work to be carried out. All aspects of the task should be considered and recorded in writing to ensure that nothing is overlooked. Typical considerations would be:

- How is the task carried out.
- Where is the task carried out.
- What is used.
- What are the current controls.
- Are the controls adequate.
- Do operators use the controls correctly.
- Behavioural factors operators/supervisors (error considerations).

The objective is to establish the hazards and controls at each stage of the procedure to ensure a safe result. How the progress of work, in particular safety arrangements, will be monitored should be considered. Any special requirements for monitoring should be specified during the planning stage, e.g. gas testing, temperature or pressure levels, measurement of emissions.

Hazard identification and risk assessment

The identification of hazards and the assessment of risks are key factors arising from the task analysis step of developing safe systems of work. From this we can build in appropriate controls to the system of work and plan to warn workers of the risks considered and how to combat them. *MHSWR, Regulation 3*, requires a suitable and sufficient risk assessment to be made of all risks to which employees and others who may be affected by them are exposed. Where a significant risk is identified through the general risk assessments a more formal detailed analysis is often required to develop a safe system of work e.g. work to inspect the lifting equipment of an office passenger lift. Considerations should be given to who does what, when and how.

Introducing controls and formulating procedures

Define the safe methods

1) Where possible, hazards should be eliminated at source. Residual hazards should be evaluated and controlled.

2) Specific responsibilities at various stages and the identity of the person in control of work should be clearly identified.

3) The need for protective or special equipment should also be identified, as should the need for the provision of temporary protection, guards or barriers.

4) Adequate emergency procedures should be in place, or developed, to control likely incidents e.g. fire, spillage.

5) If there is a possibility that injury could result during the task consider rescue methods should be considered.

6) The system should be checked against three main criteria:
   - It should adequately control hazards associated with the task.
   - It should comply with company standards.
   - It should comply with relevant legal standards.

Implementation

Once the system has been developed and agreed, preparation for implementation can proceed. Provision for the communication of relevant information to all involved or affected should be fundamental to any system of work. It is important that care be taken to ensure that controls referred to when the system of work was being developed are available to the workers when the procedure is implemented, if they are not they will devalue the procedure and cause the workers to have to work outside it, possibly in an unsafe way.

The process of implementation will involve:

- The person in charge of work must ensure that elements outlined in the Planning and Organisation stages are clearly understood and implemented.
- If problems arise which necessitate modification to the system, formal approval and documentation should be made.
- Any permanent record of any monitoring must be kept and regularly checked by a member of the management team.

Instruction and training in the operation of the system

Many organisations in the construction industry may be tempted to issue procedures without instruction and training, this can lead to a great deal of misunderstanding about what the system of work is and will often lead to people not being motivated to work to the system. This is particularly the case when the system is a change from the usual way that workers may have worked. Workers, and supervisors, can have a naturally high resistance to change. Simply providing information will not usually be sufficient to change behaviour. A more assured way to introduce the system would be to utilise such things as 'tool box' talks, the provide practical opportunity to develop the workers understanding of the operation of the system and if these are done as part of a cascade training method the supervisor or similar person will have received training from someone committed to the new system and will be better placed to get over the resistance of workers to change.

When the system of work relates to work equipment it is essential to ensure that training takes place. *The Provision and Use of Work Equipment Regulations (PUWER) 1998* require that supervisors be adequately trained to enable them to identify the hazards and control strategies associated with work equipment under their control.

Job / task analysis is not only useful for to identify the hazards and controls, but is essential for preparing written procedures and specifying the skill and knowledge content of the work to be carried out. The analysis will not only identify the sequence of work but often the work rate expected - sometimes timeliness is an important consideration, particularly in relation to certain chemical manufacturing processes. The analysis is then incorporated into job training programmes.

- For certain high risk tasks this will often involve a course to develop knowledge and understanding. This is then followed by practical application either utilising a work simulator (e.g. train driver / air craft pilot) or close one to one supervision while on the job (e.g. fork truck driver).
- Where training requirements have been identified a record of those affected should be made, this should be conducted, confirmed successful and recorded as such.

Monitoring the system

All safe systems should be formally monitored and records kept of compliance and effectiveness. This can be done by direct observation or by discussion at team meetings or safety committee meetings. SSW should not be simply imposed upon the people responsible for their operation. A system of monitoring and feedback should be implemented to ensure it is effective. Audits and accidents that occur can provide a valuable insight into whether systems of work are effective.

PERMITS TO WORK

Operation and application

Key elements
- A description of the task to be performed.
- An indication of the duration of the validity of the permit.
- The isolations that have been made and the additional precautions required.
- Details and signature of the person authorising the work.
- An acknowledgement of acceptance by the employee carrying out the task, who would then need to indicate on the permit that the work has been completed and the area made safe in order for the permit to be cancelled.

Permit to work document
- Sets out the work to be done and the precautions to be taken.
- Predetermines a safe drill
- Is a clear record that:
  - All foreseeable hazards have been considered.
  - And that all precautions are defined and taken in the correct sequence.

Requirements of the system
- Must be formal.
- Simple to operate.
- Have commitment of those who operate and are affected by it.

Operation
- Permit must provide concise and accurate information.
- Overrides any other instructions until cancelled.
- Excludes work not described within the permit.
- In the event of a change to programme must be amended or cancelled and a new permit issued.
- Only the originator may amend or cancel.
- Acceptor assumes responsibility for safe conduct of work.
- Liaison with controllers of other plant or work areas whose activities may be affected by the permit to work.
- Boundary or limits of work area must be clearly marked or defined.
- Contractors undertaking specific tasks must be included in the permit to work system, including any briefing prior to commencement.

Typical permits and circumstances in which they may be appropriate

A permit to work system is a formal safety control system designed to prevent accidental injury to personnel, damage to plant, premises and product, particularly when work with a foreseeable high hazard content is undertaken and the precautions required are numerous and complex.

Hot work

Typically involving welding operations, such as pipe work where the risk of sparks may ignite nearby flammable materials. Elimination or protection of such items will need to be considered. The provision of fire fighting equipment and trained personnel to deal with ignition is also important.

The Dangerous Substances and Explosive Atmospheres Regulations (DSEAR) 2002 specify the application of permits to work, to be used in hazardous places or involving hazardous activities.

Work on electrical equipment

Work on electrical equipment, such as a transformer, will need to consider safe isolation, access and egress, work at a height and heavy lifting.

Plant maintenance

Plant maintenance sometimes requires workers with different disciplines to work on large complex plant at the same time. This is aggravated by the fact that the plant may be spread over a number of floors in a building, such as power generation plant, flour mills or lift systems in an office block. This sort of work can have many risks involved in it - related to a variety of services and energy sources, dangerous parts of the equipment, problems with access, risk of falling or being trapped inside the plant. These risks are best controlled by a well established system of work, supported by a permit to work.

HOT WORK PERMIT

APPLIES ONLY TO AREA SPECIFIED BELOW

Part 1

Site:……………………………………….......   Floor:…………………………………………………..

Nature of the job (including exact location) ………………………………………………………..

……

The above location has been examined and the precautions listed on the reverse side have been taken.

Date:…………………………………………………

Time of issue:…………………………………………..   Time of expiry:…………………………………………..

NB. This permit is only valid on the day of issue.

Signature of person issuing permit: ………………………………………………………………....

Part 2

Signature of person receiving permit:……………………………………………………………………

Time work started:……………………………………………………….

Time work finished and cleared up:…………………………………………………………………….

Part 3   **FINAL CHECK UP**

Work areas and all adjacent areas to which sparks and heat might spread (such as floors above and below and opposite side of walls) were inspected one hour after the work finished and were found fire safe.

Signature of person carrying out final check: ……………………………………………………....

After signing return permit to person who issued it.

Figure 6-12: Hot work permit - front of form.   *Source: Lincsafe.*

HOT WORK PEMIT

PRECAUTIONS

Hot Work Area

☐   Loose combustible material cleared

☐   Non moveable combustible material covered

☐   Suitable extinguishers to hand

☐   Gas cylinders fitted with a regular and flashback arrester

☐   Other personnel who may be affected by the work removed from the area

Work on walls, ceilings or partitions

☐   Opposite side checked and combustibles moved away

Welding, cutting or grinding work

☐   Work area screened to contain sparks

Bitumen boilers, lead heaters etc.

☐   Gas cylinders at least 3mm from burner

☐   If sited on roof, heat insulating base provided

Figure 6-13: Hot work permit - reverse of form.   *Source: Lincsafe.*

© ACT

Possible Lay-Out For A Permit-To-Work Certificate
Permit-To-Work Certificate

PLANT DETAILS (Location, identifying number, etc)				ACCEPTANCE OF CERTIFICATE Accepts all conditions of certificate			
WORK TO BE DONE					Signed	Date	Time
WITHDRAWAL FROM SERVICE	Signed	Date	Time	COMPLETION OF WORK All work completed - equipment returned for use			
ISOLATION Dangerous fumes Electrical supply Sources of heat	Signed	Date	Time		Signed	Date	Time
CLEANING AND PURGING Of all dangerous materials	Signed	Date	Time	EXTENSION	Signed	Date	Time
TESTING For contamination	Contaminations tested Signed	Date	Results Time				
I CERTIFY THAT I HAVE PERSONALLY EXAMINED THE PLANT DETAILED ABOVE AND SATISFIED MYSELF THAT THE ABOVE PARTICULARS ARE CORRECT (1) THE PLANT IS SAFE FOR ENTRY WITHOUT BREATHING APPARATUS (2) BREATHING APPARATUS MUST BE WORN Other precautions necessary: Time of expiry of certificate: Delete (1) or (2)	Signed Date	Time		THIS PERMIT TO WORK IS NOW CANCELLED. A NEW PERMIT WILL BE REQUIRED IF WORK IS TO CONTINUE Signed	Date	Time	
				RETURN TO SERVICE	I accept the above plant back into service Signed	Date	Time

Figure 6-14: Example of a permit to work for entry into confined spaces.   *Source HSE Guidance note on permits to work.*

CONFINED SPACES

A failure to appreciate the dangers associated with confined spaces has led not only to the deaths of many workers, but also to the demise of some of those who have attempted to rescue them. A confined space is not only a space which is small and difficult to enter, exit or work in; it can also be a large space, but with limited/restricted access. It can also be a space that is badly ventilated e.g. a tank or a large tunnel.

Figure 6-15: Confined space - chamber.   *Source: ACT.*

Figure 6-16: Confined space - sewer.   *Source: ACT.*

Figure 6-17: Confined space - tank.   *Source: ACT.*

Figure 6-18: Confined space - open tank.   *Source: ACT.*

The Confined Spaces Regulations (CSR) define a confined space as any place, including any:

Chamber	caisson, cofferdam, or interception chamber for water
Tank	storage tanks or solid or liquid chemical
Vat	process vessel which may be open, but by its depth confines a person
Silo	may be an above the ground structure for storing cereal, crops
Pit	Below ground, such as a chamber for a pump
Pipe	concrete, plastic steel etc, fabrication used to carry liquids or gases
Sewer	brick or concrete structure for the carrying of liquid waste
Flue	exhaust chimney for disposal of waste gases
Well	deep source of water

or other similar space, in which, by virtue of its enclosed nature, there is a foreseeable risk of a 'specified occurrence'.

A "specified occurrence"

Is defined as:

a)   Fire or explosion.

b)   Loss of consciousness or asphyxiation of any person at work arising from gas, fumes, vapour or lack of oxygen.

c)   Drowning of any person at work.

d)   Asphyxiation of any person at work arising from a free flowing solid.

e)   Loss of consciousness of any person arising from a high ambient temperature.

Work in confined spaces

- No person shall work in a confined space where it is reasonably practicable for that work to be carried out without entering the space.
- No person at work shall enter, leave or carry out work in a confined space other than in accordance with a safe system of work.
- Before work in a confined space can be carried out it must be shown that it cannot be considered "reasonably practicable" to carry out the work without entering the confined space. The employer (or self-employed) must then carry out a risk assessment to identify the precautions necessary to ensure a safe system of work.

The risk assessment will in particular help to identify the need for a formal Permit to Work system which will typically involve procedures for:

- Testing the atmosphere.
- Respiratory protective equipment and other personal protective equipment for those risks which cannot be controlled by other means.
- Equipment for safe access and exit.
- Suitable and sufficient emergency rescue arrangements.

Testing the atmosphere

- Testing of the atmosphere may be needed where the atmosphere might be contaminated or abnormal.
- The appropriate choice of testing equipment will depend on particular circumstances. For example, when testing for toxic atmospheres, chemical detector tubes or portable atmospheric monitoring equipment is appropriate. However there may be cases requiring monitoring equipment specifically designed to measure for flammable atmospheres.
- Only persons experienced and competent in the practice should carry out testing and records should be kept. Personal gas detectors should be worn whenever appropriate to mitigate the hazard of local pockets of contaminant.

Safe access to and egress from confined spaces

- Openings need to be sufficiently large and free from obstruction to allow the passage of persons wearing the necessary protective clothing and equipment and to allow access for rescue purposes.
- Practice drills will help to check that the size of openings and entry procedures are satisfactory.
- Where entry to a confined space is necessary, employers will need to ensure that the necessary safety features are followed. For example, alongside openings which allow for safe access these might include a safety sign warning against unauthorised entry and platforms to enable safe working within the confined space.

Respiratory Protective Equipment (RPE)

Where RPE is provided or used in connection with confined space entry (including emergency rescue), it must be suitable. Other equipment - ropes, harnesses, lifelines, resuscitating apparatus, first aid equipment, protective clothing and other special equipment will usually need to be provided.

Figure 6-19: Entrance to a confined space.   *Source: ACT.*

Here a worker wearing full breathing apparatus is also wearing a harness with a lanyard connected to a winch so that he can be hauled to the surface in an emergency without others having to enter the manhole to rescue him.

Figure 6-20: Access to a confined space. *Source: HSG150, HSE.*

Emergency arrangements

The Regulations prohibit any person to enter or carry out work in a confined space unless there are suitable and sufficient rescue arrangements in place. Emergency arrangements shall be suitable and sufficient provided they:

■ Require the provision and maintenance of resuscitation equipment.
■ Require the provision and maintenance of such equipment as is necessary to enable the emergency rescue to be carried out effectively.
■ Restrict, so far as is reasonably practicable, the risks to health and safety of any rescuer.
■ Shall immediately be put into operation when circumstances arise requiring a rescue.

The arrangements for emergency rescue will depend on the nature of the confined space, the risks identified and consequently the likely nature of an emergency rescue. The arrangements might need to cover:

1) Rescue and resuscitation equipment.

2) Special arrangements with local hospitals (e.g. for foreseeable poisoning).

3) Raising the alarm and rescue.

4) Safeguarding the rescuers.

5) Safeguarding the third parties.

6) Fire fighting.

7) Control of plant.

8) First aid.

9) Public emergency services.

Summary of main points for confined spaces

Identify the hazards e.g.
■ Flammable substances.
■ Oxygen deficiency or enrichment.
■ Toxic gas, fume or vapour.

■ Ingress or presence of liquids.
■ Solid materials which can flow e.g. flour, grain, sugar.
■ Excessive heat

Prevent the need for entry by:
■ Use of portholes for inspection.
■ Clean from outside using water jets, long handled tools.
■ Use vibrators to clear blockages.

Develop safe working practice
■ Based on a permit to work.

Develop emergency procedures to include
■ Means of raising the alarm.
■ Safeguarding the rescuers.

■ Fire safety.
■ Notifying public emergency services.

Provide training to include
■ Awareness of CSR.
■ Need to avoid entry.
■ Hazards and precautions.

■ How emergencies arise.
■ Emergency arrangements.

LONE WORKING

Lone workers are those who work by themselves without close or direct supervision. They are found in a wide range of situations and some examples are given below.

People in fixed establishments where:

■ Only one person works on the premises e.g. petrol stations, kiosks, shops and also homeworkers.
■ People work separately from others e.g. in factories, warehouses, leisure centres or fairgrounds.

- People work outside normal hours e.g. cleaners, security, facilities management staff or contractors conducting special tasks better done at this time.

Mobile workers working away from their fixed base:

- On construction, plant installation, maintenance and cleaning work, electrical repairs, painting and decorating.
- Agricultural and forestry workers.
- Service workers e.g. rent collectors, postal staff, home helps, drivers, district nurses.

Although there is no general legal prohibition on working alone, the broad duties of the HASAWA and MHSWR still apply. These require identifying hazards of the work, assessing the risks involved, and putting measures in place to avoid or control the risks.

Control measures may include instruction, training, supervision, protective equipment etc. When the risk assessment shows that it is not possible for the work to be done safely by a lone worker, arrangements for providing help or back-up should be put in place. Where a lone worker is working at another employer's workplace, that employer should inform the lone worker's employer of any risks and the control measures that should be taken. This helps the lone worker's employer to assess the risks.

Risk assessment should help decide the right level of supervision. There are some high-risk activities where at least one other person may need to be present. Examples include some high-risk confined space working where a supervisor may need to be present, as well as someone dedicated to the rescue role, and electrical work at or near exposed live conductors where at least two people are sometimes required.

Employers need to be aware of any specific law on lone working applying in their industry; examples include supervision in diving operations, vehicles carrying explosives, fumigation work.

Establishing safe working for lone workers is no different from organising the safety of other employees. Employers need to know the law and standards which apply to their work activities and then assess whether the requirements can be met by people working alone.

Questions to ask

- Does the workplace present a special risk to the lone worker?
- Is there a safe way in and a safe way out for one person? Can any temporary access equipment which is necessary, such as portable ladders or trestles, be safely handled by one person?
- Can all the plant, substances and goods involved in the work be safely handled by one person? Consider whether the work involves lifting objects too large for one person or whether more than one person is needed to operate essential controls for the safe running of equipment.
- Is there a risk of violence?
- Are women especially at risk if they work alone?
- Are young workers especially at risk if they work alone?

Importance of training

- Where there is limited supervision.
- Experienced enough to understand the risks and precautions of lone working fully and to avoid panic reactions in unusual situations.
- Competent to deal with circumstances which are new, unusual or beyond the scope of training e.g. when to stop work and seek advice from a supervisor and how to handle aggression.
- Able to respond correctly to emergencies, also given information on established emergency procedures and danger areas.
- Able to administer first aid.

Supervision

- Helps to ensure that employees understand the risks associated with their work and that the necessary safety precautions are carried out.
- Can provide guidance in situations of uncertainty.
- Supervision can be carried out when checking the progress and quality of the work. May take the form of periodic site visits combined with discussions in which health and safety issues are raised.
- Important when an employee is new to a job, undergoing training, doing a job which presents special risks, or dealing with new situations and may need to be accompanied at first.
- Level of supervision required should be based on the findings of a risk assessment.

Procedures for monitoring purposes

- Supervisors periodically visiting and observing people working alone.
- Regular contact using either a telephone or radio.
- Automatic warning devices which operate if specific signals are not received periodically from the lone worker e.g. systems for security staff.
- Other devices designed to raise the alarm in the event of an emergency and which are operated manually or automatically by the absence of activity.
- Check returned to their base or home on completion of a task.

Medical considerations

- Check that lone workers have no medical conditions making them unsuitable for working alone.
- Consider both routine work and foreseeable emergencies which may impose additional physical and mental burdens on the individual.
- Ensure they have access to first-aid facilities and mobile workers should carry a first-aid kit suitable for treating minor injuries.

6.4 - Emergency procedures

THE IMPORTANCE OF DEVELOPING EMERGENCY PROCEDURES

Adequate emergency procedures should be in place, or developed, to control likely incidents e.g. fire, spillage, poisoning exposure to pathogens etc. Fire is a specific risk which will need regular review throughout a major build or modification project. The exit routes may need to be redefined and signed and those affected trained and drilled. Similarly, assembly points may change. Local arrangements should consider the provision of fire suppression equipment, such as extinguishers, are provided whenever contractors use equipment which may present a source of ignition.

Procedures should be in writing, and regularly tested through drills and exercises. The results of such exercises should be recorded and the procedures amended as necessary. For identified high-risk activities arrangements should be formalised with local Accident and Emergency services (A&E), for example, where there may be a need to have available special anti toxins or isolation facilities.

FIRST-AID REQUIREMENTS

Role, training and number of first-aiders and appointed persons

Principles of first aid

- Sustain life.
- Prevent deterioration.
- Promote recovery.

The Health and Safety (First-Aid) Regulations - Main requirements

Reg 2	Regulation 2 defines first aid as: '…treatment for the purpose of preserving life and minimising the consequences of injury or illness until medical (doctor or nurse) help can be obtained. Also, it provides treatment of minor injuries which would otherwise receive no treatment, or which do not need the help of a medical practitioner or nurse.'
Reg 3	Requires that every employer must provide equipment and facilities which are adequate and appropriate in the circumstances for administering first-aid to his employees.
Reg 4	An employer must inform his employees about the first-aid arrangements, including the location of equipment, facilities and identification of trained personnel.
Reg 5	Self-employed people must ensure that adequate and suitable provision is made for administering first-aid while at work.

Provision of first aid facilities

To ensure compliance with Regulation 3, an employer must make an assessment to determine the needs. Consideration of the following is required:

- Different work activities - some, such as offices, have relatively few hazards and low levels of risk; others have more or more specific hazards (construction or chemical sites). Requirements will depend on the type of work being done.
- Difficult access to treatment - an equipped first-aid room may be required if ambulance access is difficult or likely to be delayed.
- Employees working away from employer's premises - the nature of the work and its risk will need to be considered.
- Employees of more than one employer working together - agreement can be made to share adequate facilities, with one employer responsible for their provision.
- Provisions for non-employees - employers do not have to make first-aid provision for any person other than his employees. Liability issues and interpretation placed on the HASAWA may alter the situation, as, for example, in the case of a shop or other place where the public enter.
- Having made this assessment, the employer will then be able to work out the number and size of first-aid boxes required. The Approved Code of Practice outlines minimum standards for their contents and facilities - at least one will always be required. Additional facilities such as a stretcher or first-aid room may also be appropriate.

How many first aiders?

The employer must ensure that adequate numbers of "suitable persons" are provided to administer first-aid. "Suitable persons" are those who have received training and acquired qualifications approved by the HSE, All relevant factors have to be taken into account when deciding how many "suitable persons" will be needed. These include:

- Workplace hazards and risks.
- Situations where access to treatment is difficult.
- The size of the organisation.
- The organisation's history of accidents.
- Employees working on shared or multi-occupied sites.
- Employees regularly working away from the employer's premises.
- The numbers of the employees, including fluctuations caused by shift patterns. The more employees there are, the higher the probability of injury.
- Absences of first-aiders through illness or annual leave.
- Work patterns including shift work.
- Special needs e.g. young people or employees with disabilities.

A complex build or modification project will require regular review of the number of first aiders or first aid equipment and location required. This will involve liaison with contractors and the self employed to ensure adequate cover for all periods of working.

Training courses, including examinations, should be of at least four full days duration. Certificates of qualification are valid for three years. A refresher course, followed by examination, is required before re-certification.

Appointed person

In appropriate circumstances, an employer can provide an "appointed person" instead of a first-aider. The "appointed person" is someone appointed by the employer to take charge of the situation (for example, to call an ambulance) if a serious injury occurs in the absence of a first-aider. It is recommended that the "appointed person" be able to administer emergency first-aid and be responsible for the equipment provided. An appointed person is unlikely to be adequate for most construction activities, where the risk of injury may be major.

Requirements for first-aid boxes

The employer must ensure that an adequate quantity of suitable first aid equipment is provided. In deciding this similar factors when deciding how many first aiders will be used. In addition, there is the extra consideration that some people may need equipment to administer their own first aid.

There is no standard list of items to put in a first-aid box. It depends on what you assess the needs are.

However, as a guide, and where there is no special risk in the workplace, a minimum stock of first-aid items would be:

- A leaflet giving general guidance on first aid e.g. HSE leaflet Basic advice on first aid at work.
- 20 individually wrapped sterile adhesive dressings (assorted sizes).
- Two sterile eye pads.
- Four individually wrapped triangular bandages (preferably sterile).
- Six safety pins.
- Six medium sized (approximately 12 cm x 12 cm) individually wrapped sterile unmedicated wound dressings.
- Two large (approximately 18 cm x 18 cm) sterile individually wrapped unmedicated wound dressings.
- One pair of disposable gloves.

You should not keep tablets or medicines in the first-aid box.

Figure 6-21: First-aid box.   Source: ACT.

The above is a suggested contents list only - based on the guidance to the Regulations - equivalent but different items would be considered acceptable.

Shared facilities and arrangements

Where a site has multiple occupancy or a group of contracting employers exist within a site, arrangements need to be in place to identify and inform people of where first aid equipment is and who might be responsible for performing first aid duties. It is possible for an agreement to be made such that each occupier or employer does not have to make separate arrangements. This can be particularly useful in providing cover for each other's first aiders and will avoid the need for small contractors to provide their own first aid if they can obtain it from a main contractor's facilities. Where small works are going on in a hosts premises the contractor may find an acceptable agreement may be made with the host to provide first aid and other facilities. It is important that such agreements be made formally, preferably with a written agreement that will substantiate the existence of such an arrangement if it is challenged or people change their mind as the work unfolds.

ARRANGEMENTS FOR CONTACTING EMERGENCY AND RESCUE SERVICES

The employer must consider the risks arising from their undertaking and the related emergencies that could result. MHSWR require that written procedures be in place to deal with significant emergencies. In addition there is a requirement to ensure that where necessary contacts are made with external emergency and rescue services. This can include alerting them to the timing of special, high hazard tasks such as work in a confined space or where there is a significant risk that people may need to be rescued. In some cases it will mean contacting services and agreeing the boundary of what support can be expected from external services and what must be arranged by the employer.

The employer must identify and assess the nature of any injury likely to occur and consider the distance to emergency hospital facilities. It may be necessary to provide a first aid room and to train staff in specifics emergency techniques, for example resuscitation or to engage more capable staff with medical qualifications.

Part of the arrangements must ensure the means to contact the appropriate services at the time of the emergency - by telephone, radio or suitable other means.

COVERAGE IN RELATION TO SHIFT WORK AND GEOGRAPHICAL LOCATION

Additional staff will be necessary to cover for out of hours, shift working or overtime. In particular where there is a specific legal duty to provide such coverage - e.g. first aid provisions. The person with overall control of the site must ensure that coverage remains in place throughout the period work is going on. Particular care must be paid to high risk work being conducted outside normal working hours. It may be possible to maintain good emergency cover for these times by ensuring, where there is permanent security staff, that these are appropriately trained.

If the area of work is geographically large, for example, gas, electrical or telecommunication field work all staff may need to be trained and equipped with first aid equipment in order that they may administer self first aid. This may be by means of a full first aid kit in a vehicle or a personal provision in a pouch. Particular attention should be given to the likelihood and type of injuries when equipping people in this way.

General site issues - hazards & control

Overall Aims

On completion of this Unit, candidates will understand:

■ the factors particular to a construction site that may affect risk.

■ the preventive and protective measures required to take account of identified risk factors.

■ the requirements relating to welfare facilities on site.

Content

Specific Intended Learning Outcomes

The intended learning outcomes of this Unit are that candidates will be able to:

7.1   carry out an initial assessment of a site to identify key risk factors

7.2   identify the general controls shown by the initial assessment to be needed in setting up and organising a site

7.3   identify the welfare facilities required on a site

Sources of Reference

Essentials of Health and Safety at Work, HSE Books

A Guide to Managing Health and Safety in Construction, HSE Books

Protecting the Public: Your Next Move (HSG151), HSE Books

Relevant Statutory Provisions

The Construction (Design and Management) Regulations (CDM) 1994

The Construction (Health, Safety and Welfare) Regulations (CHSW) 1996

The Health and Safety (Safety Signs and Signals) Regulations (SSSR) 1996

7.1 - Initial site assessment

Factors to consider in site assessments

PREVIOUS/CURRENT USE

The previous and/ or current use of a site may present many hazards that need to be identified in an initial assessment, before construction work starts. If for example it is a "green field" (undeveloped) site, it may provide public access / right of way to members of the public or a recreation area for children. The site could be private and used for agriculture or grazing of livestock. If a "brown field" (previously used, developed) site, it could contain occupied or unoccupied buildings/ premises. Occupied premises will mean regular traffic on the site whilst unoccupied premises may be in a state of disrepair and dereliction. Any premises that are either occupied or unoccupied will, more than likely, be or have been connected to various below ground or overhead services that may require further investigation.

Figure 7-1: Site assessment - previous use.   *Source: ACT.*

Figure 7-2: Site assessment - general.   *Source: ACT.*

HISTORY OF SITE

It is important to take into account the history of a site as the site may present hazards in the form of asbestos or chemical contamination as that requires specialist land reclamation services. There may be mineshafts present or other types of underground voids such as abandoned cellars, manhole chambers or large diameter drains. Action should be taken to make site surveys and obtain current and / or historic plans that may identify any or all of the above circumstances.

AREA OF SITE AND RESTRICTIONS

The location or area of the site should be considered and any possible restrictions noted, e.g. there may be trees that are protected and unable to be felled or other natural obstacles that could cause problems to the works. If, for example, a site is bounded by a main railway line then the available space (headroom) for any construction related plant and equipment to operate, or be stored around the construction site, may be restricted once work begins.

TOPOGRAPHY AND GROUND CONDITIONS

Topography relates to the physical surface conditions of the site and is an important factor to be considered along with the ground conditions below the surface. Is the landscape flat and even or is it made up of banks, dips and hills therefore making any operations on site far more difficult to carry out? The ground conditions may be soft soil, clay or rock, each condition presenting its own individual problems and hazards. The site could have a high water table or be susceptible to becoming flooded or waterlogged.

OTHER (NON CONSTRUCTION) ACTIVITIES ON SITE

When a site is acquired, it may be necessary for other non-construction activities to be carried out prior to any construction works being authorised to begin. This could be site reclamation and clearance, installation of security fencing, lighting and signs, ground investigations, piling operation, site surveys and installation of essential utilities (power, water). Other non-construction activities usually continue when construction has started, consisting of delivery of plant, equipment or materials, site security and development of utility network around the site.

NATURE OF SURROUNDINGS

The nature of site surroundings and their proximity can have detrimental effects even if not directly associated to the site being operated. Factors to consider:

Roads

Roads and highways that surround a site boundary can be a significant source of additional hazard and are a main area for consideration as access to any site is primarily via some form of roadway. Factors such as the type of road (dual carriageway, main road, one-way system, country lane), road speed encountered, volume of traffic (high all day, cyclical, rush hour), type of traffic using the road (agricultural plant, cars, heavy goods vehicles (HGV's), well lit or unlit, capacity of road (weight, height or width restrictions). It may be that special requests or notifications are to be made with the local authority regarding access and site traffic proposals. If the site is within a residential area or in close proximity to a school, permissions or restrictions may be enforced regarding when or if surrounding roadways may or may not be used. In any of the above situations, there is a potential for danger.

Figure 7-3: Roads.   *Source: ACT.*

Figure 7-4: Footpaths.   *Source: ACT.*

Footpaths

Footpaths are a means of providing pedestrians with a safe means of travelling by foot usually alongside a highway. It should be identified how the footpath is used (e.g. for a school journey by children or by people queuing for a bus). The risk of injury may be increased at the entrance to a construction site where pedestrians cross the access opening and might encounter heavy site mobile plant or goods vehicles delivering materials to site. Footpaths may also skirt the construction site boundary, where pedestrians may also become at risk due to the activities within the site (e.g. falling objects from a scaffold structure, flying objects from cutting, drilling or hammering operations, fumes, dust, chemicals).

Railways

Railways present the hazard of heavy, high speed trains (up to and in excess of 125 mph) that do not have the ability to respond to dangerous circumstances that may arise as other transport modes are able to, i.e. quick emergency stopping, avoidance by changing direction. In addition to these hazards, there may be overhead cables carrying 25,000 volts or rails carrying 750 volts. Work near to railways requires suitable planning, as any clash between a travelling train and site equipment, plant or vehicles could, and most likely would, lead to disastrous consequences. Rail authorities have laid down strict procedures that are to be followed and any party working on railways should be in possession of a 'Personal Track Safety' certificate. High visibility clothing that is worn on or near to a railway line should be of the correct standard and colour (high visibility orange). Restrictions on colours worn on or near to a railway should be strictly followed and nothing that is red or green be worn due to the fact that it may be mistaken as a signal by a train driver. Communications should be maintained with the rail authority and notification given of any works being carried out on or near to the railway in order that all issues can be complied with correctly.

Figure 7-5: Railways.   *Source: Welsh Highland Railway.*

Figure 7-6: Waterways.   *Source: ACT.*

Waterways

Waterways located on or near construction sites present a risk of drowning; the water does not have to be fast flowing to cause a worker to get into difficulty. Other factors to consider, if waterways are in close proximity to a construction site are: the likelihood of floods occurring, environmental pollution of the waterway, damage to associated wildlife by site activities. Conversely, it is necessary to consider exposure of site staff to hygiene hazards through contaminants or disease (chemical pollutants, Weils disease) within the waterway. Waterways are used by a considerable number of boat operators that may be affected by the activities on site (e.g. falling objects from a scaffold structure, flying objects from cutting, drilling or hammering operations, fumes, dust, chemicals). Boat operators may equally affect site safety (e.g. collision of the boat with a scaffold structure, possibly noise or pollution associated with their work).

Residential/commercial/industrial properties

Construction can take place in local or immediate proximity of residential, industrial or commercial property that may be either unoccupied or occupied and fully operational. The range of hazards is wide and each concerns members of the public or others (staff, contractors). Residential property areas are usually busy areas and can include regular traffic flow, children, the elderly and animals. Commercial property areas (shops, offices) are also busy areas that include members of the public and members of staff carrying out their own duties within the work area. Industrial property areas (factories, workshops) involve people at work and present additional hazards of machinery, plant, equipment, chemicals, etc. being used that construction workers may not ordinarily be familiar with.

Figure 7-7: Commercial properties.   *Source: ACT.*

Figure 7-8: Industrial properties.   *Source: ACT.*

Schools

Schools are very busy areas and accommodate children of various ages that may have no or little perception of danger or risk and by their nature are often very inquisitive of their surroundings. In addition to children, parents or carers that deliver children to and collect children from the school create pedestrian and vehicular traffic hazards around the immediate area. Children are frequently tempted to try to gain access to construction sites and normally achieve this when site security is poor and consideration has not been given to access through small openings. Sites often underestimate the size of openings, which some small children are able to fit through, particularly when compared with that which is required to restrict adult access.

MEANS OF ACCESS

Access to a construction site should be through a controlled point and requires adequate planning to take into account the surrounding area. Restrictions and hazards relating to safe access to a construction site may include the conditions of the highway from which access is being gained (size, speed, use). The traffic that will operate on the site needs to be considered (size, type, frequency, volume).

Figure 7-9: Means of access   *Source: ACT.*

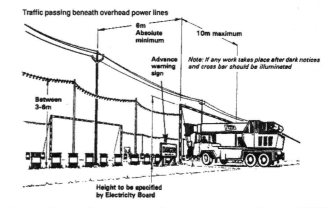

Figure 7-10: Safe distance barriers for overhead services. *Source: HSG144.*

PRESENCE OF OVERHEAD AND BURIED SERVICES

Overhead services in the form of electricity cables present the obvious risk of electrocution through either making direct contact with the electricity cable or where arcing (discharge by spark 'jumping' to a near earth point) occurs. Overhead cables should be identified prior to site works and the risk factors determined. Construction sites may involve the use of various pieces of large, mobile plant and equipment (cranes, excavators, etc) and steel scaffold systems near to power supplies. If such equipment is allowed to come too close to an overhead cable it may provide a sufficient level of earth for the power to 'leap', making the particular item of plant live. If this occurs, subsequent 'arcs' are possible to other people or plant within close proximity of the original earth point. In order to control this at points of risk the power may be isolated, cables covered or, if none of these is practicable, contact may be prevented by using barriers to set a safe distance from overhead services.

Buried services (electricity, gas, water, etc) are not obvious and the likelihood of striking a service when excavating, drilling or piling is thus increased without a site survey to identify any service present. The results of striking an underground service are varied, and the potential to cause injury or fatality is high. As with overhead power lines, any underground service should be treated as live until confirmed and documented otherwise by an authorised source. Incidents can include shock, electrocution, explosion and burns from power cables, explosion, burns or unconsciousness from gas or power cables, impact injury from dislodged stones / flooding from ruptured water mains.

7.2 - Site controls and facilities

Site planning

Following an initial site assessment that has identified hazards and risks associated with the works, control measures should be implemented to ensure the safety and well being of all those who are affected by the construction site and its activities. A plan must be assembled to takes into consideration the following factors.

ARRANGEMENTS FOR SITE ACCESS

Access to a construction site must be planned to minimise any hazards identified during the initial assessment. When a suitable location for site access has been identified, this must be controlled at a point or points that are designated as authorised access point/s and the remainder of the construction site boundary must be secure against unauthorised access. Site safety information should be displayed at access points to inform all attendees of contact names, rules and emergency procedures. Barrier systems are normal on complex undertakings, accompanied by procedures for admittance and exit of people and plant. Special rules for site safety induction and issue of any site security identification are often used to maintain control.

Figure 7-11: Site access   *Source: ACT.*

Figure 7-12: Site controls - access and roadways. *Source: ACT.*

ROADWAYS

Public roadways often extend or continue into construction sites and are subject to pedestrian and vehicular traffic. Construction site roads should be subject to site safety rules such as speed limits, safety restraints (seat belts), direction of flow (one way systems where possible), and there should be segregation of pedestrian and vehicular traffic similar to that used on the public highway. Adequate space should be provided for parking and to allow vehicles and plant to manoeuvre safely and the area should be well lit as required. Vehicles and mobile plant should never be allowed to block roadways or access points as this may prevent emergency vehicles and crews gaining access in the event of a major incident. Site slurry / mud on the road surface that can create skid hazards for site plant and vehicles should not be allowed to accumulate and there should be a system for inspection and cleaning of the surface and vehicles' wheels.

STORAGE

The storage requirements are dependent on the type of material to be stored. Different material types should be stored separately, to avoid cross contamination and the potential for a harmful adverse chemical reaction. If combined storage is permitted, it is advisable that different materials be kept separated for easy identification and retrieval. In addition to authorised access of site operatives, the storage area should be designed to allow safe access by forklift trucks and for the use of suitable mechanical lifting aids to eliminate the the need for manual handling where possible. House keeping should be of a good standard and kept clean and tidy with suitable lighting and ventilation. There should be appropriate fire precautions and provision of correct fire extinguishers. Storage areas should be restricted areas to authorised site staff only and have the correct safety information signs that warn of any dangers or mandatory signs enforcing the wearing of PPE. They should be used for solely that purpose and must not be used for any other purposes such as mixing operations or as a rest or smoking area.

Storage of flammable substances
Substances should be stored in such a way that they cannot

1) Escape and contaminate personnel or the environment   **2)** React with other substances causing explosion, fire or toxic fumes.

Requirements for storage:
- Store small quantities only in the workplace.
- Small quantities of flammables should be stored in clearly marked flameproof metal containers.
- Non-compatible chemicals should be stored apart.
- Chemicals giving off fumes should be stored and used only with suitable respiratory protection.
- Chemicals should be stored away from sources of heat, possibly refrigerated.
- Bulk storage should be outside away from other buildings and sources of heat, including sunlight.

Features of a bulk flammable substance store
- Single storey, light construction in non-combustible materials.
- Flame proof electrical equipment.
- Door sill and perimeter bunding for containment of up to 110% of the maximum storage container of the chemical.
- Interceptor pits for spillage.

Figure 7-13: Misuse of storage.   *Source: ACT.*

Figure 7-14: Loading / unloading.   *Source: ACT.*

LOADING/UNLOADING

Construction sites are constantly changing with a variety of tasks all happening at once, including continuous staff, vehicles and material movements around the site. With this in mind, it is very important that any loading and unloading of materials used on the construction site is carried out in its own dedicated area/ zone under competent supervision. The delivery of materials or equipment to a construction site should be scheduled and planned to minimise the volume of traffic at site at any one time, and drivers / operators of delivery vehicles given a site specific induction to ensure an awareness of hazards, site safety rules and procedures.

Loading and unloading of materials or equipment should be planned and organised. Materials should not be allowed to be placed too high or to lean over creating a potential risk of collapse with the possible result of major injury or a fatality. A number of people have been killed on construction sites due to carelessness in handling. Generally, loads should be kept small with goods on pallets that are in good repair. Lightweight boxes that offer no strength and can be crushed or bags of free-flowing solid (gravel) should always be palletised and never be stacked on top of each other. Different types of container should be stacked separately.

Loads should not block or be placed near emergency exits, fire points / extinguishers, vehicle routes or block light or visibility. They should be placed on firm, solid ground or floors that are strong enough to provide adequate support. Workers should be trained in the correct way to handle loads and also in the dangers associated with unsafe practices / or incorrect loading methods. Site staff should be instructed never to climb up or stand on top of racking or palletized material.

OFFICES

There should be an office available on site to house first aid facilities and equipment, emergency procedures, health and safety information, site induction documentation, health and safety plan (if The Construction (Design and Management) Regulations (CDM) apply), construction drawings and specifications. General site office equipment and records (telephone, fax, training records, visitor personal protective equipment and filing facility) are also stored in the site office. The site manager/supervisor or competent person who is in charge of the site usually attends the site office.

LIGHTING

Adequate lighting should be provided that allows safe access and egress into and around the construction site along roadways, vehicle and pedestrian routes. Attention should also be paid to sensitive areas such as scaffold structures, excavations, flammable stores or fuel bunkers / tanks. Signs warning of dangers at site should be clearly lit to allow approaching people advance notice.

SIGNS

The provision of suitable signs is an important factor in making people aware of the hazards and precautions that relate to construction work. The entrance to a construction site should have an information board that provides details of the client, architect, supervisor, contractor and any other important parties. It will also include mandatory health and safety signs such as those requiring the use of hard hats or ear protection. Other information could include a basic site layout plan and details of where to report upon arrival at the site.

Figure 7-15: Site signs.   *Source: ACT.*

Figure 7-16: Steelworks.   *Source: ACT.*

Site preparation for specialist activities

LIFTING

Lifting operations on construction sites can vary widely dependent upon the size and weight of the load required to be lifted and the lifting equipment required to carry out the lift. Specialist lifting equipment on construction sites is usually either mobile crane or tower crane type. Prior to undertaking lifting operations with any piece of lifting equipment, vital preparation is required to ensure the safety of all those affected. This includes thorough planning of the lift to include a safe system of work, method statements, risk assessments, permits to work (if required) and competent authorised persons assigned to manage the lifting operation. The ground on which the lifting equipment is to be situated should be firm and level and suitable load spreading decking provided to ensure stability. Consideration should also be given to surrounding structures and overhead power cables, ensuring the minimum safe working distances from them. Access to the area below the lifting area should be controlled or restricted to protect people at site from items falling during the lift. The equipment used for the lift must be inspected prior to use and regularly as per the specified frequencies and all test certificates made available. The Lifting Equipment and Lifting Operation Regulations (LOLER) 1998 are specifically related to mechanical lifting.

PILING

Piling is a method of creating long, straight underground cavities that are used for providing foundations for a building or structure. This is performed by either using drilling or by compacting force. The most common method of piling involves the use of a guide 'tube' in which a heavy solid 'driving piece' supported by lifting equipment is released down the guide tube causing the material it strikes to displace upon impact and thus create a cavity when withdrawn. This operation is repeated until the required depth of bore is achieved. Another method involves a steel liner being mechanically 'hammered' into the ground to the required depth. Preparations for piling works may include identifying buried services, hidden voids, the density of the material being piled and ground stability for equipment, water table levels and any local buildings or structures that may be affected by vibrations. Piling is a very noisy operation and consideration should be given to surrounding areas.

STEELWORKS

Steelwork is often used to form the basic 'skeleton' on which a structure is built. The majority of steelwork is designed and manufactured off site and is then assembled using the various pre-fabricated sections and steel beams during the build. Associated activities usually involve working at height with materials that are very heavy and difficult to manoeuvre. Site preparation involves thorough planning to include safe systems of work, risk assessments, method statements and permits to work where required. Where practicable, risks should be eliminated or reduced to the minimum possible level by combating hazards at source (e.g. use of mobile elevated work platform for access, cranes for lifting). Any lifting equipment or access equipment should only be used on firm and level ground.

Site security and means of protecting the public

PERIMETER FENCING

Construction sites must be contained within a perimeter fence. The main purpose of fencing is to keep out unauthorised persons (e.g. members of the public and children) and to prevent injury or death. Perimeter fencing also provides security against theft of materials, plant or equipment from the site. Fences should be adequate and suitable and installed at a reasonable distance from the structure to allow unrestricted movement on site of people and mobile plant, and prevent any activities being undertaken affecting the environment outside the fence. The fence should be regularly inspected to ensure there is no damage, breaks or gaps to allow unauthorised entry.

SIGNS

Signs should be fixed at regular intervals on the perimeter fence to warn of the dangers within the site and instruct people to 'keep out'. Quite often, the name of the security company that is responsible for 'out of hours' security will also be displayed with a telephone number for emergency contact or to report any trespass.

Figure 7-17: Unauthorised access.   *Source: ACT.*

Figure 7-18: Perimeter fencing and signs.   *Source: ACT.*

SAFE VIEWING POINTS

Members of the public are quite often intrigued by construction sites and can be attracted to the perimeter fence to see for themselves what is going on. This may result in injury from flying particles, dust, fumes or splashes, even though the person is outside the perimeter fence. This can be avoided by arranging for a pre-planned viewing point that consists of a wire mesh panel integrated into the fence that allows members of the public to view the site's activities. The viewing point will be planned and situated in an area that is not exposed to hazards.

MEANS OF SECURING PLANT, CHEMICALS, ETC

Plant, equipment, materials or chemicals should be suitably secured to prevent injury by unauthorised access. Plant should be locked up at all times when not in use and keys held in a secure location (site office, safe). It may be practical to house plant in an additional internal site compound. In order to improve security certain items of heavy mobile plant are provided with steel sheets or shutters fitted around the cab and padlocked in position.

MEANS OF CONTROLLING ENVIRONMENTAL DANGERS ON PUBLIC HIGHWAYS

Areas that surround a construction site are subject to mud and debris from the tyres and chassis' of vehicles that frequent the site, which creates additional hazards to other road users as highway surfaces become slippery and create skid hazards. This can be controlled by the implementation of regular highway cleaning with road sweeper vehicles. Action can also be taken at site exits prior to vehicles leaving the site by routing site traffic through a tyre and undercarriage cleaning system, which assists in preventing mud and debris leaving the site.

Arrangements with client/occupier of premises

SITE RULES

Site rules will vary at different sites or premises due to the wide range of activities that may be undertaken. Site rules provide instructions that must be followed by permanent site staff and visitors and also other important information relating to site / location specific hazards. Occupiers of premises or clients may have different standards of site rules and some may enforce them more stringently than others. Contractors should always enforce their own site rules in addition to client / occupier rules.

CO-OPERATION

Co-operation between client and occupier is a very important factor. The occupier of a premises or site will have a detailed knowledge of any site specific hazards that may or may not be obvious to a contractor undertaking construction works and this may impact upon the works. In addition, the client or occupier has the authority to place controls and restrictions on the site. The contractor should be experienced in the activities that will be carried out and will have assessed any hazards related to the activities that are to be carried out at site. It is vital that all parties co-operate and communicate in order that this knowledge and information can be assessed to determine any new hazards that may arise and to enable appropriate information to be cascaded to other people at risk on the site. Co-operation will also be required where site activities need to be controlled or access restricted or where a shared knowledge is required to undertake a task e.g. decommissioning or removal of machinery.

SHARED FACILITIES

Occupied premises will quite often have various facilities available for existing staff / occupiers (hot & cold water, toilets, communications, restroom) depending upon the type of property it is. It may be acceptable upon agreements with the party in control of the premises and its facilities for these to be shared for mutual benefit.

PROTECTION OF OTHER EMPLOYEES/ VISITORS

Construction related activities that are carried out in addition to those normally undertaken at the premises must take into account a lack of knowledge of other parties using the premises. Consideration must be paid to protecting not only those staff directly involved in the works, but also to any other person that may encounter the works including permanent site staff and / or visitors attending the site. This may require site rules to be amended, and be supported by induction, personal protective equipment issue, signs, barriers, lighting or verbal instruction.

Figure 7-19: Protection of others.   *Source: ACT.*

Figure 7-20: Sanitary conveniences.   *Source: ACT.*

Provision of welfare facilities

SANITARY CONVENIENCES

Suitable and sufficient sanitary conveniences should be made available at readily accessible places. Rooms containing sanitary conveniences should be adequately ventilated and well lit. Men and women may use the same room provided as long as it is lockable from the inside. Provision should be made for regular cleaning and replenishment of consumable toilet items.

WASHING FACILITIES

On all sites, a suitable number of wash basins big enough to allow a person to wash their hands, face and forearms should be available. All basins should have a supply of hot and cold water (warm water as a minimum). A means of drying must also be provided. Where work is particularly dirty or workers are exposed to toxic or corrosive substances, showers may also be necessary.

Figure 7-21: Washing facilities.   *Source: ACT.*

Figure 7-22: Temporary showers.   *Source: ACT.*

DRINKING WATER

An adequate supply of wholesome drinking water must be made available at suitable and readily accessible places. Drinking water supplies should be clearly marked to distinguish them from those that are not fit for human consumption. Unless the supply is in the form of a fountain, cups or other drinking vessels must be available.

CHANGING AREAS

Where a person has to wear special clothing for work, suitable facilities - separate for men and women - must be provided. Changing areas must be big enough, sufficiently warm and secure.

ACCOMMODATION FOR CLOTHING

There must be arrangements for storage and segregation of clothing not worn on site from protective clothing needed for site work. There should be somewhere to dry wet clothing and separate storage for contaminated clothes. Storage areas must be secure.

Figure 7-23: Accommodation for clothing.   *Source: ACT.*

Figure 7-24: Rest and eating facilities.   *Source: ACT.*

REST, FOOD / DRINK PREPARATION AND EATING FACILITIES

Readily accessible, suitable and sufficient rest facilities must be provided. Rest rooms and areas must include suitable arrangements for protecting non smokers from the discomfort of tobacco smoke. Suitable rest facilities must also be provided for pregnant women and nursing mothers.

Where meals are regularly eaten in the workplace suitable and sufficient facilities must be provided for their consumption. Eating facilities should include a facility for preparing or obtaining a hot drink, and where hot food cannot be readily obtained, means should be provided to enable workers to heat their own food.

VENTILATION, HEATING AND LIGHTING OF FACILITIES

All of the facilities mentioned above shall be kept clean, warm, properly ventilated and well lit.

Working at height - hazards and control

Overall Aims

On completion of this Unit, candidates will understand:

- the hazards presented by construction work where there is a risk of falling from a height.
- the precautions necessary to control these hazards and to reduce the risks they present.

Content

Specific Intended Learning Outcomes

The intended learning outcomes of this Unit are that candidates will be able to:

8.1   identify the hazards of working at height and outline the general requirements necessary to control them

8.2   describe safe working practices for common forms of access equipment and roof work

8.3   describe common types of scaffold systems and the measures necessary to ensure their stability and safe use

8.4   outline the particular requirements to ensure safety when working over water

Sources of Reference

Essentials of Health and Safety at Work, HSE Books

Safe Use of Work Equipment (ACOP) (L22), HSE Books

Health and Safety in Roof work (HSG33), HSE Books

A Guide to the Construction (Head Protection) Regulations (L102), HSE Books

Protecting the Public: Your Next Move (HSG151), HSE Books

Relevant Statutory Provisions

The Construction (Health, Safety and Welfare) Regulations (CHSW) 1996

The Construction (Head Protection) Regulations (CHPR) 1989

The Provision and Use of Work Equipment Regulations (PUWER) 1998

8.1 - Hazards and risk factors in relation to work above ground level or where there is a risk of falling a distance

Falls of persons

TYPICAL ACTIVITIES AND INJURIES ASSOCIATED WITH FALLS FROM A HEIGHT

Falls are the most common cause of fatal injuries in the construction industry. They account for more than half of those accidentally killed each year. Much of the work carried out on a building site is done above ground at a height of more than two metres. Typical activities that involve working at a height are:

- Steel erecting.
- Fixing of cladding, roof work.
- Painting and decorating.
- Demolition and dismantling

- Bricklaying.
- Scaffold erection.
- Electrical installation and maintenance.

DISTANCE (SIGNIFICANCE OF 2 METRES OR MORE)

The Construction (Health, Safety and Welfare) Regulations (CHSW) 1996, regulation 6, requires the employer or those in control of a site to take suitable and sufficient steps to prevent any person falling. In workplaces where these regulations do not apply (e.g. offices and warehouses) the Workplace (Health, Safety and Welfare) Regulations (WHSWR) 1992 require employers to take reasonably practicable steps to prevent a person from falling. The Approved Codes of Practice (ACOPs) that accompany the WHSWR state that precautions - guard rails, barriers, etc. - should be in place where a person could fall more than two metres.

Regulation 7 of the CHSW Regulations is more specific and requires suitable and sufficient steps to be taken to prevent falling through fragile material where the person might fall more than two metres. Whilst the two metre height is not seen as a safe / unsafe dividing line, experience supports the fact that falls from a height of above two metres have a particularly high risk of being fatal. Therefore legislation has tended to focus on this. This does not imply that work at a height of less than 2 metres is inherently safe; accident statistics bear out quite the contrary. It is still necessary to take measures to prevent falls from below 2 metres in height, and this is supported by general duties under the Health and Safety at Work Act etc. (HASAWA) 1974 and good practice.

FRAGILE ROOFS, ROOF-LIGHTS AND VOIDS

Almost 20% of those killed in accidents on construction sites were doing roof work. Some fall off the edge of flat or sloping roofs but many are killed by falling through fragile materials. Before work is done on and to a roof, ensure that:

- There is safe access and egress.
- Crawling boards or roof ladders are used to spread the weight of people and materials.

- Roof openings / lights are clearly identified and protected by barriers.
- People do not attempt to walk on the purlins or the roof ridge.

DETERIORATING MATERIALS

Asbestos cement, fibreglass and plastic deteriorate with age and become more fragile. Similarly, steel sheets may rust or may not be supported properly. This presents a serious risk to workers who work on these materials without means to prevent falls.

WEATHER

Adverse weather can have a significant effect on the safety of those working at a height. Rain, snow and ice increase the risk of slips and falling from a roof. When handling large objects, such as roof panels, then high wind can be a serious problem and may cause the person to be blown off the roof. Extremely cold temperatures can increase the likelihood of brittle failure of materials and therefore increase the likelihood of failure of roof supports, scaffold components and plastic roof lights.

Figure 8-1: Working above ground level. *Source: ACT.*

Materials such as old slates, tiles etc should not be thrown from the roof or scaffold - passers by may be at risk of being injured. Enclosed debris chutes should be used or debris lowered in containers.

FALLING MATERIALS

The risk of falling materials causing injury should be minimised by keeping platforms clear of loose materials. In addition, methods provided should prevent materials or other objects rolling, or being kicked, off the edges of platforms. This may be done with toe boards, solid barriers, brick guards, or similar at open edges. If working in a public place, nets, fans or covered walkways may be needed to give extra protection for people who may be passing below. High-visibility barrier netting is not suitable for use as a fall prevention device.

8.2 - Control strategies for persons working at height

Hierarchy of measures

AVOIDANCE

The first question to ask is "can the hazards be avoided?" For example, the need to paint at a height can be avoided if materials are bought ready finished. If the hazards cannot be avoided then some or all of the following precautions will have to be considered.

WORKING PLATFORMS

- Wide enough - at least 600 mm wide - to allow people to pass back and forth safely and to use any equipment or material necessary for their work at that place.
- Free of openings and traps through which people's feet could pass, causing them to trip, fall or be injured in any other way.
- Constructed to prevent materials from falling. As well as toe boards or similar protection at the edge of the platform, the platform itself should be constructed to prevent any object which may be used on the platform from falling through gaps or holes, causing injury to people working below. For scaffolds, a close-boarded platform would suffice, although for work over public areas, a double-boarded platform sandwiching a polythene sheet may be needed. If a Mobile Elevated Work Platform (MEWP) or cradle is used and it has meshed platform floors, the mesh should be fine enough to prevent materials, especially nails and bolts, from slipping through.
- Kept free of tripping and slipping hazards. Where necessary, handholds and footholds should be provided. Platforms should be clean and tidy. Do not allow mud to build up on platforms.

PERSONAL SUSPENSION EQUIPMENT

Personal suspension equipment may be used when it is impracticable to provide a working platform. An example of this is a 'Boatswains Chair / Seat'. This equipment is designed for light, short term work and generally consists of a seat with a back, a central suspension point and a carrying point (tool / equipment bucket) for tools. Other forms of personal suspension equipment include that form of abseil equipment used for access.

FALL ARREST EQUIPMENT

Fall arrest harnesses are useful when other means of fall protection are not reasonably practicable, such as work where open edges exist during steel erection. The harness itself may cause injury when the person comes to a sudden stop, therefore inertia reel harnesses (the same principle as a car seat belt) may be preferable. When using harnesses in a mobile elevating work platform (MEWP), the harness should always be fixed to the *inside* of the cradle - ***see - figure 8-25.***

Scaffolding

DESIGN FEATURES OF SCAFFOLDING

Independent tied

This type of scaffold typically uses two sets of standards; one near to the structure and the other set at the width of the work platform. It is erected so that it is independent from the structure and does not rely on it for its primary stability. However, as the name suggests, it is usual to tie the scaffold to the structure in order to prevent the scaffold falling towards or away from the structure.

Figure 8-2: Independent tied scaffold.   *Source: ACT.*

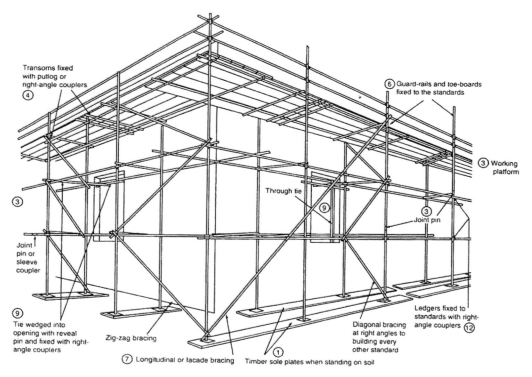

Figure 8-3: Independent tied scaffold.   *Source: HSG150 Safety in Construction.*

© ACT

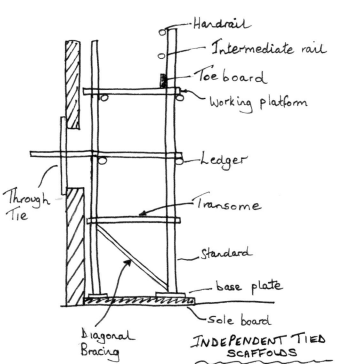

Figure 8-4: Independent tied scaffold (hand drawn example). *Source: ACT.*

Figure 8-5: Independent tied scaffold. *Source: ACT*

Figure 8-6: Tie through window. *Source: ACT*

Putlog

This type of scaffold has a single set of standards erected at the width required for the work platform. The transoms have a flat end that is inserted into the mortar gap in the wall. The structure effectively provides the inner support for the work platform and therefore an inner set of standards is not needed.

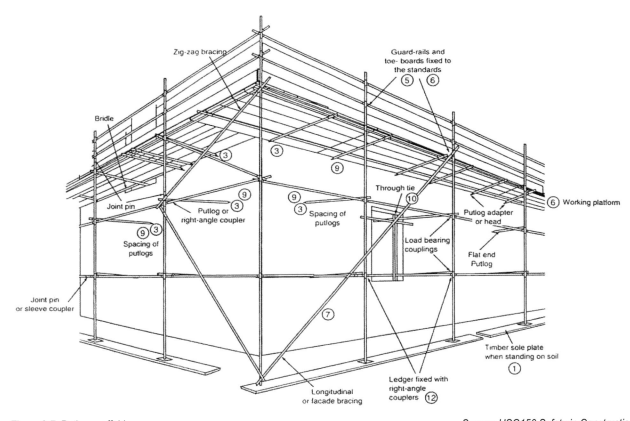

Figure 8-7: Putlog scaffold.

Source: HSG150 Safety in Construction.

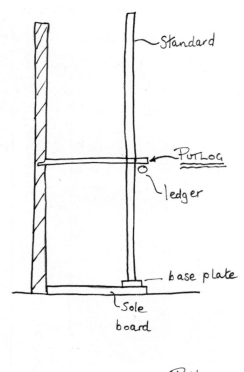

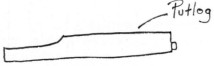

Figure 8-8: Putlog (hand drawn example). *Source: ACT.*

Figure 8-9: Putlog scaffold. *Source: ACT.*

Figure 8-10: Putlog scaffold. *Source: ACT.*

Fan

Fans are scaffold boards fixed on scaffold tubes set at an upward angle out from a scaffold in order to catch debris that may fall from the scaffold. They may be provided at the entrances to buildings to protect persons entering and leaving the building that the scaffold is erected against. They are also used where a scaffold is erected alongside a pedestrian walkway where there is a need to have an increased confidence that materials that might fall cannot contact people below. In some cases it may be necessary for horizontal barriers to be erected to direct pedestrians under the fan.

Cantilevered

A cantilever scaffold is assembled in the normal way then continued outwards by erecting a cantilever section from the inner vertical columns. Care must be taken to ensure the structure remains safe and stable. Adding stabilisers to the main scaffold or tying-in to the building are normally essential safety precautions. The use of adjustable bases either under the main scaffold or cantilever or both is usually helpful in ensuring the cantilever section rests firmly on the building.

Mobile tower scaffolds

Mobile scaffold towers are widely used as they are convenient for work which involves frequent access to a height over a short period of time in a number of locations that are spaced apart. However, they are often incorrectly erected or misused and accidents occur due to people / materials falling or the tower overturning / collapsing. They must be erected and dismantled by trained, competent personnel, strictly in accordance with the supplier's instructions. All parts must be sound and from the same manufacturer.

- The height of an untied, independent tower must never exceed the manufacturer's recommendations. A 'rule of thumb' may be:
    - outdoor use - 3 times the minimum base width
    - indoor use - 3.5 times the minimum base width.

Figure 8-11: Fans. *Source: ACT.*

Figure 8-12: Wheels with brakes. *Source: ACT.*

- If the height of the tower is to exceed these maximum figures then the scaffold MUST be secured (tied) to the structure or outriggers used.
- Working platforms must only be accessed by safe means. Use internal stairs or fixed ladders only and never climb on the outside.
- Before climbing a tower the wheels must be turned outwards, the wheel brakes "on", locked and kept locked.
- Never move a tower unless the platform is clear of people, materials, tools etc.
- Towers must only be moved by pushing them at base level. Instruct operators not to pull the tower along whilst on it. Pay careful attention to obstructions at base level and overhead.
- Never use a tower near live overhead power lines or cables.
- Working platforms must always be fully boarded out. Guard rails and toe boards must be fitted if there is a risk of a fall of more than two metres. Inspections must be carried out by a competent person - before first use, after substantial alteration and after any event likely to have affected its stability.

Figure 8-13: Mobile tower scaffold. *Source: ACT.*

Figure 8-14: Mobile tower scaffold. *Source: ACT.*

SAFETY FEATURES

Base plates & Sole boards

- A base plate must be used under every standard - it spreads the load and helps to keep the standard vertical.
- Sole boards are used to spread the weight of the scaffold and to provide a firm surface on which to erect a scaffold, particularly on soft ground. Sole boards must be sound and sufficient, and should run under at least two standards at a time.

Figure 8-15: Base plates and sole boards.   *Source: Lincsafe.*

Figure 8-16: Base plate and protection.   *Source: ACT.*

Figure 8-17: Scaffold boards - some defective.   *Source: ACT.*

Figure 8-18: Ladder access.   *Source: ACT.*

Toe boards

These are scaffold boards placed against the standards at right angles to the surface of the working platform. They help prevent materials from falling from the scaffold and people slipping under rails.

- The toe boards should be fixed to the inside of the standards with toe board clips.
- Minimum height of 150 mm.
- Joints must be as near as possible to a standard.

- Continuous around the platform where a guard-rail is required.
- Any toe board which is removed temporarily for access or for any other reason must be replaced as soon as possible.

Guardrails

These are horizontal scaffold tubes which help to prevent people falling from a scaffold.

- They must be fitted to any working platform which is two metres or more above ground level.
- They must be fixed to the *inside* of the standards, at least 910 mm from the platform.
- An intermediate rail must be no more than 470 mm between the top guardrail and the toe boards.
- Guardrails must always be fitted with load-bearing couplers.
- Joints in guard-rails must be near to a standard.

- Must be secured with sleeve couplers.
- Guardrail must go all round the work platform.
- If the gap between the structures is 300 mm or more, then a guardrail must be fitted to the inside of the working platform as well as the outside.
- Guardrails must always be carried round the end of a scaffold, to make a "stop end".

Brick guards

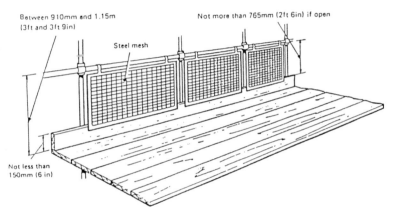

Figure 8-19: Brick guards.   *Source: HSG150 Safety in Construction.*

Boarding

Boards provide the working platform of a scaffold and landings for access ladders. Boards supported by transoms or putlogs must be close fitting, free from cracks or splits or large knots, and must not be damaged in any way which could cause weakness.

Debris netting

Debris netting is often fixed to the sides of a scaffold to limit the amount of debris escaping from the scaffold that may come from work being done on it. It provides a tough, durable and inexpensive method of helping to provide protection from the danger of falling debris and windblown waste. It allows good light transmission and reduces the effects of adverse weather. Debris netting may also be slung underneath steelwork or where roof work is being conducted to catch items that may fall. In this situation it should not be assumed that the debris netting is sufficient to hold the weight of a person who might fall.

Figure 8-20: Nets and sheets.   *Source: ACT.*

Figure 8-21: Nets.   *Source: ACT.*

REQUIREMENTS FOR SCAFFOLD ERECTORS

Scaffold erectors must erect and dismantle scaffold in a way that minimises the risk of falling. Where practicable they should erect intermediate platforms, with guard rails and toe boards, to enable them to build the next scaffold 'lift' safely. If a platform is not practicable falls must be prevented (or their effects minimised) by other means, such as the use of a safety harness or similar fall arrest equipment.

MEANS OF ACCESS

"So far as is reasonably practicable as regards any place of work under the employer's control, the maintenance of it in a condition that is safe and without risks to health and the provision and maintenance of means of access to and egress from it that are safe and without such risks"   Health and Safety at Work Act (HASAWA) 1974 S2(2)(d)).

General access must not be allowed to any scaffold until its erection has been fully completed. Access must be prevented to any subsequent sections of scaffold that are not completed and a "scaffold incomplete" sign displayed. Ladders often provide access and egress to and from scaffolds where stairs cannot be provided. Factors to be considered in the safe use of ladders for access include:

- They should be free from defect and not painted.
- The correct length used to reduce manual handling risks, flexing in use.
- Placed on a firm footing, with each stile equally supported.
- Positioned so that there is sufficient space at each rung to give an adequate foothold.
- Positioned approximately at an angle of 75^0 (1 unit horizontally to 4 units vertically).
- Extended to a height of 1 metre above the working platform (unless there is another adequate hand hold).
- When more than 3 metres in length, must be securely tied at the top or footed at the bottom to prevent slipping.
- Not be so long that it extends excessively past the stepping off point as this can cause the ladder to pivot around the tie/stepping off point and cause the user to fall.
- Positioned so that the vertical height of the ladder running between landings does not exceed 9 metres.
- Both hands should be free when climbing a ladder.

DESIGN OF LOADING PLATFORMS

Scaffold platforms that are used for loading of materials or equipment will need to be designed to take into account any concentration of heavy loads that will be placed upon them (e.g. bricks, blocks, mortar or timber). A loading platform is designed to withstand a weight that would be excessive on the normal working area of a scaffold. Often this will be a separate scaffold structure, assembled adjacent to the main working scaffold, tied to both the building and the main scaffold and will consist of additional braces and sections to provide extra support. The platform must be correctly signed as a loading area with a safe working load specified. Workers must not be allowed to access the area directly below the platform where the loading and unloading will take place.

SCAFFOLD HOISTS (PERSONS, MATERIALS)

The hoist should be protected by a substantial enclosure to prevent anyone from being struck by any moving part of the hoist or material falling down the hoist way. Gates must be provided at all access landings, including at ground level. The gates must be kept shut, except when the platform is at the landing. The controls should be arranged so that the hoist can be operated from one position only. All hoist operators must be trained and competent. The hoist's safe working load must be clearly marked. If the hoist is for materials only there should be a prominent warning notice on the platform or cage to stop people riding on it. The hoist should be inspected weekly, and thoroughly examined every six months by a competent person and the results of inspection recorded.

ENSURING STABILITY

Effects of materials

Scaffold systems are a means of providing safe access when work at a height cannot be avoided. They are not designed for storage of materials for long periods. It is however, acceptable to situate materials on scaffolds in small quantities to reflect the usage rate of the materials by the people using the scaffold. Provided the safe working load specified for the scaffold is not exceeded materials may be distributed evenly on the working platform. Care should be taken to ensure the working platform is not reduced to a width that compromises access around the scaffold, the materials are distributed evenly and the safe working load specified for the scaffold is not exceeded.

Materials (bricks, mortar, timber, etc) when placed on scaffold systems tend to be placed on the outer edge of the scaffold, creating an uneven balance and placing greater forces on the mechanical joints. These factors can contribute to failure of the joints, or buckling of the tube sections which may ultimately lead to a full or partial collapse of the structure. If this occurs, a host of other hazards become present (falls from height, falling materials).

All loading of scaffolds with materials should be well planned to prevent uneven loading and carried out under supervision. The scaffold should be checked to ensure the safe working load is adhered to at all times.

Weather

Adverse weather conditions not only affect the condition of structures and equipment but can also present dangers to those people who are exposed to them (cold weather can affect dexterity, awareness and morale). These need to be anticipated and suitable precautions taken. Rain, sleet or snow can make surfaces very slippery and in winter freeze to create ice or frost. Heavy rainfall can lead to soil being washed away from the base of the scaffold or the soil can be caused to subside leading to the scaffold becoming unstable. Scaffolds should always be inspected prior to work starting. If conditions have changed, checks should be made on whether it is safe to continue working.

A sudden gust of wind can cause loss of balance. This is usually exaggerated when working at height and/ or handling large sheets of materials. In extreme circumstances, work should be stopped during windy weather as people can easily be thrown off balance while carrying out their work. When deciding whether to continue or suspend work consider:

- Wind speed.
- The measures which have already been taken to prevent falls from the scaffold.
- The position and height of the scaffold and the work being carried out.
- The relationship of the work to other large structures as wind may be tunnelled and amplified at certain points.

Sheeting

Sheeting can be used on the outside of scaffold systems as a means of preventing materials, dust and other debris being blown from the working areas of the scaffold onto the construction site or possibly a public area, and it can also provide a means of restricting and controlling access. It is not a means of fall protection.

Whilst sheeting is relatively light and causes little stress on the scaffold system, the additional forces created by wind, rain or snow spread over the surface of the sheeting could cause sufficient force to affect the safe stability of the scaffold. It is also important that sheeting is securely fixed to the structure and not allowed to flail loosely as this could be snagged on site mobile plant resulting in the scaffold being pulled and causing it to collapse.

Protection from impact of vehicles

Construction sites quite often involve numerous types of vehicles of varying size and weight all presenting hazards to other people carrying out work within the site. Protection from impact should be applied to all aspects of work carried out, not just to scaffold structures in particular. Measures that may be implemented in order to maintain a safe environment in relation to vehicles and scaffolds may include:

- Clear lighting provided around the scaffold perimeter.
- Signs warning of scaffold, high visibility tape or sheath around scaffold standards.
- Ensuring adequate road width for the size of vehicle accessing the site.
- Provision of one-way systems around sites or turning points (away from scaffold) to minimise the need for reversing.
- Reversing vehicles properly controlled by trained banksmen. Competent drivers correctly trained.
- Concrete impact blocks strategically placed around scaffold perimeter to limit proximity.

Figure 8-22: 'Scaftag'. *Source: ACT.*

Figure 8-23: Lighting. *Source: ACT.*

Inspection requirements

Inspection requirements for scaffolds are set out in the CHSW Regulations. All scaffolds used must be inspected by a competent person before being taken into use for the first time, after any substantial addition, dismantling or other alteration, after any event likely to have affected its strength or stability and at regular intervals not exceeding 7 days since the last inspection.

Reports on inspections to include the following details:

1) Location of the place of work inspected.
2) Description of the place of work or part of that place inspected (including any plant and equipment and materials, if any).
3) Date and time of inspection.
4) Details of any matter identified that could give rise to a risk to the health and safety of any person.
5) Details of any action taken as a result of 4) above.
6) Details of any further action considered necessary.
7) Name and position of the person making the report.

MOBILE ELEVATING WORK PLATFORMS

A mobile elevating work platform (MEWP) is, as the name suggests, a means of providing a work platform at a height. The equipment is designed to be movable, under its own power or by being towed, so that it can easily be set up in a location where it is needed. Various mechanical and hydraulic means are used to elevate the work platform to the desired height, including telescopic arms and scissor lifts. The versatility of this equipment, enabling the easy placement of a platform at a height, makes it a popular piece of access equipment. Often, to do similar work by other means would take a lot of time or be very difficult. They are now widely available and, like other equipment such as fork lift trucks, there is a tendency for people to oversimplify their use and allow people to operate them without prior training and experience. This places users and others at high risk of serious injury.

Some MEWPs can be used on rough terrain. This usually means that they are safe to use on uneven or undulating ground. Always check their limitations in the manufacturer's handbook before moving onto unprepared or sloping ground and operate within the defined stability working area. Wearing a harness with a lanyard attached to the platform provides extra protection against falls especially when the platform is being raised or lowered.

Figure 8-24: Mobile elevated work platform (MEWPs). *Source: ACT.*

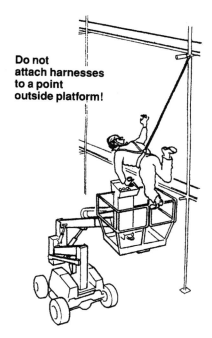

Figure 8-25: Use of harness with a MEWP.   *Source: HSG150.*

Use of Mobile Elevating Work Platforms

Mobile Elevating Work Platforms (MEWPs) can provide excellent safe access to high level work. When using a MEWP make sure:

■ Whoever is operating it is fully trained and competent.
■ The work platform is fitted with guard rails and toe boards.
■ It is used on suitable firm and level ground. The ground may have to be prepared in advance.
■ Tyres are properly inflated.
■ The work area is cordoned off to prevent access below the work platform.
■ That it is well lit if being used on a public highway in poor lighting.
■ Outriggers are extended and chocked as necessary before raising the platform.
■ All involved know what to do if the machine fails with the platform in the raised position.

Figure 8-26: Mobile elevated work platform (MEWPs). *Source: ACT.*

Figure 8-28: Scissor lift.   *Source: ACT.*

Do not

■ Operate MEWPs close to overhead cables or dangerous machinery.
■ Allow a knuckle, or elbow, of the arm to protrude into a traffic route when working near vehicles.
■ Move the equipment with the platform in the raised position unless the equipment is especially designed to allow this to be done safely (check the manufacturer's instructions).
■ Overload or overreach from the platform.

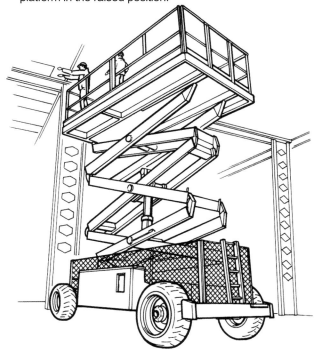

Figure 8-27: Scissor lift.   *Source: HSG150, HSE.*

Ladders

USE OF LADDERS

Ladders are primarily a means of vertical access to a workplace. However, they are often used to carry out work and this frequently results in accidents. Many accidents involving ladders happen during work lasting 30 minutes or less. Ladders are often used for short jobs when it would be safer to use other equipment, e.g. mobile scaffold towers or MEWPs. Generally, ladders should be considered as access equipment and use of a ladder as a work platform should be discouraged. There are situations when working from a ladder would be inappropriate, for example:

- When two hands are needed or the work area is large.
- Where the equipment or materials used are large or awkward.
- Excessive height.

- Work of long duration.
- Where the ladder cannot be secured or made stable.
- Where the ladder cannot be protected from vehicles etc.
- Adverse weather conditions.

Figure 8-29: Ladder as access and workplace. *Source: ACT.*

Figure 8-30: Improper use.   *Source: ACT.*

Before using a ladder to work from, consider whether it is the right equipment for the job. Ladders are only suitable as a workplace for light work of short duration, and for a large majority of activities a scaffold, mobile tower or MEWP is likely to be more suitable and safer.

- Pre-use inspection. Make sure the ladder is in good condition. Check the rungs and stiles for warping, cracking or splintering, the condition of the feet, and for any other defects. Do not use defective or painted ladders.
- Position the ladder properly for safe access and out of the way of vehicles.
- Ladders must stand on a firm, level base, be positioned approximately at an angle of 75^0 (1 unit horizontally to 4 units vertically) and extend about 1 metre above the landing place. Do not rest ladders against fragile surfaces.
- Ladders must be properly tied near the top, even if only in use for a short time. If not tied, ladders must be secured near the bottom, footed or weighted. Footing is not considered effective on ladders longer than five metres. While being tied, a ladder must be footed.
- Keep both hands free to grip the ladder when climbing or descending, with only one person on the ladder at any time. Beware of wet, greasy or icy rungs and make sure soles of footwear are clean.

Figure 8-31: Poor storage.   *Source: Lincsafe.*

Figure 8-32: Use of roof ladders. *Source: HSG150, HSE.*

STEP LADDERS

Stepladders require careful use. They are subject to the same general health and safety rules as ladders.

However, in addition, they will not withstand any degree of side loading and overturn very easily.

Over-reaching is to be avoided at all costs.

The top step of a stepladder should not be used as a working platform unless it has been specifically designed for that purpose. Ladder stays must be 'locked out' properly before use.

TRESTLES

Trestles are pre-fabricated steel, aluminium or wood supports, of approximately 500 mm - 1 metre width, that may be of fixed height or may be height adjustable by means of sliding struts with varying fixing points (pin method) or various cross bars to suit the height required. They are used to span scaffold boards from one to the other in order to make a work platform. *These can only be used where work cannot be carried out from the ground but where a scaffold would be impracticable.* A good example would be a plasterer who is installing and plastering a new ceiling. Typical working heights when using a trestle system ranges from 300 mm to 1 metre but can be up to above 4 metres. Edge protection should be fitted wherever practical. As with any work carried out above ground level, a risk assessment (as required by the Management of Health and Safety at Work Regulations (MHSWR)1999) should be carried out and the and consideration given to the application of the CHSW Regulations 1996 and/or the Workplace (Health, Safety and Welfare) Regulations (WHSWR) 1992.

Figure 8-33: Stepladder. *Source: ACT.*

STAGING PLATFORMS

Staging platforms can be made of metal alloy or wood and are often used for linking trestle systems or tower scaffolds together safely. They also provide a safe work platform for work on fragile roofs. They are produced in various lengths. The same rules apply for edge protection as with other scaffold platforms.

LEADING EDGE PROTECTION

Leading edges are created as new roof sheets are laid, or old ones are removed. Falls from a leading edge need to be prevented.

Work at the leading edge requires careful planning to develop a safe system of work. Nets are the preferred method for reducing the risk of injury from falls at the leading edge, as they provide protection to everyone on the roof. Nets should be erected by trained riggers and be strong enough to take the weight of people. Debris nets are only rigged to trap light weight debris therefore it is important to know which type is in use at a workplace.

Staging platforms fitted with guard rails or suitable barriers and toe boards, in advance of the leading edge, can provide protection in some circumstances. But these will need to be used in conjunction with harnesses attached to a suitable fixing. Close supervision of this system of work will be needed as it is difficult for the harness to remain safely clipped at all times throughout the work activity.

Other techniques for working at a height

Where it is not possible to work from the existing structure and the use of a scaffold working platform is not appropriate, a range of mobile access equipment including boatswain's chairs or seats, suspended cradles, rope access equipment and mobile elevating work platforms (MEWPs) can be used.

Those using this type of equipment should be trained and competent to operate it. They should learn emergency and evacuation procedures so that they know what to do if for example the power to the platform fails or fire breaks out in the building being worked on. With many pieces of equipment, more than one person will be needed to ensure safe operation.

BOATSWAIN'S CHAIR

Boatswain's chairs and seats can be used for light, short-term work. They should only be used where it is not practicable to provide a working platform.

Safety checklist

Before use

- Installation and use of boatswain's chair to be supervised by trained, experienced and competent person.
- Chair and associated equipment carefully examined for defects.
- Confirm test / examination certificates are valid. Establish safe working load.
- Check that user is both trained and competent in the use of the chair.
- Warning notice displayed and notification of intention to carry out work given.
- Prohibit access to the area below the chair in case materials fall.

In use
- Free of material or articles which could interfere with user's hand-hold.
- The fall rope must be properly tied off in use and always under or around a cleat to act as a brake.

After use
- Chairs and rope should be left in a safe condition:
    - Top rope secured.
    - Chair and rope secured to prevent swing.
    - Raised when out of use or for overnight storage.
- Inspected for defects.
- Ropes (and chair, if timber) dried before storage.

CRADLES (INCLUDING SUSPENSION FROM CRADLES)

Before work starts, check that:

- Equipment is installed, modified and dismantled only by competent specialists.
- There is a current report of thorough examination for the equipment.
- A handover certificate is provided by the installer. The certificate should cover how to deal with emergencies, operate, check and maintain the equipment, and state its safe working load.
- Areas of the site where people may be struck by the cradle or falling materials have been fenced off or similar. Debris fans or covered walkways may also be required.
- Systems are in place to prevent people within the building being struck by the cradle as it rises or descends and prevent the cradle coming into contact with open windows or similar obstructions which could cause it to tip.
- Supports are protected from damage (for example, by being struck by passing vehicles or by interference from vandals).
- The equipment should not be used in adverse weather. High winds will create instability. Establish a maximum safe wind speed for operation. Storms and snow falls can also damage platforms, so they should be inspected before use after severe weather.
- Only trained personnel are to operate.

At the end of each day, check that:

- All power has been switched off and, where appropriate, power cables have been secured and made dead.
- The equipment is secured where it will not be accessible to vandals or trespassers.
- Notices are attached to the equipment warning that it is out of service and must not be used.
- Check the shift report for warnings of malfunction.

ROPE ACCESS

Often known as abseiling, this technique is usually used for inspection work rather than construction work. Like a boatswain's chair, it should only be used when a working platform cannot be provided. If rope access is necessary, then check that:

- A competent person has installed the equipment.
- The user is fully trained.
- There is more than one point securing the equipment.
- Tools and equipment are securely attached or the area below cordoned off.
- The main rope and safety rope are attached to separate points.

Figure 8-34: Personal suspension equipment.   *Source: ACT.*

Fall arrest equipment

HARNESSES

There may be circumstances in which it is not practicable for guard rails etc to be provided, for example, where guard rails are taken down for short periods to land materials. In this situation if people approach an open edge from which they would be liable to fall two metres or more a suitably attached harness and temporary horizontal lifeline could allow safe working. When using harnesses and temporary horizontal lifelines, remember:

- The harness and lanyards are made of man-made fibres and as such are prone to degradation by sunlight, chemicals etc. It is important to carry out tactile pre-use checks daily, in good light, before taking harnesses and lanyards into use. If there is the slightest doubt about a harness or the lanyard, do not use it. Faults can be noticed by discolouration, little tears, nicks and grittiness to touch.
- A harness will not prevent a fall - it can only minimise the injury if there is a fall. The person who falls may be injured by the impact load to the body when the line goes tight or when they strike against parts of the structure during the fall. An energy absorber fitted to the energy-absorbing lanyard can reduce the risk of injury from impact loads.
- Where possible the energy-absorbing lanyard should be attached above the wearer to reduce the fall distance. Extra free movement can be provided by running temporary horizontal lifelines or inertia reels. Any attachment point must be capable of withstanding the impact load in the event of a fall. Consider how to recover anyone who does fall.
- Anyone who needs to attach themselves should be able to do so from a safe position. They need to be able to attach themselves before they move into a position where they are relying on the protection provided by the harness.
- To ensure that there is an adequate fall height to allow the system to operate and arrest the fall.

- A twin lanyard may be necessary in some cases where the wearer needs to move about. A twin lanyard allows the wearer to clip on one lanyard in a different position before unclipping the other lanyard.
- Installation of equipment to which harnesses will be fixed, e.g. a suitable anchor, must be inspected regularly.
- Everyone who uses a harness must be instructed in how to check, wear and adjust it before use and how to connect themselves to the structure or safety line as appropriate.
- They should be thoroughly examined at intervals of no more than every six months.

SAFETY NETS

Safety nets are used in a variety of applications where other forms of protection are reasonably practicable - such as steel erecting and roof work where site personnel are at risk of falling through fragile roofs onto solid surfaces or structures (steel work) below. Safety nets will arrest the fall of an individual preventing an impact that may cause injury or death. Safety nets must be installed beneath the work area, as a minimum, and consideration should be given to an extension of the protection to allow for people working outside the planned area. Safety nets are only to be installed under supervision by competent installers and are to be inspected weekly and checked daily. It should be remembered that nets are also used to collect debris that may fall. This may be rigged to take a lesser weight than that for protection of people. It is important to identify which type of net is in use in a workplace as reliance on the wrong type may have fatal consequences.

Figure 8-35: Safety nets.   *Source: ACT.*

AIRBAGS

Airbags are shock absorption devices that can be employed to protect against the effects of falls from a height. They are made of a toughened nylon or similar man-made material and are usually inflated using a powered fan device. They are designed so that should a person fall onto one, a volume of air is forced out of the bag creating a cushioning effect that does not bounce or deflect the person in another direction. This equipment must be matched to correspond to the fall height and as such must only be put into use by a competent person.

8.3 - Roofwork

MEANS OF ACCESS

This is usually by ladder. A ladder should extend at least 1.05 metres above the edge of the roof, and it should be securely lashed in position, preferably with wire bond or a safety tie.

EDGE AND LEADING EDGE PROTECTION

Guard rails and toe boards or suitable barriers erected at the edge or eaves level of a roof are usually needed to stop people and materials from falling off.

See also the section - leading edge protection – earlier in this unit - 8.2.

CRAWLING BOARDS

On any fragile or angled roof (greater than 30^0) or on any roof which is considered hazardous because of its condition or because of the weather, suitable crawling boards must be used. They must be correctly positioned and secure. If it is obvious that the job requires a progression along the roof, extra crawling boards must be provided and no fewer than two such boards shall be taken on any job.

Figure 8-36: Edge protection and boards   *Source: ACT.*

FALL ARREST EQUIPMENT

See also the section - Harnesses – earlier in this unit - 8.2.

8.4 - Protection of others

DEMARCATION

When working at a height is being carried out it is important to protect others from the hazards of items or objects falling onto them. A simple way of doing this is to identify hazardous zones with hazard tape and barriers. Inform those that may be affected by the work that is being undertaken and warn of the possible dangers that may arise within the demarcated area.

Clear demarcation of areas where construction work is being undertaken and where it is not will assist those not involved in the work to keep out of the area and avoid exposure to hazards. The area should be demarcated at a distance that relates to the hazards, such as materials or tools falling. A safety margin should always be built into the demarcation to ensure risks are controlled.

BARRIERS

Barriers are a physical means of preventing access to an area that is required to be restricted. As such they are particularly appropriate if people, such as the public, might stray past an area marked only with hazard tape. These can be situated at a proximity that is relative to the hazards associated with the work being carried out. If necessary to ensure a demarcation zone the barriers may be 2 metre high fencing.

'TUNNELS'

Tunnels can be used to 'isolate' others from any surrounding hazards by enclosing an area (i.e. walkway) and thus preventing any contact with likely hazards until through the danger area. An example of this could be the ground level of a scaffold on a shop front in a busy high street, being enclosed to form a tunnel that allows the public to pass through the works safely whilst allowing the work to continue above.

Figure 8-37: Nets / sheeting.   *Source: ACT.*

Figure 8-38: Marking.   *Source: ACT.*

SIGNS

Safety signs are used to provide people with information relating to the works being carried out, to control or divert people and most importantly of any dangers or hazards. Signs may be situated at a location in advance of the work area to give prior warning in addition to the works perimeter and actual work location.

MARKING

Where equipment used to gain access to a height may be collided with it should carry hazard marking. For example, the standards of a scaffold at ground level on a street may be marked with hazard tape. ***See also the sections - Demarcation and Signs - above in this unit.***

LIGHTING

Suitable and adequate lighting should be provided to allow the works being carried out and any possible hazards to be seen clearly in advance and allow people to take the required actions to avoid interference with the site. Scaffolds located near roads may be fitted with lighting to warn traffic of its presence. MEWPs and similar equipment used in poor lighting conditions on or near roads and walkways must use standard vehicle lighting.

SHEETING

Sheeting can protect others by preventing dust, materials or tools being ejected from working at height. ***See also "sheeting" in the section - Ensuring Stability - earlier in this unit.***

HEAD PROTECTION

Head protection, such as hard hats, provide the user with limited protection from objects falling from a height. Hard hats are made from toughened plastic and have an approximate life of 3 years. There is a need and legal duty to wear head protection where there is a risk of injury from falling materials; typically this includes working around people working at a height.

8.5 - Working over water

PREVENTION OF DROWNING

The CHSW Regulations state that "if there is a risk of persons falling into water and drowning, suitable steps should be taken to prevent a person from falling, and to ensure that suitable rescue equipment is provided". This means that prior to work above water being undertaken, a full risk assessment must be made that takes into account the conditions of the water being worked over or near (tidal, depth, temperature, fast flowing) and suitable control measures identified and implemented including emergency rescue plans and procedures.

Where possible and practicable, a scaffold system is the best method of safe working over water. These must be erected and inspected by competent persons with inspections required weekly. Workers who are required to work near to or over water are required to be properly trained with a provision made so that any person who does fall into water is able to float - **see also the section - Buoyancy Aids - below in this unit** and be recovered as quickly as possible. Additional means of preventing fall into water may include, floating stages, safety nets, safety harnesses and barriers.

BUOYANCY AIDS

Buoyancy aids must be provided and their use enforced when working on or near water. However, a distinction between buoyancy aids and life jackets needs to be noted. Both lifejackets and buoyancy aids are designed to keep the wearer afloat with the main difference that a buoyancy aid will provide sufficient buoyancy to keep a conscious person afloat in a reasonable flotation position. A lifejacket will support an unconscious person in a face upright flotation position, therefore reducing the likelihood of the wearer drowning.

Buoyancy aids and lifejackets can be used with safety harnesses so long as the items do not interfere with each other and reduce effectiveness. It is possible to obtain a combined piece of equipment. All staff that are required to use this equipment must be properly trained in its use and be fully aware of its functions and limitations.

Management systems must be in place that considers the use, inspection and storage of lifejackets and buoyancy aids.

The majority of drowning occurs close to the bank or waters edge, and this should be taken into account at the planning stage. Other methods of equipment available to assist someone to remain afloat are life buoys or rescue lines. Life buoys are normally attached to approximately 30 metres of lifeline but can only be thrown a short distance of 6 - 8 metres. Rescue lines are available in various forms with life lines ranging from 25 to 40 metres in length. Rescue lines work by throwing a bag or capsule to the person in the water and the line deploying as the bag / capsule goes further out. The line, bag and capsule all stay afloat and allow the person in the water to grab the line and be pulled to safety. Care must be taken that the person deploying the line is secure at the bank and unable to be pulled into the water.

In fast flowing channels that have no water borne traffic, then 'safety nets' or 'safety lines' may be stretched across the width of the channel to allow the person in the water to hang on and wait for rescue. This is only effective if the person in the water remains conscious.

SAFETY BOATS

Where works are being carried out on fast flowing, or tidal waters then a rescue boat should be made available. Requirements state that it must have a reliable engine, carry oars, and the person that is operating the boat must be competent and experienced at handling small boats on flowing water. It must be fitted with grab lines for persons who have fallen into the water and if any work is carried out in the hours of darkness, then the boat will be required to be fitted with high efficiency lighting. It may be a requirement to have two-way radio installed on the boat for communication between boat and shore.

This page is intentionally blank

This page is intentionally blank

Excavation work & confined spaces - hazards & control

Overall Aims

On completion of this Unit, candidates will understand:

- the hazards presented by excavation work and the precautions necessary to minimise risks.
- the hazards presented by work in confined spaces and the precautions necessary to minimise risks.

Content

Specific Intended Learning Outcome

The intended learning outcomes of this Unit are that candidates will be able to:

9.1   identify the hazards of excavation and describe the precautions that may be necessary to control them

9.2   recognise a confined space and describe the risks and precaution associated with confined space working

Sources of Reference

Essentials of Health and Safety at Work, HSE Books

Health and Safety in Excavations: Be Safe and Shore (HSG185), HSE Books

Avoiding Danger from Underground Services (HSG47), HSE Books

Safe Work in Confined Spaces (ACOP) (L101), HSE Books

A Guide to the Construction (Head Protection) Regulations (L102), HSE Books

Protecting the Public: Your Next Move (HSG151), HSE Books

Relevant Statutory Provisions

The Construction (Health, Safety and Welfare) Regulations (CHSW) 1996

The Confined Spaces Regulations (CSR) 1997

The Construction (Head Protection) Regulations (CHPR) 1989

The Personal Protective Equipment at Work Regulations (PUWER) 1992

9.1 - Excavations

The hazards of work in and around excavations

Work in excavations and trenches, basements, underground tanks, sewers, manholes etc., can involve high risks and each year construction workers are killed with some buried alive or asphyxiated.

Figure 9-1: Buried services.   *Source: ACT.*

Figure 9-2: Excavation hazards.   *Source: ACT.*

BURIED SERVICES

Although electricity cables provide the most obvious risk, gas pipes, water mains, drains and sewers can all release dangerous substances. Gas is particularly dangerous if there is a potential ignition source close by. Fibre-optic cables may not produce a health and safety risk but are very expensive to repair.

Buried services (electricity, gas, water, etc) are not obvious upon site survey and so the likelihood of striking a service when excavating, drilling or piling is increased. The results of striking an underground service are varied, and the potential to cause injury or fatality is high. As with overhead power lines, any underground service should be treated as live until confirmed dead by an authority. Incidents can include shock, electrocution, explosion and burns from power cables, explosion, burns or unconsciousness from gas or power cables, impact injury from dislodged stones or flooding from ruptured water mains.

FALLS OF PERSONS/EQUIPMENT/MATERIAL INTO THE EXCAVATION

When people are working below ground in excavations, the problems are very similar to those faced when people are working at a height - falls and falling objects. Particular problems arise when:

- Materials, including spoil, are stored too close to the edge of the excavation.
- The excavation is close to another building and the foundations may be undermined.
- The edge of the excavation is not clear, especially if the excavation is in a public area.
- Absence of barriers or lighting.
- Poor positioning or the absence of access ladders allowing people to fall.
- Absence of organized crossing points.
- Badly constructed ramps for vehicle access which can cause the vehicle to topple.
- No stop blocks for back filling.
- Routing of vehicles too close to the excavation.

COLLAPSE OF SIDES

Often, the soil and earth that make up the sides of the excavation cannot be relied upon to support their own weight, leading to the possibility of collapse. The risk can be made worse if:

- The soil structure is loose or made unstable by water logging.
- Heavy plant or materials are too close to the edge of the excavation.
- Machinery or vehicles cause vibration.
- There is inadequate support for the sides.

The consequences of even a minor collapse can be very serious. A minor fall of earth can happen at high speed and bring with it anything (plant and machinery) that may be at the edge. Even if the arms and head of a person are not trapped in the soil, the material pressing on the person can lead to severe crush injuries to the lower body and asphyxiation due to restriction of movement of the chest.

COLLAPSE OF ADJACENT STRUCTURES

Excavations that are carried out within close proximity to existing buildings or structures may result in their foundations becoming undermined and create the potential for significant settling damage to occur or worse still, collapse. Consideration should be given to the effects that excavation work might have on foundations of neighbouring buildings or structures, and control measures implemented to ensure that foundations are not disturbed or undermined. Building foundations that are at a distance of less than twice the excavation depth from the face of the excavation are more likely to be affected by ground movement; underpinning or shoring of such structures may be required to prevent structural damage.

WATER INGRESS

Unless a major watercourse is breached, leading to a massive ingress of water, drowning is not likely to be an issue. However, heavy rainfall, breaking into drains and digging below the natural water table can all lead to flooding. In deep excavations, where access is not readily available, the combined effect of water and mud could lead to difficulty in escape and risk of drowning. In addition, this can lead to the sides of the trench becoming soft and the integrity of the supports can be undermined.

CONTAMINATED GROUND

Digging may uncover buried materials that have the potential to be hazardous to health. The history of the site should be examined to try to identify if substances have been buried on the site during its previous use. Sites that once were used as steel works may contain arsenic and cyanide dating back many years; farmyards may have been used as graves for animals and to dispose of pesticides and organo-phosphates. There is always the presence of vermin to consider - this can increase the risk of diseases such as leptospirosis.

TOXIC AND ASPHYXIATING ATMOSPHERES

Excavations can under different circumstances be subject to toxic, asphyxiating or explosive atmospheres. Chalk or limestone deposits when in contact with acidic groundwater can release carbon dioxide, and gases such as methane or hydrogen sulphide can seep into excavations from contaminated ground or damaged services in built-up areas. These atmospheres can accumulate at the bottom of an excavation and result in asphyxiation, poisoning, explosion or potential fatalities.

Excavations should be treated with similar caution to that applied to confined spaces, and an assessment should be carried out prior to work commencing in excavations to identify the risk of toxic gas, oxygen deficiency, and fire or explosion.

It should also identify the appropriate risk control measures required, such as:

- Type of gas monitoring equipment to be provided.
- Testing of the atmosphere before entry into the excavation.
- Provision of suitable ventilation equipment.
- Training of employees.
- Use of a sufficient number of people, including one at ground level.
- Procedures and equipment needed for an emergency rescue.

Figure 9-3: Water in excavation.   Source: ACT.

MECHANICAL HAZARDS

Large pieces of mobile plant and equipment that are commonly used on construction sites have the potential to cause serious harm to site workers and members of the public. To keep people and vehicles apart, the following need to be considered:

- Exclusion zones identified by barriers.
- Warning signs and lights.

- Excavator cabs should have good visibility.
- Operators properly trained and close supervision provided.

Risk assessment

FACTORS TO CONSIDER

The type of soil being excavated

Clay presents specific risks of collapse due to it drying out or becoming more fluid when wet. If the soil is not compacted, for example because of a previous excavation near by, its strength may not be as higher as if it has had chance to settle and become compacted. Soil changes its strength significantly when it becomes wet also there is an added risk that water may make its way into the excavation and cause flooding. If the soil is chalky carbon dioxide may be liberated as part of the excavation process, similarly if it is in contaminated land there may be toxic substances and risks from methane.

The depth of the excavation

Risks increase with the depth of excavation, risks from materials falling increase with the height they may fall and there is an increased risk of collapse at greater depths as the amount of material to support (comprising the excavation wall) increases. A collapse of an excavation deeper than the head height of a worker carries a high risk of suffocation. It should be remembered that a worker may have to work low down in an excavation so a shallow excavation can present serious risks, depending on the work being carried out in it.

The type of work being undertaken

If the work to be done to create and work in the excavation is to be done manually or mechanical the risks vary significantly. The task being conducted can increase the risks, for example pipe jointing operations carried out manually will usually bring the head of the worker below the top of the excavation for a significant time. Additional risks may also be created by hot working or work in a confined space.

The use of mechanical equipment

Though this can reduce the risk to workers by not requiring them to enter the excavation to dig it they carry risks of their own. Where people work alongside this equipment there is a risk of contact or collision and as it carries a considerable amount of momentum major injuries or death would not be uncommon if contact was made.

Services

The presence or likelihood of services in the area of an excavation carries high risks of a different type. For example contact with an electrical service may be immediately fatal to a worker or damage to a gas service may cause a risk of major explosion.

Material and vehicles

If materials are placed too close to excavations or vehicles pass near by there is an increased risk of collapse or fall of materials/vehicle.

Required support equipment that may be needed

The risks from excavations may be reduced by using the correct support equipment. Care has to be taken to ensure that the right type and quantity is used if the risk is to be reduced effectively. For example there may be a need to provide close shoring of the sides of an excavation to control a particular soil condition or where the effects of water are likely.

Precautions

"All practicable steps should be taken, where necessary, to prevent danger to any person to ensure that any excavation (or part thereof) which may be in a temporary state of weakness or instability due to the carrying out of other construction work does not collapse accidentally. Suitable and sufficient steps shall be taken to prevent, so far as is reasonably practicable, any person from being trapped by a fall or dislodgement of any material."

Regulation 12 of the CHSW

IDENTIFICATION AND MARKING OF BURIED SERVICES

Excavation operations should not begin until all available service location drawings have been identified and thoroughly examined. Record plans and location drawings should not be considered as totally accurate but serve only as an indication of the likelihood of the presence of services, their location and depth. It is possible for the position of an electricity supply cable to alter if previous works have been carried out in the location due to the flexibility of the cable and movement of surrounding features since original installation of the cable. In addition, plans often show a proposed position for the services that does not translate to the ground, such that services are placed in position only approximately where the plan says.

It is important that 'service location devices' such as a cable avoidance tool (CAT) are used by competent, trained operatives to assist in the identification and marking of the actual location and position of buried services. When identified it is essential that physical markings be placed on the ground to show where these services are location.

Figure 9-4: Marking of services.   *Source: ACT.*

SAFE DIGGING METHODS

Safe digging methods should be implemented within 0.5 metres of a buried service. This involves the use of insulated hand tools such as a spade or shovel with curved edges (to be used with light force and not sudden blows). Mechanical, probing or piercing tools and equipment such as excavator's, forks, picks or drills should NOT be used when in the vicinity of buried services, as these may cause damage to any service if they strike it. Careful hand digging using a spade or shovel should be used instead.

METHODS OF SUPPORTING EXCAVATIONS

"Where it is necessary to prevent danger to anybody from falls or dislodgement of materials from the side or roof of an excavation, that excavation shall as early as practicable in the course of work be sufficiently supported so as to prevent, so far as is reasonably practicable, the fall or dislodgement of materials. Suitable and sufficient equipment for supporting an excavation shall be provided to ensure the foregoing".

Regulation 12 of the CHSW

Precautions must be taken to prevent collapse. The methods of supporting (shoring) the sides of excavations vary widely in design depending on:

- The nature of the subsoil - for example wet may require close shoring with sheets.
- Projected life of the excavation - a trench box may give ready made access where it is only needed for short duration.
- Work to be undertaken, including equipment used - for example the use of a trench box for shoring where pipe joints are made.
- The possibility of flooding from ground water and heavy rain - close shoring would be required.
- The depth of the excavation - a shallow excavation may use battering instead of shoring, particularly where shoring may impede access.
- The number of people using the excavation at any one time - a lot of space may be required so cantilever sheet piling may be preferred.

In order to ensure satisfactory support for excavations:

- Prevent collapse by battering the sides to a safe angle or supporting them with sheeting or proprietary support systems.
- Use experienced people for the erection and dismantling of timbering and other supports.
- Adequate material must be used to prevent danger from falls or falling objects.

EXAMPLE OF A PERMIT TO DIG

PERMIT TO DIG

Contract: .... Contract No: ....

Principal Contractor: .... Sub Contractor: ....

Permit No: .... Date: ....

1. Location: ....

2. Size, detail and depth of excavation: ....

    ....

3. Are Service Plans on site ?   YES / NO

    Comments: ....

4. Has cable locating equipment been used to identify services ?   YES / NO

    Comments: ....

5. Are all known services marked out ? (site inspection by relevant statutory bodies)   YES / NO

    Comments: ....

6. Are trial holes required ?   YES / NO

    Comments: ....

7. Have precautions been taken to prevent contact if overhead lines are in the vicinity of the
    operation or near approach to the operation?   YES / NO

8. Additional precautions, i.e. Shoring/Fencing/Access/Storage/Fumes/Record of setting out
    points to re-establish services routes

    Comments: ....

9. Sketch details or attach copy of plans

10. Date and time of excavation: ....

    Signed: .... Accepted by: ....
    For and on behalf of issuing party   (Work shall not commence unless all persons involved
                                              are aware of the safe systems of work)

    A new permit will be required for any further excavations. This permit is for guidance only.
    Persons carrying out work must take reasonable precautions when working around services.

Figure 9-5: Permit to dig.   *Source: Reproduced by kind permission of Lincsafe.*

Figure 9-6: Battering.   *Source: ACT.*

Figure 9-7: Trench box - for shoring.   *Source: ACT.*

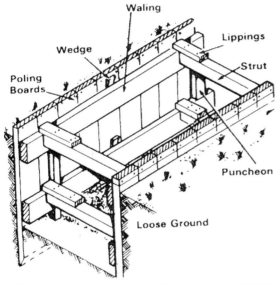

Figure 9-8: Close boarded excavation.   *Source: BS6031.*

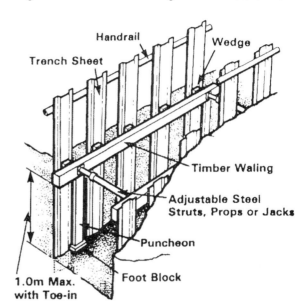

Figure 9-9: Open sheeting.   *Source: BS6031.*

Figure 9-10: Close sheeting.   *Source: ACT.*

Figure 9-11: Open sheeting.   *Source: ACT.*

MEANS OF ACCESS

Ladders are the usual means of access and egress to excavations. They must be properly secured, in good condition and inspected regularly. The ladder should extend about one metre or three rungs above ground level to give a good handhold. To allow for emergency egress, CHSW Regulations Approved Code of Practice (ACOP) recommends a minimum requirement of one ladder every 15 metres.

CROSSING POINTS

Crossing excavations should only be allowed at predetermined points. The crossing point should be able to withstand the maximum foreseeable load and be provided with guard rails and toe boards. The spacing or location of crossing points should be such that workers and others are encouraged to use them, rather than to attempt other means of crossing the excavation.

BARRIERS, LIGHTING AND SIGNS

Where people or materials can fall a distance of more than two metres, edge protection must be provided. It is also sensible to cover shallow trenches when they are left unattended. Guardrails must meet the same standards as those provided for working platforms. Concrete or wooden blocks (usually old railway sleepers) are placed some distance from the edge to prevent vehicles from getting too close, particularly when the excavation is being 'back filled', where they provide a stop block.

Signs that comply with The Health and Safety (Signs and Signals) Regulations (SSSR) 1996 should be displayed to warn people of the excavation and any special measures to be taken. If working on a public highway, the police or the local authority must be consulted over the positioning of traffic lights. Appropriate lighting should be provided; it must provide sufficient illumination for those at work but should not create glare or other distractions for passers by, especially motorists. Battery operated headlamps (to avoid trailing cables) may be considered for individual use. If excavations are present in dark conditions they must be suitably lit to prevent vehicles or people colliding or falling into them.

SAFE STORAGE OF SPOIL

Excavated material (spoil), materials, plant and vehicles should never be stored or parked close to the sides of any excavation. The additional pressure distributed on the ground from spoil, vehicles, etc significantly increases the likelihood of collapse occurring at the sides of the excavation. Though it will depend on the weight of the material it would normally be kept a minimum of 1 metre from the edge of the excavation. In addition, spoil heaps consist of loose materials that have the risk of spilling into the excavation. A means of preventing spillage of spoil into an excavation is by positioning scaffold boards as toe boards, fixed along the outside of trench sheets. This provides additional protection to combat the risk of loose materials spilling into the excavation. An alternative to this is to allow boards or sheeting to protrude above the top of the excavation sufficient to act as toe boards and prevent materials falling.

Unless sufficient control is implemented, workers can suffer injury from spoil or stored materials falling from ground level into an excavation. Head protection must be worn and this will provide protection for those working in the excavation from small pieces of materials falling either from above or from the sides of the excavation. If stored at a suitable distance away from an excavation and at a suitable height, spoil heaps can form an effective barrier against vehicles travelling around the construction site and assist in preventing falls of vehicles and plant into an excavation and onto workers.

Figure 9-12: Materials storage.   *Source: ACT.*

Figure 9-13: Preventing water ingress.   *Source: ACT.*

DE-WATERING

Ingress of water may occur through rainfall, flood (river, sea) or when an excavation continues below the natural groundwater level. Consideration must be given to the likelihood of water entering the excavation and the measures to be implemented in order to control water entering the excavation and water levels between it. Usually water is abstracted from excavations and pumped to sumps for settlement from where it can be pumped out for disposal. When an excavation is liable to water ingress the stability of walls can be undermined; this will influence the choice of shoring, for example, close shoring rather than open learning.

It is permissible to distribute pumped groundwater from within an excavation over grassy areas where any silt deposits can be absorbed and not have a detrimental effect on the environment. However, when works are within close proximity to a watercourse, within 10 metres, then advice should be sought on the disposal of groundwater and a 'Consent for Works Affecting Watercourses' should be obtained from the Environment Agency.

POSITIONING AND ROUTEING OF VEHICLES, PLANT AND EQUIPMENT

To prevent objects falling into excavations, the following precautions should be taken:

- Spoil and building materials must not be stacked near to the edge.
- The weight of stacks should not be enough to cause the sides to collapse.
- Designated operating areas for vehicles and machinery must be routed away from the excavation.
- Where vehicles have to approach, stop blocks must be provided to prevent overrunning.

PERSONAL PROTECTIVE EQUIPMENT

As well as the need for hard hats to limit the risks from falling materials, other personal protective equipment (PPE) may be necessary, such as:

- Breathing apparatus.
- Safety harnesses.
- Hearing protection.
- Clothing to protect from the rays of the sun.

- Masks and respirators.
- Face masks and gloves for welding and grinding.
- Footwear.

Particular requirements for contaminated ground

Contaminated ground can give rise to various health hazards. Exposure methods can vary and assessments should be made to determine which controls are required. Examples may include the following requirements.

SOIL TESTING

Surveys should be undertaken, and a soil-testing programme implemented prior to works beginning. As each site is different and may involve various contaminant types, the methods of testing and analysis used should be suitable to the particular local needs of each site.

Usually, specialist contractors are used to carry out this type of work. Historical information such as land deeds, maps, building plans and any other information relating to the site provide useful assistance. Contaminants will usually be found in the top 0.5 - 1m layer (strata) of ground and soil samples should be at least to the greatest depth of any excavation, remembering that contamination may seep from one part of a site to another. As a minimum precaution, any proposed control measures chosen should adequately protect against the highest concentrations of contaminant found on site.

WELFARE FACILITIES

Ensuring good hygiene standards is one of the more important elements of protective measures to be taken when working on construction sites and in particular with contaminated ground. Whilst the level of risk that is identified will establish the range of measures that are to be provided, the principles outlined should always be followed when working on a contaminated site.

Installation of a sufficiently ventilated and lit hygiene facility must be provided. This may be purpose built or a smaller standard unit may be sufficient depending upon the number of personnel involved at the site. The installation of the hygiene unit should be situated at the most convenient point to or from the dirty zone.

The hygiene facility should generally be in three stages but prior to entering the unit, a boot wash point should be provided that includes running water and fixed or hand brushes for removing contaminated matter. The hygiene facility should then be arranged in its three stages as follows:

Stage 1 Should provide storage for ordinary clothing not used whilst at work.

Stage 2 A high standard washing facility. This includes hot and cold water with taps preferably operated by the elbow foot, detergent, nail brushes and disposable towels. In certain circumstances (toxic or corrosive contamination) showers may be the necessary means of cleansing. Both men and women may use showers (at separate times) provided that it is in a separate room with a lock on the inside of the door.

Stage 3 Should provide storage for contaminated work wear such as overalls, boots, etc.

In addition to the hygiene facility, toilets should be provided. The location of toilet units on contaminated sites must be situated so workers are directed through the hygiene facility prior to reaching the toilet for use. Daily cleaning and decontamination must be carried out on toilet facilities. Everyone who works on construction sites must have access to adequate toilet and washing facilities, a place for warming up and eating their food and somewhere for storing clothing.

HEALTH SURVEILLANCE

The employer should decide about the need for health surveillance as part of the Control of Substances Hazardous to Health Regulations (COSHH) 2002 assessment. Health surveillance is appropriate where a disease or adverse effect may be related to exposure; and It is likely that this could arise in the circumstances of the work; and there are valid techniques for detecting the disease or effect. For example, work with cadmium, phenol, or arsenic, will normally need health surveillance including biological monitoring of workers.

Inspection requirements for excavation support

The CHSW Regulations require inspections and reports to be carried out for excavations. The schedule to the CHSW Regulations. specifies the frequency and circumstances for inspection of an excavation.

A competent person must inspect excavations:

- At the start of each shift before work begins.
- After any event likely to have affected the strength or stability of the excavation.
- After any accidental fall of rock, earth or other material.

The competent person must:

- Complete the inspection report before the end of the working period.
- Provide the report or a copy to the person for whom the inspection was carried out within 24 hours.
- A copy of the reports must be kept on site until the work is complete. Reports should then be kept for three months at an office of the person for whom the inspections were carried out.

Where the person carrying out the inspection is not satisfied that it is safe to work in the excavation they must inform the person who they are doing the inspection for and work must not continue until the matters identified by the inspection have been remedied.

The inspection record must include the following information:

- Name and address of person on whose behalf the inspection was carried out.
- Location of the workplace inspected.
- Description of workplace or part of workplace inspected (including any plant and equipment and materials, if any).
- Date and time of inspection.
- Details of any matter identified that could lead to a risk to the health and safety of anyone.
- Details of any action taken as a result of any matter identified in the last point.
- Details of any more action considered necessary.
- The name and position of the person making the report.

9.2 - Confined spaces

A failure to appreciate the dangers associated with confined spaces has led not only to the deaths of many workers, but also to the demise of some of those who have attempted to rescue them. *See also - Principles of control - Unit 6.*

DEFINITION

A confined space is a space which is substantially enclosed and where there will be a reasonably foreseeable risk of serious injury from substances or conditions. This therefore means not only a space which is small and difficult to enter, exit or work in but one with limited or restricted access; or it can also be a space which is badly ventilated e.g. a tank or a large tunnel.

TYPICAL CONFINED SPACES FOUND IN CONSTRUCTION WORK

The Confined Spaces Regulations (CSR) 1997 defines a confined space as any place, including:

Chamber   e.g. cellar, tunnel, chamber for a pump, oven or similar space in process machinery.

Tank   e.g. storage tanks or solid or liquid chemical.

Vat   e.g. process vessel which may be open, but by its depth confines a person.

Silo   e.g. may be an above the ground structure for storing cereal, crops.

Pit   e.g. excavations or trenches.

Pipe   e.g. concrete, plastic steel etc, fabrication used to carry liquids or gases.

Sewer   e.g. brick or concrete structure for the carrying of liquid waste.

Flue   e.g. exhaust chimney for disposal of waste gases.

Well   e.g. deep source of water.

Or other similar space, in which, by virtue of its enclosed nature, there is a foreseeable risk of a 'specified occurrence'.

Figure 9-14: Confined space - chamber.   *Source: ACT.*

Figure 9-15: Confined space - sewer.   *Source: ACT.*

A "specified occurrence" is defined as:

- Fire or explosion.
- Loss of consciousness or asphyxiation of any person at work arising from gas, fumes, vapour or lack of oxygen.
- Drowning of any person at work.
- Asphyxiation of any person at work arising from a free flowing solid.
- Loss of consciousness of any person arising from a high ambient temperature.

Figure 9-16: Confined space - closed tank.   *Source: ACT.*

Figure 9-17: Confined space - open tank.   *Source: ACT.*

Hazards associated with confined spaces

EXPOSURE TO TOXIC, EXPLOSIVE AND OXYGEN DEFICIENT ATMOSPHERES

Air in the confined space is made unbreathable either by toxic gases, fumes or by lack of oxygen. There is not enough natural ventilation to keep the air fit to breathe. In some cases the gases may be flammable, so there may also be a fire or explosion risk.

Some confined spaces are naturally dangerous, for example, because of:

- Gas build-up in sewers and manholes and pits connected to them.
- Gases leaking into trenches and pits in contaminated land such as old refuse tips and old gas works.
- Rust inside tanks and vessels which eats up the oxygen.
- Liquids and slurries which can suddenly fill the space or release gases into it when disturbed.
- Chemical reaction between some soils and air causing oxygen depletion or the action of ground water on chalk and limestone producing carbon dioxide.

Some places are made dangerous by vapours from the work done in them. Where possible, it is important to keep hazards out of confined spaces, for example, do not use petrol or diesel engines in or near to confined spaces, because exhaust gases can cause asphyxiation. Because paints and glues used in construction work processes may give off hazardous vapours it is essential to ensure the confined space has enough ventilation to make the air fit to breathe; mechanical ventilation might be needed.

HEAT

Confined spaces have limited natural ventilation and depending on the tasks being undertaken within the area may become hot and uncomfortable to work in. In extreme cases this may cause heat exhaustion which may lead to loss of consciousness. It may be necessary to implement a forced ventilation system to refresh and cool the air within the confined space.

WATER

Many confined spaces do not allow for ease of exit. If a large volume of water were to enter a confined space the consequences could be the drowning of workers due to the restrictions on space preventing rapid exit.

FREE-FLOWING SOLIDS

The term "free flowing solid" means any substance consisting of solid particles and which is of, or is capable of being in, a flowing or running consistency. This includes flour, grain, sugar, sand or other similar material. These materials are usually stored in silos (enclosed tank) that are classed as a confined space. Asphyxiation can result as a consequence of falling into a free flowing solid such as grain, due to sinking into the material as it becomes displaced as weight is applied. Because the material can appear firm, possibly because a crust of material has formed, someone may be tempted to access and walk on the crust in order to dislodge it. It is common for such a crust to break up without warning causing the person to fall into the free-flowing solid.

RESTRICTED SPACE

Working space may be restricted, bringing workers into close contact with other hazards such as moving machinery, electricity or steam vents and pipes. The entrance to a confined space, for example a small access hole, may make escape or rescue in an emergency more difficult.

Precautions for safe entry

AVOIDANCE WHERE POSSIBLE

Employers have a duty to prevent employees, or others who are to any extent within the employer's control, such as contractors, from entering or working inside a confined space where it is reasonably practicable to undertake the work without entering the space. Similarly, the self-employed should not enter or work inside a confined space where it is reasonably practicable to undertake the work without entering it.

In every situation, the employer or the self-employed must consider what measures can be taken to enable the work to be carried out without the need to enter the confined space. The measures might involve modifying the confined space itself to avoid the need for entry, or to enable the work to be undertaken from outside the space. In many cases it will involve modifying working practices.

The following are examples of modified working practices avoiding the need for entry:

- It is usually possible to test the atmosphere or sample the contents of confined spaces from outside.
- Using appropriate long tools and probes to do work.
- In some cases you can clean a confined space, or remove residues from it, from the outside using water jetting, steam or chemical cleaning, long-handled tools, or in-place cleaning systems.
- Blockages can be cleared in silos where grain or other flowing solids can 'bridge' or where voids can form by the use of remotely-operated rotating flail devices, vibrators and air purgers which avoid the need to enter the space.
- In some cases it is possible to see what is happening inside without going in by looking in through a porthole, sight glass, grille or hole. If a sight glass tends to become blocked, it can be cleaned with a wiper and washer. Lighting can be provided inside or by shining in through a window. The use of closed circuit television (CCTV) systems may be appropriate in some cases.

RISK ASSESSMENT AND PLANNING

There should be a safe system of work for operations inside confined spaces, and everyone should know and follow the system. A permit-to-work system may be required.

If entry is essential:

- Identify what work must be done in the confined space and the hazards involved.
- Consider if the space could be altered to make it permanently safe or if the work could be changed to make entry to the dangerous area unnecessary.
- Make sure workers have been trained in the dangers and precautions, including rescue procedures.

- Make sure the entrance to the space is big enough to allow workers wearing all the necessary equipment to climb in and out easily.
- Before entry, ventilate the space as much as possible, test the air inside the space and only enter if the test shows it is safe.
- After entry, continue to test the air for toxic substances, flammable gases and oxygen deficiency as necessary.
- If there is a flammable risk, the space must be ventilated until it is safe. When selecting equipment, remember heat or sparks from electrical or other equipment could ignite flammable vapours, so air-powered tools may be required. The risk from flammable vapours is very high when work is carried out on the tanks of petrol service stations and similar sites. This is work which may be safer left to a specialist contractor.
- Disturbing deposits and slurries in pipes and tanks may produce extra vapour, resulting in a greater risk, so clear deposits before entry where possible.
- If the air inside the space cannot be made fit to breath because of the presence of a toxic risk or lack of oxygen, workers must wear breathing apparatus.
- Never try to 'sweeten' the air in a confined space with oxygen as this can produce a fire and explosion risk.
- Workers inside the confined space should wear rescue harnesses, with lifelines attached, which run back to a point outside the confined spaces.
- Someone should be outside to keep watch and to communicate with anyone inside, raise the alarm in an emergency and take charge of rescue procedures if it becomes necessary. It is essential those outside the space know what to do in an emergency. They need to know how to use breathing apparatus if they are to affect a rescue. *See also - Emergency Arrangements - later in this unit.*

PERMIT TO WORK PROCEDURES AND REQUIREMENTS

A permit-to-work system is a formal written system and is usually required where there is a reasonably foreseeable risk of serious injury in entering or working in the confined space. The permit-to-work procedure is an extension of the safe system to work, not a replacement for it. The use of a permit-to-work system does not, by itself, make the job safe. It supports the safe system, providing a ready means of recording findings and authorisations required to proceed with the entry. It also contains information, for example, time limits on entry, results of the gas testing, and other information that may be required during an emergency and which, when the job is completed, can also provide historical information on original entry conditions. A permit-to-work system is appropriate, for example:

- To ensure that the people working in the confined space are aware of the hazards involved and the identity, nature and extent of the work to be carried out.
- To ensure there is a formal check undertaken confirming elements of a safe system of work are in place. This needs to take place before people are allowed to enter or work in the confined space.
- Where there is a need to coordinate or exclude, using controlled and formal procedures, other people and their activities where they could affect work or conditions in the confined space.
- If the work requires the authorisation of more than one person, or there is a time-limit on entry. It may also be needed if communications with the outside are other than by direct speech, or if particular respiratory protective and/or personal protective equipment is required.

A permit-to-work should be cancelled once the operations to which it applies have finished.

See also - Principles of control - Unit 6.

TRAINING AND THE USE OF COMPETENT PERSONS

To be competent to work safely in confined spaces, adequate training and experience in the particular work involved is essential. Training standards must be appropriate to the task, and to the individual's roles and responsibilities, so that work can be carried out safely. Where the risk assessment indicates that properly trained individuals can work for periods without supervision, you will need to check that they are competent to follow the established safe system of work and have been provided with adequate information and instruction about the work to be done. It is important that those that issue and work under a permit to work for entry into confined spaces are trained and competent to do so in general and that consideration is given to whether this training is sufficient for a specific confined space being worked in. If necessary, because of special features of the confined space, further training may be required. Anyone providing emergency rescue must be trained and competent to do so.

It is likely that general training will need to cover:

- Awareness of the CSR.
- An understanding of the work to be done, the hazards and the necessary precautions.
- An understanding of safe systems of work and permits to work, where appropriate.
- How emergencies arise and the dangers, prepared emergency arrangements.

Specific training will relate to the type of equipment used and the circumstances of use. Refresher training should be planned and conducted in order to maintain knowledge and skill.

ATMOSPHERIC TESTING

Testing of the atmosphere may be needed where the atmosphere might be contaminated or abnormal. The appropriate choice of testing equipment will depend on particular circumstances. For example, when testing for toxic atmospheres, chemical detector tubes or portable atmospheric monitoring equipment is appropriate. However there may be cases requiring monitoring equipment specifically designed to measure for flammable atmospheres.

Only persons experienced and competent in the practice should carry out testing and records should be kept.

MEANS OF ACCESS

- Openings need to be sufficiently large and free from obstruction to allow the passage of persons wearing the necessary protective clothing and equipment and to allow access and egress for rescue purposes.
- Practice drills will help to check that the size of openings and entry procedures are satisfactory.

■ Where entry to a confined space is necessary, employers will need to ensure that the necessary safety features are provided. For example, alongside openings which allow for safe access these might include a safety sign warning against unauthorised entry and platforms to enable safe working within the confined space.

Figure 9-18: Entrance to a confined space.   *Source: ACT.*

Here a worker wearing full breathing apparatus is also wearing a harness with a lanyard connected to a winch so that he can be hauled to the surface in an emergency without others having to enter the manhole to rescue him.

Figure 9-19: Confined space.   *Source: HSG150, HSE.*

PERSONAL PROTECTIVE EQUIPMENT

So far as is reasonably practicable, it should be ensured that a confined space is safe to work in without the need for personal protective equipment (PPE) and respiratory protective equipment (RPE) which should be a last resort, except for rescue work (including the work of the emergency services). Use of PPE and RPE may be identified as necessary in your risk assessment, in which case it needs to be suitable and should be provided and used by those entering and working in confined spaces. Such equipment is in addition to engineering controls and safe systems of work. The type of PPE provided will depend on the hazards identified but might include safety lines, harnesses and suitable breathing apparatus. Take account of foreseeable hazards that might arise, and the need for emergency evacuation

Wearing respiratory protective equipment and personal protective equipment can contribute to heat stress. In extreme situations cooling air may be required for protective suits.

MONITORING ARRANGEMENTS

The system of work must be monitored to ensure health and safety. This will include checking the permit to work and the practical precautions related to it. It is important that the atmosphere be monitored to ensure it stays breathable; this can be done by using specific sampler equipment or personal sampler equipment. Personal gas detectors should be worn whenever appropriate to take account of the hazard of local pockets of contaminant.

The use of personal communication equipment or a communication line will assist with monitoring the progress of the activities within the confined space and the condition of the workers. This can help decide suitable breaks, the need to stop tasks or the need to instigate emergency rescue.

It is every employers duty to ensure that any personal protective equipment provided to his employees is maintained (including replaced or cleaned as appropriate) in an efficient state, in efficient working order and in good repair. Arrangements should be in place to ensure that any PPE issued for confined spaces working is inspected, maintained and all findings recorded.

EMERGENCY ARRANGEMENTS

The CSR prohibit any person to enter or carry out work in a confined space unless there are suitable and sufficient rescue arrangements in place. Emergency arrangements shall be suitable and sufficient provided they:

■ Require the provision and maintenance of resuscitation equipment.
■ Require the provision and maintenance of such equipment as is necessary to enable the emergency rescue to be carried out effectively.
■ Restrict, so far as is reasonably practicable, the risks to health and safety of any rescuer.
■ Shall immediately be put into operation when circumstances arise requiring a rescue.

The arrangements for emergency rescue will depend on the nature of the confined space, the risks identified and consequently the likely nature of an emergency rescue.

The arrangements might need to cover:

■ Rescue and resuscitation equipment.
■ Special arrangements with local hospitals (e.g. for foreseeable poisoning).
■ Raising the alarm and rescue.
■ Safeguarding the rescuers.
■ Safeguarding the third parties.
■ Fire fighting.
■ Control of plant.
■ First aid.
■ Public emergency services.

This page is intentionally blank

This page is intentionally blank

Demolition Hazards and Control

Overall Aims

On completion of this Unit, candidates will understand:

■ the hazards presented by demolition work.

■ the precautions necessary to control these hazards and to minimise the risks they present.

Content

Specific Intended Learning Outcome

The intended learning outcomes of this Unit are that candidates will be able to:

10.1   identify the main hazards of demolition work

10.2   identify the purpose and scope of a pre-demolition survey

10.3   describe the key requirements of a demolition method statement

10.4   describe the measures necessary to minimise the specific risks posed by demolition

Sources of Reference

British Standard Code of Practice for Demolition (BS 6187), British Standards Institution

A Guide to the Construction (Head Protection) Regulations (L102), HSE Books

Protecting the Public: Your Next Move (HSG151), HSE Books

Relevant Statutory Provisions

The Construction (Health, Safety and Welfare) Regulations (CHSW) 1996

The Construction (Design and Management) Regulations (CDM) 1994

The Provision and Use of Work Equipment Regulations (PUWER) 1998

The Personal Protective Equipment at Work Regulations (PPER) 1992

10.1 - Pre-demolition investigation / survey

The Construction (Design and Management) Regulations (CDM) 1994 apply to all work that involves demolition and dismantling. Before any work begins and usually before the contract is signed, a survey is carried out to ensure that the demolition can go ahead safely and that property surrounding the site is protected from the demolition work as it progresses. It is important to know the previous use of the buildings. They may still contain toxic or flammable materials, biological hazards or even radioactive materials or sources.

TYPE OF STRUCTURE

It is the client's responsibility to ensure that any building to be demolished is adequately surveyed. The survey should clearly identify the type of structure to be worked on. The nature of the building e.g. high rise office blocks, chimneys, old buildings, etc. will have a considerable impact on the method of demolition, the hazards present and the precautions to be taken.

METHOD OF CONSTRUCTION

The method of construction also will have a similar effect. With respect to concrete or brick buildings and structures, it is essential to identify pre-stressed or post-stressed concrete beams.

Figure 10-1: Building structure.   *Source: ACT.*

Figure 10-2: Services and substances.   *Source: ACT.*

STRUCTURAL CONDITION

The structural condition of the building should be surveyed beforehand. The risk of falling during demolition work is greater when the work is of a piecemeal nature, i.e. taking it down one brick at a time. This involves the demolition worker moving about at height on materials that may be rotten and not able to sustain their weight. In this type of operation full scaffolding and other platforms should be provided and the building demolished in the reverse order of erection.

PRESENCE OF CELLARS

Basements, cellars, wells or storage tanks need to be identified. Workers may fall through into these underground areas, while tanks pose a special risk if they have held or still hold toxic or flammable materials.

IDENTIFICATION AND ISOLATION OF SERVICES

Details and location of all the public services must be known and shown on a large-scale plan. Most of these will be buried services: gas pipes, electrical cables, water pipes, sewerage, etc., and could present serious risk if damaged. It is necessary to state which of these will need to be cut off and which will need further protection. It should be made absolutely clear who is responsible for each to be sure that nothing gets overlooked.

Figure 10-3: Hazardous substances.   *Source: Stocksigns.*

Figure 10-4: Proximity of other structures.   *Source: D Hitchen.*

PRESENCE OF HAZARDOUS SUBSTANCES

There may be health hazards present which could affect the demolition worker; e.g. Weil's disease from rats, breathing difficulties from the dust of pigeon droppings or chemicals from the previous building e.g. lead, cadmium and mercury. Another risk is from the exposure to asbestos during stripping operations especially if workers are unaware of its presence and no precautions have been taken. Asbestos fibres get into the lungs and it can take many years (sometimes up to 40 years) before the symptoms of illnesses like mesothelioma (cancer of the membrane lining the lungs) become apparent. The asbestos fibres may also be released into the air and contaminate clothing which may pose an additional risk of harm to other workers and the public in the vicinity. Asbestos may be present in lagging of boilers and pipe work, fire proofing of structures and roofing materials. It is important to obtain details of any survey conducted on the building or structure for consideration before work starts. Special arrangements are required for the removal and disposal of asbestos materials.

PROXIMITY OF OTHER STRUCTURES

When work is to be carried out in close proximity to roadways or other structures, steps have to be taken to minimise the risk and nuisance to adjoining land, building or road users. Notification in good time to local residents is essential. Other safety issues such as security, selection of demolition method, dust and noise are dealt with in other sections of this unit.

10.2 - Demolition method statement

All demolition/dismantling work are covered by CDM. Part of the planning work for any project should include the development of method statements. These should consider all or some of the following issues where necessary.

Type and sequence of demolition

PIECEMEAL

Piecemeal demolition is done by hand using hand held tools and is sometimes a preliminary to other methods. It can be completed or begun by machines. For example, when demolishing a tall chimney with occupied buildings in close proximity, the job may commence with the painstaking task of dismantling by hand - brick by brick. When the structure has been reduced to about 10 metres, then conventional heavy equipment can be used.

CONTROLLED COLLAPSE AND PRE-WEAKENING

Deliberate controlled collapse involves the pre-weakening of the structure or building. This involves removing key structural members so the remaining structure collapses under its own weight.

There are several problems associated with this method of demolition:

- The structure may collapse to a greater extent than was anticipated.
- The planned collapse may only be a partial collapse and could leave the structure hazardous and insecure.
- The resultant debris may be projected over a wider area than anticipated.
- The pile of debris that is left after the collapse of the structure may be in a dangerous condition, presenting a serious risk to those who remove it.

One method of removing the key structural members is overturning by wire rope pulling. Wires are attached to the main supports, which are pulled away using a heavy tracked vehicle or a winch to provide the motive power. The area must be cleared of workers for this operation and there must be enough clearance for the vehicle to move the distance required to pull out the structural supports.

Problems associated with this method arise when the wire becomes overstressed. If it breaks, then whiplash can occur which can have the force to slice through the human body. The forces applied may be enough to overturn the winch or the tracked vehicle. Another problem can occur when the action of pulling has begun and there is inadequate power to complete it.

Use of explosives - The use of explosives requires the expertise of an experienced explosives engineer. Also, the HSE should be consulted to ensure compliance with The Control of Explosives Regulations 1991. There are a number of factors to be considered for safe demolition with the use of explosives, which include:

- The local and structural conditions must be considered when fixing the size of the charges. The structure to be blasted can be divided into a number of sections and suitable charges applied to each section.
- Shot holes should be drilled electrically. Drilling pneumatically could cause vibration, which could result in premature collapse.
- Charges should not be placed near cast iron as it easily shatters into shrapnel.
- The area around the structure being demolished and the firing point should be barricaded and unauthorised persons not allowed to enter.
- The demolition engineer must be satisfied that no dangerous situation or condition has been left or created. The danger zone must be barricaded until rendered safe.

Figure 10-5: Protection of public.   *Source: ACT.*

Figure 10-6: Disposal of waste.   *Source: ACT.*

ISOLATION OF SERVICES

It is important to isolate services at the furthest point practicable from the structure to be demolished. This may include gas or water services isolated in the pavement outside the demolition site. This will help to remove the hazard at source and is preferable to local isolation of the services within the building. It should be remembered that some systems will store energy from services and should not be presumed safe merely by isolating the service. This includes electricity stored in capacitors and batteries, stored water in tanks, and compressed oils / air in pressure systems.

See also - Identification and Isolation of Services - above, in this unit.

PROTECTION OF PUBLIC AND OTHERS

The boundaries of the demolition site need to be fenced off to exclude persons not involved with the work. These could be children, persons sleeping rough and those who wish to salvage materials, as well as people who are just passing by. The very nature of a demolition site suggests both attraction and danger. Some form of fencing or boarding about 2.5 metres high would be ideal, with warning notices set up around it. Fencing must be maintained to a good standard and checks must be made at the end of each day to ensure it is in place and up to standard.

DISPOSAL OF WASTE

Taking into account the size of the site, waste material must not be allowed to accumulate. This means controlling build up of waste at local points around the site, particularly where they impede access and egress, as well as any major accumulation points. The disposal of building materials must be controlled by consignment certificates and taken to a recognised licensed landfill site. Care must also be taken of special waste such as asbestos.

10.3 - Specific issues

AVOIDANCE OF PREMATURE COLLAPSE

The technical advances in mechanical plant have considerably reduced the risk to demolition workers of working at a height. Modern machines can be fitted with scissor jaws that can break down a wall in small pieces. Another benefit of scissor jaws is that there is less likelihood of major structural damage or premature collapse. The likelihood of premature collapse remains a consideration when using the ball and chain method or carrying out partial demolition. In some cases the façade of a building may be left intact for renovation and the rest of the structure removed, in these circumstances great care must be taken to avoid freestanding walls and to provide adequate support to the structure.

PROTECTION FROM FALLING MATERIALS

Protective screens and where appropriate fans should be set up around scaffolds set around buildings undergoing demolition, to prevent debris falling on to passers-by. In addition, brick guards, debris nets and sheeting will help to contain falling materials and prevent them falling outside the framework of a scaffold erected as part of the demolition process. There must be a clearly demarcated area where workers can tell that the specific area of the structure is being worked on and that the work in that area has a risk from falling materials. This includes buildings being demolished by hand, where a safe access route to the work place must be maintained. Warning of planned demolition stages by use of audible and visual warnings will assist in removing people from the hazards area at this time. Head protection is an essential last line of defence for workers in this environment.

Figure 10-7: Protection from falling materials.   *Source: ACT.*

Figure 10-8: Falling materials.   *Source: ACT.*

PROTECTION FROM NOISE

Demolition must take into account the public and neighbour interface, which includes noise and dust levels. Simple controls like limiting the work hours / days to those more socially acceptable will help. The choice of equipment and technique may be used to limit the effect, for example, by locating noisy plant away from those affected will also reduce exposure to noise.

CONTROL AND PROTECTION FROM DUST

Dust can be a nuisance and a risk to health to the public as well as to the workers. It may contain fungal and bacterial matter, which is pathogenic to humans. Dust can be damped down with water to keep it to a minimum. The closure of roads and pathways is a good precaution to keep people and vehicles away from the site, but this is not always possible. Prevailing winds will need to be considered in order to decide the approach and order of the demolition; it may be possible for the un-demolished parts of the structure to assist with the reduction of dust liberated from the site.

SITING AND USE OF PLANT AND MACHINERY

Access to the site should be established to enable the large plant and appliances to be taken or driven there safely. It may also be necessary to get permission to close roads or pathways for the duration of the work.

Any plant and equipment if used in the manner for which it was designed should not fall over and injure any person at work. However, there are potential hazards that can cause overturning:

1. Weak support, e.g. ground failure.
2. Operating outside the machine's capability.
3. Striking obstructions.

The key to preventing plant overturning is planning. The appointment of a competent person to organise the lifting operation is essential. It is important to restrict access to plant when it is not in use to prevent unauthorised use, by for example children. This will include securing plant in compounds, locking doors and securing keys effectively.

Care with siting of plant is essential in order to prevent accidental contact with nearby structures or the building being demolished. In restricted areas tight control of use is essential, with the addition of physical barriers to restrict movement of the plant where practicable.

Taking steps to prevent unauthorised access to the demolition site by using barriers, fencing, and increased security is the responsibility of the principal contractor.

Figure 10-9: Noise and dust.   *Source: Rollaston Council.*

Figure 10-10: Siting of plant.   *Source: ACT.*

PROTECTION OF THE ENVIRONMENT

Where lorries are being used to transport the demolition waste material to a disposal site, then provision should be made for wheel washes and the cleaning of the highway by a road sweeper. Waste substances, such as oils, must not be allowed to leak away into the soil and must be disposed of in a controlled manner. During demolition sewers may become exposed and be at risk of contamination from substances, and care should be taken to identify and protect them from entry of such materials. In the same way it may be necessary to establish interceptor pits to control water run off into water courses.

ENSURING COMPETENCE OF WORKFORCE

It is the client's responsibility to check the competence of the principal contractor. In turn, the principal contractor must ensure the competence of contractors appointed to conduct demolition and dismantling. Competence checks can include taking up references on past work and reviewing contractor's health and safety policies and procedures. It is important to recognise that demolition contractors may not be competent to act as principal contractors on larger or more complex projects.

Figure 10-11: Doubtful competence of workers. *Source: Lincsafe.*

Figure 10-12: Competence of contractors.   *Source: ACT.*

Movement of people and vehicles - hazards and control

Overall Aims

On completion of this Unit, candidates will understand:

- the hazards within the construction environment presented by the movement of people and vehicles, and the interaction between them.
- the precautions necessary to control these hazards and to reduce the risks they present.

Content

Specific Intended Learning Outcome

The intended learning outcomes of this Unit are that candidates will be able to:

11.1 identify the hazards that may cause injuries to pedestrians (both on and off site) and the control measures to reduce the risk of such injuries

11.2 suggest suitable measures to ensure the safe operation of vehicles on site and the safe passage of public vehicles during streetworks

11.3 explain the importance of site driver training as part of an overall safety programme

11.4 suggest ways of ensuring segregation of pedestrians and vehicles and the appropriate control measures when segregation is not practicable

Sources of Reference

Essentials of Health and Safety at Work, HSE Books

Safe Use of Work Equipment (ACOP) (L22), HSE Books

Lighting at Work (HSG38), HSE Books

The Traffic Signs Manual (Chapter 8: The Traffic Safety Measures and Signs for Roadworks and Temporary Situations), Department of Transport

Safety at Streetworks and Roadworks (Code of Practice), Department for Transport

Relevant Statutory Provisions

The Construction (Health, Safety and Welfare) Regulations (CHSW) 1996

The Provision and Use of Work Equipment Regulations (PUWER) 1998 - Part III in particular

The Health and Safety (Safety Signs and Signals) Regulations (SSSR) 1996

The New Roads and Street Works Act (NRSWA) 1991

11.1 - Hazards to pedestrians

Typical construction hazards

SLIPS, TRIPS AND FALLS ON THE SAME LEVEL

Slips, trips and falls on the same level are the most common causes of major injuries reported to the Health and Safety Executive (HSE) under the Reporting of Injuries, Diseases and Dangerous Occurrences Regulations (RIDDOR) 1995. Broken bones are the usual result when the following conditions are present.

- Poorly maintained surfaces - e.g. potholes in roads, site debris, excavations and poor re-instatements of road or walk ways.
- Changes in level caused by temporary road surfaces or reinstatements, excavation covers, heavy plant tracks, ramps, and kerbs or chamber lids not clearly marked.
- Slippery surfaces caused by water, oils, fuels, silt, mud, or mixed compounds - e.g. mortar, plaster, render.
- Inappropriate footwear.
- Site rules not followed - e.g. running or not taking care on site.
- General obstructions in walkways such as trailing cables, pipes and air hoses.

Figure 11-1: Slips and trips.   *Source: Lincsafe.*

Figure 11-2: Trip hazards.   *Source: Lincsafe.*

COLLISIONS WITH MOVING VEHICLES

- Poor ground conditions - e.g. loose surface, slippery, poor grip.
- Unstable ground conditions.
- Restricted space to allow for manoeuvring and passing - e.g. where there is a high volume of mobile plant and materials.
- Undefined routes to segregate site traffic - e.g. people with heavy goods vehicles, excavators, dump trucks and vans.
- Disregard for site rules concerning site vehicles - e.g. speed restrictions, competent operators.
- No or insufficient warning devices fitted to vehicles and a general lack of maintenance.

Figure 11-3: Collision with moving vehicles.   *Source: ACT.*

Figure 11-4: Falling materials.   *Source: Lincsafe.*

MOVING, FLYING OR FALLING OBJECTS

When working above ground such as on a scaffold, it is easy to concentrate on protecting people from falling. However, it is also important to consider precautions to prevent falling objects. Situations that increase the likelihood of falling objects are:

- Overloading of materials on scaffolds, roofs or mobile elevated work platforms.
- Lack of use of barriers or mesh screens to prevent materials falling from height or being blown off.
- Faulty or inappropriate means of lifting or lowering materials to the workplace.
- Unstable loads on vehicles - e.g. not correctly supported, tied or shrink wrapped.
- Unstable workplace structure - e.g. insufficient number of scaffold tie points or uneven ground.

STRIKING AGAINST FIXED OR STATIONARY OBJECTS

Whilst bumps and bruises are perceived by many as "minor" injuries, they are painful and can be distressing for the sufferer. Therefore, the following situations should be avoided.

- Low level or protruding scaffold tubing not correctly protected or highlighted with hi-visibility warning tape.
- Insufficient space for storing tools and materials causing poor access and egress.
- Poor lighting / work in enclosed areas.
- Cranes or lifting devices with hanging hooks / slings.

TREADING ON SHARP OBJECTS

It is the nature of construction sites that they have a large amount of materials moved into and around them. Sometimes the material, such as sections of trunking, is cut to length and off cuts may fall to the ground and be left there. Similarly, material comes to site with wire binding and when the binding is cut the off cuts are often left on the ground. In addition, nailed together timber is often used for improvised tasks and when it is finished with it may be broken apart and discarded, leaving nails protruding. All these sharp objects represent a hazard to pedestrians; the best way to deal with this is to ensure that people that conduct these tasks clear away the sharp objects after them. In practice this often proves difficult, as the transient nature of the work makes it difficult to enforce such rules. To strengthen the encouragement to tidy up bins for rubbish of this type can be placed around the site, supported by systems for removal and emptying. The last line in the defence against this hazard is the wearing of appropriate personal protective equipment (PPE). Stout, general work footwear will provide a degree of general protection from injury but special footwear fitted with a protective plate in the bottom of the boot affords a much higher degree of protection.

Figure 11-5: Obstructions.   *Source: Lincsafe.*

Figure 11-6: Streetworks.   *Source: ACT.*

Hazards to the public caused by construction and streetworks

The majority of the general public are attracted to construction activities and streetworks, usually out of curiosity for the project underway. The hazards and dangers present at the site are often significantly magnified due to their lack of knowledge or awareness to site issues of health and safety. On a private construction site, with controlled secure entrance facilities, exposure to hazards is minimised by restricting access to authorised, competent people (site operatives) who undergo a site specific health and safety induction. However, unless proper precautions and controls have been taken by those in charge of the project, the general public are at risk from hazards that have the potential to cross the site boundaries - for example, noise, dust, fumes, falling or flying objects from a height.

Streetworks may pose a higher risk due to activities being carried out actually within the public area resulting in an increased level of public curiosity. Due to the temporary nature of the majority of streetworks the working area is often within less secure barrier systems and security is reduced to the vigilance of staff working in the area providing enforcement of site access rules. Items of heavy plant or material deliveries often operate outside the barrier systems that are set up, thus creating increased risk to the public. Strict supervision of such operations is necessary to prevent danger to the public. Works involving scaffold structures within the highway pose an obstruction to members of the public. The risk of impact with scaffold bars must be controlled by installing horizontal tubes high enough to avoid head injury and also cladding the bars with protective foam and high visibility tape.

Consideration also has to be given to those who may gain unauthorised access outside the core working hours undertaken at the site or project. Adequate means of preventing access should be implemented and any hazards made suitably safe after work, e.g. excavations guarded, covered and lit; ladders secured and plant locked up.

11.2 - Control strategies for pedestrian hazards

General strategies

RISK ASSESSMENT

Some or all of the following issues might affect the hazards faced by pedestrians and should be considered when carrying out a risk assessment:

- Weather conditions - particularly snow and ice.
- Lighting - especially at night.
- Surfaces - the absence of potholes and the presence of mud.

- Unusually high numbers of people. Consider, for example, busy periods such as Christmas sales in department stores causing large quantities of the public to be near streetworks and fluctuations in workloads which could lead to an influx of temporary workers.
- The effectiveness of existing controls - such as barriers.
- Unexpected movements of people - such as shortcuts, entry into restricted areas, emergency evacuation.
- Special needs for certain groups of people - such as people in wheel chairs, pregnant women and elderly people.

SLIP RESISTANT SURFACES

How slip and trip hazards in the workplace might be controlled:

- Improved work layout with designated walkways.
- Using high grip surface coating.
- Highlighting changes in level with hazard warning strips.
- Providing good lighting.
- Introducing procedures for reporting defects and for dealing with spillage.
- Ensuring high standards of housekeeping to keep floors clear of obstructions, debris or spillage.
- Provision of made up roughened concrete walkways on site.
- High grip grit sheets on the edge of steps and stairs.
- Mats at entrance to buildings and cabins.

Figure 11-7: Slip resistant surfaces. *Source: ACT.*

Design features and/or safe practices intended to reduce the risk of accidents on staircases used as internal pedestrian routes within work premises:

- The removal of obstructions, paying particular attention to emergency exits and escape routes.
- The provision of non-slip surfaces, together with reflective edging.
- Adequate lighting and effective maintenance.

Important design features of a staircase (which are to a large extent defined by building standards) are its width, the provision of handrails, the dimensions of treads and risers, and the provision of landings. Thought should be given to special provisions for disabled persons and to the possibility of using a lift as an alternative. Avoid the need to carry large or heavy items up or down stairs. Site rules should address such issues as well as defining appropriate footwear.

SPILLAGE CONTROL AND DRAINAGE

A procedure for spillage response for hazardous liquids should include:

- Raise the alarm and inform emergency services and relevant authorities (e.g. fire service, water company).
- Evacuate all personnel, seal off access from danger area.
- Quickly assess the nature and extent (if possible) of the incident.
- Do not approach the liquid if you do not know what it is.
- Raise first aid treatment for those who might have been affected.
- Provide bunding or some other form of spillage containment such as sand or special granules to contain the spillage.
- Isolate any ignition sources.
- Keep people away.
- For internal spills with no fire risk, ventilate by opening windows and closing doors. Ventilate the area but isolate the material.
- For external spills, cover drains to prevent the material going into drains and watercourses. Do not wash spillage into drains.
- Issue appropriate personal protective equipment to those involved and competent in carrying out the procedure.
- Ensure safe disposal of the spilled substance and any absorbent material used.

DESIGNATED WALKWAYS

The workplace may be some distance from the ground as with construction workers working on a scaffold or several miles underground as with tunnelling operations. The duty to provide a safe place of work relates to such matters as clearly marked walkways which are free of obstruction, the maintenance of floors and staircases, a safe working environment, safe means of access and egress, together with the organisation of traffic routes (including pedestrian traffic). A critical consideration when considering traffic systems is the safety interface between pedestrians and traffic. The routes that people use should be clearly defined and marked. This is a requirement of the Construction (Health, Safety and Welfare) Regulations (CHSW) 1996 which states that every construction site shall be organised in such a way that, so far as is reasonably practicable, pedestrians and vehicles can move safely and without risks to health, and that traffic routes shall be suitable for the persons or vehicles using them, sufficient in number, in suitable positions and of sufficient size.

Good site planning should ensure the provision of designated walkways as part of the site layout. For sites that are going to be in use by a significant number of people over a period of time consideration should be made to laying formal concrete walkways for workers, particularly at parts of the site where there will be a high amount of pedestrian traffic - such as entrances, rest facilities and routes through the site. Effort should be made to segregate pedestrians from site traffic, particularly on approach roads and where vehicles manoeuvre. When arrangements are being made for designated walkways the need for emergency routes and exits need to be considered also. Routes must be clearly indicated and be adequate for the people and hazards present on site.

CONTROL OF HAZARDS RELATED TO FLOORS AND GANGWAYS

Regulation 12 of the Workplace (Health Safety and Welfare) Regulations (WHSWR) 1992 requires that floors and traffic route surfaces must be constructed so that they are suitable for the purpose for which they are used. This means such things as having no holes or being slippery or uneven. Whilst this may be difficult to achieve at times on a construction site it should not be assumed that because it is difficult it need not be done. Controls may be achieved in parts of the site such as indoor areas, storage areas and rest facilities relatively easily.

Measures to control hazards related to floors and gangways may include:

- Being kept clean and free from obstructions that may hinder passage.
- Good drainage in wet processes or wet weather.
- Suitable footwear or working platforms provided where necessary.
- Ramps kept dry and with non-skid surfaces.
- Level, even ground without holes or broken boards.
- Floor load capacities posted in lofts and storage areas.
- Salting/sanding and sweeping of outdoor routes during icy or frosty conditions.
- Steps, corners and fixed obstacles clearly marked.
- Excavations and chambers kept covered when not in use and the edges clearly marked.

FENCING AND GUARDING

The CHSW requires particular attention be taken to control hazards through the use of fencing and guarding. Fencing of the outer area of a work site, at a suitable distance, will assist in the control of movement of people and vehicles. In addition, workers and vehicles in the site need protection and in this case inner guarding using barriers may be necessary, for example to protect the edge of an excavation. It is essential that any fences or guarding (barriers) provided are stable to ensure proper protection is achieved.

"Suitable and sufficient steps shall be taken to prevent, so far as is reasonably practicable, any person falling" and

"Where necessary to prevent danger to any person, suitable and sufficient steps shall be taken to prevent, as far as is reasonably practicable, the fall of any material or object"

In any case where the steps identified above include the provision of any guard rail, toe board, barrier or other similar means of protection; or working platform, these shall comply with the provisions of schedules 1 and 2 of CHSWR.   Regulation 6 of the CHSW

Physical barriers should be erected to ensure that there is adequate protection for pedestrians who may be exposed to falls, falling objects and being struck by a moving object such as a vehicle. In addition, where pedestrians may walk into or strike an object, such as a protruding scaffold pole or a ladder the area around the objects should be guarded by means of a barrier.

Figures 11-8: Outer fencing and inner guarding. *Source: ACT.*

Figure 11-9: Protection of pedestrians. *Source: ACT.*

USE OF SIGNS AND PERSONAL PROTECTIVE EQUIPMENT

Signs must conform to the standards specified in the Health and Safety (Safety Signs and Signals) Regulations (SSSR) 1996. They must be clearly visible and be easily understood.

Safety signs should indicate the need to use personal protective equipment, such as hard hats, protective footwear or high visibility clothing, when entering certain work areas even if they are just visiting or passing quickly through. Signs to indicate the presence of a temporary hazard should be used to warn people who might be affected to keep clear of that area. Hazard signs might be used where excavations are present, a change in height occurs or for the demarcation of a hazard area to assist with the provision of diversionary routes - for example a vehicle unloading area where pedestrians are prohibited. Edges of steps, overhead obstructions and cables or pipes laid temporarily across walkways should also be clearly identified.

Good footwear is important to avoid slips or trips or puncture wounds in the workplace. The risk assessment process should consider the possibility of slips, trips and sharp material hazards, and where the decided control of this hazard includes the use of specific footwear this should be arranged.

Figure 11-10: Correct clothing & footwear. *Source: ACT.*

If the footwear has particular properties, such as anti-slip soles or steel mid-plates, this would fall under the requirements of the Personal Protective Equipment Regulations (PPER) 1992 and as such the employer should provide them to employees without charge. Where specific personal protective footwear is not required but employees need to wear suitable personal shoes to work, this should be specified and would not normally be subject to the PPER. In addition, footwear with a protective toe cap is necessary for those that may work in close proximity to vehicles.

On sites where vehicles operate and for streetworks it is essential that workers are able to be seen therefore it is essential that high visibility clothing be used. Though this is not a substitute for the separation of vehicles from people, for the many situations where workers work in close proximity to vehicles it will provide valuable assistance in preventing contact.

INFORMATION, INSTRUCTION, TRAINING AND SUPERVISION

The employer, through management, should ensure that rules, policies and procedures are followed and that people do not act irresponsibly. Certain circumstances may require specific information, instruction and training, for example, procedures for climbing ladders or wearing appropriate clothing (e.g. high visibility jackets).

The Health and Safety at Work Act (HSAWA) 1974 requires employers to provide supervision as necessary. This means that the employer must actively supervise the workplace and the work conducted in it, for example if high visibility clothing is required or walkways are to be kept clear this must be supervised. The concept requires the supervisor to increase the level of supervision on a needs basis, for example, the higher the risk related to the work or workplace hazard or the more persistent the problem, the greater is the supervision necessary. If a large number of the public are to use a route after it has been cleaned the supervisor should take special effort to ensure that it is safe. If an obstruction of a walk route keeps returning, the supervisor will need to put in extra effort to bring it under control.

Maintenance of a safe workplace

CLEANING AND HOUSEKEEPING REQUIREMENTS

"Every part of a construction site shall, so far as is reasonably practicable, be kept in good order and every part of a construction site that is used as a place of work shall be kept in a reasonable state of cleanliness". Regulation 26 of CHSW

Maintenance of a safe construction site may be achieved through the development of a housekeeping procedure. Good housekeeping implies "a place for everything and everything in its place". Laid down procedures are necessary for preventing the spread of contamination, reducing the likelihood of accidents resulting in slips, trips, and falls and reducing the chances of unwanted fire caused by careless storage of flammable waste.

ACCESS AND EGRESS

- Adequate space for easy movement, and safe plant or equipment use.
- No tripping hazards e.g. trailing cables or pipes.
- Handholds or guardrails where people might fall from floor edges.
- Emergency provision e.g. life belts/jackets for work near water or means of escape from confined spaces.
- Neat and tidy storage of tools, plant and equipment so that they do not present a hazard to passers-by.
- Identify storage areas.
- Mark areas to be kept clear.
- Pay particular attention to emergency routes.
- Vision panels in doors to avoid contact injuries.

WORK ENVIRONMENT CONSIDERATIONS

Figure 11-11: Vision panels in fire doors. *Source: ACT.*

Heating

"Suitable and sufficient steps shall be taken to ensure , so far as is reasonably practicable, that during working hours the temperature at any indoor place of work is reasonable having regard to the purpose to which the place is used". Regulation 24 of CHSW

The approved code of practice (ACOP) which accompanies (WHSWR) states that a temperature of 16^0C should be maintained for sedentary work, for example in site offices, and a temperature of 13^0C for work that requires physical effort. Because these figures are stated in an ACOP, they should be regarded as minimum figures. Construction workers can be exposed to a varying degree of conditions and resultant temperatures. The effects of excessive cold or heat can have harmful effects on employees' health and accidents can result due to fatigue or thermal stress. Work in hot environments should be undertaken in controlled systems, workers need to be acclimatised. Drinks and the provision of refuge from heat may be necessary to reduce body temperatures.

"Every place of work outdoors shall, where necessary to ensure the health and safety of persons at work there, be so arranged that, so far as is reasonably practicable and having regard to the purpose for which that place is used and any protective clothing or equipment provided for the use of any person at work there, it provides protection from adverse weather". Regulation 24 of CHSW

Where the temperatures referred to above cannot be maintained, for example when working outside, areas should be provided to enable workers who work in cold environments to warm themselves. Practical measures and adequate protection must be provided against adverse conditions, for example workers may be provided with a sheeted area to work in order to protect them from the rain and wind.

Lighting

Lighting plays an important part in health and safety. Factors to consider include:

- Good general illumination with no glare, especially where there are vehicle movements.
- Regular cleaning and maintenance of lights and windows.
- Local lighting for dangerous processes and to reduce eye strain and fatigue.
- No flickering from fluorescent tubes (it can be dangerous with some rotating machinery).
- Adequate emergency lighting which is regularly tested and maintained.
- Specially constructed fittings for flammable or explosive atmospheres e.g. during paint spraying.
- Outside areas satisfactorily lit for work and access during hours of darkness - for security as well as safety.
- Light coloured wall finishes improving brightness, or darker colours to reduce arc welding flash, for example.

"There shall be suitable and sufficient lighting in respect of every workplace and approach thereto and every traffic route, which lighting shall, so far as is reasonably practicable, be by natural light"; "The colour of any artificial lighting provided shall not adversely affect or change the perception of any sign or signal provided for the purposes of health and safety" and "Suitable and sufficient secondary lighting shall be provided in any place where there would be a risk to the heath and safety of any person in the event of failure of primary artificial lighting."
Regulation 25 of CHSW

Care should be taken, in particular where temporary lighting is rigged, to ensure that glare and shadows are minimised. Particular attention should be paid to changes in level, corners and where workers pass between the outside and inside where darkness occurs.

Noise

Noise can produce a number of types of damage to the ear. Noise levels should be assessed and appropriate controls established. Noise can cause an environmental nuisance to surrounding areas, and can have negative effects on communities in general and wildlife. Controls implemented may include barriers and screens around site boundaries to contain noise produced, the use of equipment that produces lower noise levels and restrictions on operating times to reduce the nuisance dependant upon the sensitivity of the area. *See also - Physical and Psychological Health Hazards and controls - Unit 13.*

Dust

General strategies for dust

Dust is a common hazard on construction sites and because it enters the atmosphere can easily escape past site boundaries and then have negative effects on the environment. The health hazards associated with dusts can vary but usually result in an attack on the respiratory system on humans and other living creatures. Dust can also present significant risk of eye injury and general discomfort. Other problems are layers of dust settling within the environment, causing damage to vegetation, wildlife habitats and private property. Activities creating dust include external cleaning of buildings, cutting and chasing of masonry and sanding operations.

The area where dust may be created can be watering down to minimise dust transfer into neighbouring premises. Stockpiles of material shall be damped down or otherwise suitably treated to prevent the emission of dust from the site. Stockpiles should be planned and sited to minimise the potential for dust generation. The handling of material should be kept to a minimum and when deposited onto a stockpile it should be from the minimum possible height. Dust pollution shall be minimised during demolition by:

- The complete screening, if practicable, of the building or structure to be demolished with debris screens or sheets.
- Control of cutting or grinding of materials on the site.
- Mixing of large quantities of concrete or bentonite slurries in enclosed/shielded areas.

Skips and removal vehicles shall be properly covered when leaving the site. Materials should be handled in such a way that they do not give rise to excessive dust. Watering of rubble chutes shall be undertaken where necessary to prevent dust emission.

Ensure that the area around the site, including the public highway, is regularly and adequately swept to prevent any accumulation of dust and dirt. The use of wheel cleaning facilities and road sweeping equipment may be required.

Any plant used for the crushing of materials must be authorised by a local authority under the Environmental Protection Act Part 1 (Prescribed Processes). All works shall be carried out in accordance with the conditions of such an authorisation. Where plant is used to recycle materials, the appropriate licence from the Environment Agency shall be obtained. The process operator should notify the local authority prior to the movement of the plant on to the site.

Sandblasting

- The work area shall be close-sheeted to reduce dust nuisance from grit. Routine checking is required to ensure that the sheeting remains sound and sealed during sandblasting activities.
- Particular attention shall also be given to the working platform to ensure that it is properly sheeted or sealed to contain dust.
- Non-siliceous grit shall be used to avoid long term irreversible lung damage from silica dust.
- Proper protection shall be provided for any structure painted with lead-based paint.
- In cases where water is used for large scale cleaning and blasting the requirements of the Environment Agency should be followed.
- All grit must be prevented from falling into water courses.

Measures to protect the public from construction activities

Between 1986 and 1996, construction activities killed 88 members of the public, including 27 children. More than 1,250 were seriously injured, of which over 450 were children. The importance of protecting such people cannot be emphasised enough, especially as almost all of these accidents could have been prevented.

Adopting a proper health and safety culture and providing suitable protection for those carrying out construction work will often go some way towards protecting others who may be affected by it, such as members of the public.

But the precautions which need to be taken to adequately protect the public and visitors may differ from those taken to protect those working on the site. There are good reasons for this. Members of the public may have a lower tolerance than those on site, for example, patients in a hospital which is being refurbished may be much less capable of sustaining further impairment to health than healthy people. The public are also less likely to be familiar with the risks associated with construction than those who regularly work in the industry.

Visitors - including experienced construction workers - may also require extra consideration if they are unfamiliar with the layout and particular hazards associated with the site. Certain groups such as children merit special attention because of their particular vulnerability. Certain classes of premises also need special attention because of the nature of the works.

The main measures used to protect the public include the provision of a perimeter fence with controlled access. Protection is provided by sheeting dusty operations and protection from falling materials by means of debris nets, brick guards and fans. Where ever possible the public should be placed at a suitable distance from the work activity by the use of barriers and in some cases diversions away from the work by for example crossing the road. The public should be protected from inadvertently coming into contact with the work or barriers around it, they should be supplemented by warning signs and lighting to prevent contact.

11.3 - Vehicle operations

Site vehicle hazards

Over 100 people die each year because of works transport related accidents. There is also a high incidence of accidents causing serious injury, e.g. spinal damage, amputation and crush injuries. Very few accidents involving traffic result in minor injury. In addition, transport accidents cause damage to plant, infrastructure and vehicles.

TYPICAL HAZARDS CAUSING LOSS OF CONTROL AND OVERTURNING OF VEHICLES

Various circumstances that may cause such a vehicle to overturn are insecure and unstable loads, manoeuvring with the load elevated, colliding with kerbs and other obstructions, cornering at speed, braking harshly, driving on uneven or soft ground, and mechanical failure.

Possible causes of a dumper truck overturning

- Overloading or uneven loading of the bucket.
- Cornering at excessive speed.
- Hitting obstructions.
- Driving too close to the edges of embankments or excavations.
- Mechanical defects.
- Inappropriate tyre pressures.
- Driving across slopes.

Possible causes of a fork lift truck overturning

- Driving too fast.
- Sudden braking.
- Driving on slopes.
- Driving over debris.
- Under-inflated tyres.
- Driving over holes in floor, such as drains.
- Driving with load elevated.
- Overloading - exceeding maximum capacity.
- Collisions with buildings or other vehicles.

Figure 11-12: Vehicle overturned. *Source: Lincsafe.*

COLLISIONS WITH OTHER VEHICLES, PEDESTRIANS OR FIXED OBJECTS

Because construction work involves progressive change by building, altering or demolishing things there is an increased risk of vehicles colliding with other vehicles, pedestrians and fixed objects. A scaffolding or staging may be erected that a driver is not aware of or an excavation appear in a previous route. The risk of collision is increased by the fact that scaffolds may overhang a vehicle route or power cables may run across the site. People may unexpectedly appear from a part built or demolished structure or workers intent on the work they are doing may step away from where they are working to collect materials or tools. Other factors are:

- Poor lighting.
- Poor direction signs.
- Inadequate signs or signals to identify the presence of vehicles.
- Drivers unfamiliar with site.
- Need to reverse.
- Poor visibility e.g. sharp bends, mirror / windscreen misted up.
- Poor identification of fixed objects e.g. overhead pipes, doorways, storage tanks, corners of buildings.
- Lack of separation of pedestrians and vehicles.
- Lack of safe crossing points on roads and vehicle routes.
- Lack of separate entrance / exit for vehicles and pedestrians.
- Pedestrians' misuse of doors provided for vehicle use.
- Lack of barriers to prevent pedestrians suddenly stepping from an exit/entrance into a vehicle's path.
- Poor maintenance of vehicles e.g. tyres or brakes.
- Excessive speed of vehicles.
- Lack of vehicle management e.g. use of traffic control, 'banksman'.
- Environmental conditions e.g. poor lighting, rain, snow or ice.

Figure 11-13: Collision with fixed objects. *Source: ACT.*

PROBLEMS OF SITE LAYOUT AND REFUELLING

Site layout

Construction sites are unfamiliar places due to the fact that constant development results in a dynamically changing environment on site until the project is complete. Materials, plant and operatives are concentrated in different areas of the site that also change depending upon the phase of the construction. Quite often there are no defined boundaries, roadways, or plot layouts and unless adequately controlled, traffic around a construction site can be uncoordinated and haphazard. It is important to recognise that delivery drivers of plant and materials will not be familiar with the site and that controls should be in place to guide them safely to their destination. In the first instance this can mean controlled access to the site with security staff checking where they need to go. In some larger more complicated sites this can mean controlling, directing or supervising drivers along prescribed routes that suite the vehicle and the load. Good signage will also assist in clarifying correct routes, colour coding and naming routes helps to maintain driver orientation. Remember signs are often positioned for drivers to find their way in to sites and are poorly positioned to enable smooth exit. This can result in a good driver taking a wrong turn and causing a lot of damage, injury or delay.

Road surfaces

The state and condition of road surfaces within or around construction sites can vary greatly. Poor soils surfaces can rapidly deteriorate as rain turns it to mud. Some site vehicles may be well adapted to this but visiting vehicles may fare less well, resulting in them getting bogged down or failing to stop effectively causing a collision with people or structures. Commonly, during the construction phase, the sub surface is all that provides any definition of a roadway (roadstone / hardcore). This surface offers very little grip for vehicles due to its loose nature and may be driven into the shape of ramps and dips, and this may cause a site vehicle or piece of plant to lose control. Additionally, where the final surface has not been applied, manhole access lids or stop tap boxes may be exposed which are not secured and can result in vehicle wheels falling into the opening beneath. Where a tarmac top coat has been applied, this can become wet, covered in site mud /slurry and debris and become slippery which can also result in site plant and vehicles skidding out of control.

Gradients

Gradients or slopes on a construction site can magnify the hazards already presented by the road surfaces. Extra effort is required when engaging gradients which can increase the risk of loss of control. When going down a gradient more effort is required in controlling, slowing down and stopping which can increase the risk of skidding. This may mean driving forward up a gradient and reversing downwards, particularly the case with plant such as fork lift trucks. When approaching gradients it is important that the correct method be adopted. In most circumstances and especially when carrying loads, gradients should not be engaged in a sideways manner as the centre of gravity of the vehicle may shift outside the stability base of the vehicle, this can add to the risk of material falling off or cause the plant or vehicle to overturn.

Figure 11-14: Road surface.　　　　Source: ACT.

Figure 11-15: Site layout.　　　　Source: ACT.

Excavations

Excavations pose the hazard of collapse if vehicles operate too close, this can result in plant or vehicles tipping into the excavation which could cause:

- Trapping or crushing workers.
- Trapping the driver.
- Damage to exposed buried services.

- Toppling loads may create a further crush hazard.
- Environmental hazards such as release of oils or fuels.

In addition, there is a risk of vehicles simply driving into them, for example when a dumper truck is back filling an excavation or where the edge is not protected or well identified in poor lighting. Even when excavations are filled in they remain a risk for a considerable time as the material is not well compacted and the additional weight of the vehicle, for example a mobile crane, may cause the soil to compact and the vehicle to overturn. For each of these reasons it is essential that excavations on site be well protected by barriers, fencing and lighting.

Scaffolding and falsework

Scaffolding and false work are temporary fabrications that are used in the construction of structures. Scaffolding provides the means to access and carry out work activities at height via a system of tubes and work platforms. False work provides a temporary means of support whilst casting concrete structures until the structure can support itself and is then removed. Hazards are impact from plant or vehicles that operate too close to the fabrication. Any damage sustained from an impact can result in a knock on effect causing the entire fabrication to fail. This can lead to operatives, materials or equipment falling from a height on a scaffold or heavy pieces of support materials falling from a height in a false work with the additional risk of the structure that is being formed collapsing.

Refuelling

Dependant upon the size and number of pieces of plant operating on construction sites, there may be facilities for the storage of fuel in bulk or smaller quantities. Even the smallest, most simple sites may have refuelling activities carried out via means of a suitable fuel container having its contents transferred into the fuel tank of, for example, a small generator. Hazards quite often include lack of enforcement of stringent rules and procedures that are commonplace in public fuel stations. Inexperienced operatives may be involved in refuelling processes and this may lead to various dangerous activities that may ultimately lead to fire and explosion, for example due to:

- Refuelling whilst engines are running.
- Smoking in the vicinity of fuel or refuelling activities.
- Impact from vehicles leading to leak and pollution incidents.

- Poorly maintained fuel containment, pipes, and valves.
- Inappropriately positioned / segregated fuel storage.
- Poor security attracting theft / damage / vandalism .

Public vehicle hazards during streetworks

Streetworks usually involve surface removal and renewal, line painting, excavation for exposure, renewal or installation of buried services or cleaning activities (gutters, gullies). When these operations take place, precautions often include signing, lighting and guarding the area as required by The New Roads and Street Works Act (NRSWA) 1991.

The primary hazard associated with streetworks is fast moving vehicles travelling along the highway with a large percentage of vehicle drivers possibly unaware that streetworks are present. When within the vicinity of streetworks the various hazards include:

- Lane closure causing diversionary manoeuvres often into opposing traffic flows.
- Open excavations.
- Ramps and poor road surfaces.
- Operatives involved in the streetworks.

Figure 11-16: Public vehicle hazards   *Source: ACT.*

- Diversionary measures placed on pedestrians or members of the public forcing them to cross the highway.
- Heavy plant incorporating swinging bodies / jibs (360^0 excavators, restricted swing excavators, cranes).

11.4 - Control strategies for safe vehicle operations

General site strategies

Design features of the vehicle intended to minimise the consequences of an overturn include rollover protection and seat belts. In addition, features designed to prevent overturning, include the width of the wheelbase and the position of the centre of gravity of the vehicles.

RISK ASSESSMENT

The employer, through its management, needs to consider the safe movement of vehicles and their loads as part of their overall safety policy. This includes the use of dumper trucks, lift trucks, and delivery vehicles. Consideration should be given to the following.

Suitability and sufficiency of traffic routes

- Clearly marked and signed. These should incorporate speed limits, one way systems, priorities and other factors normal to public roads. Vehicles, which are visiting the premises, should be made aware of any local rules and conditions.
- Consideration should be given to adequate lighting on routes and particularly in loading/unloading and operating areas.
- Separate routes, designated crossing places and suitable barriers at recognised danger spots. As far as is practicable pedestrians should be kept clear of vehicle operating areas and/or a notice displayed warning pedestrians that they are entering an operating area.
- Clear direction signs and marking of storage areas and buildings can help to avoid unnecessary movement, such as reversing.
- Sharp bends and overhead obstructions should be avoided where possible. Hazards that cannot be removed should be clearly marked with black and yellow diagonal stripes i.e. loading bay edges, stacks, pits etc. If reasonably practicable barriers should be installed.
- Consideration to vehicle weight and height restriction on routes - signs, barriers and weight checks may be necessary.

Factors when planning traffic routes for construction transport

- The purpose of the routes.
- The types of vehicle using the routes.
- The likely volume of traffic.
- The layout of the area.
- The possible need for one-way systems.

- Speed limits and markings.
- Crossing points and signs.
- Separating pedestrians and vehicles - physical barriers.
- Suitability of the road structure.
- Environmental issues such as lighting levels

MANAGEMENT OF VEHICLE MOVEMENTS

Many sites are complex in nature and require the careful management of vehicles in order to ensure that they are brought onto, move around and leave the site safely. This can start at the project planning stage as it can cause many problems when a vehicle is brought onto site too early when the site is at an earlier phase and is not ready for it. Conversely if it is brought in part way through the project it may be difficult to get it to where it is needed and it may be better to get it to site early. Where materials are brought to site it may be necessary to manage deliveries so that too many vehicles do not arrive at the site at the same time causing them to back up into the public highway. Site security arrangements play a significant part in the management of vehicles on site and will assist with controlling vehicles so that they are routed correctly and safely. It is not uncommon for vehicles to be sent to a site that are too big or too heavy to access the roadways, site security staff help to prevent them accessing the site and causing harm. Major vehicle movements, such as a heavy crane may be timed so that the minimum of workers are on site and that it can be conducted easily in a controlled manner.

Safe operation

- Make someone on site responsible for transport.
- Drivers properly trained.
- Ensure unauthorised people are not allowed to drive.
- Make sure visiting drivers are aware of your rules.
- Check vehicles daily and have faults rectified promptly.

- Keep keys secure when vehicles are not in use.
- Ensure safe movements - particularly when reversing.
- Keep roadways/gangways properly maintained and lit.
- Separate vehicles and pedestrians where practicable.
- Use of horns before entering doorways or at blind corners.

ENVIRONMENTAL CONSIDERATIONS

Where vehicles operate, environmental conditions such as lighting and adverse weather will make a significant impact on their safe operation by affecting **visibility**. Where reasonably practicable a suitable standard of lighting must be maintained so that operators of vehicles can see to operate and their vehicle can be seen by others. It is important to avoid areas of glare or shadow that could mask the presence of a person or vehicle. Similarly if vehicles travel from within buildings to the outside it is important that the light level is maintained at a roughly even level in order to give the driver's eyes time to adjust to the change in light. Fixed structure hazards should be made as visible as possible with additional lighting and/or reflective strips.

Roads, gangways and aisles should have sufficient width and overhead clearance for the largest vehicle. Attention should be paid to areas where they might meet other traffic e.g. the entrance to the site. If ramps (sleeping policemen) are used a by-pass for trolleys and shallow draft vehicles should be provided. A one-way traffic system should be considered to reduce the risk of collision.

Gradients and changes in ground level, such as ramps, represent a specific hazard to plant and vehicle operation. Vehicles have a limit of stability dependent on loading and their wheelbase. These conditions could put them at risk of overturning or cause damage to articulated vehicle couplings. Any gradient in a vehicle operating area should be kept as gentle as possible. Where **changes in level** are at an edge that a vehicle might approach, and there is risk of falling, it must be provided with a robust barrier or similar means to demarcate the edge. Particular care must be taken at points where loading and unloading is conducted.

On some sites weather conditions and spillages will affect the **surface condition** of the road making it difficult for vehicles to brake effectively. It is important to have a programme that anticipates this with regular cleaning or scarifying of the surface as well as means of dealing with spills. The floor surface should be in good condition, free of litter, pot holes and obstructions.

Excessive ambient noise levels can mask the sound of vehicles working in the area; additional visual warning e.g. flashing lights should be used. Sufficient and suitable parking areas should be provided away from the main work area and located where the risk of unauthorised use of the vehicles will be reduced.

Vehicle safety requirements

SUITABILITY

Construction vehicles are versatile tools but each has its own role and limitations. For example a telehandler may have some similar features to a mobile crane but it is not designed to lift large loads in the same way as a mobile crane and unlike a crane is not fitted with outriggers to maintain stability. Vehicles will have a designed load carrying capacity in order to be suitable for the work it is being put to the vehicle should not be overloaded. Some vehicles may be designed to carry passengers but for the majority they will not be and are therefore unsuitable for this task. In just the same way the forks of a rough terrain lift truck are not suitable for use as a work platform, unless a purpose designed platform is added to them.

ROLL OVER PROTECTION AND RESTRAINT SYSTEMS

In many work vehicle accidents the driver is injured because the vehicle does not offer protection when it rolls over or it does not restrain the driver to prevent them falling out of the vehicle and being injured by the fall or the vehicle falling on them. Vehicles such as dumper trucks, road rollers and forklift trucks are examples of equipment that may present this risk. PUWER Part 3 recognises the importance of this and now set out requirements for equipment to be adapted, where practicable, to provide this protection. New equipment must now be provided with protection and restraint systems, where relevant.

Figure 11-17: Roll bar and seat restraint.   *Source: ACT.*

Figure 11-18: Suitability and protection.   *Source: ACT.*

PROTECTION FROM FALLING MATERIALS

There is a risk of material falling on a vehicle driver where the vehicle is used to provide materials at a height or to remove materials from delivery vehicles. It is important that suitable protection of the driver be provided by the structure of the vehicle. Protection should also be provided where vehicles work in close proximity to areas where there is a risk from falling materials. This may be by the provision of a frame and mesh above it or by the provision of a totally enclosing cab. Safety helmets alone are unlikely to provide sufficient protection but may be a useful addition where a mesh structure is provided.

MAINTENANCE OF VEHICLES

All vehicles should be well maintained and 'roadworthy' with a formal system of checks and maintenance in place. A vehicle, such as a dumper truck, that does not usually go outside the site would be expected to be kept to the same good standard as one that was used on public roads for such critical items as tyres and brakes. Vehicle maintenance should be planned for at regular intervals and vehicles taken out of use if critical items are not up to an acceptable standard. In addition, it is important to conduct pre-use check of the vehicle. This is usually done by the driver as part of their taking it over for a period of use such as a work shift or day. This would identify the condition of critical items and provide a formal system to identify and consider problems that may affect the safety of the vehicle. If there is no nominated driver and the vehicle is for general use someone should be nominated to make these checks. A record book or card would usually be used to record the checks and the findings.

Protective measures for people and structures on site

It is important to anticipate that drivers of vehicles might misjudge a situation and collide with structures whilst operating. For this reason vulnerable plant and parts of the building should be provided with barriers that continuously surround the plant or alternatively posts can be provided at key positions. Clearly, important plant and structures that are at the same level of the vehicle should be protected. Care should also be taken of structures at a height, such as a pipe bridge, roof truss or door lintel. All of these could be damaged by tall vehicles or those that have tipping mechanisms that raise their effective height. Though it may not always be possible to protect all structures, such as a doorway, it is important to apply markings to make them more visible. In addition, signs warning of overhead structures or the presence of vehicles in the area will help increase awareness and avoid collisions. There is a need to alert people to the hazard when working in or near vehicle operating area. Signs might help and these can be supplemented by visual and audible warning systems that confirm the presence of the vehicle. These may be operated by the driver, such as a horn on a dumper truck or automatically, such as an audible reversing signal on a large road vehicle. Visibility can be improved by mounting mirrors at strategic points. Consideration should be given to the provision of protective clothing - boots, helmets and high visibility clothing - for personnel working within areas where vehicles operate.

BARRIERS

Moving vehicles, and in particular large plant, have high impact energy when they are in contact with structures or people. A glancing blow from a large vehicle may be sufficient to bring down a large section of scaffolding. It is essential that vehicles be separated from vulnerable people and structures. Because of the high energy involved the barrier used must reflect the type of thing in contact with it. If it is only people that might contact it a simple portable barrier may be adequate, but if it is heavy plant robust barriers including concrete structures may need to be considered. It is important to identify vulnerable locations that warrant protection, for example the corner of a scaffold that vehicles need to manoeuvre around, excavations where articulated vehicles may lose a trailer wheel into the hole as it corners or high risk equipment such as electrical supplies units.

Figures 11-19: Fencing and barriers at a distance. *Source: ACT.*

MARKINGS

Any structure that represents a height or width restriction should be readily identified for people and vehicle drivers. This will include low beams or doorways, pipe bridges and protruding scaffolds and edges where a risk of falling exists. These markings may be by means of attaching hazard tape or painting the structure to highlight the hazard.

SIGNS

Signs should be used to provide information, such as height restrictions, and to warn of hazards on site. Signs may direct vehicles around workers at a safe distance.

WARNINGS ON VEHICLES

Warnings may be audible or visual or a combination of each. They are used to warn that the vehicle is operating in the area, such as a flashing light on the top of a dumper truck or to warn of a specific movement, such as an audible warning that a large vehicle is reversing. These are designed to alert people in the area in order that they can place themselves in a position of safety. They do not provide the driver with authority to reverse the vehicle or to proceed in a work area without caution.

Measures to prevent accidents when pedestrians work in vehicle manoeuvring areas

- Segregated systems for vehicular and pedestrian traffic (barriers, separate doors).
- Maintaining good visibility (mirrors, transparent doors, provision of lighting, cameras etc.).
- Signs indicating where vehicles operate in this area.
- Audible warnings on vehicles and sometimes flashing lights on vehicles.
- Drawing up and enforcement of site rules.
- The provision of refuges.
- The wearing of high-visibility clothing.
- A good standard of housekeeping.
- Training for, and supervision of, all concerned, competency certificates, refresher training, trained banksmen of direct cranes.
- Provision of parking areas.
- Provision of suitable battery charging or refuelling areas if necessary.
- Careful design of traffic routes.
- Maintenance of traffic routes.
- Traffic control e.g. identification of "no go" areas.

PRECAUTIONARY MEASURES FOR REVERSING VEHICLES WITHIN A WORKPLACE

- Separation of vehicles and pedestrians.
- Warning signs.
- Audible alarms / cameras.
- Space to allow good visibility / mirrors / refuges / lighting.
- Appropriate site rules adequately enforced.
- Procedural measures such as the use of trained banksmen.
- Avoiding the need for vehicles to reverse (by the use of one-way and 'drive-through' systems or turning circles).

Site rules

It is important to establish clear and well understood site rules regarding vehicle operations. These may have to be communicated to drivers by security staff at the time they visit the site. They would often stipulate where the driver should be whilst vehicles are being loaded, where the keys to the vehicle should be, not reversing without permission and what access they have to areas of the site for such things as refreshment. Pedestrians should also know what the site rules are in order to keep themselves safe. Site rules for pedestrians might include such things as using pedestrian exits/entrances or crossing points, not entering hazardous areas or wearing personal protective equipment in hazardous areas, and not walking behind a reversing vehicle. Where sites are made up of or join a highway, such as carriageway repairs on a motorway, it is important to identify who has priority the vehicle or the worker. Site rules may clarify that once the site boundary is crossed the worker has priority, this has to be clear. The site rules may be re-enforced by the provision of additional signs to clarify a speed limit and the nature of the priority of workers.

Selection and training of drivers

No persons should be permitted to operate plant or vehicles unless they have been selected, trained and authorised to do so, or are undergoing properly organised formal training.

SELECTION

The safe usage of plant and vehicles calls for a reasonable degree of both physical and mental fitness. The selection procedure should be devised to identify people who have shown them to be reliable and mature enough to perform their work responsibly and carefully. To avoid wasteful training for workers who lack co-ordination and ability to learn, selection tests should be used.

Consideration must be given to any legal age restrictions that apply to vehicles that operate on the public road. A similar approach may be adopted for similar vehicles used on site though the law is not specific on age limitations in such cases.

Potential operators should be medically examined prior to employment/training in order to assess the individual's physical ability to cope with this type of work. They should also be examined every five years in middle age and after sickness or accident.
Points to be considered are:

a)   General - Normal agility, having full movement of trunk, neck and limbs.

b)   Vision - Good eyesight is important, as operators are required to have good judgement of space and distance.

c)   Hearing - The ability to hear instructions and warning signals with each ear is important.

TRAINING

It is essential that immediate supervisors receive training in the safe operation of plant and vehicles and that senior management appreciates the risks resulting from the interaction of vehicles and the workplace.

For the operator/driver, safety must constitute an integral part of the skill-training programme and not be treated as a separate subject. The operator/driver should be trained to a level consistent with efficient operation and care for the safety of themselves and other persons. On completion of training they should be issued with a company authority to drive and a record of all basic training, refresher training and tests maintained in the individual's personal documents file. Certification of training by other organisations must be checked.

Management systems for assuring driver competence

THE TRAINED OPERATOR/DRIVER

It should not be assumed that employees who join as trained operators/drivers have received adequate training to operate safely in their new company. The management must ensure that they have the basic skills and receive training in company methods and procedures for the type of work they are to undertake. They should be examined and tested before issue of company driving authority.

TESTING

On completion of training, the operator/driver should be examined and tested to ensure that he/she has achieved the required standard. It is recommended that at set intervals or when there is indication of the operator/driver not working to required standard, or following an accident, formal check tests be introduced.

REFRESHER TRAINING

If high standards are to be maintained, periodic refresher training and testing should be considered.

A vigorous management policy covering operator training, plant maintenance and sound systems of work, supported by good supervision will reduce personal injury and damage to equipment and materials. This in turn will lead to better vehicle utilisation and increased materials handling efficiency.

OPERATOR/DRIVER IDENTIFICATION

Many organisations operate local codes of practice and take great care to evidence the authority they have given to operators/drivers by the provision of a licence for that vehicle and sometimes a visible badge to confirm this. Access to vehicles is supervised and authority checked carefully to confirm that the actual class of vehicle is within the authority given. This is important with such things as rough terrain lift trucks that operate differently to a standard counterbalance truck. *See also - Manual and Mechanical Handling – Unit 13*. It is essential that access to keys for vehicles is restricted to those that are competent to operate/drive them, this is not just a practical point but enables compliance with PUWER.

Traffic safety measures and signs for streetworks

It is the responsibility of whoever is in control of streetworks to sign, guard light and maintain the works safely. This will require a certain amount of planning to ascertain what procedures need to be implemented and what equipment is required to ensure safety.

Measures to be taken can be found in the document, "Safety at Street Works and Road Works" that has statutory backing as a code of practice under the "New Roads and Street Works Act 1991" and the "Street Works (Northern Ireland) Order." This code of practice will help you to safely carry out temporary signing, lighting and guarding of streetworks and road works on most roads. Failure to comply with the code of practice may lead to criminal prosecution in addition to any civil proceedings. Further recommendations regarding safety measures at road works can be found in Chapter 8 of the "Traffic Signs Manual".

Prior to any works starting, and in order to ensure compliance with current health and safety legislation, an on-site risk assessment must be carried out to ensure a safe system of working is derived in respect of signing, lighting and guarding is in place at all times.

Any signs, lights or guarding equipment must be secured against being blown over or out of position by wind or passing traffic. This is usually done by the use of sand bags; hard items should not be used as these can be hazardous if struck by traffic. Signs should be placed sufficiently away from the works in order to provide drivers with adequate prior warning of the works and not present a hazard to pedestrians if placed in footpaths. Signs should also be of a reflective nature and be monitored to ensure they remain clean and visible. Any permanent signs or signals that become overridden by the temporary signing, lighting and guarding may require covering over. Consent for this will need to be received from the highway authority.

The placing of signs must consider traffic approaching from all directions, whether it is by two-way traffic or traffic at road junctions. The working area must also be demarcated with an allowance made for a safety zone (between 0.5m to 1.2m) surrounding the works, and also marked off with cones and lighting as necessary. The safety zone must never be used as a work area or for storing plant, equipment or vehicles.

Figure 11-20: Streetworks safety measures. *Source: ACT.*

When the site is not in use; but signing, lighting and guarding is in place; then arrangements must be in place to ensure regular inspections and any damaged or displaced equipment remedied immediately. Site vehicles at the works should always operate roof mounted amber beacons if fitted to the vehicles. Hazard warning indicators should not be used at road works as these confuse other road users.

Following completion of a streetworks project, all plant, equipment, materials, signs, lights and guarding should be removed immediately.

11.5 - Segregating pedestrians and vehicles

Means of segregation

'Every workplace shall be organised in such a way that pedestrians and vehicles can circulate in a safe manner".

Regulation 17(1) of WHSWR

"Every construction site shall be organised in such a way that, so far as is reasonably practicable, pedestrians and vehicles can move safely and without risks to health."

"Traffic routes shall be suitable for the persons or vehicles using them, sufficient in number, in suitable positions and of sufficient size."

Regulation 15 of CHSW

Clearly defined and marked routes should be provided for people going about their business at work. These should be provided for access and egress points to the workplace, car parks, and vehicle delivery routes. Safe crossing places should be provided where people have to cross main traffic routes. In buildings where vehicles operate, separate doors and walkways should be provided for pedestrians to get from building to building. Meshed handrails can be used to channel people into the pedestrian route. Where it is not possible to have a pedestrian route with a safe clearance from vehicle movement, because of building and plant design, then a raised pedestrian walkway could be considered to help in segregation.

- Accidents can be caused where vehicles are unsafely parked as they can be an obstruction and restrict visibility. There should be clear entrance and exit routes in parking areas and designated parking areas to allow the load and sheeting of outgoing transport to be checked safely before leaving the site.

Figure 11-21: Segregating pedestrians and vehicles. *Source: ACT.*

- There should be clear, well-marked and signposted vehicle traffic routes, which avoid steep gradients where possible, especially where fork lift trucks operate. It is important to have speed limits that are practicable and effective. Speed limit signs should be posted and traffic slowing measures such as speed bumps and ramps may be necessary in certain situations. Monitoring speed limit compliance is necessary, along with some kind of action against persistent offenders.
- Speed limits of 10 or 15 mph are usually considered appropriate, although 5 mph may be necessary in certain situations.
- Transport requires clear routes to be designated, marked with painted lines and preferably fenced off from pedestrians. Accidents can occur when plant and people collide: the pedestrian may be injured by contact and the driver injured if the vehicle overturns.
- Separate gates/doorways should be provided for vehicles entry and blind spots should be dealt with by the careful positioning of mirrors on walls, plant or storage. Routes should be wide enough to allow manoeuvrability and passing.
- Where it is unavoidable that pedestrians will come into proximity with transport, people should be reminded of the hazards by briefings, site induction and signs, so they are aware at all times.

Any traffic route which is used by both pedestrians and vehicles should be wide enough to enable any vehicle likely to use the route to pass pedestrians safely. On traffic routes in existence before 1 January 1993, where it is not practical to make the route wide enough, passing places or traffic management systems should be provided as necessary. In buildings, lines should be drawn on the floor to indicate routes followed by vehicles such as fork lift trucks.

Measures to be taken when segregation is not practicable

Where pedestrians and vehicle routes cross, appropriate crossing points should be provided and used. Where necessary, barriers or rails should be provided to prevent pedestrians crossing at particularly dangerous points and to guide them to designated crossing places. At crossing places where volumes of traffic are particularly heavy, the provision of suitable bridges or subways should be considered. At crossing points there should be adequate visibility and open space for the pedestrian where the pedestrian route joins the vehicle route.

Where segregation is not practicable and vehicles share the same workplace as pedestrians it is important to mark the work areas as being separate from vehicle routes to warn drivers to adjust their approach and be more aware of pedestrians. Audible and visual warnings of the presence of the vehicle would also assist. Where vehicles are dominant but pedestrians need to access, similar means may be used but for the opposite reason. In this situation the added use of personal protective equipment that increases the ability to see the pedestrian, and safety footwear, are usually needed. High visibility clothing is mandatory on the majority of construction projects. The reversing of large vehicles that have a restricted view should be controlled by the use of a banksman to guide them.

Figure 11-22: No segregation.   Source: ACT.

Figure 11-23: Control of vehicle movement.   Source: ACT.

SUMMARY OF MEASURES FOR SAFE MOVEMENT OF PEOPLE AND VEHICLES

- Use of barriers.
- Defined traffic routes.
- One-way systems.
- Provision of refuges.
- Speed control.
- Mirrors / cameras.
- Good lighting.
- High visibility clothing.
- A good standard of housekeeping.
- Audible warnings on vehicles.
- Training and supervision of drivers.
- Drawing up and enforcement of site rules.

Work equipment hazards & control

Overall Aims

On completion of this Unit, candidates will understand:

- the hazards and risks form the use of work equipment in construction work.
- the basic measures to be taken to minimise the risks from such equipment.

Content

Specific Intended Learning Outcome

The intended learning outcomes of this Unit are that candidates will be able to:

12.1   outline the general requirements for work equipment

12.2   outline the hazards and controls for hand-held tools, both powered and non-powered

12.3   describe the main mechanical and non-mechanical hazards of machinery

12.4   describe the main methods of protection from mechanical hazards

Sources of Reference

Safe Use of Work Equipment (ACOP) (L22), HSE Books
Safe Use of Woodworking Machinery (L144), HSE Books

Relevant Statutory Provisions

The Supply of Machinery (Safety) Regulations (SMSR) 1992 - scope and application, and relationship to CE marking
The Provision and Use of Work Equipment Regulations (PUWER) 1998 - Part II
The Personal Protective Equipment at Work Regulations (PPER) 1992

12.1 - General

Scope of work equipment

The Provision and Use of Work Equipment Regulations (PUWER) 1998 are concerned with most aspects relating to work equipment. The Regulations define work equipment as any machinery, appliance, apparatus, tool or assembly of components which are arranged so that they function as a whole. Clearly the term embraces many hand tools, power tools and machinery.

Examples of work equipment commonly used in the construction industry include:

- Air compressor.
- Air road breakers.
- Floor saws.
- Piling hammers.
- Drill rigs.
- Nail guns.
- Road breakers.

- Scabblers.
- Mobile elevating work platforms (MEWP's).
- Lifting sling.
- Mobile access platform.
- Overhead projector.
- Photocopier.
- Rough terrain fork lift truck (RTFLT).

Not work equipment:

- Livestock.
- Substances.
- Structural items (buildings).
- Private car.

Figure 12-1: Air road breakers.   *Source: Speedy Hire plc.*

Figure 12-2: Floor scabbler.   *Source: Speedy Hire plc.*

Figure 12-3: Hand held scabbler.   *Source: Speedy Hire plc.*

Figure 12-4: Lifting sling.   *Source: ACT.*

Suitability as it relates to provision of equipment

PROVISION OF WORK EQUIPMENT REGULATIONS [PUWER] 1998

PUWER Regulation 4 Suitability of work equipment

(1) Every employer shall ensure that work equipment is so constructed or adapted as to be suitable for the purpose for which it is used or provided.

(2) In selecting work equipment, every employer shall have regard to the working conditions and to the risks to the health and safety of persons which exist in the premises or undertaking in which that work equipment is to be used and any additional risk posed by the use of that work equipment.

(3) Every employer shall ensure that work equipment is used only for operations for which, and under conditions for which, it is suitable.

(4) In this regulation "suitable" means suitable in any respect which it is reasonably foreseeable will affect the health or safety of any person.

Suitability should consider:

■ Its initial integrity.
■ The place where it will be used.
■ The purpose for which it will be used.

Integrity - is equipment safe through its design, construction or adaptation? - sharp edges removed from the pen tray of a flip chart stand, 'home made' tools, equipment adapted to do a specific task.

Place - is equipment suitable for different environments (risks)? - wet or explosive. Account must be taken of the equipment causing a problem - a petrol generator used in a confined space, a hydraulic access platform used in a location with a low roof.

Use - is equipment suitable for the specific task? - a hacksaw being used to cut metal straps used to secure goods to a pallet (instead of a purpose designed tool); the use of a ladder to do work at a height (instead of a scaffold or other access platform); exceeding the safe working load of a crane or fork lift truck, a swivel chair used as a means of access to a shelf.

 ## CONFORMITY WITH RELEVANT STANDARDS, CE MARKING

Section 6 of The Health and Safety at Work Act (HASAWA) 1974 requires those involved in the supply (including design and manufacture) of equipment to ensure that it is safe and healthy, so far as is reasonably practicable. This will require them to take account of all relevant standards.

PUWER Regulation 10 Conformity with community requirements

1   Every employer shall ensure that an item of work equipment has been designed and constructed in compliance with any essential requirements, that is to say requirements relating to its design or construction in any of the instruments listed in Schedule 1 (being instruments which give effect to Community directives concerning the safety of products).

2   Where an essential requirement applied to the design or construction of an item of work equipment, the requirements of regulations 11 to 19 and 22 to 29 shall apply in respect of that item only to the extent that the essential requirement did not apply to it.

3   This regulation applies to items of work equipment provided for use in the premises or undertaking of the employer for the first time after 31st December 1992.

Work equipment provided for use after 31 December 1992 must conform with legislation made in the UK in response to EC directives relating to work equipment. Only those directives listed in schedule 1 of PUWER are to be considered and then only those that have been translated to UK law. Examples relate to:

■ The amount of noise emitted from a variety of equipment (e.g. construction equipment or lawn mowers).
■ Electro-medical equipment.
■ Simple pressure vessels.
■ Machinery safety. *See also - Supply of Machinery (Safety) Regulations - Unit 20.*
■ Personal protective equipment.

Directives, and in turn UK Regulations, tend to contain details of 'essential health and safety requirements' and a system whereby compliance may be demonstrated.   Compliance is usually demonstrated by the attachment of a CE mark and the manufacturer/supplier holding an EC declaration of conformity. This declaration may, in the early days of the legislation, be a self declaration or a third party declaration.

FIT FOR PURPOSE

Equipment used for any activity must be suitable to fulfil the exact requirements of the task. This means considering the ergonomic requirements (see paragraph below), strength, durability, power source, portability, protection against the environment, range of tasks to be carried out and the frequency and duration of use. Equipment that is designed to perform a specific task must only be used for that task and not adapted for other tasks not considered in the manufacturers design and instructions. An example of this is where a portable battery operated drill is rotated by hand or the back / butt of the drill is used as a hammer, clearly a task not meant for this equipment. Equipment used in these types of situation identifies a lack of fore thought in the planning stage of a project when the correct equipment should have been sought and used.

The equipment may be used indoors or outdoors where consideration must be given to the dangers of damp, water and electricity or explosive atmospheres within confined spaces. The grade of equipment should be industrial or commercial type for work activities and not the type of equipment designed for use by the domestic DIY sector. Whenever equipment is required, the full capacity and limitation requirements should be identified and it should be confirmed that the equipment provided can cope with the demands/limitations placed upon it. For example, construction sites use 110 volt supply it is important that workers turn up at site with equipment that suits this power supply.

ERGONOMIC CONSIDERATIONS

Ergonomic considerations involve the study of person-equipment interface, with an emphasis on adjustability of the machinery and equipment. The aim is to suit a variety of individual sizes and positions in order to provide the most comfortable position possible. In considering the ergonomic factors of a task that requires equipment to be used, it is essential to include the operator's individual attributes, and how they affect and may be affected by the process. Factors might include posture when seated or standing, height of the work station, how the equipment may be adjusted and frequency of the task being performed. It is essential that ergonomic considerations form an active part at the planning stage of a process to ensure the correct equipment is obtained and the reactive effects of poor ergonomics eliminated.

Requirement to restrict the use and maintenance of equipment

STATUTORY RESTRICTIONS ON USE OF WORK EQUIPMENT

PUWER Regulation 7 Specific risks

1) Where the use of work equipment is likely to involve a specific risk to health or safety, every employer shall ensure that:

    a) The use of that work equipment is restricted to those persons given the task of using it; and

    b) Repairs, modifications, maintenance or servicing of that work equipment is restricted to those persons who have been specifically designated to perform operations of that description (whether or not also authorised to perform other operations).

2) The employer shall ensure that the persons designated for the purposes of sub-paragraph (b) of paragraph (1) have received adequate training related to any operations in respect of which they have been so designated.

For example, in view of the specific risks, it would be appropriate to restrict the use of a nail gun, circular saw or mobile elevated work platform to those competent and authorised to use it. In the same way maintenance (replacement of a grinding wheel) of an abrasive wheel or (replacement of load bearing components) of a rough terrain fork lift truck should be restricted.

Information, instruction and training

INFORMATION AND INSTRUCTION

Whenever equipment is provided and used in the workplace there is a requirement to ensure that all operators are given adequate information and instruction in order that they can use the equipment safely. The issues covered should include the safe operation of the equipment and also the capacities ands limitations of the equipment. Specific information must be given on the particular hazards of equipment and instruction and training given on how to implement, use and maintain control measures correctly.

PUWER regulation 8 - information and instruction

"Every employer shall ensure that all persons who use work equipment have available to them adequate health and safety information and, where appropriate, written instructions pertaining to the use of the work equipment.

Every employer shall ensure that any of his employees who supervises or manages the use of work equipment has available to him adequate health and safety information and, where appropriate, written instructions pertaining to the use of the work equipment. …..information and, where appropriate, written instructions on -

a) the conditions in which and the methods by which the work equipment may be used;
b) foreseeable abnormal situations and the action to be taken if such a situation were to occur; and
c) any conclusions to be drawn from experience in using the work equipment."

TRAINING

PUWER Regulation 9 - training

"Every employer shall ensure that all persons who use work equipment have received adequate training for purposes of health and safety, including training in the methods which may be adopted when using the work equipment, any risks which such use may entail and precautions to be taken.

Every employer shall ensure that any of his employees who supervises or manages the use of work equipment has received adequate training for purposes of health and safety, including training in the methods which may be adopted when using the work equipment, any risks which such use may entail and precautions to be taken."

Training may be needed for existing staff as well as inexperienced staff or new starters (do not forget temporary staff), particularly if they have to use powered machinery. The greater the danger, the better the training needs to be. For some high risk work such as driving forklift trucks, using a chainsaw and operating a crane, training should be carried out by specialist instructors. Remember that younger people can be quite skillful when moving and handling powered equipment, but they may lack experience and judgment and may require closer supervision to begin with.

Examples:

Users - How to carry out pre-use checks, report defects, only to use equipment for the purpose designed.

Maintenance - Safe isolation recommended spares and adjustments in accordance with manufacturer's manuals.

Managers - Be aware of the hazards and controls and maintain effective supervision.

Requirement for equipment to be maintained and maintenance to be conducted safely

EQUIPMENT TO BE MAINTAINED

PUWER regulation 5 - maintenance

Equipment must be maintained in efficient working order and good repair. In order to achieve this, a system of maintenance should be in place which involves regular inspection, adjustment and testing. Maintenance logs, where they exist, must be kept up to date.

MAINTENANCE TO BE CONDUCTED SAFELY

PUWER regulation 22 - maintenance

No one should be exposed to undue risk during maintenance operations. In order to achieve this equipment should be stopped and isolated as appropriate before work starts. If it is necessary to keep equipment running then the risks must be adequately controlled. This may take the form of controlling running speed, range of movement or providing temporary guards. Consideration must be given to other legislation such as Electricity at Work (EWR) Regulations 1989 during the assessment.

Maintenance hazards

The principal sources of hazards are associated with maintenance work on:

- Heavy plant.
- Crushers.
- Cranes.
- Concrete pumps.
- Storage tanks.
- Batching plant.

Typical hazards associated with maintenance operations

Mechanical	-	Entanglement, machinery traps, contact; shearing traps, in running nips, ejection, unexpected start up.
Electrical	-	Electrocution, shock, burns.
Pressure	-	Unexpected pressure releases, explosion.
Physical	-	Extremes of temperature, noise, vibration, dust.
Chemical	-	Gases, vapours, mists, fumes, etc.
Structural	-	Obstructions and floor openings.
Access	-	Work at heights, confined spaces.

Typical accidents

- Crushing by moving machinery.
- Falls.
- Burns.
- Asphyxiation.
- Electrocution.

One or more of the following factors causes maintenance accidents:

- Lack of perception of risk by managers/supervisors, often because of lack of necessary training.
- Unsafe or no system of work devised, for example, no permit-to-work system in operation, no facility to lock off machinery and electricity supply before work starts and until work has finished.
- No co-ordination between workers, and communication with other supervisors or managers.
- Lack of perception of risk by workers, including failure to wear protective clothing or equipment.
- Inadequacy of design, installation, siting of plant and equipment.
- Use of contractors with no health and safety systems or who are inadequately briefed on health and safety aspects.

Figure 12-5: Crusher. *Source: ACT.*

Figure 12-6: Electrical isolator with hole for padlock. *Source: ACT.*

Maintenance control measures

Isolation

This does not simply mean switching off the equipment using the stop button. It includes switching the equipment off at the button and switching off the isolator of the equipment

In modern workplaces, individual isolators are the norm; i.e. each piece of equipment has its own isolator near it. In the past, one isolator often governed several items of equipment making it impossible to isolate a single piece of equipment on its own.

Lock out & tag out

Isolation alone does not afford adequate protection because there is nothing to prevent the isolator being switched back on, or fuses being replaced inadvertently, while the person who isolated the item in the first place is still working on the equipment (and still in danger).

To ensure that this does not happen, the isolator needs to be physically locked in the off position (typically using a padlock, the key to be held by the person in danger). Multiple lock out devices that can carry a number of pad locks for the different people working on the equipment, are also available. It is also a good idea to hang a *"Do not switch on..."* tag on the equipment.

Summary of control measures
- Plan work in advance - provide safe access, support parts of equipment which could fail.
- Use written safe systems of work, method statements or permit to work systems as appropriate.
- Plan specific operations using method statements.
- Use physical means of isolating or locking off plant.
- Systems of working should incorporate two-man working for high risk operations.
- Integrate safety requirements in the planning of specific high risk tasks.
- Prevent unauthorised access to the work area by using barriers and signs.
- Ensure the competence of those carrying out the work.
- Ensure the availability and use of appropriate personal protective equipment (PPE) - gloves, eye protection.
- Prevent fire or explosion - thoroughly clean vessels that have contained flammable solids or liquids, gases or dusts and check them thoroughly before hot work is carried out.

INSPECTION AND EXAMINATION

PUWER regulation 6 - inspection

"Every employer shall ensure that work equipment exposed to conditions causing deterioration which is liable to result in dangerous situations is inspected:

a)   at suitable intervals; and

b)   each time that exceptional circumstances which are liable to jeopardise the safety of the work equipment have occurred, to ensure that health and safety conditions are maintained and that any deterioration can be detected and remedied in good time.

Every employer shall ensure that the result of an inspection made under this regulation is recorded and kept until the next inspection under this regulation is recorded."

Figure 12-7: Inspection and examination.   *Source: ACT.*

Equipment must be inspected on a regular basis in order to confirm the condition that it is in. The inspection required is more than a simple daily pre use check carried out by the operator. The person using equipment, who should be confirmed as competent, should carry out operator checks prior to the use of any equipment. Operator checks should include guards, cables, casing integrity, cutting or machine parts and safety devices such as cut-outs. The inspection required under this regulation should be significant and address a list of identifiable health and safety critical parts. The purpose of an inspection sheet is to determine deterioration of specific parts, abuse and misuse and also to ensure that all items are considered at the time of inspection, by serving as an aide memoir. The results of the inspection will confirm whether or not a piece of equipment is in a safe enough condition to use. Other regulations, such as the Lifting Operations and Lifting Equipment Regulations (LOLER) 1998 require and set certain statutory inspection requirements

Examination of pressure systems - boilers and air receivers

A pressure system is, as defined in the Pressure Systems Safety Regulations, as follows:

- "a system comprising one or more pressure vessels of rigid construction, and any associated pipework and protective devices;
- the pipework with its protective devices to which a transportable gas container is or is intended to be connected, or
- a pipeline and its protective devices."

A pressure vessel is generally considered one which operates at a pressure greater than atmospheric pressure, e.g. steam boilers, receivers and air receivers.

Competent persons

The Pressure Systems Safety Regulations 2000 define the term competent person as a competent individual person (other than an employee) or a competent body of persons. There are three distinct functions of the competent person:

Figure 12-8: Air compressor.   *Source: Speedy Hire plc.*

1)   Advising the user on the scope of the written scheme of examination.

2)   Drawing up or certifying schemes of examination.

3)   Carrying out examinations under the scheme.

It is the responsibility of all users to select a competent person who is capable of carrying out his duties in a proper manner. The competent person should have relevant knowledge and experience of the system. For complex systems, the competent person may be a number of different people for different parts of the system.

The examinations should be impartial and objective with the safety considerations and use of the system in mind.

Schemes of examination

Examination means a careful and critical scrutiny of a pressure system or part of a pressure system, in or out of service as appropriate. It means using suitable techniques, including testing where appropriate, to assess its actual condition and whether, for the period up to the next examination, it will not cause danger when properly used if normal maintenance is carried out.

Normal maintenance means such maintenance as it is reasonable to expect the user (in the case of an installed system) or owner (in the case of a mobile system) to ensure is carried out independently of any advice from the competent person making the examination.

A written scheme of examination must be available before any system is used. This should be drawn up by a competent person and should include:

- Pressure vessels.
- Pipe work and valves.

- Protective devices.
- Pumps and compressors.

Examination intervals should be specified, though these may be different for different parts of the system, so that deterioration, etc. can be detected before danger arises. An initial examination should be done before use. Any repairs or modifications should be controlled. Factors to be taken into account when deciding upon the frequency of examination will include:

- Previous intervals and system records.
- Standards of supervision and routine checks.
- Type and quality of fluids in the system.

- The likelihood of creep, fatigue, etc. failures.
- Corrosion potential and effect.
- Presence of heat sources etc.

The type of examination should also be specified.

Examinations must be carried out in accordance with the written scheme and the system adequately assessed for fitness for continued use. Appropriate preparations for and precautions during examination should be arranged for by the user. A report with any conditions or limitations on use should be prepared on completion of the examination.

Where the competent person's examination identifies imminent danger then a report must be made to the user who should ensure the system is not used further and a report is sent to the relevant enforcing authority.

Anyone operating a pressure system must be given adequate and suitable instructions for safe operation and emergency action. This instruction should form part of the operating instructions for the plant and should include information on start-up, shutdown, normal operation, functions of controls, emergency procedures, etc. Doors providing routine access should be dealt with by specific instructions covering interlocking checks, opening and closing precautions, failure signs, etc. Precautions must be taken to prevent unintentional pressurisation of parts of any system not designed for pressure.

Routine and regular maintenance should be carried out including periodic checks and inspections of important parts or components.

Adequate records of examinations, repairs, modifications etc., should be kept at the premises where the system is used.

Additional safeguards for work equipment

OPERATION AND EMERGENCY CONTROLS

PUWER Regulation 14 Controls for starting or making a significant change in operating conditions

(1) Every employer shall ensure that, where appropriate, work equipment is provided with one or more controls for the purposes of -

(a) Starting the work equipment (including re-starting after a stoppage for any reason); or

(b) Controlling any change in the speed, pressure or other operating conditions of the work equipment where such conditions after the change result in risk to health and safety which is greater than or of a different nature from such risks before the change.

(2) Subject to paragraph (3), every employer shall ensure that where a control is required by paragraph (1), it shall not be possible to perform any operation mentioned in sub-paragraph (a) or (b) of that paragraph except by a deliberate action on such control.

Paragraph (1) Shall not apply to re-starting or changing operating conditions as a result of the normal operating cycle of an automatic device.

Any change in the operating conditions should only be possible by the use of a control, except if the change does not increase risk to health or safety. Examples of operating conditions include speed, pressure, temperature and power.

The controls provided should be designed and positioned so as to prevent, so far as possible, inadvertent or accidental operation. Buttons and levers should be of appropriate design, for example, including a shroud or locking facility. It should not be possible for the control to 'operate itself' such as due to the effects of gravity, vibration, or failure of a spring mechanism.

PUWER Regulation 15 Stop controls

(1) Every employer shall ensure that, where appropriate, work equipment is provided with one or more readily accessible controls the operation of which will bring the work equipment to a safe condition in a safe manner.

(2) Any control required by paragraph (1) shall bring the work equipment to a complete stop where necessary for reasons of health and safety.

(3) Any control required by paragraph (1) shall, if necessary for reasons of health and safety, switch off all sources of energy after stopping the functioning of the work equipment.

(4) Any control required by paragraph (1) shall operate in priority to any control, which starts or changes the operating conditions of the work equipment.

The primary requirement of this Regulation is that the action of the control should bring the equipment to a safe condition in a safe manner. This acknowledges that it is not always desirable to bring all items of work equipment immediately to a complete or instantaneous stop, for example, to prevent the unsafe build-up of heat or pressure or to allow a controlled run-down of large rotating parts. Similarly, stopping the mixing mechanism of a reactor during certain chemical reactions could lead to a dangerous exothermic reaction.

The Regulation is qualified by 'where necessary for reasons of health and safety'. Therefore, accessible dangerous parts must be rendered stationary. However, parts of equipment which do not present a risk, such as suitably guarded cooling fans, do not need to be positively stopped and may be allowed to idle.

PUWER Regulation 16 Emergency stop controls

(1) Every employer shall ensure that, where appropriate, work equipment is provided with one or more readily accessible emergency stop controls unless it is not necessary by reason of the nature of the hazards and the time taken for the work equipment to come to a complete stop as a result of the action of any control provided by virtue of regulation 15(1).

(2) Any control required by paragraph (1) shall operate in priority to any control required by regulation 15(1).

Emergency stops are intended to effect a rapid response to potentially dangerous situations and they should not be used as functional stops during normal operation.

Emergency stop controls should be easily reached and actuated. Common types are mushroom-headed buttons, bars, levers, kick plates, or pressure-sensitive cables.

Figure 12-9: Controls and emergency stop.   *Source: ACT.*

Figure 12-10: Controls.   *Source: ACT.*

PUWER Regulation 17 Controls

(1) Every employer shall ensure that all controls for work equipment shall be clearly visible and identifiable, including by appropriate marking where necessary.

(2) Except where necessary, the employer shall ensure that no control for work equipment is in a position where any person operating the control is exposed to a risk to his health or safety.

(3) Every employer shall ensure where appropriate:

(a) That, so far as is reasonably practicable, the operator of any control is able to ensure from the position of that control that no person is in a place where he would be exposed to any risk to his health or safety as a result of the operation of that control, but where or to the extent that it is not reasonably practicable;

(b) That, so far as is reasonably practicable, systems of work are effective to ensure that, when work equipment is about to start, no person is in a place where he would be exposed to a risk to his health or safety as a result of the work equipment starting, but where neither of these is reasonably practicable;

(c) That an audible, visible or other suitable warning is given by virtue of regulation 24 whenever work equipment is about to start.

(4) Every employer shall take appropriate measures to ensure that any person who is in a place where he would be exposed to a risk to his health or safety as a result of the starting or stopping of work equipment has sufficient time and suitable means to avoid that risk.

It should be possible to identify easily what each control does and on which equipment it takes effect. Both the controls and their markings should be clearly visible. As well as having legible wording or symbols, factors such as the colour, shape and position of controls are important.

Warnings given in accordance with regulation 17(3) (c) should be given sufficiently in advance of the equipment actually starting to give those at risk time to get clear. As well as time, suitable means of avoiding the risk should be provided. This may take the form of a device by means of which the person at risk can prevent start-up or warn the operator of his/her presence. Otherwise, there must be adequate provision to enable people at risk to withdraw, e.g. sufficient space or exits. Circumstances will affect the type of warning chosen.

PUWER Regulation 18 Control systems

(1) Every employer shall-

(a) Ensure, so far as is reasonably practicable, that all control systems of work equipment are safe; and

(b) Are chosen making due allowance for the failures, faults and constraints to be expected in the planned circumstances of use.

(2) Without prejudice to the generality of paragraph (1), a control system shall not be safe unless-

(a) Its operation does not create any increased risk to health or safety;

(b) It ensures, so far as is reasonably practicable, that any fault in or damage to any part of the control system or the loss of supply of any source of energy used by the work equipment cannot result in additional or increased risk to health or safety; (c) It does not impede the operation of any control required by regulation 15 or 16.

Failure of any part of the control system or its power supply should lead to a 'fail-safe' condition (more correctly and realistically called 'minimised failure to danger'), and not impede the operation of the 'stop' or 'emergency stop' controls. The measures, which should be taken in the design and application of a control system to mitigate against the effects of failure, will need to be balanced against the consequences of any failure, and the greater the risk, the more resistant the control system should be to the effects of failure.

STABILITY

PUWER Regulation 20 Stability

Every employer shall ensure that work equipment or any part of work equipment is stabilised by clamping or otherwise where necessary for purposes of health or safety.

Most machines used in a fixed position should be bolted or otherwise fastened down so that they do not move or rock during use. It has long been recognised that woodworking and other machines (except those specifically designed for portable use) should be bolted to the floor or similarly secured to prevent unexpected movement.

LIGHTING

PUWER Regulation 21 Lighting

Every employer shall ensure that suitable and sufficient lighting, which takes account of the operations to be carried out, is provided at any place where a person uses work equipment.

Local lighting may be needed to give sufficient view of a dangerous process or to reduce visual fatigue.

MARKINGS AND WARNINGS

PUWER Regulation 23 - Markings

Every employer shall ensure that work equipment is marked in a clearly visible manner with any marking appropriate for reasons of health and safety

There are similarities between regulation 23 and 24 covering markings and warnings. Certain markings may also serve as a warning, i.e. the maximum working speed, maximum working load or the contents being a hazardous nature (i.e. colour coded gas bottles or service mains.

PUWER Regulation 24 - Warnings

Every employer shall ensure that work equipment incorporates any warnings or warning devices which are appropriate for reasons of health and safety

Warnings given by warning devices on work equipment shall not be appropriate unless they are unambiguous, easily perceived and easily understood.

Warnings and warning devices are introduced following the implementation of markings and other physical measures have been taken and an appropriate risk to health and safety remains. Warnings are usually in the form of a notice, sign or similar. Examples of warnings being positive instructions (hard hats MUST be worn), prohibitions (no smoking) and restrictions (do not heat above 60 degrees Celsius). Warning devices are active units that give out either an audible or visual signal, usually connected to the equipment in order that it operates only when a hazard exists.

CLEAR UNOBSTRUCTED WORK SPACE

Workplace (Health, Safety & Welfare) (WHSWR) Regulations 1992

Regulation 11 - Room dimensions and space

Every room where persons work shall have sufficient floor area, height and unoccupied space for purposes of health, safety and welfare.

Workrooms should have enough free space to allow people to get to and from workstations and to move within the room with ease. Workrooms should be of sufficient height (from floor to ceiling) over most of the room to enable safe access to workstations. In older buildings with obstructions such as low beams, the obstruction should be clearly marked.

The total volume of the room, when empty, divided by the number of people normally working in it, should be at least 11 cubic metres. In making this calculation a room or part of a room which is more than 3.0 m high should be counted as 3.0 m high. The figure of 11 cubic metres per person is a minimum and may be insufficient if, for example, much of the room is taken up by furniture.

Where work equipment, such as a circular saw, is used in a workplace care should be taken to ensure that adequate space is around the equipment to ensure it is not overcrowded and does not cause risk to operators and those passing by the equipment when it is operating.

Responsibilities of users

MANAGEMENT OF HEALTH AND SAFETY AT WORK- REGULATION 14 EMPLOYEES DUTIES

Every employee shall use any machinery, equipment, dangerous substance, transport equipment, means of production or safety device provided to him by his employer in accordance both with any training in the use of the equipment concerned which has been received by him and the instructions respecting that use which have been provided to him by the said employer in compliance with the requirements and prohibitions imposed upon that employer by or under the relevant statutory provisions.

Employees have a duty under section 7 of the HASAWA 1974 to take reasonable care for their own health and safety, and for that of others who, may be affected by their acts or omissions and to co-operate with the employer to enable him to comply with statutory duties for health and safety. Employees should notify any shortcomings in the health and safety arrangements, even when no immediate danger exists, so that employers can take remedial action if needed. The duties placed on employees do not reduce the responsibility of the employer to comply with his own duties.

12.2 - Hand-held tools

Hand tools

HAZARDS AND MISUSE OF HAND TOOLS

Hand tools are tools powered manually i.e. axes, hammers, screwdrivers; therefore the biggest hazard would arise from errors made by the user e.g. striking a finger whilst using a hammer or cuts from a saw.

REQUIREMENTS FOR SAFE USE

Hammers   Avoid split, broken or loose shafts and worn or chipped heads. Heads should be properly secured to the shafts.

Files   These should have a proper handle. Never use them as levers.

Chisels   The cutting edge should be sharpened to the correct angle. Do not allow the head of cold chisels to spread to a mushroom shape - grind off the sides regularly. Use a hand guard on the chisel.

Screwdrivers   Never use them as chisels, and never use hammers on them. Use the correct size and type of screwdriver for the screw. Split handles are dangerous.

Spanners   Avoid splayed jaws. Scrap any which show signs of slipping. Have enough spanners of the right size. Do not improvise by using pipes, etc., as extensions to the handle.

SUITABILITY FOR PURPOSE AND LOCATION

Use of alloy or bronze hammers or spanners to prevent sparks, and damping with water, in areas where there is a flammable atmosphere.

Portable power tools

HAZARDS AND CONTROLS

Figure 12-11: Eye injury & sparks.   *Source: Speedy Hire plc.*

Figure 12-12: Impact injury. *Source: Speedy Hire plc.*

Pneumatic drill/chisel

Pneumatic drills or chisels are used commonly where heavy duty tasks are performed such as penetrating tarmac or concrete surfaces. This equipment is usually very heavy and labour intensive, resulting in manual handling hazards and risks. The pneumatic energy is usually delivered through mobile industrial compressors that are capable of supplying adequate power. The compressor is a separate piece of equipment that introduces its own specific hazards. Perhaps the most obvious hazard is the drill or chisel piece which, when operating presents a risk of impact injury to the operator's, and others nearby, feet. During normal operation, the drill or chisel tool produces high frequency and intensity noise from impact with the surface. Other noise includes the exhausting of the pneumatic pressure from the internal drive of the equipment as the tool operates. The noise sources are located very close to the operator's ears and are at a level that is damaging to the ear and requires the user to wear protective hearing protection. The operation of the chisel produces the hazard of flying debris in the form of dust and fragments that pose the risk of abrasion, cuts or eye damage. In order to control this risk the surface may be damped down and protective goggles worn by the user. The energy produced by the compressor is converted into vibration. Vibration introduces the risk of injuries such as hand arm vibration syndrome (HAVS) with possible long term effects including damage to the nervous system beginning at the fingertips. Precautions for vibration include using well maintained equipment, using equipment with lower vibration levels, taking frequent breaks or job rotation, exercise to improve circulation and warm the hands and seeking suitable personal protective gloves. There are risks associated with high pressure air lines becoming broken or damaged resulting in pipes lashing freely. Equipment should always be inspected as safe to use with certification for pressure lines. Screens can be used as a final measure to protect others at the site of the works.

Electric drill

Electric drills are used for penetrating various materials and in construction are usually of a medium to heavy-duty nature. This equipment involves rotating shafts and tool bits, sharp tools, electricity and flying debris. Obvious hazards include shock and electrocution leading to possible fatalities, however this potential is reduced by using 110 volt or battery operated equipment. Other hazards include entanglement hazards, noise and dust. Control measures include using only equipment that is suitable for the task, ensuring equipment is tested and inspected as safe to use, suitable shut off and isolation measures, goggles, hearing protection. Care should be taken to ensure the drill bits are kept sharp as injuries can occur when the rotating drill bit gets stuck in material and the drill is caused to kick and rotate in the operator's hands.

Disc-cutter

Disc cutters consist of a motor providing power to a circular cutting disc (made of stone or steel). Power is provided by petrol, diesel, electricity or pneumatic energy. This equipment is used for slicing materials into sections or cutting grooves into surfaces. Hazards include initially the power of the equipment which may result in shock and electrocution, fire, inhalation of fumes or absorption of hazardous substances. When in operation the disc of the cutter may spin at speeds ranging from 2900 revolutions per minute. Hazards arising from cutting operations or due to cutter discs exploding following misuse include flying debris, sparks and dust. Goggles must be worn when operating this equipment, due to the velocity of the flying debris they must be grade 1 impact resistant and totally enclose the eye region of the face. Dust masks must also be worn when using this equipment, however the area being cut into may be damped down to minimise the production of dust clouds into the atmosphere. Vacuum attachments are available that make these operation almost dust-less when working correctly. Sparks arising from cutting operations can result in a fire and in order to control this risk, good housekeeping practice is essential, sources of fuel must be removed from the work area. Misuse of this equipment includes using the side of the cutting disc, using over worn discs, using the incorrect disc for the material being cut, leaving the cutter with the disc still spinning and not wearing the appropriate personal protective equipment (PPE). The disc when spinning may provide cuts to cables, hands and legs; entanglement with rotating parts; noise and hearing damage.

Sander

Sanding equipment is used to provide a finished surface to various materials. This occurs through application of friction from an abrasive surface to give a desired 'polished' effect. The operation produces heat at the source, which may be fuel (wood). This may lead to a fire in severe circumstances. Sanding equipment is typically electrical and of the 110 volt power type. Cables can be damaged by abrasion by the sanding surface, particularly as the sander is placed on the ground while still rotating. This hazard can also cause abrasions to the operator that lead to grazing of various levels. The action of the equipment removes the top layer of the material it is in contact with and converts this to dust. When using sanding equipment, suitable personal respiratory protective equipment (RPE) is required to protect the user from the dust in the atmosphere. Where possible, local exhaust ventilation equipment should be used to minimise dust in the atmosphere. Vibration is produced whilst in operation this presents a risk of HAVS. In order to protect against vibration injuries, the operator should be given regular breaks and the equipment maintained at intervals, including the renewal of sanding media to prevent the need for over exertion by the operator.

Nail gun

Nail guns are used in many activities in construction including carpentry, steelwork, plastering and surveying. Power sources range from battery power, electrical low voltage, pneumatic and explosive cartridge. They are used for shooting nails or pins into or through materials in order to secure a section. The noise produced is high intensity impact noise which may be amplified by the material it is vibrating through. Personal hearing protection must be worn at all times due to the risk of hearing damage from the high intensity impact noise. Vibrations produced by the use of this equipment, which is grasped by hand, may risk possible effects of HAVS in sustained use. There is a significant risk of flying debris from nailing operations and impact injuries to eyes or flesh, in addition to the risk of puncture wounds from nails released incorrectly from the gun.

Procedures for defective equipment

Under section 7 of the HASAWA, employees have a duty and should notify any shortcomings in the health and safety arrangements, even when no immediate danger exists, so that employers can take remedial action if needed. The duties placed on employees do not reduce the responsibility of the employer to comply with his own duties.

Under Regulation 5 of the PUWER, "every employer shall ensure that work equipment is maintained in an efficient state, in efficient working order and in good repair" Regulation 6 of PUWER lays down requirements for inspecting work equipment to ensure that health and safety conditions are maintained and that any deterioration can be detected and remedied in good time. With duties being placed upon both the employer and the employee to ensure the use of safe equipment, when identified in the workplace, faulty equipment should be isolated until such a time repaired by a competent party.

12.3 - Machinery

Main mechanical and non-mechanical hazards

MECHANICAL HAZARDS

Entanglement

The mere fact that a machine part is revolving can in itself constitute a very real hazard. Loose clothing, jewellery, long hair, etc. increase the risk of entanglement. Examples of rotating action hazards include: couplings, drill chucks/ bits, flywheels, spindles & shafts (especially those with keys/bolts).

Friction and abrasion

Friction burns and encountering rough surfaces moving at high speed e.g. sanding machine, grinding wheel etc. can cause abrasion injuries.

Figure 12-13: Auger drill - entanglement. *Source: STIHL.*

Figure 12-14: Abrasion.　　　　　　*Source: ACT.*

Cutting

Saw blades, knives and even rough edges, especially when moving at high speed, can result in serious cuts and even amputation injuries. The dangerous part can appear stationary! Examples of cutting action hazards include saws, slicing machines, abrasive cutting discs, chains (especially chainsaws) etc.

Figure 12-15: Chop saw - cutting.　　*Source: Speedy Hire plc.*

Figure 12-16: Shear.　　　　　　*Source: ACT.*

Shear

When two or more machine parts move towards/past, one another a "trap" is created. This can result in a crush injury or even an amputation. Examples of shearing/crushing action hazards include: scissor lifts, power presses, guillotines etc.

Stabbing and puncture

The body may be penetrated by sharp pieces of equipment, or material contained in the equipment, e.g. fixing materials such as nails fired into a part of the body, or a drill bit puncturing the hand.

Impact

Impact is caused by objects that strike the body, but do not penetrate it. They may cause the person or part of the person to be moved, sometimes violently, resulting in injury e.g. struck by the jib of a crane/excavator or materials on a hoist or the moving platter of a machine like a surface grinder.

Figure 12-17: Stabbing & puncture.　　*Source: Speedy Hire plc.*

Figure 12-18: Impact.　　　　　　*Source: ACT.*

Crushing

Caused when part of the body is caught between either two moving parts of machinery or a moving part and a stationary object e.g. the platform of hoist closing together with the ground or an overhead beam; moving parts of piling equipment or the calipers of a spot welding machine.

Figure 12-19: Crushing.   *Source: ACT.*

Figure 12-20: Drawing-in.   *Source: ACT.*

Drawing-in

When a belt runs round a roller an in-running nip is created between them (in the direction of travel); this inward movement draws in any part of the body presented to it. Examples of drawing-in (in-running / nip) hazards are V-belts - such as on the drive from a motor to the drum of a cement mixer, meshing gears and conveyors.

Ejection

When pieces of the material being worked on or components of the machinery are thrown or fired out of the equipment during operation they represent an ejection hazard. For example parts of a shattered grinding wheel, sparks, swarf or a nail from a nail gun.

Injury by compressed air or high pressure fluid injection

Injection of fluids through the skin may lead to soft tissue injuries similar to crushing. Air entering the blood stream through the skin may be fatal. Examples are diesel injectors, spray painting, compressed air jets for blast cleaning the outside of a building and a high pressure lance for cutting concrete.

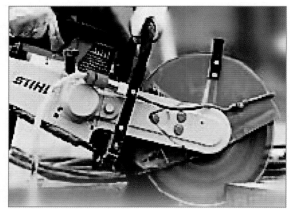

Figure 12-21: Disc saw - ejection.   *Source: STIHL.*

Figure 12-22: Fluid injection.   *Source: ACT.*

NON MECHANICAL HAZARDS

Machinery may also present other hazards. The nature of the hazard will determine the measures taken to protect people from them.

The various sources of non-mechanical hazards include the following:

- Electricity - shock and burns.
- Hot surfaces / fire.
- Noise and vibration.
- Biological - viral and bacterial.
- High/low temperatures.
- Chemicals that are toxic, irritant, flammable, corrosive, explosive.
- Ionising and non ionising radiation.
- Access - slips, trips and falls; obstructions and projections.
- Manual handling.

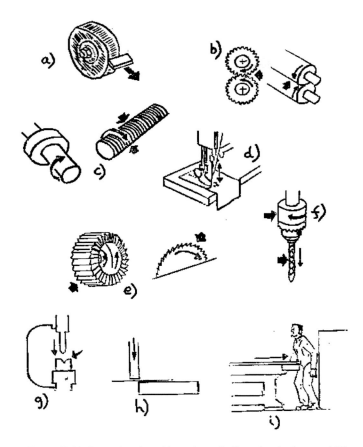

Figure 12-23: Examples of machinery hazards (Questions). *Source: ACT.*

SUMMARY - MACHINERY HAZARDS

Mechanical		Non Mechanical
Entanglement	e.g. Auger Drill	Electricity
Friction and abrasion	e.g. Grinding wheel	Hot surfaces / fire
Cutting	e.g. Sharp edges of circular saw	Noise
Shear	e.g. Scissor lift mechanism	Vibration
Stabbing and Puncture	e.g. Nail gun	Extremes of temperature
Impact	e.g. Moving arm of an excavator	Chemicals
Crushing	e.g. Platform of a hoist	Radiation
Drawing in	e.g. Belt drive of a cement mixer	Access
Injection	e.g. High pressure water lance	Manual handling
Ejection	e.g. Disc saw - sparks	

Hazards presented by a range of equipment

OFFICE MACHINERY

Photocopier

Hazards are drawing-in, hot surfaces, fumes, toner, electrical, manual handling, and noise, glare.

Document shredder

Main hazards are drawing-in, cutting or crushing, also cuts from paper handling and electrical dangers.

WORKSHOP MACHINERY

Bench-top grinder

Bench top grinders are typically found in workshops (indoor use) and operators are required to be trained, competent and formally appointed in order to dress (re-surface) or change grinding wheels. Positioning of grinders should be at a suitable height to avoid poor posture whilst using them and they must be permanently fixed or bolted in position. Grinders may be used on construction sites when installed in a site mobile workshop. Tasks involve sharpening of tool bits (drills, chisels, blades), shaping steel, and de burring cut steel components. Hazards include friction and abrasion from contact with the spinning wheel which can revolve at speeds in excess of 2900 revolutions per minute. Entanglement or drawing in (of fingers, gloves or other items being pulled between the rotating parts of the abrasive wheel and rest) and possible ejection when parts of the wheel or work piece break and sparks are thrown off. Other hazards are electricity, heat and noise. Control measures include an adjustable fixed guard that is fitted and in good working order, trained and competent operatives, grade1 impact resistant goggles, respiratory protective equipment (depending on task) and personal hearing protection.

Pedestal drill

Hazards in setting up the equipment include failure to remove chuck-key before use and failure to secure guard to drive pulleys.

Hazards when the equipment is in use include entanglement, puncture and flying swarf.

Bench-mounted circular saw

Cutting is the main hazard together with electricity, noise and sawdust.

Hand-fed power planer

Hazards include noise, cuts and severs, dust, impact from flying debris, fire and electrocution.

Spindle moulding machine

Hazards include noise, cuts, entanglement and fire.

Figure 12-24: Abrasive wheel (grinder).   *Source: ACT.*

Figure 12-25: Pedestal drill.   *Source: ACT.*

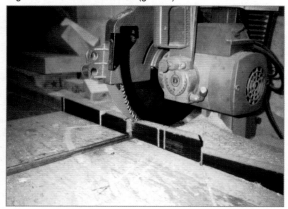

Figure 12-26: Bench cross-cut circular saw.   *Source: ACT.*

Figure 12-27: Cement mixer.   *Source: ACT.*

CONSTRUCTION SITE MACHINERY

Pneumatic compressor

Pneumatic compressors are a source of power for a variety of portable equipment used in construction activities. Tools that can source power from compressors include drills and chisels, saws, nail guns, mixing equipment and plasterer's surface scotchers. Whilst this list of tools is not exhaustive, the principle remains the same in that power is delivered through a high pressure air line to the tool and converted into mechanical power. Pneumatic compressors are typically large pieces of mobile plant that attach to the towing bar of a road going works vehicle. When at site, a compressor is free standing, only attached to the tool by the pressure air line.

Hazards arise from the fuelling of the plant (normally diesel) where contact with the skin can occur, splashes into eyes, inhalation of fumes and the possible risk of fire where hot temperatures are involved. In operation, the compressor produces exhaust gases from the motor which may, in addition to the fuel, require an assessment in compliance with the Control of Substances Hazardous to Health (COSHH) Regulations 2002. Noise and vibration at high levels may be produced from the compressor although these levels may vary dependant upon the effectiveness of the soundproofing material incorporated into the plant in addition to the condition of the equipment and frequency of maintenance programmes that may exist. This equipment also involves pressure lines that provide a trip hazard.

Cement mixer

Cement mixers are portable construction plant used for mixing a variety of aggregates and cement used in the construction process. The main benefit of this equipment is removing a significant volume of the manual labour aspect of the mixing process although a significant amount of labour intensive activities remain. The equipment consists of a motor (electric, petrol or diesel) linked through a gear box and drive shaft to a rotating drum that incorporates internal mixing blades to aid the mixing process. The assembly may vary from a complete unit that pivots on a central bar or a two part system where the mixer is seated onto a plinth or stand and pivots forward to enable emptying of the drum when the mixture is complete. Hazards arise from the source of power when electricity is combined with the water used in the mixing process. In order to control this risk, a low voltage power supply should be used, with suitable heavy duty cable and cable covers when there is a risk of running over them with vehicles or plant. Used with a residual current device a good level of protection can be obtained. When the fuel source is diesel or petrol there is a risk of fire, which increases during refuelling operations when the exhaust system may still be hot or people may be smoking in the close vicinity of the equipment.

The rotating drum and drive shaft poses an entanglement risk with personal protective equipment and other tools. If covers are removed they can expose drive belts or gearing with the associated risk of drawing in. Operatives loading mixers should be warned of the dangers of shovels and trowels becoming caught in the mixer blades and snatching the hand tool out of the operatives hand with force, which may result in personal injury to limbs and muscles. Loading the mixer is a manual task which can result in injury from repetitive, twisting motion when emptying shovels or gauging buckets into the mixer. Job rotation should be planned. Assessments as required by the COSHH regulations may be required for the fumes and dusts involved in the mixing process. Whilst the mixing activity is not a quick process, operatives tend to leave the mixer running alone until the mix is ready. The equipment when running should, at all times, be attended to prevent unauthorised access and injuries to third parties. As the mixing process proceeds there is a likelihood of build up of materials on the floor, leading to a risk of slips and trips and a possibility of falling onto the moving equipment.

Figure 12-28: Cement mixer.   *Source: ACT.*

Figure 12-29: Ground consolidation equipment.   *Source: ACT.*

Plate compactor

Plate compactors are a simple machine used for consolidating aggregates or loose materials. They are also used for securing block paviors into position by applying a heavy downward force through a flat plate where the force is increased by the vibrating motion. They operate on the principle of a motor that rotates a cam through a drive belt which provides the vibration force. Upon first appearances from a distance, operators would appear to look as though they are operating a lawn mower as the equipment is walked up and down the surface to be compacted, with the vibration providing the drive, assisted by the operator. Hazards arise from the source of power, typically petrol, which has associated fire risks that are increased through refuelling operations when the exhaust system is still hot. This equipment, because of its purpose, has to be heavy which brings a risk of manual handling strain injuries when loading or unloading from a vehicle. A safe system of work for handling this equipment may be required which could include a hoist on site vehicles and a trolley to manoeuvre around the site.

Ground consolidation equipment

Ground consolidation equipment serves the same purpose as a plate compactor. However, a plate compactor is generally for lighter duty than the large types of ground consolidation equipment such as man riding rollers or manual rollers. This heavy duty type of equipment requires competence and authorisation in order to use it on site. Ground consolidation equipment moves at a greater speed than lighter duty equipment and its power drives the equipment directly through the roller wheel. The potential harm from the drawing in / crush hazards are high, a crush sustained from a piece of this plant could more easily lead to a major injury or fatality. Control measures include segregation of pedestrians and plant using barriers, warning signs and close supervision.

Road-making equipment

Road making equipment includes all of the previously described equipment in addition to heavy duty items such as road planers, excavators, piling equipment etc. This equipment requires special training and authorisation for its safe use. Where this equipment is being used, barriers, warning signs and lighting is to be used, in addition to supervision. Hazards posed from this type of equipment include impact and crush of pedestrians, impact and collision with other plant or site vehicles, contact with buried services, contact with or arc (electrical discharge) from overhead cables and possible collapse of the ground at excavations, voids or sewers. When this equipment is being used it is normally a requirement to have refuelling facilities available on site. When this is the case suitable isolation from sources of heat should be ensured, with only authorised operatives allowed to carry out refuelling activities. The equipment may have other forms of specific hazard, including - entanglement in drive shafts, impact from flying fragments, fumes and exhaust gases, shear or cutting risk and falls from the equipment.

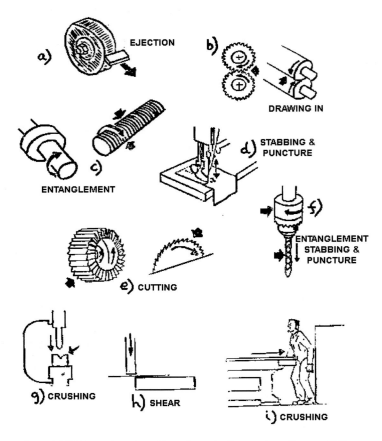

Figure 12-30: Examples of machinery hazards (Answers).   *Source: ACT.*

Protection from machinery hazards

MACHINERY GUARDING

Objective of machinery guarding
- To prevent workpeople from coming into contact with dangerous parts of machinery.
- To prevent physical injury from power driven and manually operated machines.
- To enable machines to be operated safely without interference with production.

PUWER Regulation 11 Dangerous parts of machinery

Every employer shall ensure that measures are taken in accordance with paragraph (2) which are effective - to prevent access to any dangerous part of machinery or to any rotating stock-bar; or

(b) To stop the movement of any dangerous part of machinery or rotating stock-bar before any part of a person enters a danger zone.

(2) The measures required by paragraph (1) shall consist of-

(a) the provision of fixed guards enclosing every dangerous part or rotating stock-bar where and to the extent that it is practicable to do so, but where or to the extent that it is not, then

(b) The provision of other guards or protection devices where and to the extent that it is practicable to do so, but where or to the extent that it is not, then

(c) The provision of jigs, holders, push-sticks or similar protection appliances used in conjunction with the machinery where and to the extent that it is practicable to do so, but where or to the extent that it is not, then

(d) The provision of information, instruction, training and supervision.

(3) All guards and protection devices provided under sub-paragraphs (a) or (b) of paragraph (2) shall -

(a) Be suitable for the purpose for which they are provided;

(b) Be of good construction, sound material and adequate strength;

(c) Be maintained in an efficient state, in efficient working order and in good repair;

(d) Not give rise to any increased risk to health or safety;

(e) Not be easily bypassed or disabled;

(f) Be situated at sufficient distance from the danger zone;

(g) Not unduly restrict the view of the operating cycle of the machinery, where such a view is necessary;

(h) Be so constructed or adapted that they allow operations necessary to fit or replace parts and for maintenance work, restricting access so that it is allowed only to the area where the work is to be carried out and, if possible, without having to dismantle the guard or protection device.

(4) All protection appliances provided under sub-paragraph c) of paragraph (2) shall comply with sub-paragraphs (a) to (d) and (g) of paragraph (3).

(5) In this regulation - "danger zone" means any zone in or around machinery in which a person is exposed to a risk to health or safety from contact with a dangerous part of machinery or a rotating stock-bar; "stock-bar" means any part of a stock-bar which projects beyond the headstock of a lathe.

THE PRINCIPLES OF MACHINE GUARDING

Fixed guard

Fixed guard/fence can be fitted and has to have screws / bolts undone in order to remove it. A fixed guard is the preferred option and should be used when access to the danger area is required only for maintenance or inspection purposes.

Merits of fixed guards
- Create a physical barrier.
- Require a tool to remove.
- Can protect against non-mechanical hazards such as dust and fluids which may be ejected.
- No moving parts therefore require very little maintenance.

Limitations of fixed guards
- Does not disconnect power when not in place therefore machine can still be operated without guard.
- May cause problems with visibility for inspection.
- If enclosed, may create problems with heat.

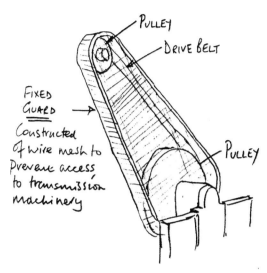

Figure 12-31: Fixed guard (hand drawn example). *Source: ACT.*

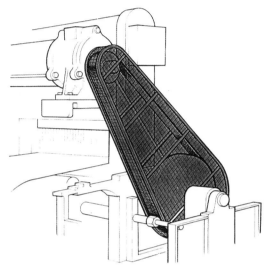

Figure 12-32: Total enclosure fixed guard. *Source: BS 5304: 1988.*

Adjustable (fixed) Guard

A fixed guard which incorporates an adjustable element (which remains fixed for the duration of a particular operation).

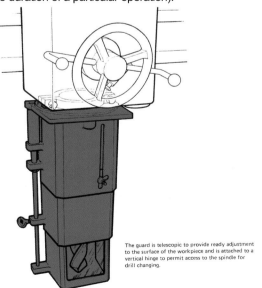

The guard is telescopic to provide ready adjustment to the surface of the workpiece and is attached to a vertical hinge to permit access to the spindle for drill changing.

Figure 12-33: Adjustable (fixed) guard. *Source: BS 5304: 1988.*

Self adjusting (fixed) guard

Guards which prevents accidental access by the operator, but allows entry of the material to the machine in such a way that the material actually forms part of the guarding arrangement itself. For example a hand held circular saw.

Figure 12-34: Self adjusting (fixed) guard. *Source: ACT.*

Distance (fixed) guard

Fixed guards which do not completely cover the danger point but place it out of normal reach? The larger the opening (to feed in material) the greater must be the distance from the opening to the danger point.

Figure 12-35: Fixed guard - not full enclosure.   *Source: ACT.*

Figure 12-36: Fixed guard over fan - holes too big. *Source: ACT.*

Interlocking guards

An interlocking guard is similar to a fixed guard, but has a movable (usually hinged) part, so connected to the machine controls that if the movable part is in the open/lifted position the dangerous moving part at the work point cannot operate. This can be arranged so that the act of closing the guard activates the working part (to speed up work efficiently), e.g. the front panel of a photocopier. Interlocked guards are useful if operators need regular access to the danger area.

Merits of interlocking guards
- Connected to power source, therefore, machine cannot be operated with guard open,
- Allow regular access.

Limitations of interlocking guards
- Have moving parts therefore need regular maintenance.
- Can be over-ridden.
- If interlock is in the form of a gate, a person can step inside and close gate behind them (someone else could re-activate machine),
- Dangerous parts of machinery may not stop immediately the guard is opened. A delay timer or brake might need to be fitted as well, e.g. the drum on a spin drier does not stop instantly when the door is opened.

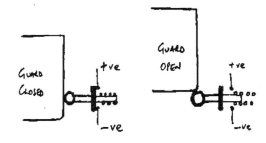

Fig 12-37: Interlock guard (hand drawn example). *Source: ACT.*

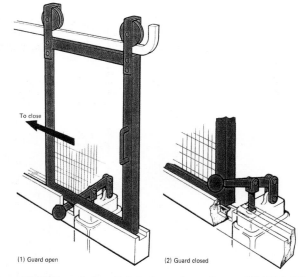

Figure 12-38: Open & closed interlock guard.   *Source: BS 5304: 1988.*

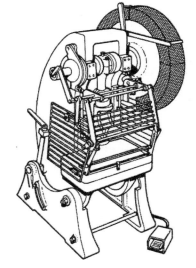

Figure 12-39: Power press - interlock guard. *Source: BS 5304: 1988.*

Automatic guard (not usually found in construction workplaces)

A guard, which operates as the machine, goes through its cycle. In some cases it physically moves the operator away from danger and is therefore only suitable for slow cycling equipment. e.g. on a guillotine or large panel press.

Trip device

A sensitive rod, cable or other mechanism, which causes the device to activate a further mechanism either stops or reverses the machine. It is important to note that this is not classed as a guard. A guard is something that physically prevents access to the hazard whereas a trip device detects the person in the danger zone and responds to this. e.g. pressure sensitive mats.

Two-hand control (2HC) device

They provide a level of protection where other methods are not practicable, helping to ensure the operators' hands remain outside the danger area. A two handed control is a device that requires both hands to operate it. Note that '2HC' devices protect only the operator and then, only provided the assistance of a colleague is not solicited to activate one control e.g. hedge trimmer, garment press.

Protection appliances

When the methods of safeguarding mentioned above are not practicable then protection appliances such as jigs, holders and push-sticks must be provided. They will help to keep the operator's hands at a safe distance from the danger area. There is no physical restraint to prevent the operator from placing their hands in danger.

Figure 12-40: Fixed guard.   *Source: ACT.*

Figure 12-41: Fixed guard and push stick.   *Source: Lincsafe.*

HIERARCHY OF MEASURES FOR DANGEROUS PARTS OF MACHINERY (PUWER)

Prevent access to dangerous parts by means of *F* ixed guard (preferably fully enclosing).

When the above is not practicable protect by other guards (*I* nterlock, *A* utomatic) or safety devices (e.g. *T* rip device).

When the above is not practicable protect by using safety appliances

(e.g. push stick or jig).

When the above is not practicable protect by information, instruction and training.

The various guards and safety devices can be summarised as follows:

F	ixed
I	nterlock
A	utomatic
T	rip devices

PERSONAL PROTECTIVE EQUIPMENT (PPE)

The Personal Protective Equipment at Work (PPER) Regulations 1992 governs the provision of PPE. PPE is as a last resort and should only be relied upon when other controls do not adequately control risks. The use of machinery presents a number of mechanical hazards and care has to be taken that PPE is not used in situations where they present an increased risk of entanglement or drawing in to machinery, such as might happen with loose overalls and gloves. Main examples are:

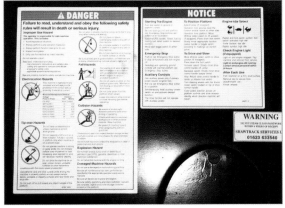

Figure 12-42: Information and instruction.   *Source: ACT.*

Figure 12-43: PPE and supervision.   *Source: ACT.*

- Eye protection (safety spectacles / glasses, goggles and face shields) - protection for the eyes and face from flying particles, welding glare, dust, fumes and splashes.
- Head protection (safety helmets or scalp protectors i.e. bump caps) - protection from falling objects.
- Protective clothing for the body (overalls) - protection from a wide range of hazards.
- Gloves (chain mail gloves and sleeves) - protection against cuts and abrasions when handling machined components, raw material or machinery cutters.
- Footwear (steel in-soles and toe-caps) - protection against sharp objects that might be stood on or objects dropped while handling them.
- Ear protection for noisy machine operations.

See also - Personal Protective Equipment - Unit 12.

INFORMATION, INSTRUCTION, TRAINING AND SUPERVISION

PUWER requires every employer to ensure that all persons who use work equipment and any of his employees who supervises or manages the use of work equipment have available to them adequate health and safety information and, where appropriate, written instructions pertaining to the use of the work equipment. This includes information and, where appropriate, written instructions that are comprehensible to those concerned on:

- The conditions in which and the methods by which the work equipment may be used.
- Foreseeable abnormal situations and the action to be taken if such a situation were to occur.
- Any conclusions to be drawn from experience in using the work equipment.

Similarly PUWER requires employers to ensure that all persons who use work equipment and any of his employees who supervises or manages work equipment have received work equipment, any risks which such use may entail and precautions to be taken. It is a requirement of the HASAWA 1974 that supervision be provided as necessary to ensure the health and safety of employees (and others).

Basic requirements for guards and safety devices

PUWER REGULATION 11 PARAGRAPH 3 - EFFECTIVE GUARDS AND DEVICES

All guards and protection devices provided under sub-paragraphs (a) or (b) of paragraph (2) shall :

a)   Be *suitable* for the purpose for which they are provided.

b)   Be of *good construction*, sound material and adequate strength.

c)   Be *maintained* in an efficient state, in efficient working order and in good repair.

d)   Not give rise to any *increased risk* to health or safety.

e)   Not be *easily bypassed* or disabled.

f)   Be situated at *sufficient distance* from the danger zone.

g)   Not unduly *restrict the view* of the operating cycle of the machinery, where such a view is necessary.

h)   Be so constructed or adapted that they allow operations necessary to fit or replace parts and for maintenance work, restricting access so that it is allowed only to the area where the work is to be carried out and, if possible, without having to dismantle the guard or protection device.

COMPATIBLE WITH PROCESS

Compatibility with the material being processed - this is particularly important in the food processing industry where the guard material should not constitute a source of contamination of the product. Its ability to maintain its physical and mechanical properties after coming into contact with potential contaminants such as cutting fluids used in machining operations or cleaning and sterilising agents used in food processing machinery is also very important. In selecting an appropriate safeguard for a particular type of machinery or danger area, it should be borne in mind that a fixed guard is simple, and should be used where access to the danger area is not required during operation of the machinery or for cleaning, setting or other activities. As the need for access arises and increases in frequency, the importance of safety procedures for removal of a fixed guard increases until the frequency is such that interlocking should be used.

ADEQUATE STRENGTH

Guard mounting should be compatible with the strength and duty of the guard. In selecting the material to be used for the construction of a guard, consideration should be given to the following:

- Its ability to withstand the force of ejection of parts of the machinery or material being processed, where this is a foreseeable danger.
- Its ability to provide protection against hazards identified. In many cases, the guard may fulfil a combination of functions such as prevention of access and containment of hazards. This may apply where the hazards include ejected particles, liquids, dust, fumes, radiation, noise, etc. and one or more of these considerations may govern the selection of guard materials.

MAINTAINED

All guards must be maintained in effective order to perform their function. This will require a planned approach to checks on guards and work such as checking the security of fixed guards.

ALLOW MAINTENANCE WITHOUT REMOVAL

Its weight and size are factors to be considered in relation to the need to remove and replace it for routine maintenance.

NOT INCREASE RISK OR RESTRICT VIEW

Any guard selected should not itself present a hazard such as trapping or shear points, rough or sharp edges or other hazards likely to cause injury.

Power operated guards should be designed and constructed so that a hazard is not created. Power operated guards should be designed and constructed so that a hazard is not created.

NOT EASILY BY-PASSED

Guards or their components must not be easily by-passed, in particular by operators. There is always a temptation to do so when under production or similar pressures. When siting such things as interlock switches it is best to locate them away from the operator and preferably within the guard.

Unit 13

Manual & mechanical handling hazards & control

Overall Aims

On completion of this Unit, candidates will understand

- the hazards involved in the movement of loads by physical and mechanical effort.
- the risk reduction and preventive measures available.
- the risks involved in the use of lifting and moving equipment on construction sites.

Content

Specific Intended Learning Outcomes

The intended learning outcomes of this Unit are that candidates will be able to:

13.1 describe the main types of injury associated with manual handling

13.2 carry out a manual handling assessment

13.3 suggest ways of minimising manual handling risks on a construction site

13.4 explain the training requirements for those who are required to manually lift loads

13.5 explain the precautions and procedures necessary to ensure safety in the use and maintenance of materials handling and lifting equipment used in construction

13.6 identify the legal requirements for the inspection and examination of lifting equipment

13.7 describe the requirements to ensure safety in lifting operations.

Sources of Reference

Manual Handling (Guidance) (L23), HSE Books

Backs for the Future: Safe Manual Handling in Construction (HSG149), HSE Books

Safe Use of Work Equipment (ACOP) (L22), HSE Books

Safe Use of Lifting Equipment (L113), HSE Books

Safety in Working with Lift Trucks (HSG6), HSE Books

Rider-operated Lift Trucks - Operator Training (ACOP) (L117), HSE Books

British Standard Code of Practice on Safe Use of Cranes (BS 7121), British Standards Institution

Relevant Statutory Provisions

The Manual Handling Operations Regulations (MHOR) 1992

The Provision and Use of Work Equipment Regulations (PUWER) 1998

The Lifting Operations and Lifting Equipment Regulations (LOLER) 1998

13.1 - Manual handling hazards

Typical manual handling hazards and injuries

Manual handling operations can cause many types of *injury*. The most common injuries are:

- Rupture of intervertebral discs ('slipped disc') in the lower spine.
- Muscle strain and sprain.
- Tendons and ligaments can also be over-stretched and torn.
- Rupture of a section of the abdominal wall can cause a hernia.
- Loads with sharp edges can cause cuts.
- Dropped loads can result in bruises, fractures and crushing injuries.

Around 25% of all injuries reported to the appropriate enforcing authority have been attributed to the manual lifting and handling of loads. The injuries arise from such *hazards* as stooping while lifting, holding the load away from the body, twisting movements, frequent or prolonged effort, heavy / bulky / unwieldy / unstable loads, sharp / hot / slippery surfaces of loads, space constraints, and lack of capability of the individual.

The assessment of manual handling risks

FACTORS TO CONSIDER

MHOR specify that the four factors to which the employer must have regard and questions he must consider when making an assessment of manual handling operations are:

- The **L**oad
- **I**ndividual Capability
- The **T**ask
- The Working **E**nvironment

Each factor in turn should be looked at to determine whether there is a risk of injury. When this has been completed the information can then be processed giving a *total* risk assessment.

FACTORS	QUESTIONS	Level of Risk:		
		High	Med	Low

The Task	Does it involve:
	
	■ Holding load at distance from trunk?
	■ Unsatisfactory bodily movement or posture?
	  • Twisting the trunk.
	  • Stooping.
	■ Excessive movement of load?
	  • Excessive lifting or lowering distances.
	  • Excessive pushing or pulling distances.
	  • Risk of sudden movement of load.
	  • Frequent or prolonged physical effort.
	  • Insufficient rest or recovery periods.			

The Load	Is it: ■ Heavy? ■ Bulky or Unwieldy? ■ Difficult to grasp? ■ Unstable, or with contents likely to shift? ■ Sharp, hot or otherwise potentially damaging?			
The Working Environment	Are there: ■ Space constraints preventing good posture? ■ Uneven, slippery or unstable floors? ■ Variations in level of floors or work surfaces? ■ Extremes of temperature, humidity or air movement? ■ Poor lighting conditions?			
Individual Capability	Does the job: ■ Require unusual strength, height, etc.? ■ Create a hazard to those who have a health problem? ■ Require special knowledge or training for its safe performance?			

Figure 13-1: Manual handling risk assessment.   *Source: HSE Manual handling (Manual Handling Operations Regulations 1992) Guidance L23.*

The detailed consideration of each factor is necessary to achieve a suitable and sufficient risk assessment. The process of risk assessing includes observing the task as it is actually done; recording the factors that contribute to risk; assessing the level of risk that each factor represents (taking account of the circumstances and controls in place); and considering if the risks are different at different times and for different people. The following considerations are offered to assist in making a risk assessment.

The L oad

- Consideration should be given to reducing the weight although this may mean increasing the frequency of handling.
- If there is a great variety of weight to be handled it may be possible to sort the loads into weight categories so that precautions can be applied selectively.
- Where the size, surface texture or nature of a load makes it difficult to grasp, consideration should be given to the provision of handles, hand grips, indents etc. to improve the grasp.
- Loads in packages should be such that they cannot shift unexpectedly while being handled.
- Any loads to be handled should not have sharp corners, jagged edges, rough surfaces and the like.

Figure 13-2: Manual handling.   Source: ACT.

I ndividual capability

- The individual's state of health, fitness and strength can significantly affect the ability to perform a task safely.
- An individual's physical capacity can also be age-related, typically climbing until the early 20's and declining gradually from the mid 40's.
- It is clear then that an individual's condition and age could significantly affect the ability to perform a task safely.

The T ask

- Ensure work and components in regular use are stored at waist height. Storage above or below this height should be used for lighter or less frequently used items.
- Layout changes should avoid the necessity for frequent bending, twisting, reaching, etc. and the lessening of any travel distances.
- Pay attention to the work routine i.e. fixed postures dictated by sustained holding or supporting loads, frequency of handling loads, with particular emphasis on heavy and awkward loads.
- Fixed breaks are generally less effective than those taken voluntary within the constraints of the work organisation.
- Handling while seated also requires careful consideration. Use of the powerful leg muscles is precluded and the weight of the handler's body cannot be used as a counterbalance. For these reasons, the loads that can be handled in safety by a person who is seated are substantially less than can be dealt with while standing.
- Team handling could be a solution for some tasks that are beyond the capability of one person. However team handling can create additional problems. The proportion of the load carried by each member of the team will vary; therefore, the load that can be handled in safety will be less than the sum of the loads with which an individual could cope.

The working E nvironment

- Adequate gangways, space and working area should be provided in order to allow room to manoeuvre during handling.
- Lack of headroom could cause stooping and constrictions caused by a poor workstation, adjacent machinery etc. should also be avoided.
- In many cases problems are simply caused by lack of attention to good housekeeping.
- Whenever possible all manual handling tasks should be carried out on a single level. If tasks are to be carried out on more than one level, access should preferably be by a gentle slope, or failing that, properly positioned and well maintained stairs/steps. Steep slopes should be avoided.
- Workbenches should be of a uniform height, thus reducing the need for raising or lowering loads.
- Finally, look at the general working environment. A comfortable working environment (e.g. heating, ventilating and lighting) will help to reduce the risk of injury.

REVIEWING ASSESSMENTS

The assessment should be kept up to date. It should be reviewed whenever there is a reason to suppose that it is no longer valid, for example, because the working conditions or the personnel carrying out the operations have changed. It should also be reviewed whenever there has been a significant change in the manual handling operations, for example, affecting the nature of the task or load.

GUIDELINES FOR ASSESSMENT OF MANUAL HANDLING OPERATIONS

Lifting

The Manual Handling Operations Regulations (MHOR) 1992 set no specific requirements such as weight limits. The following guidelines set out an *approximate* boundary within which manual handling operations are unlikely to create a risk of injury sufficient to warrant assessment that is more detailed. This should enable assessment work to be concentrated where it is most needed.

The guideline figures are not weight or force limits. They may be exceeded where a more detailed assessment shows it is safe to do so. However, the guideline figures should not normally be exceeded by more than a factor of about two. The guideline figures for weight and force will give reasonable protection to nearly all men and between one half and two thirds of women.

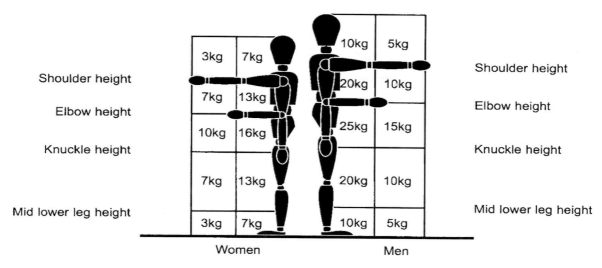

Figure 13-3: Guideline figures.   *Source: HSE Manual Handling (Manual Handling Operations Regs 1992) Guidance L23.*

Carrying

The guideline figures for manual handling operations involving carrying are similar to those given for lifting and lowering. It is assumed that the load is held against the body and is carried no further than about 10 metres without resting.

If the load is carried over a longer distance without resting the guideline figures may need to be reduced. Where the load can be carried securely on the shoulder without attendant lifting (e.g. unloading sacks from a lorry) a more detailed assessment may show that it is safe to exceed the guideline figure.

Pushing and pulling

Guideline figures for manual handling operations involving pushing and pulling, whether the load is slid, rolled or supported on wheels, are as follows:

■ The guideline figure for starting or stopping the load is a force of about 250 newtons (i.e. a force of about 25 Kg as measured on a spring balance).

■ The guideline figure for keeping the load in motion is a force of about 100 newtons.

■ No specific limit is intended as to the distances over which the load is pushed or pulled provided there are adequate opportunities for rest or recovery.

Handling while seated

The guideline figure for handling operations carried out while seated is given below and applies only when the hands are within the box zone indicated. If handling beyond the box zone is unavoidable, a more detailed assessment should be made.

Twisting

The basic guideline figures for lifting and lowering should be reduced if the handler twists to the side during the operation. As a rough guide, the figures should be reduced by about 10% where the handler twists through 45° and by about 20% where the handler twists through 90°.

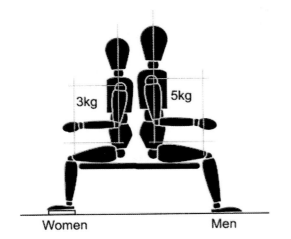

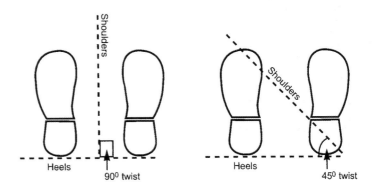

Figure 13-4: Handling while seated. *Source: HSE: Manual Handling (Manual Handling Operations Regs 1992) Guidance L23*

Figure 13-5: Twisting. *Source: HSE: Manual Handling (Manual Handling Operations Regs 1992) Guidance L23*

Assumptions

The guideline figures should not be regarded as precise recommendations and should be applied with caution, noting particularly that they are based on the following assumptions:

- The handler is standing or crouching in a stable body position with the back substantially upright.
- The trunk is not twisted during the operation.
- Both hands are used to grasp the load.
- The hands are not more than shoulder width apart.
- The load is positioned centrally in front of the body and is itself reasonably symmetrical.
- The load is stable and readily grasped.
- The work area does not restrict the handler's posture.
- The working environment (heat, cold, wet, condition of floor) and any personal protective equipment used do not interfere with performance of the task.

Means of minimizing the risks from manual handling

GENERAL APPROACH

Practical measures that can be taken to reduce the risk of injury can also be based on *LITE*. For example:

L oad   Changing the load by lightening, reducing in size, provision of handles, elimination of sharp edges etc.

I ndividual   Address the individual factors such as selection, provision of information and training, provision of appropriate protective equipment and clothing.

T ask   Redesign the task so that manual handling is eliminated or reduced by mechanisation, reducing carrying distances, team lifting, job rotation, etc.

E nvironment   Improving the working environment e.g. optimum heights of surfaces, improving floor conditions, increasing workspace, improving lighting, avoidance of changes in floor level etc.

MINIMISING THE RISK FROM MANUAL HANDLING

Each manual handling operation should be examined and appropriate steps taken to minimise the risk of injury to the lowest level reasonably practicable. Wherever reasonably practicable, manual handling should be replaced or reduced by using mechanical handling aids, examples of which are shown below.

Mechanical assistance

This involves the use of handling aids. Although this may retain some elements of manual handling, bodily forces are applied more efficiently.

Examples are:

Levers	Reduces bodily force to move a load. Can avoid trapping fingers.
Hoists	Can support weights, allowing handler to position load.
Trolley, sack truck, truck roller or hoist	Reduces effort to move loads horizontally.
Chutes	A way of using gravity to move loads from one place to another.
Handling devices	Hand-held hooks or suction pads can help when handling a load that is difficult to grasp.

Figure 13-6: Mechanical assistance.   *Source: ACT.*

Ergonomic approach

Emphasis must be given to all the factors involved in manual handling operations, task, load, working environment and individual capability. This should be carried out with a view to fitting the operation to the individual rather than the other way round.

Involving the workforce

Effort should be made to seek contributions from employees and, where applicable, safety representatives or representatives of employee safety.

Training

Employers should ensure that all employees who carry out manual handling operations receive the necessary training to enable them to carry out the task in a safe manner.

A training programme should include:

- How potentially hazardous loads may be recognised.
- How to deal with unfamiliar loads.
- The proper use of handling aids.
- The proper use of personal protective equipment.
- Features of the working environments that contribute to safety.

- The importance of good housekeeping.
- Factors affecting individual capability.
- Good handling techniques.

It should always be remembered that training is not a "one off situation"; it should be on-going and monitored, for it is only by doing this that organisations can ensure that they will cope with the requirements of good health and safety practices.

Techniques for manually lifting loads

LIFTING TECHNIQUES USING KINETIC HANDLING PRINCIPLES

In order to avoid musculoskeletal disorders due to lifting, poor posture and repetitive awkward loads it is important to use recognised techniques. Many of these techniques use a kinetic handling approach, which seeks to use the body's natural movement to the advantage of lifting.

1. Stop and think

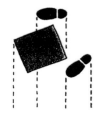
2. Place the feet

3. Adopt a good posture

4. Get a firm grip

5. Don't jerk

6. Move the feet

7. Keep close to the load

8. Put down, *then* adjust

Figure 13-7: Basic lift principles.   *Source: Ambiguous.*

Putting it all into practice

a)   Begin with the *load between the feet*, the leading foot should be in line with the side of the load, pointing in the direction of movement.

b)   Bend your knees, tuck your chin in *and keep your back straight* (not vertical).

c)   Generally grip the load at the upper outer corner on the side of the leading foot, tilt it slightly and grip the opposite corner with the other hand. *(Ensure the palm, not fingers, take the weight).*

d)   Keep your *arms close to your body*, move rear hand forward along the lower edge of the load. Stand up in one movement, keeping the load in contact with the body at all times.

e)   To lower the load reverse the procedure, *bending your knees* whilst tilting the load to avoid trapping fingers.

Always remember:

■   Assess the Load.
■   Lift the load smoothly - do not jerk.
■   Avoid twisting and stretching.

Poor posture

Injuries that are received as a result of carrying out activities that include manual handling operations need not necessarily arise solely from lifting large, awkward or heavy items. Poor posture can greatly increase the likelihood of suffering manual handling injuries. Examples of poor posture can include over-stretching, twisting, lifting with the spine (in bending position) or lifting whilst seated. Many construction tasks can encourage the worker to take up a poor posture so they are bent over for a period of time, for example laying a floor. Training should be given in correct manual handling techniques, adoption of the correct posture and ensuring that the 'kinetic' lifting method is used (feet slightly apart, straight back and use of the leg muscles to lift).

Guidance published by the Health & Safety Executive (HSE), indicates values of weights and ideal positions for these given weight values that should be adopted when manually handling *(see also - Figure 13-3: Guideline figures - earlier in this unit).* It can be seen from the guidance that the ideal position for manually handling is waist height whilst standing; also to be noted is the different values given for the male and female gender. These figures are not strict and are quoted as maximum under guidance only and allowances must be made for individual differences in capability.

Whilst standing is seen to give the more suitable posture for lifting, it should also be noted that movements made in the standing position can also reduce individual weight values and lifting zones significantly. A twisting motion of the spine of 45 degrees will result in a 10% reduction in lifting capability, whilst a twisting motion of 90 degrees will result in a 20% reduction.

Manually handling whilst seated also reduces individual weight values and lifting zones significantly, with guidance stating 5kg for a male and 3kg for a female as maximum weights whilst seated. Sitting, something done more frequently during work activities can result in back injuries. Research has found that pressure exerted on the spine and discs of the spine are increased by approximately 40% whilst seated, this pressure increases to 90% when leaning forward.

Repetitive movements

The aim of the regulations is to reduce the risk of injury from manual handling operations. One of the main methods used to reduce the load being manually lifted is to package smaller weights or break the bulk load down into smaller batches. This solution avoids the need to lift heavy items, however it will introduce increased frequency.

Injuries received from manual handling operations can either be immediate, resulting from over exertion and poor posture or also occur over time as a result of performing the manual handling task repeatedly, for example digging an excavation or laying bricks. Whilst acute, painful injuries are typically more immediately noticeable, long-term effects from cumulative muscle strain can prove equally detrimental to individual health.

Where frequency is increased, in addition to training in the correct lifting method, regular breaks or job rotation must be introduced in order to share the workload suitably throughout the workforce. Mechanical assistance may also be introduced to prevent twisting or bending under strain (rollers, conveyors, air suction devices, and waist height benches).

Awkward movements

Training should be given in the correct lifting method (the kinetic method), that if used correctly, should eliminate incorrect posture and provide a means for lifting safely in most positions (floor level, waist height, not stretching). Awkward movements that should be avoided include, stretching, bending at the waist using the spine, twisting, lifting whilst seated, sudden movements, jerky movements, over exertion whilst pushing or pulling. It should be remembered that many construction tasks require a person to hold awkward positions for a period of time, for example the fitting of overhead lights or tiles. These awkward movements can lead to cumulative strain and it is important that there are sufficient rest periods or work rotation built into the work activity to allow relief of the muscles likely to be affected.

13.2 - Mechanical Handling

Forklift trucks

FORKLIFT TRUCK HAZARDS

Although the forklift truck (FLT) is a very useful machine for moving materials in many industries, it features prominently in industrial accidents. Every year about 20 deaths and 5000 injuries can be attributed to forklift trucks and these can be analysed as follows:

- Injuries to driver   40%
- Injuries to assistant   20%
- Injuries to pedestrians   40%
- Fractures   80%
- Injury to ankles & feet   60%

Unless preventative action is taken these accidents are likely to increase as forklift trucks are increasingly used in industry.

As about 45% of the accidents can be wholly or partly attributed to operator error, the need for proper operator training is underlined. There are, however, many other causes of accident including inadequate premises, gangways, poor truck maintenance, lighting etc.

- Overturning:
  - Driving too fast.
  - Sudden braking.
  - Driving on slopes.
  - Driving with load elevated.
- Collisions:
  - With buildings.
  - With pedestrians.
  - With other vehicles.

- Loss of load:
  - Insecure load.
  - Poor floor surface.
  - Passengers should not be carried.
- Overloading:
  - Exceeding maximum capacity.
- Failure:
  - Load bearing part (e.g. chain).

SAFE USE AND MAINTENANCE

Selection of equipment

There are many types of truck available for a range of activities. There are many situations when specialist trucks such as reach trucks, overhead telescopic or rough terrain trucks are required. Many accidents happen due to the incorrect selection and/or use of forklift trucks.

When choosing the right truck for the job the following factors should be taken into account:

- Power source - the choice of battery or diesel will depend on whether the truck is to be used indoors or outdoors.
- Tyres - solid or pneumatic depending on the terrain.
- Size and capacity - dependent on the size and nature of loads to be moved.
- Height of the mast.
- Audible and/or visual warning systems fitted according to the proximity of pedestrians.
- Protection provided for the operator dependent on rough terrain which might increase the likelihood of overturning or the possibility of falling objects say from insecure racking.
- Training given to operators must be related specifically to the type of truck.

ROUGH-TERRAIN FORK LIFT TRUCK

Rough terrain fork lift trucks operate similarly to traditional fork lift truck equipment found within industry, the main difference being the surface on which they operate is typically unmade and not hard standing. The design employed on construction sites is usually of a heavier duty design. Typical design differences include:

- Diesel fuelled engines to provide the greater power required.
- Increased load / lifting capacity.
- Enclosed operator cab for protection against the elements.
- Higher chassis position for uneven terrain.
- Large diameter wheels with deep tread, pneumatic traction tyres for muddy, rough terrain.
- Increased security for external siting of the vehicle

The same stringent rules and procedures should be in place for rough terrain FLT's as there are for industrial types. Operators must be competent and licensed, loads must not exceed the safe working load and should be palletised when loading, unloading or moving.

Figure 13-8: Rough-terrain forklift truck.   *Source: ACT.*

Telehandlers

Tele-handlers are all-purpose pieces of plant that can be used for construction site preparation, material handling, scaffold erection, as elevated work platforms and for final site cleanup. A tele-handler consists of a heavy duty chassis, body and lifting gear on large diameter wheels and deep treads, pneumatic traction tyres. Materials handling is through various attachments fixed to a boom that enables vertical, horizontal and diagonal reach. Construction sites are finding various uses for tele-handlers, and with the different attachments available, greater flexibility is provided for the variety of jobs that may be encountered.

Hazard and control

Hazards include the generic hazards associated with all heavy plant. Increased power required to cope with the demands of construction sites is transferred through larger drive shafts / wheels and generally larger and heavier duty mechanical ancillary items. In the case of a telehandler, hazards include moving large hydraulic rams that actuate the front forks or bucket with hydraulic hoses attached that are under high pressure. There are various mechanical hazards involved, such as impact, crush, trap, and shear. In addition to these there are non-mechanical hazards such as heat, fumes, chemicals and noise. Control measures should include barriers to segregate pedestrians from machinery to a safe distance, good visibility with the assistance of mirrors, high visibility clothing for those working nearby, seat restraints for the operator who should be enclosed in a protective cage that can also act as a guard against contact with moving machinery and the effects of overturning.

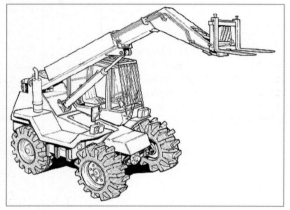

Figure 13-9: Telehandler.   *Source: HSG6, HSE books.*

Figure 13-10: Dumper truck.   *Source: ACT.*

Dumper trucks

General piece of plant consisting of a heavy-duty chassis, body and tipping bucket on large diameter wheels and deep tread, traction tyres, used for transporting materials around a construction site or street works. The equipment is generally used as a large mechanised wheelbarrow.

Hazard and control

Hazards include the generic hazards associated with mobile equipment. Specific hazards associated with dumper trucks are impact with pedestrians or vehicles, trap and crush beneath the tipping bucket as it discharges its contents, falling items or objects from the bucket, high pressure hydraulic lines and tipping over on unstable ground or into excavations. Other hazards include noise, chemicals and fumes produced by the running of the machinery which may find their way into places like excavations. Control measures should include trained, authorised, operatives; maintenance and inspection; segregation of pedestrians to a safe distance by the provision of suitable barriers and signs advising of the dangers of operating plant; stop blocks for tipping into excavations; seat restraints and rollover protection for the operator.

Excavators

Consisting of a heavy duty chassis, fixed or rotating body and digging gear (jib arms & bucket) on either large diameter wheels and deep tread, pneumatic traction tyres or caterpillar track system.

Figure 13-11: Excavator hazards   *Source: ACT.*

Figure 13-12: Excavator.   *Source: ACT.*

Hazard and control

Specific hazards associated with excavators are impact with pedestrians or vehicles by swinging jibs and booms, trap and crush beneath the excavator bucket as it digs into the ground or discharges its contents, falling items or objects from the bucket, high pressure hydraulic lines and tipping over on unstable ground or into excavations. Other hazards include noise, chemicals and fumes produced by the running of the equipment. Excavation equipment is generally adapted and used for a variety of different purposes that it may not specifically be designed for, including towing /shunting, lifting, loading / unloading / transport of articles and equipment. The fact that these are improvised activities increases the risk of injury. Control measures should include trained and authorised operatives; not overloading the bucket; maintenance and inspection; segregation of pedestrians to a safe distance by the provision of suitable barriers and signs advising of the dangers of operating plant; good visibility with the assistance of mirrors where necessary, high visibility clothing for those working nearby, seat restraints for the operator who should be enclosed in a protective cage that can also act as a guard against contact with moving machinery and the effects of overturning.

Manually operated load moving equipment

WHEELBARROW

A wheelbarrow is a low-tech fabrication, generally consisting of a shallow hopper style bucket supported on a single wheel at the front and two legs at the rear with handle bars for grip and use when moving. In use, the load being carried is pivoted and supported over the front wheel. There is still a need to manually handle materials when loading and unloading the wheel barrow, with speed of operation and the capacity of the truck governed by the individual that uses the equipment.

Hazard and control

Wheel barrows are typically manually driven pieces of equipment and the hazards arising from their use are generally of an ergonomic nature relating to posture and over exertion. Mechanical hazards are restricted to the single wheel of the barrow that only moves when moved by the operator. Other associated hazards are tripping and falling whilst using the equipment or ejecting the contents of the barrow. Control measures include indicating a safe working load for the equipment and the provision of information / instruction in the safe loading and use of the equipment for the operator. A manual handling assessment may be required when using this equipment.

Figure 13-13: Wheelbarrow. *Source: ACT.*

Figure 13-14: Sack truck. *Source: ACT.*

SACK TRUCK

A sack truck is a simple, 'low-tech' fabrication fitted with two wheels on which the load is pivoted and supported when the truck is tilted back and pushed manually. A risk assessment must be made of manual handling operations associated with using equipment of this type. As with the wheelbarrow there is still a need to manually handle materials when using a sack truck.

Hazard and control

Sack trucks are typically manually driven and like the wheelbarrow the hazards arising from their use are generally of an ergonomic nature relating to posture and over exertion through manual handling. Mechanical hazards are restricted to the wheels of the truck that only moves when moved by the operator. Other associated hazards are tripping and falling whilst using the equipment and manual handling back and strain injuries. Control measures include indicating a safe working load for the equipment and the provision of information / instruction in the safe loading and use of the equipment for the operator. A manual handling assessment may be required when using this equipment.

THE PALLET TRUCK

This truck has two elevating fingers for insertion below the top deck of a pallet. When the 'forks' are raised the load is moved clear of the ground to allow movement. This truck may be designed for pedestrian or rider control. It has no mast and cannot be used for stacking. Pallet trucks may be powered or non-powered.

Hazard and control

Pallet trucks can be driven both manually or by quiet running electric motor. Hazards include crush from moving loads or momentum of the equipment when stopping, crush and trap in the forks of the equipment, manual handling strain injuries and electricity hazards from battery power points. In addition, some pallet trucks have a lifting mechanism to raise and lower the load. Control measures should include trained and authorised operatives; identification of safe working loads; inspection and maintenance; and designated areas for parking the equipment.

General means of minimising mechanical handling risk

MECHANICAL HANDLING EQUIPMENT OPERATORS

No person should be permitted to drive a forklift truck or mobile plant unless they have been selected, trained and authorised to do so, or is undergoing properly organised formal training.

Selection of personnel

The safe use of forklift trucks calls for a reasonable degree of both physical and mental fitness and of intelligence. The selection procedure should be devised to identify people who have shown themselves reliable and mature during their early years at work.

Training

Training should consist of three stages, the last being the one in which the operator is introduced to his future work environment. This is illustrated by the stages of training of a fork lift truck operator.

Stage one - should contain the basic skills and knowledge required to operate the forklift truck safely, to understand the basic mechanics and balance of the machine, and to carry out routine daily checks.

Stage two - under strict training conditions closed to other personnel. This stage should include:

- Knowledge of the operating principles and controls.
- Use of the forklift truck in gangways, slopes, cold-stores, confined spaces and bad weather conditions etc.
- The work to be undertaken e.g. loading and unloading vehicles.

Stage three - after successfully completing the first two stages, the operator should be given further instruction in the place of work.

Testing - on completion of training, the operator should be examined and tested to ensure that he/she has achieved the required standard.

Refresher Training - if high standards are to be maintained, periodic refresher training and testing is essential good practice.

TRAFFIC ROUTES

1) Separate routes, designated crossing places and suitable barriers at recognised danger spots.

2) Roads, gangways and aisles should have sufficient width and overhead clearance for the largest forklift truck.

3) Clear direction signs.

4) Sharp bends and overhead obstructions should be avoided.

5) The floor surface should be in good condition.

6) Any gradient in a forklift truck operating area should be kept as gentle as possible.

PARKING AREAS

Sufficient and suitable parking areas should be provided away from the main work area.

PROTECTION OF PERSONNEL

There is a need to alert people to the hazard when working in or near a mechanical handling plant operating area. This is achieved by putting up signs and/or fitting audible warnings to vehicles.

SUMMARY OF CONTROLS

- Make someone responsible for transport.
- Select and train drivers thoroughly.
- Daily vehicle checks.
- Keep keys secure. **Do not leave in the ignition.**
- Maintain and light gangways.
- Separate vehicles and pedestrians.

A vigorous management policy covering operator training, vehicle maintenance and sound systems of work, supported by good supervision will reduce personal injury and damage to equipment and materials. This in turn will lead to better utilisation of plant and increased materials handling efficiency. ***See also Unit 11 - Movement of people and vehicles - hazards and control.***

Figure 13-15: Width of traffic route   *Source: ACT.*

Figure 13-16: Warning of traffic   *Source: ACT.*

Hoists

HAZARDS

In general, the hazards associated with lifts and hoists are the same as with any other lifting equipment.

- The lift / hoist may overturn or collapse.
- The lift / hoist can strike persons, during normal operations, who may be near or under the platform or cage.
- The supporting ropes may fail and the platform/cage fall to the ground.
- The load or part of the load may fall.
- The lift / hoist may fail in a high position.
- Persons being lifted may become stranded if the lift or hoist fails.

SAFE USE AND MAINTENANCE

Lifts and hoists for movement of goods require:

- Statutory safety devices.
- Holdback gears (for rope failure).
- Overrun tip systems.
- Guards on hoist machinery.
- Landing gates (securely closed down during operation).

In addition, passenger hoists require more sophisticated controls:

- Operating controls inside the cage.
- Electromagnetic interlocks on the cage doors.
- The enclosing shaft must be of fire-proof construction, if within a building.

Safe use of lifts and hoists depends on:

- Adequate design.
- Competent operation.
- Sound construction.
- Regular inspection.
- Correct selection.
- Adequate maintenance.
- Correct installation.

The legislation governing the construction, use and thorough examination of lifts and hoists, is the Lifting Operations and Lifting Equipment Regulations (LOLER) 1998.

For further details see later in this unit and also - Relevant Statutory Provisions – Unit 20.

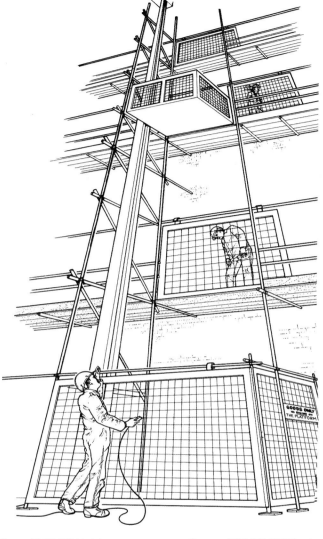

Figure 13-17: Lift / hoist.   *Source: HSG150, HSE books.*

Conveyors

HAZARDS

Drawing in	-	Clothing or limbs being drawn in to in-running nips caused by moving parts.
Contact	-	With moving parts (cut and abrasion).
Entanglement	-	With rollers.
Striking	-	Falling objects, especially from overhead conveyors.
Manual Handling	-	Loading and unloading components / packages.
Noise	-	From mechanical movement.

TYPES OF CONVEYOR

The three basic types of conveyor are belt, roller and screw.

Belt

Materials are transported on a moving belt. Trapping points are created between the belt and the rotating drum. The 'head and tails' pulleys create the main risks. Guards can be fitted enclosing the sides or at each drawing in point (in-running nip).

Roller

- Power Driven Rollers: guards are required on power drives and in-running nips.
- Powered and Free Running Rollers: guards are required between each pair of powered and free running rollers.
- Free Running Rollers: no nips occur on these, but injuries can occur when people try to walk across them. Providing walkways can solve this problem.

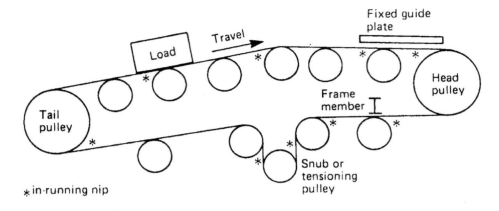

Figure 13-18: Diagrammatic layout of belt conveyor showing in-running nips. *Source: J Ridley; Safety at Work; Fourth Edition.*

Figure 13-19: Preventing free running roller trap.
Source: J Ridley; Safety at Work; Fourth Edition - Courtesy HSE.

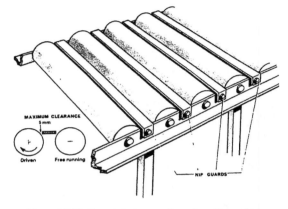

Figure 13-20: Guards between alternative drive-rollers.
Source: J Ridley; Safety at Work; Fourth Edition - Courtesy HSE.

Figure 13-21: Roller conveyor.   *Source: ACT.*

Figure 13-22: Belt conveyor guard.   *Source: ACT.*

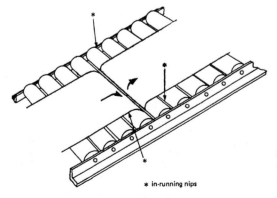

Figure 13-23: Nip points on roller conveyor with belts.
Source: J Ridley; Safety at Work; Fourth Edition - Courtesy HSE.

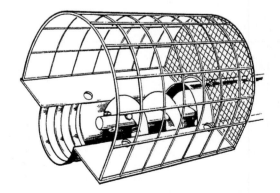

Figure 13-24: Screw conveyor guarding.
Source: J Ridley; Safety at Work; Fourth Edition - Courtesy HSE.

Screw

Materials are pushed forward by a rotating screw. Screw conveyors can cause terrible injuries and should be guarded or covered at all times. A locking-off system is required for maintenance and repairs.

SAFE USE AND MAINTENANCE

- Fixed guards on drums.
- Enclosure of conveyed items by side guards.
- Trip wires, if necessary, along the full length of the conveyor.
- Emergency stop buttons.
- Safe access at regular intervals.
- Avoid loose clothing.
- Restrict access.
- Wearing bump caps.
- Regular maintenance by competent people.

13.3 - Lifting operations and lifting equipment

Cranes

GENERAL CRANE HAZARDS

The principal hazards associated with any lifting operation are:

- **Overturning** which can be caused by weak support, operating outside the capabilities of the machine and by striking obstructions.

- **Overloading** by exceeding the operating capacity or operating radii, or by failure of safety devices.

- **Collision** with other cranes, overhead cables or structures.

- **Failure of load bearing part** - placing over cellars and drains, outriggers not extended, made-up or not solid ground, or of structural components of the crane itself.

- **Loss of load** from failure of lifting tackle or slinging procedure.

No matter what the type of crane, the main issues are the same:

- The ground the crane stands on - is it capable of bearing the load? Is it level? Are there any underground caverns or cellars?

- The load bearing capacity of the crane - is it sufficient for the task?

- Positioning the crane - is there enough room for the lift? Are there any overhead power lines, nearby buildings or other cranes? Will there be personnel or members of the public nearby? Is the tower crane near an airport or in a flight path?

- Adverse weather conditions.

- Structural integrity of the crane - are there signs of corrosion?

- Erecting and dismantling the crane - will other cranes be used?

Figure 13-25: Hook with safety latch.   *Source: Corel Clipart.*

SAFE USE AND MAINTENANCE

Crane selection

Cranes used within the construction industry vary from road going mobile cranes, to static tower type cranes. The type of crane selected will depend on a number of factors including the weight of the load to be lifted, the radius of operation, the height of the lift, the time available, and the frequency of the lifting activities. Hazards include impact with pedestrians or other vehicles when moving the crane or from moving parts of the crane, for example swinging jibs or loads. This equipment is often very heavy, which means the weight of the crane can cause the ground underneath the crane to sink or collapse. Other factors like height and size may have to be considered as there may be limitations in site roads that are placed between structures or where overhead restrictions exist. Careful consideration of these factors must be made when selecting the correct crane. Selecting a crane to carry out a lifting activity should be done at the planning stage, where the most suitable crane can be identified that is able to meet all of the lifting requirements and the limitations of the site.

Crane siting

Detailed consideration must be given to the location of any heavy piece of plant on construction sites, and in particular crane equipment, due to the fact that additional weight is distributed to the ground through the loading of the crane when performing a lift. Surveys must be carried out to determine the nature of the ground, whether soft or firm and what underground hazards are present such as buried services or hollow voids. If the ground proves to be soft, then this can be covered in timber, digger mats or hard core to prevent the crane or its outriggers sinking when under load. The surrounding environment must also be taken into consideration and factors may include highways, railways, electricity cables, areas of public interest. The area around where a crane is sited should be securely fenced, including the extremes of the lift radius, with an additional factor of safety to allow for emergency arrangements such as emergency vehicle access or safety in the event of a collapse or fall.

Stability of cranes

Cranes must be secured so that they do not tip over when in use. This anchoring can be achieved by securing with guy ropes, bolting the structure to a foundation, using ballast as counterweights or using outriggers to bring the centre of gravity down to the base area.

Cranes should be sited on firm ground with the wheels or outrigger feet having their weight distributed over a large surface. Care should be taken that the crane is not positioned over cellars or underground cavities, or positioned near excavations.

Sloping ground should be avoided as this can shift the load radius out or in, away from the safe working position.

In the uphill position, the greatest danger occurs when the load is set down. This can cause the crane to tip over. In the downhill position, the load moves out of the radius, which may cause the crane to tip forwards.

Operating area

Lifting equipment or a load must be positioned or installed in such a way as to reduce the risk, so far as is reasonably practicable, of it:

- Striking a person.
- Drifting from the load.
- Falling freely.
- Being released unintentionally.

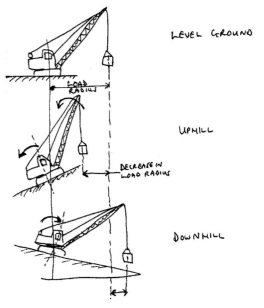

Figure 13-26: Stability of cranes (hand drawn example).
Source: ACT.

The load must be otherwise safe. Suitable devices must be in place to prevent a person from falling down a shaft or hoist way. All nearby hazards, including overhead cables and bared power supply conductors, should be identified and removed or covered by safe working procedures such as locking-off and permit systems. The possibility of striking other cranes or structures should be examined.

Operation of equipment

Lifting operations must be properly planned by a competent person, appropriately supervised and carried out in a safe manner.

No matter what type of crane, there are a number of common measures for safe operation that apply, including crane identification and capacity marking safe working load (SWL), and maintenance (preventative maintenance, as well as statutory implications).

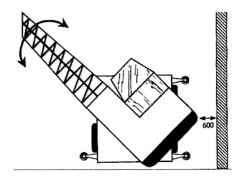

Figure 13-27: Danger zone - crane & fixed item. *Source: ACT.*

The main safety measures that should be incorporated for the safe operation of a crane include:

- Pre-use check by operator.
- Lifting equipment must be of adequate strength and stability for the load. Stresses induced at mounting or fixing points must be taken into account. Similarly every part of a load, anything attached to it and used in lifting must be of adequate strength.
- The safe working load (SWL) must be clearly marked on lifting machinery, equipment and accessories in order to ensure safe use. Where the SWL depends on the configuration of the machinery, it must be clearly marked for each configuration used and kept with the machinery. Equipment which is not designed for lifting persons, but which might be used as such, must have appropriate markings to the effect that it is not to be used for passengers.
- Load indicators - two types - a requirement with jib cranes, but beneficial if fitted to all cranes.
  - ✓ Load/radius indicator - shows the radius the crane is working at and the safe load for that radius. Must be visible to the driver.
  - ✓ Automatic safe load indicator - providing visible warning when SWL is approached and audible warning when SWL is exceeded.
- Controls - should be clearly identified and of the "hold to run" type.
- Over travel switches - limit switches to prevent the hook or sheave block being wound up to the cable drum.
- Access - safe access should be provided for the operator and for use during inspection and maintenance/emergency.
- Operating position - should provide clear visibility of hook and load, with the controls easily reached.
- Passengers - should not be carried without authorisation, and never on lifting tackle.
- Lifting tackle - chains, slings, wire ropes, eyebolts and shackles should be tested / examined.

Accessories

Mechanical lifting accessories include slings, hooks, chains eyes and cradles. This equipment is designed with the aim of assisting in lifting items without the need for manual force. Because these accessories are in a constantly changing environment and are in and out of use they need to be protected from damage, a failure of any one item could have fatal effects. For example, lifting eyes needed to be correctly fitted, slings have to be used with the correct technique and all equipment must be stored properly. Accessories must be attached correctly and safely to the load by a competent person, and then the lifting equipment takes over the task of providing the necessary required power to perform the lift. As with all lifting equipment, accessories must be regularly inspected and certificated and only used by trained authorised persons.

Figure 13-28: Lifting operation.   *Source: ACT.*

Figure 13-29: Lifting points on load.   *Source: ACT.*

Figure 13-30: Accessories.   *Source: Lincsafe.*

Figure 13-31: Accessories.   *Source: ACT.*

Operator training and practices

Crane operators and slingers should be fit and strong enough for the work. Training should be provided for the safe operation of the particular equipment.

A safe system of work should be developed and communicated to all those involved. The planning should involve selecting competent persons including the mobile crane driver and appointed person who will supervise the lifting operation.

A number of safety rules are suggested as a basis of a Code of Practice for the safe operation of mobile cranes. Circumstances differ from site to site and additional rules should be inserted to cover individual cases and conditions.

For example, before taking over a mobile crane the driver must always check around the crane, and check the pressure of tyres, the engine for fuel, lubrication oil, water and the compressed air system. All controls, such as clutches, brakes and safe load indicator, should be tested to see that all ropes run smoothly and check limit switches, where fitted.

The driver of a *mobile crane* should carry out the following:

- To travel unladen, lower jib onto its rest (if fitted) or to the lowest operating position and point in the direction of travel, but beware of steep hills.
- Learn the signalling system and observe the signals of the appointed banksman.
- Do not permit unauthorised persons to travel on the crane.
- Do not use the crane to replace normal means of transport, or as a towing tractor.
- Before lifting, check that the crane is on firm and level ground, and that spring locks and out-riggers (where fitted) are properly in position.
- Keep a constant watch on the load radius indicator. The driver may refuse to lift any suspected overload. Overloads are forbidden.
- All movements must be made with caution. Violent handling produces excess loading on the crane structure and machinery.
- Make allowances for adverse weather conditions.
- Do not attempt to drag loads or cause loads to swing. Always position the crane so that the pull on the hoist rope is vertical.
- Satisfy yourself that the load is properly slung. A load considered unsafe should not be lifted.
- Satisfy yourself that all persons are in a safe position before any movement is carried out.
- Make certain before hoisting that the hook is not attached to any anchored load or fixed object.
- Do not drag slings when travelling.
- If the crane is slewing, the jib, hook or load must be in a position to clear any obstruction, but the load must not be lifted unnecessarily high.
- Be on a constant lookout for overhead obstructions, particularly electric cables.
- Never tamper with or disconnect safe load indicators.
- Should the hoist or jib ropes become slack or out of their grooves, stop the crane and report the condition.
- Report all defects to the supervisor and never attempt to use a crane with a suspected serious defect until rectified or certified by a competent person that it is not dangerous.
- When leaving a crane unattended, see that the power is off, the engine stopped, the load unhooked, and the hook taken up to a safe position.

- Where using special devices; e.g. magnets, grabs, etc. they must be used only for the purpose intended and in accordance with the instruction given.
- Keep the crane clean and tidy.
- When parking a crane after use, remember to apply all brakes, slew locks, and secure rail clamps when fitted. Some cranes, however, particularly tower cranes, must be left to weather vane and the manufacturers instructions must be clearly adhered to. Park the crane where the weather vaning jib will not strike any object. Lock the cabin before leaving the crane.
- When it is necessary to make a report this must be done promptly through supervision.
- Drive smoothly - drive safely. Remember that cranes are safe only when they are used as recommended by the makers. This applies in particular to speciality cranes.

Rules for safe operation of a crane

Always	Ensure operators/slingers are trained and competent.
Always	Select the right appliance and tackle for the job.
Always	Ensure the appliance is stable when lifting - e.g. not outside lifting radius, firm, level ground, outriggers.
Always	Use correct slinging methods.
Always	Protect sling from sharp edges - pack out and lower onto spacers.
Always	Ensure the sling is securely attached to the hook.
Always	Ensure load is lifted to correct height and moved at an appropriate speed.
Always	Use standard signals - refer to the Health and Safety (Safety Signs & Signals) Regulations (SSR) 1996.
Never	Use equipment if damaged (check before use) - e.g. stretched or not free movement, worn or corroded, outside inspection date.
Never	Exceed the safe working load.
Never	Lift with sling angles greater than 120^0.
Never	Lift a load over people.
Never	Drag a load or allow sudden shock loading.

Figure 13-32: Crane operation.   *Source: ACT.*

Statutory examination of lifting equipment

Statutory requirements are set out in Regulation 9 of the LOLER.

Used lifting equipment must be thoroughly examined before being put into service for the first time by a new user. This does not apply to new lifting equipment (unless its safety depends on installation conditions) or equipment that conforms to European Community requirements and has been certified as being examined within the previous 12 months. Suppliers of used lifting equipment are obliged to certify that a thorough examination has been carried out.

Where the safety of lifting equipment depends on the installation conditions it must be thoroughly examined prior to first use, after assembly and on change of location in order to ensure that it has been installed correctly and is safe to operate.

Lifting equipment exposed to conditions causing deterioration that is liable to result in dangerous situations is to be thoroughly examined by a competent person:

a) At least every 6 months - lifting equipment for lifting persons and lifting accessories.

b) At least every 12 months - other lifting equipment or

c) In either case, in accordance with an examination scheme and

d) On each occurrence of exceptional circumstances liable to jeopardise the safety of the lifting equipment.

Figure 13-33: Marking of equipment.   *Source: ACT.*

Where appropriate to ensure health and safety, inspections must be carried out at suitable intervals between thorough examinations. Examinations and inspections must ensure that the good condition of equipment is maintained and that any deterioration can be detected and remedied in good time.

Control of lifting operations

GENERAL REQUIREMENTS

Under regulation 8 of the LOLER employers have a duty to ensure that every lifting operation involving lifting equipment for the purposes of lifting or lowering of a load is organised safely. This will include ensuring the following:

a) Lifting operations to be properly planned by a competent person.

b)　　　Provision of appropriate supervision.

c)　　　Work is to be carried out in a safe manner.

There are various appointments with specified responsibilities in order to ensure the safety of lifting operations on site, these are as follows.

- Competent person　-　Appointed to plan the operation.
- Load handler　-　Attaches and detaches the load.
- Authorised person　-　Ensures the load safely attached.
- Operator　-　Appointed to operate the equipment.
- Responsible person　-　Appointed to communicate the position of the load (banksman).
- Assistants　-　Appointed to relay communications.

Lifting equipment and accessories should be subject to a pre-use check. In addition, care should be taken to ensure the lifting accessories used are compatible with the task and that the load is protected or supported such that it does not disintegrate when lifted. The lifting operation should be organised to prevent the lifting equipment being operated until movement has been authorised by the person attaching or detaching the load.

If the operator cannot observe the full path of the load an appointed person (and assistants as appropriate) should be used to communicate the position of the load and directions to avoid striking anything or anyone.

Where practicable, loads should not be carried or suspended over areas occupied by people. Where this is necessary appropriate systems of work should be used to ensure it is done safely.

Lifting operations should not be carried on where adverse weather conditions occur, such as fog, lightning, wind or where heavy rainfall is making ground conditions unstable. It is important that measures be used to prevent lifting equipment overturning and that there is sufficient room for it to operate without contacting other objects. Lifting equipment should not be used to drag loads and should not be overloaded. Special arrangements need to be in place when lifting equipment not normally used for people is used for that purpose, e.g. de-rating the working load limit, ensuring communication is in place between the people and operator, and ensuring the operation controls are manned at all times.

Figure 13-34: Lifting operations.　　*Source: ACT.*

Figure 13-35: Lifting operations.　　*Source: ACT.*

PLANNING

The type of lifting equipment that is to be used and the complexity of the lifting operations will dictate the degree of planning required for the lifting operation. Planning combines two parts:

1)　　Initial planning to ensure that lifting equipment is provided which is suitable for the range of tasks that it will have to carry out.

2)　　Planning of individual lifting operations so that they can be carried out safely with the lifting equipment provided.

Factors that should be considered when formulating a plan include:

- The load that is being lifted - weight, shape, centres of gravity, surface condition, lifting points.
- The equipment and accessories being used for the operation and suitability - certification validity.
- The proposed route that the load will take including the destination and checks for obstructions.
- The team required to carry out the lift - competencies and numbers required.
- Production of a safe system of work, risk assessments, permits to work.
- The environment in which the lift will take place - ground conditions, weather, local population.
- Securing areas below the lift - information, restrictions, demarcation and barriers.
- A suitable trial to determine the reaction of the lifting equipment prior to full lift.
- Completion of the operation and any dismantling required.

Figure 13-36: Siting and stability.　　*Source: ACT.*

SELECTION OF EQUIPMENT

Lifting equipment and any accessories used for lifting are pieces of work equipment under the PUWER. Regulation 4 states that

'every employer shall ensure that work equipment is used only for operations for which, and under conditions for which, it is suitable in order to avoid any reasonably foreseeable risk to the health and safety of any person'.

In order for lifting equipment to be suitable it must be of the correct type for the task, have a safe working load limit in excess of the load being lifted, and have the correct type and combination of lifting accessories attached.

Certification of equipment

Regulation 9 of the LOLER places duties on employers to ensure that lifting equipment is thoroughly examined and specifies the different circumstances and periods of time under which the examinations need to take place. *See also the section - Requirements for the statutory examination of lifting equipment - earlier in this unit.*

Regulation 10 of LOLER requires those persons carrying out the thorough examination as specified under regulation 9 to, as soon as is practicable, make a written report of the results of the examination. This is to be signed by the competent person carrying out this task.

Regulation 11 of LOLER concerns the keeping of information in relation to examinations and specifies that any report written by a competent person following an examination must be kept available for inspection and the periods of validity for which the report must be kept.

Competence of operators and signallers

The Health and Safety at Work etc Act (HASAWA) 1974 places a duty on employers to their employees for the provision of information, instruction, training and supervision as is necessary to ensure, so far as is reasonably practicable, the health and safety at work of his employees. In addition to this general duty, a further duty exists under The Provision and Use of Work Equipment Regulations (PUWER) 1998. Employers must ensure that any person who uses a piece of work equipment has received adequate training for purposes of health and safety, including training in the methods which may be adopted when using work equipment, any risks which such use may entail and precautions to be taken.

Drivers / operators of cranes and other lifting appliances, including others involved in lifting operations (e.g. signallers), must be adequately trained, experienced and aged 18 years or over. The only exception is when under the direct supervision of a competent person for training requirements.

Electrical hazards & control

Overall Aims

On completion of this Unit, candidates will understand:

- the hazards and risks associated with the use of electrical equipment and systems operating at mains voltages.
- the measures that should be taken to minimise the risks.
- the measures needed to protect against contact with overhead power lines.

Content

Specific Intended Learning Outcomes

The intended learning outcomes of this Unit are that candidates will be able to:

14.1   identify the hazards and evaluate the consequential risks from the use of electricity in the workplace

14.2   advise on the control measures that should be taken when working with electrical systems or using electrical equipment

14.3   outline the measures to be taken when working near or under overhead power lines

Sources of Reference

Electricity at Work - Safe Working Practices (HSG85), HSE Books

Maintaining Portable and Transportable Electrical Equipment (HSG107), HSE Books

Electrical Safety on Construction Sites (HSG141), HSE Books

Relevant Statutory Provisions

The Electricity at Work Regulations (EWR) 1989

Health and Safety (First-Aid) Regulations (FAR) 1981

14.1 - Principles of electricity

Basic circuitry

ELECTRICAL EQUIPMENT SAFETY

Electricity is a facility that we have all come to take for granted, whether for lighting, heating, as a source of motive power or as the driving force behind the computer. Used properly it can be of great benefit to us, but misused it can be very dangerous and often fatal.

Electricity is used in most industries, offices and homes and our modern society could now not easily function without it. Despite its convenience to the user, it has a major danger. The normal senses of sight, hearing and smell will not detect electricity. Making contact with exposed conductors at our domestic supply voltage, 240V can be lethal.

Unlike many other workplace accidents, the actual number of electrical notifiable accidents is small. However, with a reported 10-20 fatalities each year, the severity is high. Accidents are often caused by complacency, not just by the normally assumed ignorance. It must be recognised by everyone working with electricity that over half of all electrical fatal accidents are to skilled/competent persons. In order to avoid the causes of electric injury, it is necessary to understand the basic principles of electricity, what it does to the body and what controls are necessary.

BASIC PRINCIPLES OF ELECTRICITY

The flow of electrons through a conductor is known as a current. Electric current flows due to differences in electrical "pressure" (or potential difference as it is often known), just as water flows through a pipe because of the pressure behind it. Differences in electrical potential are measured in volts.

In some systems the current flows continually in the same direction. This is known as direct current (DC). However the current may also constantly reverse its direction of flow. This is known as alternating current (AC). Most public electricity supplies are AC. The UK system reverses its direction 50 times per second and it is said to have a frequency of 50 cycles per second or 50 Hertz (50Hz). DC is little used in standard distribution systems but is sometimes used in industry for specialist applications. Although there are slight differences in the effects under fault and shock conditions between AC and DC it is a safe approach to apply the same rules of safety for the treatment and prevention of electric shock.

As a current passes round a circuit under the action of an applied voltage it is impeded in its flow. This may be due to the presence in the circuit of resistance, inductance or capacitance, the combined effect of which is called impedance and is measured in ohms.

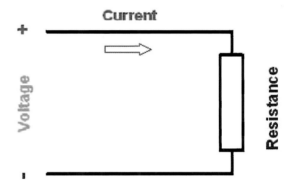

Figure 14-1: A basic electrical circuit.   *Source: ACT.*

RELATIONSHIP BETWEEN VOLTAGE, CURRENT AND RESISTANCE

There is a simple relationship between electrical pressure (Volts), current (measured in Amperes or milliamperes) and resistance (measured in Ohms) represented by Ohm's Law:

Voltage **(V)** = current **(I)** multiplied by the circuit resistance **(R)**. $V = I \times R$ or $I = \dfrac{V}{R}$

Hence, given any two values the third can be calculated. Also, if one value changes the other two values will change accordingly.

This basic electrical equation can be used to calculate the current that flows in a circuit of a given resistance.

This will need to be done to determine, for example, the fuse or cable rating needed for a particular circuit. Similarly, the current that will flow through a person who touches a live conductor can be calculated.

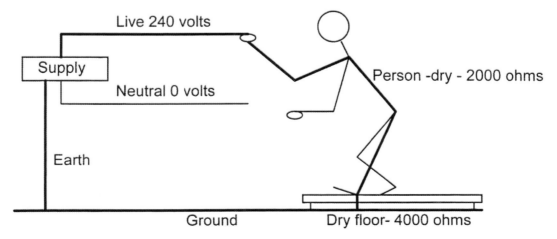

Figure 14-2: An electric circuit under fault conditions showing resistances in the path of a fault current.   *Source: R. Gilmour.*

By Ohm's law:

Current = $\dfrac{\text{Voltage}}{\text{Resistance}}$ or $I = \dfrac{V}{R}$

Resistance in a circuit is dependent on many factors. Most metals, particularly precious metals, allow current to pass very easily. These have a low resistance and are used as conductors. Other materials such as plastics, rubber and textiles have a high resistance and are used as insulators.

If the person is on, say, a dry concrete floor, resistance in the body will only be about 2000 Ohms and the resistance in the floor about 4000 Ohms, therefore the combined resistance would be 6000 Ohms. Presuming the person is in contact with a live electrical supply at 240 Volts the current flowing through the person in this fault condition can be calculated.

$I = \dfrac{V}{R} = \dfrac{240 \text{ Volts}}{2000+4000 \text{ Ohms}} = 0.04 \text{ Amperes}$

The current flowing through the operator will be about 0.04 Amperes or 40mA (40 milliAmperes). This could result in a fatal shock.

14.2 - Hazards of electricity

The consequences of contact with electricity are:

- **Shock**
- **Electrical burns**   -   resulting from the heating effect of the current which burns the body tissue.
- **Electrical fires**   -   caused by overheating or arcing apparatus in contact with a fuel.
- **Explosions**   -   from sparks in a flammable atmosphere.
- **Secondary injuries**   -   falling from a ladder.

Electric shock and its effect on the body

FACTORS INFLUENCING SEVERITY

The severity of electric shock or the amount of current which flows for a given voltage will depend on the frequency of the supply voltage, on the level of the voltage which is applied and on the state of the point of contact with the body, particularly the moisture condition.

CURRENT

The current that flows through the body provides the energy to do the harm, the more current flowing the more harm likely to be done. The body can tolerate small levels of current flowing through it, but as the level increases the current is able to have a greater effect on the body, in particular the muscles. As such, low currents tend to influence only the smaller muscles and the larger muscles need a larger current to influence them. The effects on the muscle will be to cause it to spasm, therefore small muscles in the hand may contract causing the hand to close or at higher current flow larger muscles in the chest may contract restricting breathing. When the heart is affected by the current flow its normal beat may be disrupted and it attempts to beat in a discordant manner, this effect is known as fibrillation. It should be remembered that the level of current necessary to cause harm to the body is much less than that required to run most equipment and is in mA rather than Amperes.

FREQUENCY

The frequency of current flow in an alternating current supply, such as the mains supply in an office block, operates at 50 cycles per second. This frequency is close to that of the heart when functioning normally. It can have the effect of disrupting the operation of the heart causing it to beat in a discordant manner, to fibrillate.

DURATION

For an electric shock to have an effect a person needs to be in contact with the current for sufficient time. At low current levels the body tolerates the current so the time is not material, however at higher current levels e.g. 50mA the person has to remain in contact for sufficient time to affect the heart, in the order of milliseconds. In general, the longer a person is in contact with the current more harm may be caused.

RESISTANCE

The amount of resistance in a circuit influences the amount of current that is allowed to flow, as explained above by Ohm's law. It is possible for a person to be in contact with a circuit and to present sufficiently high resistance that very little current is allowed to flow through their body. The example shown above illustrates this. It should be noted that the level of current is also dependent on the voltage; at high voltages an enormous amount of resistance is needed to ensure current flow will remain at a safe level. The human body contributes part of the resistance of a circuit, the amount it contributes depends on the current path taken and other factors such as personal chemical make-up (a large portion of the body is water), dryness and thickness of skin, and any clothing that is being worn, such as shoes and gloves.

CURRENT PATH

The effect of an electric shock on a body is particularly dependent on the current path through the body. Current has to flow through from one point to another as part of a circuit. If the flow was between two points on a finger the effect on the body would be concentrated between the two points. If the current path is between one hand and another across the chest this means the flow will pass through major parts of the body, such as the heart, and may have a specific effect on it. In a similar way a contact between hand and foot (feet) can have serious effects on a great many parts of the body, including the heart. These latter current paths tend to be the ones leading to fatal injuries.

An important message to be put over to employees is that, though many may experience shock from 240 volts this may not be fatal if they were, for example, standing on or wearing some insulating material. This may be a matter of fortune and should not be relied on.

EFFECTS OF CURRENT FLOWING IN THE HUMAN BODY

CURRENT (mA)	LENGTH OF TIME	LIKELY EFFECTS
0-1	Not Critical	Threshold of feeling. Undetected by person.
1-15	Not Critical	Threshold of cramp. Independent loosening of the hands no longer possible.
15-30	Minutes	Cramp-like pulling together of the arms, breathing difficult. Limit of tolerance
30-50	Seconds to minutes	Strong cramp-like effects, loss of consciousness due to restricted breathing. Longer time may lead to fibrillation.
50-500	Less than one heart period (70 mS)	No fibrillation. Strong shock effects.
	Greater than one heart period	Fibrillation. Loss of consciousness. Burn marks
Over 500	Less than one heart period	Fibrillation. Loss of consciousness. Burn marks

Figure 14-3: Effects of current flowing in the human body.

mA = milliAmperes   mS = milliseconds

CAUSES OF ELECTRIC SHOCK

Direct shock. Contact with a charged or energised conductor that is intended to be so charged or energised. In these circumstances the installation is operating in its normal or proper condition.

Indirect shock. Contact with a conductor or exposed conductive parts e.g. casing of the apparatus that is normally safe to touch but which, under fault conditions, could become dangerously live.

Common causes of electric shock
- Work on electrical circuits by unqualified persons.
- Work on live circuits.
- Replacement of fuses and light bulbs on supposedly dead circuits.
- Working on de-energised circuits that could accidentally be re-energised.

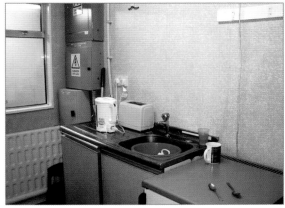

Figure 14-4: Electrical equipment near water.   *Source: ACT.*

Figure 14-5: Contact with high voltage buried cable. *Source: ACT.*

FIRST AID TREATMENT FOR ELECTRIC SHOCK

Statistically, reportable accidents run at about 200,000 per year of which some 200 are fatal. With electricity, of some 550 reported accidents each year, 75 per year are thought to be fatal. The severity of accidents involving electricity therefore merits detailed study of their causes and development in order to prevent them. The first aid treatment points listed in this section below are for guidance only and are not a substitute for a qualified first aider with knowledge of the workplace.

In case of electrical shock:

Do
- Switch off or remove the plug.
- Check that there is no remaining connection to the supply and, if possible, prove that the system is discharged and dead.
- Assess the situation and any remaining danger to yourself or the casualty.
- Call for qualified support which may mean the 999 emergency services.
- If safe, check the casualty's response (What is the degree of consciousness?).

Check

A - Airway   -   Is it open?

B - Breathing   -   Is the casualty breathing normally?

C - Circulation   -   Does the casualty have a normal pulse?

Action

If airway obstructed by teeth, food etc., remove; if tongue tilt head back to clear, and then provide cardio pulmonary resuscitation (CPR).

If trained, place in the recovery position and/or apply resuscitation as required. Cool any burns with cold water.

Keep the casualty under observation for secondary effects until you hand him over to a medically qualified person.

Do not

Do not go near the casualty until the electricity supply is proven to be off. This is especially important with overhead high voltage lines: keep yourself and others at least 18 metres away until the electricity supply company personnel advise otherwise.

Do not delay - after 3 minutes without blood circulation irreversible damage can be done to the casualty.

Figure 14-6: First aid sign.   *Source: ACT.*

Do not wait for an accident to happen - train in emergency procedures and first aid now, plan procedures for an emergency (calling for help, making 999 calls, meeting ambulances and leading them to the casualty) as seconds saved may save a life. Hold emergency drills.

Electrical burns

DIRECT

There will be a heating effect along the route taken by electric current as it passes through body tissue. Whilst there are likely to be burn marks on the skin at the point of contact there may also be a deep seated burning within the body which is painful and slow to heal. As the outer layer of skin is burnt the resistance decreases and so the current will increase. The current flowing through the body can cause major injury to internal organs and bone marrow as it passes through them.

INDIRECT

If while working on live equipment the system is short-circuited by, for example, an un-insulated spanner touching live and neutral this will result in a large and sudden current flow through the spanner. This current will cause the spanner to melt and may throw molten metal out from the points of contact. When this molten metal contacts the parts of a person in the vicinity of the spanner, for example the hands or face, serious burns can take place as the molten metal hits and sticks to the person. With high voltages and the very low resistance of the spanner very large currents can flow. This rapid discharge of energy that follows contact with high voltages not only causes the rapid melting of the spanner but does so with such violent force that the molten particles of metal are thrown off with huge velocity. It is not necessary to have high voltages to melt a spanner in this way - it can also occur with batteries with sufficient stored energy, such as those on a fork lift truck. There are many experiences of people suffering injury in this way when servicing lift truck batteries as a spanner falls out of their overall top pocket.

Electrical fires

COMMON CAUSES

Much electrical equipment generates heat or produces sparks and this equipment should not be placed where this could lead to the uncontrolled ignition of any substance.

The principal causes of electrical fires are:

- Wiring with defects such as insulation failure due to age or poor maintenance.
- Overheating of cables or other electrical equipment through overloading with currents above their design capacity.
- Incorrect fuse rating.
- Poor connections due to lack of maintenance or unskilled personnel.

Electrical equipment may itself explode or arc violently and it may also act as a source of ignition of flammable vapours, gases, liquids or dust through electric sparks, arcs or high surface temperatures of equipment. Other causes are heat created by poorly maintained or defective motors, heaters and lighting.

Figure 14-7: Used coiled up - risk of overheating. *Source: ACT.*

Figure 14-8: Max current capacity exceeded.   *Source: ACT*

Portable electrical equipment

CONDITIONS AND PRACTICES LIKELY TO LEAD TO ACCIDENTS

Unsuitable equipment
- Unsuitable apparatus for the duty or the conditions.
- Misuse.
- Failure to follow operating instructions.
- Wrong connection of system - supply phase, neutral or earth reversed.
- Wrong voltage or rating of equipment.

Figure 14-9: Hazard - fuse wired out.   *Source: ACT.*

Figure 14-10: Hazard - defective apparatus. *Source: ACT*

Inadequate maintenance
- Inadequate maintenance of the installation and the equipment.
- Wrong or broken connection to portable apparatus.
- Inadequate earthing.
- Poor maintenance and testing.
- No defect reporting system.

Use of defective apparatus
- Faulty cables, notably extension leads.
- Plugs and sockets.
- Damaged plug or socket.
- Protection devices, such as fuses or circuit breaker, incorrect rating, damaged or missing.
- Overloaded leading to damage or over-heating.
- Short circuit leading to damage, overheating or movement
- Isolation procedures or systems of work wrong.
- Bad circuit connections.

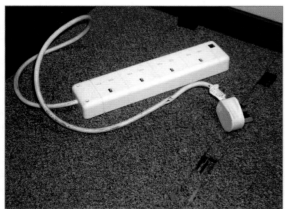

Figure 14-11: Hazard - damaged cable.   *Source: ACT.*

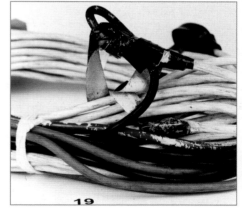

Figure 14-12: Hazard - taped joints.   *Source: ACT.*

General
- Lack of competence.　■ Poor access, lighting and emergency procedures.　■ No work planning, e.g. permit-to-work.

Secondary hazards

These occur where the injury results from the flow of electricity through the body's nerves, muscles and organs and causes abnormal function to occur. Muscular spasm may be severe, particularly if the leg muscles are affected, causing a person to be thrown several metres. Injuries may result from dislocation, impact with surrounding objects or fall from a height. In addition, a tool may be dropped causing such injuries as burns or impact injury to the user or others near by.

14.3 - Control measures

Selection and suitability of equipment

The British Standard BS 7671, the Institute of Electrical Engineers (IEE) 16th edition requirements, Chapter 13 - 'Fundamental requirements for safety' - specifies the following needs. Good workmanship and proper materials shall be used. Construction, installation, inspection, testing and maintenance shall be such as to prevent danger. Equipment shall be suitable for the power demanded and the conditions in which it is installed. Additions and alterations to installations shall comply with regulations. Equipment, which requires operation or attention, shall be accessible.

The Low Voltage (Safety) Regulations place a duty on the supplier of equipment to ensure that equipment using between 50 and 100 volts AC is safe.

Construction, including flexible cables and cords, must be to European Union (EU) accepted good engineering practice standards. The Regulations are deemed satisfied if the equipment bears a recognised standard mark, certificate or other acceptable authorisation. Supply of unsafe equipment or components is prohibited.

It is important to ensure that all electrical equipment is suitable. For example, if it is to be used for outdoor work on a construction site in conditions that it might get wet, equipment providing protection from the ingress of water must be selected. Many tools are designed and provided for use in a domestic situation and they may not be suitable for use in the more arduous conditions of a construction site, for example, cable entry grips may be more secure and outer protection of cables thicker on equipment designed for construction work. Part of the selection process is to determine situations where low voltage, such as 110 volt systems, can be used in preference to 240 volts.

CABLES AND LEADS

Insulation appropriate to the environment should be used to give resistance to abrasion, chemicals, heat and impact. The insulation must be in good condition. Flexible, multi-strand cables are required for portable tools and extension leads. Extension leads must be fused.

Cables must be secured by the outer sheath at their point of entry into the apparatus, including plugs. The individual conductor insulation should not show through the sheath and conductors certainly must not be exposed even through cuts may only be opened when the cable is bent.

Temporary wiring should be used in compliance with standards and properly secured, supported and mechanically protected against damage. Attention to cables in offices is particularly important to avoid tripping hazards with phone, computer, calculator and kettle leads growing in number.

Taped joints in cables are not allowed and proper line connectors must be used to join cables. Connectors should be kept to a minimum to reduce earth path impedance.

Conductors across roads or pedestrian ways should be covered to protect them from damage. Where they are to cross a doorway this is usually best done by taking it around the door instead of trailing it across the floor. Overhead cables likely to be hit by vehicles or persons carrying ladders, pipes etc. should be highlighted by the use of appropriate signs. Where necessary to protect them cables should be protected in armoured sheath or run in protective conduit or trunking. Many cables are set up on a temporary basis but get left for a considerable time with improvised arrangements. Care should be taken to identify true short term temporary arrangements and those that warrant full longer term arrangements such as placing in trunking.

Regular examination should be made for deterioration, cuts, kinks or bend damage (particularly near to the point of entry into apparatus), exposed conductors, overheat or burn damage, trapping damage, insulation brittling or corrosion.

Site electrical systems

PLANNING AND INSTALLATION

Electricity in construction brings numerous hazards that require stringent planning and control systems. Prior to starting construction activities at the planning stage consideration must be given to factors including buried services, electricity sub-stations or proximity to overhead cables. A site may have existing buildings and tests must be made to determine whether existing services are live or dead. At the planning stage, a full site survey will include identifying the location of any electrical sources or conductors.

Planning also provides the ideal opportunity to ensure that where electricity is involved, the correct measures are implemented to control risk. This may include location of plant, planning cable runs or ducts, whether high or low voltage is required, control features when in use (switch panels, isolation, and lock off), protection devices (earthing arrangements, trip switches, residual current devices, panel housings, warnings and instructions). Maintenance should play a key part in the planning stage, with consideration given to access, isolation, lock-off and security.

When construction activities start heavy mechanical plant will be introduced that may operate in close proximity to sources of electricity. Safe systems should be introduced to include ensuring that sufficiently safe distances are maintained from overhead cables to prevent electrical 'arc' (discharge) from the uninsulated cables. Safe systems may include permits-to-work, 'goal post' type visual barriers, information for site workers and signs. There may be activities that involve explosive atmospheres that require intrinsically safe equipment to be used (e.g. work is sewers or chambers).

Most industrial installations work on high voltage systems due to increased consumption of electricity during the many different processes. Owing to economic advantages, industrial sites commonly include their own dedicated power sub-stations that operate at voltages typically in ranges of 11kV. This high voltage is then transformed down into values more commonly in the range of 415v. When working with high voltage circuitry, staff must be 'high voltage' trained and work under a permit to work system.

Figure 14-13: Construction site generator.   *Source: ACT.*

Figure 14-14: Construction site power supply panel. *Source: ACT*

It is essential that the planning and installation of electrical systems reflect not only the power needs but the lighting needs of the site as well. The plan should include anticipated needs or demand as the site changes, for example extending provision as a structure is built or orderly withdraw of provision as a structure is demolished. Planning should ensure power is available at key points as close to where work is carried out that requires it, thus minimising the need for extension cables to run for long distances. Planning should take account of where it is not practicable to provide a permanent system and where local power generation is more suitable. In this case the same planning a thought is required to ensure the system provided is adequate for the demands. In some cases this will require the provision of a quantity of small generators to ensure the right amount of power is available where it is needed.

Figure 14-15: 110v generator.   *Source: ACT.*

Figure 14-16: 110v extension lead.   *Source: ACT.*

If work is to be conducted in someone else's building that is occupied and power is to be obtained by adapting the system within the building consideration has to be given to the effects on the host's power supply of this additional demand. Care should be taken to ensure that power is drawn from agreed points and at agreed, safe voltages. Where practicable systems provided for construction work should run at 110V or lower and should be set into place at the earliest safe opportunity, in many cases this can be integrated into ground works that is planned for the site. If systems are to be left in place at the end of the work, and they do not form part of the system for the structure constructed, care should be taken to identify them on plans and if they are to be left 'dead' they should be checked to ensure this is the case. This data would be provided as part of the safety file provided as a Construction (Design and Management) Regulations (CDM) 1994 requirement.

PERMIT TO WORK PROCEDURES AND REQUIREMENTS

A permit to work is an official, documented safe system of work that is used for controlling high risk activities. Implementation is required prior to work beginning to ensure that all precautions are taken and are securely in place to prevent danger to the workforce. When managed correctly, a permit to work prevents any mistakes or deviations through poor communication; by stating the specific requirements of the task. For electrical systems, a permit to work is typically used for those rated at or in excess of 240v or where there is more than one point or means of isolation.

The authorised person issues the permit to work and will sign the document to declare that all isolations are made and remain in place throughout the duration of the task. In addition to this, the authorised person will make checks to ensure that all controls to be implemented by the acceptor are in place before work begins

The acceptor of the permit to work assumes responsibility for carrying out the work on the electrical system. The acceptor signs the document to declare that the terms and conditions of the permit to work are understood and will be complied with fully at all times by the entire work team. Compliance with a permit to work system includes ensuring the required safeguards are implemented and that the work will be restricted to only the equipment stated within the document.

Items included in the electrical permit to work are;

- Permit issue number.
- Authorised person identification.
- Points at which isolation is made.
- Test procedure & confirmation of dead circuitry.
- Warning information sign locations.
- Earth connection points.
- Details of the work to be carried out.
- Signature of authoriser.
- Signature of Acceptor.
- Signature for works clearance / extension / handover.
- Signature for cancellation.
- Other precautions (risk assessments, method statements, and personal protective equipment).

Figure 14-17: Power supply isolation. *Source: ACT.*

Advantages and limitations of protective systems

FUSE

This is a device designed to automatically cut off the power supply to a circuit within a given time when the current flow in that circuit exceeds a given value. A fuse may be a rewirable tinned copper wire in a suitable carrier or a wire or wires in an enclosed cartridge.

In effect it is a weak link in the circuit that melts when heat is created by too high a current passing through the thin wire in the fuse case. When this happens the circuit is broken and no more current flows. They tend to have rating in the order of Amperes rather than mA which means it has **limited usefulness in protecting people from electric shock.** This may also act slowly if the current is just above the fuse rating. Using too high a fuse means that the circuit will remain intact and the equipment will draw power. This may cause it to overheat leading to a fire or if a fault exists the circuit will remain live and the fault current may pass through the user of the equipment when they pick it up or operate it.

The following formula should be used to calculate the correct rating for a fuse:

Current (Amperes) = $\frac{\text{Power (watts)}}{\text{Voltage (volts)}}$

For example, the correct fuse current rating for a 2-kilowatt kettle on a 240-volt supply would be:

$\frac{2000 \text{ W}}{240 \text{ V}} = 8.33\text{A}$

Typical fuses for domestic appliances are 3,5,10 and 13 Ampere ratings.

The nearest fuse just above this current level is 10A.

	Typical examples of power ratings are:	Suitable fuses at 240 Volts:
■ Computer processor. ■ Electric kettle. ■ Dishwasher. ■ Refrigerator.	■ 350 Watts. ■ 1850-2200 Watts. ■ 1380 Watts. ■ 90 Watts.	■ 3 Amperes. ■ 10 - 13 Amperes. ■ 10 Amperes. ■ 3 Amperes.

Summary

- A weak link in the circuit that melts slowly when heat is created by a fault condition. However, this usually happens too slowly to protect people.
- Easy to replace with wrong rating.
- Needs tools to replace.
- Easy to override by replacing a fuse with one of a higher rating or putting in an improvised 'fuse', such as a nail, that has a high rating.

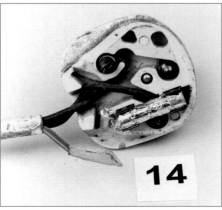

Figure 14-18: Plug-foil fuse no earth. *Source: ACT.*

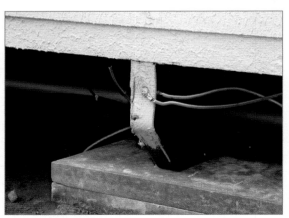

Figure 14-19: Earthing. *Source: ACT.*

EARTHING

A conductor called an earth wire is fitted to the system; it is connected at one end to a plate buried in the ground and the other end connected to the metal casing of the equipment. If for any reason a conductor touches the casing so that the equipment casing becomes 'live' the current will flow to the point of lowest potential, the earth. The path to this point (earth) is made easier as the wire is designed to have very little resistance. This *may prevent electric shock* provided it is used in association with a correctly rated fuse, or better still a residual current device (RCD), and no one is in contact with the equipment at the time the fault occurs. It should be remembered that earthing is provided where the casing can become live. If the equipment is designed so that this cannot be the case, such as double insulated equipment where the user touches non-conducting surfaces, earthing of the equipment is no advantage. In summary, earthing provides a path of least resistance for "stray" current and provides protection against indirect shock.

ISOLATION

Isolation of an electrical system is an excellent way of achieving safety for those that need to work on or near the system; for example, isolation of a power supply into a building that is to be refurbished or isolation of plant that is to be maintained. In its simplest form it can mean switching off and unplugging a portable appliance at times it is not in use. Care must be taken to check that the isolation has been adequate and effective before work starts; this can include tests on the system. It is also important to ensure the isolation is secure; 'lock off' and 'tag out' systems will assist with this.

REDUCED VOLTAGE

One of the best ways to reduce the risk from electricity is to reduce the voltage. This is frequently achieved by the use of a transformer (step down) which will reduce the voltage. A common reduction is from the usual mains voltage of 240V to 110V. Normally, transformers that are used to reduce voltage are described as "centre tapped to earth". In practice this means that any voltage involved in an electrical shock will be 55V.

Using the earlier example of Ohms Law, if the voltage is 240V then:

$$I = \frac{V}{R} = \frac{240 \text{ Volts}}{2000+4000 \text{ Ohms}} = 0.04 \text{ Amperes or 40 mA}$$

However, if a centre tapped to earth transformer is used then,

$$I = \frac{V}{R} = \frac{55 \text{ Volts}}{2000+4000 \text{ Ohms}} = 0.009 \text{ Amperes or 9 mA}$$

Reference to figures 14.2 and 14.3 will clearly show how this *reduces the effects of electric shock* on the body.

An alternative to reduction in voltage by means of a transformer is to provide battery-powered equipment; this will commonly run on 12V-24V but may be higher. The common method is to use a rechargeable battery to power the equipment which eliminates the need for a cable to feed power to the equipment and gives a greater flexibility of use for the user, e.g. for drills and power drivers.

Figure 14-20: 110V centre tapped earth transformer. *Source: ACT*

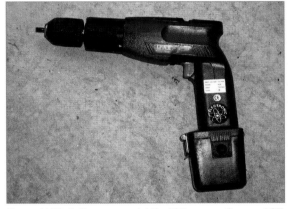

Figure 14-21: Battery powered drill - 12V. *Source: ACT.*

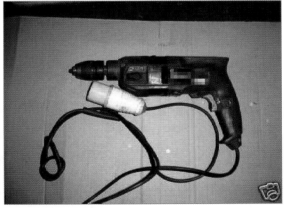

Figure 14-22: 110V powered drill. *Source: ACT.*

Figure 14-23: 110V powered drill. *Source: ACT.*

RESIDUAL CURRENT DEVICE (RCD)

An electro-mechanical switching device is used to automatically isolate the supply when there is a difference between the current flowing into a device and the current flowing from the device. Such a difference might result from a fault causing current leakage, with possible fire risks or the risk of shock current when a person touches a system and provides a path to earth for the current. RCDs can be designed to operate at low currents and fast response times (usually 30 mA and 30 mSeconds) and thus they *reduce the effect of an electric shock.* Though they do not prevent the person receiving an electric shock they are very sensitive and operate very quickly and reduce some of the primary effects of the shock. It is still possible for a person to receive injury from the shock, not least some of the secondary injuries referred to earlier. But the use of this type of device means the fault current should be isolated before sustained shock, and therefore fibrillation, occurs. The equipment needs to be de-energised from time to time in order to be confident it will work properly when needed. This can easily be done by a simple test routine before use, as equipment is plugged into it the RCD.

Summary

- Rapid and sensitive.
- Difficult to defeat.
- Easy and safe to test and reset.
- Does not prevent shock, but reduces the effect of a shock.

Figure 14-24: Residual current device.   *Source: ACT.*

Figure 14-25: Plug-in residual current device.   *Source: ACT.*

DOUBLE INSULATION

This is a common protection device and consists of a layer of insulation around the live electrical parts of the equipment and a second layer of insulated material around this, commonly the casing of the equipment. Since the casing material is an insulator and does not conduct electricity, equipment having this type of protection does not normally have an earth wire.

Each layer of insulation must be sufficient in its own right to give adequate protection against shock.

Equipment, which is double insulated, will carry the symbol shown opposite.

Double insulated equipment has two layers of insulating material between the live parts of the equipment and the user. If a fault occurs with the live parts and a conductor touches the insulating material surrounding it no current can pass to the user, therefore *no shock occurs.*

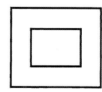

Figure 14-26: Double insulation symbol.   *Source: HSG107.*

Inspection and maintenance strategies

USER CHECKS

The user of electrical equipment should be encouraged, after basic training, to look critically at apparatus and the source of power. If any defects are found, the apparatus should be marked and not be used again before examination by a competent person. Obviously, there must be a procedure by which the user brings faults to the attention of a supervisor and/or a competent person who might rectify the fault.

Checks by the user are the first line of defence but should never be the only line taken. Such inspections should be aimed at identifying the following:

- ✓ Damaged cable sheaths.
- ✓ Damaged plugs. Cracked casing or bent pins.
- ✓ Taped or other inadequate cable joints.
- ✓ Outer cable insulation not secured into plugs or equipment.
- ✓ Faulty or ineffective switches.
- ✓ Burn marks or discolouration.
- ✓ Damaged casing.
- ✓ Loose parts or screws.
- ✓ Wet or contaminated equipment.
- ✓ Loose or damaged sockets or switches.

FORMAL INSPECTON AND TESTS

Inspection

The maintenance system should always include formal visual inspection of all portable electrical equipment and electrical tests.

The frequency depends on the type of equipment and where it is used. The inspection can be done by a member of staff who has been trained in what to look for and has basic electrical knowledge. They should know enough to avoid danger to themselves or others. Visual inspections are likely to need to look for the same types of defects as user checks but should also include the following:

Opening plugs of portable equipment to check for:

- ✓ Use of correctly rated fuse.
- ✓ Effective cord grip.
- ✓ Secure and correct cable terminations.

Inspection of fixed installations for:

- ✓ Damaged or loose conduit, trunking or cabling.
- ✓ Missing broken or inadequately secured covers.
- ✓ Loose or faulty joints.
- ✓ Loose earth connections.
- ✓ Moisture, corrosion or contamination.
- ✓ Burn marks or discolouration.
- ✓ Open or inadequately secured panel doors.
- ✓ Ease of access to switches and isolators.
- ✓ Presence of temporary wiring.

User checks and a programme of formal visual inspections are found to pick up some 95% of faults.

Testing

Faults such as loss of earth or broken wires inside an installation or cable cannot be found by visual inspection, so some apparatus needs to have a combined inspection and test. This is particularly important for all earthed equipment and leads and plugs connected to hand held or hand operated equipment.

The system should be tested regularly in accordance with Institute of Electrical Engineers (IEE) requirements; tests may include earth continuity and impedance tests and tests of insulation material.

FREQUENCY OF INSPECTION AND TESTING

Question: "I have been told that I have to have my desk lamp tested every six months. Is this correct?"

Answer: No. The law requires it to be maintained. It does not require any elaborate or rigorous system of frequent electrical testing.

Source: HSE Note INDG 160L

The legal duty for inspection and maintenance

The Electricity at Work Regulations (EWR) 1989, Regulation 4(2) requires that the owner shall 'as may be necessary to prevent danger, *maintain* all systems so as to prevent, so far as is reasonably practicable, such danger'. Danger is defined as the risk of injury from electric shock, electric burn, fire of electrical origin, electric arcing or explosion initiated or caused by electricity.

Deciding the frequency

Many approaches to establishing frequency suggest that they should be done regularly. As can be seen above, the word 'regularly' is not specified in terms of fixed time intervals for all systems; a management judgment must be made to specify an appropriate timetable. In effect, the frequency will depend on the condition the system is used in; for example, a test of office portable equipment may be sufficient if conducted every 3 years, whereas equipment used on a construction site may need to be tested every 3 months. The system as a whole rather that just portable equipment must also be tested periodically and again this will depend on the conditions of use and may vary from 10 years to 6 months. Factors to be considered when deciding the frequency include:

- ✓ Type of equipment.
- ✓ Whether it is hand held.
- ✓ Manufacturer's recommendations.
- ✓ Its initial integrity and soundness.
- ✓ Age.
- ✓ Working environment.
- ✓ Likelihood of mechanical damage.
- ✓ Frequency of use.
- ✓ Duration of use.
- ✓ Foreseeable use.
- ✓ Who uses it.
- ✓ Modifications or repairs.
- ✓ Past experience.

RECORDS OF INSPECTION AND TESTING

In order to identify what systems and equipment will need inspection and testing they should be listed. This same listing can be used as a checklist recording that the appropriate checks, inspections and tests have been done. It would be usual to include details of the type of the equipment, its location and its age. It is important that a cumulative record of equipment and its status is held available to those that are responsible for using the equipment as well as those that are conducting the inspection or test.

In addition, it is common practice to add a label to the system or part of the system (e.g. portable appliances) to indicate that an inspection and / or test has taken place and its status following this. Some labels show the date that this took place; others prefer to show the date of next inspection or test.

Figure 14-27: PAT labels. *Source: ACT.*

There is a growing trend, especially in offices, for employees to bring to work their own electrically powered equipment including calculators, radios, kettles and coffee makers. The number of electrical accidents has grown accordingly and fires from calculator chargers left on overnight are growing in number. All such equipment should be recorded, inspected and tested by a competent person before use and at regular intervals, as if it were company property.

PURPOSE AND LIMITATIONS OF PORTABLE APPLIANCE TESTING (PAT)

The purpose of portable appliance testing is to periodically confirm the critical aspects of electrical integrity of portable appliances. This is done by subjecting the equipment to tests that prove the integrity of such things as earth continuity, impedance and insulation. At the same time the equipment is subject to a visual examination for defects and items such as security of cable grips and fuse ratings are checked.

The limitation with portable appliance testing is that people may have an over-reliance on the apparent assurance that the test indicates. They may be tempted to see it as a permanent assurance that the equipment is safe. This can lead to users not making their own pre-use checks of the appliance. In effect it is only a test, and therefore assurance, at a point in time. It does not assure that someone has not, for example, altered the fuse and put one in with an incorrect rating or that the cable grip has not come loose.

It must also be recognised that there is little benefit in having perfect portable appliances if it is plugged into a defective socket which may be without proper insulation, with a switch that does not work properly, with the polarity reversed or with a high resistance earth connection.

Means of protecting against contact with overhead power lines

The local electricity company should be consulted before any work commences and a safe system of work should be developed and implemented from this.

Practical steps that can be taken to prevent danger from any live electrical cable include the placing of barriers. If there is a danger to people carrying scaffold poles then the barrier must exclude people and vehicles.

Any ground level barriers should consist of:

- Stout rail or posts.
- Tension wire earthed at both ends.
- Large steel drums filled with rubble.

- An earth bank at least 1 metre high.
- Timber baulks to act as wheel stops.

Fences posts and steel drums should be made as distinctive as possible, utilising hazard warning colours.

There should be a general rule prohibiting the storage of materials between overhead lines and barriers. Precautions are necessary even though work in the vicinity may be of short duration.

Where it is necessary to work underneath the power lines, additional requirements may be needed to prevent the upward movement of ladders, scaffold poles, excavator buckets, etc. Specific advice should be sought from the electricity company, including safe distances from the power lines.

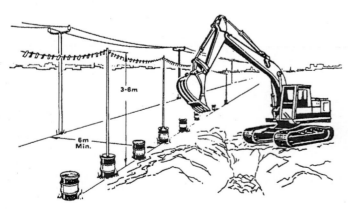

Figure 14-28: Working near power lines. *Source: HSG144.*

Figure 14-29: Overhead power lines. *Source: Lincsafe.*

Fire hazards & control

Overall Aims

On completion of this Unit, candidates will understand:

■ basic fire hazards and consequential risks in construction workplaces.

■ the main measures that should be taken to minimise fire risks.

Content

Specific Intended Learning Outcomes

The intended learning outcomes of this Unit are that candidates will be able to:

15.1   identify basic fire hazards in a construction workplace

15.2   evaluate the main fire risks in a construction workplace, and the additional fire risks caused by construction work in an existing workplace

15.3   advise on measures to prevent fire and fire spread during construction work

15.4   identify appropriate fire alarm systems and fire-fighting equipment for construction work

15.5   assess the adequacy and maintenance of existing means of escape in a workplace

15.6   implement a successful evacuation of a construction workplace in the event of a fire

Sources of Reference

Fire Safety: an Employer's Guide (HSE, Home Office, Scottish Executive, DoE Northern Ireland), The Stationery Office

Fire Safety in Construction Work (HSG168), HSE Books

Safe Use and Handling of Flammable Substances (HSG140), HSE Books

The Storage of Flammable Liquids in Containers (HSG51), HSE Books

Relevant Statutory Provisions

The Fire Certification (Special Premises) Regulations (FCSPR) 1976

The Fire Precautions (Workplace) Regulations (FPWR) 1997 (in relation to occupied premises)

The Construction (Health, Safety and Welfare) Regulations (CHSW) 1996

The Management of Health and Safety at Work Regulations (MHSWR) 1999

The Health and Safety (Safety Signs and Signals) Regulations (SSSR) 1996

The Dangerous Substances and Explosive Atmospheres Regulations (DSEAR) 2002

15.1 - Basic principles of fire

Definitions

FIRE PREVENTION

The concept of preventing outbreaks of fire or reducing the risk of fire spread and avoiding danger from fire to people or property.

FIRE PRECAUTIONS

The measures taken and the fire protection provided in a building to minimise the risk to occupants, contents and structure from an outbreak of fire.

FIRE PROTECTION

Design features, systems or equipment in a building provided to reduce the danger to persons and property by detecting, extinguishing or containing fires.

Combustion principles

THE FIRE TRIANGLE

In order for combustion to take place the three essential elements of a fire have to be brought together - fuel, oxygen and source of ignition (heat) - this is called the fire triangle.

In order to prevent fires these elements, particularly the fuel and ignition sources, are kept apart. When they are brought together in the right proportions combustion takes place. Remember it is only the vapour from a fuel that burns. A solid or liquid must be heated to a temperature where the vapour given off can ignite before combustion takes place.

This principle is important when considering combustible dusts as this combustion process happens so quickly it is an explosion. This explosion can be caused by just a spark; similarly a small *dust explosion* can disturb more dust and create bigger explosions.

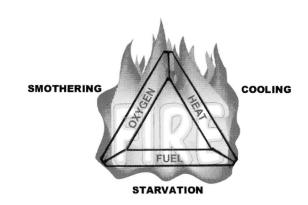

Figure 15-1: Fire triangle.   *Source: Corel.*

The other important aspect of this combustion principle is that if one or more of these elements of the fire is removed the fire will be extinguished.

This can be done by:

Cooling   -   the fire to remove the heat - by applying water to a fire.

Starving   -   the fire of fuel - by moving material from the area of a fire or closing off an area of combustible material from a fire.

Smothering   -   the fire by limiting its oxygen supply - by closing a lid on a metal bin that contained a fire, covering a fire with a fire blanket or applying an extinguishing medium such as foam.

SOURCES OF IGNITION

Any source of heat is a possible ignition source. Examples could be:

- Smokers' materials.
- Naked flames.
- Fixed or portable heaters.
- Hot processes e.g. welding.

- Cooking.
- Electrical equipment or machinery.
- Static electricity.

Figure 15-2: Welding.   *Source: Speedy Hire Plc.*

Figure 15-3: Combustible materials.   *Source: ACT.*

SOURCES OF FUEL

Anything that burns is a fuel for a fire:

- Flammable liquids.
- Flammable gases.
- Flammable chemicals.
- Wood.

- Paper and card.
- Plastics, rubber and foam.
- Insulating materials.
- Waste materials.

SOURCES OF OXYGEN

- Oxygen supplies e.g. cylinders or piped supply.
- Ventilation systems e.g. windows, doors, vents, air conditioning.
- Chemicals e.g. oxidising agents.

Classification of fires

A basic understanding of the classes of fire needs to be understood because many fire extinguishers state the classes of fire on which they may be used.

Class A	-	Fire involving solids - wood, paper or plastics (usually material of an organic nature).
Class B	-	Fires involving liquids or liquefiable solids - petrol, oil, paint, fat or wax.
Class C	-	Fires involving gases - liquefied petroleum gas, natural gas or acetylene.
Class D	-	Fires involving metals - sodium, magnesium, aluminium and many metal powders.
Electrical Fires	-	There is not a class for electrical fires, but obviously we need to consider fires in electrical apparatus. In many cases, electricity is a source of heat.
Class F	-	Fires involving cooking oils and fats.

Basic principles of heat transmission and fire spread

There are four methods by which heat may be transmitted:

Convection	-	the movement of hotter gases up through the air (hot air rises).
	e.g.	Smoke and hot gases rising up a staircase through an open door.
Control measure	-	Protection of openings by fire doors and the creation of fire resistant compartments in buildings.
Conduction	-	the movement of heat through a material (usually solid).
	e.g.	A metal beam or pipe transmitting heat through a solid wall.
Control measure	-	Insulating the surface of a beam or pipe with heat resistant materials.
Radiation	-	transfer of heat as invisible waves through the air (the air or gas is not heated but solids and liquids in contact with the heat are).
	e.g.	Items or waste containers stored too near to a building may provide enough radiant heat to transfer the fire to the building.
Control measure	-	separation distances or fire resistant barriers.
Direct Burning	-	combustible materials in direct contact with naked flame.
	e.g.	Curtains or tiles may be consumed by combustion and enable fire to be transferred along them to other parts of a building.
Control measure	-	the use of fire retardant materials.

15.2 - Causes and consequences of fires during construction work

Common causes

Causes may be split into four main groups. These are:

CARELESS ACTIONS AND ACCIDENTS

e.g. hot works, discarded lighted cigarette end or match, smouldering waste, unattended burning or poor electrical connections.

MISUSING EQUIPMENT

e.g. overloading electrical circuits and using fuses of too high a rating failure to follow servicing instructions, failure to repair faulty machinery/equipment promptly.

DEFECTIVE MACHINERY OR EQUIPMENT

e.g. electrical short circuits, electrical earth fault can cause local overheating and electrical insulation failure may occur when affected by heat, damp or chemicals.

DELIBERATE IGNITION

e.g. insurance fraud, aggrieved persons, concealment of another crime, political activists or vandalism.

Figure 15-4: Careless action.   *Source: ACT.*

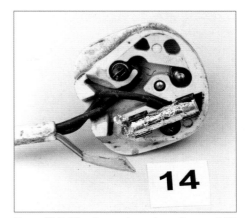

Figure 15-5: Misusing equipment.   *Source: ACT.*

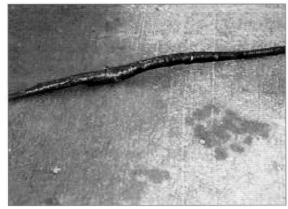

Figure 15-6: Defective electrical equipment.   *Source: ACT.*

Figure 15-7: Deliberate ignition of materials.   *Source: ACT.*

Reasons why fires spread

FAILURE OF EARLY DETECTION

- No detection system or patrols.
- No alarm system in place.
- People not knowing or confusing the sound of an alarm.
- Not promptly extinguished due to no hoses or extinguishers.
- Fire starts in unoccupied area.
- Fire starts out of normal work hours.
- Building material waste may be being burnt as a normal routine and smoke and other signs of fire may not be seen as unusual.
- Numerous hot working tasks conducted - therefore smells of burning ignored.
- Frequent occurrence of small, local fires caused by hot work, and not seen as significant.

ABSENCE OF COMPARTMENTS IN BUILDING STRUCTURE

- Open plan office.
- False ceilings.
- The structure under construction or demolition is incomplete and has reduced separation between levels and/or sections on a level.

Figure 15-8: Not knowing the sound of an alarm. *Source: ACT.*

Figure 15-9: Compartment undermined-holes cut. *Source: ACT.*

COMPARTMENTS UNDERMINED

- Fire doors wedged open.
- Poor maintenance of door structure.
- Holes may be designed to pass through compartments and are waiting fitment of services and subsequent sealing.
- Holes cut for ducts or doorways or to provide temporary access to locate/remove equipment.
- Compartments may be progressively created in buildings under demolition, thus increasing the risk of fire spread.

MATERIALS INAPPROPRIATELY STORED

- Flammable liquids not controlled - too much or in unsuitable containers.
- Boxes in corridors.
- Off cuts of wood and sawdust left in the area that work was done.
- Packing from materials used in the construction process, such as fittings for toilets or cupboards.
- Pallets and plastic covering left near to where materials were used.
- Part empty pots or tubes of adhesives.

Figure 15-10: Fire door held open. *Source: ACT.*

Figure 15-11: Materials inappropriately stored. *Source: ACT.*

Fire risk assessment

THE REQUIREMENT FOR A FIRE RISK ASSESSMENT

The purpose of a fire risk assessment (FRA) is to identify where fire may start in the workplace, the people who would be put at risk, and to reduce the risk where possible.

Specific legal duties to conduct risk assessments are set out in the Management of Health and Safety at Work Regulations (MHSWR) 1999, which require the following.

Every employer must make a suitable and sufficient assessment of:

- The risks to the health and safety of his *employees* to which they are exposed whilst they are at work; and
- The risks to the health and safety of *persons not in his employment* arising out of or in connection with the conduct by him of his undertaking.

Similarly every self-employed person must make a suitable and sufficient assessment of:

- The risks to his *own* health and safety to which he is exposed whilst he is at work; and
- The risks to the health and safety of *persons not in his employment* arising out of or in connection with the conduct by him of his undertaking.

The assessments must, at least, identify the measures needed to comply with relevant statutory provisions, in the case of construction work, the Construction (Health, Safety and Welfare) Regulations (CHSW) 1996 Regulations. These regulations require fire and other emergency provisions to be in place on construction sites; as such, risk assessments must be conducted to determine fire risks and the provisions necessary. Where part of the site is set aside for non-construction work, for example, significant office facilities for managing a large construction project, these regulations would not apply and therefore compliance with the Fire Precautions (Workplace) Regulations (FPWR) 1997 is the requirement.

Where the employer employs five or more employees they must record the significant findings of the assessment and any group of his employees identified by it as being especially at risk.

Assessments must be reviewed by the employer or self-employed person who made it if there is reason to suspect that it is no longer valid or there has been a significant change in the matters to which it relates. In view of the changing nature of construction work and construction sites it could be anticipated that assessments would be under frequent review on a large complex site.

"EXCEPTED WORKPLACES" UNDER THE FIRE PRECAUTIONS (WORKPLACE) REGULATIONS

Construction sites which are within the meaning of the CHSW Regulations are excepted workplaces from the FPWR. An implication of this exception is that the Health and Safety Executive (HSE) are the enforcers of all fire precautions on construction sites that are separate from other work activities - for example, building on a 'green field' site or construction of a road or bridge. However the *Fire Authority* is the enforcer of fire precautions when the construction site is not the principal activity in that it is *not fully separated* from another premises activity - for example extending or maintaining a shop or office structure.

Where a place, being a construction site, is excepted from the FPWR, the CHSW Regulations apply. The requirements of the CHSW Regulations are similar to those in the FPWR and therefore meet the overall intent to have appropriate fire precaution measures in place at construction sites. It should be remembered that where part of the site is set aside for non-construction work, for example, significant office facilities for managing a large construction project, these regulations would not apply and therefore compliance with the FPWR is the requirement to be met.

Some construction premises may require a fire certificate as they come under the Fire Certificates (Special Premises) Regulations (FCSPR) 1976. The regulations apply to buildings, or parts of a building, that meet the occupancy criteria set out below and have been constructed (or were in existence when work commenced) for temporary occupation for the purposes of building, construction or civil engineering operations. Occupancy criteria are more than 20 people at any one time or more than 10 elsewhere than on the ground floor or where flammable / explosive material is stored. A fire certificate may also be required for lesser occupancy levels where basic fire precautions are not met. The HSE enforce these regulations, a fire certificate is applied for and obtained from the HSE before premises are occupied.

MATTERS TO BE ADDRESSED IN CARRYING OUT THE ASSESSMENT

When undertaking a fire risk assessment there are five steps that need to be taken: -

Step 1 - Identify potential fire hazards.

Step 2 - Decide who may be in danger, and note their locations.

Step 3 - Evaluate the risks and carry out any necessary improvement measures.

Step 4 - Record findings and action taken.

Step 5 - Keep assessment under review.

Step 1 - Identify fire hazards

- *Identify sources of ignition* - Smokers' materials, naked flames, heaters, hot processes, cooking, machinery, boilers, faulty or misused electrical equipment, lighting equipment, hot surfaces, blocked vents, friction, static electricity, metal impact and arson.
- *Identify sources of fuel* - Flammable liquids, flammable chemicals, wood, paper and card, plastics, foam, flammable gases, furniture, textiles, packaging materials, waste materials including shavings, off cuts and dust.
- *Identify sources of oxygen* - Natural ventilation, doors, windows, forced ventilation systems, air conditioning, oxidising materials, oxygen cylinders or piped oxygen systems.
- *Identify structural features that may spread fire* - Combustible wall, floor or ceiling linings, open voids, open ducts, breeches in fire resistance.

Step 2 - Decide who could be harmed

- Consider people in the workplace - staff, visitors, contractors, public, old, young, disabled, and their level of discipline and training.
- How could fire, heat or smoke spread to areas that people occupy - convection, conduction, radiation or direct burning.
- Who and where are the people that may be at risk? - people carrying out noisy tasks, placed high at the top of a building or in confined spaces conducting work, nearby workers or the public.
- How will people be warned of fire and could people be trapped by fire?

Step 3 - Evaluate the risks and carry out necessary improvements

Risk reduction by prevention

- *Reduce sources of ignition* - Remove unnecessary sources of heat or replace with safer alternatives, ensure electrical fuses etc are of the correct rating, ensure safe and correct use of electrical equipment, enforcing a 'hot work' permit system, safe smoking policy, arson reduction measures.
- *Minimize potential fuel for a fire* - Remove or reduce amount of flammable materials, replace materials with safer alternatives, ensure safe handling, storage and use of materials, safe separation distances between flammable materials, use of fire resisting storage, repair or replace damaged or unsuitable furniture, control and removal of flammable waste, care of external storage due to arson, good housekeeping.
- *Reduce sources of oxygen* - Close all doors and windows not required for ventilation particularly out of working hours, shutting down non essential ventilation systems, not storing oxidizing materials near heat sources or flammable materials, controlling the use of oxygen cylinders and ensuring ventilation to areas where they are used.
- *Reducing unsatisfactory structural features* - Remove, cover or treat large areas of combustible wall and ceiling linings, improve fire resistance of workplace, install fire breaks into open voids.

Risk reduction by protection

Consider existing fire safety measures, risk reduction by protection (controls), in the workplace and consider possible improvements.

- Fire detection and warning.
  - Can fire be detected quickly enough to allow people to escape?
  - Can means of warning be recognized and understood?
  - Do staff know how to operate the system?
  - Will staff know what to do if the alarm operates?
  - Are fire notices posted around workplace?
- Means of escape.
  - How long will it take for people to escape once they are aware of a fire?
  - Is this time reasonable?

- Are there enough exits?
- Are exits in the right places?
- Do you have suitable means of escape for all people, including disabled?
- Could a fire happen that would affect all escape routes?
- Are escape routes easily identifiable?
- Are exit routes free from obstructions and blockages?
- Are exit routes suitably lit at all times?
- Have staff been trained in the use of the escape routes?

■ Means of fighting fire.
  - Is the fire fighting equipment suitable for the risk?
  - Is it suitably located?
  - Is it signed where necessary?
  - Have people been trained to use equipment where necessary?

■ Maintenance and testing.
  - Do you regularly check all fire doors, escape routes, lighting and signs?
  - Do you regularly check all fire fighting equipment?
  - Do you regularly check all fire detectors and alarms?
  - Do you regularly check any other equipment provided to help means of escape arrangements?
  - Are there relevant instructions to staff regarding maintenance and testing?
  - Are those who carry out maintenance and testing competent?

■ Fire procedures and training.
  - Do you have an emergency plan?
  - Does the emergency plan take account of all reasonably foreseeable circumstances?
  - Are all employees familiar with the plan, trained in its use, and involved in testing it?
  - Is the emergency plan made available to staff?
  - Are fire procedures clearly indicated throughout the workplace?
  - Have you considered all people likely to be present?

Step 4 - Record findings and action taken

If you employ more than 5 staff you must keep a written record of the findings of your risk assessment, together with details of any people identified as being at particular risk. You also need to keep a record of action taken. Suitable headings of the record are:

Significant Hazard	People at risk	Existing control measures	Further action needed	Projected completion date	Responsible person

Emergency plans

Following completion of the fire risk assessment, an emergency plan should be devised. The plan should include the following:

■ Action on discovery of fire.
■ Action on hearing alarm.
■ Details of the fire warning system.
■ Details of the evacuation process.
■ Means of escape - travel distances.
■ Location of assembly points.
■ Identification of escape routes - signs, emergency lighting.
■ Details of fire fighting equipment.
■ Specific staff duties.
■ Safe evacuation of people who need assistance to escape.
■ Safe working practices in high risk areas.
■ Procedures for calling Fire Service.
■ Staff training needs and arrangements for providing training.

Step 5 - Review and monitor

You must review the fire risk assessment and your fire safety measures on a regular basis.

This should definitely be done if:

■ Changes to workplace are proposed.
■ Changes to work process / activity are proposed.
■ Changes to number or type of people present are proposed.
■ A near miss or a fire occurs.

See also - Principles of Control - Unit 6, for more details on risk assessment technique.

THE IMPLICATIONS OF CONSTRUCTION WORK WITH RESPECT TO A FIRE RISK ASSESSMENT IN EXISTING PREMISES

Many serious fires occur in existing buildings during maintenance and construction work. Due to the increased fire risks during these periods of time, additional fire precautions may be needed.

Dependant upon the nature of the work to be carried out and the size and use of the workplace, it may be necessary to carry out a new fire risk assessment to include all the new hazards that will be created during the construction work. In some cases the increased risk will be due to the increase of sources of ignition or additional materials. In other cases it will be due to the effect on the controls in place at the premises. Some work may require the isolation of smoke detectors or an alarm system. Normally well controlled escape routes may become cluttered by equipment, materials or workers.

Attention should be paid to :

- Accumulation of flammable waste and building materials.
- The obstruction or loss of exits and exit routes.
- Fire doors being propped open, wedged open or removed.
- Openings created in fire resisting structures.
- Isolation of fire detection, or fixed fire fighting systems.
- Introduction of additional electrical equipment, or other sources of ignition.
- Use of hot work process.
- Introduction of flammable products e.g. adhesives or flammable gases.
- The addition of new people to the premises that may be unfamiliar with fire arrangements e.g. alarm, routes, roll calls, assembly points.
- People working in unusual locations e.g. the roof, basement or duct areas.
- People working outside normal working hours.

Figure 15-12: Materials in escape route. *Source: Lincsafe.*

15.3 - Control measures to minimise the risk of fire in a workplace

Use and storage of flammable and combustible materials

Where possible we should seek to eliminate the use of flammable materials in the workplace, for example, replacing adhesives that have a flammable content with those that are water based. Where this is not possible the amount used should be kept to the minimum. Quantities of material stored in the workplace must be in suitable containers and controlled to the minimum for immediate work needs. Flammable materials not in use should be removed to a purpose designed store in a well ventilated area, preferably outside the building but in a secure area. Lids should be kept on containers at all times when they are not in immediate use. Any waste containers, contaminated tools or materials should be treated in the same way and removed to a store in fresh air, until dealt with. Containers and contaminated materials need to be disposed of in a controlled manner so that they do not present a risk of fire.

Care has to be taken to control the delivery and therefore the storage of flammable and combustible materials to site. There is a temptation to have large quantities all delivered at the same time, but where possible deliveries should be staggered to reflect the rate of use in order to minimise the amount stored on site.

TERMS USED WITH FLAMMABLE AND COMBUSTIBLE MATERIALS

Flashpoint

The flammability of a liquid is related to its 'flash point', i.e. the minimum liquid temperature at which vapour above the liquid will ignite in air. The lower the flash point of a liquid the more flammable it is.

Flammable

Liquids with a flash point between 32°C and 55°C are classified as flammable.

Highly flammable

Liquids with a flash point below 32°C are classified as highly flammable.

GENERAL PRINCIPLES FOR STORAGE AND USE OF FLAMMABLE LIQUIDS

When considering the storage or use of flammable liquids, the following safety principles should be applied:

V Ventilation - plenty of fresh air.

I Ignition - control of ignition sources.

C Containment - suitable containers and spillage control.

E Exchange - try to use a less flammable product to do task.

S Separation - keep storage away from process areas, by distance or a physical barrier e.g. a wall or partition.

Control of ignition sources

WELDING

- Only use competent trained staff.
- Regulators should be of a recognised standard.
- Colour code hoses   - blue   - oxygen
                             - red   - acetylene
                             - orange - propane.
- Fit non-return valves at blowpipe/torch inlet on both gas lines.
- Fit flashback arrestors incorporating cut-off valves and flame arrestors fitted to outlet of both gas regulators.
- Use crimped hose connections not jubilee clips.
- Do not let oil or grease contaminate oxygen supply due to explosion hazard.
- Check equipment visually before use, and check new connections with soapy water for leaks.
- Secure cylinders in upright position.
- Keep hose lengths to a minimum.
- Follow a permit to work system.

Figure 15-13: Welding equipment.   *Source: ACT.*

HOT WORK

Hot work has been responsible for causing many fires during construction works. One of the most tragic fires due to hot work was Dusseldorf Airport Fire in 1996. The fire was started by welding on an open roadway and resulted in damage in excess of £200 million, several hundred injuries and 17 deaths.

It is imperative that good safe working practices are utilised. Combustible materials must be removed from the area or covered up. Thought must be given to the effects of heat on the surrounding structure, and where sparks, flames, hot residue or heat will travel to. It is often necessary to have a fire watcher to spot any fires that may be started. Fire extinguishers need to be immediately available and operatives must know how to use them. The work area must be checked thoroughly for some time after the completion of work to ensure there are no smouldering fires. Strong consideration should be given to the use of hot work permits.

SMOKING

Prohibition of smoking may be unreasonable and will lead to illicit smoking, but prohibition is essential where hazardous materials are dealt with, or processes are carried on which involve the release of ignitable or explosive dusts or vapours or the production of readily combustible waste. Smoking should be prohibited in stock rooms and other rooms not under continuous supervision. Any area where 'no smoking' is imposed should have the rule strictly enforced. Where smoking is allowed, provide easily accessible, non-combustible receptacles for cigarette ends and other smoking material and empty daily. Smoking should cease half an hour before closing down.

ARSON

Simple but effective ways to deter the arsonist are by giving attention to security, both external and internal, which should encompass the following:

External security

- Control of people having access to the building/site.
- Use of patrol guards.
- Lighting the premises at night.
- Safety of keys.
- Structural protection.
- Siting of rubbish bins at least 8m from buildings.

Internal security

- Good housekeeping.
- Inspections.
- Clear access routes.
- Visitor supervision.
- Control of sub-contractors.
- Audits.

Figure 15-14: Control arson by external security. *Source: ACT.*

Figure 15-15: Control arson by housekeeping. *Source: ACT.*

Systems of work

Systems of work combine people, equipment, materials and the environment to produce the safest possible climate in which to work. In order to produce a safe system of work, it is essential to make an assessment of the area to determine where the hazards and risks arise and how best to control them.

The requirement to carry out a risk assessment should address the following:

■   Identify potential fire hazards.
■   Decide who may be in danger, and note their locations.
■   Evaluate the risks and carry out any necessary improvement measures.
■   Record findings and action taken.
■   Keep assessment under review.

In addition to the risk assessment carried out, other measures may include implementing the following strategies.

1) A safe place

A safe place begins with ensuring that the fabric of the building is designed or planned in a way that will prevent ignition, suppress fired spread and allow for safe, speedy unobstructed evacuation with signs to direct people. Factors to consider will include compartmentalisation, fire resistant materials, proper and suitable means of storage, means of detection, means of raising the alarm good housekeeping and regular monitoring and review.

2) Safe person

A safe person begins with raising awareness to individuals of any risk of loss resulting from outbreak of fire. Information can be provided that will identify where to raise the alarm, what the alarm sounds like, how to evacuate and where to muster, responsibility for signing in and out of the site register, fire drill procedures, trained authorised fire appointed persons, use and storage of flammable materials, good housekeeping and use of equipment producing heat or ignition (including hot processes i.e. welding).

3) Safe materials

Safe materials begin with providing information and ensuring safe segregation and storage for materials and sources of ignition / heat. In addition, providing information on the correct way to handle materials and substances including a COSHH register that will detail methods of tackling a fire involving hazardous substances.

4) Safe equipment

Safe equipment begins with user information and maintenance to ensure good working and efficient order. Information should also provide the user with a safe method for use and the limitations of and risks from the equipment. Supervision may be necessary to ensure correct use and prevent misuse that may lead to short circuiting or overheating that could result in fire. Where work involves hot processes by nature (welding, grinding, casting, etc) then permit-to-work procedures may be necessary in order to tightly control the operations.

Other equipment required in relation to fire hazards and control may include smoke or heat detection equipment, alarm sounders / bells, alarm call points and appropriate fire extinguishing apparatus. It should be noted that in the event of a fire alarm, all the passenger lifts should not be used. Under normal circumstances the lift will drop to the ground floor and remain in that position with the doors locked in the open position. All equipment should be regularly tested to ensure its conformity and be accompanied with a suitable certificate of validity.

Safe systems must also include consideration for who is at risk, including those persons with special needs such as the young, elderly, infirm or disabled. There may be a requirement to prevent smoking in the workplace or employ appointed persons to take control of the situation and co-ordinate emergency responses in the event of an alarm. If the building relies solely on internal artificial lighting, then the requirement to install emergency back-up lighting will be needed. All systems must be regularly monitored in order to reflect changes to the environment and put remedies in place to ensure full preparedness in the event of a fire.

PERMIT TO WORK PROCEDURES

A permit to work is an official, documented safe system of work that is used for controlling high risk activities. Implementation is required prior to work beginning to ensure that all precautions are taken and securely in place to prevent danger to the workforce. When managed correctly, a permit to work prevents any mistakes or deviations through poor verbal communication by stating the specific requirements of the project. For fire control, a permit to work is typically used where there is a requirement to use flammable materials or when hot work or processes are being carried out.

The authorised person shall issue the permit to work and will sign the document to declare that all isolations are made and remain in place throughout the duration of the project. In addition to this, the authorised person will make checks to ensure that all controls to be implemented by the acceptor are in place before work begins

The acceptor of the permit to work shall assume responsibility for carrying out the works. The acceptor shall sign the document to declare that the terms and conditions of the permit to work are understood and will be complied with fully at all times by the entire work team. Compliance with a permit to work system includes ensuring the required safeguards are implemented and that the work will be restricted to the equipment only stated within the document.

Items included in the electrical permit to work are;

■   Permit issue number.
■   Authorised person identification.
■   Locations of fire fighting equipment.
■   Locations of flammable materials.
■   Warning information sign locations.
■   Emergency muster points.

■   Details of the work to be carried out.
■   Signature of authoriser.
■   Signature of acceptor.
■   Signature for works clearance / extension / handover.
■   Signature for cancellation.
■   Other precautions (risk assessments, method statements, PPE).

HOT WORK PERMITS

Hot work permits are formal management documents that control and implement a safe system of work whenever methods of work that utilise heat or flame systems are used. If the risk of fire is low, it may not be necessary to implement a hot work permit; however they should always be considered.

The hot work permit should be issued by an Authorised Person who ensures that the requirements stated in them are complied with before the permit is issued, and during duration of the work. Hot work permits should be issued for a specific time, for a specific place, for a specific task, and are issued to a designated competent person.

See also - Principles of Control - Unit 6

Figure 15-16: Hot work.   *Source: Speedy Hire Plc.*

Good housekeeping

HOUSEKEEPING

By 'housekeeping' we mean the general tidiness and order of the building. At first sight, this may seem a strange matter to discuss when considering fire safety, but as housekeeping affects so many different aspects of this subject, it cannot be ignored.

Housekeeping and its effect on fire safety

Fires need fuel. A build up of redundant combustible materials, rubbish and stacks of waste materials provide that fuel. We cannot eliminate all combustible materials, but we can control them. Any unnecessary build-up of rubbish and waste should be avoided. If a fire starts in a neatly stacked pile of timber pallets, around which there is a clear space, the fire may be spotted and extinguished before it can spread. However, if the same pile were strewn around in an untidy heap, along with adjacent rubbish, the likelihood is that fire would spread over a larger area and involve other combustible materials.

Bad housekeeping can also lead to

- Blocked fire exits.
- Obstructed escape routes.
- Difficult access to fire alarm call points / extinguishers / hose reels.
- Obstruction of vital signs and notices.
- A reduction in the effectiveness of automatic fire detectors and sprinklers.

CHECKLISTS

Fire Prevention is a matter of good routine and the checklists shown below are a guide as to what to look out for:

List A   Routine checks

Daily at the start of business - including:

- Doors which may be used for escape purposes - unlocked and escape routes unobstructed.
- Free access to hydrants, extinguishers and fire alarm call points.
- No deposits on electric motors.

List B   Routine checks

Daily at close-down - including:

- Inspection of whole area for which you are responsible - to detect any incipient smouldering fires.
- Fire doors and shutters closed.
- All plant and equipment safely shut down.
- Waste bins emptied.
- No accumulation of combustible process waste, packaging materials or dust deposits.
- Safe disposal of waste.
- Premises left secure from unauthorised access.

List C   Periodic inspection

During working hours - weekly/monthly/quarterly as decided:

- Goods neatly stored so as not to impede fire fighting.
- Clear spaces around stacks of stored materials.
- Gangways kept unobstructed.
- No non-essential storage in production areas.
- Materials clear of light fittings.
- Company smoking rules known and enforced.

Small quantities of highly flammable or flammable liquids

The objective in controlling the risk from these materials is to remove all unnecessary quantities from the workplace to a recognised storage area outside the building. This may be done as part of a close down routine at the end of the day. It is accepted that quantities of this material may need to be available in a workplace during normal working. This should not exceed 50 litres in any work area unless a full scale purpose constructed store is used. In other cases local small scale storage of up to 50 litres of highly flammable or flammable liquid may be kept within the workplace provided it is controlled and placed in a suitable store container. Highly flammable or flammable liquids removed from storage must be in suitable containers to prevent spills and loss of vapours.

STORAGE IN THE WORKPLACE

- In a suitable sealed container.
- In a suitable cabinet, bin or other store container.
- In a designated area of the workplace.
- Away from ignition sources, working or process areas.
- Capable of containing any spillage.
- It is a 30 min fire resistant structure.
- Provided with hazard warning signs to illustrate the flammability of the contents.
- Prohibition signs for smoking and naked flame.
- Not contain other substances or items.

STORAGE IN OPEN AIR

- Formal storage area on a concrete pad, with a sump for spills.
- Bunded all around to take content of largest drum plus an allowance of 10%.
- Away from other buildings.
- Secure fence and gate 2m high.
- Marked by signs warning of flammability.
- Signs prohibiting smoking or other naked flames.
- Protection from sunlight.
- If lighting is provided within store it must be flameproof.
- Provision for spill containment materials.
- Fire extinguishers located nearby - consider powder type.
- Full and empty containers separated.
- Clear identification of contents.

Figure 15-17: Poor storage of flammable liquids. *Source: ACT.*

Figure 15-18: Storage of flammable materials. *Source: ACT.*

Liquefied petroleum and other gases in cylinders

Liquefied Petroleum Gas (LPG) is a term that relates to gas stored in a liquefied state under pressure; common examples are propane and butane. LPG and other gas cylinders should be stored in line with the principles detailed below:

STORAGE

- Storage area should preferably be in clear open area outside.
- Stored in a secure compound - 2m high fence.
- Safe distance from toxic, corrosive, combustible materials, flammable liquids or general waste.
- Stored safe distance from any building.
- If stored inside building, keep away from exit routes, consider fire resisting storage.
- Well ventilated area - 2.5% of total floor and wall area as vents, high and low.
- Oxygen cylinders at least 3m away from flammable gas cylinders.
- Acetylene may be stored with LPG if quantity of LPG less than 50Kg.
- Control access to stores to prevent LPG etc being distributed all around site & keep locked.
- More than one exit (unlocked) may need to be available from any secure storage compound where distance to exit is greater than 12m.
- Lock storage compound when not in use.
- Protect from sunlight.
- Flameproof lighting.
- Empty separate from full.
- Fire extinguishers located nearby - consider powder and water types.

TRANSPORT

- Upright position.
- Secured to prevent falling over.
- Protection in event of accident e.g. position on vehicle.
- Transport in open vehicle preferably.
- Avoid overnight parking while loaded.
- Park in secure areas.
- 'Trem card' and warning signs.
- Driver training.
- Fire fighting equipment.

USE

General use

- Cylinder connected for use plus spare in building if necessary - no more unless in a formal purpose built store.
- Fixed position to prevent falling over, or on wheeled trolley - chained.
- Well ventilated area.
- Away from combustibles.
- Keep upright unless used on equipment specifically designed for horizontal use - e.g. gas powered lift truck.
- Handle carefully - don't drop.
- Allow to settle after transport and before use.
- Consider manual handling and injury prevention.
- Turn off cylinder before connecting, disconnecting equipment.
- Check equipment before use.
- Any smell of gas during use, turn off cylinder and investigate.
- Use correct gas regulator for equipment/task.
- Use equipment in line with manufacturers' instructions.

Use in huts

- Only allow cylinders in a hut if it is part of a heater (cabinet heater).
- Pipe into site huts from cylinder located outside where possible.
- If cylinder is outside the hut use the shortest connecting hose as possible.
- Hut to be adequately ventilated high and low.
- Heaters fitted with flame failure devices.
- Turn off heater and cylinder after use and overnight.
- Be aware of danger of leaks inside huts, especially overnight as a severe risk of fire or explosion may occur.
- Keep heaters away from clothing and other combustibles.

Figure 15-19: Gas cylinders for huts.   Source: ACT.

15.4 - Fire precautions

Structural measures to prevent spread of fire and smoke

COMMON BUILDING MATERIALS

Brickwork / blockwork

Both brickwork and blockwork perform well in fires. Dependent upon the materials, workmanship, thickness, and the load carried, fire resistance of 30 minutes to 2 hours may be achieved.

Steelwork

Steel and other metals are extensively used in modern building structures. Generally they can be affected by fire at relatively low temperatures unless they are protected from the effects of the fire by some form of fire retardant materials. This may be done by encasing in concrete; fire retardant boards or spray coatings.

Timber

Timber performs very well in fires as long as it is of sufficient size that, as its outer coat burns away, there is still sufficient strength to do its task. Generally timber does not fail rapidly in a fire, unlike steel.

Glass

Glass generally performs poorly in a fire unless it is fire resistant glass. At high temperatures glass will melt and sag, which is why the traditional fire resistant glass has wire within it.

OPENINGS AND VOIDS

Consideration should be given to the protection of openings and voids by the use of fire barriers such as fire shutters, cavity barriers and fire curtains. It is important that construction work be managed to minimise the effect on the structure being worked on to keep fire precautions intact as much as possible. This will involve planning for the prompt re-instatement of protection of openings and voids as soon after their breach to do work as is possible. The temptation to leave all breaches to the end of work and then re-instate them should be avoided - the longer that breaches are left open the higher the risk from fires. Where openings or voids are created as part of the construction process they should be considered as part of the fire risk assessment and consideration be given to the timeliness of their protection. If cavity barriers made from vulnerable or delicate material are to be used they may have to have temporary covering to protect them. This is a good example of the sort of thing that a designer should be considering and making arrangements for as part of the construction design.

STRATEGIC APPROACH TO FIRE PRECAUTIONS

The principles used for the control of fire spread within buildings have undergone dramatic changes within the last few years.

Traditional means

- Fire resisting structures.
- Fire stopping of ducts, flues and holes in fire resistant structures.
- Fire resisting doors.
- Smoke seals and intumescent materials on doors.
- Compartmentalisation to confine the fire to a predetermined size.
- Sprinklers in large compartments.

Figure 15-20: Magnetic door holder linked to alarm. *Source: ACT.*

Figure 15-21: Door stop with automatic release. *Source: ACT.*

New concepts in fire safety

Modern systems now revolve around 3 aspects:

- Early and rapid detection of a fire by use of 'intelligent' fire alarm systems.
- Limitation of the size of fire by use of 'rapid response' sprinkler system.
- Control of smoke and toxic fumes by ventilation systems, so that clear air is maintained at head height level, to enable persons to escape.

Common fire detection and alarm systems

FIRE DETECTION

Heat detection

Sensors operate by the melting of a metal (fusion detectors) or expansion of a solid, liquid or gas (thermal expansion detectors).

Radiation detection

Photoelectric cells detect the emission of infra-red/ultra-violet radiation from the fire.

Smoke detection

Using ionising radiations, light scatter (smoke scatters beams of light), obscuration (smoke entering a detector prevents light from reaching a photoelectric cell).

Flammable gas detection

Measures the amount of flammable gas in the atmosphere and compares the value with a reference value.

Figure 15-22: Smoke detector.   *Source: ACT.*

ALARM SYSTEMS

The purpose of a fire alarm is to give an early warning of a fire in a building for two reasons:

- To increase the safety of occupants by encouraging them to escape to a place of safety.
- To increase the possibility of early extinction of the fire thus reducing the loss of or damage to the property.

TYPES OF FIRE ALARMS

Voice - Simplest and most effective type but very limited because it is dependent upon the size of the workplace and background noise levels.

Manual alarms - Rotary gong, hand bell or triangle and sounder but limited by the scale of the building.

Call points with sounders - Standard system, operation of one call point sounds alarm throughout workplace.

Automatic system - System as above, with added fire detection to initiate the alarm.

Single stage alarm

The alarm sounds throughout the whole of the building and calls for total evacuation.

Two-stage alarm

In certain large / high rise buildings it may be better to evacuate the areas of high risk first, usually those closest to the fire or immediately above it. In this case, an evacuation signal is given in the affected area, together with an alert signal in other areas. If this type of system is required, early consultation with the Fire Service is essential.

Figure 15-23: Easy operation alarm call point.   *Source: ACT.*

Figure 15-24: Alarm point identified & well located. *Source: ACT.*

Staff alarms

In some premises, an immediate total evacuation may not be desirable, e.g. nightclubs, shops, theatres, cinemas. A controlled evacuation by the staff may be preferred, to prevent distress and panic to the occupants. If such a system is used, the alarm must be restricted to the staff and only used where there are sufficient members of staff and they have been fully trained in the action of what to do in case of fire. Alarms must make a distinctive sound, audible in all parts of the workplace (sound levels should be 65 dB (A) or 5dB (A) above any other noise - which ever is the greater). The meaning of the alarm sound must be understood by all. They may be manually or automatically operated.

Portable fire fighting equipment

Figure 15-25: Extinguishers sited at correct height. *Source: ACT.*

Figure 15-26: Siting of fire extinguishers.   *Source: ACT.*

SITING

Portable fire extinguishers should always be sited:

- On the line of escape routes.
- Near, but not too near, to danger points.
- Near to room exits inside or outside according to occupancy and/or risk.
- In multi-storey buildings, at the same position on each floor e.g. top of stair flights or at corners in corridors.

- Where possible in groups forming fire points.
- So that no person need travel more than 30 metres to reach an extinguisher.
- With the carrying handle about one metre from the floor to facilitate ease of handling, removal from wall bracket, or on purpose designed floor stand.
- Away from excesses of heat or cold.

MAINTENANCE AND INSPECTION

The CHSW Regulations require that any fire fighting equipment provided must be properly maintained and subject to examination and test at intervals such that it remains effective.

Maintenance

This means service of the fire extinguisher by a competent person. It involves thorough examination of the extinguisher, its testing, and is usually done annually.

Inspection

A monthly check should be carried out to ensure that extinguishers are in their proper place and have not been discharged, lost pressure or suffered obvious damage. It may be necessary to increase the frequency of checks made for fire extinguishers on a construction site to a weekly basis, due to the less structured or controlled work environment that they are sited in. This could mean that there is a higher risk of them being damaged or used without notification.

FIRE FIGHTING EQUIPMENT TRAINING

The CHSW Regulations requires that every person at work on a construction site, so far as is reasonably practicable, be instructed in the correct use of any fire fighting equipment which it may be necessary for them to use. This may mean that all workers on a site will need to know basic information but that some key people may need more detailed instruction. Though the regulations do not use the term "training" it would be good practice to make sure that those that may need to take a lead in operating fire extinguishers can do this competently and for most people this would mean practising how to use them in a situation that reproduces the circumstances of a fire. Training should include:

- Understanding of principles of combustion and classification of fires.
- Identification of the various types of fire extinguisher available to them.
- Principles of use and limitations of extinguishers.
- Considerations for personal safety and the safety of others.
- How to identify if the extinguisher is appropriate to the fire and ready to use.
- How to attack fires with the appropriate extinguisher(s).
- Any specific considerations related to the environment the extinguishers are kept or used in.

Training has to clarify the general and specific rules for use of extinguishers:

General - aim at the seat of the fire and move the extinguisher across the fire to extinguish it - this is particularly appropriate for class A fires.

Specific - if using a foam extinguisher for class B fires the foam is allowed to drop onto the fire by aiming just above it. If this is for a flammable liquid fire contained in an open tank it is possible to get good results by this process or aiming it to the back of the tank and allowing the foam to float over the liquid. For other specific limitations or approaches to the use of individual types of extinguisher see section below.

Extinguishing media

FIRE EXTINGUISHERS

The familiar coding of the whole body of an extinguisher in a single discernible colour has now disappeared under the new British/European standard BS EN 3. From 1st January 1997 all types of new certified fire extinguishers should have a red body like the existing water-type extinguisher. In addition, BS EN 3 allows manufacturers to use up to 5% of the extinguisher casing in another colour in order to differentiate between extinguishers that use a different extinguishing medium. A new British Standard (BS 7863) recommends that manufacturers affix different colour coded panels (for example, labels or bands) using the existing colour code scheme noted below when describing the different extinguishers. The changes introduced by BS EN 3 are not legal requirements and existing extinguishers do not have to be replaced, but may be replaced as they become unserviceable.

Figure 15-27: Colour coding by label and sign. *Source: ACT.*

Figure 15-28: Whole body colour coded. *Source: ACT.*

Water (Colour code - Red)

Water extinguishers should only be used on Class A fires - those involving solids like paper and wood. Water works by cooling the burning material to below its ignition temperature, therefore removing the heat part of the fire triangle, and so the fire goes out. Water is the most common form of extinguishing media and can be used on the majority of fires involving solid materials.

Must not be used on liquid fires or in the vicinity of live electrical equipment.

Foam (Colour code - Cream)

Foam is especially useful for extinguishing Class B fires - those involving burning liquids and solids which melt and turn to liquids as they burn. Foam works in several ways to extinguish the fire, the main way being to smother the burning liquid, i.e. to stop the oxygen reaching the combustion zone. Foam can also be used to prevent flammable vapours escaping from spilled volatile liquids and also on Class A fires. It is worth noting that the modern spray foams are more efficient than water on a Class A fire.

Must not be used in the vicinity of live electrical equipment, unless electrically rated.

Dry powder (Colour code - Blue)

Designed for Class A, B and C fires but may only subdue Class A fires for a short while. One of the main ways in which powder works to extinguish a fire is the smothering effect, whereby it forms a thin film of powder on the burning liquid thus excluding air. The extinguisher is also excellent for the rapid knock down (flame suppression) of flammable liquid spills.

Powders generally provide extinction faster than foam, but there is a greater risk of re-ignition and this should always be borne in mind. If used indoors, a powder extinguisher can cause problems for the operator due to the inhalation of the powder and obscuration of vision. This type of extinguisher may be used on live electrical equipment.

Vaporising liquids (e.g. Halogenated Hydrocarbon or Halon) (Colour code - Green)

Note: Halons are no longer recommended, for environmental reasons.

Gaseous - Carbon Dioxide (CO_2) (Colour code - Black)

May also be used for small Class B fires in their early stages, indoors or outdoors with little air movement. CO_2 extinguishers are safe and excellent for use on live electrical equipment. Carbon dioxide replaces the oxygen in the atmosphere surrounding the fuel and the fire is extinguished. As most carbon dioxide extinguishers last only a few seconds, only small fires should be tackled with this type of extinguisher. CO_2 is an asphyxiant and should not be used in confined spaces. It does not remove the heat - therefore beware of the possibility of re-ignition. CO_2 extinguishers are very noisy due to the rapid expansion of gas as it is released; this can surprise people when they operate the extinguisher. This expansion causes severe cooling around the discharge horn and can freeze the skin if the operator's hand is in contact with the horn.

Special fires

Class C Fires

Except in very small occurrences, a Class C fire involving gas should not normally be extinguished. If a gas fire is to be extinguished, then isolation of the gas supply must also take place.

Class D Fires

Class D metal fires are a specialist type of fire and they cannot be extinguished by the use of any of the traditional fire extinguishers. In fact, it may be dangerous to attempt to fight a metal fire with such an extinguisher as an explosion of the metal may take place or toxic fumes may be produced. Metal fires can be extinguished by smothering them with dry sand. However, the sand must be absolutely dry or an explosion may occur. Extinguishers specifically designed for metal fires are produced; the extinguishing agents used may be pyromet, graphite, talc or salt. All of these extinguishers basically operate by the smothering principle.

Class F Fires

New style wet chemical extinguishers have been designed to specifically deal with Class F **cooking oil** fires. This type of extinguisher congeals on top of the oil and excludes the oxygen. They may also be used on Class A fires depending upon the manufacturer's instructions.

SUMMARY MATRIX - FIRE EXTINGUISHERS

	METHOD	CLASS 'A'	CLASS 'B'	CLASS 'C'	CLASS 'D'	ELECTRIC	CLASS 'F'
WATER	Cools	Yes	No	No	No	No	No
SPRAY FOAM	Smothers	Yes	Yes	No	No	No	Special Forms
DRY POWDER	Smothers & Chemical	Limited	Yes	Yes & Isolate	Special Powders	Yes - Low Voltage	No
HALON	Chemical & Smothers	NOT RECOMMENDED					
CARBON DIOXIDE	Smothers	Surface Fires Only	Yes - Small Fires	No	No	Yes	No

HOSEREELS

Hosereels are designed for use on Class A - Carbonaceous fires. The hosereel acts as a replacement for water fire extinguishers and it is said that one hosereel equates to 4 x 9 litre water extinguishers. Modern hosereels have an adjustable nozzle and can be adjusted to give a jet of water, water spray or a combination of both. The water jet is normally used for its "striking power" in attacking the seat of a fire. The jet of water should be "played" across the fire surface and into the heart of the fire to extinguish embers etc. The water spray can be used if the burning material is easily disturbed with the possibility of spreading the fire. The spray pattern produced allows larger areas to be covered in one go than if the water jet has been used and, as it has less pressure behind it, it does not spread materials such as dusts or paper as easily.

Advantages

- Continuous supply of water - no time constraint.
- Greater quantity of water is delivered than from an extinguisher, and this has a better effect at extinguishing the fire.
- The person who is attempting to extinguish the fire does not need to get as close as when using extinguishers.
- A spray pattern can be produced to protect the user from radiated heat.

Disadvantages

■ Considerable physical effort may be required to pull the hosereel to the fire, especially if the route is twisting and has lots of obstructions.

■ Any doors through which the hosereel is pulled will become wedged open by the reel.

■ The user may stay in the vicinity of the fire too long.

■ The extended hosereel may create an additional tripping hazard.

Limitations

■ Hosereels should be connected to a permanent water supply so they are not limited by discharge time factors as are extinguishers.

■ The hosereel itself should comply with current standards which permit up to 30 metres of hosereel to be used. This does limit the use of a hosereel by virtue of the distance that it is located away from a fire.

■ Considerable physical strength is required to pull 30 metres of hose, and for this reason consideration should be given to shorter lengths of hosereel being provided in more frequent locations.

■ A limiting factor is the likely route through which the hosereel will need to pass. If this route includes a lot of corners, turns or doors, then hosereels may not be the most suitable fire equipment to be provided.

Requirements for fire plans for means of escape

An adequate means of escape is essential for all premises, regardless of whether a fire certificate is required. A fire certificate will make specific requirements regarding the means of escape for a particular building. The following general factors should be taken into consideration when planning means of escape.

TRAVEL DISTANCES

Travel distance is a significant component of a successful means of escape plan. Travel distances are judged on the basis of distance to a place of safety in the open air and away from the building; the distance needs to be kept to the minimum. The distance includes travel around obstructions in the workplace and may be greatly affected by any work in progress on a construction site. If someone is outside on a scaffold it is unlikely to be considered as a place of safety and the distance would usually be taken as that to reach the ground away from the building (for example, at an assembly point).

■ The route must be sufficiently wide and of sufficiently short distance to allow speedy and safe evacuation.

■ There should normally be alternative routes leading in different directions.

■ Everyone should be able to escape unaided (if able bodied).

■ The distance between work stations and the nearest fire exit should be minimised.

Figure 15-29: Fire escape - hazard. *Source: ACT.*

STAIRS

Staircases form an integral part of the means of escape from fire in most buildings. If they are to be part of the escape route, the following points must be ensured:

■ Fire resistant structure.

■ Fitted with fire doors.

■ Doors must not be wedged open.

■ Wide enough to take the required number of people.

■ Must lead direct to fresh air, or to two totally separate routes of escape.

■ Non slip/trip and in good condition.

■ No combustible storage within staircase.

PASSAGEWAYS

■ The route should lead directly to the open air via a protected route (where necessary).

■ Route to be kept unobstructed.

DOORS

■ Exit doors are to open outwards easily (unless small numbers of people involved).

■ Provide fire doors along the escape route.

■ Fire doors along with fire resistant structures serve two purposes:

   • Prevent the spread of fire.

   • Ensure that there is means of escape for persons using the building.

■ They should not be wedged open.

■ Lead to open air - safety.

EMERGENCY LIGHTING

Emergency lighting should be considered if escape is likely to be required in dark conditions. This could mean late afternoon in winter time, not just at night time.

EXIT AND DIRECTIONAL SIGNS

The escape route should be adequately signposted and easy to follow (see also Safety Signs).

ASSEMBLY POINTS

The assembly point is a place of safety where staff wait whilst any incident is investigated, and where confirmation can be made that all persons have evacuated the premises. The main factors to consider are:

- Safe distance from building.
- Sited in a safe position.
- Not sited so that staff will be in the way of Fire Brigade.
- Must be able to walk away from assembly point and back to a public road.
- Clearly signed.
- More than one provided to suit numbers and groups of people.
- Communications should be provided between assembly points.
- Measures provided to decide if evacuation successful.
- Person must be in charge of assembly point and identified.
- Person to meet / brief the Fire Brigade clear and identified.

Figure 15-30: Assembly point.   *Source: ACT.*

NEED FOR CONTINUAL REVIEW AS WORK PROGRESSES

In all workplaces there is a need to constantly review and revise the fire risk assessment and the fire safety measures that apply. This aspect of fire safety is absolutely vital in construction sites.

By the nature of the business within the construction world, building layouts will constantly be changing, or escape routes may be restricted due to other building works or for safety reasons. Dependant upon the state of the built environment, fire safety should be inspected on a weekly basis but it may need to be checked on a daily basis. Checks and assessment should be made to ensure that the fire plan for means of escape is still appropriate and that the following fire safety measures are not being compromised:

- Escape routes.
- Access to Fire alarms.
- Audibility of fire alarm systems.
- Access and availability of fire fighting equipment.
- Suitability of fire safety signage.
- Need for and suitability of escape lighting.
- Fire protection / fire resistant structures within the building.
- Introduction of new fire hazards e.g. hot works.
- Correct storage / use of flammable materials.
- Site security / arson prevention.
- New staff and the need for 'fire induction'.

If, as a result of the works that need to be carried out, fire safety standards will be reduced then additional compensating factors may need to be introduced. For example, if detector heads need to be covered to prevent false alarms a fire watch system of patrols may be introduced to compensate. As can be seen, fire safety is a constantly changing factor which must be integral to the everyday management of site safety.

Evacuation procedures

The danger which may threaten persons if an emergency occurs at work depends on many different factors; consequently it is not possible to construct one model procedure for action in the event of fire and emergency for all premises. Evacuation procedures need to reflect the type of emergency, the people affected and the premises involved. Many of the different issues to consider for different emergencies have common factors, for example, evacuation in an efficient / effective manner, an agreed assembly location (which may be different for different emergencies) and checks to ensure people are safe. These factors are considered below with regard to fire emergencies.

APPOINTMENT OF FIRE MARSHALS

In all premises a person should be nominated to be responsible for co-ordinating the fire evacuation plan. This may be the same person that organises fire instruction and training and drills and co-ordinates the evacuation at the time of the fire. They may appoint persons such as fire marshals to assist them in fulfilling the role. This involves the appointment of certain staff to act as fire marshals to assist with evacuation. The way in which they assist will vary between organisations; for example, some will check areas of the building in event of a fire to ensure no person is still inside and others will lead the evacuation to show where to go. In complex construction situations the nomination of active fire marshals to encourage people to evacuate some of whom may be at an important stage in their work or conducting noisy operations, is very important. The fire marshals' appointment should be made known to workers and they should be clearly identifiable at the time of emergency so that those that are asked to evacuate understand the authority of the person requiring them to do so. The appointment of fire marshals contributes to an employer's compliance with the MHSWR requirement to establish competent persons to assist with health and safety.

FIRE INSTRUCTION NOTICES

At conspicuous positions in all parts of the location, and adjacent to all fire alarm actuating points (e.g. break glass operated call points), printed notices should be exhibited stating, in concise terms, the essentials of the action to be taken upon discovering a fire and on hearing the fire alarm. It is usual to also state what someone must do when they discover a fire.

Fire action

The action in the event of a fire and upon discovery needs to be immediate, and a simple fire action plan should be put into effect. A good plan of action would include the following points.

On discovering a fire

- Sound the fire alarm (to warn others).
- Call the fire service.
- Go to the assembly point.

On hearing the alarm

- Leave the building by the nearest exit.
- Close doors behind you.
- Go to the assembly point.
- Get out of the building and stay out.

On evacuation

- Do not take risks.
- Do not stop for personal belongings.
- Do not use lifts.
- Do not return to the building unless authorised to do so.
- Report to assembly point.

Figure 15-31: Fire instruction notice. *Source: ACT.*

Note: You must consider the wording on notices that are posted and ensure that workers are instructed and trained to do what you are asking of them.

FIRE TRAINING

Typical issues to be included in a fire training programme relating to emergency action are:

- Fire prevention.
- Recognition of fire alarms and the actions to be taken.
- Understanding the emergency signs.
- Location of fire escape routes and assembly points.
- Requirements for safe evacuation (e.g. non-use of lifts, do not run etc.).
- Location and operation of call points and other means of raising the alarm.
- How the fire service is called.
- Location, use and limitations of fire fighting equipment.
- Consideration of people with special needs.
- Identity and role of fire marshals.

FIRE DRILLS

A fire drill is intended to ensure, by means of training and rehearsal, that in the event of fire:

- The people who may be in danger act in a calm, orderly and efficient manner.
- Those designated with specific duties carry them out in an organised and effective manner.
- The means of escape are used in accordance with a predetermined and practised plan.
- An opportunity for management leadership.

The fire drill enables all people involved in the evacuation to practice and learn under as near realistic circumstances as possible. This can identify what works well in the evacuation procedure and what does not. Practice in the form of a drill helps people to respond quickly to the alarm and, because they have done it before, to make their way efficiently to the assembly point. At least once a year a practice fire drill should normally be carried out simulating conditions in which one or more of the escape routes from the building are obstructed. This will assist in developing an awareness of the alternative exits that can be taken and assist in ensuring people understand the unpredictability of fires.

ROLL CALLS

The traditional method of undertaking a roll call is by use of a checklist of names. Very few workplaces can now operate this system as they do not have such a static workforce as this system requires. Where they can operate they will provide a speedy and efficient means of identifying who has arrived at the assembly point and who has not. Where strict security control to a construction site is used, with signing in and out, this may make this process more viable. This requires people on site to report to their allocated assembly point and for someone (e.g. a Fire Marshal) to confirm that they have arrived safely and determine if anyone is missing.

If it is not known exactly who is in a building a system of Fire Marshals who can make a check of the building at the time of their own evacuation (without endangering their own safety) may be employed. This can assist with the process and may identify people that have not evacuated. However, this system may not be able to provide an absolute confirmation that everyone has evacuated as there may be limited opportunity for the Fire Marshal to check the whole of the area allocated to them. Any doubt or confirmed missing persons should be reported to the person nominated to report to the fire service, who in turn will provide a report to the fire service as soon as they arrive.

PROVISIONS FOR THE INFIRM AND DISABLED

When planning a fire evacuation system we need to consider who may be in the workplace, their abilities and capabilities. Any disability e.g. hearing, vision, mental or mobility impairment must be catered for.Some of the arrangements may be to provide the person with a nominated assistant(s) to support their speedy escape, for example, with the use of a specially designed evacuation chair to enable them to make their way out of a building down emergency exit stairs. Part of the provision is to make sure they are capable of knowing that an emergency exists. This may mean providing them with special alarm arrangements that cater for their disability, for example, a visual and or vibrating alert for the hearing impaired.

This page is intentionally blank

Chemical & biological health hazards & control

Overall Aims

On completion of this Unit, candidates will understand:

■ the ill-health effects of exposure to chemical and biological hazards.

■ the options to control these hazards in the construction workplace.

Content

Specific Intended Learning Outcomes

The intended learning outcomes of this Unit are that candidates will be able to:

16.1   recognise chemical and biological hazards in a construction workplace

16.2   explain the significance of the physical form of a substance to the related health hazards and the relationship between the route of entry into the body of a hazardous substance and its associated risk

16.3   distinguish between acute and chronic ill-health effects

16.4   explain the difference between a maximum exposure limit and an occupational exposure standard and the purpose of long term and short term exposure limits

16.5   make a preliminary assessment of the health risks from substances and biological agents commonly encountered in construction workplaces utilising:

- a basic survey to determine the presence and nature of ill-health risks
- suppliers' safety data sheets to assist in health risk assessments
- simple environmental monitoring and testing using stain tube detectors and smoke tubes (including the relative merits and limitations of these techniques)
- the need for expert guidance where necessary

16.6   apply a hierarchy of control measures to reduce the risk of ill-health caused by exposure to chemical or biological agents

16.7   outline the basic requirements relating to the disposal of waste and effluent and the control of atmospheric pollution from construction activities

Sources of Reference

Step by Step Guide to COSHH Assessment (HSG97), HSE Books

Occupational Exposure Limits (EH40), HSE Books (updated annually)

General COSHH ACOP, Carcinogens ACOP and Biological Agents ACOP (L5), HSE Books

Personal Protective Equipment at Work (L25), HSE Books

An Introduction to Local Exhaust Ventilation (HSG37), HSE Books

The Selection, Use and Maintenance of Respiratory Protective Equipment (HSG53), HSE Books

Health Risks Management: A Guide to Working with Solvents (HSG188), HSE Books

Introduction to Asbestos Essentials (HSG213), HSE Books

Asbestos Essentials Task Manual (HSG210), HSE Books

Controlled Asbestos Stripping Techniques for Work Requiring a Licence (HSG189/1), HSE Books

Working with Asbestos Cement (HSG189/2), HSE Books

Relevant Statutory Provisions

The Control of Substances Hazardous to Health Regulations (COSHH) 2002

The Control of Asbestos at Work Regulations (CAWR) 2002

The Asbestos (Licensing) Regulations (ASLIC) 1983

The Control of Lead at Work Regulations (CLAW) 2002

Chemicals (Hazard Information and Packaging for Supply) Regulations (CHIP) 2002

The Personal Protective Equipment at Work Regulations (PPER) 1992

The Environmental Protection Act (EPA) 1990

16.1 - Forms of agents

Chemical agents

The form taken by a hazardous substance is a contributory factor to its potential for harm. Principally the form affects how easily a substance gains entry to the body, how it is absorbed into the body and how it reaches a susceptible site.

Chemical agents take many forms, the most common being as follows:

Dusts	These are solid airborne particles, often created by operations such as grinding, crushing, milling, sanding or demolition - e.g. silica.
Fumes	Are solid particles formed by condensation from the gaseous state - e.g. lead fume, welding fume.
Smoke	Particles that result from incomplete combustion. These can be either solid or liquid state.
Gases	Formless fluids usually produced by chemical processes involving combustion or by the interaction of chemical substance. A gas will normally seek to fill the space completely into which it is liberated - e.g. chlorine gas.
Mists and aerosols	Are finely dispersed liquid droplets suspended in air. Mists are mainly created by spraying, foaming, pickling and electro-plating - e.g. mist from a water pressure washer.
Vapour	Is the gaseous form of a material normally encountered in a liquid or solid state at normal room temperature and pressure; typical examples are solvents - e.g. trichloroethylene which releases vapours when the container is opened.
Liquids	Substances which are liquid at normal temperature and pressure.
Solids	Are materials which are solid at normal temperature and pressure.

Biological agents

FUNGAL

Fungi are a variety of organisms that act in a parasitic manner, feeding on organic matter. Most are either harmless or positively beneficial to health; however a number cause harm to humans and may be fatal. Examples of the fungi organism are aspergillosis (farmer's lung), ringworm and athlete's foot.

ALGAE

Microscopic plants deposited in pool or spa water by wind, rain, and dust. They thrive in sunlight and warm water, clogging filters, increasing the need for sanitizers and oxidizers, and causing slippery surfaces. The presence of algae can increase the risk of Legionella.

BACTERIAL

Bacteria are single cell organisms. Most bacteria are harmless to humans and many are beneficial. The bacteria that can cause disease are called pathogens. Examples of bacteria are leptospira (causing Weil's disease), bacillus anthracis (causing anthrax), and legionella pneumophila (causing legionnaires disease).

VIRUSES

Viruses are the smallest known type of infectious agent. They invade the cells of other organisms, which they take over and make copies of themselves and while not all cause disease many of them do. Examples of viruses are hepatitis which can cause liver damage and the Human Immunodeficiency Virus (HIV) which causes acquired immune deficiency syndrome (AIDS).

16.2 - Main classification of substances hazardous to health

Indication of danger	Symbol (orange background)	Category of danger	Characteristic properties and body responses
Irritant		Irritant	A non-corrosive substance which, through immediate, prolonged or repeated contact with the skin or mucous membrane, can cause inflammation e.g. butyl ester, a severe irritant which can cause abdominal pain, vomiting and burning of the skin and eyes.
		Sensitising (by contact)	May cause an allergic skin reaction which will worsen on further exposures (allergic dermatitis), e.g. nickel or epoxy resin.

Corrosive

| Corrosive | May destroy living tissues on contact e.g. sulphuric (battery) acid or sodium hydroxide (caustic soda). |

Harmful

| Harmful | If inhaled or ingested or it penetrates the skin, has an adverse effect on health e.g. some solvents causing narcosis or central nervous system failure. |

Figure 16-1: Harmful, toxic.   *Source: ACT.*

Sensitising (by inhalation)	May cause an allergic respiratory reaction, which will progressively worsen on further exposures (asthma), e.g. flour dust, isocyanates.
Carcinogenic (category 3)	Only evidence is from animals, which is of doubtful relevance to humans, e.g. benzyl chloride.
Mutagenic (category 3)	Evidence of mutation in Ames Test and possible somatic cell mutation.
Toxic to reproduction (category 3)	Animal data, not necessarily relevant.

Toxic

| Toxic | If inhaled or ingested or it penetrates the skin, may involve serious acute or chronic health risks and even death e.g. arsenic, a systemic poison. |

Figure 16-2: Toxic.   *Source: ACT.*

Carcinogenic (categories 1 & 2)	May, if inhaled or it penetrates the skin, induce uncontrolled cell division (cancer) or increase its incidence, e.g. benzene affects the bone marrow causing leukaemia.
Mutagenic (categories 1 & 2)	May cause genetic defects, e.g. 2-Ethoxyethanol may impair fertility.
Toxic to reproduction (categories 1 & 2)	May cause harm to the unborn child, e.g. lead suspected of causing restricted development of the brain of the foetus.

Very Toxic

If inhaled or ingested or it penetrates the skin, may involve extremely serious acute or chronic health risks and even death e.g. cyanide, a severe irritant and systemic poison.

Source: The Chemicals (Hazard Information & Packaging for Supply) Regulations (CHIP 3) 2002.

16.3 - Difference between acute and chronic health effects

The effect of a substance on the body depends not only on the substance, but also on the dose, and the susceptibility of the individual. No substance can be considered non-toxic; there are only differences in degree of effect.

Toxicology	Is the study of the body's responses to substances. In order to interpret toxicological data and information, the meaning of the following terms should be understood.
Toxicity	The ability of a chemical substance to produce injury once it reaches a susceptible site in or on the body. A poisonous substance (e.g. organic lead), which causes harm to biological systems and interferes with the normal functions of the body. The effects may be acute or chronic, local or systemic.
Dose	Is the level of environmental contamination multiplied by the length of time (devotion) of exposure to the contaminant.
Acute effect	Is an immediate or rapidly produced, adverse effect, following a single or short term exposure to an offending agent, which is usually reversible.
Chronic effect	Is an adverse health effect produced as a result of prolonged or repeated exposure, with a gradual or latent, and often irreversible, effect that may often go unrecognised for a number of years.

Local effect   Is usually confined to the initial point of contact. Possible sites affected include the skin, mucous membranes or the eyes, nose or throat. Examples are burns to the skin by corrosive substances (acids and alkalis), asbestos scarring lung tissue.

Systemic effect   Occurs in parts of the body other than at the point of initial contact. Frequently the circulatory system provides a means to distribute the substance round the body to a target organ/system.

Target organs   An organ within the human body on which a specified toxic material exerts its effects e.g. lungs, liver, brain, skin, bladder or eyes.

Target systems   Central nervous system, circulatory system, reproductive system.

Examples of substances that have a systemic effect and their target organs are:

Alcohol - central nervous system, liver.

Lead - bone marrow and brain damage.

Mercury - central nervous system.

16.4 - The health hazards of specific agents

AMMONIA

Ammonia is a gas used extensively as a refrigerant or as an aqueous solution used in cleaning materials. It is a gas usually stored under pressure.

Contact with liquid - it has a corrosive action that will burn the skin on contact and it will severely irritate or burn the cornea.

Gas - it is lighter than air and has a local effect on the lungs. In small concentrations it is an acute irritant but is recoverable; in larger concentrations it can result in pneumonia and pulmonary failure.

Aqueous - (alkaline liquor) can cause skin damage on contact and the vapours from the liquor are an acute respiratory irritant.

CHLORINE

It is usually stored under pressure in its liquid state. If a leak occurs a small amount of liquid will give rise to a large amount of gas. It is an acute respiratory irritant; small quantities may lead to chronic lung disease, large quantities result in pneumonia and pulmonary failure. It is a highly reactive chemical gas which supports violent combustion. It is used extensively in water treatment processes, for example, where water is required for human consumption. Compounds of chlorine include sodium hypochlorite e.g. domestic bleach. These compounds liberate chlorine gas readily when mixed with acids, therefore creating a risk to workers who use mixtures of bleaches and acid cleaners.

ORGANIC SOLVENTS

Include highly volatile / flammable cleaning agents such as acetone, organo chlorides such as trichloethylene (used for commercial degreasing) or carbon tetrachloride used in dry cleaning processes. In the construction industry they may be encountered as residual contents of storage tanks or may be used as convenient cleaning substances to remove adhesives. Trichloethylene is capable of absorption through the skin and it is a narcotic - classified "Harmful" by CHIP. If the vapours are inhaled, it can cause drowsiness very quickly, depress the central nervous system and lead to liver failure and death if exposure is for prolonged periods.

CARBON DIOXIDE

A simple asphyxiant produced as a by-product of the brewing processes. As a simple asphyxiant it displaces oxygen in the air that we breathe and means insufficient oxygen goes to the brain, leading to collapse and death. Available commercially as a frozen solid 'dry ice' used as a refrigerant or to generate 'smoke' in theatre productions. Provides the constituent part of a carbon dioxide fire extinguisher and may be encountered in fixed fire fighting installations in buildings. It may be encountered in confined spaces, such as trenches, in areas with chalky soil as carbon dioxide is evolved naturally; it is heavier than air and tends to gather in low areas.

CARBON MONOXIDE

Is a chemical asphyxiant produced as a by-product of incomplete combustion of carbon fuels e.g. gas water heaters, compressors, pumps, dumper trucks or generators. It is a particular risk when operated in poorly ventilated confined areas where workers are forced to breathe it. Carbon monoxide has a great affinity (200 times that of oxygen) for the haemoglobin red blood cells which means it will inhibit oxygen uptake by red blood cells resulting in chemical asphyxiation, leading to collapse and death.

ISOCYANATES

Isocyanates are used in the manufacture of resins and urethane foams; common compounds are toluene di-isocyanate (TDI) and methylene bisphenyl di-isocyanate (MDI). TDI is an extremely volatile vapour and is evolved during the manufacture of foams. TDI and MDI are highly toxic in very small amounts (parts per billion) and inhalation will result in a severe respiratory reaction. Isocyanates are sensitising agents; in particular they sensitise the lungs.

LEAD

Lead poisoning results from the inhalation of fumes produced from the heating of lead, or certain solders containing lead, at temperatures above 500^0C. In construction activities this will include exposure to lead by oxyacetylene cutting of metal coated with paint containing lead. In addition, lead poisoning may result from the inhalation of organic lead compounds e.g. tetraethyl lead. Chronic (cumulative) lead poisoning may result in anaemia, mental dullness and is often accompanied by the presence of a blue line around the gums. Acute lead poisoning is often fatal; symptoms include muscular twitch, hallucinations and violent behaviour.

ASBESTOS

Asbestos is a general term used to describe a range of mineral fibres (commonly referred to by colour i.e. white, brown and blue). Asbestos was mainly used as an insulating and fire resisting material. Asbestos fibres readily become air borne when disturbed and may enter the lungs, where they cause fibrosis (scarring and thickening) of the lung tissue, asbestosis or mesothelioma (thickening of the pleural lining). Asbestosis typically takes more than 10 years to develop. Research suggests that 50 per cent of asbestos sufferers will also develop cancer of the lung or bronchus.

SILICA

Silica exists naturally as crystalline minerals (tridymite, cristobalite). A common variety is quartz. Industrially silica is used in the morphous (after heating) form e.g. fumed silica, silica gel. In construction activities it may be encountered in stone work or work with quartz based tiles. Inhalation of silica can result in silicosis, a fibrosis of the lung. Nodular lesions are formed which ultimately destroy lung structure reducing the capacity of the lungs.

Figure 16-3: Asbestos label. *Source: Scaftag.*

CEMENT

Cement can cause ill health by skin contact, eye contact or inhalation. The hazards of wet cement are due to its caustic, abrasive and drying properties, which in their mildest form may cause dermatitis, or in more severe cases damage shown below.

Skin contact

Continuous contact between skin and wet cement allows alkaline compounds to penetrate and burn the skin. When wet cement is trapped against the skin - for instance by falling inside a worker's gloves or boots - the result can be first, second or third degree burns or skin ulcers depending on the duration of exposure.

Some workers may develop skin and respiratory allergies to the traces of hexavalent chromium in cement.

Eye contact

Depending on the level of exposure, effects may range from redness to chemical burns and blindness.

Inhalation

In the short term, exposure irritates the nose and throat and causes choking and difficulty in breathing. Prolonged or repeated exposure can lead to the disabling and often fatal disease silicosis. Portland cement has an occupational exposure standard (OES).

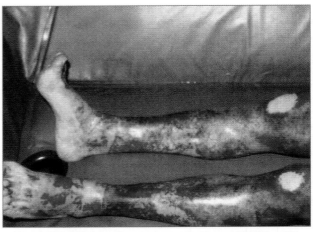

Figure 16-4: Skin burns from wet cement. *Source: SHP (Aug 03).*
This man's right leg had to be amputated owing to the severe burns he sustained from kneeling in wet cement for three hours.

WOOD DUST

Skin irritation and skin sensitisation

Skin irritation can be caused by contact with the wood itself, dust, bark, sap or lichens growing on the bark. Symptoms subside once the irritant is removed.

Sensitization dermatitis is usually caused by exposure to the fine dust from certain wood species. This exposure produces symptoms similar to skin irritation. Once sensitized, the body sets up an allergic reaction, and will react severely when exposed even to a small amount of wood dust.

Allergic and non-allergic respiratory effects

The most commonly reported allergic respiratory effect due to wood dust exposure is asthma. It may occur alone or in conjunction with dermatitis. Occupational asthma and rhinitis due to exposure to Western Red Cedar has been well documented.

Exposure to wood dust can cause chronic obstructive lung disease. Exposure to saw fumes containing terpenes, a constituent of wood, also causes chronic obstructive impairment in lung function.

Nasal effects

Chronic exposure to wood dust can cause impaired nasal mucociliary clearance. A major portion of airborne wood dust is contributed by particles larger than 10-μm size, which can be trapped effectively in the nasal passage.

Nasal cancer is a significant hazard of woodworking and is particularly associated with hardwoods.

Biohazards

Exposure to micro-organisms that grow on wood can also cause potential health effects. Endotoxins from bacteria and allergenic fungi growing on wood are the main biohazards found in wood processing workplaces.

TETANUS

A life-threatening disease caused by toxins produced by the bacterium Clostridium tetani, which often grow at the site of a cut or wound. Muscles first become stiff, then rigidly fixed (lockjaw). Vaccination against tetanus should be done every 10 years or at the time of injury.

LEPTOSPIRA

The bacteria Leptospira, spiral shaped bacteria, penetrates the skin and causes leptospirosis (Weil's Disease). Rodents represent the most important reservoir of infections, especially rats (also gerbils, voles, and field mice). Other sources of infection are dogs, hedgehogs, foxes, pigs, and cattle. These animals are not necessarily ill, but carry leptospires in their kidneys and excrete it in their urine. Infection can be transmitted directly via direct contact with blood, tissues, organs or urine of one of the host animals or indirectly by contaminated environment.

Infection enters through broken skin or mucous membrane. Symptoms vary but include flu-like illness, conjunctivitis, liver damage (including jaundice), kidney failure and meningitis. If untreated infection may be fatal.

Construction workers most at risk are those who work where rats prevail and will include water and sewage work, demolition or refurbishment of old unoccupied buildings, and those working on sites adjoining rivers and other watercourses. The bacteria's survival depends on protection from direct sunlight, so it survives well in water courses and ditches protected by vegetation.

HEPATITIS

Hepatitis is inflammation of the liver; there are a number of types of hepatitis the B variety being the most serious. Hepatitis is caused by a virus and is passed from human to human. Hepatitis A is spread by ingesting the virus from the faeces of an infected person, from food or water contaminated by the faeces of a contaminated person or from eating raw or undercooked shellfish harvested from contaminated water. The hepatitis B virus, which is very resilient in that it remains viable for weeks in the environment outside the human body, is resistant to common antiseptics and is not affected by boiling for less than thirty minutes.

Symptoms vary, but typically the sequence is: flu-like illness with aches and pains in the joints, general tiredness, anorexia, nausea and high fever, jaundice and the liver enlarged and tender.

Workers most at risk are: those in health care: hospital personnel, dentists, laboratory staff, domestic staff, teachers, prison officers, ambulance staff, police and customs officers. Intravenous drug abusers are also seriously at risk; therefore workers who are responsible for keeping streets, parks and toilets clean are at risk from discarded needles. Construction workers carrying out work on old derelict property and those clearing ground that may have been used by intravenous drug users are particularly at risk.

16.5 - Routes of entry and the body's reaction

Routes of entry

INHALATION

The most significant industrial entry route is inhalation. It has been estimated that at least 90% of industrial poisons are absorbed through the lungs. Harmful substances can directly attack the lung tissue causing a local effect or pass through to the blood system, to be carried round the body and affect target organs such as the liver.

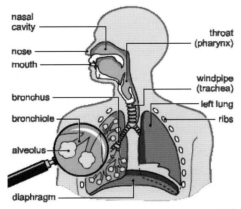

Figure 16-5: Respiratory system. *Source: BBC.*

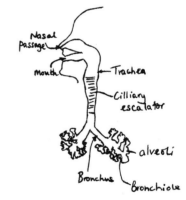

Figure 16-6: Hand drawn respiratory system. *Source: ACT.*

Typical effects of entry are:

Local effect - Silicosis

Dust causes scarring leading to inelastic fibrous tissue to develop reducing lung capacity.

Systemic effect - Anoxia

Carbon monoxide replaces oxygen in the bloodstream affecting the nervous system.

INGESTION

This route normally presents the least problem as it is unlikely that any significant quantity of harmful liquid or solid will be swallowed without deliberate intent. However, accidents will occur where small amounts of contaminant are transferred from the fingers to the mouth if eating, drinking or smoking in chemical areas is allowed or where a substance has been decanted into a container normally used for drinking. The sense of taste will often be a defence if chemicals are taken in through this route, causing the person to spit it out. If the substance is taken in, vomiting and/or excretion may mean the substance does not cause a systemic problem, though a direct effect, like burns, may occur.

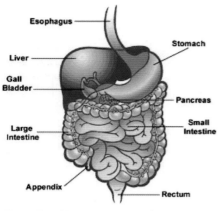

Figure 16-7: Digestive system.   *Source: STEM.*

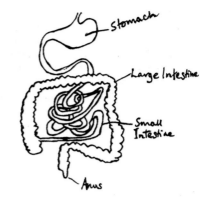

Figure 16-8: Hand drawn digestive system. *Source: ACT.*

ABSORPTION (SKIN CONTACT)

Substances can enter through the skin, cuts or abrasions and conjunctiva of the eye. Solvents such as organic solvents, e.g. toluene and trichloroethylene, can enter either accidentally or if used for washing. The substance may have a local effect, such as de-fatting of the skin, or pass through into the blood system.

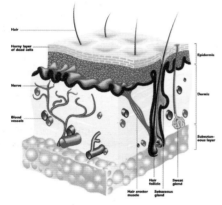

Figure 16-9: Skin layer.   *Source: SHP.*

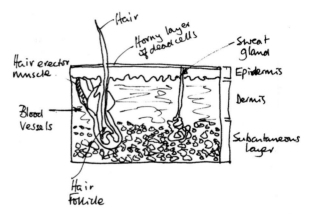

Figure 16-10: Hand drawn skin layer.   *Source: ACT.*

Contact dermatitis

Caused by contact with substances which interfere with normal skin physiology leading to inflammation of skin, usually on the hands, wrists and forearms. The skin turns red and in some cases may be itchy. Small blisters may occur and the condition may take the form of dry and cracked skin. There are many chemicals which may irritate the skin; including cement, soaps, detergents, industrial chemicals, some metals, cosmetics and plants. For babies, contact with urine causes nappy rash. Removal from exposure allows normal cell repair. A similar level of repeat exposure results in the same response. This class of dermatitis is called contact dermatitis.

Sensitisation dermatitis

A second form of dermatitis is called sensitisation dermatitis.   In this case a person exposed to the substance develops dermatitis. When taken away the dermatitis repairs, but the body gets ready for later exposures by preparing the body's defence mechanisms. A subsequent small exposure is enough to cause a major response by the immune system. The person will have become sensitised and will no longer be able to tolerate exposure to the substance without a reaction occurring.

Figure 16-11: Dermatitis.   *Source: SHP.*

Dermatitis can be prevented by:

- Clean working conditions and properly planned work systems.
- Careful attention to skin hygiene principles.
- Prompt attention to cuts, abrasions and spillages onto the skin.
- Use of protective equipment.
- Barrier cream can help.
- Pre-employment screening for sensitive individuals.

INJECTION

A forceful breach of the skin, perhaps as a result of injury, can carry harmful substances through the skin barrier; for example handling broken glass which cuts the skin and transfers a biological or chemical agent. On construction sites there are quite a few items that present a hazard of penetration, such as nails in broken up falsework that might be trodden on and penetrate the foot presenting a risk of infection from tetanus. In addition, some land or buildings being worked on may have been used by intravenous drug users and their needles may present a risk of injection of a virus, such as hepatitis. The forced injection of an agent into the body provides an easy route past the skin, which usually acts as the body's defence mechanism and protects people from the effects of many agents that do not have the ability to penetrate.

Body response to agents and protective mechanisms

The body's response against the invasion of substances likely to cause damage can be divided into external or superficial defences and internal or cellular defences.

SUPERFICIAL DEFENCE MECHANISMS

Respiratory (inhalation):

Nose
On inhalation many substances and minor organisms are successfully trapped by nasal hairs, for example, the larger wood dust particles.

Respiratory tract
The next line of defence against inhalation or substances harmful to health begin here, where a series of reflexes activate the coughing and sneezing mechanisms to forcibly expel the triggering substances.

Ciliary escalator
The passages of the respiratory system are also lined with mucus and well supplied with fine hair cells which sweep rhythmically towards the outside and pass along large particles. The respiratory system narrows as it enters the lungs where the ciliary escalator assumes more and more importance as the effective defence. Smaller particles of agents, such as some lead particles, are dealt with at this stage. The smallest particles, such as organic solvent vapours, reach the alveoli and are either deposited or exhaled.

Gastrointestinal (ingestion):

Mouth
For ingestion of substances. Saliva in the mouth provides a useful defence to substances which are not excessively acid or alkaline or in large quantities.

Gastrointestinal tract
Acid in the stomach also provides a useful defence similar to saliva. Vomiting and diarrhoea are additional reflex mechanisms which act to remove substances or quantities that the body is not equipped to deal with.

Skin (absorption):

Skin
The body's largest organ provides a useful barrier against the absorption of many foreign organisms and chemicals (but not against all of them). Its effect is, however, limited by its physical characteristics. The outer part of the skin is covered in an oily layer and substances have to overcome this before they can damage the skin or enter the body. The outer part of the epidermis is made up of dead skin cells. These are readily sacrificed to substances without harm to the newer cells underneath. Repeated or prolonged exposure could defeat this. The skin, when attacked by substances, may blister in order to protect the layers beneath. Openings in the skin such as sweat pores, hair follicles and cuts can allow entry and the skin itself may be permeable to some chemicals, e.g. toluene.

CELLULAR MECHANISMS

The cells of the body possess their own defence systems.

Scavenging action

A type of white blood cell called macrophages attack invading particles in order to destroy them and remove them from the body. This process is known as phagocytosis.

Secretion of defensive substances

Is done by some specialised cells. Histamine release and heparin, which promotes availability of blood sugar, are examples.

Prevention of excessive blood loss

Reduced circulation through blood clotting and coagulation prevents excessive bleeding and slows or prevents the entry of germs.

Repair of damaged tissues

Is a necessary defence mechanism which includes removal of dead cells, increased availability of defender cells and replacement of tissue strength, e.g. scar tissue caused by silica.

The lymphatic system

Acts as a 'form of drainage system' throughout the body for the removal of foreign bodies. Lymphatic glands or nodes at specific points in the system act as selective filters preventing infection from entering the blood system. In many cases a localised inflammation occurs in the node at this time.

16.6 - Occupational exposure limits

Maximum exposure limits and occupational exposure standards

MAXIMUM EXPOSURE LIMITS

A Maximum Exposure Limit (MEL) is the maximum concentration of an airborne substance, averaged over a reference period to which employees may be exposed by inhalation under any circumstances. The reference periods used are 8 hours (LTEL - long term exposure limit) or 15 minutes (STEL - short term exposure limit). Substances are assigned either a LTEL or a STEL or both. Those substances assigned only a STEL have acute effects.

The limits must never be exceeded.

In the event of a MEL being exceeded the following actions should be taken immediately:

- Evacuate, isolate and ventilate the affected area.
- Curtail the process producing the contaminant.
- Provide medical treatment for those exposed.

In the longer term:

- Commence an investigation.
- Implement and assess the effectiveness of extra control measures.
- Possible health surveillance.

Examples of substances assigned a MEL:

- Trichloroethylene.
- Arsenic.
- Isocyanates.
- Wood dust.
- Benzene.
- Formaldehyde.

OCCUPATIONAL EXPOSURE STANDARD

An Occupational Exposure Standard (OES) is the concentration of an airborne substance, averaged over a reference period (usually 8 hours) at which, according to current knowledge, there is no evidence that it is likely to be injurious to employees if they are exposed by inhalation, day after day, to that concentration.

Levels should not be exceeded, but if this does occur then steps should be taken as soon as is practicable to reduce the exposure.

Examples of substances assigned an OES:

- Portland Cement.
- Sulphur Dioxide.
- Sulphuric acid.
- Paracetamol.
- Carbon Monoxide.
- Ammonia.

OCCUPATIONAL EXPOSURE LIMITS (OELS) – GENERAL POINTS

The absence of a substance from the lists of MELs and OESs does not indicate that it is safe. In these cases exposure should be controlled to a level to which nearly all the working population could be exposed, day after day at work, without adverse effects on health.

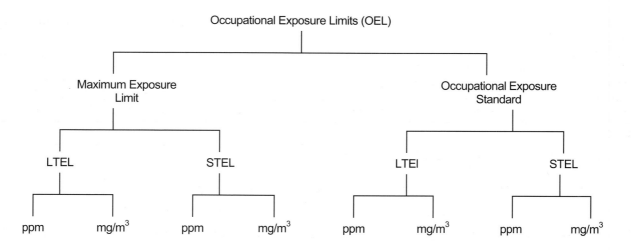

EH40 is primarily concerned with airborne contaminants which includes vapours, fumes and dusts. Certain substances listed are annotated "Sk" to denote that they can be absorbed through the skin. This warns that additional controls, in addition to respiratory protection, may be required.

TOTAL INHALABLE DUST AND RESPIRABLE DUST

OELs may be expressed in total inhalable dust and respirable dust and it is important to understand the difference in the terms. 'Total inhalable dust' approximates to the fraction of airborne material which enters the nose and mouth during breathing and is, therefore, available for deposition in the body. 'Respirable dust' approximates to the fraction which penetrates to the gas exchange region of the lung.

Where dusts contain components for total inhalable dust and respirable dust that have their own assigned occupational exposure limits, all the relevant limits should be complied with.

LONG-TERM AND SHORT-TERM EXPOSURE LIMITS

Long-term exposure limits

LTEL Concerned with the total intake averaged over a reference period (usually 8 hours) and is therefore appropriate for protecting against the effects of long term exposure (chronic effects).

Short-term exposure limits

STEL Aimed primarily at avoiding the acute effects or at least reducing the risk of occurrence. They are averaged over a 15 minute reference period.

LIMITATIONS OF EXPOSURE LIMITS

There are many reasons why control of exposure should not be based solely on OELs:

- **Inhalation only.** Many substances (e.g. trichloroethylene) have the ability to absorb through the skin. OELs do not account for these compound routes of entry.
- **Personal susceptibility.** The majority of the work has been based on the average male physiology from the countries in which studies were conducted. Some work has been done where specific health related effects have been noted amongst females e.g. exposure to lead compounds.
- **Adopted from American TLV.** Work done to date has been based upon exposure to individuals in the developed countries e.g. Europe and USA.
- **Variations in control.**
- **Errors in monitoring.** Measuring microscopic amounts of contamination requires very accurate and sensitive equipment. Lack of maintenance and mis-use can lead to inaccuracies in monitoring.
- **Synergistic effects.** The standards that are available relate to single substances and the effects of multiple substances in the workplace need to be considered.

REDUCING EXPOSURE LEVELS TO 'AS LOW AS IS REASONABLY PRACTICABLE'

Though OELs may be set for substances the Health and Safety at Work Act (HASAWA) 1974 and COSHH require reduction to as low as is reasonably practicable. Existing data on exposure limits may not reflect the safe levels that should be achieved to ensure the health of people exposed to substances in the workplace. It is important to review work practices and control strategies to reduce levels of exposure whenever possible. For MELs there is a statutory obligation to constantly review control strategies to ensure the lowest levels of exposure are achieved. If workplace levels of exposure are to be controlled below OELs, with confidence, it will be necessary to work below them sufficiently to account for changes in work situation. This is particularly important with MELs which must not be exceeded. An effective working limit should be set to achieve this e.g. 25% of the MEL.

16.7 - Sources of information

PRODUCT LABELS

All substances available for use in the workplace should be labelled in accordance with the Chemicals (Hazard Information Packaging for Supply) Regulations (CHIP) e.g. toxic, harmful, irritant, and corrosive.

Where a dangerous chemical is supplied in a package, the package must be labelled. Packaging must be safe and able to withstand the conditions. The label must state the hazards and precautions required.

More useful information to help ensure the safe use of dangerous substances comes in the form of risk phrases and safety phrases. These are often displayed either on the container label (if it is large enough) or in the safety data sheet. There are currently 48 risk phrases and 53 safety phrases, some examples are given below and detailed information can be found in the ACOP to C(HIP) 2.

Risk Phrase		Safety Phrase	
R3	Extreme risk of explosion by shock, friction, fire or other sources of ignition	S2	Keep out of reach of children
R20	Harmful by inhalation	S20	When using do not eat or drink
R30	Can become highly flammable in use	S25	Avoid contact with eyes
R45	May cause cancer	S36	Wear suitable protective clothing
R47	May cause birth defects	S41	In case of fire and/or explosion do not breathe fumes

Absence of hazard symbols or risk and safety advice does not mean the item is harmless.

Figure 16-12: Product labels.   *Source: Stocksigns.*

HSE GUIDANCE NOTE EH40

EH40, which is prepared and published annually by the Health and Safety Executive (HSE), contains the lists of Occupational Exposure Limits (OEL) for use with the Control of Substances Hazardous to Health Regulations (COSHH), a description of the limit setting process, technical definitions and explanatory notes. EH40 is mostly guidance but does contain sections of special legal status, some sections have been approved by the Health and Safety Commission (HSC) and are statutory requirements that must be complied with.

MANUFACTURERS' HEALTH AND SAFETY DATA SHEETS

Section 6 of HASAWA requires manufacturers, importers and suppliers to provide information on substances for use at work; this is usually provided in the form of a data sheet.   CHIP sets out the content of data sheets for substances, the content must include the following.

- Identification of the substance/preparation and the company.
- Composition/information on ingredients.
- Hazards identification.
- First-aid measures.
- Fire fighting measures.
- Accidental release measures.
- Handling and storage.
- Exposure controls/personal protection.
- Physical and chemical properties.
- Stability and reactivity.
- Toxicological information.
- Ecological information.
- Disposal considerations.
- Transport information.
- Regulatory information.

See also - Unit 17 - Physical and psychological health hazards and control - for more detail.

USE AND LIMITATIONS OF INFORMATION IN ASSESSING RISKS TO HEALTH

Information provided by manufacturers and contained within the HSE Guidance Note EH40 may be very technical and require a specialist to explain its relevance to a given construction activity.   Some substances have good toxicological information, usually gained from past experience of harm; many others have a limited amount of useful toxicological information available to guide us as to the harm it may produce.   This can lead to a reliance on data that is only our best understanding at the time and this may have to be revised as our knowledge on the substance changes.   This is reflected in the use of MELs and OESs. Individual susceptibility of workers differs by, for example, age, gender or ethnic origin.   Exposure history varies over the working life of an individual and although current exposure may not indicate, the individual may suffer due to a cumulative effect. For example, an individual may have been or be engaged in a number of processes within a variety of workplaces or personal pastimes.

16.8 - Surveys for health risks

Basic surveys

As discussed previously, the health effects of exposure to toxic substances can be acute or chronic. It will therefore be necessary to distinguish appropriate methods of measurement. When embarking upon a monitoring campaign to assess the risk to which an individual may be exposed, it is necessary to ask several questions.

1)   What to sample?

This involves a review of the materials, processes and operating procedures being used within a plant, coupled with discussions with management and health and safety personnel.   A brief 'walk-through' survey can also be useful as a guide to the extent of monitoring that may be necessary.

Hazard data sheets are also of use.   When the background work has been completed it can then be decided what is to be measured.

2)   On whom?

This depends on the size and diversity of the group that the survey relates to.   From the group of workers being surveyed the sample to be monitored should be selected; this must be representative of the group and the work undertaken.   Selecting the individual with the highest exposure can be a reasonable starting point.   If the group is large then random sampling may have to be employed, but care has to be exercised with this approach.   The group should also be aware of the reason for sampling.

3)   How long do we sample for?

There are many considerations when answering this question: what are the control limits; is the hazard acute or chronic; what is our limit of detection; or simply what resources do we have at our disposal?

4)   How do we monitor?

The particular sampling strategy, based on the hazard presented, is outlined in the following table:

Measurements to determine	Suitable types of measurement
Chronic hazard	Continuous personal dose measurement.
	Continuous measurements of average background levels.
	Short term readings of containment levels at selected positions and times.
Acute hazard	Continuous personal monitoring with rapid response.
	Continuous background monitoring with rapid response.
	Short term readings of background contaminant levels at selected positions and times.
Environmental control status	Continuous background monitoring.
	Short term readings of background contaminant levels at selected positions and times.
Whether area is safe to enter	Direct reading instruments.

Basic monitoring equipment

SHORT TERM SAMPLERS

Stain tube detectors (multi-gas/vapour)

Simple devices for the measurement of contamination on a grab (short term) sampling basis. It incorporates a glass detector tube, filled with inert material. The material is impregnated with a chemical reagent which changes colour ('stains') in proportion to the quantity of contaminant as a known quantity of air is drawn through the tube.

There are several different manufacturers of detector tubes including Dräger and Gastec.

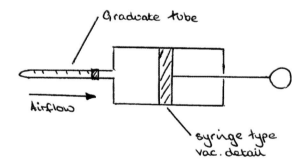

Figure 16-13: Detector tube example (hand drawn).   *Source: ACT.*

It is important that the literature provided with the pumps and tubes is followed.

These provide a quick and easy way to detect the presence of a particular airborne contaminant. However they possess inherent inaccuracies and tube manufacturers claim a relative standard deviation of 20% or less (i.e. 1ppm in 5ppm).

Types of tube construction
- Commonest is the simple stain length tube, but it may contain filter layers, drying layers, or oxidation layers.
- Double tube or tube containing separate ampoules, avoids incompatibility or reaction during storage.
- Comparison tube.
- Narrow tube to achieve better resolution at low concentrations.

The above illustrates the main types of tubes; however there are more variations and therefore it can only be re-emphasised that the manufacturer's operating instructions must be read and fully understood before tubes are used.

Pumps

There are four types:
- Bellows pump.
- Piston pump.
- Ball pump.
- Battery operated pump.

Never mix pumps and tubes of different manufacturers.

How to use Tubes
- Choose tube to measure material of interest and expected range.
- Check tubes are in date.
- Check leak tightness of pump.

- Read instructions to ensure there are no limitations due to temperature, pressure, humidity or interfering substances.
- Break off tips of tube, prepare tube if necessary and insert correctly into pump. Arrows normally indicate the direction of air flow.
- Draw the requisite number of strokes, to cause the given quantity of air to pass through the tube.
- Immediately, unless operating instructions say otherwise, evaluate the amount of contaminant by examining the stain and comparing it against the graduations on the tube.   If there is any doubt when reading the tube, always err on the safe side.
- Remove tube and discard according to instructions.
- Purge pump to remove any contaminants from inside the pump.

Advantages of short term samplers:
- Quick and easy to use.
- Instant reading without further analysis.
- Does not require much expertise to use.
- Relatively inexpensive.

Disadvantages of short term samplers:
- Tubes can be cross sensitive to other contaminants.
- Accuracy varies - some are only useful as an indication of the presence of contaminants.
- Is only a grab sample.
- Relies on operator to accurately count pump strokes (manual versions).
- Only suitable for gases and vapours (not dusts).

Direct reading dust sampler

(e.g. Tyndall Lamp)

Simple methods are by direct observation of the effect of the dust on a strong beam of light e.g. using a Tyndall Lamp. High levels of small particles of dust show up under this strong beam of light. Other ways are by means of a direct reading instrument. This establishes the level of dust by, for example, scattering of light. Some also collect the dust sample. The advantages and disadvantages are:

Advantages of direct reading dust samplers:
- Instant reading.
- Continuous monitoring.
- Can record electronically.
- Can be linked to an alarm.
- Suitable for clean room environments.

Disadvantages of direct reading dust samplers:
- Some direct reading instruments can be expensive.
- Does not differentiate between dusts of different types.
- Most effective on dusts of a spherical nature.

LONG TERM SAMPLERS

Personal samplers

Passive personal samplers

Passive samplers are so described to illustrate the fact that they have no mechanism to draw in a sample of the contaminant but instead rely on passive means to sample. As such they take a time to perform this function, for example, acting as an absorber taking in contaminant vapours over a period of a working day. Some passive samplers, like gas badges, are generally fitted to the lapel and change colour to indicate contamination.

Active personal samplers

Filtration devices are used for dusts, mists and fumes. A known volume of air is pumped through a sampling head and the contaminant filtered out. By comparing the quantity of air with the amount of contaminant a measurement is made. The filter is either weighed or an actual count of particles is done to establish the amount, as with asbestos. The type of dust can be determined by further laboratory analysis. Active samplers are used in two forms, for personal sampling and for static sampling.

Sampling head in consistent position (eg mid point on shoulder seam)

Battery operated sampling pump

Figure 16-14: Personal sampling equipment. *Source: Ambiguous.*

accuro gas detector pump
OPERATING INSTRUCTIONS

Dräger

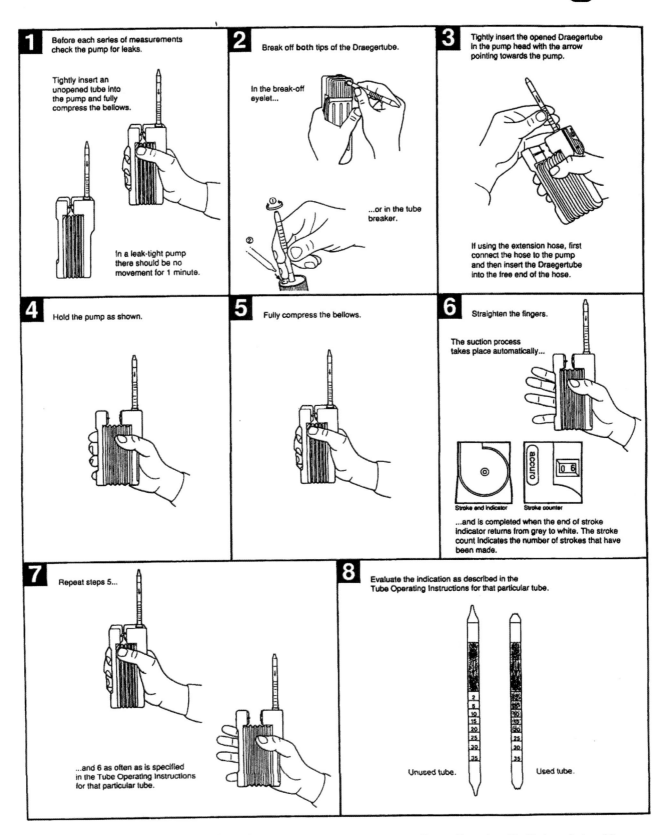

Figure 16-15: Stain tube detector operating instructions.

Source: Reproduced by kind permission of Dräger.

Static sampling

These devices are stationed in the working area. They sample continuously over the length of a shift, or longer period if necessary. Mains or battery operated pumps are used. Very small quantities of contaminant may be detected. The techniques employed include absorption, bubblers, and filtration; they are similar in principle to personal samplers, but the equipment is tailored to suit static use.

Advantages of long term samplers:
- Will monitor the workplace over a long period of time.
- Will accurately identify 8 hour time weighted average.

Disadvantages of long term samplers:
- Will not generally identify a specific type of contaminant.
- Does not identify personal exposure.
- Will not identify multiple exposure i.e. more than one contaminant.
- Unless very sophisticated, will not read peaks and troughs.

SMOKE TUBES

Smoke tubes are simple devices that generate a 'smoke' by means of a chemical reaction. A tube similar in type to those used in stain tube detectors is selected, its ends broken (which starts the chemical reaction) and it is inserted into a small hand bellows. By gently pumping the bellows smoke is emitted. By watching the smoke air flow can be studied. This can be used to survey extraction and ventilation arrangements to determine their extent of influence.

16.9 - Control measures

In the control of occupational health hazards many approaches are available, the use of which depends upon the severity and nature of the hazard. The principal control strategies are outlined below and follow the general strategy:

- Elimination or substitution.
- Process change.
- Reduced time exposure.
- Enclosure of hazards, process or people.
- Local exhaust ventilation.
- Dilution ventilation.
- Respiratory protective equipment.
- Other personal protective equipment.
- Personal hygiene.
- Health surveillance.

Elimination or substitution of hazardous substances or form of substance

ELIMINATION

This represents an extreme form of control and is appropriately used where high risk is present from such things as carcinogens. It is usually achieved through the prohibition of use of these substances. Care must be taken to ensure that all stock is safely disposed of and that controls are in place to prevent their re-entry, even as a sample or for research. If this level of control is not achievable then another must be selected.

REDUCTION

By substitution

The substitution of a less toxic substance in place of a more highly toxic one, e.g. toluene for benzene, glass fibre for asbestos, or water based adhesives for solvent based adhesives is a frequently used technique. It is also possible to substitute the form of the substance in that a substance that requires mixing from dry products, such as cement, may be ordered pre-prepared thus avoiding the additional contact with the substance in the mixing process and in the dry state where dust may be liberated. In the same way dust generated in a demolition process may be watered down so that the dust becomes liquid slurry.

Quantity

A useful approach is to reduce the actual quantity of the substance presenting the hazard. This may be achieved by limiting the amount used or stored. It may be possible to use a more dilute form than is presently being used, for example, with acids. In the case of disposal it is possible to reduce the quantity by neutralisation.

Process changes

The role of the occupational hygienist is to identify peaks in exposure to operators during their normal working day e.g. when charging or discharging process equipment - at this time higher than normal background levels of contamination may occur in the general work area. Whenever process changes occur through plant failure or maintenance, consideration needs to be given to exposure to those affected at these times. It may be necessary to re-assess the process / maintenance arrangements to ensure adequacy of health controls.

Figure 16-16: Reduced exposure – bulk supply.   *Source: ACT.*

Reduced time exposure

There is a close relationship between exposure and time. At a fixed level of contamination the effect will be proportional to the time exposed. This is the basis of occupational exposure limits, i.e. long-term exposure limits (8 hours time weighted average value) and short-term exposure limits (15 minutes weighted average value). The strategy is also encompassed in the approach to control noise exposure whereby the total noise dose over an eight hour day, 5-day week, must not exceed 90 dB(A). It may be possible to organise work so that exposure to any one person is controlled by means of job/task rotation.

Enclosure

ENCLOSURE OF HAZARDS

In its simplest sense this can mean putting lids on substances that have volatile vapours, such as tins of solvent based products. In this way the strategy is to enclose the hazard so that vapours are not given off. In this case, this is best done when the substance is not in use, this does not just mean at the end of the day but at intervals when the substance is not actually in use. It makes a very simple and effective control of exposure to hazards.

SEGREGATION OF PROCESS

This strategy is based on the containment of an offending substance or agent to prevent its free movement in the working environment. It may take a number of forms, e.g. acoustic enclosures, pipelines, closed conveyors, laboratory fume cupboards. In construction situations this is used in processes such as asbestos removal where the work being done is enclosed in plastic sheeting in order to segregate the work from the surrounding areas. In a similar way this may be for building cleaning processes using shot or for spray protection being applied to a structure.

SEGREGATION OF PEOPLE

Segregation is a method of controlling the risks from toxic substances and physical hazards such as noise and radiation. It can take a number of forms:

By distance

This is a relatively simple method where a person is separated from a source of danger by distance. It can appropriately be used in the case of noise where the risk of occupational deafness decreases as the distance from the source increases.

By age

The protection of young workers in certain trades is still valid today, a good example being lead. In this case the CLAW 2002 Regulations excludes the employment of young persons in lead processes.

By time

This involves the restriction of certain hazardous operations to periods when the number of persons present is at its smallest, for instance at weekends. An example might be the radiation of an item for non-destructive test.

By Sex

There remains the possibility of sex linked vulnerability to certain toxic substances such as lead; segregation affords a high level of control in these circumstances.

Local exhaust ventilation

GENERAL APPLICATIONS AND PRINCIPLES

Various local exhaust ventilation (LEV) systems are in use in the workplace, for example:

- Receptor hoods such as are used in fume cupboards and kilns,
- Captor hoods (used for welding and milling operations) and
- High velocity low volume flow systems e.g. as used on a grinding tool.

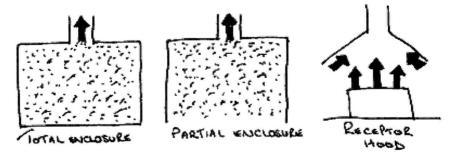

Figure 16-17: Receptor systems (hand drawn).   *Source: ACT.*

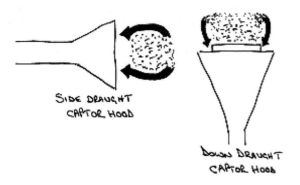

Figure 16-18: Captor systems (hand drawn). *Source: ACT*

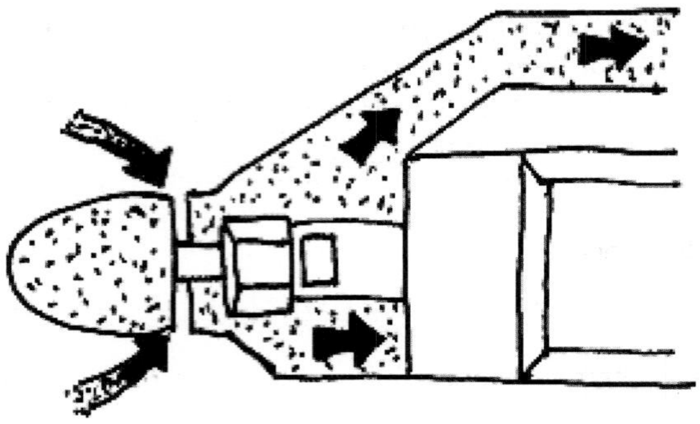

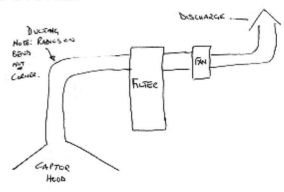

Figure 16-19: High velocity low volume system (hand drawn). *Source: ACT.*

COMPONENTS OF A BASIC SYSTEM

Figure 16-20: Components of a basic system (hand drawn). *Source: ACT.*

FACTORS THAT REDUCE A LEV SYSTEM'S EFFECTIVENESS

The efficiency of LEV systems can be affected by many factors including the following:

- Damaged ducting.
- Unauthorised alterations.
- Process changes leading to overwhelming amounts of contamination.
- Incorrect hood location.
- Fan strength or incorrect adjustment of fan.
- Too many bends in ducts.
- Blocked or defective filters.
- Leaving too many ports open.
- The cost of heating make up air.

It is vital that the pre and post ventilation contamination levels are determined and the required reduction should be part of the commissioning contract.

REQUIREMENTS FOR INSPECTION

COSHH Regulation 9(2)a and schedule 4 set out requirements for inspection of LEV systems. A thorough examination and test must take place once every 14 months (more frequently for those processes listed in schedule 4). Records must be kept available for at least 5 years from the date on which it was made.

The majority of ventilation systems, although effective in protecting workers' health from airborne contaminants, can create other hazards. One of the main hazards that needs to be considered when designing LEV systems is that of noise. Even if it has been considered as a design feature when establishing LEV systems, it should be monitored on a periodic basis.

Use and limitations of dilution ventilation

Dilution ventilation is a system designed to induce a general flow of clean air into a work area. This may be done by driving air into a work area, causing air flow around the work area, dilution of contaminants in the work area and then out of the work area through general leakage or through ventilation ducts to the open air. A variation on this is where air may be forcibly removed from the work area, but not associated with a particular contaminant source, and air is allowed in through ventilation ducts to dilute the air in the work area. Sometimes a combination of these two approaches is used, an example may be general air conditioning provided into an office environment. A particularly simple approach to providing dilution ventilation is to open a window and door and allow natural air flow to dilute the workplace air. This is not a reliable means of dealing with toxic contaminants and may be over relied on in the construction industry. On its own it may prove inadequate but supported by respiratory protection equipment it may be acceptable for some substances.

Because it does not target any specific source and it relies on dispersal and dilution instead of specific removal, it can only be used with nuisance contaminants that are themselves fairly mobile in air. Dilution ventilation systems will only deal with general contamination and will not prevent contaminants entering a person's breathing zone. Local exhaust ventilation is the preferred means of controlling a person's exposure to substances.

Dilution ventilation may only be used as the sole means of control in circumstances where there is:

- Non toxic contaminant or vapour (not dusts).
- Contaminant which is uniformly produced in small, known quantities.
- No discrete point of release.
- No other practical means of reducing levels.

Respiratory protective equipment

This equipment includes two main categories of respiratory protection:

1) Respirators.

2) Breathing Apparatus.

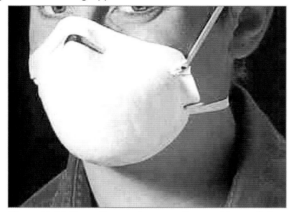

Figure 16-21: Paper filter respirator. *Source: Haxton Safety.*

Figure 16-22: Mis-use of respirator. *Source: ACT.*

Figure 16-23: Full face canister respirator. *Source: Haxton Safety.*

Figure 16-24: Breathing apparatus. *Source: Haxton Safety.*

RESPIRATORS

Respirators filter the air breathed but do not provide additional oxygen. There are a number of types of respirator that provide a variety of degrees of protection from dealing with nuisance dusts to high efficiency respirators for solvents or asbestos. Some respirators may be nominated as providing non-specific protection from contaminants whereas others will be designed to protect from a very specific contaminant such as solvent vapours.

There are five main types of respirators:

1) Filtering face piece.

2) Half mask respirator.

3) Full face respirator.

4) Powered air purifying respirator.

5) Powered visor respirator.

Advantages

- Unrestricted movement.
- Often lightweight and comfortable.
- Can be worn for long periods.

Limitations

- Purify the air by drawing it through a filter to remove contaminants. Therefore, can only be used when there is sufficient oxygen in the atmosphere.
- Requires careful selection by a competent person.
- Requires regular maintenance.
- Knowing when a cartridge is at the end of its useful life
- Requires correct storage facilities.
- Can give a 'closed in' / claustrophobic feeling.
- Relies on user for correct fit/use etc.
- Incompatible with other forms of personal protective equipment (PPE).
- Performance can be affected by beards and long hair.
- Interferes with other senses, e.g. sense of smell.

BREATHING APPARATUS

Breathing Apparatus provides a separate source of supply of air (including oxygen) to that which surrounds the person. Because of the self-contained nature of breathing apparatus it may be used to provide a high degree of protection from a variety of toxic contaminants and may be used in situations where the actual contaminant is not known or there is more than one contaminant.

There are three types of breathing apparatus:

1) Fresh air hose apparatus - clean air from uncontaminated source.

2) Compressed air line apparatus from compressed air source.

3) Self-contained breathing apparatus - from cylinder.

Advantages

- Supplies clean air from an uncontaminated source. Therefore, can be worn in oxygen deficient atmospheres.
- Has high assigned protection factor (APF). Therefore may be used in an atmosphere with high levels of toxic substance.
- Can be worn for long periods if connected to a permanent supply of air.

Limitations

- Can be heavy and cumbersome which restricts movement.
- Requires careful selection by competent person.
- Requires special training.
- Requires arrangements to monitor / supervise user and for emergencies.
- Requires regular maintenance.
- Requires correct storage facilities.
- Can give a 'closed in' / claustrophobic feeling.
- Relies on user for correct fit/use etc.
- Incompatible with other forms of PPE.
- Performance can be affected by e.g. long hair.
- Interferes with other senses. e.g., sense of smell.

SELECTION

There are a number of issues to consider in the selection of respiratory protective equipment (RPE) not least the advantages and limitations shown above. A general approach must not only take account of the needs derived from the work to be done and the contaminant to be protected from but must include suitability for the person. This will include issues such as face fit and the ability of the person to use the equipment for a sustained period, if this is required. One of the important factors is to ensure that the equipment will provide the level of protection required. This is indicated by the assigned protection factor given to the equipment by the manufacturers - the higher the factor the more protection provided. With a little knowledge it is possible to work out what APF is needed using the following formula.

$$APF = \frac{\text{Concentration of contaminant in the workplace}}{\text{Concentration of contaminant in the face-piece}}$$

It is important to understand that this factor is only an indication of what the equipment will provide. Actual protection may be different due to fit and the task being conducted.

USE

Every employee must use any personal protective equipment provided in accordance with the training and instructions that they have received.

MAINTENANCE

Where respiratory protective equipment (other than disposable respiratory protective equipment) is provided the employer must ensure that thorough examination, and where appropriate testing, of that equipment is carried out at suitable intervals.

Other protective equipment and clothing

EYE PROTECTION

When selecting suitable eye protection, some of the factors to be considered are:

Type and nature of hazard (impact, chemical, ultra violet (UV) light, etc.), type/standard/quality of protection, comfort and user acceptability issues, compatibility, maintenance requirements, training requirements and cost.

Figure 16-25: Eye and ear protection. *Source: Speedy Hire plc.*

Figure 16-26: Arc welding visor – UV reactive. *Source: ACT.*

Types	Advantages	Limitations
Spectacles	■ Lightweight, easy to wear. ■ Can incorporate prescription lenses. ■ Do not 'mist up'.	■ Do not give all round protection. ■ Relies on the wearer for use.
Goggles	■ Give all round protection ■ Can be worn over prescription lenses. ■ Capable of high impact protection. ■ Can protect against other hazards e.g. dust, molten metal.	■ Tendency to 'mist up' ■ Uncomfortable when worn for long periods. ■ Can affect peripheral vision.
Face shields (visors)	■ Gives full face protection against splashes. ■ Can incorporate a fan which creates air movement for comfort and protection against low level contaminants. ■ Can be integrated into other PPE e.g. head protection.	■ Require care in use, otherwise can become dirty and scratched. ■ Can affect peripheral vision. ■ Unless the visor is provided with extra sealing gusset around the visor, substances may go underneath the visor to the face.

PROTECTIVE CLOTHING

1) Head protection - safety helmets or scalp protectors (bump caps) - scalp protectors give limited protection and are unsuitable for confined spaces. Safety helmets have a useful life of three years and this can be shortened by prolonged exposure to ultra-violet light. There is specific legal requirement on construction sites where there is risk of injury from falling objects.

2) Protective outer clothing - normally PVC, often high visibility to alert traffic.

3) Protective inner clothing - overalls.

Figure 16-27: Gloves. *Source: Speedy Hire plc.*

Figure 16-28: Protective clothing. *Source: ACT.*

HAND / ARM PROTECTION

This area of protection is vast. There are numerous types of glove and gauntlet available that offer protection from hazards:

- Chemical hazards such as acids, alkalis etc.
- Thermal hazards such as hot surfaces.
- Mechanical hazards in the form of splinters and sharp edges.

The materials used in the manufacture of these products are an essential feature to consider when making the selection. There are several types of rubber (latex, nitrile, PVC, butyl) all giving different levels of protection against aqueous chemicals; leather affords protection against heat , splinters and cuts; space age technology in the form of kevlar (a tough, lightweight material) protects against cuts from knife blades and is used in the sleeves of jackets for those using chainsaws.

FOOTWEAR - SAFETY BOOTS / SHOES

The importance of foot protection is illustrated by the fact that around 21,000 foot and ankle injuries were reported in 1996/97. Inadequate protection and a lack of discipline on the part of the wearer commonly cause these. There are many types of safety footwear on the market, many of them offering different types of protection. It is vital that the nature of the hazard is considered when selecting appropriate footwear. Here are some common examples:

- Falling objects   -   steel toe-caps.
- Sharp objects   -   steel in-soles.
- Flammable atmospheres   -   anti-static footwear.
- Spread of contamination   -   washable boots.
- Electricity   -   rubber soles.
- Wet environments   -   impermeable wellingtons.
- Slippery surfaces   -   non-slip soles.
- Cold environments   -   thermally insulated soles.

Figure 16-29: Personal protective equipment.   *Source: ACT.*

EAR PROTECTION

See also - Unit 17 - Physical and psychological health hazards and control - for details of ear protection.

Personal hygiene and protection regimes

Personal hygiene and good housekeeping have an important role in the protection of the health and safety of the people at work. Laid down procedures and standards are necessary for preventing the spread of contamination. The provision of adequate washing / showering facilities is important to remove contamination from the body.

The provision of laundry facilities for overalls and PPE reduces the effect of contamination. Barrier creams and suitable hand protection are important considerations for chemical and biological risks.

Where personal hygiene is critical, for example, when stripping asbestos, a 'three room system' is employed. Workers enter the 'clean end' and put work clothes on, leaving by means of the 'dirty end'. When work has been completed they return by means of the 'dirty end', carry out personal hygiene and leave by means of the 'clean end'.

VACCINATION

Certain occupations, such as water treatment / sewage workers, medical profession, have a higher than average risk from some biological hazards. Staff from these occupations may need to be immunised against common high risks e.g. hepatitis B. Whilst vaccination can be an effective way of preventing ill health as a result of exposure to biological agents, it is important that employers are aware of problems that can arise. In the first instance, vaccination is intrusive.

Employers need the permission of employees before adopting this method – this may not always be forthcoming. Secondly, it is possible that some people will suffer adverse effects from the vaccination. Finally, not all diseases are treatable by vaccination and, for those that are, vaccination might not be available.

Health surveillance

The Management of Health and Safety at Work Regulations (MHSWR) 1999, Regulation 6, deals with health surveillance and gives employers a duty to provide it where it is appropriate. Further details on health surveillance are contained in other Regulations e.g. COSHH, Approved Code of Practice schedule 6.

Other than the cases stated in the COSHH schedule, surveillance may be appropriate where exposure to hazardous substances is such that an identifiable disease or adverse health effect may be linked to the exposure. There must be a reasonable likelihood that the disease or effect may occur under the particular conditions of work prevailing and that valid techniques exist to detect such conditions and effects.

The employer must keep records of surveillance in respect of each employee for at least 40 years. This requirement still applies where companies cease to trade, in which case the records must be offered to the HSE.

As part of health surveillance, noise levels and its effects should be considered. Audiometry testing should be carried out on individuals to monitor hearing levels and to scrutinise results for any signs of hearing deficiency. This means preventative action can be taken early to protect the individual and it can also highlight problems with equipment that can be corrected before any other workers are affected.

Substances for which health surveillance is appropriate		Processes
Vinyl Chloride Monomer (VCM)		In manufacturing, production, reclamation, storage, discharge, transport, use or polymerization.
Nitro or amino derivatives of phenol and of benzene or its homologues		In the manufacture of nitro or amino derivatives of phenol and of benzene or its homologues and the making of explosives with the use of any of these substances
1-Napthylamine and its salts Orthotolidine and its salts	Dianisidine and its salts Dichlorbenzidene and its salts	In manufacture, formation or use of these substances
Auramine	Magenta	In manufacture
Carbon Disulphide Disulpher Dichloride Benzene, including benzol	Carbon Tetrachloride Tricholoroethylene	Process in which these substances are used, or given off as a vapour, in the manufacture of indiarubber or of articles or goods made wholly or partially of indiarubber
Pitch		In manufacture of blocks of fuel consisting of coal, coal dust, coke or slurry with pitch as a binding substance.

Figure 16-30: Schedule 6 medical surveillance

Source: COSHH AcoP.

16.10 - Control of asbestos

Identification

Asbestos is a generic term for a number of silicates of iron, magnesium, calcium, sodium and aluminium which appear naturally in fibrous form. Asbestos is defined as any of the following minerals ... "crocidolite, amosite, chrysotile, fibrous anthophyllite, fibrous actinolite, fibrous tremolite and any mixture containing any of the said minerals".

The three common forms are often referred to by colour;

- Chrysotile, known as "white asbestos", which in the pure form looks like dirty cotton wool.
- Crocidolite, or "blue asbestos", because of its sky blue appearance in the pure form.
- Amosite, a dirty grey/brown coloured fibrous mineral, also known as "brown" asbestos.

Assessment

Before any work with asbestos is started the employer must ensure a thorough assessment of the likely exposure is carried out. Such an assessment must identify the type of asbestos involved in the work, or to which the employees are likely to be exposed. For the purposes of the identification requirement the employer may assume that the asbestos is asbestos other than chrysotile alone, i.e. can assume the worst case scenario and provide for the situation accordingly. The assessment must also determine the nature and degree of any exposure and the steps required to prevent or reduce the exposure to the lowest level reasonably practicable.

Assessments must be reviewed regularly and when there is reason to suspect that the original assessment is invalid or there is a significant change in the work to which the original assessment related, assessments should be revised accordingly to take account of any such changes.

Figure 16-31: Asbestos label. *Source: Scaftag.*

Requirements for removal

NOTIFICATION

The enforcing authority must be notified of any work to which these Regulations apply at least 28 days prior to commencement of the work (a lesser time may be agreed by mutual consent). Significant changes must also be notified, although work carried out in accordance with *ASLIC Regulations 1983* is exempt from this provision, as are work situations where the exposure is not likely to exceed the 'action level'.

In these Regulations 'action level' is defined as "one of the following cumulative exposures to asbestos over a continuous 12 week period", when measured or calculated by a method approved by the Health and Safety Commission (HSC):

a) Where the exposure is solely to chrysotile, 72 fibre hours per millilitre of air.

b) Where exposure is to any other form of asbestos either alone or in mixtures (including chrysotile mixtures), 48 fibre hours per millilitre of air.

c) Where both types of exposure occur separately during the 12 week period, a proportionate number of fibre hours per millilitre of air.

PLAN OF WORK

Employers must also prepare a suitable 'plan of work' before any work involving asbestos removal from buildings, structures, plant or installations (including ships) is undertaken. Such 'plans of work' must be retained for the duration of the work. The 'plan of work' should address the location, nature, expected duration and asbestos handling methods involved with the work, and the characteristics of the protection and decontamination equipment for the asbestos workers and the protection equipment for any others who may be affected by such work. The asbestos risk assessment and plan of work must be kept on site.

LICENSING

Any work involving asbestos is subject to the CAWR. However, if the work involves thermal insulation boards or asbestos coatings then it must be licensed by the Health and Safety Executive.

Control measures

RESPIRATORY EQUIPMENT AND PROTECTIVE CLOTHING

Employers must ensure that any measures provided to control the risks of exposure from asbestos are properly used or applied so far as is reasonably practicable. Likewise employees have a duty to use any control measures provided in the proper manner and to report any defects immediately. All control measures, including respiratory protective equipment (RPE), must be maintained in a clean and efficient condition and a suitable record of the work carried out in accordance with this provision must be kept for five years. RPE must be tested and examined and should be face-fit tested to the user (ACOP requirement).

Where protective clothing is required to be provided to reduce the risks of exposure it must be either safely disposed of as asbestos waste, or adequately cleaned at certain intervals, after use in the specified manner. The spread of asbestos from one place to another must be prevented or reduced to the lowest level that is reasonably practicable.

It must be remembered that personal protective equipment is last in the hierarchy of controls and that exposure must, wherever reasonably practicable, be controlled by engineering methods.

AIR MONITORING

A monitoring programme must be set up to record the efficiency of the control measures in reducing or preventing exposure to asbestos. Suitable records of the monitoring results must be kept for at least five years.   Laboratories carrying out clearance tests and personal sampling must be accredited to EN 45001.

MEDICAL SURVEILLANCE

Where employees are exposed to asbestos above the 'action level', the employer is obliged to keep health records for the affected persons. Such records must be kept for at least 40 years. Employees who are exposed to asbestos above the 'action level' are also required to undergo medical surveillance. Medical examinations prior to employment and then at intervals not exceeding two years must be provided by the employer who will keep a certificate issued by the Employment Medical Adviser or appointed doctor of all such examinations in the individual's file. The employer is also obliged to provide the appropriate facilities that enable medical examinations to be carried out. Original medical certificates (not copies) must be given to workers.

REQUIREMENTS FOR DISPOSAL

Only carriers who are licensed by the Environment Agency (EA) may carry asbestos waste. Carriers must give the EA three days notice of the intention to move the waste. On receipt of a small fee, the EA will issue a consignment note to authorise the movement of the waste directly to the landfill site. (Note - unless the carrier is authorised to do so, the waste must not be stored en route to the disposal site). Landfill sites must have a licence issued by the EA to receive asbestos waste.

16.11 - Environmental issues

BASIC ENVIRONMENT ISSUES

A definition of pollution

"The introduction into the environment of substance or energy liable to cause hazards to human health, harm to living resources and to ecological systems, damage to structures or amenity or interference with the legitimate use of the environment."

Environmental pollution is a major issue today with the industrialised countries of the world concerned about the long term effects on Earth's resources and on plant, animal and human life. Major concerns on health are often blamed on pollution and there are many pressure groups that focus on environmental issues, particularly pollution.

The problem of pollution is not new, it has been with us since Roman times and the land around old lead mines is still contaminated with the heavy metal today. Since the industrial revolution industry has relied on the capacity of the environment to dilute and disperse pollutants by discharging them to the ground, water and air. This has left a legacy of polluted areas, land pollution being the most persistent, but the discharges to air and water are more global in their effect.

An example of an intentional release of pollution is the emission of sulphur dioxide (SO_2) and nitrogen oxides (NOx) into the atmosphere by coal-fired power stations. This example also illustrates the global, as well as local, impact that such emissions have which, in this case, results in acid rain falling in Scandinavia, a country which emits very little sulphur dioxide itself. A further impact by the same power station is caused by the carbon dioxide emissions that lead to global warming.

The local effects of the emission of particulates and sulphur dioxide is illustrated by the London smogs of the 1950s, and more recently by the increase in road traffic - many cities in Britain now have pollutants above recommended limits, especially in warm, still conditions.

Plant failure and accidents can lead to abnormal releases following higher than expected temperatures and pressures.   This has led to a loss of process control with uncontrolled venting to the environment. Lack of control can lead to losses e.g. overfilling.

Waste disposal, effluent and atmospheric pollution control

PHYSICAL AND CHEMICAL WASTE TREATMENT

The aim of physical and chemical treatment of wastes is to minimise the environmental impact. Physical treatment techniques include settling, sedimentation, filtration, flotation, evaporation and distillation (e.g. the separation of oil and water using settlement lagoons or the recovery of solvents by distillation). Chemical conversion processes, such as flue gas desulphurisation, change the chemical make-up of the substance making it more compatible with the environment. In this latter case, the conversion of sulphur dioxide into gypsum can render the waste inert with little or no environmental impact. Other techniques include:

- Making soluble wastes insoluble.
- Destroying toxicity (e.g. oxidation of cyanides).
- Neutralisation of acids and alkalis.

The majority of waste techniques of this type relate to waterborne contamination and particularly the Water Industry. It should be noted that treated wastes will still require final disposal of solid residues (e.g. water treatment residues).

Landfill and land raising sites

Landfill sites play a crucial role in waste management alongside other methods such as incineration, waste minimisation and recycling techniques. A landfill site is a complex engineering, technical and commercial project that requires thorough planning and high standards of management to ensure that it is successful throughout its lifetime, which may be up to 50 years or more. A land-raising site involves the filling of a natural geographical depression such as a valley. Land raising sites can have all the problems, which are discussed below, as can occur with a landfill site.

Legislation relating to landfill sites

Any person wishing to operate a landfill site must comply with the relevant legislation and also obtain a waste management licence from the Environment Agency.

Sections 33, 35-43 and 54 of the EPA 1990 provide for a new system of waste management licensing. The objective of the waste management licensing system is to ensure that waste management facilities do not cause pollution of the environment, do not cause harm to human health and do not become seriously detrimental to the amenities of the locality.

Incineration

Incineration falls under two main categories; the burning of:

1. Municipal solid wastes (MSW).
2. Hazardous wastes.

The principle of incineration of MSW is to reduce the volume of waste by burning it under controlled conditions in order to reduce volume/mass for final disposal. The heat produced can also be used as an energy source (as a fuel MSW wastes are about 30-40% that of industrial bituminous coal). Incineration is the only really secure environmental option for most pathogens, inflammable liquids and carcinogens such as PCBs or dioxins. Thus this option represents a suitable treatment/disposal for a waste stream if combustion or application of high temperature destroys or transforms it. Thus its potential as an environmental hazard is reduced. About 2% of controlled waste destined for disposal in the UK is incinerated. There are two main types of incinerator-thermal and catalytic.

Recycling or composting

The National Waste Strategy published in May 2000 sets a target of recovering 40% of municipal waste by 2005 and of recycling or composting 17% of household waste by 2003, rising to 25% by 2005. The EPA 1990 requires waste collection authorities to draw up plans for recycling household and commercial waste and empowers waste disposal authorities to pay recycling credits as a result of waste collected for recycling by waste collection authorities.

RELEASE AND DISPERSION OF TOXIC SUBSTANCES TO GROUND, WATER OR AIR

Releases to ground

The surface of the planet is made up of materials including rocks, gravels, sands, clays and soils, which are present in many combinations. Superimposed on these are the various ecosystems which combine to produce a complex system which is therefore not easy to characterise. Glacial action has formed the landscape as the ice age retreated. Rivers, floods, earthquakes, volcanoes, winds, and all forms of life shape the surface of the planet. Each country has unique forms and habitats which provide for the great diversity of life on the planet. Human life results in waste being generated and depending on how these are deposited pollution of the land can occur. As we have mainly populated the land masses, it is these that have traces of pollution dating back to ancient times. Some typical pollutants and their effects include the following:

Contaminant	Hazard Pathway	Harmful Effects
Heavy metals	Ingestion	May cause respiratory cancers, emphysema and other lung disorders, kidney dysfunction and birth defects (teratogenicity).
Zinc, copper, nickel	Phytotoxicity	Can stunt plant growth, cause discoloration, shallow root system and die back.
Sulphate and sulphides	Contact with buildings	Can corrode and accelerate the weathering of services and structural components.

Releases to water

Water is present on the planet in all three of its phases; that is, as a solid, liquid and gas. Most water vapour is found within the atmosphere; the oceans store most of the water in its liquid phase and the poles and high alpine regions store water in the form of ice. Water moves between each of these three states by processes such as evaporation, condensation, melting and freezing. Operating together these are known as the hydrological cycle and these processes make a major contribution to the weather of the planet. Over 97% of all water on Earth is salt water. Of the 3% that is fresh water 77.5% is locked up in the ice caps and glaciers. The atmosphere, rivers, lakes and underground stores hold less than 1%. The largest volumes of freshwater are held in the Great Lakes of North America.

In terms of water pollution it is the water in its liquid phase that is of most interest. This water appears in the oceans of the world, rivers, lakes, streams and lochs. Water is also stored in its liquid phase in the ground and is referred to as **groundwater**. It is defined as water which occupies the earth's mantle and which forms the sub surface section of the hydrological cycle. An aquifer is a layer of permeable rock, sand or gravel that absorbs water and allows it free passage through the interstices of the rock.

Water pollutants

One way of thinking about pollution is too much of something in the wrong place and therefore there are many potential water pollutants. This fact is recognised within the European Community by the listing of **Black** and **Grey List** materials, sometimes called List I and List II substances. Black List or List I substances are considered to be so toxic, persistent or bio accumulative in the environment that priority should be given to eliminating pollution by them. This includes substances such as organohalogens, organophosphorous, cyanide, cadmium and mercury and their compounds. Sheep-dip and solvents are included in this list. The Grey List or List II covers those substances considered less harmful when discharged to water. Included here are metals such as zinc, nickel, chromium, lead, arsenic and copper. Also included are various biocides and substances such as phosphorus and its compounds and ammonia (which is present in sewage effluent).

Diffuse and point sources

A diffuse source of pollution is one which is spread over a wide area, an example of which is the use of fertilisers over wide areas. Nitrate pollution from fertilisers represent a significant pollutant to rivers, coastal areas and seas. A discharge from an industrial sewer represents an example of a point source. Pollution from diffuse sources is more significant than from point sources and is much more difficult to control.

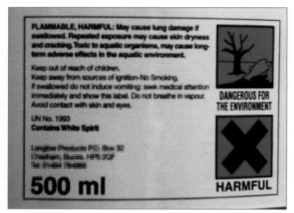

Figure 16-32: Hazard label - environment. *Source: ACT.*

Figure 16-33: Environmental hazard controlled. *Source: ACT.*

Figure 16-34: Measures to control pollution. *Source: ACT.*

Figure 16-35: Measures to control pollution. *Source: ACT.*

Releases to air

The atmospheric system

The atmosphere of the planet is a complex fluid system of gases and suspended particles. Five gases - nitrogen, oxygen, argon, carbon dioxide and water vapour make up 99.9% of the total volume of the atmosphere. The balance is made up of suspended particles such as water droplets, dust and soot, and the minor gases. Into this system a range of pollutants are released.

Atmospheric pollutants

Sulphur dioxide The major source of sulphur dioxide is the combustion of fossil fuels containing sulphur. These are predominantly coal and fuel oil, since natural gas, petrol and diesel fuels have a relatively low sulphur content.

Suspended particulate matter The main source of primary man-made particulate pollutants is combustion of fossil fuels, especially coal. Power stations use large tonnages of coal. There has been a massive decrease in urban concentrations of smoke. The main source of black smoke in urban air in the UK is diesel engined road vehicles.

Oxides of nitrogen The most abundant nitrogen oxide in the atmosphere is nitrous oxide, N_2O, and this is formed by natural microbiological processes in the soil. It is not normally considered as a pollutant, although it does have an effect upon stratospheric ozone concentrations and there is concern that use of nitrogenous fertilisers may be increasing atmospheric levels of nitrous oxide. The main concerns are nitric oxide, NO, and nitrogen dioxide, N_2O, which together are called NOx. The major source of NOx is in high temperature combustion processes.

Carbon monoxide The main source of this pollutant is petrol engined road vehicles. Car exhaust gases contain several per cent carbon monoxide under normal running conditions, and greater amounts when cold and choked.

Hydrocarbons The major sources of hydrocarbons in air are the evaporation of solvents and fuels, and the partial combustion of fuels.

Carbon dioxide Increasingly CO_2 is viewed as an air pollutant because of its importance as a "greenhouse gas". Its source lies in animal and plant respiration, and anoxic decomposition processes. It may be both absorbed and released by the oceans. Fossil fuel combustion receives a lot of attention but it is a minor source. However a small imbalance in the CO_2 cycle is leading to a steady increase in atmospheric concentration.

Ozone: Ozone is a naturally occurring gas in the atmosphere and is important in the upper reaches because it forms a protective layer (the ozone layer) to filter out potentially harmful rays from the sun.

"Holes" in the ozone layer have been discovered at both North and South poles and severe thinning over large parts of North America and Europe - people living in these areas suffer from a greater risk of skin cancer due to increased ultra violet exposure. In addition plant and aquatic life can be affected with corresponding problems for the whole food chain. A range of chemicals containing chlorine or bromine primarily causes the ozone depletion. ***Chlorofluorocarbons (CFCs)*** are in this group and, when they react with radiation from the sun, release chlorine that reacts with and destroys ozone. However the chlorine is not destroyed and can go on to repeat the process up to 100,000 times. Other ozone depleting gases include Halons and Carbon tetrachloride.

Principal duties of Parts I & II of the Environmental Protection Act

The main legislation relating to environmental protection and management is the EPA and the key parts are:

Part 1: Integrated Pollution Control and Air Pollution Control   Part II: Waste on Land

The EPA was introduced in 1990 partially in response to European Union pressures but partly because of perceived needs in the UK to update the Control of Pollution Act 1974 (CoPA) (much of which has never been implemented) and to introduce 'prior approval' together with a more integrated approach.

The main features of the EPA affecting industry are:

- The introduction of Integrated Pollution Control (IPC) and Air Pollution Control by Local Authorities (LAAPC).
- The classification of Part A - EA and Part B - LAAPC processes, depending on the type of material being processed and size of facility.
- Provision to make regulations defining prescribed substances.
- Best Available Techniques Not Entailing Excessive Cost (BATNEEC) EPA s.7.
- Best Practicable Environmental Option (BPEO). In IPC Applications operators must show that their chosen abatement technique represents the BPEO.

The powers of the EA are affected by:

1)   Part B processes in regard to air pollution control being dealt with by local authorities.

2)   Their relationship with the HSE - there are potential problems over the COSHH Regulations and extracting workplace pollutants and venting to atmosphere directly.

MEANING OF ENVIRONMENTAL TERMS

The Environmental Protection Act introduced the concepts of ***Integrated Pollution Control (IPC)*** and ***Local Authority Air Pollution Control (LAAPC)***. The aim is to ensure that wastes are disposed of so as to minimise the impact on all three environmental media (air, water and ground), by achieving the optimum environmental solution. This approach is the basis of the term ***'Best Practicable Environmental Option' (BPEO)*** which is a key element of Integrated Pollution Control. As a first step towards a new system of IPC, HM Inspectorate of Pollution (HMIP) was established in April 1987.

The new framework provided a centralised control regime by HMIP for the most polluting industrial processes and a system of Local Authority Air Pollution Control (LAAPC) for smaller, less polluting industries and businesses. Under IPC, pollution from industries with the potential to produce significant harmful discharges is considered as a whole and is subject to a single authorisation. The authorisation originally granted by HMIP is now granted by the Environment Agency body, which was set up to develop a consistent and cohesive approach to all media.

The main objectives of IPC are:

- To prevent or minimise the release of prescribed substances and to render harmless any such substances which are released
- To develop an approach to pollution control that considers discharges from industrial processes to all media in the context of the effect on the environment as a whole.

Thus it provides for a "one stop shop" on pollution control.

IPC applies to any process that is a prescribed process as listed in the ***Environmental Protection (Prescribed Processes and Substances) Regulations***. These are deemed to be the most potentially harmful or polluting when released into the environment. These fall into the broad industry sectors as follows:

- Fuel and power industry.
- Waste disposal industry.
- Minerals industry.
- Chemical industry.
- Metals industry.
- Other.

No prescribed process may be operated without an authorisation from the Environment Agency (EA). The prescribed processes are categorised as either Part A processes for which EA authorisation is required, or Part B processes for smaller, less polluting processes which emit pollutants to the air and which are authorised by the Local Authority. In setting the conditions within an authorisation, S.7 of the EPA places the EA under a duty to ensure that the following objectives are met:

■ That the **Best Available Technique Not Entailing Excessive Cost (BATNEEC)** is used to prevent, or if that is not practicable, to minimise the release of prescribed substances, and to render harmless prescribed substances that are released.
■ That releases do not cause, or contribute to, the breach of any EU or international obligations relating to environmental protection, or any statutory environmental quality standards or objectives.
■ BPEO is achieved.

The conditions in the authorisation must ensure that all these objectives are met and conditions imposed may include training, abatement techniques and other conditions relating to the operation. Releases are regulated by conditions that explicitly limit the substances that can be released both in terms of their concentration and the total amount.

Guidance on what constitutes BATNEEC for each description of a prescribed process is given in the Chief Inspector's Guidance Notes. These notes have a common format and include:

■ Introduction and definition of the process.
■ General requirements for new and existing plant.
■ Release limits to air, water and land which can be achieved by the application of BATNEEC and BPEO to the process.

Annexes cover:

■ A description of the process and plant used.
■ A list of the most likely prescribed substances.
■ The techniques for pollution abatement.
■ Monitoring necessary to demonstrate compliance with discharge consents.
■ Additional requirements e.g. training, contingency planning.

Releases are regulated and consents given explicitly limiting the substances that can be released both in terms of their concentration in the releases and the total amount of the substances released.

EPA includes requirements for public involvement in the decision-making process. There is a provision that requires consultation with statutory bodies. All applications must be advertised locally and representations made by the public must be taken into account. The Act provides for a system of public registers containing the applications and authorisations, together with any additional detail. These are located at regional EA offices. The EA may initiate a variation of an authorisation, which, if substantial, will normally require public participation. S.4(9) places a duty on the Chief Inspector to keep abreast of new developments in pollution abatement technology. If the operator introduces any plant changes or modifications, the EA must be notified so as to ascertain any changes in the type or amounts of substances released. The EA must also be notified if an accidental release or problem occurs. Enforcement notices can be served on an operator.

Local Authority (LA) Air Pollution Control

LAAPC applies to prescribed processes which can potentially pollute the air, but which are not prescribed for IPC. As these controls are concerned only with air pollution, BPEO does not apply. The basic controls are the same as for IPC, but the regulatory body is the local authority. In granting authorisations, local authorities are required to set conditions requiring the use of BATNEEC.

The **Pollution Prevention Control Act** repealed Part I of the EPA.

In essence, there are three tiers of control. Companies which have processes designated as Part B (LAAPC) have seen the biggest changes, as their processes are now to be listed as Part A(2) and they will have to apply for integrated permits covering all three media. They will continue to deal with the LA for air emissions, but they will also need to obtain authorisation from the EA for emissions to water. The new definitions are as follows:

Process to be designated as	Currently called	Regulator under IPPC
Part A(1)	Part A	EA
Part A(2)	Part B (LAAPC), but now covered by IPPC Directive Annex I	LAs/EA
Part B	Part B (LAAPC) not in Directive Annex 1	Las

Part B processes under the new regulations will continue much as before, maintaining the scope and requirements of the existing LAAPC regime. Those processes which come under Part A (2) are larger Part B processes, and are capable of more pollution emissions to different mediums.

There are a number of other major changes relating to noise, emissions which "cause offence to any human senses" (e.g. odours), waste sites including site contamination reports as well as other proposals covering enforcement powers, charging mechanisms, triviality arrangements and standard permit conditions.

Physical & psychological health hazards & control

Overall aims

On completion of this unit, candidates will understand:

■ the ill-health effects of the physical process of work and of the working environment.

■ the available control options to combat these risks in the workplace.

Content

Specific Intended Learning Outcomes

The intended learning outcomes of this Unit are that candidates will be able to:

17.1 explain the term 'ergonomics' and the contribution that ergonomic design can make to health, safety and efficiency at work

17.2 identify work processes and practices that may give rise to musculoskeletal health problems (in particular work-related upper limb disorders - WRULDs) and suggest appropriate control measures

17.3 describe the health effects associated with exposure to noise and suggest appropriate control measures

17.4 describe the health effects associated with exposure to vibration and suggest appropriate control measures

17.5 describe the principal health effects associated with ionising and non-ionising radiation and outline basic protection techniques

17.6 explain the causes and effects of stress, violence and drug use at work and suggest appropriate control actions

Sources of Reference

A Pain in Your Workplace? Ergonomic Problems and Solutions (HSG121), HSE Books

Safe Use of Work Equipment (ACOP) (L22), HSE Books

The Workplace (Health, Safety and Welfare) Regulations 1992 (ACOP) (L24), HSE Books

Personal Protective Equipment at Work (L25) HSE Books

Guidance on the Noise at Work Regulations (L108), HSE Books

Lighting at Work (HSG38), HSE Books

Work-related Upper Limb Disorders - A Guide (HSG60)-HSE Books

Hand-arm Vibration (HSG88), HSE Books

Tackling Work-related Stress (HSG218), HSE Books

Relevant Statutory Provisions

The Construction (Health, Safety and Welfare) Regulations (CHSW) 1996

The Health and Safety (Display Screen Equipment) Regulations (DSE) 1992

The Provision and Use of Work Equipment Regulations (PUWER) 1998

The Noise at Work Regulations (NWR) 1989

The Personal Protective Equipment at Work Regulations (PPER) 1992

The Ionising Radiations Regulation (IRR) 1999

17.1 - Task and workstation design

The principles of ergonomics as applied to the workplace

The study of ergonomics is essential to good job design. It can be defined as 'the study of the relationship between man, the equipment with which he works and the physical environment in which this man-machine system operates'.

It is a broad area of study that includes the disciplines of psychology, physiology, anatomy and design engineering. Ergonomics has man at the centre of the study where his capabilities and fallibilities are considered in order to, ultimately, eliminate the potential for human error. It is also the study of ways to prevent the so-called 'ergonomic illnesses' - work-related musculoskeletal disorders. These areas of ill health may lead to disability. They stem from poorly designed machines, tools, task and workplace. Research has shown that there are about one million cases of work-related musculoskeletal disorders annually in England and Wales.

Man works within certain boundaries which must be recognised for all situations. However, even when human beings work within their limitations, there will still be degradation in performance. Why, when and how degradation occurs needs to be understood in order to make allowances for or to remedy the situation.

The aims of ergonomics, therefore, are to design the equipment and the working environment to fit the needs and capabilities of the individual, i.e. fitting the task to the individual, and to ensure that the physical and mental well-being of the individual are being met. This involves a consideration of psychological and physical factors, including the work system, training, body dimensions, intelligence, noise, temperature and lighting.

The design of the human body is basically uniform, allowing for differences of sex. The spine, joints, tendons and muscles work in the same way and will suffer also the same abuse, although to a varying extent. Individuals, therefore, have different physical capabilities due to height, weight, age and levels of fitness. They also have different mental capabilities, memory retention and personalities.

The ill-health effects of poorly designed tasks and workstations

The body will be affected, more or less, by tasks, which involve bending, reaching, twisting, repetitive movements and poor posture. These can lead to a variety of effects commonly known as work related upper limb disorders or WRULDS.

Some common WRULDs are:

Carpel Tunnel Syndrome	CTS occurs when tendons or ligaments in the wrist become enlarged, often from inflammation, after being aggravated. The narrowed tunnel of bones and ligaments in the wrist pinches the nerves that reach the fingers and the muscles at the base of the thumb. The first symptoms usually appear at night. Symptoms range from a burning, tingling numbness in the fingers, especially the thumb and the index and middle fingers, to difficulty gripping or making a fist, to dropping things.
Tenosynovitis	An irritation of the tendon sheath. It occurs when the repetitive activity becomes excessive and the tendon sheath can no longer lubricate the tendon. As a result, the tendon sheath thickens and becomes aggravated.
Tendinitis	Tendinitis involves inflammation of a tendon, the fibrous cord that attaches muscle to bone. It usually affects only one part of the body at a time, and usually lasts a short time, unless involved tissues are continuously irritated. It can result from an injury, activity or exercise that repeats the same movement.
Peritendinitis	Inflammation of the area where the tendon joins the muscle.
Epicondylitis	Tennis Elbow or Lateral Epicondylitis is a condition when the outer part of the elbow becomes painful and tender, usually because of a specific strain, overuse, or a direct bang. Sometimes no specific cause is found. Tennis Elbow is similar to Golfer's Elbow (Medial Epicondolytis) which affects the other side of the elbow.

The aches, pains and fatigue suffered doing certain tasks will eventually impair the operator's ability and lead to degradation in performance. It is therefore essential to consider the task in order to match it to the individual so the level of general comfort is maximised. For example, when carrying out manual handling assessments it is important to look at the relationship between the individual, the task, the load and the environment.

WORK RELATED UPPER LIMB DISORDERS [WRULD]

Were first defined in medical literature as long ago as the 19th century as a condition caused by *forceful, frequent, twisting and repetitive movements*. WRULD covers well-known conditions such as tennis elbow, flexor tenosynovitis and carpal tunnel syndrome. It is usually caused by the conditions detailed above and aggravated by excessive workloads, inadequate rest periods and sustained or constrained postures, the result of which is pain or soreness to the inflammatory conditions of muscles and the synovial lining of the tendon sheath. Present approaches to treatment are largely effective, provided the condition is treated in its early stages. Clinical signs and symptoms are local aching pain, tenderness, swelling, crepitus (a grating sensation in the joint).

The factors and risk activities giving rise to ill-health conditions

TASKS

Tasks should be assessed to determine the health risk factors.

If the task is *repetitive* in nature, i.e. the same series of operations are repeated in a short period of time, such as ten or more times per minute, then injury may occur to the muscles and ligaments be affected.

Similarly, work of a *strenuous* nature, such as moving heavy or difficult shaped objects, perhaps in limited space or hot environments, will cause fatigue, strains and sprains.

ENVIRONMENT

Poor working environments. Working in *extremes of temperature* or handling hot or cold items will make simple work more strenuous. Long hours of work in cold conditions causes problems with blood circulation which, in turn, may increase the likelihood of hand arm vibration syndrome. Fatigue will also occur to the eyes if the *lighting* levels are low, typically below 100-200 lux. or bright, typically greater than 800 lux. Other lighting factors may need to be considered such as the stroboscopic effects associated with moving machinery, which may appear to be stationary when viewed under fluorescent light powered by alternating current.

The risk of injury increases with the *length of time* that a task is carried out. However, injury may occur over a short period if the work requires a lot of effort.

Working in *uncomfortable positions* such as working above head height or holding something in the same place for a long period of time increases the risk of injury.

There is robust scientific evidence of an association of increases in selected respiratory health effects with building dampness or visible mould. These health effects are asthma exacerbation in sensitized individuals, and cough, wheeze, and upper respiratory symptoms in otherwise healthy individuals.

Dampness in buildings is a concern because it often leads to growth of molds and bacteria and to increased emissions of chemicals. In addition, dampness causes structural degradation on buildings. Building dampness problems have a number of causes. The report argues that the way to reduce these problems and the risk of associated health effects is to improve the design, construction, operation, and maintenance of buildings.

Poor posture. The position of the body and the way it has to move to carry out a particular function. This can be affected by such things as: badly designed work methods (e.g. the need for regular bending or twisting), and poor layout of the workplace (e.g. having to kneel or stretch to put articles in a cupboard).

Figure 17-1: Posture. *Source: Speedy Hire Plc.*

EQUIPMENT

All work factors that influence health issues should be under the influence of the operator as much as possible, such as the ability to adjust temperature and lighting, and the opportunity to take rest breaks. If this is not possible with continuous automated lines, such as with car assembly, then work should be designed to provide facilities for operators' work patterns to be rotated to reduce these effects. Consideration to automation should be given whenever possible.

Equipment design should take into account the ergonomic requirements of the operator and, where possible, allow the user to adjust any settings to suit his/her needs. Such things as workbench height and positioning of switches and buttons should be in the operator's control.

Preventative and precautionary measures

PREVENTATIVE

Control measures
- Improved design or working areas.
- Provision of special tools.

PRECAUTIONARY

General
- Better training and supervision.
- Adjustment of workloads and rest periods.
- Health surveillance aimed at early detection.

Figure 17-2: Working area. *Source: ACT.*

Information and Training

(Regulations 6 and 7 - Health and Safety (Display Screen Equipment) Regulations

Should include:
- Risks to health.
- Precautions in place (e.g. the need for regular breaks).
- How to recognise problems.
- How to report problems.

17.2 - Noise

The effects on hearing of exposure to noise

The ear senses **Sound**, which is transmitted in the form of pressure waves travelling through a substance, e.g., air, water, metals etc. Unwanted sound is generally known as **Noise.**

The ear has 3 basic regions (see Figure 13.1):

a)   The **outer** ear channels the sound pressure waves through to the ear drum.

b)   In the **middle** ear, the vibrations of the eardrum are transmitted through three small bones (hammer, anvil and stirrup) to the inner ear.

c)   The cochlea in the **inner** ear is filled with fluid and contains tiny hairs (nerves) which respond to the sound. Signals are then sent to the brain via the acoustic nerve.

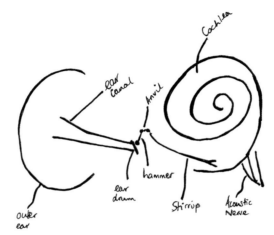

Figure 17-3: The ear.   *Source: ACT.*

Excessive noise over long periods of time can cause damage to the hairs (nerves) in the cochlea of the ear. This results in **noise induced hearing loss (deafness)**, which can be of a temporary or permanent nature. Also, a single high pressure event can damage the ear, by dislocation of a bone or rupturing the ear drum.   It has been shown that high levels of noise can cause, or increase the onset of, **tinnitus** ('ringing in the ears').

The meaning of common sound measurement terms

SOUND POWER AND PRESSURE

For noise to occur power must be available. It is the sound power of a source (measured in Watts) which causes the sound pressure (measured in Pascals) to occur at a specific point.

INTENSITY AND FREQUENCY

The amplitude of a sound wave represents the intensity of the sound pressure. When measuring the **amplitude** of sound there are two main parameters of interest, as shown in Figure 17-2. One is related to the energy in the sound pressure wave and is known as the 'root mean square' (rms) value, and the other is the 'peak' level. We use the rms sound pressure for the majority of noise measurements, apart from some impulsive types of noise when the peak value is also measured.

Sound (noise) waves travel through air at the **'speed of sound'** which is approximately equal to 344 m/s. A sound can have a **'frequency'** or **'pitch'**, which is measured in cycles per second (Hz).

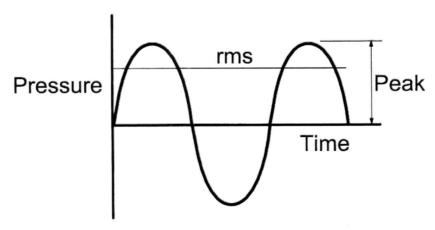

Figure 17-4: Rms and peak levels of a sound wave.   *Source: ACT.*

THE DECIBEL SCALE

The ear can detect pressures over a very wide range, from 20 µPa to 20 Pa (Pascals). To help deal with this wide range, the **deciBel (dB)** is used to measure noise. A decibel is a unit of sound pressure (intensity) measured on a logarithmic scale from a base level taken to be the threshold of hearing (0dB). Typical noise levels include:

Source	dB
Disco	110
Smoke detector at 1 metre	105
Machine Shop	90
Radio in average room	70
Library	30
Threshold of Hearing	0

A problem with deciBels is that they are based on a logarithmic scale and cannot be added together in the conventional way, for example:

$$2 \, dB + 2 \, dB = 5 \, dB \qquad \text{(deciBel Arithmetic)} \textbf{ and}$$

$$90 \, dB + 90 \, dB = 93 \, dB \qquad \text{(deciBel Arithmetic)}$$

The term dB(A)

The human ear can hear sound over a range of frequencies, from 20 Hz up to approximately 20000 Hz (20 kHz). However, the ear does not hear the same at all frequencies; it naturally reduces (attenuates) low frequencies and very high frequencies. To take account of the response of the ear measured sound levels are usually **'A weighted'**. A weighted is a weighting added to a noise meter reading (by electronic filters) to represent the way the ear hears sound of different frequencies. Hence, the term **dB(A).** The majority of measurements are made in terms of dB(A), although there are other weightings that are used in some circumstances.

The range of frequencies that we encounter is often divided into **Octave Bands**. A noise can be measured in each octave band and these levels can be used when assessing the attenuation of hearing protectors, or when diagnosing noise problems.

Other noise units

In most situations the noise level varies with time. When measuring noise we need to determine the average, or 'equivalent continuous level', over a period of time. This is known as the **Leq**. Not all noise meters include an **Leq** function. Other noise units commonly encountered are also listed below:

L_{eq} the average, or 'equivalent continuous level'

$L_{EP,d}$ daily personal exposure level, dB(A). This is equivalent to the L_{eq} over an 8 hour working day. The $L_{EP,d}$ is directly related to the risk of hearing damage.

L_{peak} peak pressure - pascals or dB

Action levels and simple noise measurement techniques

FIRST ACTION LEVEL

Where the $L_{EP,d}$ is above 85dB(A) but below 90 dB(A), the employer should ensure that:

- Regular assessments of noise levels are carried out by a competent person.
- Employees are informed about the risks to hearing, how to minimise those risks and the use of PPE.
- Ear protectors must be freely available on demand. (It is not a legal duty for employees to use ear protection below the second action level but there is a duty on employers to make it available).

SECOND ACTION LEVEL

Where the $L_{EP,d}$ is above 90 dB(A), the employer should ensure that:

- Regular assessments of noise levels are carried out by a competent person.
- Employees are informed about the risks to hearing and how to minimise those risks.
- Ear protection zones are identified and clearly marked.
- Employees (and others entering the marked zones) are provided with ear protection and are compelled to wear it.

In addition, where the action levels apply, employers must seek to reduce noise levels at source by engineering means. (See "Noise Control Techniques")

Figure 17-5: Noise hazard sign.   *Source: ACT.*

Figure 17-6: Mandatory signs.   *Source: Stocksigns.*

SIMPLE NOISE MEASUREMENT TECHNIQUES

Noise is measured using a sound level meter, which works in simple terms by converting pressure variations into an electric signal. This is achieved by capturing the sound with a microphone, pre-amplification of the resultant voltage signal and then processing the signal into the information required dependent on the type of meter (e.g. 'A' weighting, integrating levels, fast or slow response). The microphone is the most important component within the meter as its sensitivity and accuracy will determine the accuracy of the final reading. Meters can be set to fast or slow response depending on the characteristics of the noise level. Where levels are rapidly fluctuating, rapid measurements are required and the meter should be set to fast time weighting.

Sound level meters should be calibrated using a portable acoustic calibrator and batteries checked before, during and after each measurement session. Laboratory calibration should be carried out annually or according to the manufacturer's instructions. Meters are used to measure the:

- Sound pressure level (L_p) - the intensity of sound at a given moment in time at a given position (i.e. the instantaneous level): an unweighted linear measurement dB (L_{in}).
- Equivalent continuous sound level (L_{eq}) - an average measure of intensity of sound over a reference period, usually the period of time over which the measurement was taken. Measured in dB(A). As the intensity and spacing of the noise levels usually vary with time, an integrating meter is used. This meter automatically calculates the L_{eq} by summing or integrating the sound level over the measurement period.
- Peak pressure level - some sound level meters produce peak pressure values for impulsive noise or where a fast time weighting reading exceeds 125 dB(A).

The expense and time consuming nature of personal dosimetry means that they should only be used when other techniques are unsuitable. It is used in situations where the task of the worker involves movement around the workplace and exposure is likely to vary.

Typical sources of high levels of noise in construction work

PNEUMATIC DRILL

This is a heavy-duty piece of equipment that produces high intensity and pitch vibrations commonly used in construction or street works for operations that involve breaking up hard surfaces made of tarmac or concrete. When in use the noise generated is amplified by the chisel impacting against the material being drilled. An additional factor associated with pneumatic drilling equipment is the plant required providing the power source, usually diesel-powered compressors. This additional item of plant produces noise and vibrations from the engine, exhaust system, high pressure air release and quite often loose body shells. Exposure is partly controlled by the fact that this equipment is usually operated out-doors so noise dissipates easily. Users of pneumatic drills and its associated equipment should wear hearing protection.

WOODWORKING MACHINERY

Woodworking machinery can be in the form of heavy duty fixed workshop equipment or also portable / mobile equipment for use on site. It is used for cutting, moulding, drilling or sanding various types of wood. Noise is generated through rotating parts originating from electrical motors, bearings, spindles and cutting tools. When in use the noise is amplified by cutting tools coming into contact with the material being worked upon and resulting in high frequency vibrations. Noise can also be amplified through poorly maintained equipment / cutting tools, equipment cases, or bases that are not dampened. Woodworking machinery would usually be accompanied with signs enforcing the mandatory requirement to wear ear protection in defined ear protection zones. Operators should wear hearing protection.

Figure 17-7: Noise from pneumatic drill. *Source: Speedy Hire Plc.*

PILING

Piling operations take place on construction sites for the purposes of providing deep foundations for steel structures. The most common method of piling involves the use of a guide 'tube' in which a heavy solid 'driving piece' supported by lifting equipment is released down the guide tube causing the material it strikes to displace upon impact and thus create a cavity when withdrawn. This operation is repeated until the required depth of bore is achieved. Another method involves a steel liner being mechanically 'hammered' into the ground to the required depth. Noise is generated through impact between the driving piece and the ground or steel liner tube resulting in a low frequency, high magnitude noise for short momentary bursts. The noise can be amplified through the driving tool striking the steel liner tube, and the vibrations passing through the ground. An additional factor associated with piling equipment is the plant required providing the power source, usually diesel-powered engines. This additional item of plant produces noise and vibrations from the engine, exhaust system, associated motors and quite often, loose body shells. Operatives involved with piling equipment should wear hearing protection.

CONSTRUCTION PLANT

Construction plant is varied but all types produce noise of differing magnitudes and frequencies as indicated in the previous paragraphs. Typically the types of plant found on construction sites are as follows:

- Excavation equipment - restricted movement excavators, 360 degree excavators, piling equipment.
- Materials handling equipment - all terrain fork lift truck, dumper trucks.
- Manual operations with plant - compactors, pneumatic drills, disc saw.
- Mixing equipment.
- Heavy goods vehicles and site traffic - supplier lorries, concrete mixers, vans.
- Generator, compressor and pumping equipment.
- Demolition equipment - pincer jaws, demolition ball, crusher.

The noise produced by the items of plant identified above have various generation sources that can include rotating shafts or tools, impact, engine and exhaust vibration, intended vibration (compaction equipment), electrical motors, crushing. Operators of plant in general will wear ear defenders due to their proximity to the noise source. The environment should be considered when implementing techniques for noise control due to noise being carried through the atmosphere and causing nuisance to the general population. Construction sites can have site boundary fences installed to act as a barrier to the noise. However it is always better to combat the noise hazard at source.

Figure 17-8: Crusher.   *Source: ACT.*

Figure 17-9: Disc saw.   *Source: ACT.*

Basic noise control techniques

NOISE CONTROL TECHNIQUES

Noise can be controlled at different points in the following 'chain':

1)   The source (e.g., a noisy machine).

2)   The path (e.g., through the air).

3)   The receiver (e.g., the operator of a machine).

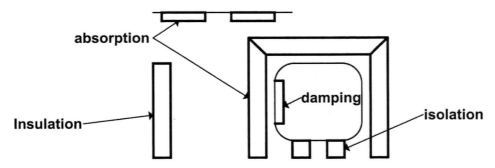

Figure 17-10: Basic layout of the main control methods.   *Source: ACT.*

The main methods of noise control are listed below:

Isolation   Positioning an elastic element (e.g. rubber mount etc.) in the path of vibration can isolate a noise radiating area from a vibration input.

Absorption   When noise passes through porous materials (e.g. foam, mineral, wool etc.) some of its energy is absorbed.

Insulation   Imposing a barrier (e.g., a brick wall, lead sheet etc.) between the noise source and the receivers will provide noise insulation.

Damping   Mechanical vibration can be converted into heat by damping materials (e.g. metal/plastic/metal panels).

Silencers   Pipe/boxes can be designed to reduce air/gas noise (e.g. engine exhaust silencers, duct silencers, etc.).

Other specialist control methods (NOT examinable):

Force Reduction - Reduce impacts by using rubber pads or lower drop heights.

Air exhaust and jet silencers - Proprietary silencers can be used.

Active - Equal but opposite phase noise can cancel a problem noise

In addition to controlling the amplitude of noise the **exposure level** can be reduced by minimising the amount of time an employee is exposed to noise, for example, by job rotation. Increasing the distance between noisy equipment and a work location can reduce the noise to which an employee is exposed. When buying new plant and equipment employers should adopt a purchasing policy which results in the quietest machines being bought.

Figure 17-11: Silenced diesel welder.   *Source: Speedy Hire Plc.*

Personal hearing protection

All types of personal ear protector should carry a CE marking.

PURPOSE

The purpose of personal hearing protection is to protect the user from the adverse effects on hearing caused by exposure to high levels of noise. All hearing protection must be capable of reducing exposure to below the second action level. (90dB over 8 hours).

APPLICATION AND LIMITATIONS OF VARIOUS TYPES

Earmuffs:

1)   Banded.

2)   Helmet mounted.

3)   Communication muffs.

Advantages:

- Worn on the outside of the ear so less chance of infection.
- Clearly visible therefore easy to monitor.
- Can be integrated into other forms of PPE e.g. head protection.

Limitations:

- Can be uncomfortable when worn for long periods.
- Incompatibility with other forms of PPE.
- Effectiveness may be compromised by e.g. long hair, spectacles etc.
- Requires correct storage facilities and regular maintenance.

Ear Plugs:

1)   Pre-moulded.

2)   User formable.

3)   Custom moulded.

4)   Banded plugs.

Advantages:

- Easy to use and store - but must be inserted correctly.
- Available in many materials and designs, disposable
- Relatively lightweight and comfortable. Can be worn for long periods.

Limitations:

- They are subject to hygiene problems unless care is taken to keep them clean.
- Correct size may be required. Should be determined by a competent person.
- Interferes with communication.
- Worn inside the ear, difficult to monitor.

Figure 17-12: Ear defenders.   *Source: ACT.*

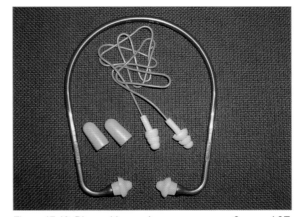

Figure 17-13: Disposable ear plugs.   *Source: ACT.*

SELECTION

When selecting personal hearing protectors employers must take into consideration several factors, including:

- Provision of information and training.
- Readily available.
- Comfort and personal choice.

- Issue to visitors.
- Care and maintenance.
- Noise reduction.

USE

All PPE should be used in accordance with employer's instructions, which should be based on manufacturer's instructions for use. PPE should only be used after adequate training has been given. Also, adequate supervision must be provided to ensure that training and instructions are being followed. Personal ear protection may not provide adequate protection due to any of the following reasons:

a)   Long hair, spectacles, earrings etc, may cause a poor seal to occur.

b)   Ear protectors are damaged, e.g., cracked.

c)   Not fitted properly - due to lack of training.

d)   Not wearing ear protectors all of the time.

e)   Specification of protectors does not provide sufficient attenuation.

MAINTENANCE

Employers have a legal duty to ensure that any PPE is maintained in an efficient state, efficient working order and good repair. Simple maintenance can be carried out by the trained wearer, but more intricate repairs should only be done by specialist personnel.

ATTENUATION FACTORS

The attenuation (noise reduction) associated with personal ear protectors must be supplied with the product. The information required is in terms of:

1) Octave band mean attenuation and the standard deviation.   **2)** HML (High, Medium and Low) values.   **3)** SNR (Single Number Rating) values.

Control of environmental noise nuisance

Construction sites are naturally noisy workplaces due to the wide range and volume of operations taking place involving both light and heavy plant and equipment. Operations can include demolition, excavation & piling, compressors, generators, mixing equipment, manual operations, power tools, etc. Noise generated can vary in frequency and magnitude and due to the open nature of construction sites can escape outside the site boundaries. Employers have a duty to control noise and protect workers and any other person from its effects including causing noise nuisance to the local environment.

Noise should be as far as is reasonably practicable reduced at source in order to reduce exposure to the wider population. Prior planning should include identifying potential sources of noise that will be situated at site in order to implement counter measures to eliminate or reduce the impact. The following should be considered:

- Design of the project and all processes involved.
- Alternative methods and processes.
- Phasing of operations to take into account different trade operations.
- Requirements and restrictions imposed by local authorities.
- Location of the construction, boundaries, and sensitivity of surrounding area.
- Layout of the site including entrances, plant & equipment, fixed processes etc.
- Hours of work, shift patterns and duration of noisy periods.
- Noise control measures (site screens, relocation of noisy operations, time restrictions, ppe).

17.3 - Vibration

Effects of exposure to vibration

HARM TO HEALTH

Occupational exposure to vibration may arise in a number of ways, often reaching workers at intensity levels disturbing to comfort, efficiency and health and safety. There are two routes of vibration energy transmission. In the case of whole body vibration it is transmitted to the worker through a contacting or supporting structure which is itself vibrating, e.g. a ship's deck, the seat or floor of a vehicle (tractor or tank), or a whole structure shaken by machinery (e.g. in the processing of coal, iron ore or concrete), where the vibration is intentionally generated for impacting. By far the most common route of entry to the human body is through the hands, wrists and arms of the subject - so called segmental vibration, where there is actual contact with the vibrating source.

Figure 17-14: Use of road drill - vibration.   *Source: ACT.*

Prolonged intense vibration transmitted to the hands and arms by vibrating tools and equipment can lead to a condition known as **hand-arm vibration syndrome (HAVs).** These are a range of conditions relating to long term damage to the circulatory system, nerves, soft tissues, bones and joints. Probably the best known of these conditions is known as vibration white finger (VWF). Here the fingers go white and numb (known as ***Raynaud's phenomenon***), leading to 'pins and needles' and an often painful deep red flush. This seems to occur in response to a change in metabolic demand in the fingers induced, for example, by temperature change. It seems that the blood vessels are unable to dilate either at all or rapidly enough because of the thickened tissues that then become anoxic (lacking in oxygen).

CONTRIBUTORY FACTORS

As with all work-related ill health there are a number of factors which when combined result in the problem occurring. These include:-

- Vibration frequency - frequencies ranging from 2- 1500 Hz are potentially damaging but the most serious is the 5-20 Hz range.
- Duration of exposure - this is the length of time the individual is exposed to the vibration.
- Contact Force - this is the amount of grip or push used to guide or apply to the tools or work piece. The tighter the grip the greater the vibration to the hand.
- Factors affecting circulation - including temperature and smoking.
- Individual susceptibility.

Examples of risk activities

- The use of hand-held chain saws in forestry.
- The use of hand-held rotary tools in grinding or in the sanding or polishing of metal, or the holding of material being ground, or metal being sanded or polished by rotary tools.
- The use of hand-held percussive metal-working tools, or the holding of metal being worked upon by percussive tools in riveting, caulking, chipping, hammering, fettling or swaging.
- The use of hand-held powered percussive drills or hand-held powered percussive hammers in demolition, or on roads or footpaths, including road construction.

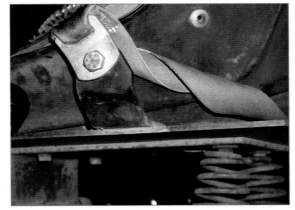

Figure 17-15: Dumper truck seat.　　　*Source: ACT.*

The medical effects are in the main more serious and permanent and are summarised below:

a) Vascular changes in the blood vessels of the fingers.

b) Neurological changes in the peripheral nerves.

c) Muscle and tendon damage in the fingers, hands, wrists and forearms.

d) Suspected bone and joint changes.

e) Damage to the autonomic centres of the central nervous system in the brain influencing the endocrine, cardiac, vestibular and cochlear functions (not proven).

WHOLE BODY VIBRATION (WBV)

WBV is caused by machinery vibration passing through the buttocks of seated people or the feet of standing people. The most widely reported WBV injury is back pain. Prolonged exposure can lead to considerable pain and time off work and may result in permanent injury and having to give up work. High-risk activities include driving site vehicles (e.g. dumper trucks) and the prolonged use of compactors.

Preventative and precautionary measures

Protective measures are the only means of protecting people who work with vibrating machinery. The following controls should be considered:

PREVENTIVE

- The need for such machinery should be reviewed so as to eliminate unnecessary operations.
- Consideration should be given to the automation of processes.
- Wearing gloves is recommended for safety and for retaining heat. They will not absorb a significant fraction of the vibration energy which lies within the 30-300Hz range. There is also the danger that the absorbent material used in glove manufacture may introduce a resonance frequency and therefore the total energy input to the hands may be increased (Bednall, Health and Safety Executive 1988). There have been recent reports of patented composite materials that, when moulded into hand-grips and fitted onto vibrating power tools, reduce vibration by 45%.
- The greater the coupling (hand and tool interface), the more energy enters the hand. Increasing grip force increases the coupling. There are working techniques for all tools and the expertise developed over time justifies an initial training period for new starters.
- Operators with established HAVS should avoid exposure to cold and thus minimise the number of blanching attacks. Operators with advanced HAVS who are deteriorating (as measured by annual medical checks) should be removed from further exposure. The medical priority is to prevent finger tip ulceration (tissue necrosis).

PRECAUTIONARY

- The vibration characteristics of the hand tools in the works should be assessed and reference made to the BSI and ISO Guidelines.
- The work schedule should be examined to reduce vibration exposure either by alternating with non-vibration work or avoiding continuous vibration by, for example, scheduling ten minute breaks every hour.
- Carry out a detailed ergonomic assessment of hazardous tasks (e.g. breaking asphalt with a road breaker). This should include duration and frequency of the task.
- Development of a purchasing policy to include consideration of vibration and, where necessary, vibration isolating devices.
- Training of all exposed employees on the proper use of tools and the minimisation of exposure.
- Establish a routine health surveillance programme. Operators of vibrating equipment should be trained to recognise the early symptoms of HAVS and WBV and how to report them.

- Tools should be maintained to their optimum performance thereby reducing vibration to a minimum (e.g. the bearings of grinders).
- A continuous review with regard to the redesigning tools, rescheduling work methods, or automating the process until such time as the risks associated with vibration are under control.
- As with any management system, the controls in place for vibration should include audit and review.

17.4 - Temperature and radiation

The body generates heat energy by the conversion of foodstuffs; energy is generated through muscle action. At rest, typically 80 watts of energy is produced, whereas during heavy physical exercise perhaps 500 watts is produced. The body loses (exchanges) heat energy by the process of sweat evaporation, conduction contact of the feet with the floor and by radiation (infra red energy loss).

Extremes of temperature

Exposure to the effects of cold temperature relies on high calorie diet, physical exercise and suitable protective clothing. Clothing should have a high tog rating 20 - 25 tog, and prevent absorption of water and be suitably fastened to reduce the effects of wind chill. The feet should be insulated to avoid loss through conduction. The head should be covered to the maximum extent to avoid excessive heat loss. Clothing should be light and white in colour to prevent heat loss through radiation.

Exposure to the effects of heat may be minimised by suitable clothing, such as light and loose or reflective clothing if working with very hot sources of heat. Issues such as conduction from hot surfaces and movement of heat will need to be considered. Consideration will need to be given to humidity levels and workload.

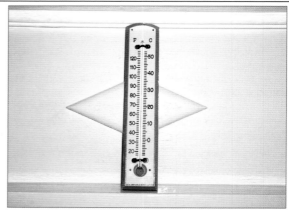

Figure 17-16: Workplace temperature.   *Source: ACT.*

EFFECTS

People working outside their thermal comfort range can suffer a dramatic loss of efficiency e.g. hot metal process working, working in refrigerated warehouses, working outdoors. The precise effects will depend upon the type of work being carried out, the rate of air movement (wind chill) and temperature and humidity. The main effects of working at high and low temperatures are outlined as follows:

General Effects

Cold
- Loss of concentration in mental work.
- Reduced manipulative powers in manual work.
- Discomfort caused by shivering.

Hot
- Loss of concentration.
- Reduced activity rate.
- Discomfort caused by sweating.

Heat Stress

Heat syncope	-	fainting due to vasodilation
Heat rash or 'prickly heat'	-	skin disorder
Heat exhaustion	-	fatigue, nausea, headache, giddiness
Anhidrotic heat exhaustion	-	insufficient moisture to sweat
Heat cramps	-	painful spasms of muscles - insufficient salt
Heat stroke	-	breakdown of control mechanisms, body temperatures soar, immediate cooling of body temperature required, otherwise death ensues

Cold

- Hypothermia.
- Frost bite.

- Trench foot.
- Violent shivering.

RELEVANT FACTORS

One of the fundamental mechanisms by which the body regulates its temperature is by perspiration. Key factors which aid or hinder this process are airflow and humidity. Humidity relates to the moisture content in the air. Air with a relatively high humidity has little capacity to cool the body by 'wicking' away sweat whereas low relative humidity can cause dry skin and has been identified as a possible factor in facial dermatitis (occasional itching or reddened skin) reported by some Display Screen Equipment users. Industries and occupations particularly susceptible to extremes of temperature include foundries, cold stores, those who carry out hot work (e.g. burning and welding) or work in confined spaces where temperatures are often uncomfortably high. Likewise, those who work outdoors can be subject to extreme weather conditions. In winter the strength of the wind can significantly affect the temperature (windchill).

PREVENTIVE MEASURES

Steps that employers should consider to reduce the effects of extremes of temperature should include: regular work breaks with fluid intake. Improved ventilation and humidity control, screening, suitable clothing. In the case of cold stores, removal of ice, improved lighting and the provision of anti-locking in devices.

Ionising and non-ionising radiation

IONISING RADIATION

Radiation is emitted by a wide range of sources and appliances used throughout industry, medicine and research. It is also a naturally occurring part of the environment.

All matter is composed of **atoms**. Different atomic structures give rise to unique **elements**. Examples of common elements, which form the basic structure of life, are hydrogen, oxygen and carbon.

Atoms form the building blocks of nature and cannot be further sub divided by chemical means. The centre of the atom is called the **nucleus**, which consists of **protons** and **neutrons**. Electrons take up orbit around the nucleus.

Protons - Have a unit of mass and carry a positive electrical charge.

Neutrons - These also have mass but no charge.

Electrons - Have a mass about 2000 times less than that of protons and carry a negative charge.

In an electrically neutral atom the number of electrons equals the number of protons (the positive and negative charges cancel out each other). If the atom loses an electron then a positively charged atom is created. The process of losing or gaining electrons is called **ionisation**. If the matter which is ionised is a human cell, the cell chemistry will change and this will lead to functional changes in the body tissue. Some cells can repair radiation damage, others cannot. The cell's sensitivity to radiation is directly proportional to its reproductive function; bone marrow, and reproductive organs are the most vulnerable.

"Ionising radiation is that radiation which has sufficient energy to produce ions by interacting with matter".

Figure 17-17: Ionising radiation.   *Source: ACT*

Ionising radiation found in industry are alpha, beta and gamma, and X-rays. Whilst X-rays may occur in nature generally they are created in the work place either with knowledge, e.g. X-ray machines or sometimes without knowledge from high voltage equipment. The human body absorbs radiation readily from a wide variety of sources, mostly with adverse effects.

Types of ionising radiation

(Note. For the purpose of the NEBOSH National Certificate in Construction Safety and Health, you do not need to understand the differences between types of ionising radiation.)

There are a number of different types of ionising radiation each with their different powers of penetration and effects on the body. Therefore, the type of radiation will determine the type and level of protection.

Alpha particles

Are comparatively large. Alpha particles travel short distances in dense materials, and can only just penetrate the skin. The principal risk is through ingestion or inhalation of a source e.g. radon of alpha particles which might place the material close to vulnerable tissue; when this happens the high localised energy effect will destroy tissue of the organ/s affected.

Beta particles

Are much faster moving than alpha particles. They are smaller in mass than alpha particles, but have longer range, so they can damage and penetrate the skin. Whilst they have greater penetrating power than alpha, beta particles are less ionising and take longer to effect the same degree of damage.

Gamma rays

Have great penetrating power. Gamma radiation passing through a normal atom will sometimes force the loss of an electron, leaving the atom positively charged; this we call an **ion**.

X-rays

Are very similar in their effects to gamma rays. X-rays are produced by sudden acceleration or deceleration of a charged particle, usually when high-speed electrons strike a suitable target under controlled conditions. The electrical potential required to accelerate electrons to speeds where X-ray production will occur is a minimum of **15,000 volts**. X-rays and gamma rays have **high energy**, and **high penetration** power through fairly dense material. In low density substances, including air, they may travel long distances.

Potential health effects

The effects on the body of exposure to ionising radiation will depend on the type of radiation, the frequency and duration of exposure. Acute effects will include nausea, vomiting, diarrhoea and burns (either superficial skin burns or deep, penetrating burns causing cell damage). Long term (chronic) effects such as dermatitis, skin ulcers, cataracts and cancers can also be expected.

NON IONISING RADIATION

Generally, non-ionising radiation does not possess sufficient energy to cause the ionisation of matter. Radiation of this type includes ultraviolet, visible, infra-red, micro and radio waves. Artificially-produced laser beams are a special case.

Types of non-ionising radiation

Ultraviolet

Possible sources. There are many possible sources of Ultra Violet (UV) radiation to which people may be exposed at work

- The sun.
- Electric arc welding.
- Insect killers.
- Sunbeds and sunlamps.
- Crack detection equipment.

- Tanning and curing equipment.
- Forgery detectors.
- Some lasers.
- Mercury vapour lamps.
- Tungsten halogen lamps.

Potential effects. Much of the natural ultraviolet in the atmosphere is filtered out by the ozone layer. Sufficient penetrates to cause sunburn and even blindness. Its effect is thermal and photochemical, producing burns and skin thickening, and eventually skin cancer. Electric arcs and ultraviolet lamps can produce an effect by absorption on the conjunctiva of the eyes, resulting in "arc-eye" and cataract formation.

Visible light (including lasers)

Possible sources. Any high intensity source of visible light can cause problems. Lasers are an obvious danger but so are light beams, powerful light bulbs and the sun. The danger is always due to direct or reflected radiation.

Potential health effects. Light in the visible frequency range can cause damage if it is present in sufficiently intense form. The eyes are particularly vulnerable but skin tissue may also be damaged. Indirect danger may also be created by employees being temporarily dazzled.

Infra-red

Possible sources. Anything that glows is likely to be a source of IR radiation, for example:

- Furnaces or fires.
- Molten metal or glass.
- Burning or welding.
- Heat lamps.
- Some lasers.
- The sun.

Potential health effects. Exposure results in a thermal effect such as skin burning and loss of body fluids (heat exhaustion and dehydration). The eyes can be damaged in the cornea and lens which may become opaque (cataract). Retinal damage may also occur if the radiation is focused.

RADIO-FREQUENCY AND MICROWAVES

Possible sources. This type of radiation is produced by radio/television transmitters. It is used industrially for induction heating of metals and is often found in intruder detectors.

Potential health effects. Burns can be caused if persons using this type of equipment allow parts of the body which carry jewellery to enter the radio frequency field. Intense fields at the source of transmitters will damage the body and particular precautions need to be taken to isolate radio/television transmitters to protect maintenance workers. Microwaves can produce the same deep heating effect in live tissue as they can produce in cooking.

Figure 17-18: UV - from welding. *Source: Speedy Hire Plc.*

Figure 17-19: Radio mast. *Source: ACT*

Typical occupational sources of ionising and non-ionising radiation

SOURCES OF IONISING RADIATION

The most familiar examples of ionising radiation in the workplace are in hospitals, dentist surgeries and veterinary surgeries where X-rays are used extensively. X-ray machines are used for security purposes at baggage handling points in airports. In addition, Gamma rays are used in non-destructive testing of metals, for example, site radiography of welds in pipelines.

In other industries ionising radiation is used for measurement, for example, in the paper industry the thickness of paper, and in the food processing industry for measuring the contents of sealed tins.

SOURCES OF NON-IONISING RADIATION

- Infra-red (any hot body gives off this type of radiation):
  - The sun.
  - Molten steel or steel processes.
  - Oxyacetylene welding and cutting.
  - Road and road marking burning equipment.
  - Bitumen heating equipment.
  - Brick ceramic manufacture.

- Ultra-violet
  - The sun.
  - Arc welding and cutting.
  - Adhesive curing processes.
  - Water treatment.
- Microwave
  - Telecommunications.
  - Cooking equipment.
- Visible radiation
  - Lasers, for example, in surveying or level alignment equipment
  - and other high intensity lights such as photocopiers and printers.
- Radio frequency
  - Overhead power lines.
  - Plastic welding.
  - High powered transmitters.

The basic means of controlling exposures to ionising and non-ionising radiation

CONTROLS FOR IONISING RADIATION

Preventive measures

Reduced time

Reducing the duration of exposure through redesigning work patterns. Giving consideration to shift working, job rotation etc. The dose received will also depend upon the time of the exposure. These factors must be taken into account when devising suitable operator controls.

Increased distance

Radiation intensity is subject to the inverse square law. Energy received *(dose)* is inversely proportional to the square of the distance from the source.

Shielding

The type of shielding required to give adequate protection will depend on the penetration power of the radiation involved. For example, it may vary from thin sheets of silver paper to protect from Beta particles through to several centimetres of concrete and lead for protection against Gamma or X-rays. In addition to the previous specific controls, the following general principles must be observed:

- Radiation should only be introduced to the work-place if there is a positive benefit.
- Safety information must be obtained from suppliers about the type(s) of radiation emitted or likely to be emitted by their equipment.
- Safety procedures must be reviewed regularly.
- Protective equipment provided must be suitable and appropriate, as required by relevant Regulations. It must be checked and maintained regularly.
- Emergency plans must cover the potential radiation emergency.
- Written authorisation by permit should be used to account for all purchase/use, storage, transport and disposal of radioactive substances.

Precautionary measures

Basic radiation protection strategies include the application of the principles of time, distance and shielding. Exposure should be limited to as few as possible and those individuals should be monitored and exposure levels maintained within limits. Where possible only sealed sources should be used and a system developed to minimise dose levels to individuals. This work must be under the control of the radiation protection advisor.

Radiation protection advisers (RPA)

With the exception of the operations specified in Schedule 1 of the IRR, at least one radiation protection adviser (RPA) must be appointed in writing by employers using ionising radiation. The numbers of RPA appointed must be appropriate to the risk and the areas where advice is needed is to be stated. Employers must consult the RPA on:

- The implementation of controlled and supervised areas.
- The prior examination of plans for installations and the acceptance into service of new or modified sources of ionising radiation in relation to any engineering controls, design features, safety features and warning devices provided to restrict exposure to ionising radiation.
- The regular calibration of equipment provided for monitoring levels of ionising radiation and the regular checking that such equipment is serviceable and correctly used.
- The periodic examination and testing of engineering controls, design features, safety features and warning devices and regular checking of systems of work provided to restrict exposure to ionising radiation.

Adequate information and facilities must be provided by the employer to the RPA in order to allow them to fulfil their functions.

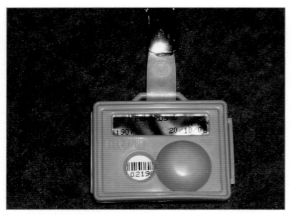

Figure 17-20: Personal dose monitor.   *Source: ACT.*

Figure 17-21: Contamination monitoring.   *Source: ACT.*

CONTROLS FOR NON-IONISING RADIATION

Ultra-violet

Protection is relatively simple; sunbathers may use simple barrier creams. That emitted from industrial processes can be isolated by physical shielding such as partitions or plastic curtains; some plastic materials differ in their absorption abilities and care needs to be taken in selection. Users of emitting equipment, such as welders, can protect themselves by the use of goggles and protective clothing - the latter to avoid "sunburn". Assistants often fail to appreciate the extent of their own exposure, and require similar protection.

Visible light

Is detected by the eye which has two protective control mechanisms of its own, the eyelids and the iris. These are normally sufficient, as the eyelid has a reaction of 150 milliseconds. There are numerous sources of high-intensity light which could produce damage or damaging distraction, and sustained glare may also cause eye fatigue and headaches. Basic precautions include confinement of high-intensity sources, matt finishes to nearby paint-work, and provision of optically-correct protective glasses for outdoor workers in snow, sand or near large bodies of water.

Infra-red

Radiation problems derive from thermal effects and include skin burning, sweating and loss of body salts leading to cramps, exhaustion and heat stroke. Clothing and gloves will protect the skin, but the hazard should be recognised so that effects can be minimised without recourse to personal protective equipment.

Radio-frequency and microwaves

Radiation can usually be shielded to protect the users. If size and function prohibits this, restrictions on entry and working near an energised microwave device will be needed. Metals, tools, flammable and explosive materials should not be left in the electromagnetic field generated by microwave equipment. Appropriate warning devices should be part of the controls for each such appliance.

17.5 - Stress violence and drugs at work

Stress

CAUSES

Causes of stress can be divided into two groups:

1)   Environmental.   **2)**   Psychological.

Environmental stressors are things such as

- Bodily injury.
- Noise.
- Extremes of temperature.
- Poor lighting.

Psychological stressors include

- Periods of intense mental activity.
- Being unable to achieve what is required.
- Physical or social isolation.
- Conflicting demands.
- Personal problems.

EFFECTS OF STRESS

Being exposed to stressful situations brings about changes in behaviour and also physical well being.

Physical effects
- Increased heart rate.
- Increased sweating.
- Headache.
- Dizziness.
- Blurred vision.
- Aching neck and shoulders.
- Skin rashes.
- Lowered resistance to infection.

Behavioural effects
- Increased anxiety.
- Irritability.
- Increased alcohol intake.
- Increased smoking.
- Erratic sleep patterns.
- Poor concentration.
- Feeling of inability to cope with everyday tasks.

This can result in

- Lack of motivation.
- Lack of commitment.
- Poor timekeeping.
- Increase in mistakes.
- Increase in sickness absence.
- Poor decision making.
- Poor planning.

Stress is reflected in relationships at work as

- Tension between colleagues/supervisors.
- Poor service to clients.
- Deterioration in industrial relations.
- Increase in disciplinary problems.

PREVENTION STRATEGIES

General management and culture

- Clear company objectives.
- Close employee involvement.
- Training and development of staff.
- Good communication.
- Good management support.

Relationships at work

- Training in interpersonal skills.
- Effective systems for dealing with conflict, harassment etc.

Job design

- Well defined tasks and responsibilities.
- Proper use of skills.
- Targets that are stretching but achievable.
- Plenty of variety.
- Proper hazard control.
- Planned and agreed work areas.

Violence

RISK FACTORS

People who deal directly with the public may face aggressive or violent behaviour. They may be sworn at, threatened or even attacked. In addition, it is necessary to consider possible violence between employees. Construction activities can carry quite a lot of pressure to conduct work within strict, often pressured, time tables. This can lead to a good deal of tension that might result in violence.

"any incident in which a person is abused, threatened or assaulted in circumstances relating to their work".

Figure 17-22: Definition of work related violence. *Source: HSE*

Verbal abuse and threats are the most common types of incident. Physical attacks are comparatively rare. Those most at risk are engaged in caring, education, cash handling, representing authority.

Find out if you have a problem

- Ask staff informally through managers and safety representatives.
- Keep detailed records.
- Classify all incidents according to their severity of outcome.
- Try to predict what might happen.

PREVENTION STRATEGIES

Decide what action to take

- Decide who might be harmed and how. Who is most vulnerable? Where appropriate identify potentially violent people in advance.
- Evaluate the risk. Check existing arrangements. Train your employees to recognise early signs of violence.
- Provide information - case histories, etc.
- Improve the environment - better seating, lighting, etc.
- Improve security - video cameras, coded locks, wider counters.
- Redesign the job - use credit cards rather than cash, bank money more frequently, check arrangements for lone workers.
- Arrange safe transport or secure car parking for people who work late at night.

Take action

The policy for dealing with violence should be written into the safety policy statement so that all employees are aware of it. This will encourage employees to cooperate with the policy and report further incidents.

Check what you have done

Check regularly to see if the arrangements are working by consulting employees and safety representatives. If violence is still a problem, go back to stages one and two.

What about the victims

If there is a violent incident involving your workplace you might like to consider the following:

- Debriefing - victims might need to talk through their experience as soon as possible.
- Time off work - individuals may need differing times to recover. In some cases they might need counselling.
- Legal help - legal assistance may be appropriate in serious cases.
- Other employees - may need guidance or counselling to help them react appropriately.

Source: HSE INDG69 (rev)

Health and safety of drugs and alcohol

EFFECTS

Drugs and alcohol are becoming increasingly commonplace in society. People who start consuming alcohol or drugs usually have a nil or low dependency and do so for recreational reasons. This however can escalate quickly into abuse when larger quantities of alcohol are consumed more frequently and become habitual. The effects of alcohol or drugs can vary dependant upon the individual's state of health and fitness, and resilience to the chemicals. Alcohol and drugs can remain in the body for a considerable time after consumption and its effects still be present the next day when at work. Effects on health and safety include;

- Poor co-ordination and balance.
- Perception ability reduced.
- Overall state of poor health including fatigue, poor concentration and stress.
- Poor attitude, lack of adherence to rules, violence to fellow workers.

CONTROL STRATEGIES

The use of alcohol and drugs is a personal choice over which employers usually have little or no control. However employers should have a policy to deal with the issue should it start to impact on the employees' performance at work.

Control strategies often start with the identification of safety critical work, where the influence of drugs and alcohol would have a significant effect. It is usual that strategies do not presume use or non-use of drugs and alcohol for those that conduct safety critical work, treating them all equally. In a simple approach all workers that come on to a construction site might be considered to be in safety critical work. All would work to the same rules banning them being under the influence while at work and offering them opportunities to talk to someone about how this affects them, coupled with carrying out random drugs and alcohol tests. When accidents occur it is common to consider drugs and alcohol as factors. It may not always be possible to test an injured party for causing their own accident by being under the influence of drugs and alcohol, but it may be possible to test a driver of a dumper truck that ran into someone for example.

Strategies need to be supported by education and the opportunity to get help for people with a problem.

Incident investigation, recording & reporting

Overall aims

On completion of this unit, candidates will understand:

- the process and purpose of investigating incidents (accidents, cases of work-related ill-health and other occurrences including near-misses) associated with construction work.

- the legal and organisational requirements for recording and reporting such incidents.

Content

Specific Intended Learning Outcomes

The intended learning outcomes of this Unit are that candidates will be able to:

18.1   explain the purpose of and procedures for investigating incidents at work

18.2   describe the legal requirements for the notification and/or the reporting of injuries (including fatal injuries), diseases/ill-health conditions and dangerous occurrences

18.3   utilise records of accident and ill-health experience to improve standards of health and safety within a construction organisation

Sources of Reference

Guide to the Reporting of Injuries, Diseases and Dangerous Occurrences Regulations 1995 (L73), HSE Books

Relevant Statutory Provisions

The Reporting of Injuries, Diseases and Dangerous Occurrences Regulations (RIDDOR) 1995

18.1 - Role and function of accident and incident investigation

WHY INVESTIGATE?

The reasons for investigating accidents are the same as for accident prevention, i.e.

- Humane.
- Economic.
- and Legal - including need to report under the RIDDOR.

The findings should be applied to prevent recurrence by improving work place standards, procedures and training requirements.

ROLE OF INVESTIGATION

The role of investigation includes:

- Discovery of underlying causes.
- Prevention of recurrence.
- Establish legal liability.
- Data gathering.
- Identification of trends.

FUNCTION OF INVESTIGATION

Ideally all accidents should be investigated. A study of minor injuries and near misses can often reveal a major hazard, as the occurrence and severity of injury is a random happening. The degree of investigation may well vary with the degree of injury or damage, but should be based on the worst possible case of injury which is reasonably foreseeable as a result of the accident in question.

The objectives of any investigation will vary according to the circumstances, but it will always include the following points:

- The need to establish the causes of an accident, both immediate and underlying, in order that appropriate preventative action can be taken.
- Identify weaknesses in current systems so that standards can be improved.
- Determine economic losses.
- Recommend actions to prevent a recurrence.
- Determine compliance with statutory requirements or with company regulations.
- Improve staff relations by demonstrating commitment to health and safety.
- Acquire statistics.
- Prepare for civil action/insurance date.

The role and directive for the investigation of this nature should *never* seek to blame any individual or group of individuals.

If human error is believed to be a significant cause, the reasons for this must be investigated. Lack of knowledge, training or unsuitability for the job may be the causes of this error. These are *management* and not operator *failings*. Only when these have been evaluated can the conclusion of willful and intentional acts or omissions be considered.

18.2 - Basic accident investigation procedures

Investigation Techniques

PREPARING FOR THE INVESTIGATION

- Determine who should be involved in order that the investigation team has all the necessary skills and expertise.
- Ensure that the accident scene remains undisturbed insofar as it is reasonable and safe to do so.
- Collate all relevant existing documents such as previous incident reports, maintenance records, risk assessments etc.
- Identify the persons (witnesses) who will need to be interviewed during the investigation.
- Check that legal reporting requirements have been met.
- Ascertain the equipment that will be needed e.g. measuring tape, camera.
- Determine the style and depth of the investigation. This will depend on a number of factors.

TRAINING FOR THE REPORTING OF ACCIDENTS/INCIDENTS

To ensure that the investigation team has all the necessary information, training in some of these areas may be required for some employees:

- The importance of reporting accidents and incidents for legal, investigative and monitoring reasons.
- The types of incident that the organisation requires to be reported.
- The lines of reporting.
- How to complete internal documents and forms.
- Responsibilities for completing the accident book.

SCOPE AND DEPTH OF INVESTIGATION

Ideally all accidents should be investigated. A study of minor injuries and near misses can often reveal a major hazard, as the occurrence and severity of injury is a random happening. The depth of investigation should depend on the severity of actual or potential loss, whichever is the greater.

TYPES OF INVESTIGATIONS

Supervisory Investigations

As the person in immediate operating control of an area or activity it is logical to expect the supervisor to gather information on all accidents that happen in his sphere of responsibility. This investigation is normally all that is necessary for the majority of accidents. It should result in swift remedial actions being implemented, and underlines the supervisor's responsibility for safety on a day to day basis.

Formal Investigation

In some cases a formal investigation will be convened to carry out the functions described above.

The committee should include the following people:

- A senior manager to sit as chairperson.
- A manager at a lower level than the chairperson e.g. supervisor/team leader.
- A person competent to give technical advice e.g. an electrical engineer in the case of electrocution.
- The safety professional, who may sometimes act as secretary.
- An employee representative.

Any person whose responsibilities or actions may have been involved in the incident being investigated should be excluded from sitting on the committee, but would, of course, be valuable witnesses.

INVESTIGATION GUIDELINES

- The scene of the accident may still be highly hazardous. Anyone wishing to assist the injured party must take care, so that they too do not become victims.
- The investigation must begin as soon as possible after the accident.
- Keep the objective clearly in mind - this is, of course, to discover the causes in order to initiate remedial action, not to find a scapegoat.
- Witnesses must be interviewed one at a time and not in the presence of any other witnesses to avoid influencing subsequent statements.
- Identify the root causes of the accident, not immediate ones.
- Ask probing questions - these should not put words in the witnesses' mouths.
- Avoid jumping to conclusions.
- Approach the witness with an open mind.
- Notes should be taken, so that the investigator is not relying on memory.
- Interviews are of critical importance. The witnesses may be on guard and very defensive, feeling that blame could be directed their way, so it is important to put the person being interviewed at ease - state that the purpose of the interview is to help determine the facts to prevent a re-occurrence.

INTERVIEWING TIPS

- Record details: names of the interviewers and interviewee; place, data and time of the interview; and any significant comments or actions during the interview.
- Conduct the interview in private with no interruptions.
- Do not interview more than one person at a time.
- Protect the reputation of the people you interview.
- Set a casual, informal tone during the interview to put the individual at ease.
- Summarise your understanding of the matter.
- Express appreciation for the witnesses' information.
- Translate conclusions into effective action.

INVESTIGATION REPORT FORMS

Investigation report forms vary in design, layout and content. Many organisations recognise that a different report form may be necessary for first line managers' initial investigations (a level 1 report) and those done by other managers and health and safety professionals (a level 2 report), the main difference being in the section relating to causes of the accident. The version used by other managers and professionals often has more analysis in this area and causes greater investigation of underlying causes. In the same way, reports prepared by an investigation team would not tend to be on a pre-printed format, but would be designed around agreed headings and the content/extent of the report would depend on the matter being investigated and findings (a level 3 report).

Common structure of a report tends to determine:

- *What happened* - the loss.
- *How it happened* - the event.
- *Why it happened* - the causes.
- *Recommendations* - remedial (and preventive) action.

Drawing and photographs and statements as appendices usually support the report.

Identifying immediate and (root) underlying causes

IDENTIFYING IMMEDIATE CAUSES

The cause of injury should be identified. Injuries are caused by:

Unsafe acts by individuals e.g. not wearing the correct personal protective equipment such as goggles to prevent an eye injury.

Unsafe conditions in the workplace e.g. an electrical cable, supplying energy to a power tool, trailing across a busy walkway and presenting a trip hazard.

ROOT OR UNDERLYING CAUSES

The cause of the accident is often the result of many underlying or root causal failures.

Typical root or underlying causes result:

- When people lack understanding or training, they are in a hurry and they are poorly supervised.
- When the wrong equipment is provided or the equipment is inadequate, not maintained or regularly inspected.

These are known as ***management system failures*** and occur when the organisation does not establish an adequate safety policy, incorporating an appropriate approach to risk identification and control for the organisation activities.

Research by Frank Bird and others into accident causation has led them to put forward an accident causation model based on a row of dominoes standing on one end. If any of the earlier dominoes fall, a chain reaction follows which results in a loss.

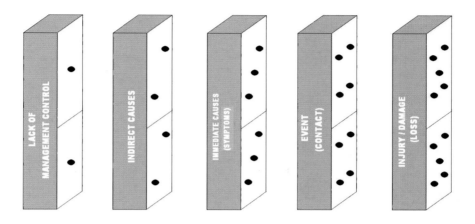

Figure 18-1: Domino theory of accident causation.   *Source: Frank Bird.*

Considering each stage separately:

"Loss"

This is the consequence of the accident and can be measured in terms of people (injuries), property (damage) or loss to the process (failed telecommunication) and hence loss of profit.

"Event (accident or incident)"

The event producing the loss involving contact with a substance or source of energy above the threshold limits of the body or structure.

"Immediate (direct) causes"

These are the substandard (unsafe) ***acts*** (e.g. using tools and equipment for tasks they were not designed to do) and substandard (unsafe) ***conditions*** (e.g. a trailing telephone cable in an office) which gives rise to an accident. These are physical symptoms which can be seen or sensed. Whilst these symptoms cannot be ignored, action solely at this level will not, by itself, ensure that recurrence is not prevented. Unsafe acts and conditions may be considered as workplace ***hazards.***

"Indirect (root or underlying) causes"

These are the underlying or root causes of accidents. Identifying the root causes will explain why the substandard act happened or the condition arose. They are not always easy to identify. Indirect causes fall into three major categories:

1)   Organisational Factors

2)   Job Factors

3)   Personal Factors

Organisational factors:

- Work standards and procedures.
- Communication.
- Co-ordination.
- Supervision.

Personal Factors include:

- Physical capability.
- Mental capability.
- Physical stress.
- Mental stress.

Job Factors:

- Design of equipment and layouts.
- Maintenance.
- Purchase of materials and equipment.

- Knowledge.
- Skill.
- Motivation.
- Information.

"Lack of management control"

This is the initial stage, centred around the management functions of:

- Policy.
- Planning.
- Organising.
- Controlling.
- Monitor.
- Review.

It should be remembered that accident investigation experience confirms that there is usually more than one causative factor. Therefore each of the multiple causation factors may be seen as one domino in its own line of dominoes [just as the **roots** of a tree branch out].

EXAMPLE

An accident involving an operator coming into contact with dangerous machinery could be the result of any of the following:

Immediate cause	*Root (underlying) cause*
Inadequate or non-existent safety devices.	Inadequate training, instruction and / or supervision.
Poor housekeeping.	Poor maintenance.
Loose clothing.	Inadequate risk assessment.
Machine malfunction.	A range of personal factors i.e. stress, fatigue, influence of drugs and alcohol.
Operator error.	Poor design of guard.

Identifying remedial actions

ACTION FOLLOWING A SERIOUS ACCIDENT

Immediately after an accident

- Attend to the victim.
- Notify the next of kin.
- Secure the scene of the accident.
- Report to enforcing authority if necessary.

Longer-term actions will include

- Identifying witnesses.
- Undertaking an investigation.
- Reviewing work procedures.

Reporting a death at work following an accident should include informing:

- The senior manager.
- Health and safety specialist.
- Coroner.
- Enforcing authority.
- Next of kin.
- Employee representatives.
- Other employees.
- Insurance company.

REPORTS AND FOLLOW-UP

The report should include a summarised version of the facts and recommendations together with discussion of controversial points, and if necessary appendices containing specialist reports (medical and technical), photographs and diagrams.

This virtually finishes the work of the investigator, but management is still responsible for seeing that the necessary remedial actions are implemented and monitored to ensure that the causes are satisfactorily controlled. The line manager, health and safety professional and health and safety committee/members will monitor these actions.

SUMMARY

Throughout the process of investigation it must be clearly borne in mind that the object is to prevent a recurrence of the accident, not to apportion blame. It is important to identify the true causes of the accident, not superficial ones. This cannot be achieved without the whole-hearted assistance of witnesses and other persons who work in that area.

It follows that recommendations must be put into action and this itself may be a protracted business. However, if this is thoroughly carried out it may well trigger off further measures of inspection and training or other positive measures that will amply justify the effort spent in trying to extract some degree of improvement from the occurrence.

18.3 - Requirements for statutory recording and reporting

Reasons for reporting

There are many important reasons why employers need to ensure that accidents and incidents are reported. Among them are the following:

- It is a clearly implied requirement of the Management of Health and Safety at Work Regulations (MHSWR) 1999 (regulation 5).
- The report should be the trigger for an investigation.
- The investigation, in turn, should help to identify flaws with existing controls and therefore assist in the implementation of improved controls.
- Analysis of reports may identify trends or patterns that may emerge.
- Gathering statistical evidence to enable the employer to compare health and safety performance with industry and other standards (benchmarking).
- To provide evidence for use in legal actions that may ensue.
- An increase in the number of reported incidents should prompt a review of risk assessments.
- The report will help the employer to identify if the incident is reportable under RIDDOR.

Accident book

It is a requirement of the Social Security (Claims and Payment) Act that all employees keep an Accident Book available to employees. It is not necessary that the employer use the book designed specifically for this purpose, the BI 510, so long as the same headings are used. The purpose of the book is to enable the employee to record accidents that have occurred to them at work and for which (industrial Injury) benefit may be payable. It is a duty placed on the employer that he investigate all recorded accidents to determine if they were accidents at work (for which benefit may be payable). Following this it is the duty of the employer to provide information to government organisations investigating an employee's claim for benefit. Accident record books (e.g. BI 510) must be kept for three years after the last entry and kept available for inspection.

Procedures for notifying and / or reporting

RIDDOR covers the requirement to report certain categories of injury and disease sustained at work, along with specified dangerous occurrences and gas incidents, to the relevant enforcing authority. These reports are used to compile statistics to show trends and to highlight problem areas, in particular industries or companies.

THE MAIN POINTS OF RIDDOR

Reporting

1) When a person *dies or suffers any serious condition* specified in Schedule 1 *(Reporting of Injuries)* and Schedule 2 *(Reporting of Dangerous Occurrences)* a responsible person is to notify by the quickest possible means (usually by telephone) the enforcing authorities and must send them a written report within 10 days (F2508).

2) In cases of diseases which are linked to work activities listed in Schedule 3 *(Reporting of Diseases)* a responsible person must notify by the quickest possible means (usually by telephone) the enforcing authorities and must send them a written report forthwith (F2508A).

3) If personal injury results in *more than 3 days incapacity* from work away from normal duties, but does not fall in the category of "major", the written report alone is required. The day of the accident is not counted.

4) The enforcing authority is either the Health and Safety Executive or the Local Authority. The approved form for reporting is F2508 for injuries and dangerous occurrences and F2508A for diseases.

Note:

"Accident" includes:

- An act of non-consensual physical violence done to a person at work.
- An act of suicide which occurs on or in the course of the operation of a relevant transport system.

Road traffic accidents

Road traffic accidents only have to be reported if:

- Death or injury results from exposure to a substance being conveyed by a vehicle.
- Death or injury results from the activities of another person engaged in the loading or unloading of an article or substance.
- Death or injury results from the activities of another person involving work on or alongside a road.
- Death or injury results from an accident involving a train.

Non Employee

The responsible person must not only report non-employee deaths, but also cases that involve major injury or hospitalisation.

Recording

In the case of an accident at work, the following details must be recorded:

- Date.
- Time.
- Name.
- Occupation.
- Nature of injury.
- Place of accident.
- Brief description of the event.

Copies of F2508 or suitable alternative records must be kept for at least 3 years. There may be held electronically provided they are printable.

Defences

A person must prove that he was not aware of the event and that he had taken all reasonable steps to have such events brought to his notice.

Typical examples of major injuries, diseases and dangerous occurrences within the construction industry

MAJOR INJURIES (RIDDOR - SCHEDULE 1)

The list of major injuries includes:

- Any fracture, other than the finger or thumbs or toes.
- Any amputation.
- Dislocation of the shoulder, hip, knee or spine.
- Permanent or temporary loss of sight.
- Chemical, hot metal or penetrating eye injury.
- Electrical shock, electrical burn leading to unconsciousness or resuscitation or admittance to hospital for more than 24 hours.
- Loss of consciousness caused by asphyxia or exposure to a harmful substance or biological agent.
- Acute illness or loss of consciousness requiring medical attention due to any entry of substance by inhalation, ingestion or through the skin.
- Acute illness where there is a reason to believe that this resulted from exposure to a biological agent or its toxins or infected material.
- Any other injury leading to hypothermia, heat-induced illness or unconsciousness requiring resuscitation, hospitalisation greater than 24 hours.

DISEASES (RIDDOR - SCHEDULE 3)

Conditions due to physical agents and the physical demands of work, e.g.

- Inflammation, ulceration or malignant disease of the skin due to ionising radiation.
- Decompression illness.
- Subcutaneous cellulitis of the hand (beat hand).
- Carpal tunnel syndrome.
- Hand-arm vibration syndrome.

Infections due to biological agents, e.g.

- Anthrax.
- Hepatitis.
- Legionellosis.
- Leptospirosis.
- Tetanus.

Conditions due to chemicals and other substances e.g.

- Arsenic poisoning.
- Ethylene Oxide poisoning.
- Cancer of a bronchus or lung.
- Folliculitis.
- Acne.
- Pneumoconiosis.
- Asbestosis.
- Occupational dermatitis.

DANGEROUS OCCURRENCES (RIDDOR - SCHEDULE 2)

Dangerous occurrences are events that have the potential to cause death or serious injury and so must be reported whether anyone is injured or not. Examples of dangerous occurrences that must be reported are:

- The failure of any load bearing part of any lift, hoist, crane or derrick etc.
- The failure of any pressurised closed vessel.
- The failure of any freight container in any of its load bearing parts.
- Any unintentional incident in which plant or equipment either
  - comes into contact with an uninsulated overhead electric line, or
  - causes an electrical discharge from such an electric line by coming into close proximity to it.
- Electrical short-circuit or overload attended by fire or explosion which results in the stoppage of the plant involved for more than 24 hours.

Note: This information is a brief summary only. For full details consult HSE document L73 A Guide to RIDDOR 95.

18.4 - Internal systems for collecting, analysing and communicating data

COLLECTING DATA

Report form types

A number of report forms are utilised to identify and inform that accidents and ill-health have occurred. These include:

- Accident book, in the form of BI 510.
- First aid treatment reports.
- Medical treatment reports.
- Medical (doctor) reports of ill-health.
- Sickness absence reports.
- Event (accident) reports.
- Event (near miss) reports.
- Maintenance/repair reports.
- Insurance reports.
- RIDDOR reports - F2508, F2508A.

Reporting Routes

Reporting of an accident or ill-health may be by a number of means and includes:

- Person receiving harm.
- Person causing loss.
- Person discovering loss.

Person receiving harm

This person is often the source of first reporting of less serious events. The reporting system must make available to them the means to make a report. They have a right to report in an 'accident book' BI 510 (or equivalent) any event that may cause them to claim Social Security benefit. This might be fulfilled by using: a copy of the BI 510 book or first aid/medical treatment documents/event report forms that are adapted to contain the same data. These reports should be under the control of a responsible person who would then initiate an investigation; this would usually require the completion of an event (e.g. accident) report.

Person causing loss

This person would be expected to bring the loss to the attention of a line manager who would fill in the appropriate event (e.g. accident) report and initiate an investigation to complete the remainder of the report that the person reporting the loss may not be able to do.

Person discovering the loss

If this person were not the manager responsible for the location in which the loss took place they would have to bring the loss to the attention of a line manager, as above. If the person were the line manager they would initiate an investigation and report on the appropriate event form.

ANALYSING AND COMMUNICATING DATA

Reports from first line managers may be copied to the next line manager (middle manager), health and safety professional, employee representative. It is important that the originator retains a copy until action to prevent is complete, to encourage ownership and continued involvement.

The copy passed to the next line manager is usually seen as the primary document. The manager confirms/adds to the investigation, retains a copy and passes the report to a central record point.

Clearly this may be done in part or whole as a computer or paper system.

Records held by the line manager/health and safety professional may be held for varying periods depending on their role. Central records are usually maintained in accordance with the organisation's own practices. A minimum period is usually 3 years for accident (in order to respond to civil claims) and 40 years for events resulting in ill-health (in order to deal with the long lived nature of the problem).

COLLECTION OF RELEVANT INFORMATION AND ITS AVAILABILITY IN A CIVIL CLAIM

Any accident may result in a claim. It is essential that organisations anticipate this and at the earliest opportunity, assemble data necessary to consider whether a claim may be defended. The line manager plays an important role in promptly investigating accidents, and copying relevant data to file as part of the accident investigation.

It is important to note that although one of the reasons that this data is being assembled is in readiness to defend a claim, its primary use is in providing a thorough accident investigation. This and the identification of any prevent measures comes before defending a claim.

Data prepared for accident investigation purposes remains discoverable in any legal action. Indeed, since the introduction of revised civil proceedings it is necessary to disclose to the other party evidence that will be relied on in court. This means that evidence may not be introduced at a later date. This reinforces the need to assemble all material data promptly.

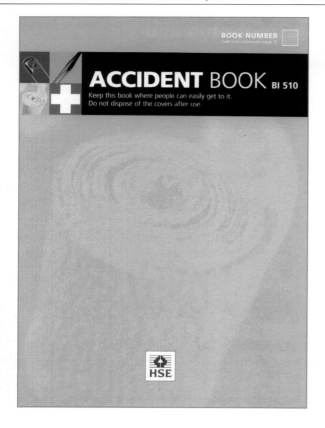

Figure 18-2: Examples from an accident book.

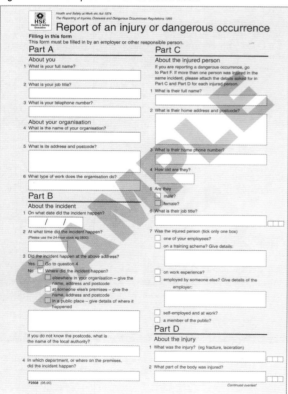

Figure 18-3: Example F2508 Forms.

Monitoring, review & audit

Overall aims

On completion of this unit, candidates will understand:

■ the process and purpose of investigating incidents (accidents, cases of work-related ill-health and other occurrences including near-misses) associated with construction work.

■ the legal and organisational requirements for recording and reporting such incidents.

Content

Specific Intended Learning Outcomes

The intended learning outcomes of this Unit are that candidates will be able to:

19.1   use a variety of proactive and reactive monitoring procedures

19.2   carry out an inspection of a construction site (and other premises associated with a construction organisation) in order to set priorities and time scales for action and to assign action points to relevant personnel

19.3   communicate inspection findings in the form of an effective and persuasive report

19.4   differentiate between safety inspections, sampling and tours and explain their roles within a monitoring regime

19.5   explain the purpose of regular reviews of health and safety performance, the means by which reviews might be undertaken and the criteria that will influence the frequency of such reviews

19.6   explain the meaning of the term 'health and safety audit' and describe the preparations that may be needed prior to an audit and the information that may be needed during an audit

Sources of Reference

Successful Health and Safety Management (HSG65), HSE Books

Relevant Statutory Provisions

Management of Health and Safety at Work Regulations (MHSWR) 1999

19.1 - Monitoring

Purpose of health and safety monitoring

Organisations need to monitor their health and safety performance to find out the degree to which they are being successful, just like finance, production or sales. Monitoring is an essential component of good management. An old maxim is "what gets measured tends to get done".

In modern, active and changing organisations it is essential to identify and confirm what is working and why in order to prevent these successful management actions being 'lost' at a time when resources are being reviewed.

Monitoring provides the opportunity and information to enable:

- The assessment of the effectiveness and appropriateness of health and safety objectives and arrangements, including control measures.
- The making of recommendations for review of the current management systems.

It is essential for organisations to learn from their experiences and take the opportunity to decide how to improve performance. Audits, by an organisation's own staff or people from outside the organisation, complement other monitoring activities by looking to see if the Policy, Organisations and Arrangements (systems) are actually achieving the right results.

The MHSWR 1999 (Reg. 5) require employers employing five or more employees to record their arrangements for the effective monitoring of preventive and protective measures.

MONITORING SYSTEMS

There is a need for a range of both proactive and reactive measures to determine whether objectives have been met.

A balanced approach to monitoring seeks to learn from all available sources. Hence two forms of monitoring system are required:

proactive (active) monitoring, before the event, involves identification through regular, planned observations of workplace conditions, systems and the actions of people, to ensure that standards are being implemented and management controls are working e.g. workplace inspections.

reactive monitoring, after the event, involves learning from mistakes, whether they result in injuries, illness, property damage or near misses e.g. accident investigation.

Organisations need to ensure that information from both active and reactive monitoring is used to identify situations that create risks, and to do something about them. Priority should be given where risks are greatest.

Both monitoring methods require an understanding of the immediate and the underlying causes of events.

Proactive monitoring measures

OBJECTIVES OF PROACTIVE MONITORING

The primary objectives of proactive (active) monitoring are to:

- Check that health and safety plans have been implemented, and
- Monitor the extent of compliance with the organisation's systems/procedures, and with its legislative/technical standards.

The assessment of the appropriateness, implementation and effectiveness of health and safety standards (in the form of objectives and arrangements, including Risk Control Systems (RCSs)). This includes the operation of the current management systems.

Organisations need to know:

- Where they are.
- Where they want to be.
- What is the difference - and why.

Active monitoring will tell the organisation about the reliability and effectiveness of its systems. This provides a good basis from which decisions and recommendations for maintenance and improvement may be made.

Active monitoring also provides an opportunity for management to confirm commitment to health and safety objectives. In addition it also reinforces a positive health and safety culture by recognising success and positive actions, instead of 'punishing' failure after an undesired event.

Organisations must see active monitoring as an integral (and normal) part of the management (work) function. As such it must take place at all levels and opportunities in the organisation. Managers should be given responsibility for the monitoring of objectives and compliance with standards for which they and their subordinates are responsible. The actual method of monitoring will depend on the situation and the position held by the person monitoring.

METHODS OF PROACTIVE MONITORING

The various methods and levels of active monitoring include the following *(source HSG 65)*

- Routine procedures to monitor specific objectives, e.g. quarterly or monthly reports or returns.
- Periodic examination of documents to check that systems relating to the promotion of the health and safety culture are complied with, e.g. the way objectives for managers are established or appraised, assessment of records of training needs and delivery of training.
- Systematic inspection of premises, plant, and equipment by supervisors, maintenance staff, management, safety representatives and other employees to ensure continued effective operation of workplace precautions.
- Environmental monitoring and health surveillance to check on the effectiveness of health control measures and to detect early signs of harm to health.

- Systematic direct observation of work and behaviour by first-line supervisors to assess compliance with risk control systems (RCSs) and associated procedures and rules, particularly those concerned with risk control.
- The operation of audit systems.
- Consideration of regular reports on health and safety performance by the board of directors.

Active monitoring effort should be applied on a risk basis. Monitoring of workplace precautions would typically be more detailed and frequent than management system activities that carry a low risk if misapplied.

MONITORING PERFORMANCE STANDARDS

Health and safety performance in organisations that manage health and safety effectively is measured against established standards. This enables confirmation of compliance with standards and where improvement is required. By establishing standards of expectation it enables deficiencies to be quickly translated into improvement actions.

The success of action to manage risks is assessed through active monitoring involving a range of techniques. This includes techniques which examine technical measures (equipment, premises and substances), procedural measures (systems of work, method statements, safety cases, and permits to work), and behavioural measures (motivation, attitudes, and competencies).

Deficiencies in control measures are assessed through reactive monitoring which requires the thorough investigation of accidents, ill health or events with the potential to cause harm or loss.

In both active and reactive monitoring, the objectives are not only to determine the immediate causes of sub-standard (at risk) performance but, more importantly, to identify the underlying causes and the implications for the structure and operation of the health and safety management system.

Reactive monitoring measures

OBJECTIVES OF REACTIVE MONITORING

The primary objectives of reactive monitoring are to analyse data relating to:

- Accidents.
- Ill-health.
- Other downgrading events.

In order to carry out reactive monitoring effectively systems must be in place to identify the event, record it and report it. Without this nothing may be learnt. Indeed, what little data that is communicated might serve to reinforce that there is no need to put in a great deal of health and safety effort. If reporting etc. is planned and encouraged it is not uncommon to find a large increase in recorded events. This does not necessarily mean an increase in events, merely an increase in reporting.

Events contribute to the 'corporate memory', helping to prevent a repeat in another part of the organisation or at a later time. Though it should be remembered that the 'corporate memory' is said to be short, in the average organisation (one undergoing some change) it is said to be 4 years.

Data may be gained from other organisations to reinforce or extend experience of events and the hazards involved.

METHODS OF REACTIVE MONITORING

These methods are deemed to be after the event and are therefore reactive monitoring measures:

- Identification.
- Reporting.
- Investigation.
- Collation of data and statistics, on the events.

The events monitored include those resulting in:

- Injuries.
- Cases of illness (including sickness absence).
- Property damage.
- Near misses.
- Dangerous occurrences.
- Complaints by the workforce.
- Enforcement actions.

It is important to identify, in each case, why performance was sub-standard. Trends and common features may be identified, such as when, where and how these events occur. This provides an opportunity to learn and put into place improvements to the overall management system and to specific risk controls.

Figure 19-1: Accident statistics.   *Source: ACT.*

ACCIDENT STATISTICS

Many organisations spend considerable time developing data on their health and safety performance based on the accidents they have. Whilst there is value in doing so it has the limitation of being a little after the event. Accidents must occur to get the data, thus tending to reflect what is done to prevent a recurrence rather than what was being done prior to the event. A more complete approach to monitoring will tend to include 'before the event' actions like audits and inspections to indicate what is currently being done to prevent accidents.

A low injury accident rate is not a guarantee that risks are being effectively controlled. In some cases this might be a matter of good fortune, or the fact that incidents are not being reported rather than effective management.

If organisations wait until an event occurs to determine where health and safety effort is required then some sort of loss must have occurred. In order to gain sufficient management attention this could be an event resulting in personal injury to someone. Clearly this is an undesirable way of learning, particularly as, with an amount of effort, planning and thought, the event could have been foreseen and prevented. The more mature organisation seeks to learn most from activities (e.g. risk assessment) before the event or, at the very least, learn from those events that result in no personal injury, e.g. near misses.

The obvious use of accident data is to identify specific problem areas by recording instances where control measures have failed. However, analysis of the data allows general trends to be shown in order perhaps to identify common root causes, as well as comparisons to be made with others in order to learn from successes elsewhere. Accident data can also help to raise awareness in the minds of both managers and employees of health and safety in general, and of specific problems in particular. In addition, collection of data allows costs to be calculated, which can increase the likelihood of resources being allocated.

Examples of statistical analysis in common usage is:

Frequency rate = $\dfrac{\text{Number of accidents in the period}}{\text{Total hours worked during the period}}$ x 100 000

Incidence rate = $\dfrac{\text{Number of accidents in the period}}{\text{Average number employed during the period}}$ 1 000

For statistics derived to be of value their limitations have to be understood. Variables in work methods, hours of work, hazard controls and management system effort make it fundamentally difficult to make comparisons outside the organisation deriving the data. Indices such as these, are best suited to comparison of performance of the same organisation over similar periods of time, for example, yearly. In this way trends may be observed and conclusions drawn. If comparisons are to be made outside the organisation, it should be remembered that other organisations might have a different understanding of the following:

- Definition of an accident (lost time or reportable).
- Hours worked may not be actual (contracted minimum hours - easier to work out).
- Who is included (are contractors included or excluded?).
- What multiplier is used (International Labour Office and HSE use 1,000,000 for the frequency rate, USA use 200,000).

Workplace inspections

ROLE OF INSPECTIONS

The role of safety is to identify areas where improvements are needed. Inspections may also affect the organisational safety culture, particularly where employees' views are sought as part of the inspection. In this way, employers' commitment to health and safety can be demonstrated, ownership of health and safety can be shared and employee morale can be increased by simple improvements being implemented at the time of the inspection.

Inspections involve examination of the workplace or items of equipment in order to identify hazards and determine if they are effectively controlled. Four different types of inspections are common:

- General workplace inspections - carried out by local first-line managers and employee representatives.
- Statutory inspections (thorough examination) of equipment, e.g. boilers, lifting equipment - carried out by specialist Competent Persons.
- Preventive maintenance inspections of specific (critical) items - carried out by maintenance staff.
- Pre-use 'checks' of equipment, e.g. vehicles, fork lift trucks, access equipment - carried out by the user.

An important aid used by anyone carrying out an inspection is a checklist, i.e. a list of "the way things ought to be". When a work area or item of equipment fails this test it is considered substandard and represents a hazard. Each substandard condition should be assessed and corrective action carried out and details recorded. Issues to be considered when creating a checklist should include: substances or materials being used, condition of traffic routes and means of access and egress, work equipment, work practices (manual handling, etc.), work environment, electricity, fire precautions, welfare provision including first aid arrangements and workstation ergonomics.

Inspections will not improve health and safety performance unless corrective measures are set out (where a deficiency is identified) and fully implemented. This will not happen on its own or by default; indeed, the opposite is likely to occur. Standards will continue to deteriorate where employees/managers find that their efforts to identify improvement needs are "a waste of time". It is, however, equally important to avoid putting in "any old solution" as this is bound to result in a waste of company resources (time, equipment, money etc.). The trick is therefore, to get the right solution implemented and this can take a quantity of management time and effort. If the risk is significant clearly this is warranted. Whenever a sub-standard (at risk) situation is identified two important steps must be taken:

- Each situation must be evaluated as to its risk potential.
- The underlying cause(s) of the situation must be identified.

The first step ensures that resources are allocated on a worst first basis, and the second step ensures that the appropriate corrective action will reduce the risk and prevent its return to the same level.

A simple approach to risk evaluation levels (rating) and allocation of time for actions may follow the method below:

- High risk (likely to cause a major loss) - complete within 24 hours.
- Moderate risk (likely to cause a serious loss) - complete within 7 days (1 month if preferred).
- Low risk (will possibly cause a minor loss) - complete within 30 days (3 months if preferred).

A common approach is to refer to the three categories above as Class A, Class B and Class C risks respectively, class A being the highest.

Once situations that require most urgent attention are identified and what measures are needed, the best approach is to assign a maximum time period by which the action is to be completed (tied to the risk rating). A structured approach is necessary to ensure that the actions needed are initiated and followed up (monitored) in such a way that they are not simply forgotten about.

THE REQUIREMENTS FOR EFFECTIVE REPORT WRITING

The primary purpose of written information is to communicate. The writer should, therefore, always bear the reader in mind when producing the text. The use of plain English must be encouraged-this is particularly important for safety related material.

One useful vehicle for conveying information is the *report.*

One simple structure is as follows:

- Introduction and background.
- Summary.
- Main body of the report.
- Recommendations.
- Conclusions.

Introduction and background

This section includes the title page which should clearly identify the writer and the document. It should contain a brief explanation of the subject described in the document title and the reason for the document. Consider the aim of the report and inform the reader of the problems it intends to address.

Summary

Most reports benefit from a summary, which seeks to provide the reader with an overview of the strengths and weaknesses of the subject being reported on. It should be sufficient to motivate the reader to read the rest of the report with an idea of what it is going to cover.

Main body of the report

This section deals with details, facts and findings. Keep the style simple and to the point. Avoid the use of jargon or embellishment. Inaccuracy, inadequate and sloppy presentation can distract the reader and lessen the impact.

Recommendations

These should flow logically from the main body of the report. Recommendations should consist of a plain statement of action without repeating the arguments of the preceding section. In short, in simple reports the recommendation may follow each of the findings and therefore appear in the main body of the report.

Conclusions

This section should contain a summary of the main findings and inferences. Ideally, the writer should end on a positive note.

Other proactive monitoring methods

SAFETY SAMPLING

Sampling is where only a partial amount of a potential group/area is examined to establish facts that can indicate the standard of compliance of the whole.

A very small sample, such as the examination of three pieces of lifting tackle, may only give a rough, but acceptable, indication of the situation relating to lifting tackle as a whole.

When a representative sample is taken this may be considered to reasonably represent the situation for the whole group.

Sampling is conducted relating to the following:

- Specific hazards - such as noise or dust - typically conducted by staff trained in appropriate hygiene techniques.
- Good practice - such as the wearing of personal protective equipment - typically conducted by first-line managers.
- General workplace hazards - such as those identified during a defined walk through a work area - typically conducted by first-line managers, employee representatives and employees.

TOURS

Tours provide opportunity for management to explore the effectiveness of risk control measures through planned visits to the workplace to observe and discuss the controls in use.

It is important, when developing a positive health and safety culture, that management commitment be visible. The conducting of planned tours to workplaces to meet work groups is one effective way of achieving this. As such it is a monitoring method that senior and middle managers would find useful. It has the advantage of enabling direct contact and communication between employees and senior management. This gives an accurate picture of work conditions and the understanding of employees. It can indicate deficiencies or success in managers carrying the organisation's objectives through to action. It also provides a forum for gaining the viewpoint of employees directly, without the translation that takes place through formal management channels.

In order to be planned there must be an intended outcome e.g. to communicate or review a topic, even if this includes some free time for other comment. Details of the tour and outcomes, including improvement actions, must be recorded to be effective.

SURVEYS

A summary may be described as an examination of a narrow field of the health and safety programme on an exploratory basis, with no fixed expectation of findings. The term 'survey' is usually applied to an exercise that involves a limited number of critical aspects, for example:

- Noise survey - usually with the aid of noise measuring equipment.
- Lighting survey - usually with the aid of a light meter.
- Temperature survey (to measure both high & low temperature levels) - usually with the aid of a thermometer.
- Personal protective equipment needs survey - usually involving review of standards and workplace conditions/activities.

The term 'survey' is also used to define an exercise in which managers/employees are interviewed in order to identify knowledge, understanding, and details of specific needs within the working environment.   Examples of these might be:

■ Training needs - usually involving written questionnaires to managers and employees.
■ Attitudes to health and safety - usually involving written questionnaires to managers and employees.
■ The need for specific health and safety rules for specific tasks - usually involving review of standards and workplace conditions/activities.

Should these exercises seek to identify details from only a small number of people within a subject group or small geographical area it would cease to be a survey and would become a sample.

Review

Learning from all relevant experience (including that of the organisation and of other organisations) needs to be done systematically, through regular reviews of performance. The review draws on data from monitoring activities and from independent audits. These form the basis of continuous improvement, necessary to maintain compliance and effectiveness. This helps to maintain a management system that is fresh, dynamic, appropriate and effective.

For example, it is a well established principle that things like health and safety policy and risk assessments are reviewed. This is done when something it is believed may affect them has changed. For example, legislation may change and cause a review, or an accident may occur leading to a review to determine if the arrangements and controls in place are effective.

Auditing health and safety management systems

SCOPE AND PURPOSE OF AUDITING

Audits are concerned with assessing systems and management controls.   Whereas inspections are concerned with hazard identification in the workplace, auditing relates to the confirmation of controls and, where they are not sufficient, the putting into place of remedial action.

An audit is a systematic, critical examination of an organisation's systems to determine the extent to which there is compliance with a set of agreed standards.

The entire health and safety management system should be subjected to a comprehensive audit from time to time.   Individual elements of the health and safety programme can, of course, be subjected to individual audits for example:

■ Evaluation of compliance with health and safety programme procedures.
■ Evaluation of compliance with set occupational health standards.
■ Evaluation of compliance with physical safeguards (health and safety hardware).
■ Evaluation of compliance with fire prevention/control standards.

PRE-AUDIT PREPARATIONS

The audit must be structured and co-ordinated in its assessment of the systems. This is best achieved by utilising audit checklists developed or obtained before the audit. The audit involves assessment of documents, interview of people and observations in the workplace.

The outcome from an audit should be a detailed report of findings and recommendations to improve or maintain the health and safety management system.

RESPONSIBILITY FOR AUDITS

The responsibility to ensure audits take place rests with the organisation in question. Conducting audits will assist the organisation in complying with the MHSWR requirement to have in place arrangements to monitor. In addition it will help confirm the level of compliance with general duties under the Health and Safety at Work Act (HASAWA) 1974 and specific regulations. Audits should be conducted by people that are both independent and competent. Health and safety specialists that have received specific training in health and safety auditing techniques would usually be able to carry out this function.

Audits can be carried out by the management of the organisation, provided that the managers do not audit their own efforts directly (bias must be eliminated) and that the managers concerned have been trained in audit technique.   Often a small team will be commissioned to conduct the exercise, in order to widen the experience base and establish some degree of independence. A team may comprise three essential groups of people:

■ a manager   ■ a representative from the workforce   ■ a health and safety professional.

Extra individuals with specific skills may join the team when specific topics are under assessment. A more independent approach would be to conduct an audit using auditors from outside the organisation or location.

ADVANTAGES AND DISADVANTAGES OF EXTERNAL AND INTERNAL AUDITS

	Advantages	Disadvantages
Internal audits	Internal audits ensure local buy-in to recommendations and actions. The auditor often has intimate knowledge of the hazards and existing work practices.	The auditor may also be responsible for implementation of any proposed changes and this might inhibit recommendations because of the effect on workload.
External audits	External audits are usually impartial, with often wide experience of a number of different types of work practices. May be able to offer solutions to what might be considered unsolvable problems within.	Need to plan well to identify nature and scope of the organisation; individuals may not be forthcoming, be nervous or resistant to discussing their workplace with an outsider.

(Sample) # Overall Compliance  AUDIT 123
(Single Location)

These marks are obtained from totalling the (total achieved marks and total maximum mark) from audit check list matrix (by location) for each section heading or directly from audit check list (whole organisation) for each section heading, depending on which is used.

Enter the totalled achieved marks in column 1 for each section heading (total achieved marks). Enter the totalled maximum obtainable marks in column 2 for each section heading (total maximum marks).

This compliance matrix is used to show the overall compliance of the organisation by section headings only.

Determine the percentage : $$\frac{\text{Total Achieved Marks}}{\text{Maximum Obtainable Marks}} \times 100$$

and enter in column 3 (Percentage).

	Column 1	Column 2	Column 3
Main Section Heading	**Total Achieved Marks**	**Maximum Obtainable Marks**	**Percentage**
Administration and Procedures	78	160	49
Legislation Compliance	90	210	75
Environment	58	110	53
Equipment	60	120	50
Materials Handling	80	100	80
Facilities	88	90	98
Special Risks	75	100	75
External	76	120	63
Environment - Office	70	90	78
Facilities - Office	60	110	55
Special Risks - Office	N/A	N/A	N/A
Totals	735	1210	
Organisation Compliance			61

Figure 19-2: Sample page from the ACT / RMS Audit 123 system.   *Source: ACT.*

Relevant Statutory Provisions

Content

Asbestos (Licensing) Regulations (ASLIC) 1983

Law considered in context / more depth in Unit 16.

Outline of key points

The **Asbestos (Licensing) Regulations (ASLIC) 1983** as amended by the Asbestos (Licensing) (Amendment) Regulations 1998 provide that an employer or self employed person who undertakes work with asbestos insulation or asbestos coating may only do so in accordance with a licence issued to him by the Health and Safety Executive (HSE).

This means that in many cases if work is being carried out with asbestos insulation, asbestos coating or asbestos insulating board a licence will be needed. In addition, a licence will be needed when using a scaffold to create an enclosure for working with asbestos. A licence will only be provided to those who plan to do work.

"Work with asbestos insulation or asbestos coating" means work in which asbestos insulation or coating is removed, repaired or disturbed and includes such work in any supervision or ancillary capacity. From the 1 August 1999 work with Asbestos Insulation Board (AIB) also requires a licence from the HSE.

A licence is not required if there is *no intention* of working with asbestos. In addition, no licence is required to work with asbestos if it is short duration work (within any 7-day period a single job lasts less than one hour per worker or two hours in total) and the following provisions are made:

- Air monitoring is done.
- Bulk samples to identify asbestos are collected.
- Clearance inspections are done.

Also, *no* licence is required if you are working with asbestos within your own premises using your own employees - although you still need to notify the relevant Enforcing Authority (either HSE or you local authority) at least 14 days before you start the work.

Although a licence may not be required to carry out a particular job, you will still need to make sure that you comply with general rules detailed under the Control of Asbestos at Work Regs (CAWR) 2002 to prevent exposure to asbestos.

The application process has 3-stages

1) Application - complete an application form (FOD ASB1) and send it to the HSE, together with the appropriate fee.

2) Assessment - an inspector assesses the organisation's operation.

3) Decision - a licence issued or explanation provided of what further action is necessary to gain a licence.

The HSE may refuse to issue a licence and may impose conditions in any licence it issues. The HSE can revoke an asbestos licence if the licence holder is found to be in breach of any health and safety legislation (not just asbestos related legislation).

Chemicals (Hazard Information and Packaging for Supply) Regulations (CHIP 3) 2002

Law considered in context / more depth in Unit 16.

Arrangement of Regulations

1) Citation and commencement.

2) Interpretation.

3) Application of these Regulations.

4) Meaning of the approved supply list.

5) Classification of substances and preparations dangerous for supply.

6) Safety data sheets for substances and preparations dangerous for supply.

7) Advertisements for substances dangerous for supply.

8) Packaging of substances and preparations dangerous for supply.

9) Labelling of substances and preparations dangerous for supply.

10) Particular labelling requirements for certain preparations.

11) Methods of marking or labelling packages.

12) Child resistant fastenings and tactile warning devices.

13) Retention of classification data for substances and preparations dangerous for supply.

14) Notification of the constituents of certain preparations dangerous for supply to the poisons advisory centre.

15) Exemption certificates.

16) Enforcement, civil liability and defence.

17) Transitional provisions.

18) Extension outside Great Britain.

19) Revocations and modifications.

Schedule 1   Classification of substances and preparations dangerous for supply.

Schedule 2   Indications of danger and symbols for substances and preparations dangerous for supply.

Schedule 3   Classification provisions for preparations dangerous for supply.

Schedule 4   Classification provisions for preparations intended to be used as pesticides.

Schedule 5   Headings under which particulars are to be provided in safety data sheets.

Schedule 6   Particulars to be shown on labels for substances and preparations dangerous for supply and certain other preparations.

Schedule 7   British and International Standards relating to child resistant fastenings and tactile warning devices.

Schedule 8   Modifications to certain enactments relating to the flashpoint of flammable liquids.

The Chemicals (Hazard Information and Packaging for Supply) Regulations (CHIP 3) 2002 apply to those who supply dangerous chemicals. They are based on European Directives, which apply to all EU and European Economic Area (EEA) Countries. The Directives are constantly reviewed and changed when necessary. When changes do occur to the Directives, CHIP is changed as well (about once a year). CHIP may be changed by amending Regulations or if there are major changes, the principal Regulations are revised.

The Regulations are designed to protect people's health and the environment by:

- Identification of the hazardous properties of materials (classification).
- Provision of health and safety information to users (safety data sheet and label).
- Packaging of materials safely.

CHIP introduces a new scheme to classify products based upon a calculation method.

Outline of key points

REGULATION 6 (1)

'The supplier of a substance or preparation dangerous for supply **shall** *provide the recipient of that substance or preparation with a safety data sheet containing information under the headings specified in Schedule 5 to enable the recipient of that substance or preparation to take the necessary measures relating to the protection of health and safety at work and relating to the protection of the environment and the safety data sheet shall clearly show its date of first publication or latest revision as the case may be.'*

The test of adequacy of the information provided in a safety data sheet is whether the information enables the recipient to take the necessary measures relating to the protection of health and safety at work and relating to the protection of the environment.

This does not mean that the safety data sheet will take the place of a risk assessment which would require specific detail of the circumstances in which the chemical is to be used.

GUIDANCE ON THE CONTENTS OF SAFETY DATA SHEETS

The headings shown here are those specified in Schedule 5 of C(HIP) 2. However, information given here is indicative of the issues to be addressed by the person compiling the safety data sheet and do not impose an absolute requirement for action or controls.

Identification of the substance/preparation and the company
- Name of the substance.
- Name, address and telephone number (including emergency number) of supplier.

Composition/information on ingredients
- Sufficient information to allow the recipient to identify readily the associated risks.

Hazards identification
- Important hazards to man and the environment.
- Adverse health effects and symptoms.

First-aid measures
- Whether immediate attention is required.
- Symptoms and effects including delayed effects.
- Specific information according to routes of entry.
- Whether professional advice is advisable.

Fire fighting measures
- Suitable extinguishing media.
- Extinguishing media that must not be used.
- Hazards that may arise from combustion e.g., gases, fumes etc.
- Special protective equipment for fire fighters.

Accidental release measures
- Personal precautions such as removal of ignition sources, provision of ventilation, avoid eye/skin contact etc.
- Environmental precautions such as keep away from drains, need to alert neighbours etc.
- Methods for cleaning up e.g. absorbent materials. Also, "Never use…."

Handling and storage
- Advice on technical measures such as local and general ventilation.
- Measures to prevent aerosol, dust, fire etc.
- Design requirements for specialised storage rooms.
- Incompatible materials.
- Special requirements for packaging/containers.

Exposure controls/personal protection

- Engineering measures taken in preference to personal protective equipment (PPE) 1992.
- Where PPE is required, type of equipment necessary e.g. type of gloves, goggles, barrier cream etc.

Physical and chemical properties

- Appearance, e.g. solid, liquid, powder, etc.
- Odour (if perceptible).
- Boiling point, flash point, explosive properties, solubility etc.

Stability and reactivity

- Conditions to avoid such as temperature, pressure, light, etc.
- Materials to avoid such as water, acids, alkalis, etc.
- Hazardous by-products given off on decomposition.

Toxicological information

- Toxicological effects if the substance comes into contact with a person.
- Carcinogenic, mutagenic, toxic for reproduction etc.
- Acute and chronic effects.

Ecological information

- Effects, behaviour and environmental fate that can reasonably be foreseen.
- Short and long term effects on the environment.

Disposal considerations

- Appropriate methods of disposal e.g. land-fill, incineration etc.

Transport information

- Special precautions in connection with transport or carriage.
- Additional information as detailed in the Carriage of Dangerous Goods by Road Regs (CPL) 1994 may also be given.

Regulatory information

- Health and safety information on the label as required by C(HIP) 2.
- Reference might also be made to Health and Safety at Work etc Act (HASAWA) 1974 and Control of Substances Hazardous to Health Regulations (COSHH) 2002.

Other Information

- Training advice.
- Recommended uses and restrictions.
- Sources of key data used to compile the data sheet.

RISK PHRASES AND SAFETY PHRASES

More useful information to help ensure the safe use of dangerous substances comes in the form of risk phrases and safety phrases. These are often displayed either on the container label or in the safety data sheet. There are currently 48 risk phrases and 53 safety phrases. Some examples are given below and detailed information can be found in the ACOP to C(HIP) 2.

Risk Phrase		*Safety Phrase*	
R3	*Risk of explosion by shock, friction, fire or other sources of ignition.*	*S2*	*Keep out of reach of children.*
R20	*Harmful by inhalation.*	*S20*	*When using do not eat or drink.*
R30	*Can become highly flammable in use.*	*S25*	*Avoid contact with eyes.*
R45	*May cause cancer.*	*S36*	*Wear suitable protective clothing.*
R47	*May cause birth defects.*	*S41*	*In case of fire and/or explosion do not breathe fumes.*

Absence of hazard symbols or risk and safety advice does not mean the item is harmless.

Confined Spaces Regulations (CSR) 1997

Law considered in context / more depth in Unit 6.

Arrangement of Regulations

1) Citation, commencement and interpretation.
2) Disapplication of Regulations.
3) Duties.
4) Work in confined spaces.
5) Emergency arrangements.
6) Exemption certificates.
7) Defence in proceedings.

8)   Extension outside Great Britain.

9)   Repeal and revocations.

Outline of key points

The Confined Spaces Regulations (CSR) 1997 repeal and replace earlier provisions contained in s.30 of the Factories Act 1961.

A failure to appreciate the dangers associated with confined spaces has led not only to the deaths of many workers, but also to the demise of some of those who have attempted to rescue them.

A confined space is not only a space which is small and difficult to enter, exit or work in; it can also be a large space, but with limited/restricted access. It can also be a space which is badly ventilated e.g. a tank or a large tunnel.

The Confined Spaces Regulations (CSR) 1997, define a confined space as any place, including any chamber, tank, vat, silo, pit, pipe, sewer, flue, well, or other similar space, in which, by virtue of its enclosed nature, there is a foreseeable risk of a 'specified occurrence'.

Construction (Design and Management) Regulations (CDM) 1994

Arrangement of Regulations

1)   Citation and commencement.

2)   Interpretation.

3)   Application of regulations.

4)   Clients and agents of clients.

5)   Requirements on developer.

6)   Appointments of planning supervisor and principal contractor.

7)   Notification of project.

8)   Competence of planning supervisor, designers and contractors.

9)   Provision for health and safety.

10)   Start of construction phase.

11)   Client to ensure information is available.

12)   Client to ensure health and safety file is available for inspection.

13)   Requirements on designer.

14)   Requirements on planning supervisor.

15)   Requirements relating to the health and safety plan.

16)   Requirements on and powers of principal contractor.

17)   Information and training.

18)   Advice from, and views of, persons at work.

19)   Requirements and prohibitions on contractors.

20)   Extension outside Great Britain.

21)   Exclusion of civil liability.

22)   Enforcement.

23)   Transitional provisions.

24)   Repeals, revocations and modifications.

Schedule 1   Particulars to be notified to the Executive.

Schedule 2   Transitional provisions.

Outline of key points

The Construction (Design & Management) Regulations (CDM) 1994 came into force on 31 March 1995, with the aim of raising standards of construction site health and safety.

METHOD

The method the CDM Regulations take are to:

1.   Plan health and safety into construction at the design stage by improving management and co-ordination of health and safety issues.

2.   Create two instruments for managing and co-ordinating health and safety:

    a.   The Health and Safety Plan

       ■   Pre tender stage and,

       ■   Construction Phase

    b.   The Structure Health and Safety File.

3.   Allocate adequate time and resources so that duties imposed by these and other health and safety legislation can be met.

4.   Involve all participants in the achievement of safe working environments to minimise risks during construction work.

APPLICATION OF CDM

The Regulations do not apply to projects where fewer than five people at any one time are expected to carry out construction work and where the local authority is the enforcing authority. Only the HSE enforce CDM, where the Local Authority is the enforcing authority, they hand over to the HSE as soon as CDM applies.

The Regulations apply to projects where five or more people at any one time are carrying out construction and where demolition or dismantling of a structure is taking place regardless of time or numbers.

Projects with a construction phase longer than 30 days or involving more than 500 person days of construction work, are also notifiable to the Health and Safety Executive (HSE). Notification must be in writing and can be made using the form F10(rev).

Where there are fewer than five people CDM will still apply if the project is notifiable, e.g. a construction phase lasting 40 days with a workplace of 4.

CIVIL LIABILITY

The right to civil action is excluded under CDM except for:

- The Client's duty to ensure that a health and safety plan is prepared before construction starts [Regulation 10].
- The Principal Contractor's duty to take reasonable steps to control access to site [Regulation 16(1)(c)].

RESOURCES AND COMPETENCE

The Client must be reasonably satisfied as to the competence and resources of the Planning Supervisor and Principal Contractor. In this context competency and resources relate to dealing with risks to health and safety. Similar duties are imposed on anyone appointing designers or contractors such as:

- Designers appointing other designers to assist in design work.
- The Principal Contractor appointing contractors.

REQUIREMENTS ON DEVELOPERS

When commercial developers sell domestic premises before the project is complete (e.g. 30 houses on an estate of 100 houses are released for occupation whilst work on the remainder continues) then the developer must comply with the following:

- Appointment of planning supervisor and principal contractor.
- Ensure the competence of the planning supervisor, designers and contractors.
- Be reasonably satisfied that the planning supervisor, designers and contractors has allocated or will allocate adequate resources to enable them to comply with their functions/duties etc.
- Ensure the construction phase does not start unless a construction phase health and safety plan has been prepared.
- Ensure information is available to the planning supervisor.
- Ensure the structure health and safety file is available for inspection and if their entire interest in the property has been disposed of, the person acquiring the property is aware of the nature and purpose of the file.

KEY PARTIES

A number of key parties identified in the regulations have specific duties:

Client:

a. Prompt (as soon as practicable) appointment of competent Planning Supervisor and Principal Contractor.
b. Ensure adequate provision of resources and time to achieve a safe working environment.
c. Preparation of the pre-tender health and safety plan.
d. Make reasonable site enquiries.
e. Make relevant health and safety information available.
f. Keep health and safety file available for inspection.

The Client may appoint an agent to undertake his duties under CDM provided that he is reasonably satisfied that the agent is competent and that the HSE are notified in writing of the appointment.

Designer:

a. Ensure that structures are designed to avoid risks to health and safety while they are being built and maintained.
b. Ensure where it is not possible to avoid risks that they are minimised.
c. Provide adequate information about materials used in the design that could affect the health and safety of persons carrying out construction work.
d. To co-operate with the planning supervisor and other designers.

Planning Supervisor:

a. Ensure that a health and safety plan for the pre-tender stage is prepared.
b. Ensure that designers include among the design considerations, adequate regard to health and safety.
c. Ensure co-operation between different designers.
d. Be in a position to give advice to clients and contractors.
e. Ensure that a health and safety file is prepared.
f. Ensure that a health and safety file is delivered to the client.

Principal Contractor:

a.   Take account of health and safety issues when preparing tenders.

b.   Develop the construction phase health and safety plan.

c.   Ensure co-operation between all contractors to ensure they comply with health and safety legislation.

d.   Take reasonable steps to ensure only authorised persons are allowed on site.

e.   Provide information to the Planning Supervisor for inclusion in the health and safety file.

f.   Enable employed persons to discuss health and safety issues.

g.   Arrange for the co-ordinating the views of employed persons where this is important for health and safety.

Contractors:

a.   Must co-operate with the Principal Contractor.

b.   Provide relevant information to the Principal Contractor on the health and safety risks created by their works and how they will be controlled.

c.   Comply with directions given by the Principal Contractor and any rules in the Health and safety Plan.

d.   Provide the Principal Contractor with any Reporting of Injuries, Disease and Dangerous Occurrences Regulations (RIDDOR) reports.

INSTRUMENTS

The Pre-tender Health and Safety Plan

The contents of the pre-tender plan will depend on the nature of the project, however, the following areas should be considered:

- Description of project.
- Client's considerations and management requirements.
- Environmental restrictions and existing on-site risks.
- Significant design and construction hazards.
- The health and safety file.

THE CONSTRUCTION PHASE HEALTH AND SAFETY PLAN

The plan is developed by the principal contractor and is the foundation on which the health and safety management of the construction work is based. The contents of the pre-tender stage health and safety plan will depend on the nature of the project itself. However, the following areas should be considered.

a.   The management structure and responsibilities of the various members of the project team, whether based at site or elsewhere.

b.   The health and safety standards to which the project will be carried out. These may be set in terms of statutory requirements or high standards that the client may require in particular circumstances.

c.   Means for informing contractors about risks to their health and safety arising from the environment in which the project is to be carried out and the construction work itself.

d.   All contractors, the self employed and designers to be appointed by the principal contractor are properly selected (i.e. they are competent and will make adequate provision for health and safety).

e.   Means for communicating and passing information between the project team (including the client and any client's representatives) the designers, the planning supervisor, the principal contractor, other contractors, workers on site and others whose health and safety may be affected.

f.   Arrangements for the identification and effective management of activities with risks to health and safety, by carrying out risk assessments, incorporating those prepared by other contractors, and also safety method statements which result. These activities may be specific to a particular trade or to site-wide issues.

g.   Emergency arrangements for dealing with and minimising the effects of injuries, fire and other dangerous occurrences.

h.   Arrangements for passing information to the principal contractor about accidents, ill health and dangerous occurrences that require to be notified to the Health and Safety Executive (HSE) under RIDDOR.

i.   Arrangements for the provision and maintenance of welfare facilities.

j.   Arrangements to ensure the principal contractor checking that people on site have been provided with health and safety information and safety training.

k.   Arrangements that have been made for consulting and co-ordinating the views of workers or their representatives.

l.   Arrangements for making site rules and for bringing them to the attention of those affected.

m.   Arrangements for passing on information to the planning supervisor for the preparation of the health and safety file.

n.   Arrangements should be set out for the monitoring systems to achieve compliance with legal requirements; and the health and safety rules developed by the principal contractor.

THE HEALTH AND SAFETY FILE

The health and safety file should include information about all the following topics, where this may be relevant to the health and safety of any future construction work. The level of detail should be proportionate to the risks likely to be involved in such work.

1. A brief description of the work to be carried out.

2. Residual hazards and how they have been dealt with (e.g. surveys or other information concerning asbestos, contaminated land, water bearing strata, buried services).

3. Key structural principles incorporated in the design of the structure (e.g. bracing, sources of substantial stored energy – including pre- or post- tensioned members) and safe working loads for floors and roofs, particularly where these may preclude placing scaffolding or heavy machinery there.

4. Any hazards associated with the materials used (e.g. hazardous substances, lead paint, special coatings which should not be burnt off).

5. Information regarding the removal or dismantling of installed plant and equipment (e.g. lifting arrangements).

6. The nature, location and markings of significant services, including fire-fighting services.

7. Information and as-built drawings of the structure, its plant and equipment (e.g. the means of safe access to and from service voids, fire doors and compartmentation).

Control of Asbestos at Work Regulations (CAWR) 2002

Law considered in context / more depth in Unit 16.

Arrangement of Regulations

1) Citation and commencement.

2) Interpretation.

3) Duties under these Regulations.

4) Duty to manage asbestos in non-domestic premises.

5) Identification of the type of asbestos.

6) Assessment of work which exposes employees to asbestos.

7) Plans of work.

8) Notification of work with asbestos.

9) Information, instruction and training.

10) Prevention or reduction of exposure to asbestos.

11) Use of control measures etc.

12) Maintenance of control measures etc.

13) Provision and cleaning of protective clothing.

14) Arrangements to deal with accidents, incidents and emergencies.

15) Duty to prevent or reduce the spread of asbestos.

16) Cleanliness of premises and plant.

17) Designated areas.

18) Air monitoring.

19) Standards for air testing.

20) Standards for analysis.

21) Health records and medical surveillance.

22) Washing and changing facilities.

23) Storage, distribution and labelling of raw asbestos and asbestos waste.

24) Supply of products containing asbestos for use at work.

25) Exemption certificates.

26) Extension outside Great Britain.

27) Revocations, amendments and savings.

28) Defence.

Schedule 1   Particulars to be included in a notification.

Schedule 2   The labelling of raw asbestos, asbestos waste and products containing asbestos.

Outline of key points

The Control of Asbestos at Work Regulations (CAWR) 2002 emphasis is placed on assessment to exposure; exposure prevention, reduction and control; adequate information, instruction and training for employees; monitoring and health surveillance. The regulations also clearly apply to incidental exposure.

Identification and assessment

Before any work with asbestos is started the employer must ensure a thorough assessment of the likely exposure is carried out. Such an assessment must identify the type of asbestos involved in the work, or to which the employees are likely to be exposed. For the purposes of the identification requirement the employer may assume that the asbestos is asbestos other than chrysotile alone, I.E. can assume the worst case scenario and provide for the situation accordingly. The assessment must also determine the nature and degree of any exposure and the steps required to prevent or reduce the exposure to the lowest level reasonably practicable.

Assessments must be reviewed regularly and when there is reason to suspect that the original assessment is invalid or there is a significant change in the work to which the original assessment related. Assessments should be revised accordingly to take account of any such changes, etc.

Plan of work

Employers must also prepare a suitable 'plan of work' before any work involving asbestos removal from buildings, structures, plant or installations (including ships) is undertaken. Such 'plans of work' must be retained for the duration of the work. The 'plan of work' should address the location, nature, expected duration and asbestos handling methods involved with the work, and the characteristics of the protection and decontamination equipment for the asbestos workers and the protection equipment for any others who may be affected by such work.

The asbestos risk assessment and plan of work must be kept on site.

Notification

The enforcing authority must be notified of any work to which these Regulations apply at least 28 days prior to commencement of the work (a lesser time may be agreed by mutual consent). Significant changes must also be notified, although work carried out in accordance with the *Asbestos (Licensing) Regulations 1983* is exempt from this provision, as are work situations where the exposure is not likely to exceed the 'action level'.

In these Regulations 'action level' is defined as "one of the following cumulative exposures to asbestos over a continuous 12 week period, when measured or calculated by a method approved by the HSC:

a.   where the exposure is solely to chrysotile, 72 fibre hours per millilitre of air, or

b.   where exposure is to any other form of asbestos either alone or in mixtures (including chrysotile mixtures), 48 fibre hours per millilitre of air, or

c.   where both types of exposure occur separately during the 12 week period, a proportionate number of fibre hours per millilitre of air."

Information, instruction and training

Employees exposed to asbestos must be provided with adequate information, instruction and training to understand the risks associated with asbestos and the necessary precautions. Employees who carry out work in connection with the employer's duties under these Regulations should also be given adequate information, instruction and training to do their work effectively. Under Regulation 7, refresher training must also be provided.

Prevention or reduction of exposure

Wherever possible the employer must prevent exposure of asbestos to the employees. Where this is not reasonably practicable the employer must reduce the exposure to the lowest level reasonably practicable other than by using respiratory protective equipment (RPE). If the asbestos exposure is in connection with a manufacturing process or the installation of a product, then the prevention of such exposure should be achieved by the substitution of asbestos for a less harmful substance, where practicable. RPE, where used, must reduce exposure to as low as is reasonably practicable below Control Limits.

Any personal protective equipment (respiratory protective equipment and protective clothing must comply with the health and safety requirements of any relevant design or manufacturing EU Directives applicable to such personal protective equipment and which are implemented in the UK.

Control limits

Under these Regulations 'control limits' (equivalent to 'maximum exposure limits' under COSHH) are defined as follows:

"(a)   for chrysotile

(i)   0.3 fibres per millilitre of air averaged over any continuous period of four hours

(ii)   0.9 fibres per millilitre of air averaged over any continuous period of 10 minutes

(b)   for any other form of asbestos either alone or in mixtures (including mixtures of chrysotile)

(i)   0.2 fibres per millilitre of air averaged over any continuous period of four hours

(ii)   0.6 fibres per millilitre of air averaged over any continuous period of 10 minutes."

In the event of a unexpected escape of asbestos in the workplace at a concentration that is liable to exceed any relevant control limit, the employer must ensure that only persons necessary to deal with the situation are permitted into the affected area and that such persons are provided with the appropriate personal protective equipment (respiratory protective equipment and protective clothing). Employees and other persons who may have been affected by the escape should be informed immediately.

Control measures

Employers must ensure that any measures provided to control the risks of exposure from asbestos are properly used or applied so far as is reasonably practicable. Likewise employees have a duty to use any control measures provided in the proper manner and to report any defects immediately. All control measures, including respiratory protective equipment (RPE), must be maintained in a clean and efficient condition and a suitable record of the work carried out in accordance with this provision must be kept for five years. RPE must be tested and examined and should be face-fit tested to the user (ACOP requirement).

Local exhaust ventilation equipment must be regularly examined and tested at suitable intervals by a competent person.

Where protective clothing is required to be provided to reduce the risks of exposure it must be either safely disposed of as asbestos waste, or adequately cleaned at certain intervals, after use in the specified manner. The spread of asbestos from one place to another must be prevented or reduced to the lowest level that is reasonably practicable.

Cleanliness

Any areas where asbestos work is carried out, or any plant/machinery used in connection with that work, must be kept in a clean state and be capable of being thoroughly cleaned. When considering work which creates asbestos dust, regard should be made as to the design and construction of the building to facilitate cleaning. Provision should be made for a suitable and adequate fixed vacuum system.

Provision and Cleaning of Protective Clothing

Adequate and suitable protective clothing shall be provided where necessary. Disposable overalls should be treated as asbestos waste and non-disposable protective clothing should be washed after every shift and the wastewater filtered.

Arrangements to deal with accidents, incidents and emergencies

Employers should have emergency procedures in place for any accident, incident or emergency relating to asbestos. Information should be provided to the emergency services so that when they attend an incident, they can protect themselves against the risks from asbestos.

Duty to prevent or reduce the spread of asbestos

Contaminated plant or equipment should be thoroughly decontaminated before it is moved for use elsewhere or for disposal. Persons should also be decontaminated every time they leave the work area.

Cleanliness of premises and plant

Asbestos dust and debris must be cleaned up as work progresses and not allowed to accumulate. Dustless methods, e.g. vacuuming with a type H vacuum should be used. When work comes to an end, all traces must be removed before handing the workplace over.

Designated areas

Work areas where the 'action level' is likely to be exceeded must be designated as 'asbestos areas'. Similarly, areas where the 'control limits' are likely to be exceeded must be designated as 'respirator zones'. Both such areas must be clearly marked and demarcated by means of suitable notices and only permitted persons allowed to enter. Employees must not eat, drink or smoke in these areas.

Monitoring

A monitoring programme must be set up to record the efficiency of the control measures in reducing or preventing exposure to asbestos. Suitable records of the monitoring results must be kept. Health records are required to be kept for 40 years, while other records must be retained for at least five years. Laboratories carrying out clearance tests and personal sampling must be accredited to EN 45001.

Health records

Where employees are exposed to asbestos above the 'action level', the employer is obliged to keep health records for the affected persons. Such records must be kept for at least 40 years. Employees who are exposed to asbestos above the 'action level' are also required to undergo medical surveillance. Medical examinations prior to employment and then at intervals not exceeding two years must be provided by the employer who will keep a certificate issued by the Employment Medical Adviser or appointed doctor of all such examinations in the individual's file. The employer is also obliged to provide the appropriate facilities which enable medical examinations to be carried out. Original medical certificates (not copies) must be given to workers.

Washing and changing facilities

Where employees are exposed to asbestos at work, the employer must provide suitable and adequate washing and changing facilities. Such facilities would include the provision of somewhere to store protective clothing and personal clothing not used at work. There must also be somewhere to store respiratory protective equipment.

Storage and labelling

Raw asbestos and asbestos waste must always be stored and transported in sealed, properly labelled containers.

Supply of products containing asbestos

No one may supply a product, which contains asbestos, for use at work unless the product is labelled in accordance with the provisions contained in the Schedule to these Regulations.

Approved Code of Practice

The regulations are accompanied by an Approved Code of Practice and Guidance - "Work with asbestos which does not normally require a licence".

Boards, insulation and coating

The *Asbestos (Licensing) Regulations (ASLIC) 1983* as amended by the Asbestos (Licensing) (Amendment) Regulations 1998 provide that an employer or self employed person who undertakes work with asbestos insulation or asbestos coating may only do so in accordance with a licence issued to him by the Health and Safety Executive (HSE). "Work with asbestos insulation or asbestos coating" means work in which asbestos insulation or coating is removed, repaired or disturbed and includes such work in any supervision or ancillary capacity. From the 1 August 1999 work with Asbestos Insulation Board (AIB) also requires a licence from the HSE.

Control of Lead at Work Regulations (CLAW) 2002

Law considered in context / more depth in Unit 16.

Arrangement of Regulations

1) Citation and commencement.
2) Interpretation.
3) Duties under these Regulations.
4) Prohibitions.
5) Assessment of the risk to health created by work involving lead.
6) Prevention or control of exposure to lead.
7) Eating, drinking and smoking.
8) Maintenance, examination and testing of control measures.
9) Air monitoring.
10) Medical surveillance.
11) Information, instruction and training.
12) Arrangements to deal with accidents, incidents and emergencies.
13) Exemption certificates.
14) Extension outside Great Britain.
15) Revocation and savings.

Schedule 1   Activities in which the employment of young persons and women of reproductive capacity is prohibited.

Schedule 2   Legislation concerned with the labelling of containers and pipes.

Outline of key points

The **Control of Lead at Work Regulations (CLAW) 2002** aims to protect people at work exposed to lead by controlling that exposure. The Regulations, which are summarised below, apply to any work which exposes people to lead.

Exposure to lead must be assessed by employers so that they may take adequate measures to protect both employees and anyone else who may be exposed to lead at work. Once the level of exposure has been assessed, then adequate measures can be taken ranging from simple maintenance of good washing facilities through to the provision of control measures such as respiratory equipment and constant medical surveillance. The Regulations prohibit the employment of young persons and women of reproductive capacity from some manufacturing, smelting and refining processes (specified in Schedule 1).

WORK WITH LEAD

The Regulations apply to any work which exposes employees or others to lead. In practical terms, this means any work from which lead arises:

a.   in the form of lead dust, fume or vapour in such a way as it could be inhaled.
b.   in any form which is liable to be ingested such as powder, dust, paint or paste.
c.   in the form of lead compounds such as lead alkyls and compounds of lead, which could be absorbed through the skin.

Employers' duties under the 2002 Regulations extend to any other people at work on the premises where work with lead is being carried on.

Lead assessment

Before employers (or a self employed person) can take adequate measures to protect people from lead at work, they need to know exactly what the degree of risk of lead exposure is. The level of risk dictates the measures to be taken. The employer's first duty, therefore, is to assess whether the exposure of any employee is liable to be significant. The next step is to determine the nature and degree of exposure. The assessment must be made before the work is commenced and revised where there is a reason to suspect that it is incorrect.

The purpose of the assessment is to determine whether or not exposure to lead is significant. Where exposure is significant then the employer must, so far as is reasonably practicable, ensure the prevention or adequate control of exposure by means other than the provision of personal protective equipment (PPE). Where control measures are not sufficient by themselves and PPE is issued then it must comply with the PPE Regulations or be of a type approved by the Health and Safety Executive (HSE).

When deciding controls the employer must take reasonable steps to ensure that they are being used and employees are under a duty to make full and proper use of control measures, PPE or any other measures dictated by the Regulations.

Control measures

Employers must, so far as is reasonably practicable, provide such control measures for materials, plant and processes as will adequately control the exposure of their employees to lead otherwise than by the use of respiratory protective equipment or protective clothing by those employees. Again, personal protective equipment and clothing should be used as a last resort. Employers are under a duty to restrict access to areas to ensure that only people undertaking necessary work are exposed.

If other control measures are inadequate, respiratory protective equipment must be provided for employees exposed to airborne lead. Employees must also be provided with protective clothing where they are significantly exposed to lead.

Respiratory protective equipment (RPE) or protective clothing should comply with any UK legislation which implements relevant EU 'design and manufacture' Directives.

Employers must also carry out an assessment before selecting RPE or protective clothing to ensure it will satisfy the necessary requirements and provide adequate protection. The assessment should define the characteristics required by the RPE or protective clothing in order to be suitable, and compare these characteristics against those of the protective equipment actually available. RPE must be examined and tested at appropriate intervals and records kept for a minimum period of 5 years.

Control measures, respiratory equipment and protective clothing must be maintained in an efficient state, in efficient working order and good repair. Employers should ensure that employees use the measures provided properly and employees must make full and proper use of all respiratory protective equipment or protective clothing provided, report defects immediately to the employer and take all reasonable steps to ensure RPE or protective clothing is returned to its storage accommodation after use.

Eating, drinking and smoking are prohibited in any place that is, or is liable to be, contaminated with lead.

Occupational exposure limits

Control limits for exposure to lead in atmosphere are:

- For lead other then lead alkyls, a concentration of lead in air which any employee is exposed of 0.15 mg per m^3 (8 hour TWA).
- For lead alkyls a concentration of lead of 0.10 mg per m^3 (8 hour TWA).

Air monitoring in relevant areas must be carried out at least every 3 months. This interval can be increased to 12 months providing that there are no material changes to the workplace and lead in air concentrations have not exceeded 0.10 mg per m^3 on two previous consecutive occasions.

Medical surveillance

Employees subject to, or liable to be, significantly exposed (or for whom a relevant doctor has certified that they should be) must be placed under medical surveillance by an employment medical adviser or appointed doctor. The Regulations set down action levels for blood-lead concentrations, which are:

- 20 g/dl for women of reproductive capacity, or
- 35 g/dl for any other employee.

Levels for urinary lead concentration are also specified. The adviser or doctor can certify that employees should not be employed on work which exposes them to lead or can only be employed under certain conditions. An investigation must be made when blood-lead action levels are exceeded.

Employees exposed to lead at work are under a duty to present themselves, in normal working hours, for medical examination or such biological tests as may be required. Employers and employees have a right to appeal against decisions made by relevant doctors.

Information, instruction and training

Every employer must ensure that adequate information, instruction and training is given to employees who are liable to be exposed to lead so that they are aware of the risks from lead and the precautions which should be observed. Information must also be given about the results relating to air monitoring and health surveillance and their significance. Adequate information, instruction and training must also be given to anyone who is employed by the employer to carry out lead assessments, air monitoring, etc.

Records

Adequate records must be kept of assessments, examination and testing of controls, air monitoring, medical surveillance and biological tests. Those records should be made available for inspection by employees (although not health records of identifiable individuals). Specific recording requirements are made in respect of female employees who are, or who are likely to be, exposed to significant levels of lead. Air monitoring records must be kept for at least 5 years and individual medical records for 40 years.

Control of Substances Hazardous to Health Regulations (COSHH) 2002

Law considered in context / more depth in Unit 16.

Arrangement of Regulations

1) Citation and commencement.
2) Interpretation.
3) Duties under these Regulations.
4) Prohibitions on substances.
5) Application of regulations 6 to 13.
6) Assessment of health risks created by work involving substances hazardous to health.
7) Control of exposure.
8) Use of control measures etc.
9) Maintenance of control measures.
10) Monitoring exposure.
11) Health surveillance.
12) Information etc.
13) Arrangements to deal with accidents, incidents and emergencies.
14) Exemption certificates.

15) Extension outside Great Britain.

16) Defence in proceedings for contravention of these Regulations.

17) Exemptions relating to the Ministry of Defence etc.

18) Revocations, amendments and savings.

19) Extension of meaning of "work".

20) Modification of section 3(2) of the Health and Safety at Work etc Act 1974.

Schedule 1   Other substances and processes to which the definition of "carcinogen" relates.

Schedule 2   Prohibition of certain substances hazardous to health for certain purposes.

Schedule 3   Special provisions relating to biological agents.

Schedule 4   Frequency of thorough examination and test of local exhaust ventilation plant used in certain processes.

Schedule 5   Specific substances and processes for which monitoring is required.

Schedule 6   Medical surveillance.

Schedule 7   Legislation concerned with the labelling of containers and pipes.

Schedule 8   Fumigations excepted from regulation 14.

Schedule 9   Notification of certain fumigations.

Appendix 1   Control of carcinogenic substances.

Annex 1   Background note on occupational cancer.

Annex 2   Special considerations that apply to the control of exposure to vinyl chloride.

Appendix 2   Additional provisions relating to work with biological agents.

Appendix 3   Control of substances that cause occupational asthma.

NOTE the main impact to the latest version of the COSHH Regulations concern the control of substances that cause occupational asthma.

Outline of key points

REGULATIONS

Reg. 2   **Interpretation**

"Substance hazardous to health" includes:

1)   Substances which under The Chemicals (Hazard Information and Packaging) Regulations (CHIP 3) 2002 are in categories of very toxic, toxic, harmful, corrosive or irritant.

2)   A substance listed in Schedule 1 to the Regs or for which the HSC have approved a maximum exposure limit or an occupational exposure standard.

3)   A biological agent.

4)   Dust in a concentration in air equal to or greater than:

■   10 mg/m^3 inhalable dust as an 8hr TWA, or
■   4mg/m^3 respirable dust as an 8hr TWA.

5)   Any other substance which creates a health hazard comparable with the hazards of the substances in the other categories above.

Reg. 3   **Duties**

Are on employer to protect:

Employees

Any other person who may be affected, except:

■   Duties for health surveillance do not extend to non-employees.
■   Duties to give information may extend to non-employees if they work on the premises.

Reg. 4   **Prohibitions on Substances**

Certain substances are prohibited from being used in some applications. These are detailed in Schedule 2 to Regs.

Reg. 5   **Application of Regs. 6 - 13**

Regs. 6 - 13 are made to protect a person's health from risks arising from exposure. They do not apply if:

The following Regs already apply:

■   The Control of Lead at Work Regulations (CLAW) 2002.
■   The Control of Asbestos at Work Regulations (CAWR) 2002.

The hazard arises from one of the following properties of the substance:

■   Radioactivity, explosive, flammable, high or low temperature, high pressure.
■   Exposure is for medical treatment.
■   Exposure is in a mine.

Reg. 6 ## Assessment

Employer must not carry out work which will expose employees to substances hazardous to health unless he has made an assessment of the risks to health and the steps that need to be taken to meet the requirements of the Regs.

The assessment must be reviewed if there are changes in the work and at least once every 5 years.

A suitable and sufficient assessment should include:

- An assessment of the risks to health.
- The practicability of preventing exposure.
- Steps needed to achieve adequate control.

An assessment of the risks should involve:

- Types of substance including biological agents.
- Where the substances are present and in what form.
- Effects on the body.
- Who might be affected.
- Existing control measures.

Reg. 7 ## Control of Exposure

1) Employer shall ensure that the exposure of employees to substances hazardous to health is either prevented or, where this is not reasonably practicable, adequately controlled.

2) So far as is reasonably practicable (1) above except to a carcinogen or biological agent shall be by measures other than personal protective equipment (PPE).

3) Where not reasonably practicable to prevent exposure to a carcinogen by using an alternative substance or process, the following measure shall apply:

- Total enclosure of process.
- Use of plant, process and systems which minimise generation of, or suppress and contain, spills, leaks, dust, fumes and vapours of carcinogens.
- Limitation of quantities of a carcinogen at work.
- Keeping of numbers exposed to a minimum.
- Prohibition of eating, drinking and smoking in areas liable to contamination.
- Provision of hygiene measures including adequate washing facilities and regular cleaning of walls and surfaces.
- Designation of areas/installations liable to contamination and use of suitable and sufficient warning signs.
- Safe storage, handling and disposal of carcinogens and use of closed and clearly-labelled containers.

4) If adequate control is not achieved, then employer shall provide suitable PPE to employees in addition to taking control measures.

5) PPE provided shall comply with The Personal Protective Equipment at Work Regulations, 2002 (dealing with the supply of PPE).

6&7) For substances which have a maximum exposure limit (MEL), control of that substance shall, so far as inhalation is concerned, only be treated if the level of exposure is reduced as far as is reasonably practicable and in any case below the MEL.

Where a substance has an occupational exposure standard (OES), control of that substance shall, so far as inhalation is concerned, only be treated as adequate if the OES is not exceeded or if it is, steps are taken to remedy the situation as soon as reasonably practicable.

8) Respiratory protection must be suitable and of a type or conforming to a standard approved by the HSE.

9) In the event of failure of a control measure which may result in the escape of carcinogens, the employer shall ensure:

- Only those who are responsible for repair and maintenance work are permitted in the affected area and are provided with PPE.
- Employees and other persons who may be affected are informed of the failure forthwith.

Reg. 8 Employer shall take all reasonable steps to ensure control measures, PPE, etc. are properly used/applied.

Employee shall make full and proper use of control measures, PPE etc. and shall report defects to employer.

Reg. 9 ## Maintenance of Control Measures

Employer providing control measures to comply with Reg.7 shall ensure that it is maintained in an efficient state, in efficient working order and in good repair and in the case of PPE in a clean condition, properly stored in a well-defined place checked at suitable intervals and when discovered to be defective repaired or replaced before further use.

- Contaminated PPE should be kept apart and cleaned, decontaminated or, if necessary destroyed.
- Engineering controls - employer shall ensure thorough examination and tests.
- Local exhaust ventilation (LEV) - Once every 14 months unless process specified in Schedule 4.
- Others - At suitable intervals.
- Respiratory protective equipment - employer shall ensure thorough examination and tests at suitable intervals.
- Records of all examinations, tests and repairs kept for 5 years.

Reg. 10   ## Monitoring Exposure

Employer shall ensure exposure is monitored if

- Needed to ensure maintenance of adequate control.
- Otherwise needed to protect health of employees.
- Substance/process specified in Schedule 5.

Records kept if:

- There is an identified exposure of identifiable employee - 40 years.
- Otherwise - 5 years.

Reg. 11   ## Health Surveillance

1) Where appropriate for protection of health of employees exposed or liable to be exposed, employer shall ensure suitable health surveillance.

2) Health surveillance is appropriate if:

- Employee exposed to substance/process specified in Schedule 6.
- Exposure to substance is such that an identifiable disease or adverse health effect can result, there is a reasonable likelihood of it occurring and a valid technique exists for detecting the indications of the disease or effect.

3) Health records kept for at least 40 years.

4) If employer ceases business, HSE notified and health records offered to HSE.

5) If employee exposed to substance specified in Schedule 6, then health surveillance shall include medical. surveillance, under Employment Medical Adviser (EMA) at 12 monthly intervals - or more frequently if specified by EMA.

6) EMA can forbid employee to work in process, or specify certain conditions for him to be employed in a process.

7) EMA can specify that health surveillance is to continue after exposure has ceased. Employer must ensure.

8) Employees to have access to their own health record.

9) Employee must attend for health/medical surveillance and give information to EMA.

10) EMA entitled to inspect workplace.

11) Where EMA suspends employee from work exposing him to substances hazardous to health, employer of employee can apply to HSE in writing within 28 days for that decision to be reviewed.

Reg. 12   ## Information etc.

Employer shall provide suitable and sufficient information, instruction and training for him to know:

- Risks to health.
- Precautions to be taken.

This should include information on:

- Results of monitoring of exposure at workplace.
- Results of collective health surveillance.

If the substances have been assigned a maximum exposure limit, then the employee/Safety Representative must be notified forthwith if the MEL has been exceeded.

Reg. 13   ## Arrangements to deal with accidents, incidents and emergencies.

To protect the health of employees from accidents, incidents and emergencies, the employer shall ensure that:

- Procedures are in place for first aid and safety drills (tested regularly).
- Information on emergency arrangements is available.
- Warning, communication systems, remedial action and rescue actions are available.
- Information made available to emergency services: external and internal.
- Steps taken to mitigate effects, restore situation to normal and inform employees.
- Only essential persons allowed in area.

These duties do not apply where the risks to health is slight or measures in place Reg 7(1) are sufficient to control the risk.

The employee must report any accident or incident which has or may have resulted in the release of a biological agent which could cause severe human disease.

NOTE the main impact to the latest version of the COSHH Regulations concern the control of substances that cause occupational asthma.

APPENDIX 3 CONTROL OF SUBSTANCES THAT CAUSE OCCUPATIONAL ASTHMA

This relates certain regulations specifically to substances with the potential to cause asthma.

- Regulation 6 - assessment of risk to health created by work involving substances hazardous to health, (i.e. substances that may cause asthma).
- Regulation 7 – prevention or control of exposure to substances hazardous to health, (i.e. substances that may cause occupational asthma).
- Regulation 11 – health surveillance, (for employees who are or may be exposed to substances that may cause occupational asthma).
- Regulation 12 – information, instruction and training for persons who may be exposed to substances hazardous to health, to include: typical symptoms of asthma, substances that may cause it, the permanency of asthma and what happens with subsequent exposures, the need to report symptoms immediately and the reporting procedures.

Training should be given, including induction training before they start the job.

SCHEDULE 3 ADDITIONAL PROVISIONS RELATING TO WORK WITH BIOLOGICAL AGENTS

Regulation 7(10)

Part I Provision of general application to biological agents

1   Interpretation.

2   Classification of biological agents.

The HSC shall approve and publish a "Categorisation of Biological Agents according to hazard and categories of containment" which may be revised or re-issued.

Where no approved classification exists, the employer shall assign the agent to one of four groups according to the level of risk of infection.

Group 1 - unlikely to cause human disease.

Group 2 - can cause human disease.

Group 3 - can cause severe disease and spread to community.

Group 4 - can cause severe disease, spread to community and there is no effective treatment.

3   Special control measures for laboratories, animal rooms and industrial processes

Every employer engaged in research, development, teaching or diagnostic work involving Group 2, 3 or 4 biological agents; keeping or handling laboratory animals deliberately or naturally infected with those agents, or industrial processes involving those agents, shall control them with the most suitable containment.

4   List of employees exposed to certain biological agents

The employer shall keep a list of employees exposed to Group 3 or 4 biological agents for at least 10 years. If there is a long latency period then the list should be kept for 40 years.

5   Notification of the use of biological agents

Employers shall inform the HSE at least 20 days in advance of first time use or storage of Group 2, 3 or 4 biological hazards. Consequent substantial changes in procedure or process shall also be reported.

6   Notification of the consignment of biological agents

The HSE must be informed 30 days before certain biological agents are consigned.

Part II Containment measures for health and veterinary care facilities, laboratories and animal rooms.

Part III Containment measures for industrial processes.

Part IV Biohazard sign.

The biohazard sign required by regulation 7(6)(a) shall be in the form shown below -

Part V Biological agents whose use is to be notified in accordance with paragraph 5(2) of Part I of this Schedule

- Any Group 3 or 4 agent, or
- Certain named Group 2 agents.

Construction (Head Protection) Regulations (CHPR) 1989

Law considered in context / more depth in Units 8 and 9.

Arrangement of Regulations

1)   Citation, commencement and interpretation.

2)   Application of these Regulations.

3)   Provision, maintenance and replacement of suitable head protection.

4)   Ensuring suitable head protection is worn.

5)   Rules and directions.

6)   Wearing of suitable head protection.

7)   Reporting the loss of, or defect in, suitable head protection.

8)   Extension outside Great Britain.

9)   Exemption certificates.

Outline of key points

ENSURING SUITABLE HEAD PROTECTION IS WORN

Reg. 4(1)   Every employer shall ensure so far as is reasonably practicable that each of his employees who is at work on operations or works to which these Regulations apply wears suitable head protection, unless there is no foreseeable risk to injury to his head other than by his falling.

4(2)   Every employer, self-employed person or employee who has control over any other person who is at work on operations or works to which these Regulations apply shall ensure so far as is reasonably practicable that each such other person wears suitable head protection, unless there is no foreseeable risk of injury to that other person's head other than by his falling.

RULES AND DIRECTIONS

Reg.5(1)   The person for the time being having control of a site where operations or works to which these Regulations apply are being carried out may, so far as is necessary to comply with regulation 4 of these Regulations, make rules regulating the wearing of suitable head protection on that site by persons at work on those operations or works.

5(2)   Rules made in accordance with paragraph (1) of this regulation shall be in writing and shall be brought to the notice of persons who may be affected by them.

5(3)   An employer may, so far as is necessary to comply with regulation 4(1) of these Regulations, give directions requiring his employees to wear suitable head protection.

5(4)   An employer, self-employed person or employee who has control over any other self-employed person may, so far as is necessary to comply with regulation 4(2) of these Regulations, give directions requiring each such other self-employed person to wear suitable head protection.

WEARING OF SUITABLE HEAD PROTECTION

Reg.6(1)   Every employee who has been provided with suitable head protection shall wear that head protection when required to do so by rules made or directions given under regulation 5 of these Regulations.

6(2)   Every self-employed person shall wear suitable head protection when required to do so by rules made or directions given under regulation 5 of these Regulations.

6(3)   Every self-employed person who is at work on operations or works to which these Regulations apply, but who is not under the control of another employer or self-employed person or of an employee, shall wear suitable head protection unless there is no foreseeable risk of injury to his head other than by his falling.

6(4)   Every employee or self-employed person who is required to wear suitable head protection by or under these Regulations shall do so properly.

REPORTING THE LOSS OF, OR DEFECT IN, SUITABLE HEAD PROTECTION

Reg. 7   Every employee who has been provided with suitable head protection by his employer shall take reasonable care of it and shall forthwith report to his employer any loss of, or obvious defect in, that head protection.

Construction (Health, Safety and Welfare) Regulations (CHSW) 1996

Law considered in context / more depth in Units 7, 8, 9 and 10.

Arrangement of Regulations

1) Citation and commencement.
2) Interpretation.
3) Application.
4) Persons upon whom duties are placed by these Regulations.
5) Safe places of work.
6) Falls.
7) Fragile material.
8) Falling objects.
9) Stability of structures.
10) Demolition or dismantling.
11) Explosives.
12) Excavations.
13) Cofferdams and caissons.
14) Prevention of drowning.
15) Traffic routes.
16) Doors and gates.
17) Vehicles.
18) Prevention of risk from fire etc.
19) Emergency routes and exits.
20) Emergency procedures.
21) Fire detection and fire-fighting.
22) Welfare facilities.
23) Fresh air.
24) Temperature and weather protection.
25) Lighting.
26) Good order.
27) Plant and equipment.
28) Training.
29) Inspection.
30) Reports.
31) Exemption certificates.
32) Extension outside Great Britain.
33) Enforcement in respect of fire.
34) Modifications.
35) Revocations.

Schedule 1.   Requirements for guard-rails etc.
Schedule 2.   Requirements for working platforms.
Schedule 3.   Requirements for personal suspension equipment.
Schedule 4.   Requirements for means of arresting falls.
Schedule 5.   Requirements for ladders.
Schedule 6.   Welfare facilities.
Schedule 7.   Places of work requiring inspection.
Schedule 8.   Particulars to be included in a report of inspection.
Schedule 9.   Modifications.
Schedule 10.   Revocations.

Outline of key points

DUTY HOLDERS UNDER THE REGULATIONS

The main duty-holders under these Regulations are employers, the self-employed and those who control the way in which construction work is carried out. Employees too have duties to carry out their own work in a safe way. Also, anyone doing construction work has a duty to co-operate with others on matters of health and safety and report any defects to those in control.

SAFE PLACES OF WORK (REGULATION 5)

A general duty to ensure a safe place of work and safe means of access to and from that place of work

This Regulation sets out a general requirement which applies to all construction work. It applies equally to places of work in the ground, at ground level and at height. In essence it requires that 'reasonably practicable' steps should be taken to provide for safety and to ensure risks to health are minimised. This means that action to be taken should be proportionate to the risk involved.

PRECAUTIONS AGAINST FALLS (REGULATIONS 6 AND 7)

- Prevent falls from height by physical precautions or, where this is not possible, provide equipment that will arrest falls.
- Ensure there are physical precautions to prevent falls through fragile materials.
- Erect scaffolding, access equipment, harnesses and nets under the supervision of a competent person.
- Ensure there are criteria for using ladders.

Falls account for more than half of the fatal accidents in construction. The aim of the Regulations is to prevent falls from any height, but there are specific steps to be taken for work at heights of two metres or more.

1) At or above two metres, where work cannot be done safely from the ground, the first objective is to provide physical safeguards to prevent falls. Where possible, means of access and working places should be of sound construction and capable of safely supporting both people and the materials needed for the work. Guard rails and toe boards or an equivalent standard of protection should be provided at any edge from which people could fall.

2) If it is either not possible to provide the above safeguards or the work is of such duration or difficulty that it would not be reasonably practicable to do so consider using properly installed personnel equipment such as rope access or boatswain's chairs.

3) If, for the same reasons these methods of work cannot be used, it will be necessary to consider equipment which will arrest falls, i.e. safety harnesses or nets with associated equipment. Scaffolds, personnel harnesses and net equipment have to be erected or installed under the supervision of a competent person.

FALLING OBJECTS (REGULATION 8)

- Where necessary to protect people at work and others, take steps to prevent materials from falling.
- Where it is not reasonably practicable to prevent falling materials, take precautions to prevent people from being struck, e.g. covered walkways.
- Do not throw any materials or objects down from a height if they could strike someone.
- Store materials and equipment safely.

The first objective is to prevent materials or objects from falling in circumstances where they could strike someone. Only where it is not reasonably practicable to do so, should other means, e.g. covered walkways, be used.

WORK ON STRUCTURES (REGULATIONS 9, 10 AND 11)

- Prevent accidental collapse of new or existing structures or those under construction.
- Make sure any dismantling or demolition of any structure is planned and carried out in a safe manner under the supervision of a competent person.
- Only fire explosive charges after steps have been taken to ensure that no one is exposed to risk or injury from the explosion.

Every year there are structural collapses which have the potential to cause serious accidents. The CHSW Regulations set a high standard to prevent collapses which involves taking into account the hazard during the planning stage. Demolition or dismantling are recognised as high risk activities. In any cases where this work presents a risk of danger to anyone, it should be planned and carried out under the direct supervision of a competent person.

EXCAVATIONS, COFFERDAMS AND CAISSONS (REGULATIONS 12 AND 13)

- Prevent collapse of ground both in and above excavations.
- Identify and prevent risk from underground cables and other services.
- Ensure cofferdams and caissons are properly designed, constructed and maintained.

From the outset, and as work progresses, any excavation which has the potential to collapse unless supported, should have suitable equipment immediately available to provide such support. Underground cables and services can also be a source of danger. These should be identified before work starts and positive action taken to prevent injury.

PREVENTION OR AVOIDANCE OF DROWNING (REGULATION 14)

- Take steps to prevent people from falling into water or other liquid so far as is reasonably practicable.
- Ensure that personal protective and rescue equipment is immediately available for use and maintained, in the event of a fall.
- Make sure safe transport by water is under the control of a competent person.

TRAFFIC ROUTES, VEHICLES, DOORS AND GATES (REGULATIONS 15, 16 AND 17)

- Ensure construction sites are organised so that pedestrians and vehicles can both move safely and without risks to health.
- Make sure routes are suitable and sufficient for the people or vehicles using them.
- Prevent or control the unintended movement of any vehicle.
- Make arrangements for giving a warning of any possible dangerous movement, e.g. reversing vehicles.
- Ensure safe operation of vehicles including prohibition of riding or remaining in unsafe positions.
- Make sure doors and gates which could present danger, e.g. trapping risk of powered doors, have

suitable safeguards.

PREVENTION AND CONTROL OF EMERGENCIES (REGULATIONS 18, 19, 20 AND 21)

- Prevent risk from fire, explosion, flooding and asphyxiation.
- Provide emergency routes and exits.
- Make arrangements for dealing with emergencies, including procedures for evacuating the site.
- Where necessary, provide fire-fighting equipment, fire detectors and alarm systems.

These Regulations require the prevention of risk as far as it is reasonably practicable to achieve. However, there are times when emergencies do arise and planning is needed to ensure, for example, that emergency routes are provided and evacuation procedures are in place.

These particular Regulations (as well as those on traffic routes, welfare, cleanliness and signing of sites) apply to construction work which is carried out on construction sites. However, the rest of the Regulations apply to all construction work.

The HSE continues to be responsible for inspection of means of escape and fire-fighting for most sites. However, fire authorities have enforcement responsibility in many premises which remain in normal use during construction work. This continues the sensible arrangement which ensures that the most appropriate advice is given.

WELFARE FACILITIES (REGULATION 22)

- Provide sanitary and washing facilities and an adequate supply of drinking water.
- Provide rest facilities.
- Provide facilities to change and store clothing.

There is an important additional duty in this Regulation. Anybody in control of a site has to ensure that there are reasonable welfare facilities available at readily accessible places. This does not necessarily mean, for example, that the main contractor has to provide these facilities, but they should check that others who have duties are making this provision.

A number of the Regulations are supported by explanatory Schedules. For welfare, the Schedule is fairly detailed and explains what is a reasonable standard of welfare in line with the duration of work and site activities.

SITE-WIDE ISSUES (REGULATIONS 23, 24, 25, AND 26)

- Ensure sufficient fresh or purified air is available at every workplace, and associated plant is capable of giving visible or audible warning of failure.
- Make sure a reasonable working temperature is maintained at indoor work places during working hours.
- Provide facilities for protection against adverse weather conditions.
- Make sure suitable and sufficient emergency lighting is available.
- Make sure suitable and sufficient lighting is available, including providing secondary lighting where there would be a risk to health or safety if primary or artificial lighting failed.
- Keep construction sites in good order and in a reasonable state of cleanliness.
- Ensure the perimeter of a construction site to which people, other than those working on the site could gain access, is marked by suitable signs so that its extent can be easily identified.

Note that **Regulation 27** (the duty to ensure that plant and equipment is safe, of sound construction and to ensure maintenance and safe use) has been revoked and replaced by the Provision and Use of Work Equipment Regulations (PUWER) 1998. All of these duties (with the exception of those for lighting) are governed by the term 'so far as it is reasonably practicable'.

TRAINING, INSPECTION AND REPORTS (REGULATIONS 28, 29 AND 30)

- Ensure construction activities where training, technical knowledge or experience is necessary to reduce risks of injury are only carried out by people who meet these requirements or, if not, are supervised by those with appropriate training, knowledge or experience.
- Before work at height, on excavations, cofferdams or caissons begins, make sure the place of work is inspected, (and at subsequent specified periods), by a competent person, who must be satisfied that the work can be done safely.
- Following inspection, ensure written reports are made by the competent person.

Lack of training has been identified as one of the major contributory factors in accidents and ill health in construction. Many activities are made safe simply by ensuring that those doing the work have knowledge of and understand the importance of safe practices.

The frequency of inspections depends on the nature and place of work. For example, following the initial inspection, work at places over two metres in height require weekly inspections. In contrast, for work in excavations (including shafts and tunnels), inspections are necessary at the beginning of every shift. Inspections help to ensure that safety is monitored during changing site conditions.

Reports detailing inspections are generally required every time an inspection is carried out, but there are exceptions. For example, weekly reports only are needed for inspections of excavation work, and unless the tower scaffold remains erected in the same place for seven days or more, inspections of tower scaffolds do not have to be recorded.

[Source HSE]

Dangerous Substances and Explosive Atmospheres Regulations (DSEAR) 2002

Law considered in context / more depth in Unit 15.

Arrangement of Regulations

1) Citation and commencement.
2) Interpretation.
3) Application.
4) Duties under these Regulations.
5) Risk assessment.
6) Elimination or reduction of risks from dangerous substances.
7) Places where explosive atmospheres may occur.
8) Arrangements to deal with accidents, incidents and emergencies.
9) Information, instruction and training.
10) Identification of hazardous contents of containers and pipes.
11) Duty of co-ordination.
12) Extension outside Great Britain.
13) Exemption certificates.
14) Exemptions for Ministry of Defence etc.
15) Amendments.
16) Repeals and revocations.
17) Transitional provisions.

Schedule 1. General safety measures.
Schedule 2. Classification of places where explosive atmospheres may occur.
Schedule 3. Criteria for the selection of equipment and protective systems.
Schedule 4. Warning sign for places where explosive atmospheres may occur.
Schedule 5. Legislation concerned with the marking of containers and pipes.
Schedule 6. Amendments.
Schedule 7. Repeal and revocation.

Outline of key points

These new regulations aim to protect against risks from fire, explosion and similar events arising from dangerous substances that are present in the workplace.

DANGEROUS SUBSTANCES

These are any substances or preparations that due to their properties or the way in which they are being used could cause harm to people from fires and explosions. They may include petrol, liquefied petroleum gases, paints, varnishes, solvents and dusts.

APPLICATION

DSEAR applies in most workplaces where a dangerous substance is present. There are a few exceptions where only certain parts of the regulations apply, for example:

- Ships.
- Medical treatment areas.
- Explosives/chemically unstable substances.
- Mines.
- Quarries.
- Boreholes.
- Offshore installations.
- Means of transport.

MAIN REQUIREMENTS

You must::

- Conduct a risk assessment of work activities involving dangerous substances.
- Provide measures to eliminate or reduce risks.
- Provide equipment and procedures to deal with accidents and emergencies.
- Provide information and training for employees.
- Classify places into zones and mark zones where necessary (to be phased in) -

Workplace in use by July 2003	-	Meet requirements by July 2006
Workplace modified before July 2006	-	Meet requirements at time of modifications
New workplace after 30 June 2003	-	Meet requirements from start.

The risk assessment should include:

- The hazardous properties of substance.
- The way they are used or stored.
- Possibility of hazardous explosive atmosphere occurring.
- Potential ignition sources.
- Details of zoned areas (July 2003).
- Co-ordination between employers (July 2003).

SAFETY MEASURES

Where possible eliminate safety risks from dangerous substances or, if not reasonably practicable to do this, control risks and reduce the harmful effects of any fire, explosion or similar event.

Substitution - Replace with totally safe or safer substance (best solution).

Control measures - If risk cannot be eliminated apply the following control measures in the following order:

- Reduce quantity.
- Avoid or minimise releases.
- Control releases at source.
- Prevent formation of explosive atmosphere.
- Collect, contain and remove any release to a safe place e.g. ventilation.
- Avoid ignition sources.
- Avoid adverse conditions e.g. exceeding temperature limits.
- Keep incompatible substances apart.

Mitigation measures - Apply measures to mitigate the effects of any situation.

- Prevent fire and explosions from spreading to other plant, equipment or other parts of the workplace.
- Reduce number of employees exposed.
- Provide process plant that can contain or suppress an explosion, or vent it to a safe place.

ZONED AREAS

In workplaces where explosive atmospheres may occur, areas should be classified into zones based on the likelihood of an explosive atmosphere occurring. Any equipment in these areas should ideally meet the requirements of the Equipment and Protective Systems Intended for Use in Potentially Explosive Atmospheres Regulations (ATEX) 1996. However equipment in use before July 2003 can continue to be used providing that the risk assessment says that it is safe to do so. Areas may need to be marked with an 'Ex' warning sign at their entry points. Employees may need to be provided with appropriate clothing e.g. anti static overalls. Before use for the first time, a person competent in the field of explosion protection must confirm hazardous areas as being safe.

ACCIDENTS, INCIDENTS AND EMERGENCIES

DSEAR builds on existing requirements for emergency procedures, which are contained in other regulations. These may need to be supplemented if you assess that a fire, explosion or significant spillage could occur, due to the quantities of dangerous substances present in the workplace. You may need to arrange for:

- Suitable warning systems.
- Escape facilities.
- Emergency procedures.
- Equipment and clothing for essential personnel who may need to deal with the situation.
- Practice drills.
- Make information, instruction and training available to employees and if necessary liaise with the emergency services.

Electricity at Work Regulations (EWR) 1989

Law considered in context / more depth in Unit 14.

Arrangement of Regulations

PART I
Introduction

1) Citation and commencement.
2) Interpretation.
3) Persons on whom duties are imposed by these Regulations.

PART II
General

4) Systems, work activities and protective equipment.
5) Strength and capability of electrical equipment.
6) Adverse or hazardous environments.
7) Insulation, protection and placing of conductors.
8) Earthing or other suitable precautions.
9) Integrity of referenced conductors.
10) Connections.

11) Means for protecting from excess of current.

12) Means for cutting off the supply and for isolation.

13) Precautions for work on equipment made dead.

14) Work on or near live conductors.

15) Working space, access and lighting.

16) Persons to be competent to prevent danger and injury.

PART III
Regulations Applying to Mines Only

17) Provisions applying to mines only.

18) Introduction of electrical equipment.

19) Restriction of equipment in certain zones below ground.

20) Cutting off electricity or making safe where firedamp is found either below ground or at the surface.

21) Approval of certain equipment for use in safety-lamp mines.

22) Means of cutting off electricity to circuits below ground.

23) Oil-filled equipment.

24) Records and information.

25) Electric shock notices.

26) Introduction of battery-powered locomotives and vehicles into safety-lamp mines.

27) Storage, charging and transfer of electrical storage batteries.

28) Disapplication of section 157 of the Mines and Quarries Act 1954.

PART IV
Miscellaneous and General

29) Defence.

30) Exemption certificates.

31) Extension outside Great Britain.

32) Disapplication of duties.

33) Revocations and modifications.

Schedule 1.   Provisions applying to mines only and having effect in particular in relation to the use below ground in coal mines of film lighting circuits.

Schedule 2.   Revocations and modifications.

Outline of key points

SYSTEMS, WORK ACTIVITIES AND PROTECTIVE EQUIPMENT (REGULATION 4)

The system and the equipment comprising it must be designed and installed to take account of all reasonably foreseeable conditions of use.

- The system must be maintained so as to prevent danger.
- All work activities must be carried out in such a manner as to not give rise to danger.
- Equipment provided to protect people working on live equipment must be suitable and maintained.

STRENGTH AND CAPABILITY OF ELECTRICAL EQUIPMENT (REGULATION 5)

Strength and capability refers to the equipment's ability to withstand the effects of its load current and any transient overloads or pulses of current.

ADVERSE OR HAZARDOUS ENVIRONMENTS (REGULATION 6)

This regulation requires that electrical equipment is suitable for the environment and conditions that might be reasonably foreseen. In particular, attention should be paid to:

- *Mechanical damage* caused by for example; vehicles, people, vibration, etc.
- Weather, natural hazards, temperature or pressure. Ice, snow, lightning, bird droppings, etc.
- *Wet, dirty, dusty or corrosive conditions.* Conductors, moving parts, insulators and other materials may be affected by the corrosive nature of water, chemicals and solvents. The presence of explosive dusts must be given special consideration.
- *Flammable or explosive substances.* Electrical equipment may be a source of ignition for liquids, gases, vapours etc.

INSULATION, PROTECTION AND PLACING OF CONDUCTORS (REGULATION 7)

The purpose of this regulation is to prevent danger from direct contact. Therefore, if none exists, no action is needed. Conductors though will normally need to be insulated and also have some other protection to prevent mechanical damage.

EARTHING OR OTHER SUITABLE PRECAUTIONS (REGULATION 8)

The purpose of this regulation is to prevent danger from indirect contact. Conductors such as metal casings may become live through fault conditions. The likelihood of danger arising from these circumstances must be prevented by using the techniques described earlier in this section i.e. earthing, double insulation, reduced voltages etc.

INTEGRITY OF REFERENCED CONDUCTORS (REGULATION 9)

In many circumstances the reference point is earthed because the majority of power distribution installations are referenced by a deliberate connection to earth at the generators or distribution transformers. The purpose of this regulation is to ensure that electrical continuity is never broken.

CONNECTIONS (REGULATION 10)

As well as having suitable insulation and conductance, connections must have adequate mechanical protection and strength. Plugs and sockets must conform to recognised standards as must connections between cables. Special attention should be paid to the quality of connections on portable appliances.

MEANS FOR PROTECTING FROM EXCESS CURRENT (REGULATION 11)

Faults or overloads can occur in electrical systems and protection must be provided against their effects. The type of protection depends on several factors but usually rests between fuses and circuit breakers.

MEANS FOR CUTTING OFF THE SUPPLY AND FOR ISOLATION (REGULATION 12)

Means must be provided to switch off electrical supplies together with a means of isolation so as to prevent inadvertent reconnection.

PRECAUTIONS FOR WORK ON EQUIPMENT MADE DEAD (REGULATION 13)

Working dead should be the norm. This regulation requires that precautions be taken to ensure that the system remains dead and to protect those at work on the system. Any or all of the following steps should be considered:

- Identify the circuit. Never assume that the labelling is correct.
- Disconnection and isolation. These are the most common methods: isolation switches, fuse removal and plug removal.
- Notices and barriers.
- Proving dead. The test device itself must also be tested before and after testing.
- Earthing.
- Permits to work.

WORK ON OR NEAR LIVE CONDUCTORS (REGULATION 14)

Live work must only be done if it is unreasonable for it to be done dead. If live work must be carried out then any or all of the following precautions should be taken:

- Competent staff (see reg. 16).
- Adequate information.
- Suitable tools. Insulated tools, protective clothing.
- Barriers or screens.
- Instruments and test probes. To identify what is live and what is dead.
- Accompaniment.
- Designated test areas.

WORKING SPACE, ACCESS AND LIGHTING (REGULATION 15)

Space. Where there are dangerous live exposed conductors, space should be adequate to:

- Allow persons to pull back from the hazard.
- Allow persons to pass each other.

Lighting. The first preference is for natural lighting then for permanent artificial lighting.

PERSONS TO BE COMPETENT TO PREVENT DANGER AND INJURY (REGULATION 16)

The object of this regulation is to 'ensure that persons are not placed at risk due to a lack of skills on the part of themselves or others in dealing with electrical equipment'.

In order to meet the requirements of this regulation a competent person would need:

- An understanding of the concepts of electricity and the risks involved in work associated with it.
- Knowledge of electrical work and some suitable qualification in electrical principles.
- Experience of the type of system to be worked on with an understanding of the hazards and risks involved.
- Knowledge of the systems of work to be employed and the ability to recognise hazards and risks.
- Physical attributes to be able to recognise elements of the system e.g. colour blindness and wiring.

Advice and queries regarding qualifications and training can be directed to the IEE - Institute of Electrical Engineers, London.

DEFENCE (REGULATION 29)

In any Regulation where the absolute duty applies, a defence in any criminal proceedings shall exist where a person can show that:
"He took all reasonable steps and exercised due diligence to avoid the commission of the offence."

Is there a prepared procedure (steps), is the procedure being followed (diligence) and do you have the records or witness to prove it retrospectively?

Environmental Protection Act (EPA) 1990

Law considered in context / more depth in Unit 16.

Outline of key points

"An Act to make provision for the improved control of pollution arising from certain industrial and other processes;

to re-enact the provisions of the Control of Pollution Act 1974 relating to waste on land with modifications as respects the functions of the regulatory and other authorities concerned in the collection and disposal of waste and to make further provision in relation to such waste;

to restate the law defining statutory nuisances and improve the summary procedures for dealing with them, to provide for the termination of the existing controls over offensive trades or businesses and to provide for the extension of the Clean Air Acts to prescribed gases;

to amend the law relating to litter and make further provision imposing or conferring powers to impose duties to keep public places clear of litter and clean;

to make provision conferring powers in relation to trolley abandoned on land in the open air; to amend the Radioactive Substances Act 1960;

to make provision for the control of genetically modified organisms; to make provision for the abolition of the Nature Conservancy Council and for the creation of councils to replace it and discharge the functions of that Council and, as respects Wales, of the Countryside Commission; to make further provision for the control of the importation, exportation, use, supply or storage of prescribed substances and articles and the importation, exportation, use, supply or storage of prescribed substances and articles and the importation or exportation of prescribed descriptions of waste; to confer powers to obtain information about potentially hazardous substances; to amend the law relating to the control of hazardous substances on, over or under land;

to amend section 107(6) of the Water Act 1989 and sections 31 (7)(a), 31 A(2) (c)(i) and 32(7)(a) of the Control of Pollution Act 1974;

to amend the provisions of the Food and Environmental Protection Act 1985 as regards the dumping of waste at sea;

to make further provision as respects the prevention of oil pollution from ships; to make provision for and in connection with the identification and control of dogs;

to confer powers to control the burning of crop residues;

to make provision in relation to financial or other assistance for purposes connected with the environment;

to make provision in relation to financial or other assistance for purposes connected with the environment;

to make provision as respects superannuation of employees of the groundwork Foundation and for remunerating the chairman of the Inland Waterways Amenity Advisory Council; and

for purposes connected with those purposes." [1st November 1990].

The EPA 1990 has 9 main Parts plus 16 Schedules, The main Parts are as follows:

Part I   Integrated Pollution Control and Air Pollution Control by Local Authorities.

Part II   Waste on Land.

Part III   Statutory Nuisances and Clean Air.

Part IV   Litter etc. (provisions relating to litter and abandoned trolleys).

Part V   Amendment of the Radioactive Substances Act 1960.

Part VI   Genetically Modified Organisms.

Part VII   Nature Conservation in Great Britain and Countryside Matters in Wales

Part VIII   Miscellaneous (Other controls on substances, articles or waste, Pollution at sea, Control of dogs, Straw and stubble burning and Environmental expenditure)

Part IX   General

Schedules:

Schedule 1	Authorisations for Processes: Supplementary Provisions.	
	Part I	Grant of Authorisations.
	Part II	Variation of Authorisations.
Schedule 2	Waste Disposal Authorities and Companies.	
	Part I	Transition to Companies.
	Part II	Provisions regulating Waste Disposal Authorities and Companies.
Schedule 3	Statutory Nuisances: Supplementary Provisions.	
Schedule 4	Abandoned Shopping and Luggage Trolleys.	
Schedule 5	Further Amendments of the Radioactive Substances Act 1960.	
	Part I	Miscellaneous and Consequential Amendments.
	Part I	Amendments relating to Scotland and Northern Ireland.
Schedule 6	The Nature Conservancy Councils for England and Scotland and the Countryside Council for Wales: Constitution.	
Schedule 7	The Joint Nature Conservation Committee.	
Schedule 8	Amendment of Enactments relating to Countryside Matters.	
Schedule 9	Amendment of Enactments conferring Nature Conservancy Functions.	

Schedule 10	Transfer Schemes and Staff of Existing Councils.	
	Part I	Transfer Schemes: Nature Conservancy Council.
	Part II	Transfer Schemes: The Countryside Commission.
	Part III	Employment of staff of Existing Bodies.
Schedule 11	Transitional Provisions and Savings for Part VII	
	Part I	Countryside Functions.
	Part II	Nature Conservation Functions.
	Part III	Supplementary.
Schedule 12	Injurious or Hazardous Substances: Advisory Committee.	
Schedule 13	Amendments of Hazardous Substances Legislation.	
	Part I	England and Wales.
	Part II	Scotland.
Schedule 14	Amendments of the Prevention of Oil Pollution Act 1971.	
Schedule 15	Consequential and Minor Amendments of Enactments.	
Schedule 16	Repeals.	
	Part I	Enactments relating to Processes.
	Part II	Enactments relating to Waste on Land.
	Part III	Enactments relating to Statutory Nuisances.
	Part IV	Enactments relating to Litter.
	Part V	Enactments relating to Radioactive Substances.
	Part VI	Enactments relating to Nature Conservation and Countryside Matters.
	Part VII	Enactments relating to Hazardous Substances.
	Part VII	Enactments relating to Deposits at Sea.
	Part IX	Miscellaneous Enactments.

Fire Precautions Act (FPA) 1971

Law considered in context / more depth in Unit 15.

Outline of key points

The FPA requires that a fire certificate be issued for certain premises based on the concept of "designated use". These include:

FACTORY, OFFICES AND SHOPS

Where:

- There are more than 20 persons at work in total.
- There are more than 10 persons (in total) on anything other than the ground floor.
- Adjoining premises, which are not fire separated, accumulate to more than these numbers.
- There are explosives or flammable liquids stored or used.

HOTELS AND BOARDING HOUSES

Where sleeping accommodation is provided for staff or guests:

- For more than six people.
- At basement level.
- Above the first floor level.

Fire Certificates may also be required for premises defined as special premises under the Fire Certification (Special Premises) Regulations 1976.

CONTENTS OF A FIRE CERTIFICATE

Include the specification of:

- Use of premises.
- Means of escape.
- Means of securing safe escape. i.e. provision of suitable extinguishers, alarms, fire doors etc.
- Special requirements for explosives, flammables etc.
- Maintenance of fire escape routes.
- Training of employees in fire safety, use of extinguishers etc.
- Maximum number of people in the building at any one time.

Fire Certificates (Special Premises) Regulations (FCSPR) 1976

Law considered in context / more depth in Unit 15.

Outline of key points

It was recognised, when the Fire Precautions Act (FPA) 1971 was compiled, that there are special industrial and commercial installations and processes which present particularly significant hazards, not only to people at work, but also to members of the public. In these types of premises, expertise in the administration and enforcement of safety provisions derives from the technical knowledge of the materials and processes in question and their potential hazards, including the risk of fire and explosion. It was decided, therefore, that the additional fire regulations to be made due to the certification under the FPA, should be administered by the same enforcing authority who should control other safety issues within the site. It is for this reason that these regulations are enforced by the Health and Safety Executive (HSE).

It is estimated that between 1,000 and 2,000 premises come under these regulations.

The system laid down in the regulation for the application for, issue of, contents, conditions and amendment to fire certificates is similar to that prescribed under the FPA. However, the variations are highlighted under the requirements for the types of premises that need fire certificates under the Special Premises Regulations.

The main types of premises requiring fire certificates under the Special Premises Regulations are those which:

1. Have more than 50 tonnes of a flammable liquid which is at a pressure greater than atmospheric pressure, and above it boiling point.
2. Manufacture expanded cellular plastics and have quantities of 50 tonnes or more per week.
3. Store 100 tonnes or more of L. P. G.s unless it is for use as a fuel or for heat treatment methods.
4. Store 100 tonnes or more of liquefied natural gas unless it is solely for use as a fuel at the premises themselves.
5. Store 100 tonnes or more of liquefied flammable gas predominantly of methyl acetylene unless it is solely to be used as a fuel at the premises.
6. Store 135 tonnes or more of oxygen or liquid oxygen.
7. Store 50 tonnes or more of chlorine, unless it is solely stored for the purpose of water purification.
8. Storage of 250 tonnes or more of ammonia at premises which manufacture artificial fertilisers.
9. The following quantities or more of materials are in process, manufacture, use or storage:

Phosgene	5 tonnes
Ethylene Oxide	20 tonnes
Carbon Disulphide	50 tonnes
Acrylonitrile	50 tonnes
Hydrogen Cyanide	50 tonnes
Ethylene	100 tonnes
Propylene	100 tonnes
Any highly flammable liquid	4,000 tonnes

10. Explosive factories or magazines licensed under the Explosives Act 1875.
11. Any building on the surface of any mine under the Mines and Quarries Act 1954.
12. Certain sites which involve nuclear installations.
13. Certain sites involving radioactive substances.

Fire Precautions (Workplace) Regulations (FPWR) 1997

Law considered in context / more depth in Unit 15.

Arrangement of Regulations

PART I
PRELIMINARY

1) Citation, commencement and extent.
2) Interpretation.

PART II
FIRE PRECAUTIONS IN THE WORKPLACE

3) Application of Part II.
4) Fire-fighting and fire detection.
5) Emergency routes and exits.
6) Maintenance.

PART III

AMENDMENT OF THE MANAGEMENT OF HEALTH AND SAFETY AT WORK REGULATIONS 1992

7)   Amendment of the 1992 Management Regulations: general provisions.

8)   Amendment of the 1992 Management Regulations.

PART IV

ENFORCEMENT AND OFFENCES

9)   Disapplication of the 1974 Act.

10)   Enforcement.

11)   Serious cases: offence.

12)   Serious cases: prohibition notices.

13)   Serious cases: enforcement notices.

14)   Enforcement notices: rights of appeal.

15)   Enforcement notices: offence.

16)   Enforcement orders.

PART V

FURTHER, CONSEQUENTIAL AND MISCELLANEOUS PROVISIONS

17)   Application of the 1971 Act.

18)   Application to the Crown.

19)   Application to visiting forces, etc.

20)   Application to premises occupied by the UK Atomic Energy Authority.

21)   Employee consultation.

22)   Disapplication of section 9A of the 1971 Act.

Outline of key points

INTRODUCTION

The Fire Precautions (Workplace) Regulations (FPWR) 1997 came into force on the 1st December 1997, and have been amended on 1st December 1999.

APPLICATION

There are few additional responsibilities for the majority of employers. However the Regulations do differ slightly from traditional fire legislation. The main difference is that the regulations apply to all workplaces (with a few exceptions), regardless of the number of employees that work there, unlike the Fire Precautions Act (FPA) 1971.

OBLIGATIONS

The regulations require employers to provide minimum fire safety standards in workplaces.

Where an employer does not have control over parts of the workplace, there is a responsibility on the occupier, owner or landlord to ensure compliance with the regulations.

MAIN REQUIREMENTS

The main requirements of the regulations are as follows:

■   Employers to assess the fire risks in the workplace (either as part of existing risk assessment requirements or as a separate area. This is a requirement of the Management of Health and Safety at Work Regulations (MHSWR) 1999.

■   Employers must check that a fire can be detected in reasonable time and that people can be warned.

■   Employers are to ensure that people who may be in the building can evacuate safely.

■   Provide reasonable fire fighting equipment.

■   Employers are to check that people in the workplace know what to do if there is a fire.

■   Fire safety equipment in the workplace is to be maintained and monitored, to ensure it is in a safe working condition.

■   Employer has to nominate employees to implement fire-fighting measures as necessary, and to ensure there are sufficient numbers, equipment, and training.

■   Arrange necessary contacts with emergency services, particularly with regard to rescue work and fire fighting.

Health and Safety (Consultation with Employees) Regulations (HSCER) 1996

Law considered in context / more depth in Unit 3.

Arrangement of Regulations

1) Citation, extent and commencement.

2) Interpretation.

3) Duty of employer to consult.

4) Persons to be consulted.

5) Duty of employer to provide information.

6) Functions of representatives of employee safety.

7) Training, time off and facilities for representatives of employee safety and time off for candidates.

8) Amendment of the Employment Rights Act 1996.

9) Exclusion of civil liability.

10) Application of health and safety legislation.

11) Application to the Crown and armed forces.

12) Disapplication to sea-going ships.

13) Amendment of the 1977 Regulations.

Outline of key points

1) The HSCER come into force on 1 October 1996 and are made under the European Communities Act 1972.

2) "Employees" do not include persons employed in domestic service in private households. Workplaces are defined as "any place where the employee is likely to work, or which he is likely to frequent in the course of his employment or incidentally to it."

3) Where there are employees not represented by the Safety Representatives and Safety Committee Regulations (SRSCR), the employer shall consult those employees in good time on matters relating to their health & safety at work. In particular they must be consulted on:

■ The introduction of any new measures which may affect their safety and health.

■ Arrangements made by the employer for appointing or nominating competent persons in accordance with regs. 6(1) and 7(1) of the Management of Health and Safety at Work Regs 1999 (MHSWR).

■ Any safety information the employer is legally obliged to provide to workers.

■ The planning and organisation of any health and safety training required under particular health and safety laws.

■ The health and safety consequences for employees of the introduction of new technologies into the workplace.

4) Employers can consult either directly with employees or, in respect of any group of employees, one or more elected representatives of that group. These are referred to as "representatives of employee safety" (RES). If the latter option is chosen, then employers must tell the employees the name of the representative and the group he/she represents. An employer which has been consulting a representative may choose to consult the whole workforce. However, the employer must inform the employees and the representatives of that fact.

5) If the employer consults employees directly then it must make available such information, within the employers' knowledge, as is necessary to enable them to participate fully and effectively in the consultation. If a representative is consulted, then the employer must make available all necessary information to enable them to carry out their functions, and of any record made under the Reporting of Injuries, Diseases and Dangerous Occurrences Regs 1995 which relates to the represented group of employees.

6) Representatives of employee safety have the following functions:

■ To make representations to the employer on potential hazards and dangerous occurrences at the workplace which affect, or
■ could affect the represented employees.
■ Make representations to the employer on general matters of health and safety.
■ To represent the employees in workplace consultations with HSE or local authority inspectors.

7) Representatives of employee safety must be given reasonable training in order to carry out their duties. Employers must meet the costs of the training and any travel and subsistence. They must also permit the representatives to take time off with pay during working hours in order for them to carry out their functions. Time off shall also be given, with pay, where this is required for any person standing as a candidate for election as a representative. Employers must also provide suitable facilities for the representatives to carry out their duties.

8) The Employment Rights Act 1996, which gives protection against unfair dismissal or discrimination on grounds of health and safety, is amended to protect representatives of employee safety and candidates for their election.

9) A breach of the HSCER does not confer any right of action in any civil proceedings.

10) Ensures that certain provisions of health and safety legislation (including enforcement provisions) operate in respect of the HSCER. The Regulations are made under the European Communities Act 1972. Enforcement is by the enforcing authorities appointed under the Health & Safety at Work Act 1974.

11) The HSCER will apply in respect of the armed forces. However, the representatives of employee safety will be appointed by the employer, rather than elected. Furthermore, representatives in the armed forces will not be entitled to time off with pay under reg.7.

12) The HSCER do not apply to the master or crew of a seagoing ship.

13) The SRSCR are amended so that they now include employees of coal mines.

Health and Safety (Display Screen Equipment) Regulations (DSE) 1992

Law considered in context / more depth in Unit 17.

Arrangement of Regulations

2) Every employer shall carry out suitable and sufficient analysis of workstations.

3) Employers shall ensure that equipment provided meets the requirements of the schedule laid down in these Regulations.

4) Employers shall plan activities and provide such breaks or changes in work activity to reduce employees' workload on that equipment.

5) For display screen equipment (DSE) users, the employer shall provide, on request, an eyesight test carried out by a competent person.

6 & 7) Provision of information and training.

Outline of key points

WORKSTATION ASSESSMENTS (REG 2)

Should take account of:

- Screen   -   positioning, character definition, character stability etc.
- Keyboard   -   tilt able, character legibility etc.
- Desk   -   size, matt surface etc.
- Chair   -   adjustable back and height, footrest available etc.
- Environment   -   noise, lighting, space etc.
- Software   -   easy to use, work rate not governed by software.

INFORMATION AND TRAINING (REGS 6 & 7)

Should include:

- Risks to health.
- Precautions in place (e.g. the need for regular breaks).
- How to recognise problems.
- How to report problems.

Health and Safety (First-Aid) Regulations (FAR) 1981

Law considered in context / more depth in Unit 6.

Arrangement of Regulations

1) Citation and commencement.

2) Interpretation.

3) Duty of employer to make provision for first-aid.

4) Duty of employer to inform his employees of the arrangements.

5) Duty of self-employed person to provide first-aid equipment.

6) Power to grant exemptions.

7) Cases where these Regulations do not apply.

8) Application to mines.

9) Application offshore.

10) Repeals, revocations and modification.

Schedule 1   Repeals.

Schedule 1   Revocations.

Outline of key points

2) Regulation 2 defines first aid as: '…treatment for the purpose of preserving life and minimising the consequences of injury or illness until medical (doctor or nurse) help can be obtained.   Also, it provides treatment of minor injuries which would otherwise receive no treatment, or which do not need the help of a medical practitioner or nurse.'

3) Requires that every employer must provide equipment and facilities which are adequate and appropriate in the circumstances for administering first-aid to his employees.

4) An employer must inform his employees about the first-aid arrangements, including the location of equipment, facilities and identification of trained personnel.

5) Self-employed people must ensure that adequate and suitable provision is made for administering first-aid while at work.

Health and Safety Information for Employees Regulations (IER) 1989

Law considered in context / more depth in Unit 4.

Arrangement of Regulations

1) Citation and commencement.
2) Interpretation and application.
3) Meaning of and revisions to the approved poster and leaflet.
4) Provision of poster or leaflet.
5) Provision of further information.
6) Exemption certificates.
7) Defence.
8) Repeals, revocations and modifications.

The Schedule   Repeals, revocations and modifications.

Part I - Repeals.

Part II - Revocations.

Part III - Modifications.

Outline of key points

The Health And Safety (Information for Employees) Regulations 1989 require that information relating to health and safety at work to be furnished to all employees by means of posters or leaflets in a form approved by the Health and Safety Executive.

The approved poster *"Health and Safety Law - what you should know"* should be placed in a prominent position and should contain details of the names and addresses of the enforcing authority and employment medical advisory service (EMAS). Since the modification to these Regulations (see below), the name(s) of the competent person(s) and the names and locations of trade union or other safety reps and the groups they represent must also be included. Any change of name or address should be shown within 6 months of the alteration.

The Health and Safety Executive (HSE) may approve a particular form of poster or leaflet for use in relation to a particular industry or employment and, where any such form has been approved, the HSE shall publish it. If a poster is used, the information must be legible and up to date. The poster must be prominently located in an area which all employees have access. If a leaflet is used, revised leaflets must be issued to employees when any similar changes occur.

MODIFICATION TO THE REGULATIONS

The Health and Safety Information for Employees (Modifications and Repeals) Regulations 1995 amended these regulations, this allows the HSE to approve an alternative poster to the basic 'Health and Safety Law' poster. The basic poster required updating in order to take account of European directives and recent legal developments.

The updated poster includes two new sections which allows employers to personalise information. There is now a box for the names and location of safety representatives, and a similar one for details of competent people appointed by the employer and their health and safety responsibilities.

The earlier version of the poster could have been used until the end of June 2000. After that, the new version of the poster must be displayed and the new leaflet used.

Health and Safety (Safety Signs and Signals) Regulations (SSSR) 1996

Law considered in context / more depth in Unit 6.

Arrangement of Regulations

1) Citation and commencement.
2) Interpretation.
3) Application.
4) Provision and maintenance of safety signs.
5) Information, instruction and training.
6) Transitional provisions.
7) Enforcement.
8) Revocations and amendments.

Outline of key points

The Regulations require employers to provide specific safety signs whenever there is a risk which has not been avoided or controlled by other means, e.g. by engineering controls and safe systems of work. Where a safety sign would not help to reduce that risk, or where the sign is not significant, there is no need to provide a sign.

They require, where necessary, the use of road traffic signs within workplaces to regulate road traffic.

They also require employers to:

- Maintain the safety signs which are provided by them.
- Explain unfamiliar signs to their employees and tell them what they need to do when they see a safety sign.

Regs cover 4 main areas of signs:

1) **PROHIBITION** - circular signs, prime colours red and white. e.g. no pedestrian access.

2) **WARNING** - triangular signs, prime colours black on yellow. e.g. overhead electrics.

3) **MANDATORY** - circular signs, prime colours blue and white e.g. safety helmets must be worn.

4) **SAFE CONDITION** - oblong/square signs, prime colours green and white e.g. fire exit, first aid etc.

Supplementary signs provide additional information.

Supplementary signs with yellow/black or red/white diagonal stripes can be used to highlight a hazard, but must not substitute for signs as defined above.

Fire fighting, rescue equipment and emergency exit signs have to comply with a separate British Standard.

Health and Safety at Work etc. Act (HASAWA) 1974

Law considered in context / more depth in Unit 1 – 4 and 6.

Arrangement of Act

Preliminary

1) Preliminary.

General duties

2) General duties of employers to the employees.

3) General duties of employers and self-employed to persons other than their employees.

4) General duties of persons concerned with premises to persons other than their employees.

5) [repealed].

6) General duties of manufacturers etc. as regards articles and substances for use at work.

7) General duties of employees at work.

8) Duty not to interfere with or misuse things provided pursuant to certain provisions.

9) Duty not to charge employees for things done or provided pursuant to certain specific requirements.

The Health and Safety Commission and the Health and Safety Executive

10) Establishment of the Commission and the Executive.

11) General functions of the Commission and the Executive.

12) Control of the Commission by the Secretary of State.

13) Other powers of the Commission.

14) Power of the Commission to direct investigations and Inquiries.

Health and safety regulations and approved codes of practice

15) Health and safety regulations.

16) Approval of codes of practice by the Commission.

17) Use of approved codes of practice in criminal proceedings.

Enforcement

18) Authorities responsible for enforcement of the relevant statutory provisions.

19) Appointment of inspectors.

20) Powers of inspectors.

21) Improvement notices.

22) Prohibition notices.

23) Provisions supplementary toss. 21 and 22.

24) Appeal against improvement or prohibition notice.

25) Power to deal with cause of imminent danger.

26) Power of enforcing authorities to indemnify their inspectors.

Obtaining and disclosure of information

27)   Obtaining of information by the Commission, the Executive, enforcing authorities etc.

28)   Restrictions on disclosure of information.

Special provisions relating to agriculture

29-32)   [repealed].

Provisions as to offences

33)   Offences.

34)   Extension of time for bringing summary proceedings.

35)   Venue.

36)   Offences due to fault of other person.

37)   Offences by bodies corporate.

38)   Restriction on institution of proceedings in England and Wales.

39)   Prosecutions by inspectors.

40)   Onus of proving limits of what is practicable etc.

41)   Evidence.

42)   Power of court to order cause of offence to be remedied or, in certain cases, forfeiture.

Financial provision

43)   Financial provisions.

Miscellaneous and supplementary

44)   Appeals in connection with licensing provisions in the relevant statutory provisions.

45)   Default powers.

46)   Service of notices.

47)   Civil liability.

48)   Application to Crown.

49)   Adaptation of enactments to metric units or appropriate metric units.

50)   Regulations under the relevant statutory provisions.

51)   Exclusion of application to domestic employment.

52)   Meaning of work and at work.

53)   General interpretation of Part I.

54)   Application of Part I to Isles of Scilly.

Outline of key points

AIMS

1)   To protect people.

2)   To protect the public from risks which may arise from work activities.

THE MAIN PROVISIONS - SECTION 1

a)   Securing the health, safety and welfare of people at work.

b)   Protecting others against risks arising from workplace activities.

c)   Controlling the obtaining, keeping, and use of explosive and highly flammable substances.

d)   Controlling emissions into the atmosphere of noxious or offensive substances.

Duties imposed on:

a)   The employer.

b)   The self employed.

c)   Employees.

d)   Contractors and subcontractors.

e)   Designers, manufacturers, suppliers, importers and installers.

f)   Specialists - architects, surveyors, engineers, personnel managers, health and safety specialists, and many more.

EMPLOYER'S DUTIES - [TO EMPLOYEES]

Section 2(1)

To ensure, so far as *reasonably practicable*, the health, safety and welfare at work of employees.

Section 2(2)

Ensuring health, safety and welfare at work through:

a)   Safe plant and systems of work e.g. provision of guards on machines.

b)   Safe use, handling, storage and transport of goods and materials e.g. good manual handling of boxes.

c)   Provision of information, instruction, training and supervision e.g. provision of induction training.

d)   Safe place of work including means of access and egress e.g. aisles kept clear.

e)   Safe and healthy working environment e.g. good lighting.

Further duties are placed on the employer by:

Section 2(3)

Prepare and keep up to date a written safety policy supported by information on the organisation and arrangements for carrying out the policy. The safety policy has to be brought to the notice of employees. If there are fewer than five employees, this section does not apply.

Section 2(4)

Recognised Trade Unions have the right to appoint safety representatives to represent the employees in consultations with the employer about health and safety matters.

Section 2(6)

Employers must consult with any safety representatives appointed by recognised Trade Unions.

Section 2(7)

To establish a safety committee if requested by two or more safety representatives.

EMPLOYER'S DUTIES - [TO PERSONS NOT HIS EMPLOYEES]

Section 3

a)   Not to expose them to risk to their heath and safety e.g. contractor work barriered off.

b)   To give information about risks which may affect them e.g. location induction for contractors.

Figure 20-1: Risks from road side work.   *Source: ACT.*

Figure 20-2: Risks from street light repair or tree felling. *Source: ACT.*

SELF EMPLOYED DUTIES

Section 3

a)   Not to expose themselves to risks to their health and safety e.g. wear personal protection.

b)   Not to expose other persons to risks to their health and safety e.g. keep shared work area tidy.

Some of the practical steps that an organisation might take in order to ensure the safety of visitors to its premises are:

- Identify visitors by signing in, badges etc.
- Provide information regarding the risks present and the site rules and procedures to be followed, particularly in emergencies.
- Provide escorts to supervise visitors throughout the site.
- Restrict access to certain areas.

PEOPLE IN CONTROL OF PREMISES

Section 4

This section places duties on anyone who has control to any extent of non-domestic premises used by people who are not their employees. The duty extends to the provision of safe premises, plant and substances, e.g. maintenance of a boiler in rented out property.

MANUFACTURERS, DESIGNERS, SUPPLIERS, IMPORTERS, INSTALLERS

Section 6

This section places specific duties on those who can ensure that articles and substances are as safe and without risks as is reasonably practicable. The section covers:

- Safe design, installation and testing of equipment (including fairground equipment).
- Safe substances tested for risks.
- Provision of information on safe use and conditions essential to health and safety.
- Research to minimise risks.

EMPLOYEES' DUTIES

Section 7

a) To take reasonable care for themselves and others that may be affected by their acts / omissions e.g. wear eye protection, not obstruct a fire exit.

b) To co-operate with the employer or other to enable them to carry out their duty and/or statutory requirements e.g. report hazards or defects in controls, attend training, provide medical samples.

Additional duties created by the Management of Health and Safety at Work

Regulations employees' duties:

- Every employee shall use any equipment, material or substance provided to them in accordance with any training and instruction.
- Every employee shall inform (via supervisory staff) their employer of any (a) risk situation or (b) shortcoming in the employer's protection arrangements.

OTHER DUTIES

Section 8

No person to interfere with or misuse anything provided to secure health and safety - e.g. wedge fire door open, remove first aid equipment without authority, breach lock off systems.

Section 9

Employees cannot be charged for anything done or provided to comply with a specific legal obligation e.g. personal protective equipment, health surveillance or welfare facilities.

OFFENCES COMMITTED BY OTHER PERSONS

Section 36

- Where the commission by any person of the breach of legislation is due to the act or default of some other person, that other person shall be guilty of the offence and may be charged with and convicted of the offence whether or not proceedings are taken against the first mentioned person.
- Case law indicates that 'other person' refers to persons lower down the corporate tree than mentioned in section 37, e.g.
- middle managers, safety advisors, training officers; and may extend to people working on contract e.g. architects, consultants or a planning supervisor.

OFFENCES COMMITTED BY THE BODY CORPORATE

Section 37

Where there has been a breach of legislation on the part of a body corporate (limited company or local authority) and the offence can be proved to have been committed with the consent or connivance of or to be attributable to any neglect on the part of any director, manager, secretary or similar officer of the body corporate, he, as well as the body corporate, can be found guilty and punished accordingly.

ONUS OF PROOF

Section 40

In any proceedings for an offence under any of the relevant statutory involving a failure to comply with a duty or requirement:

- to do something so far as is practicable or
- to do something so far as is reasonably practicable.

it shall be for the accused to prove that the requirements were met rather than for the prosecution to prove that the requirements were not met.

Ionising Radiations Regulations (IRR) 1999

Law considered in context / more depth in Unit 17.

Arrangement of regulations

Schedule 3.   Additional particulars that the Executive may require.

Schedule 4.   Dose limits.

Schedule 5.   Matters in respect of which radiation protection adviser must be consulted by a radiation employer.

Schedule 6.   Particulars to be entered in the radiation passbook.

Schedule 7.   Particulars to be contained in a health record.

Schedule 8.   Quantities and concentrations of radionuclides.

Schedule 9.   Modifications.

Outline of key points

These Regulations supersede and consolidate the Ionising Radiations Regulations 1985 and the Ionising Radiation (Outside Workers) Regulations 1993.

The Regulations impose duties on employers to protect employees and other persons against ionising radiation arising from work with radioactive substances and other sources of ionising radiation and also impose certain duties on employees.

The Regulations are divided into 7 Parts.

Lifting Operations and Lifting Equipment Regulations (LOLER) 1998

Law considered in context / more depth in Unit 13.

Arrangements of Regulations

1)   Citation and commencement.

2)   Interpretation.

3)   Application.

4)   Strength and stability.

5)   Lifting equipment for lifting persons.

6)   Positioning and installation.

7)   Marking of lifting equipment.

8)   Organisation of lifting operations.

9)   Thorough examination and inspection.

10)   Reports and defects.

11)   Keeping of information.

12)   Exemption for the armed forces.

13)   Amendment of the Shipbuilding and Ship-repairing Regulations 1960.

14)   Amendment of the Docks Regulation 1988.

15)   Repeal of provisions of the Factories Act 1961.

16)   Repeal of section 85 of the Mines and Quarries Act 1954.

17)   Revocation of instruments.

Schedule 1.   Information to be contained in a report of a thorough examination.

Schedule 2.   Revocation of instruments.

Outline of key points

The Lifting Operations and Lifting Equipment Regulations (LOLER) 1998 impose health and safety requirements with respect to lifting equipment (as defined in regulation 2(1)). They are not industry specific and apply to almost all lifting operations.

The Regulations place duties on employers, the self-employed, and certain persons having control of lifting equipment (of persons at work who use or supervise or manage its use, or of the way it is used, to the extent of their control (regulation 3(3) to (5)).

The Regulations make provision with respect to:

■   The strength and stability of lifting equipment (regulation 4).

■   The safety of lifting equipment for lifting persons (regulation 5).

■   The way lifting equipment is positioned and installed (regulation 6).

■   The marking of machinery and accessories for lifting, and lifting equipment which is designed for lifting persons or which might so be used in error (regulation 7).

■   The organisation of lifting operations (regulation 8).

■   The thorough examination (defined in (regulation 2(1)) and inspection of lifting equipment in specified circumstances, (regulation 9(1) to (3)).

■   The evidence of examination to accompany it outside the undertaking (regulation 9(4)).

■   The exception for winding apparatus at mines from regulation 9 (regulation 9(5)).

■   Transitional arrangements relating to regulation 9 (regulation 9(6) and (7)).

■   The making of reports of thorough examinations and records of inspections (regulation 10 and Schedule 1).

■   The keeping of information in the reports and records (regulation 11).

Management of Health and Safety at Work Regulations (MHSWR) 1999

Law considered in context / more depth in Units 3, 5 & 6.

Arrangement of Regulations

1) Citation, commencement and interpretation.
2) Disapplication of these Regulations.
3) Risk assessment.
4) Principles of prevention to be applied.
5) Health and safety arrangements.
6) Health surveillance.
7) Health and safety assistance.
8) Procedures for serious and imminent danger and for danger areas.
9) Contacts with external services.
10) Information for employees.
11) Co-operation and co-ordination.
12) Persons working in host employers' or self-employed persons' undertakings.
13) Capabilities and training.
14) Employees' duties.
15) Temporary workers.
16) Risk assessment in respect of new or expectant mothers.
17) Certificate from a registered medical practitioner in respect of new or expectant mothers.
18) Notification by new or expectant mothers.
19) Protection of young persons.
20) Exemption certificates.
21) Provisions as to liability.
22) Exclusion of civil liability.
23) Extension outside Great Britain.
24) Amendment of the Health and Safety (First-Aid) Regulations 1981.
25) Amendment of the Offshore Installations and Pipeline Works (First-Aid) Regulations 1989.
26) Amendment of the Mines Miscellaneous Health and Safety Provisions Regulations 1995.
27) Amendment of the Construction (Health, Safety and Welfare) Regulations 1996.
28) Regulations to have effect as health and safety regulations.
29) Revocations and consequential amendments.
30) Transitional provision.

Schedule 1. General principles of prevention.
Schedule 2. Consequential amendments.

Outline of key points

Management of Health and Safety at Work Regulations (MHSWR) 1999 set out some broad general duties which apply to almost all kinds of work. They are aimed mainly at improving health and safety management. You may already be familiar with broad health and safety law of this kind - as it is the form taken by the Health and Safety at Work Act (HASAWA) 1974. The Regulations work in a similar way, and in fact they can be seen as a way of fleshing out what is already in the HASAWA. The 1999 Regulations replace the Management of Health and Safety at Work Regulations 1992, the Management of Health and Safety at Work (Amendment) Regulations 1994, the Health and Safety (Young Persons) Regulations 1997 and Part III of the Fire Precautions (Workplace) Regulations 1997. The Principal Regulations are discussed below.

RISK ASSESSMENT (REGULATION 3)

The regulations require employers (and the self-employed) to assess the risk to the health and safety of their employees and to anyone else who may be affected by their work activity. This is necessary to ensure that the preventive and protective steps can be identified to control hazards in the workplace.

A *hazard* is defined as something with the potential to cause harm and may include machinery, substances or a work practice.

A *risk* is defined as the likelihood that a particular hazard will cause harm. Consideration must be given to the population, i.e. the number of persons who might be exposed to harm and the consequence of such exposure.

Where an employer is employing or about to employ young persons (under 18 years of age) he must carry out a risk assessment which takes particular account of:

- The inexperience, lack of awareness of risks and immaturity of young persons.
- The layout of the workplace and workstations.
- Exposure to physical, biological and chemical agents.
- Work equipment and the way in which it is handled.
- The extent of health and safety training to be provided.
- Risks from agents, processes and work listed in the Annex to Council Directive 94/33/EC on the protection of young people at work.

Where 5 or more employees are employed, the significant findings of risk assessments must be recorded in writing (the same threshold that is used in respect of having a written safety policy). This record must include details of any employees being identified as being especially at risk.

PRINCIPLES OF PREVENTION TO BE APPLIED (REGULATION 4)

Regulation 4 requires an employer to implement preventive and protective measures on the basis of general principles of prevention specified in Schedule 1 to the Regulations. These are:

1) Avoiding risks.
2) Evaluating the risks which cannot be avoided.
3) Combating the risks at source.
4) adapting the work to the individual, especially as regards the design of workplaces, the choice of work equipment and the choice of working and production methods, with a view, in particular, to alleviating monotonous work and work at a predetermined work-rate and to reducing their effect on health.
5) Adapting to technical progress.
6) Replacing the dangerous by the non-dangerous or the less dangerous.
7) Developing a coherent overall prevention policy which covers technology, organisation of work, working conditions, social relationships and the influence of factors relating to the working environment.
8) Giving collective protective measures priority over individual protective measures.
9) Giving appropriate instructions to employees.

HEALTH AND SAFETY ARRANGEMENTS (REGULATION 5)

Appropriate arrangements must be made for the effective planning, organisation, control, monitoring and review of preventative and protective measures (in other words, for the management of health and safety). Again, employers with five or more employees must have their arrangements in writing.

HEALTH SURVEILLANCE (REGULATION 6)

In addition to the requirements of specific regulations such as Control of Substances Hazardous to Health (COSHH) and Asbestos regulations, consideration must be given to carry out health surveillance of employees where there is a disease or adverse health condition identified in risk assessments.

HEALTH AND SAFETY ASSISTANCE (REGULATION 7)

The employer must appoint one or more competent persons to assist him in complying with the legal obligations imposed on the undertaking (including Part II of the Fire Precautions (Workplace) Regulations (FPWR) 1997). The number of persons appointed should reflect the number of employees and the type of hazards in the workplace.

If more than one competent person is appointed, then arrangements must be made for ensuring adequate co-operation between them. The Competent person(s) must be given the necessary time and resources to fulfil their functions. This will depend on the size the undertaking, the risks to which employees are exposed and the distribution of those risks throughout the undertaking.

The employer must ensure that competent person(s) who are not employees are informed of the factors known (or suspected) to affect the health and safety of anyone affected by business activities.

Competent people are defined as those who have sufficient training and experience or knowledge and other qualities to enable them to perform their functions.

Persons may be selected from among existing employees or from outside. Where there is a suitable person in the employer's employment, that person shall be appointed as the 'competent person' in preference to a non-employee.

PROCEDURES FOR SERIOUS AND IMMINENT DANGER AND FOR DANGER AREAS (REGULATION 8)

Employers are required to set up emergency procedures and appoint **competent persons** to ensure compliance with identified arrangements, to devise control strategies as appropriate and to limit access to areas of risk to ensure that only those persons with adequate health and safety knowledge and instruction are admitted.

The factors to be considered when preparing a procedure to deal with workplace emergencies such as fire, explosion, bomb scare, chemical leakage or other dangerous occurrence should include:

- The identification and training requirements of persons with specific responsibilities.
- The layout of the premises in relation to escape routes etc.
- The number of persons affected.
- Assessment of special needs (disabled persons, children etc.).
- Warning systems.
- Emergency lighting.

- Location of shut-off valves, isolation switches, hydrants etc.
- Equipment required to deal with the emergency.
- Location of assembly points.
- Communication with emergency services.
- Training and/or information to be given to employees, visitors, local residents and anyone else who might be affected

CONTACTS WITH EXTERNAL SERVICES (REGULATION 9)

Employers must ensure that, where necessary, contacts are made with external services. This particularly applies with regard to first-aid, emergency medical care and rescue work.

INFORMATION FOR EMPLOYEES (REGULATION 10)

Employees must be provided with relevant information about hazards to their health and safety arising from risks identified by the assessments. Clear instruction must be provided concerning any preventative or protective control measures including those relating to serious and imminent danger and fire assessments. Details of any competent persons nominated to discharge specific duties in accordance with the regulations must also be communicated as should risks arising from contact with other employer's activities (see Regulation 11).

Before employing a child (a person who is not over compulsory school age) the employer must provide those with parental responsibility for the child with information on the risks that have been identified and preventative and protective measures to be taken.

CO-OPERATION AND CO-ORDINATION (REGULATION 11)

Employers who work together in a common workplace have a duty to co-operate to discharge their duties under relevant statutory provisions. They must also take all reasonable steps to inform their respective employees of risks to their health or safety which may arise out of their work. Specific arrangements must be made to ensure compliance with fire legislation (i.e. the Fire Precautions (Workplace) Regulations (FPWR) 1997).

PERSONS WORKING IN HOST EMPLOYERS' OR SELF EMPLOYED PERSONS' UNDERTAKINGS (REGULATION 12)

This regulation extends the requirements of regulation 11 to include employees working as sole occupiers of a workplace under the control of another employer. Such employees would include those working under a service of contract and employees in temporary employment businesses under the control of the first employer.

CAPABILITIES AND TRAINING (REGULATION 13)

Employers need to take into account the capabilities of their employees before entrusting tasks. This is necessary to ensure that they have adequate health and safety training and are capable enough at their jobs to avoid risk. To this end consideration must be given to recruitment including job orientation when transferring between jobs and work departments. Training must also be provided when other factors such as the introduction of new technology and new systems of work or work equipment arise.

Training must

- Be repeated periodically where appropriate.
- Be adapted to take account of any new or changed risks to the health and safety of the employees concerned.
- Take place during working hours.

EMPLOYEES' DUTIES (REGULATION 14)

Employees are required to follow health and safety instructions by using machinery, substances, transport etc. in accordance with the instructions and training that they have received.

They must also inform their employer (and other employers) of any dangers or shortcoming in the health and safety arrangements, even if there is no risk of imminent danger.

TEMPORARY WORKERS (REGULATION 15)

Consideration is given to the special needs of temporary workers. In particular to the provision of particular health and safety information such as qualifications required to perform the task safely or any special arrangements such as the need to provide health screening.

RISKS ASSESSMENT IN RESPECT OF NEW OR EXPECTANT MOTHERS (REGULATION 16)

Where the work is of a kind which would involve risk to a new or expectant mother or her baby, then the assessment required by regulation 3 should take this into account.

If the risk cannot be avoided, then the employer should take reasonable steps to:

- Adjust the hours worked, or
- Offer alternative work, or
- Give paid leave for as long as is necessary.

CERTIFICATE FROM A REGISTERED MEDICAL PRACTITIONER IN RESPECT OF NEW OR EXPECTANT MOTHERS (REGULATION 17)

Where the woman is a night shift worker and has a medical certificate identifying night shift work as a risk then the employer must put her on day shift or give paid leave for as long as is necessary.

NOTIFICATION BY NEW OR EXPECTANT MOTHERS (REGULATION 18)

The employer need take no action until he is notified in writing by the woman that she is pregnant, has given birth in the last six months, or is breastfeeding.

PROTECTION OF YOUNG PERSONS (REGULATION 19)

Employers of young persons shall ensure that they are not exposed to risk as a consequence of their lack of experience, lack of awareness or lack of maturity.

No employer shall employ young people for work which:

- Is beyond his physical or psychological capacity.
- Involves exposure to agents which chronically affect human health.
- Involves harmful exposure to radiation.
- Involves a risk to health from extremes of temperature, noise or vibration.
- Involves risks which could not be reasonably foreseen by young persons.

This regulation does not prevent the employment of a young person who is no longer a child for work:

- Where it is necessary for his training.
- Where the young person will be supervised by a competent person.
- Where any risk will be reduced to the lowest level that is reasonably practicable.

(Note: Two HSE publications give guidance on the changes. HSG122 - New and expectant mothers at work: a guide for employers and HSG165 - Young people at work: a guide for employers.)

EXEMPTION CERTIFICATES (REGULATION 20)

The Secretary of State for Defence may, in the interests of national security, by a certificate in writing exempt the armed forces, any visiting force or any headquarters from certain obligations imposed by the Regulations.

PROVISIONS AS TO LIABILITY (REGULATION 21)

Employers cannot submit a defence in criminal proceedings that contravention was caused by the act or default either of an employee or the competent person appointed under Regulation 7.

EXCLUSION OF CIVIL LIABILITY (REGULATION 22)

Breach of a duty imposed by these Regulations shall not confer a right of action in any civil proceedings for those other than employees.

REVOCATIONS AND AMENDMENTS (REGULATIONS 24-29)

The Regulations:

- Revoke regulation 6 of the Health and Safety (First-Aid) Regulations (FAR) 1981 which confers power on the Health and Safety
  Executive to grant exemptions from those Regulations.
- Amend the Offshore Installations and Pipeline Works (First-Aid) Regulations 1989.
- Amend the Mines Miscellaneous Health and Safety Provisions Regulations 1995.
- Amend the Construction (Health, Safety and Welfare) Regulations 1996.

The Regulations provide that, with some exceptions, the Fire Precautions (Workplace) Regulations (FPWR) 1997 are to be considered as health and safety regulations within the meaning of the Health and Safety at Work etc Act (HASAWA) 1974. The Regulations also make amendments to the statutory instruments as specified in Schedule 2.

TRANSITIONAL PROVISION (REGULATION 30)

The Regulations contain a transitional provision (regulation 30). The substitution of provisions in the 1999 Regulations for provisions of the Management of Health and Safety at Work Regulations (MHSWR) 1992 shall not affect the continuity of the law; and accordingly anything done under or for the purposes of such provision of the 1992 Regulations shall have effect as if done under or for the purposes of any corresponding provision of these Regulations.

Manual Handling Operations Regulations (MHOR) 1992

Law considered in context / more depth in Unit 13.

Arrangement of Regulations

1) Citation and commencement.
2) Interpretation.
3) Disapplication of Regulations.
4) Duties of employers.
5) Duty of employees.
6) Exemption certificates.
7) Extension outside Great Britain.
8) Repeals and revocations.

Outline of key points

1)   **Citation and commencement**

2)   **Interpretation.**

"Injury" does not include injury caused by toxic or corrosive substances which:

- Have leaked/spilled from load.
- Are present on the surface but not leaked/spilled from it.
- Are a constituent part of the load.

"Load" includes any person or animal.

"Manual Handling Operations" means transporting or supporting a load including:

- Lifting and putting down.
- Pushing, pulling or moving by hand or bodily force.
- Shall as far as is reasonably practicable.

3)   **Disapplication of regulations**

4)   **Duties of employers**

4) (1)(a)   **Avoidance of manual handling**

The employer's duty is to avoid the need for manual handling operations which involve a risk of their employees being injured - as far as is reasonably practicable.

4) (1)(b)(i)   **Assessment of risk**

Where not reasonably practicable make a suitable and sufficient assessment of all such manual handling operations.

4) (1)(b)(ii)   **Reducing the risk of injury**

Take appropriate steps to reduce the risk of injury to the lowest level reasonably practicable.

4) (1)(b)(iii)   **The load - additional information**

Employers shall provide information on general indications or where reasonably practicable precise information on:

- The weight of each load.
- The heaviest side of any load whose centre of gravity is not central.

4) (2)   **Reviewing the assessment**

Assessment review:

- Where there is reason to believe the assessment is no longer valid.
- There is sufficient change in manual handling operations.

5)   **Duty of employees**

Employees shall make full and proper use of any system of work provided for his use by his employer.

6)   **Exemption certificates**

7)   **Extension outside Great Britain**

8)   **Repeals and revocations**

Schedule 1   Factors to which the employer must have regard and questions he must consider when making an assessment of manual handling operations.

Schedule 2   Repeals and revocations.

Appendix 1   Numerical guidelines for assessment.

Appendix 2   Example of an assessment checklist.

Thus the Regulations establish a clear hierarchy of measures:

1. Avoid hazardous manual handling operations so far as is reasonably practicable.
2. Make a suitable and sufficient assessment of any hazardous manual handling operations that cannot be avoided.
3. Reduce the risk of injury so far as is reasonably practicable.

New Roads and Street Works Act (NRSWA) 1991

Refer to Unit 11 Movement of people and vehicles – hazards and control.

Noise at Work Regulations (NWR) 1989

Law considered in context / more depth in Unit 17.

Arrangement of Regulations

1)   Citation and commencement.

2)   Interpretation.

3)   Disapplication of duties.

4)   Assessment of exposure.

5)   Assessment records.

6)   Reduction of risk of hearing damage.

7)   Reduction of noise exposure.

8)   Ear protection.

9)   Ear protection zones.

10)   Maintenance and use of equipment.

11)   Provision of information to employees.

13)   Modification of duties of manufacturers etc. of articles for use at work and articles of fairground equipment.

14)   Exemptions.

15)   Modifications relating to the Ministry of Defence etc.

16)   Revocation.

Schedule 1   Daily personal noise exposure of employees.

Schedule 2   Weekly average of daily personal noise exposure of employees.

Outline of key points

1)   **Citation and Commencement**

The Noise at Work Regulations 1989 came into force on 1st January 1990 and implemented the requirements of the European Directive 86/188/EEC.

2)   **Interpretation**

Defines 'daily personal exposure level' ($L_{EP,d}$) and Action Levels.

- ■   'First Action Level' is a $L_{EP,d}$ of 85 dB(A).
- ■   'Second Action Level' is a $L_{EP,d}$ of 90 dB(A).
- ■   'Peak Action Level' is a peak sound pressure of 200 Pa (140 dB).

3)   **Application**

Apply to all in Great Britain, with the exception of master and crew of sea going ships, crew of aircraft and ships.

4)   **Assessment Of Exposure**

Employers must ensure that a competent person assesses the exposure of employees likely to be subjected to the First Action Level or above or the Peak Action Level or above. Assessments must be reviewed to ensure that they are valid.

5)   **Assessment Records**

An adequate record of the assessment must be made and kept until a further assessment is made.

6)   **Reduction**
Of risk of hearing damage

Employers shall reduce the risk of damage to the hearing of employees from exposure to noise to the lowest level reasonably practicable.

7)   **Of noise exposure**

Employers shall reduce noise exposure of employees exposed to the Second or Peak Action Levels, where reasonably practicable.

8)   **Ear protection**

Employers shall ensure that employees exposed to the First Action Level are provided, at their request, with suitable ear protectors. When employees are exposed to the Second or Peak Action levels ear protectors must be provided, and worn, which reduce the exposure to below the Second or Peak Action levels.

9)   **Ear protection zones**

Employers shall designate areas as Ear Protection Zones where any employee is likely to be exposed to the Second or Peak Action level. All that enter these zones must wear ear protection.

10) **Maintenance and use of equipment**

Employers shall ensure that equipment supplied by them is used and maintained. Also, there is a duty for employees to use equipment provided by the employer and to report any defects.

11) **Provision of information to employees**

Employers must provide information, instruction and training for all employees likely to be exposed to the First or Peak Action levels, or above, as follows:

- Risk of damage to hearing from exposure to noise.
- What steps an employee can take to minimise the risk.
- How employees can obtain ear protectors.
- The employee's obligations under the Regulations.

12) **Modifications of duties of manufacturers etc. of articles for use at work and articles of fairground equipment**

Adequate information must be provided by manufacturers of equipment which is likely to subject employees to the First or Peak Action levels or above. This information is in the form of sound pressure levels (L_{eq} and peak) at the work stations, and the sound power levels when the sound pressure level exceeds 85 dB(A).

13) **Exemptions** - The HSE may exempt employers from Regs 7 and 8 under certain circumstances.

14) **Modifications For MOD** - Secretary of State for Defence may exempt MOD forces, in the interests of national security.

15) **Revocation** - Reg. 44 of the Woodworking Machines Regulations 1974 is revoked.

Personal Protective Equipment at Work Regs (PPER) 1992

Law considered in context / more depth in Units 6, 8 -10, 12, 16 & 17.

Arrangement of Regulations

1) Citation and commencement.
2) Interpretation.
3) Disapplication of these Regulations.
4) Provision of personal protective equipment.
5) Compatibility of personal protective equipment.
6) Assessment of personal protective equipment.
7) Maintenance and replacement of personal protective equipment.
8) Accommodation for personal protective equipment.
9) Information, instruction and training.
10) Use of personal protective equipment.
11) Reporting loss or defect.
12) Exemption certificates.
13) Extension outside Great Britain.
14) Modifications, repeal and revocations directive.

Schedule 1	Relevant Community.
Schedule 2	Modifications.
Part I	Factories Act 1961.
Part II	The Coal and Other Mines (Fire and Rescue) Order 1956.
Part III	The Shipbuilding and Ship-Repairing Regulations 1960.
Part IV	The Coal Mines (Respirable Dust) Regulations 1975.
Part V	The Control of Lead at Work Regulations 1980.
Part VI	The Ionising Radiations Regulations 1985.
Part VII	The Control of Asbestos at Work Regulations 1987.
Part VIII	The Control of Substances Hazardous to Health Regulations 1988.
Part IX	The Noise at Work Regulations 1989.
Part X	The Construction (Head Protection) Regulations 1989.
Schedule 3	Revocations.

Outline of key points

2) Personal protective equipment (PPE) means all equipment (including clothing provided for protection against adverse weather) which is intended to be worn or held by a person at work and which protects him against risks to his health or safety.

3) These Regulations do not apply to:

- Ordinary working clothes/uniforms.
- Offensive weapons.
- Portable detectors which signal risk.
- Equipment used whilst playing competitive sports.

■   Equipment provided for travelling on a road.

The Regulations do not apply to situations already controlled by other Regulations i.e.

- ■   Control of Lead at Work Regulations 1998.
- ■   Ionising Radiation Regulations 1999.
- ■   Control of Asbestos at Work Regulations 1987 (and as amended 1999).
- ■   CoSHH Regulations 1999.
- ■   Noise at Work Regulations 1989.
- ■   Construction (Head Protection) Regulations 1989.

4)   Suitable PPE must be provided when risks cannot be adequately controlled by other means. Reg. 4 shall ensure suitable PPE:

- ■   Appropriate for the risk and conditions.
- ■   Ergonomic requirements.
- ■   State of health of users.
- ■   Correctly fitting and adjustable.
- ■   Complies with EEC directives.

5)   Equipment must be compatible with any other PPE which has to be worn.

6)   Before issuing PPE, the employer must carry out a risk assessment to ensure that the equipment is suitable.

- ■   Assess risks not avoided by other means.
- ■   Define characteristics of PPE and of the risk of the equipment itself.
- ■   Compare characteristics of PPE to defined requirement.
- ■   Repeat assessment when no longer valid, or significant change has taken place.

7)   PPE must be maintained.

- ■   In an efficient state.
- ■   In efficient working order.
- ■   In good repair.

8)   Accommodation must be provided for equipment when it is not being used.

9)   Information, instruction and training must be given on:

- ■   The risks PPE will eliminate or limit.
- ■   Why the PPE is to be used.
- ■   How the PPE is to be used.
- ■   How to maintain the PPE.

Information and instruction must be comprehensible to the wearer/user.

10)   Employers shall take reasonable steps to ensure PPE is worn.

- ■   Every employee shall use PPE that has been provided.
- ■   Every employee shall take reasonable steps to return PPE to storage.

11)   Employees must report any loss or defect.

The Guidance on the Regulations points out:

"Whatever PPE is chosen, it should be remembered that, although some types of equipment do provide very high levels of protection, none provides 100%"

PPE includes the following when worn for health and safety reasons at work:

- ■   Aprons.
- ■   Adverse weather gear.
- ■   High visibility clothing.
- ■   Gloves.
- ■   Safety footwear.
- ■   Safety helmets.
- ■   Eye protection.
- ■   Life-jackets.
- ■   Respirators.
- ■   Safety harness.
- ■   Underwater breathing gear.

Provision and Use of Work Equipment Regulations (PUWER) 1998

Law considered in context / more depth in Unit 12.

Arrangement of Regulations

PART I - INTRODUCTION

1)   Citation and commencement.

2)   Interpretation.

3)   Application.

PART II - GENERAL

4)   Suitability of work equipment.

5)   Maintenance.

6)   Inspection.

7)   Specific risks.

8)   Information and instructions.

9)   Training.

10)   Conformity with Community requirements.

11)   Dangerous parts of machinery.

12)   Protection against specified hazards.

13)   High or very low temperature.

14)   Controls for starting or making a significant change in operating conditions.

15)   Stop controls.

16)   Emergency stop controls.

17)   Controls.

18)   Control systems.

19)   Isolation from sources of energy.

20)   Stability.

21)   Lighting.

22)   Maintenance operations.

23)   Markings.

24)   Warnings.

PART III - MOBILE WORK EQUIPMENT

25)   Employees carried on mobile work equipment.

26)   Rolling over of mobile work equipment.

27)   Overturning of fork-lift trucks.

28)   Self-propelled work equipment.

29)   Remote-controlled self-propelled work equipment.

30)   Drive shafts.

PART IV - POWER PRESSES

31)   Power presses to which Part IV does not apply.

32)   Thorough examination of power presses, guards and protection devices.

33)   Inspection of guards and protection devices.

34)   Reports.

35)   Keeping of information.

PART V - MISCELLANEOUS

36)   Exemption for the armed forces.

37)   Transitional provision.

38)   Repeal of enactment.

39)   Revocation of instruments.

Schedule 1   Instruments which give effect to Community directives concerning the safety of products.

Schedule 2   Power presses to which regulations 32 to 35 do not apply.

Schedule 3   Information to be contained in a report of a thorough examination of a power press, guard or protection device.

Schedule 4   Revocation of instruments.

Outline of key points

These Regulations impose health and safety requirements with respect to the provision and use of work equipment, which is defined as 'any machinery, appliance, apparatus, tool or installation for use at work (whether exclusively or not)'. These regulations:

■   Place general duties on employers.

■   Certain persons having control of work equipment, of persons at work who use or supervise or manage its use or of the way it is used, to the extent of their control.

■   List minimum requirements for work equipment to deal with selected hazards whatever the industry.

'Use' includes any activity involving work equipment and includes starting, stopping, programming, setting, transporting, repairing, modifying, maintaining, servicing and cleaning.

The general duties require you to:

■   Make sure that equipment is suitable for the use that will be made of it.

■   Take into account the working conditions and hazards in the workplace when selecting equipment.

■   Ensure equipment is used only for operations for which, and under conditions for which, it is suitable.

■   Ensure that equipment is maintained in an efficient state, in efficient working order and in good repair.

■   Ensure the inspection of work equipment in specified circumstances by a competent person; keep a record of the result for specified periods; and ensure that evidence of the last inspection accompany work equipment used outside the undertaking.

■   Give adequate information, instruction and training.

■   Provide equipment that conforms with EU product safety directives.

SPECIFIC REQUIREMENTS COVER
- Guarding of dangerous parts of machinery.
- Protection against specified hazards i.e. falling/ejected articles and substances, rupture/disintegration of work equipment parts, equipment catching fire or overheating, unintended or premature discharge of articles and substances, explosion.
- Work equipment parts and substances at high or very low temperatures.
- Control systems and control devices.
- Isolation of equipment from sources of energy.
- Stability of equipment.
- Lighting.
- Maintenance operations.
- Warnings and markings.

MOBILE WORK EQUIPMENT MUST HAVE PROVISION AS TO:
- Its suitability for carrying persons and its safety features.
- Means to minimise the risk to safety from its rolling over.
- Means to reduce the risk to safety from the rolling over of a fork-lift truck.
- The safety of self-propelled work equipment and remote-controlled self propelled work equipment.
- The drive shafts of mobile work equipment.

This did not apply to existing mobile work equipment (in use before 5 Dec 1998) until 5 Dec 2002 for existing mobile work equipment.

PUWER ALSO APPLIES TO CERTAIN POWER PRESSES

The Regulations provide for:
- The thorough examination (defined in regulation 2(1)) of power presses and their guards and protection devices (regulation 32).
- Their inspection after setting, re-setting or adjustment of their tools, and every working period (regulation 33).
- The making (regulation 34 and Schedule 3) and keeping (regulation 35) of reports.
- The regulations implement an EC directive aimed at the protection of workers. There are other directives setting out conditions which much new equipment (especially machinery) will have to satisfy before it can be sold in EC member states.

Reporting of Injuries, Diseases and Dangerous Occurrences Regulations (RIDDOR) 1995

Law considered in context / more depth in Unit 18.

Arrangement of Regulations

1) Citation and commencement.
2) Interpretation.
3) Notification and reporting of injuries and dangerous occurrences.
4) Reporting of the death of an employee.
5) Reporting of cases of disease.
6) Reporting of gas incidents.
7) Records.
8) Additional provisions relating to mines and quarries.
9) Additional provisions relating to offshore workplaces.
10) Restrictions on the application of regulations 3, 4 and 5.
11) Defence in proceedings for an offence contravening these Regulations.
12) Extension outside Great Britain.
13) Certificates of exemption.
14) Repeal and amendment of provisions in the Regulation of Railways Act 1871, the Railway Employment (Prevention of Accidents) Act 1900 and the Transport and Works Act 1992.
15) Revocations, amendments and savings.

Schedule 1   Major Injuries.
Schedule 2   Dangerous Occurrences.
Schedule 3   Reportable Diseases.
Schedule 4   Records.
Schedule 5   Additional provisions relating to mines and quarries.
Schedule 6   Additional provisions relating to offshore workplaces.
Schedule 7   Enactments or instruments requiring the notification of events which are not required to be notified or reported under these Regulations.
Schedule 8   Revocations and amendments.

Outline of key points

The Reporting of Injuries, Diseases and Dangerous Occurrences Regulations (RIDDOR) 1995 cover the requirement to report certain categories of injury and disease sustained at work, along with specified dangerous occurrences and gas incidents, to the relevant enforcing authority. These reports are used to compile statistics to show trends and to highlight problem areas in particular industries or companies.

REPORTING

1)   When a person *dies or suffers any serious condition* specified in Schedule 1 *(Reporting of Injuries)* and Schedule 2 *(Reporting of Dangerous Occurrences)* a responsible person is to notify by the quickest possible means (usually by telephone) the enforcing authorities and must send them a written report within 10 days (F2508).

2)   In cases of diseases which are linked to work activities listed in Schedule 3 *(Reporting of Diseases)* a responsible person is required to notify by the quickest possible means (usually by telephone) the enforcing authorities and must send them a written report forthwith (F2508A).

3)   If personal injury results in *more than 3 days incapacity* from work off from normal duties, but does not fall in the category of "major", the written report alone is required. The day of the accident is not counted.

4)   The enforcing authority is either the Health and Safety Executive or the Local Authority. The approved form for reporting is F2508 for injuries and dangerous occurrences and F2508A for diseases.

"Accident" includes:

■   An act of non-consensual physical violence done to a person at work.
■   An act of suicide which occurs on or in the course of the operation of a relevant transport system.

ROAD TRAFFIC ACCIDENTS

Road traffic accidents only have to be reported if:

■   Death or injury results from exposure to a substance being conveyed by a vehicle.
■   Death or injury results from the activities of another person engaged in the loading or unloading of an article or substance.
■   Death or injury results from the activities of another person involving work on or alongside a road.
■   Death or injury results from an accident involving a train.

NON EMPLOYEE

The responsible person must not only report non-employee deaths, but also cases that involve major injury or hospitalisation.

RECORDING

In the case of an accident at work, the following details must be recorded:

■   Date.   ■   Time.
■   Name.   ■   Occupation.
■   Nature of injury.   ■   Place of accident.
■   Brief description of the event.

Copies of F2508 or suitable alternative records must be kept for at least 3 years. This may be held electronically provided it is printable.

DEFENCES

A person must prove that he was not aware of the event and that he had taken all reasonable steps to have such events brought to his notice.

Typical examples of major injuries, diseases and dangerous occurrences

MAJOR INJURIES (RIDDOR - SCHEDULE 1)

The list of major injuries includes:

■   Any fracture, other than the finger or thumbs or toes.
■   Any amputation.
■   Dislocation of the shoulder, hip, knee or spine.
■   Permanent or temporary loss of sight.
■   Chemical, hot metal or penetrating eye injury.
■   Electrical shock, electrical burn leading to unconsciousness or resuscitation or admittance to hospital for more than 24 hours.
■   Loss of consciousness caused by asphyxia or exposure to a harmful substance or biological agent.
■   Acute illness or loss of consciousness requiring medical attention due to any entry of substance by inhalation, ingestion or through the skin.
■   Acute illness where there is a reason to believe that this resulted from exposure to a biological agent or its toxins or infected material.
■   Any other injury leading to hypothermia, heat-induced illness or unconsciousness requiring resuscitation, hospitalisation greater than 24 hours.

DISEASES (RIDDOR - SCHEDULE 3)

Conditions due to physical agents and the physical demands of work
- Inflammation, ulceration or malignant disease of the skin due to ionising radiation.
- Decompression illness.
- Subcutaneous cellulitis of the hand (beat hand).
- Carpal tunnel syndrome.
- Hand-arm vibration syndrome.

Infections due to biological agents
- Anthrax.
- Hepatitis.
- Legionellosis.
- Leptospirosis.
- Tetanus.

Conditions due to chemicals and other substances
- Arsenic poisoning.
- Ethylene Oxide poisoning.
- Cancer of a bronchus or lung.
- Folliculitis.
- Acne.
- Pneumoconiosis.
- Asbestosis.
- Occupational dermatitis.

DANGEROUS OCCURRENCES (RIDDOR - SCHEDULE 2)

Dangerous occurrences are events that have the potential to cause death or serious injury and so must be reported whether anyone is injured or not. Examples of dangerous occurrences that must be reported are:

- The failure of any load bearing part of any lift, hoist, crane or derrick etc.
- The failure of any pressurised closed vessel.
- The failure of any freight container in any of its load bearing parts.
- Any unintentional incident in which plant or equipment either comes into contact with an uninsulated overhead electric line causes an electrical discharge from such an electric line by coming into close proximity to it.
- Electrical short circuit or overload attended by fire or explosion which results in the stoppage of the plant involved for more than 24 hours.

Note: This information is a brief summary only. For full details consult HSE document L73 A Guide to RIDDOR 95.

Safety Representatives and Safety Committees Regulations (SRSC) 1977

Law considered in context / more depth in Unit 3.

Arrangement of Regulations

1) Citation and commencement.
2) Interpretation.
3) Appointment of safety representatives.
4) Functions of safety representatives.
5) Inspections of the workplace.
6) Inspections following notifiable accidents, occurrences and diseases.
7) Inspections of documents and provision of information.
8) Cases where safety representatives need not be employees.
9) Safety committees.
10) Power of Health and Safety Commission to grant exemption.
11) Provision as to industrial tribunals.

Outline of key points

The Safety Representatives and Safety Committees Regulations (SRSC) 1977 are concerned with the appointment by recognised trade unions of safety representatives, the functions of the representatives and the establishment of safety committees.

Representatives are appointed when a recognised trade union notifies the employer in writing. Representatives must have been employed throughout the preceding 2 years or, where this is not reasonably practicable, have had at least 2 years' experience in similar employment.

Similarly, employees cease to be representatives when:

- The employer has be notified in writing by the trade union.
- The representative ceases to be employed.
- He/she resigns.

FUNCTIONS OF TRADE UNION - APPOINTED SAFETY REPRESENTATIVES

The SRSCR grant safety representatives the right to carry out certain functions as outlined below.

Functions are activities that safety representatives are permitted to carry out by legislation, but do not have a 'duty' to perform and therefore are treated as advisory actions. As a consequence the representatives cannot be held accountable for failing to carry out these activities or for the standard of the advice given, when performing their functions. They are, however, still employees and have the same consequent duties as any other employee (for example their duties under HASAW Ss 7and 8). Their functions as safety representatives are:

a) To take all reasonably practical steps to keep themselves informed of:

- The legal requirements relating to the health and safety of persons at work, particularly the group or groups of persons they directly represent.
- The particular hazards of the workplace and the measures deemed necessary to eliminate or minimise the risk deriving from these hazards and the health and safety policy of their employer and the organisation and arrangements for fulfilling that policy;

b) To encourage co-operation between their employer and his employees in promoting and developing essential measures to ensure the health and safety of employees, and in checking the effectiveness of these measures.

c) To carry out investigations into:

- Hazards and dangerous occurrences (incl. accidents) at the workplace.
- Complaints, by any employee he represents, relating to that employee's health, safety or welfare.

d) To carry out inspections of the workplace.

e) To bring to the employer's notice, normally in writing, any unsafe or unhealthy conditions, or unsafe working practices, or unsatisfactory arrangements for welfare at work, which comes to their attention whether during an inspection/investigation or day to day observation.

The report does not imply, that all other conditions and working practices are safe and healthy or that the welfare arrangements are satisfactory in all other respects. Making a written report does not preclude the bringing of such matters to the attention of the employer or his representative by a direct oral approach in the first instance, particularly in situations where speedy remedial action is necessary. It will also be appropriate for minor matters to be the subject of direct discussion, without the need for a formal written approach.

f) To represent the employees they were appointed to represent in consultation at the workplace with inspectors of the Health and Safety Executive and of any other enforcing authority within the Act.

g) To receive information from inspectors in accordance with section 28(8) of the 1974 Act.

h) To attend meetings of safety committees during which he/she attends in his capacity as a safety representative in connection with any of the above conditions.

EMPLOYERS DUTIES

The Regulations require employers to make any known information available to safety representatives which is necessary to enable them to fulfil their functions. This should include:

a) Information about the plans and performances of the undertaking and any changes proposed, in so far as they affect the health and safety at work of their employees.

b) Information of a technical nature about hazards to health and safety and precautions deemed necessary to eliminate or minimise them, in respect of machinery, plant, equipment, processes, systems of work and substances in use at work. This should include any relevant information provided by consultants or designers or by the manufacturer, importer or supplier of any article or substance used, or proposed to be used, at work by their employees.

c) Information which the employer keeps relating to the occurrence of any accidents, dangerous occurrences or notifiable industrial disease and any statistical records relating to such accidents, dangerous occurrences or cases of notifiable industrial disease.

d) Any other information specifically related to matters affecting the Health and Safety at work of his employees, including the result of any measurements taken by persons acting on his behalf in the course of checking the effectiveness of his health and safety arrangements.

e) Information on articles or substances which an employer issues to homeworkers.

f) Any other suitable and relevant reasonable facility to enable the representatives to carry out their functions.

TRAINING

The basis of Trades Union Congress (TUC) policy is that the union appointed safety representative will be trained on TUC approved courses. However, there is much to be gained by the employer approaching the trades unions active in his workplace with the objective of holding joint company/industry based courses. In any event it is prudent for the employer to carry out company/industry orientated training to supplement the wide industry based TUC course. The functions and training of the safety representatives should be carried out during normal working hours. The representative must receive normal earnings, this taking into consideration any bonuses which would have been earned if carrying out their normal work activities.

FUNCTIONS OF HEALTH AND SAFETY COMMITTEES

If two or more appointed safety representatives request in writing the formation of a safety committee, the employer must implement this request within three months. Consultation must take place with the representatives making the request and the appointing trade union. A basic requirement for a successful safety committee is the desire of both employee and management to show honest commitment and a positive approach to a programme of accident prevention and the establishment of a safe and healthy environment and systems of work. For any committee to operate effectively, it is necessary to determine its objectives and functions.

Objectives

a)   The promotion of safety, health and welfare at work by providing a forum for discussion and perhaps a pressure group.

b)   To promote and support normal employee/employer systems for the reporting and control of workplace problems.

Functions

a)   To review accident and occupational health trends.

b)   To review recurring problems revealed by safety audits.

c)   To consider enforcing authority reports and information releases.

d)   To consider reports on matters arising from previous safety committee meetings.

e)   To assist in the development of safety rules and systems of work and procedures.

f)   To review health and safety aspects of future development and changes in procedure.

g)   To review health and safety aspects of purchasing specifications of equipment and materials.

h)   To review renewal/maintenance programmes.

i)   To monitor safety training programmes and standards achieved.

j)   To monitor the effectiveness of safety and health communications within the workplace.

k)   To monitor the effectiveness of the Safety Policy.

This may be summarised as review and recommend on the overall direction of the health and safety programme, on specific aspects of the programme, on difficulties encountered in its implementation and to monitor the programme in both a specific and overall manner.

Composition

The membership and structure of the safety committee should be settled in consultation between management and the trade union representatives concerned. This should be aimed at keeping the total size as compact as possible, compatible with the adequate representation of the interests of management and employees. Management representatives will naturally be appointed by the management. Employee representatives will either be appointed by a recognised Trade Union (HASAW 2(4)) or, in a non-union company, elected by their colleagues. The committee suggested in HASAW section 2 (7) will probably be the 'Company Safety Committee.' There is nothing to prevent the formation of 'works' or 'office' committees as required in order to maintain the company safety committee at a reasonable size.

Supply of Machinery (Safety) Regulations (SMSR) 1992

Law considered in context / more depth in Unit 12.

Outline of key points

GENERAL ADVICE

The Supply of Machinery (Safety) Regulations (SMSR) 1992 came into force on 1 January 1993 and implement the EC Machinery Directive (89/392/EEC) and its first amendment (91/368/EEC). Duties are placed upon those who supply machinery. 'Supply' is given a broad definition and those covered by the Regulations include manufacturers, importers and others in the supply chain. There is a transitional period from January 1993 to January 1995, during which time suppliers can either meet the users' national laws in force before 1993 or these Regulations. Machinery first supplied after 1 January 1995 must comply with these Regulations. These Regulations are being mirrored in other EC countries and also those not in the EC but within the European Economic Area (EEA) (EC and EFTA countries except Switzerland), so that there will eventually be uniformity in legislation, and legal barriers to trade within the EEA will be removed. The machinery covered is very wide ranging. There are some exclusions, however, such as most manually powered machines, machinery for medical use and most means of transport (see Schedule 5 of the Regulations). Machinery whose risks are mainly electrical are also excluded.

AMENDING REGULATIONS

In 1994 the Supply of Machinery (Safety) Regulations were extended so as to implement two more recent European Directives. The principal effect of this has been to apply the above requirements, as from 1 January 1995, to safety components, as defined, and widens the scope to include a greater range of lifting machines (but not classical passenger lifts and other specified exclusions). There is a further two year transitional period from January 1995, during which time compliance with the new requirements is optional with certain conditions.

MEETING THE REQUIREMENTS

The duty to meet the requirements mainly falls to the 'responsible person' who is defined as the manufacturer or the manufacturer's representative. If the manufacturer is not established in the EEA, the person who first supplies the machinery in the EEA may be the responsible person, which can be a user who manufactures or imports a machine for his/her own use.

There are basically three steps to dealing with the requirements.

Step 1 - Conformity assessment

The responsible person should ensure that machinery and safety components satisfy the essential health and safety requirements (EHSRs), and that appropriate conformity assessment procedures have been carried out. The EHSRs are laid out in the Directive and repeated in the Regulations (Schedule 3). This can be done either by reference directly to these requirements or to a relevant transposed harmonised standard where one exists. Harmonised standards are currently being prepared by the European Standards Organisations, CEN and CENELEC, before formal adoption by the European Commission. Harmonised standards will be available for a wide range of industrial machinery, including agricultural, textiles, engineering, construction, machinery. In addition, the responsible person must draw up a technical file (see below).

For certain classes if dangerous machine and safety component, a more rigorous procedure is required. Such products are listed in Annex 4 of the Directive and reproduced in Schedule 4 of the Regulations. In additional to the above requirements, the responsible person must arrange for type-examination of these produces by an approved body if there are no harmonised standards formally adopted by the EC for them, or if they are not manufactured to such standards. The Department of Trade and Industry (DTI) has appointed approved bodies in the UK for this purpose. Details are available from: DTI, Technology and Innovation Policy Division, 151 Buckingham Palace Road, London SW1W 9SS (Tel: 0171 215 5000).

Step 2 - Declaration procedure

The responsible person must issue one of two forms of declaration.

Declaration of conformity

This declaration should be issued with the finished product so that it is available to the user. It will contain various details such as the manufacturer's address, the machinery type and serial number, and Harmonised European or other Standards used in design.

Declaration of Incorporation

Where machinery is intended for incorporation into other machinery, the responsible person can draw up a declaration of incorporation. This should state that the machinery must not be put into service until the machinery into which it is to be incorporated has been given a Declaration of Conformity. A CE mark is not affixed at this intermediate stage.

Step 3 - Marking

When the first two steps have been satisfactorily completed, the responsible person or the person assembling the final product should affix the EC mark.

ENFORCEMENT

In this country the Health and Safety Executive is responsible for enforcing these Regulations in relation to machinery designed for use at work. Trading Standards Officers are responsible for enforcing these Regulations in relation to consumer goods. *After 1 January 1995 it is an offence for the responsible person to supply machinery which does not comply with these requirements. It is also an offence for any supplier to supply machinery which is not safe (and which was not first supplied before 1 January 1995).*

Detailed advice for the designer and manufacturer.

TECHNICAL FILE CONTENTS

The responsible person (defined above) is required to draw up a technical file for all machinery and safety components covered by these Regulations. The file or documents should comprise:

a)   An overall drawing of the product together with the drawings of the control circuits.

b)   Full detailed drawings, accompanied by any calculation notes, test results etc. required to check the conformity of the product   with the essential health and safety requirements.

c)   A list of the essential health and safety requirements, transposed harmonised standards, national standards and other technical specifications which were used when the product was designed.

d)   A description of methods adopted to eliminate hazards presented by the machinery or safety component.

e)   If the responsible person so desires, any technical report or certificate obtained from a component body or laboratory.

f)   If the responsible person declares conformity with a transposed harmonised standard, any technical report giving the results of tests.

g)   A copy of the instructions for the product.

For series manufacture, the responsible person must also have available documentation on the necessary administrative measures that the manufacturer will take to ensure that the product meets requirements.

TECHNICAL FILE PROCEDURE

The technical file document need not be on a permanent file, but it should be possible to assemble and make them available to an enforcement authority. The technical file documents should be retained and kept available for at least ten years following the date of manufacture of the product or of the last unit produced, in the case of a series manufacture. If the technical file documents are drawn up in the United Kingdom, they should be in English unless they are to be submitted to an Approved/Notified Body in another Member State, in which case they should be in a language acceptable to that approved Body. In all cases the instructions for the machinery should be in accordance with the language requirements of the EHSRs.

Workplace (Health, Safety and Welfare) Regulations (WHSWR) 1992

Law considered in context / more depth in Unit 17.

Arrangement of Regulations

1) Citation and commencement.
2) Interpretation.
3) Application of these Regulations.
4) Requirements under these Regulations.
5) Maintenance of workplace, and of equipment, devices and systems.
6) Ventilation.
7) Temperature in indoor workplaces.
8) Lighting.
9) Cleanliness and waste materials.
10) Room dimensions and space.
11) Workstations and seating.
12) Condition of floors and traffic routes.
13) Falls or falling objects.
14) Windows, and transparent or translucent doors, gates and walls.
15) Windows, skylights and ventilators.
16) Ability to clean windows etc. safely.
17) Organisation etc. of traffic routes.
18) Doors and gates.
19) Escalators and moving walkways.
20) Sanitary conveniences.
21) Washing facilities.
22) Drinking water.
23) Accommodation for clothing.
24) Facilities for changing clothing.
25) Facilities for rest and to eat meals.
26) Exemption certificates.
27) Repeals, saving and revocations.

Schedule 1   Provisions applicable to factories which are not new workplaces, extensions or conversions.
Schedule 2   Repeals and revocations.

Outline of key points

SUMMARY

The main requirements of the Workplace (Health, Safety and Welfare) Regs 1992 are:

1) **Maintenance** of the workplace and equipment.
2) **Safety** of those carrying out maintenance work and others who might be at risk (e.g. segregation of pedestrians and vehicles, prevention of falls and falling objects etc.).
3) Provision of **welfare** facilities (e.g. rest rooms, changing rooms etc.).
4) Provision of a safe **environment** (e.g. lighting, ventilation etc.).

ENVIRONMENT

Reg 1	New workplaces, extensions and modifications must comply now. Older workplaces have until 1 January 1996 to get up to standard.
Reg 4	Requires employers, persons in control of premises and occupiers of factories to comply with the regulations.
Reg 6	Ventilation - enclosed workplaces should be ventilated with a sufficient quantity of fresh or purified air (5 to 8 litres per second per occupant).
Reg 7	Temperature indoors - This needs to be reasonable and the heating device must not cause injurious fumes. Thermometers must be provided. Temperature should be a minimum of 16oC or 13oC if there is physical effort.

Reg 8	Lighting - must be suitable and sufficient. Natural light if possible. Emergency lighting should be provided if danger exists.
Reg 10	Room dimensions and space - every room where persons work shall have sufficient floor area, height and unoccupied space (min 11 cu.m per person).
Reg 11	Workstations and seating have to be suitable for the person and the work being done.

SAFETY

Reg 12	Floors and traffic routes must be of suitable construction. This includes absence of holes, slope, uneven or slippery surface. Drainage where necessary. Handrails and guards to be provided on slopes and staircases.
Reg 13	Falls or falling objects - suitable and effective measures shall be taken to prevent persons falling or being struck by falling objects. Tanks and pits must be covered or fenced.
Reg 14	Windows and transparent doors, where necessary for health and safety, must be of safety material and be marked to make it apparent.
Reg 15	Windows, skylights and ventilators must be capable of opening without putting anyone at risk.
Reg 17	Traffic routes for pedestrians and vehicles must be organised in such a way that they can move safely.
Reg 18	Doors and gates must be suitably constructed and fitted with any necessary safety devices.
Reg 19	Escalators and moving walkways shall function safely, be equipped with any necessary safety devices and be fitted with emergency stop.

HOUSEKEEPING

Reg 5	Workplace and equipment, devices and systems must be maintained in efficient working order and good repair.
Reg 9	Cleanliness and waste materials - workplaces must be kept sufficiently clean. Floors, walls and ceilings must be capable of being kept sufficiently clean. Waste materials shall not be allowed to accumulate, except in suitable receptacles.
Reg 16	Windows etc. must be designed so that they can be cleaned safety.

FACILITIES

Reg 20	Sanitary conveniences must be suitable and sufficient and in readily accessible places. They must be adequately ventilated, kept clean and there must be separate provision for men and women.
Reg 21	Washing facilities must be suitable and sufficient. Showers if required (a table gives minimum numbers of toilets and washing facilities).
Reg 22	Drinking water - an adequate supply of wholesome drinking water must be provided.
Reg 23	Accommodation for clothing must be suitable and sufficient.
Reg 24	Facilities for changing clothes must be suitable and sufficient, where a person has to use special clothing for work.
Reg 25	Facilities for rest and eating meals must be suitable and sufficient. Non smokers must be protected from discomfort caused by tobacco smoke.

Summary of relevant forthcoming legislation

Current at time of publication

The Control of Noise at Work Regulations 2005 (Draft)

The Noise at Work Regulations were established in 1989 and have had a significant effect on the reduction of exposure to workplace noise. Recent European Union directives have established an opportunity to review the regulations. This has resulted in the introduction of the Control of Noise at Work Regulations 2005.

OUTLINE OF KEY POINTS

Regulation 2 sets out the definition of 'daily average noise exposure' as the time weighted average of the levels of noise to which a worker is exposed over an 8 hour working day, taking account of levels of noise and duration of exposure and including impulsive noises. Weekly noise exposure level means the average of daily noise exposure levels over a week and normalised to five working days.

'Exposure limit value' (ELV) is the daily or weekly noise exposure level of 87dB (A) and a peak sound pressure level of 140 dB (C). 'Lower exposure action value' (LEAV) means a daily or weekly noise exposure level of 80 dB (A) and a peak sound pressure level of 135 dB (C). 'Upper exposure action value' (UEAV) means a daily or weekly noise exposure level of 85 dB (A) and a peak sound pressure level of 137 dB (C).

Regulation 3 states that the duty for health surveillance, information, instruction and training does not extend to who are not employees.

Regulation 4 states the determination of exposure limit values and action values. Under this regulation, if the noise levels in the workplace vary greatly, then the employer can choose to use weekly noise exposure levels instead of daily noise exposure levels. The exposure can take into account personal hearing protection provided to the employee.

Regulation 5 of the regulations states that any employer that carries out work which is likely to expose any employees to noise must make a suitable and sufficient assessment of the risk to health and safety created by noise at the workplace. In conducting the risk assessment the employer should assess the level of noise the employees are exposed to.

Regulation 6 complies with the general principles of prevention set out in the Management of Health and Safety at Work Regulations. Employers shall ensure that risk from the exposure of his employees to noise is either eliminated at source or, where this is not reasonably practicable, reduced to a minimum.

Regulation 7 states that any employer who caries out work which is likely to expose any employees to noise at or above a lower action value shall make hearing protection available upon request. If any area of the workplace is likely to be exposed to noise at or above an upper exposure action value the employer shall ensure that the area is designated a hearing protection zone and fitted with mandatory hearing protection signs.

Regulation 8 states that employers shall ensure that equipment provided in compliance with the regulations is used properly and maintained in an efficient state, in efficient working order and in good repair. The employee is required to use equipment properly and report any deficiencies as soon as is possible.

Regulation 9 states that if a risk assessment indicates a risk to the health and safety of any employees, due to their exposure to noise, then they must be put under suitable health surveillance, including testing of their hearing. The employer shall keep and maintain a suitable health record and the employee will be informed of any health problems.

Regulation 10 states that where employees are exposed to noise which is likely to be at or above the LEAV the employer must provide the employees and their representatives with suitable and sufficient information, instruction and training.

Control of Vibration at Work Regulations 2005 (Draft)

Hand-arm vibration (HAV) and whole body vibration (WBV) are caused by the use of work equipment and work processes that transmit vibration into the hands, arms and bodies of employees in many industries and occupations. Long-term, regular exposure to vibration is known to lead to permanent and debilitating health effects such as vibration white finger, loss of sensation, pain, and numbness in the hands, arms, spine and joints. These effects are collectively known as hand-arm or whole body vibration syndrome. These Regulations will introduce controls, which aim substantially to reduce ill health caused by exposure to vibration.

OUTLINE OF KEY POINTS

Regulation 4 states the personal daily exposure limits and daily exposure action values, normalised over an 8-hour reference period.

	Daily exposure limits	Daily exposure action values
Hand arm vibration	5 m/s^2	2.5 m/s^2
Whole body vibration	1.15 m/s^2	0.5 m/s^2

Regulation 5 requires the employer to make a suitable and sufficient assessment of the risk created by work that is liable to expose employees to risk from vibration. The assessment must observe work practices, make reference to information regarding the magnitude of vibration from equipment and if necessary measurement of the magnitude of the vibration.

Consideration must also be given to the type, duration, effects of exposure, exposures limit / action values, effects on employees at particular risk, the effects of vibration on equipment and the ability to use it, manufacturers' information, availability of replacement equipment, and extension of exposure at the workplace (e.g. rest facilities), temperature and information on health surveillance. The risk assessment should be recorded as soon as is practicable after the risk assessment is made and reviewed regularly.

Regulation 6 states that the employer must seek to eliminate the risk of vibration at source or, if not reasonably practicable, reduce it to a minimum. Where the personal daily exposure limit is exceeded the employer must reduce exposure by implementing a programme of organisational and technical measures. Measures include the use of other methods of work, ergonomics, maintenance of equipment, design and layout, information, instruction and training, limitation by schedules and breaks and the provision of personal protective equipment.

Regulation 7 states that health surveillance must be carried out if there is a risk to the health of employees liable to be exposed to vibration. This is in order to diagnose any health effect linked with exposure to vibration. A record of health shall be kept of any employee who undergoes health surveillance. If health surveillance identifies a disease or adverse health effect, considered by a doctor to be a result of exposure to vibration, the employer shall ensure that a qualified person informs the employee and provides information and advice. In addition the employer must also review risk assessments and the health of any other employee who has been similarly exposed and consider alternative work.

Regulation 8 states that employers must provide information, instruction and training to all employees who are exposed to risk from vibration. This includes any organisational and technical measures taken, exposure limits and values, risk assessment findings, why and how to detect injury, health surveillance entitlement and safe working practices. The requirement for information, instruction and training extends to persons whether or not an employee, but who carries out work in connection with the employers duties.

Regulatory Reform (Fire Safety) Order 2004

INTRODUCTION

At present we have to consider 5 principal pieces of legislation when considering fire safety in the workplace:

- Fire Precautions Act (FPA).
- Fire Precautions (Workplace) Regulations (FPWR).
- Management of Health and Safety at Work Regulations (MHSWR).
- Dangerous Substances & Explosive Atmosphere Regulations (DSEAR).
- Regulatory Reform Fire Safety Order (RRO) – due to be introduced in 2005.

In addition to the above we would also need to consider common law.

Fire Precautions Act

This legislation is due to be repealed when the RRO is introduced in 2005.

Fire Precautions Workplace Regulations

This regulation outlines the fire safety measures that need to be achieved via the risk assessment of fire and management of fire safety within a workplace. These regulations will be repealed when RRO is implemented however they have been incorporated within the RRO.

Management of Health and Safety at Work Regulations

It is this regulation that makes the legal requirement for fire risk assessments, at present. In addition, it makes various requirements for the management of fire safety within workplaces. This regulation will continue as a stand alone health and safety regulation in the future. Again the relevant fire aspects of this regulation have been incorporated within the RRO.

Dangerous Substances & Explosive Atmosphere Regulations

This regulation outlines the safety and control measures that need to be taken if dangerous or flammable / explosive substances are present. This regulation will continue as a stand alone health and safety regulation in the future. Again the relevant fire aspects of this regulation have been incorporated within the RRO.

Regulatory Reform (Fire Safety) Order 2004 (RRO)

This is a new, all encompassing, fire safety order is due to be implemented in 2005. As shown above it will have aspects of other legislation within it and has been compiled in such a way as to present a 'one stop shop' for fire safety legislation.

The order is split into 5 parts:

- Part 1   General
- Part 2   Fire Safety Duties
- Part 3   Enforcement
- Part 4   Offences and appeals
- Part 5   Miscellaneous

Each part is then subdivided into the individual points or articles as they are called in the order.

OUTLINE OF KEY POINTS

Part 1 General

This part covers various issues such as the interpretation of terminology used, definition of responsible person, definition of general fire precautions, duties under the order, and its application.

Part 2 Fire Safety Duties

This part imposes a duty on the responsible person to carry out a fire risk assessment to identify what the necessary general fire precautions should be. It also outlines the principles of prevention that should be applied and the necessary arrangements for the management of fire safety. The following areas are also covered:

- Fire-fighting and fire detection.
- Emergency routes and exits.
- Procedures for serious and imminent danger and for danger areas.
- Additional emergency measures re dangerous substances.
- Maintenance.
- Safety assistance.
- Provision of information to employees, employers and self employed.
- Capabilities and training.
- Co-operation and co-ordination.
- General duties of employees.

Part 3 Enforcement

This part details who the enforcing authority is, (which in the main is the Fire Authority), and it states they must enforce the order. It also details the powers of inspectors. It also details the different types of enforcement that can be taken:

- Alterations notice.
- Enforcement notice.
- Prohibition notice.

Part 4 Offences and appeals

This part details the 13 offences that may occur and the subsequent punishments and appeals procedure. It also explains that the legal onus for proving that an offence was not committed is on the accused. A new disputes procedure is also outlined within this part.

Part 5 Miscellaneous

Various matters are covered within this part the principal points being:

- 'Fire-fighters switches' for luminous tube signs etc.
- Maintenance of measures provided for the protection of fire-fighters.
- Civil liability.

■ Duty to consult employees.
■ Special provisions for licensed premises.
■ Application to crown premises.

There is then a schedule that covers the risk assessment process, plus details of the various legislation that will be repealed or amended.

Working at Height Regulations 2004 (Draft)

Falls from height at work are the most common cause of fatality and the second most common cause of major injury to workers and during the period between 2001/2002 resulted in 68 fatalities and approximately 4,000 serious injuries.

Health and Safety Commission (HSC) consultation on these regulations ended in April 2004, resulting in the production of a draft regulation entitled The Working at Height Regulations. An additional consultative document was issued concerning retention of the above 'two metre rule', consultation on this ended in December 2004. Issue of the final version of the regulations is anticipated around March 2005.

Under the WHR the interpretation of 'work at height' includes any place of work at ground level, above or below ground level that a person could fall a distance liable to cause personal injury and includes places for obtaining access or egress, except by staircase in a permanent workplace. The regulations will replace regulations in the Workplace (Health and Safety) Regulations and the Construction (Health, Safety and Welfare) Regulations and some of the terminology used in the latter regulations.

OUTLINE OF KEY POINTS

Regulation 4 states that all work at height must be properly planned, supervised and be carried out so far as is reasonably practicably safely. Planning must include the selection of suitable equipment, take account of emergencies and give consideration to weather conditions impacting on safety.

Regulation 5 states that those engaged in any activity in relation to work at height must be competent , if under training, is supervised.

Regulation 6 states that work at height must only be carried out when it is not reasonably practicable to carry out the work otherwise. If work at height does take place suitable and sufficient measures must be taken to prevent a fall of any distance, to minimise the distance and the consequences of any fall liable to cause injury. Employers must also make a risk assessment, as required by regulation 3 of the Management of Health and Safety at Work Regulations.

Regulation 7 states that when selecting equipment for use in work at height the employer shall take account of working conditions and any risk to persons in connection with the place where the equipment is to be used. Other particular equipment for use during work at height must have a guardrail, toe board, barrier or other means of protection as required by regulation 8.

Regulation 8 sets out requirements for particular equipment to conform to standards expressed in schedules to the regulations. It includes guard-rails, toe-boards, working platforms, nets, airbags, personal fall arrest equipment rope access and ladders.

Regulation 9 states that every employer shall ensure that suitable and sufficient steps are taken to prevent any person at work falling through any fragile surface and that no work on or from fragile surfaces shall be permitted when it is reasonably practicable to carry out work without doing so. If work has to be from a fragile roof then suitable and sufficient means of support must be provided that can sustain foreseeable loads. No person at work should be allowed to pass or work near a fragile surface unless suitable and sufficient guard rails and other means of fall protection is in place. Signs must be situated at a prominent place at or near to works involving fragile surfaces.

Regulation 10 states that every employer shall take reasonably practicable steps to prevent injury to any person from the fall of any material or object and that no material is thrown or tipped from height in circumstances where it is liable to cause injury to any person. Materials and objects must be stored in such a way as to prevent risk to any person arising from the collapse, overturning or unintended movement of the materials or objects.

Regulation 11 states that every employer shall ensure that where an area presents a risk of falling from height or being struck from an item falling at height that the area is equipped with devices preventing unauthorised persons from entering such areas and the area is clearly indicated.

Regulation 12 states that every employer shall inspected at suitable intervals and each time exceptional circumstances that are liable to affect the equipment occur. Specific requirements exist for periodic (every 7 days) inspection of a scaffold where someone could fall more than 2 metres.

Regulation 13 states that every employer shall ensure that fall protection measures of every place of work at height are visually inspected before use.

Regulation 14 states the duties of persons at work to report defects and use equipment in accordance with training / instruction.

Schedule 1	Requirements for existing places of work and means of access or egress at height.
Schedule 2	Requirements for guard rails, etc.
Schedule 3	Requirements for working platforms.
Schedule 4	Requirements for collective safeguards for arresting falls.
Schedule 5	Requirements for personal fall protection systems.
Schedule 6	Requirements for ladders.
Schedule 7	Particulars to be included in a report of inspection.
Schedule 8	Revocation of instruments.

This page is intentionally blank.

Assessment

Content

Written assessments - Papers A1 and A2

At every examination a number of candidates - including some good ones - perform less well than they might because of poor examination technique. It is essential that candidates practice answering both essay-type and short answer questions and learn to budget their time according to the number of marks allocated to questions (and parts of questions) as shown on the paper.

Each written paper is 2 hours duration and contains 2 sections:

Section 1 has one question carrying 20 marks requiring quite an 'in-depth' answer. This question should be allocated 30 minutes in total. If time (e.g. 5 minutes) is given to reading, planning and checking, the time available for writing is 25 minutes. Two pages are allowed for this answer; candidates should produce approximately 1½ sides for an average answer.

Section 2 has 10 questions each carrying 8 marks. If time (e.g. 10 minutes) is allowed for reading, planning and checking then there are 8 minutes to answer each question. One page is allowed for each of these answers, candidates should produce approximately ½ a side for an average answer.

A common fault is that candidates may fail to pay attention to the action verb in each question. The most common 'action verbs' used in examination questions are:

define	provide a generally recognised or accepted definition
state	a less demanding form of 'define', or where there is no generally recognised definition
sketch	provide a simple line drawing using labels to call attention to specific features
explain	give a clear account of, or reasons for
describe	give a word picture
outline	give the most important features of (less depth than either 'explain' or 'describe', but more depth than 'list'.)
list	provide a list without explanation
give	provide without explanation (used normally with the instruction 'give an example [or examples] of…')
identify	select and name

Other questions may start with 'what, when, how' etc. In such cases the examiners are expecting candidates to give their own explanations.

NEBOSH questions will progressively change to reflect practical issues that need to be managed in the workplace. Questions will increasingly reflect more than one unit of knowledge, for example "electrical fires" which could require an understanding of Unit 14 and Unit 15 to answer adequately.

We have chosen questions of this type to enable you to better apply your knowledge and approach, to meet the future requirements.

NEBOSH sample questions

Section 1

1   A sewer connection for a new housing estate is to be made in an existing 4 metre deep manhole. The manhole is 2 metres from the kerbside on a 40 mph single carriageway road. The road opening notice specifies that the work can be carried out only between the hours of 9.30 am and 4.30 pm.

  Describe the main features that must be covered to ensure the health and safety of the workforce and the public. Illustrate your answer with sketches of (a) the road layout and (b) the excavation. *(40)*

  Dec 2000 Sec 1 Question 4

2   A mobile tower scaffold is to be used in the re-pointing of external brickwork on the gable end wall of a building, which is 10 metres high at its highest point.

  (i)   *Explain* the possible dangers associated with this operation. *(20)*

  (ii)   *Outline* the precautions to be taken to minimise the risks. *(20)*

  Dec 1999 Sec 1 Question 6

Section 2

1   *Describe* the measures to be taken to prevent falls associated with stairwells and other holes in floors during the construction of a multi-storey building. *(8)*

  Dec 1999 Sec 2 Question 13

2   *Outline* the main areas to be addressed in a demolition method statement. *(8)*

  Dec 2000 Sec 2 Question 14

3   *Identify* ways of minimising the risk of accidents to children who might be tempted to gain access to a construction site. *(8)*

  June 2000 Sec 2 Question 12

4   *Outline* a hierarchy of measures to be considered when a construction worker is likely to fall a distance of 2 metres or more. *(8)*

  June 2000 Sec 2 Question 11

5   *Outline* a hierarchy of measures to minimise the risks from reversing vehicles on a construction site. *(8)*

  Dec 2000 Sec 2 Question 7

6   *Identify*, by means of a labelled sketch, the main requirements for a loading bay on a scaffold in order that materials for bricklayers and roofers can be safely placed on the bay by a fork-lift truck. *(8)*

  June 2000 Sec 2 Question 14

7   (a)   *Identify* the main risks to health and safety associated with kerb-laying. *(3)*

  (b)   *Outline* the steps to be taken to minimise the risks identified in (a). *(5)*

  Dec 2000 Sec 2 Question 12

8   A major hazard on a refurbishment project is fire.

  (i)   *List THREE* activities that represent an increased fire risk in such a situation. *(3)*

  (ii)   *Outline* the precautions that may be taken to prevent a fire from occurring. *(5)*

  Dec 1999 Sec 2 Question 8

PLEASE REFER TO BACK OF UNIT FOR ANSWERS

Practical assessment - Paper B

The practical assessment must be carried out under the control of the accredited centre and will normally be carried out on a working construction site identified by the practical assessor. The assessment must take place within 14 days of (before or after) the date of the written papers (date of the examination). Please make sure you are clear about when you will carry out the assessment and that your assessment invigilator has set the time aside.

Aims

The aim of the practical assessment is to test a candidate's ability to complete a health and safety assessment of a construction site. In particular, the assessment requires candidates to:

- Carry out unaided a health and safety inspection of a construction site (or part of a site), identifying the more common hazards, deciding whether they are adequately controlled and, where necessary, suggesting appropriate and cost effective remedial action.

- Prepare a report that persuasively urges site management to take appropriate action, explaining why such action is needed (including reference to possible breaches of legislation) and identifying, with due consideration of reasonable practicability, the remedial measures that should be taken.

Procedure

A report form / observation sheet should be used during your inspection. There are four columns on the form; observations, priority / risk, timescales; and brief notes on actions. The forms must be completed during the inspection and must be included with your covering management report for marking by the assessor.

The maximum time allocated to the practical assessment is 2 hours. You should spend 45 minutes making an assessment of the site, covering as wide a range of hazards as possible. The remaining time should be allocated to write a report to management in your own handwriting.

You are expected to recognise physical, health and environmental hazards - good, as well as bad, work practices. While only short notes on each hazard are required, it is important that the assessor is able to subsequently identify the following:

- Where the hazard was located.
- The nature of the hazard.
- In what way, if any, the hazard is being controlled.
- The remedial action, where appropriate.
- Preventative action required.

You should, however, note that the assessment is not intended to be a pure hazard spotting exercise and consideration should be given to other matters such as:

- Availability and standard of washing and toilet facilities.
- Adequacy of heating, lighting and ventilation.
- General condition of floors and gangways.
- Cleanliness of structures.
- If staff are present, are they aware of the actions to take in the event of an emergency?

On completion of the inspection, you should use lined paper to produce a report, consulting your own (and only your own) notes made during the inspection. The report should be in your own handwriting. The marking sheet will be used by the assessor when marking your paper, it is not confidential and you should bear it in mind when you are writing your report.

Sample practical assessment

Site Inspection Report for _____ Store

Introduction

This report looks at the building site area of the ____ Store in Tamworth. The work covers the construction of a full cover mezzanine with lifts, escalators and associated services. The purpose of the report is to identify hazards and good practice with the aim of preventing accidents and identifying areas for continuous improvement. The inspection sheets (attached in appendix) and report were completed by J. Bloggs, Health and Safety Manager.

Summary

I was particularly pleased to see very good fire precautions in place with high quality temporary systems and knowledgeable operatives. Equally pleasing was the high standard of the welfare facilities provided.

However there were some high risks areas that were unacceptable and needed immediate action. These concerned the building of the mezzanine which seems to be unplanned. There was a risk of operatives falling, heavy boards being dropped onto operatives below and no proper access to the mezzanine. There was also risk of electric shock from untested tools and bare wires.

Main Findings

Please not that the numbered observations relate to the numbered hazards on the inspection sheets.

Hazard 8,
The lift shaft pit was unguarded which could have resulted in operatives falling into it. This could lead to major injuries or fatalities. This shaft should be guarded, which could be done with strong plywood boards (8 x 4 ft) at a cost of £50-£100. It is a breach of the Construction (Health, Safety and Welfare) Regs 1996 and the Health and Safety at Work act 1974 to allow falls from a height.

Hazard 9,
The goods loading area on the mezzanine floor was unguarded with operatives working on the mezzanine close to the edge. The chance of a fatality if someone was to fall is high. The loading area should have toe boards, top and intermediate guard rails when it is not in use. Alternatively an 'up and over' pallet gate can be installed. Guard rails would cost £100-£200 while a pallet gate (much the preferred option) could cost up to £750. Breach of legislation here comes under the Construction Health and Safety and Welfare Regs 1996, The Health and safety at Work Act 1974 and the Construction, Design and Management Regs 1994 (no suitable health and safety plan).
The whole mezzanine installation was poor – see hazards 10 and 11.

Hazard 12,
The operative bolting the partitions to the mezzanine was being pushed while on top of a tower scaffold. This was to allow him to bolt both ends of the portion without climbing down. The tower scaffold could easily overturn resulting in a major injury or fatality. This action was stopped immediately and information and instructions must be given to operatives through tool box talks. Provision of a suitable mobile / scissor lift would prevent this problem. Ongoing hire of a scissor lift would only be in the low hundreds of pounds. Legislation breached here includes the Construction Health, Safety and Welfare Regs 1996, The Health & Safety at Work Act 1974 and the Provision and Use of Work Equipment Regs 1998,

Hazard 15,

There was a 5 gallon jerry can of petrol stored inside the building for the disc cutter. Petrol is highly flammable and so increases the risk of fire dramatically. The can was removed to stores outside the building. Supervisory controls to ensure the cutter is filled outside the building costs nothing. Renting an electrically operated cutter would be less than £100 per week. Legislation breached here includes the Construction Health and Safety at Welfare Regs 1996 and the Health and Safety at Work Act 1974.

Hazard 18,
Portable tools were found with no unique identification on them. This means there was no way of checking if they had been PAT tested (portable appliance testing). Electrical equipment that is not maintained or tested can develop faults that can lead to electrocution and death. All portable tools should have a unique number, be inspected and tested at regular intervals. The results of the testing should be entered into a log. The frequency of testing depends on usage / environment. Costs of setting up this system are initially high in terms of time but become less when ongoing. The Electricity at Work Regs 1989 were breached here.

Conclusion

The costs of safety far outweigh the costs of being safe and these costs are not only measured in monetary terms.

Morally we do not want to harm anyone, be it friends, family or employees. A guilty conscience is hard to live with. A safe and healthy workforce will have a high morale and work better.

Legally we have duties under Acts of Parliament and Regulations. Breaches of these duties can and will lead to prosecution followed by fines and / or imprisonment. This applies to both the company and employees. Further, breaches can lead to civil claims with high damages.

Financially, lack of safety can be very costly. These are not only the fines mentioned above. High absenteeism and staff turnover result. Repairs for damage are incurred. Insurance premiums can increase and business can be lost through bad publicity.

All of these reasons put together far outweigh the effort in correcting the problems identified in this report.

NEBOSH NATIONAL GENERAL AND CONSTRUCTION CERTIFICATES **FORM C**

Candidate's observation sheet No 1 of 6

Candidate's Name: _J. Bloggs_ and number: _F_

Place inspected: _Store in Tamworth_ Date of Inspection: _XX/XX/200X_

Observations List hazards, unsafe practices and good practices	Priority / risk (H,M,L)	Actions to be taken (if any) List any immediate *and* longer-term actions required	Timescale (immediate, 1 week, etc.)
1, Risk of fire control, e.g. Fire Plan, Fire points, emergency lighting and fire alarm systems. One exit partially blocked – three others available.	L	Remove items partially blocking fire exit Provide proper storage for 12V batteries and herras fence bases Daily checks on exits – weekly checks on systems	I M L
2, Risk of poor welfare controlled by site cabins with hot / cold water, kettle, toaster and microwave. Facilities for storing clothes and PPE	L	No immediate actions Weekly checks on condition of facilities Ensure confirmed provision of washing up liquids, clean tea towels, enough storage	I M L
3, Risk of poor welfare controlled by provision of toilet block – clean soap, hot and cold water	L	Clean facilities – no immediate action Provide ample supplies of toilet paper Weekly inspection and daily cleaning schedule.	I M L
4, Risk of poor welfare due to no barrier cream, moisturising cream or towels	M	Provide barrier and moisturizing creams & towels Weekly inspection to ensure adequate supplies Regular tool box talks about dermatitis hazards	I M L

NEBOSH NATIONAL GENERAL AND CONSTRUCTION CERTIFICATES   **FORM C**

Candidate's observation sheet No 2 of 6

Candidate's Name: J. Bloggs   and number: F

Place inspected: Store in Tamworth   Date of Inspection: XX/XX/200X

Observations List hazards, unsafe practices and good practices	Priority / risk (H,M,L)	Actions to be taken (if any) List any immediate *and* longer-term actions required	Timescale (immediate, 1 week, etc.)
5, Risk of fire from propane bottles, controlled by storage in mesh cage in yard, but due to cage too close to building	M	Move cage away from building to reduce risk of explosion in case of fire	I
		Ensure bottles are stored in cage at the end of each shift / day	M
		Use electric fork lift truck	L
6, Risk of trips / falls due to strapping from bundles of materials left on floor in yard	M	Clear yard	I
		Daily / weekly site inspections to check housekeeping	M
		Tool box talks on housekeeping – skips emptied regularly	L
7, Risk of electric shock from bare wires (conductors) trailing by main distribution board	H	Electrician to make safe / remove cables	I
		Instruct strip out electricians to strip cables back	M
		H&S Plan under CDM to cover this risk?	L
8, Risk of fall from height into unguarded lift shaft at ground level (deep pit)	H	Guard entrance to lift shaft	I
		Daily checks on guarding	M
		Lift installers to devise safe method of guarding lift shaft while installing the lift	L

NEBOSH NATIONAL GENERAL AND CONSTRUCTION CERTIFICATES **FORM C**

Candidate's observation sheet No 3 of 6

Candidate's Name: J. Bloggs and number: F

Place inspected: Store in Tamworth Date of Inspection: XX/XX/200X

Observations List hazards, unsafe practices and good practices	Priority / risk (H,M,L)	Actions to be taken (if any) List any immediate **and** longer-term actions required	Timescale (immediate, 1 week, etc.)
9, Risk of fall from height from unguarded mezzanine edge at goods loading point.	H	Work stopped straight away	I
		Install edge protection along mezzanine edge	M
		Provide 'pallet gate' or similar at loading point	L
10, Risk of being struck by falling mezzanine floor boards as area under leading edge not barricaded	H	Work under leading edge stopped	I
		Barricade area under the leading edge	M
		Control access under the edge as the mezzanine is built	L
11, Risk of falling while accessing / egressing the mezzanine as no proper access. Only incorrectly assembled tower scaffold.	H	Work on mezzanine stopped	I
		Provide suitably tied ladder	M
		Provide temporary stairs until permanent stairs installed	L
12, Risk of tower scaffold overturning as tower being pushed with man on top landing.	H	Stopped this taking place	I
		Toolbox talks on use of tower scaffolds	M
		Provide mobile scissor lift to mezzanine floor erectors	L

NEBOSH NATIONAL GENERAL AND CONSTRUCTION CERTIFICATES   FORM C

Candidate's observation sheet No 4 of 6

Candidate's Name: J. Bloggs   and number: F

Place inspected: Store in Tamworth   Date of Inspection: XX/XX/200X

Observations List hazards, unsafe practices and good practices	Priority / risk (H,M,L)	Actions to be taken (if any) List any immediate *and* longer-term actions required	Timescale (immediate, 1 week, etc.)
13, -Risk of dermatitis from cement while mixing mortar. No PPE in use	M	Provide suitable gloves to operative Tool box talks on risks from cement Inspect and monitor use of gloves	I M L
14, Risk of health problems whilst using disc cutter on lift shaft blocks. No dust mask used	M	Provide dust mask to operative Information /Instruction and supervision re Hazards Look at different cutting methods e.g. wet or dust collection	I M L
15, Risk of fire from 5 gallon jerry can of petrol for disc cutter in the building	H	Remove petrol can from building to yard store Control filling of cutter to outside the building Provide electrically powered tools	I M L
16, Risk of injury from saw bench as emergency stop button damaged and will not operate immediately	H	Take saw out of use Ensure daily /weekly inspections done and faults reported / recorded Repair faulty equipment	I H M

NEBOSH NATIONAL GENERAL AND CONSTRUCTION CERTIFICATES   FORM C

Candidate's observation sheet No 5 of 6

Candidate's Name: J. Bloggs   and number: F

Place inspected: Store in Tamworth   Date of Inspection: XX/XX/200X

Observations List hazards, unsafe practices and good practices	Priority / risk (H,M,L)	Actions to be taken (if any) List any immediate *and* longer-term actions required	Timescale (immediate, 1 week, etc.)
17, Risk of noise induced hearing loss whilst using portable tools to bolt portions into place. Only operative using tool has hearing protection	M	Provide all operatives in the immediate area with hearing protection. Carry out regular checks to ensure hearing protection is worn Information / instruction / supervision – tool box talks / posters	I M L
18, Risk of electric shock from portable tools. Not labelled and no PAT Test on angle grinder and electric drill.	H	Take tools out of use. Have them tested Set up labelling, testing, inspection, and recording system for PAT	I M L
19, Risk of severe cuts from petrol driven disc cutter that continues to run whilst not in use.	H	Stop using this cutter Provide electrical cutter with a 'dead mans switch' Inspect / test / maintain the equipment	I M L
20, Risk from handling of cement and sand. Controlled by delivery in IBC for sand and pallet for cement.	L	No immediate action Continue to order bulk materials in containers that can be moved by a FLT Regular checks to maintain the system	I M L

NEBOSH NATIONAL GENERAL AND CONSTRUCTION CERTIFICATES **FORM C**

Candidate's observation sheet No 6 of 6

Candidate's Name: J. Bloggs   and number: F

Place inspected: Store in Tamworth   Date of Inspection: XX/XX/200X

Observations List hazards, unsafe practices and good practices	Priority / risk (H,M,L)	Actions to be taken (if any) List any immediate **and** longer-term actions required	Timescale (immediate, 1 week, etc.)
21, Risk of collision of fork lift truck with people and plant / building as keys left in ignition	H	Instruct steel erectors to remove ignition key	I
		Instruction / Information / supervision in hazards of FLT	M
		Daily checks on use of FLT and competent driver	L
22, Risk of hand / arm vibration from floor scabbler and angle grinder. No PPE in use.	M	Provide suitable gloves for operative	I
		Plan work so that equipment used short term or intermittently	M
		Source equipment which provides lower vibration levels	L
23, Risk of slips / trips due to site rubbish	M	Clean site	I
		Schedule for daily site cleaning	M
		Inspections and tool box talks to operatives	L
24, Risk of fall into escalator pit as poorly boarded with gaps and bowing boards	H	Replace wooden boarding with metal plates	I
		Signs for danger of falling into pit	M
		Provide secure fence around pit	L

NEBOSH sample questions - answers

Section 1

1   A sewer connection for a new housing estate is to be made in an existing 4 metre deep manhole. The manhole is 2 metres from the kerbside on a 40 mph single carriageway road. The road opening notice specifies that the work can be carried out only between the hours of 9.30 am and 4.30 pm.

   Describe the main features that must be covered to ensure the health and safety of the workforce and the public. Illustrate your answer with sketches of (a) the road layout and (b) the excavation. *(40)*

Dec 2000 Sec 1 Question 4

To answer this question you should consider the health and safety implications of making a sewer connection in an urban road. To provide a comprehensive answer you should have some knowledge of the requirements of Chapter 8 of the Traffic Signs Manual, the New Roads and Street Works Act (NRSWA) 1991, the Confined Spaces Regulations (CSR) 1997 and the Construction (Health, Safety and Welfare) Regulations (CHSW) 1996. Good sketches of the road layout should show temporary signs in the correct order and cones set out with lead-in and exit tapers and an indication of a safety zone between the cones and the work area. Means of controlling traffic, either by the use of traffic lights or stop/go boards, are also important as is the provision of barriers for pedestrian safety. Sketches of the excavation should show adequate support for the sides, means of preventing falls into the excavation and a safe means of access. Additionally, for the operation as a whole, you should point out the need to draw up a method statement, to use trained and competent employees, to provide and ensure use of personal protective equipment (e.g. high visibility clothing), and to ensure adequate precautions are taken (such as gas testing, venting and the use of a permit- to-work system) before employees are allowed to enter a confined space.

2   A mobile tower scaffold is to be used in the re-pointing of external brickwork on the gable end wall of a building, which is 10 metres high at its highest point.

   (i)   *Explain* the possible dangers associated with this operation. *(20)*

   (ii) *Outline* the precautions to be taken to minimise the risks. *(20)*

Dec 1999 Sec 1 Question 6

For part (i), candidates should note that an explanation of the dangers are required. In order to explain the dangers it was not enough, for example, to state simply that there is a danger of persons falling from the tower; an explanation requires some description of the circumstances that may lead to such a danger, such as over-reaching or the scaffold becoming unstable because it has been erected on soft or uneven ground, is not tied in or not provided with outriggers, has been struck by a vehicle, or has been moved with persons on the working platform.

For Part (ii) Precautions that could be taken to minimize the risks could include:
- *The erection of the scaffold by trained and competent personnel.*
- *Provision of a fully boarded working platform (complete with guard rails and toe boards).*
- *Insuring that wheels are locked while the tower is in use.*

Additionally, identification of the problem of dust in part (i) could invariably lead to suggestions for eye and respiratory protection.

There are also many precautions that should be mentioned in relation to preventing the scaffold from becoming unstable, protecting persons from falling materials and the safe use of equipment.

Section 2

1   *Describe* the measures to be taken to prevent falls associated with stairwells and other holes in floors during the construction of a multi-storey building. *(8)*

Dec 1999 Sec 2 Question 13

Most serious injuries on construction sites are as a result of falls. The risk of falls from a height is present on almost all sites at some stage. It is important, therefore, that those with responsibilities for safety have a good understanding of the measures needed to minimise this particular risk. It should be recognised that the provision of guard rails for stairwells and lift shafts, and hand rails on stairs, are important measures to be taken as well as identifying that other holes in floors need to be covered over. It is also important to ensure that adequate levels of lighting are provided or that good housekeeping and a high standard of supervision and control are also essential if falls are to be prevented.

2   *Outline* the main areas to be addressed in a demolition method statement. *(8)*

June 2002 Sec 2 Question 14

The method statement essentially sets out the sequence of work and the methods to be employed for each part of the work. In this case, particular emphasis would need to be placed on preparation work (such as pre-weakening, temporary propping and the isolation of existing services) protection of the public, control of noise and dust, and the removal of waste from the site. The statement would additionally need to address issues such as dealing with hazardous or flammable materials, the provision of temporary services, emergency procedures, control and co-ordination on site, and the competencies of the personnel involved in the demolition work.

3   *Identify* ways of minimising the risk of accidents to children who might be tempted to gain access to a construction site. *(8)*

June 2000 Sec 2 Question 12

Ways of minimizing the risk of accidents to children who might be tempted to gain access to a construction site could include:

- *The need to provide secure hoardings and fences to prevent access.*
- *Signs to warn of the dangers.*
- *Ensure that the site is safe should children breach the outer defences.*
- *Removing access ladders.*
- *Providing trench supports.*

- *Securing fuel storage tanks.*
- *Covering holes.*
- *Immobilizing plant.*
- *Isolating electrical supplies.*
- *Reducing the heights of stacked materials.*
- *Locking away equipment and chemicals.*
- *Campaigning and educational measures – such as visiting local schools to warn children of the dangers of using construction site as playgrounds.*

4   **Outline** a hierarchy of measures to be considered when a construction worker is likely to fall a distance of 2 metres or more. *(8)*

June 2000 Sec 2 Question 11

The Construction (Health, Safety and Welfare) Regulations (CHSW) 1996 call for a hierarchy of preventive measures to be considered in situations where there is a risk of workers falling a distance of 2 metres or more. The initial measure in the hierarchy is the provision of a properly constructed working platform, complete with guard rails and toe boards. If this is not practicable, or where the work is of short duration, then suspension equipment should be used and, only when this is considered impracticable, should reliance be placed on fall arrest equipment.

5   **Outline** a hierarchy of measures to minimise the risks from reversing vehicles on a construction site. *(8)*

June 2002 Sec 2 Question 7

Many accidents on construction sites involve site transport and a number of these are caused by reversing vehicles. One of the first measures to be considered would be to eliminate or reduce the need for reversing by introducing a one-way system and providing turning circles or loading /unloading areas. In circumstances where this might not be possible, it would be necessary to ensure that safe systems of work are in place and followed. Such systems would include the exclusion of pedestrians from site traffic areas, the use of banks men, the provision of information, instruction and training for site personnel and the mandatory wearing of high visibility clothing. Finally, the vehicles should be fitted with audible/visual reversing warning devices and features such as CCTV and fresenel lens mirrors to ensure adequate driver visibility.

6   **Identify**, by means of a labelled sketch, the main requirements for a loading bay on a scaffold in order that materials for bricklayers and roofers can be safely placed on the bay by a fork-lift truck. *(8)*

June 2000 Sec 2 Question 14

To answer this question you need to identify that a loading bay, because of the weight it is expected to carry, should be constructed to a higher specification than an ordinary scaffold. Standards should therefore be closer together than normal and extra bracing should be provided to improve rigidity. The loading platform would also need to be fully boarded, fitted with guard rails and toe boards and with gates to allow the platform to be loaded while at the same time affording the user of the scaffold some protection from falling. Safe access routes and stop blocks for vehicles should have been identified in candidates' sketches, as should a suitable footing for the scaffold.

7   (a)   **Identify** the main risks to health and safety associated with kerb-laying. *(3)*

(b)   **Outline** the steps to be taken to minimise the risks identified in (a). *(5)*

Dec 2000 Sec 2 Question 12

Answers to part (a) includes:
- *The risk of strained backs.*
- *Pulled muscles.*
- *Trapped fingers.*

- *Dust and noise arising from the use of cutting tools.*
- *Those associated with handling concrete, such as dermatitis and cement burning.*
- *The risks that may arise from working in close proximity to vehicular traffic.*

Answers to part (b) for steps to minimise the identified risks should include the completion of a manual handling assessment, together with assessments required by the Control of Substances Hazardous to Health Regulations (CAWR) 1999 and the Noise at Work Regulations (NWR) 1989, the provision and use of the appropriate personal protective equipment such as footwear, respiratory, eye and hearing protection and high visibility clothing. Other important aspects are training, information and supervision.

8   A major hazard on a refurbishment project is fire.

(i)   **List THREE** activities that represent an increased fire risk in such a situation. *(3)*

(ii)   **Outline** the precautions that may be taken to prevent a fire from occurring. *(5)*

Dec 1999 Sec 2 Question 8

Hot work such as cutting and welding, the use of flammable or highly flammable materials, electrical work, individuals smoking and burning rubbish on site are all examples of activities that can be used in answer to part (i).

In part (ii), precautions should cover all eventualities and include inspection and testing of electrical systems, hot work permit systems, inspection of the work area after the completion of hot work, regular clearing away of accumulated rubbish, the proper storage of flammable and combustible materials, the control of smoking and the avoidance of burning of rubbish on the site.

Index

G

Generic risk assessment, 61
Giving priority to collective protective measures, 69
Good housekeeping and fire, 218
Guard rails, 104
Guards and safety devices, 172

H

Hand tools, 161
Hazard, 4, 57
    confined spaces, 125
    equipment, 165
    excavations,117
    machinery, 162
    manual handling, 175
    electricity
    pedestrians, 137
    site vehicle, 143
    to the public from street works, 138
Hazardous substances in demolition, 131
Health and safety
    Arrangements, 24
    culture, 39
    external influences, 41
    framework management, 19
    Internal influences,.40
    legal framework for regulating 14
    management framework, 19
    management HSG65, 19
    moral, legal and financial argument, 7
    multi-disciplinary nature of, 3
    organising, 23
    performance, 39
    policy, 23
    size of the problem, 7
    sources of information, 17
Health and Safety (Consultation with Employees) Regs. (HSCER) 1996, 321
Health and Safety (Display Screen Equipment) Regulations (DSE) 1992, 322
Health and Safety (First-Aid) Regulations (FAR) 1981, 322
Health and Safety (Safety Signs and Signals) Regulations (SSSR) 1996, 323
Health and Safety at Work etc. Act (HASAWA) 1974, 324
Health and Safety Information for Employees Regulations (IER) 1989, 323
Health, 3
    hazards of specific agents, 233
    risk categorisation, 59
    surveillance, 250
Hierarchy of control, 75
    elimination/substitution, 75
    engineering control, 75
    isolation/segregation, 75
    personal protective equipment, 75
    reducing exposure, 75
Hierarchy of measures
    machinery, 171
    working at height, 99
Highly flammable or flammable liquids, 218
Hoists, 185
HSG65 - Successful Health and Safety Management, 19
Human behaviour, 42
    attitude, aptitude and motivation, 44
    effects of age and experience, 47
    errors and violations, 46
    individual, job and organisational factors, 42
    peers, 48
    perception of risk, 45

I

Ignition sources, 216
Incidence rate, 17
Incident types, 57
Independent tied scaffolding, 100
Indicators of culture, 39
Indirect costs of accidents and ill-health, 13
Individual factors, 42
Influence and role of the European Union, 14
Information
    employees, 52
    work equipment, 155
Information, instruction, training and supervision, 141
Injuries from manual handling, 175
Inspection, 106
    electrical equipment, 204
    excavations, 123
    work equipment, 156
Inspectors' powers under HASWA, 16
Instructions for work equipment, 155

Internal influences on health and safety, 40
Ionising Radiations Regulations (IRR) 1999, 328
Isolation of services, 133, 203
Isolation/segregation, 75

J

Job factors, 42
Joint occupation
    co-operation and co-ordination, 32
    premises, 32
    shared responsibilities, 32

L

Ladders, 108
Legal & organisational roles & responsibilities, 27
Legal framework for regulating health and safety, 14
Liabilities
    civil, 11
    criminal, 8
Lifting equipment, 187
Lifting operations and lifting equipment 187
    accessories, 188
    certification of equipment, 192
    competence of operators and signallers, 192
    control of lifting operations, 190
    cranes, 187
    statutory examination of lifting equipment, 190
Lifting Operations and Lifting Equipment Regulations (LOLER) 1998, 329
Lifting techniques for manual handling, 179
Liquefied petroleum and other gases in cylinders, 219
Local exhaust ventilation, 245
Lone working, 84

M

Machinery guards
    automatic, 170
    fixed adjustable, 169
    fixed distance, 169
    self adjusting, 169
    fixed, 169
    interlocking, 170
Machinery, 62
    guards and safety devices, 172
    hierarchy of measures, 171
    mechanical hazards, 165
    non-mechanical hazards, 162
    protection from hazards, 168
    protective appliances, 170
    trip device, 170
Maintenance
    conducted safely for work equipment, 156
    electrical equipment, 204
    equipment, 155
    safe workplace, 141
Management of Health and Safety at Work Regulations (MHSWR) 1999, 330
Management systems for driver competence, 148
Manual handling, 175
    hazards, 175
    injuries, 175
    means of minimizing the risks from, 178
    risks assessment, 175
    techniques for manually lifting loads, 179
Manual Handling operations Regulations (MHOR) 1992, 333
Manually operated load moving equipment, 182
Maximum exposure limits, 238
Mean duration rate, 17
Meanings of common terms, 3
Means of escape, 225
Measures to protect the public from construction activities, 142
Mechanical handling, 181
    dumper trucks, 182
    excavators, 182
    forklift trucks, 181
    hoists, 185
    manually operated load moving equipment, 182
    means of minimising mechanical handling risk, 183
    telehandlers, 182
Mechanical hazards, 162
Method of construction, 131
Minimising
    fire risk, 215
    manual handling risks, 178
    mechanical handling risk, 183
Mobile elevating work platforms (MEWP), 106
Mobile tower scaffolding, 102

© ACT